BITBURG
AND
BEYOND

A Shapolsky Book

For any additional information, contact:
Shapolsky Publishers, Inc.
56 East 11th Street, NY, NY 10003

First Edition 1987

1 2 3 4 5 6 7 8 9 10

Library of Congress Cataloging in Publication Data

Levkov, Ilya I.
Bitburg And Beyond

Includes index.
1. Holocaust, Jewish (1939-1945) – Anniversaries, etc.
2. Reagan, Ronald – Journeys – Germany (West).
3. Visits of state – Germany (West).
4. Bitburg (Germany) – Politics and government.
5. Holocaust, Jewish (1939-1945) – Public opinion.
6. Reagan, Ronald – Journeys – Germany (West) – Bitburg – Public opinion
I. Levkov, Ilya I., 1943-

D810.J4B496   1986   940.53'15'03924   86-27950

ISBN 0-933503-94-6

BITBURG

AND

BEYOND

Encounters In American, German and Jewish History

Edited by Ilya Levkov

Shapolsky Publishers
New York

ACKNOWLEDGMENTS

The preparation of a book such as this one is made possible only by the generous assistance of many individuals and institutions. I would like to thank Elan Steinberg, executive director of the American section of the world Jewish Congress; Dr. Harris Schoenberg, director of B'nai-Brith International's delegation to the United Nations; Abraham Foxman of the ADL; Marc Tanenbaum of the American Jewish Committee; Dr. Pearl Laufer of the Jewish War Veterans of America; and Ms. Kohler of the German Information Center in New York for granting me the opportunity to peruse their archives and for introducing me to additional sources of information and to other helpful persons.

I am especially grateful to Menachem Z. Rosensaft, the founder of the International Network of Children of Jewish Holocaust Survivors, who exposed me to the turbulence and agonies that the members of his organization felt during the period of the Bitburg crisis. He gave most generously of his time, rendering professional advice and sharing personal experiences.

I would like to extend my thanks to the contributors and to the organizations that graciously allowed me to reprint their copyrighted material. I am also indebted to Mr. George H. Asher for his skillful translations of the French and German materials.

No book can see the light without an editor who molds the material until it is fully formed and ready for the reader to understand and enjoy. Malcolm Jordan-Robinson literally moved mountains of papers to achieve this goal.

And to my publisher, Mr. Ian Shapolsky, I owe a deep sense of gratitude. Over nine months of "creation" he stoically watched this project grow threefold in size and expense . . . and, believing in its importance, voiced no objections nor even once compared this growth with the rate of Brazil's inflation.

Despite the valuable assistance of those mentioned here, I alone am responsible for the ideas presented in this work and any errors of omission.

DEDICATION

This work is lovingly dedicated to my father, Yitzhak, and to the memory of my mother, Emma, who instilled in me the values of truth and the bitter consequences of its absence.

To my wife Ruth, whose support was invaluable; and to my seven year–old–son, Benjamin, for whom Bitburg meant a year of weekends bicycling without a father.

"Greetings, my friend," said President Reagan as he was greeted by Chancellor Kohl on arrival in West Germany to visit the Bitburg cemetery and the former German concentration camp Bergen-Belsen.

BITBURG AND BEYOND

Table of Contents

6. Bonn Reacts   94

PART II:
REAGAN PROCEEDS WITH GERMAN VISIT

7. May 5th At Bergen-Belsen — Reagan and Kohl   130

8. May 5th At Bergen-Belsen — Protest   136

9. May 5th At Bitburg   166

16. The American Press   440

Before Bitburg

PART V: THE GERMAN RESPONSE

17. The Response Of Religious Leaders 490

18. The Response of Theologians 498

19. The Response of Jewish Leaders 521

Introduction

In the spring of 1985, a decision that had been made in a quiet conversation in a private White House drawing room between President Reagan of the United States and Chancellor Kohl of the Federal Republic of Germany erupted into a fierce public debate. Before it was executed, the decision drew vigorous dissent from bipartisan political groups, organizations of Nazi camp survivors, senators, congressmen, veterans, and religious and ethnic groups of every shade and color in the United States, as well as comment in all major countries, including many behind the Iron Curtain.

The conflict stemmed from the announcement that President Reagan would accept an invitation from West Germany's Chancellor Kohl to engage in a symbolic act of reconciliation between the United States and the Federal Republic of Germany. The decision of the leaders of these two powerful countries was the first in the modern history of American-German relations to cause such a fundamental political questioning and soul-searching. And this seemingly friendly encounter between two allies evolved into a web of political errors, misstatements and gaffes, charges and countercharges by these two leaders and bureaucratic mishandling of such magnitude that the affair became known as "the Watergate of symbols." Later, it was called "the Bitburg affair."

Mistakes abounded from the start. The first report was that the selected site for this reconciliation, which also would recognize the fortieth anniversary of the ending of World War II, would be a German concentration camp. Debate erupted when the site was dropped in favor of a military cemetery in a small town in Germany, and was heightened when it was learned that the cemetery contained the graves of 47 or 49 (the exact figure has never been determined) members of the Waffen SS.

Requests were made for President Reagan to alter his itinerary; and protests poured forth when the president refused to do this. As a result, a major battle gathered momentum in the Congress of the United States, spilled over into the media, and before it was finalized, the actual event threatened existing relationships between Jews, Christians, politicians, veterans, and the governments of the two countries involved.

The genesis of this conflict dates back to November 30, 1984, in the White House, when Chancellor Kohl invited President Reagan to visit Germany during the upcoming Economic Summit in May. The West German chancellor was the first head of state to be received at the White House after President Reagan's historical victory in the 1984 Presidential election. The president — probably still flushed from his success at carrying 49 states — did not hesitate to accept Kohl's idea of staging a symbolic act of reconciliation between the United States and the Federal Republic of Germany during the visit.

The act of reconciliation was to consist of a handshake and the laying of a wreath at the site of a military cemetery where American and German soldiers are buried. (Apparently, no one involved knew that there are no American soldiers buried in the Bitburg cemetery.)

'The idea was to have a symbolic act of peace and reconciliation over the graves," Kohl later explained to the Bundestag [the German parliament].

During their friendly chat, Kohl presented the President and Secretary of State George Shultz with a list of sites that would be on the agenda for the state visit. One of the suggestions made by the chancellor was a visit to Dachau concentration camp; and the president had no objection to this idea.

A few days later the American planners received a message from their German counterparts that upon reflection of the agenda it was deemed unwise to visit Dachau. The German planning team was composed of political advisers in the chancellor's office, and did not include professionals from the Ministry of Foreign Affairs. While the itinerary had not been announced, the trip had been and Reagan's team would not accede to the request for a cancellation. They continued to hold to the original agenda over the next several months despite the hints, signs, and histrionics that multiplied from West Germany.

The West German *Der Spiegel* reported on January 20, 1985, that president Reagan's visit to Dachau would be against the wishes of Chancellor Kohl. What had started out as a suggestion from Chancellor Kohl was now being viewed as President Reagan's idea.

Sensitive to the change, and mindful of the intended purpose of "reconciliation," White House Press Officer Larry Speakes stated on behalf of the president four days later that "Dachau is a place that the President would like not to visit."

Yet Dachau was still not off the agenda. In February Michael Deaver of the president's White House staff inspected several Holocaust sites, *including Dachau,* and found the latter "worthy for the president to visit."

The West Germans were furious. In examining this it is difficult to pinpoint the specific reason for Chancellor Kohl's first suggesting Dachau as part of the itinerary and then opposing the plan. Two possible reasons can be offered:

1. He made the initial overture without thinking through the idea. Kohl may have not considered the fact that worldwide press coverage of President Reagan and Chancellor Kohl visiting the crematorium ovens in Dachau would include graphic film coverage and photographs that would not lend themselves to the mosaic picture of reconciliation nor contribute to the sought-after image of a new rehabilitated Germany.

2. He may also have later realized that he would have to share the visit by President Reagan with his conservative political rival, Franz Josef Strauss, the prime minister of Bavaria, where Dachau is located.

Whatever the reasons behind the German objection, on March 19, the White House advance team left for a second look at itinerary sites as well as possible sites for a state visit to Spain, Portugal, and France.

While they were on their fact-finding mission, President Reagan decided that he would not visit a concentration camp and stated publicly on March 21 that such a visit "would reawaken the memories . . . and the passions of the time." Ever public-relations-minded, the president did not present his decision as having been a result of pressure from West Germany. For some reason, at the same time, the president stated that most present German citizens were young and would not remember the war. Further inflaming passions that lie smoldering below the surface where this issue is concerned, in an interview with the *Washington Post* he reaffirmed that he would not visit a concentration camp. He said that, of course, "we should never forget that Holocaust," but added that the bulk of German citizens had not gone through the experience of World War II.

Why this was mentioned boggled the mind of many who read the story. What was transpiring became clearer several days later.

On April 11 the California White House staff, happy that the problem of Dachau had been solved, announced from Santa Barbara that President Reagan would not visit the Dachau concentration camp but would visit a military cemetery. President Reagan was determined to have his public-relations wreath-laying.

As the president was making his historic statement about not visiting a concentration camp and adding that current West Germans were not of an age to be held responsible for the actions of the Third Reich, Deaver's advance team was engaged in finding a suitable German military cemetery. They were assured by the Kohl team that there were "no painful surprises" in the Bitburg cemetery.

Had Deaver's advance team and Kohl's advisers researched the site, they would have discovered the fact which would upset Holocaust survivors, Jews in general, veterans, politicians, and concerned men and women around the world. It was learned later from a non-White House source that located in the cemetery in the small town of Bitburg were the graves of members of the infamous Waffen SS.

Such bungled planning by the staffs of the leaders of two of the world's powerful nations resulted in an outcry that did not cease even after the visit had taken place.

It is possible that had President Reagan not gone along with Kohl's wishes to eliminate the visit to Dachau, his eventual visit to Bitburg would not have caused such a furor. As it was, it looked as if the president was willing to substitute for a visit to a concentration camp a wreath-laying in a cemetery which contained the graves of the Third Reich's specially trained killers.

Four days after Reagan's team had announced the Bitburg visit, Kohl's team stated that the chancellor had suggested the visit to Dachau "because we knew it would be a political necessity," but that Reagan had rejected it.

By now the visit was evolving into a political tug-of-war with both sides attempting to place the blame on the other. On April 19 President Reagan announced that he would visit a concentration camp. His choice this time was Bergen-Belsen. Elaborating on this, Reagan said: "I thought there was no way that I, as a guest of the government [of the Federal Republic of Germany] . . . could on my own take off and go some place and, then, run the risk of appearing as if I was trying to say to Germans, 'Look what you did,' and all this when most of the people in Germany today weren't even alive or were very small children when this was happening."

The scope of this last statement about German responsibility was expanded at a state dinner for Algerian President Schadli, when President Reagan explained that most of the Waffen SS buried in Bitburg were just 17 or 18 years old at the time and thus were as much victims of Nazism as the inmates of the concentration camps.

The shock of hearing the president equating criminals and victims was felt around the world.

On April 15, 53 U.S. senators appealed to President Reagan to drop the intended visit to Bitburg.

Four days later on April 19, at a ceremony at the White House where he was receiving the Congressional Gold Medal, the chairman of the U.S. Holocaust Memorial Council, Elie Wiesel, implored the president not to visit Bitburg.

Two days later, Menachem Rosensaft, the leader of the sons and daughters of the Holocaust survivors, received an overwhelming ovation from several thousand survivors gathered at Philadelphia when he denounced Reagan's trip to Bitburg as obscene. If the President insisted on going through with the Bitburg visit, Rosensaft said, he was neither needed nor wanted at Bergen-Belsen.

Four days later, 257 members of the House of Representatives signed a letter to Chancellor Kohl urging him to withdraw his invitation.

The next day the Senate passed a resolution urging President Reagan to reconsider his itinerary.

In spite of this gathering storm, the president remained unshaken in his determination not to back down from the planned itinerary. Moreover, to the surprise of his remaining supporters, on April 23 he stated that the visit to the cemetery in Bitburg was "morally right." He would maintain his full assurance that he was doing to the right thing up to and after his visit to Bitburg.

Thus, the incubation of this thorny affair called Bitburg had three distinct stages:

1. The earliest phase, from November 30, 1984, through mid-March 1985 involved manipulative moves on the part of Chancellor Kohl and his team, and the Reagan team's acquiescence.

2. A middle phase from March 21 through May 3, 1985 included Reagan's remarks equating criminals and victims, his decision to drop Dachau and add Bergen-Belsen, and his absolute determination not to give in on Bitburg.

3. In the culminating visit of May 5-7, President Reagan made speeches in Germany in which he reasserted his political and moral position.

President Reagan chose to resolve this conflict in the traditional compromise of politics. He made a painful compromise about the site of the symbolic reconciliation, and then stood in two controversial places to side with the angels by speaking out against the Holocaust.

The escalating furor touched on three major issues which had never been exposed to such intense international scrutiny:

1. The involvement of the United States in the commemoration of the Holocaust issue.

2. The clash between conventional politics and a moral issue.

3. The clash between two national memories — that of the Jews and that of the Germans.

These conflicts were magnified by the setting in which they were decided and the degree of mobilization and response aroused in so many people in so many different countries. Therefore, a clarification of these three issues is of paramount importance in the understanding of the encompassing nature and consequences of the Bitburg affair.

For various reasons, the government of the United States, which took part in the defeat of Nazi Germany and conducted the process of denazification and the bringing to trial of the leading Nazis, was not involved, domestically, in the commemoration of the Holocaust until the late 1970's.

Why this did not take place before is not the subject of this book. Suffice it to state that in 1977 Mark Siegel, the special liason to the Jewish community at the White House, initiated an inquiry into a Holocaust memorial and instructed Ellen Goldstein, his assistant, to prepare a survey. In her report, Ms. Goldstein noted that unlike numerous other western democracies, the United States did not have such a national memorial. But before he was able to bring to fruition any plans, Siegel resigned in protest over President Carter's decision to sell military aircraft to Saudi Arabia.

Nine months later, the concept was reintroduced by Ms. Goldstein, who was now an assistant to Stuart Eizenstat, the special adviser on domestic affairs to President Carter. Her resurrection of the idea was sparked by a column by William Safire in **The New York Times** of March 27, 1978, when he discussed the Nazis' right to march in Skokie, Illinois. He noted that "America has no vivid reminder to the horror of the Final Solution. But we have a reminder not even Israelis can boast: our own homegrown handful of Nazis."

The idea gained power through the TV mini-series *Holocaust.* Americans were awakened to the horrors of the Holocaust as never before. More fuel for a memorial was heaped on during the visit of Prime Minister Menachem Begin to Washington, which also coincided with Israel's 30th anniversary. And it finally became a viable idea as (ironically enough) a peace offering to the Israeli prime minister, counterbalancing the sale of F-15s to Saudi Arabia.

During Begin's time in the U.S., presidential advisers Robert Lipshutz and Stuart Eizenstat sent a memorandum to President Carter concerning the establishment of an official U.S. memorial to the Holocaust on April 28, 1978. This memo was endorsed by Secretary of State Cyrus Vance and Special Adviser to the President on International Affairs Zbigniew Brzezinski.

On May 1 President Carter announced the establishment of a President's Commission on the Holocaust at a reception jointly honoring Prime Minister Begin and Israel's 30th anniversary.

This did much to appease the prime minister, still angry about the sale of F-15s, and was definitely responsible for creating a working atmosphere at Camp David.

Thus, political compromise where the issue of the Holocaust is concerned was established early. At the cradle of American involvement in commemorating the Holocaust were President Carter and his political officials. Seven years later there would be a new set of seasoned political officials and a different president. However, in each case, advice and a decision concerning the Holocaust were based more upon political considerations than on moral imperatives.

The second issue that lay smoldering under the Bitburg visit was the inherent difficulty in bridging a state's (or country's) political behavior with that of a group's claim for absolute morality.

Whereas conventional political behavior is based upon premises of mutual compromise, moral absulutism negates any such notion. For this simple reason the visit was destined to fail in the minds of many.

Part of the Bitburg conflict centered around the issue of the deeds of Nazi Germany — the epitome of evil — as they were relegated to the realm of conventional politics. President Reagan's call for reconciliation above the military graves was an effort to stage a symbolic act of reconciliation with the present Germans without regard for any inherent responsibility on their part for the Nazi atrocities. However, this staging — which was questionable in its need and timing — took place over the symbols of the Nazi regime, and thus contributed to the dilution of the absolute evil and the incorporation of this act into the realm of conventional politics.

There was ample interest by both state leaders in expanding and consolidating this realm of conventional politics. President Reagan desired the support of the Federal Republic for the Strategic Defense Intiative ("Star Wars"); Chancellor Kohl sought a much-needed victory in his upcoming state elections in North Rhineland Westphalia. With these two conventional political goals in mind, one opposed a visit to Dachau, the other allowed the site to be changed to Bitburg and later added Bergen-Belsen. In each case, conventional politics hinged upon an issue within the realm of moral absolutism.

The clash, then, was inevitable, even invited.

The third underlying issue was the hovering clash between the Jewish national memory and the Geman memory. By their very nature, the one demands the negation of the other.

In any situation where a group has been maligned by a country, memory of the pain always lies ready to be ignited. In the case of Jews, the value of memory constitutes the basis of Jewish heritage in general and of the modern Jewish nationhood in particular. It is inconceivable to detach the Holocaust phenomenon from the national/ethnic experience. As Rabbi Irving Greenberg wrote, "To be a Jew is to have a memory — a Jewish memory." Consequently, any manipulation of that memory on the international level is perceived as a direct assault against Jewish history and thus against the heritage it was built upon.

The proposed visit to Bitburg, then, was perceived by many as the legitimization of the atrocities performed by the Third Reich against the Jews.

But as the Jews have a historical memory, so, too, do the Germans. The former hold dear to what has gone before; the latter wish not to be reminded of it. Contemporary Germany came into being in 1949 upon the basis of a lowering of the threshold of German history. Since then the populace and the politicians constantly remind themselves that they should bury what has passed, and that they were not guilty or responsible for what was done in the name of Hitler, the Nazis, or the Third Reich. Though rarely voiced, the notion is always present that only a small minority — Jews — have some kind of veto over this treatment of German history and the German moral fabric of today.

This so-called "denial" of the German memory does not conflict with the existence and the legitimacy of the Federal Republic of Germany (FRG). However, it does inhibit the growing expression of a political patriotism which is being supported by a larger and larger segment of the population. (For a more detailed analysis of German patriotism, see Walter Laqueur's article in the Epilogue section.) Nationalism and patriotism are generally acceptable in any country, but in Germany they are tinged by the atrocities committed by the Third Reich.

This, then, pits Germans against Jews. The Jews will never be able to erase from their memory the traumatic experience of the German effort to annihilate them — in all European countries. The Germans, on the other hand, want their memory, upon which they would base their contemporary society, not to include the actions of the Third Reich or their murders of 6 million Jews.

The visit to Bitburg encapsulated all three of these themes. Future social and political historians will undoubtedly question why President Reagan agreed to a state visit the outcome of which was doomed from the start. But, then, social and political historians do not make up the agendas of visiting heads of state — politicans do.

While President Reagan and Chancellor Kohl acted out of motives of political compromise, there were luminaries in this tragedy who found themselves in a role not of their choosing.

Chief among these was the U.S. ambassador to the Federal Republic of Germany, Arthur Burns. An elder statesman completing his tour of duty and facing the final chapter in his long and distinguished career in government, he realized at the outside the complications in the assumptions on which the Bitburg visit was based. Ambassador Burns has long been respected by those in government service. Indeed, his service in West Germany had earned him the highest marks from all of Germany's political leaders, including respect and admiration from the former chancellor, Helmut Schmidt.

The ambassador was deeply affected by the intended visit. Born in Romania, and a Jew well-versed in Yiddish, he was unable to make his peace with the visit, nor was he able to persuade the president to reconsider the political decision. As the president's representative in West Germany, he knew that opposition from him would not be in the best interests of the United States.

Possibly, as he outlines in his article in this book, no other single person might have been in the position to discourage the president from the Bitburg visit. His decision not to oppose the president still haunts him.

Another ambassador to toss and turn at night pondering his role in the Bitburg affair, Yitzhak Ben Ari, was under the strict instructions of the Israeli government to participate in the ceremonies at Bergen-Belsen, as he explains in his story.

Thus, at the ceremony were two Jewish ambassadors, whose inner drive was to oppose the visits on political and moral grounds, but who had to attend because of dictates from their respective governments — while around them Jews and non-Jews demonstrated.

A third luminary in this scenario was President of the Federal Republic of Germany Richard von Weizsaecker. Although of the same political party as Chancellor Kohl, his frame of reference is too broad for him not to clash with Kohl over the responsibility of Germany for the actions of the Third Reich. As can be seen in his speech to the Bundestag and others (in this book), he accepts that Germany's past is most relevant to the present German political culture. This former mayor of Berlin, educated in religion and contemporary politics, was also faced with a moral dilemma that reached into his childhood and one which involved his family.

As a young man, von Weizsaecker had defended his father, Ernst von Weizsaecker, the one-time director-general of the Ministry of Foreign Affairs of the Third Reich and later German ambassador to the Vatican, against the charge of responsibility for crimes committed by the Nazis. Although there was no evidence linking him with any direct participation in Nazi crimes, he was found guilty.

This experience in personal and collective guilt so early in his political life left an indelible mark upon him. His call for understanding, tolerance, and historical responsibility from his fellow Germans was stated unequivocally in his March 2, 1986 speech during Brotherhood Week, which can be found in the Epilogue.

This book is long. Maybe to some minds too long. Yet I felt that such a subject, because of its one-time-only nature, should be as far-reaching as possible, gathering all the information together — the magazine stories, newspaper articles, cartoons. I found that many leading Jews and non-Jews had important views to express. This is not a work on the Holocaust, but on a specific type of international conflict.

To make the perusal of the material as clear and easy as possible, I have divided the book into several sections.

The first part covers the chronological development of the decision made by the two state leaders. The second part concerns the response of President Reagan and Chancellor Kohl and other participants in the two ceremonies. In the third part, the three issues are gathered together in the numerous speeches, debates, and analyses. The last part covers the response on a geographical basis.

After the reader has gone through the material, he or she will be in a much better position to face the question I have wrestled with since I first heard of the proposed visit to Bitburg. Should a president and his advisers have an intense dialogue before decisions of state are made, and should there be intense political mobilization to help change the mind of a president? Presidential decisions must at all times be in the best interests of national goals. When a decision collides with moral principles, is there a time when the president must act immorally?

The Effect Kohl Desired...

... Was a handshake of reconciliation with President Reagan before a World War II memorial similar to the one he exchanged with French President Francois Mitterrand (left) at a ceremony for the war dead in Verdun. (For what happened at Bitburg, see page 166.)

Part I

Planning A Reconciliation Across The Graves

In the contemporary history of international summits, there is none that went astray with so much publicity as when President Reagan accepted the invitation to visit the Federal Republic of Germany (West Germany) in May 1985.

The mistake was in the selection of a military cemetery in the small town of Bitburg as a site for a ceremonious "act of reconciliation" between the United States and West Germany.

Much hot air was generated between Bonn and Washington before it was decided to hold the wreath-laying ceremony at the cemetery instead of at Dachau, a German concentration camp.

This was a tragic and foolish choice, it turned out, because within a few days it was determined that no American soliders were buried at Bitburg, but there were 47 or 49 graves of the infamous Waffen SS. (See Chapter 1 for the buildup of criticism).

While it would be diffiult to deny that some of the American criticism was of a partisan nature, overall both pro- and anti-Reagan factions joined in a call for the president to cancel Bitburg from his agenda. (See examples in Chapter 20). This was particularly true of politicians in general and the Congress in particular. Thus, Senate Resolution 143 of April 26, 1985, commends the president for this goal of reconciliation, but requests him not to journey to Bitburg. The same resolution in the House, No. 130, , was passed on April 29 by 325 votes. Congressman Dante Fascell attempted to inject specific wording calling upon the president not to visit Bitburg. In this form the motion was declined. Although it is difficult at this time to estimate the political price Republican senators and representatives will pay, their support of a bipartisan condemnation of a decision by President Reagan is without precedent during his six years in office. (See Chapter 3.)

Even those who would normally be supportive of any action by the president did not all line up behind him this time. (See Chapter 4 for a response from veterans' groups.)

While the focus on a cemetery that contined graves of those who were responsible for the deaths of millions of Jews was not regarded as an indication of anti-Semitism on the part of President Reagan, the Jewish press and intellectuals were outraged. (See Chapter 4.)

A brief survey of Reagan's political career reveals no specific actions that might hint of any animosity toward Jews or the Holocaust. During his tenure in the White House, Reagan has twice received Austrian Nazi hunter Simon Wiesenthal and has participated in several Holocaust ceremonies at the White House. Therefore, one can only conjecture that the erroneous statements made about German responsiblity for World War II spoke more about his lack of sensitivity and limited proficiency in dealing with this subject than of any prejudice disclosed to the world. (See the article by Morris B. Abram.)

Still, there is a haunting question: Why did the president not drop Bitburg from his itinerary once he knew of the double fact that the cemetery contained no graves of American soldiers and did contain graves of members of the Waffen SS?

A look at the previous U.S. Administrations and their dealings with West Germany might provide a clue. Chancellor Helmut Schmidt was re-elected in 1976 on the strength of his statement in the Bundestag that it was his advice to President Ford — that the U.S. administration not abandon New York City — that saved that city from bankruptcy. So highly was this coziness with Washington regarded that he won by one vote when he was expected to lose badly. This coziness, however, was not carried over into the term of the Carter administration, when Schmidt allegedly called Zbigniew Brzezinski "ZBig" and Brzezinski would not refer to the chancellor by title.

Whatever the conflict between the personalities, it was the overall relationship between Bonn and Washington that mattered. And this, too, was not entirely successful. When President Carter was planning to station neutron weapons in West Germany as a deterrent to Soviet superiority in Europe, he needed the approval of the West German Bundestag. After Schmidt had achieved this goal and thereby demonstrated his loyalty, Carter abandoned the plan without first informing the chancellor.

It was perceived that the U.S. administration neither felt any need to reward the loyalty of the chancellor nor regarded him highly.

This set of circumstances must have been at the back of Reagan's mind when he resisted the pressure to back off from visiting Bitburg. Needing West German support for "Star Wars," Reagan could not afford to antagonize the chancellor. Moreover, Reagan had not yet received the backing of Congress. A unified European Support of "Star Wars" would ensure congressional endorsement.

The chancellor's role in representing European support seems highlighted when one considers that the CDU/CSU-FDP coalition in the Bundestag had passed a resolution calling for government support for free "space." Kohl had already officially stated that Europe must be able to participate in the program upon which Reagan would hinge his two terms in the White House. (The fact that such participation would also furnish West German firms — such as Zeiss and Leitz — with several hundreds of millions of dollars for work In optics and electronics was also a factor.) Reagan, therefore, could not upset his major supporter in West Germany and Europe.

The matter of West German support hung especially in the balance, because at the same time, leading West German politicans such as Minister of Foreign Affairs Genscher and former Chancellor Willi Brandt went to Moscow to discuss non-"Star Wars" arrangements for European security.

These facts must have all been under consideration when the President made the fateful decision to go ahead with his planned visit to Bitburg. (See Chapter 6 for the reaction in Bonn.)

Chapter 1

The Eye Of The Hurricane

President Will Not Go To Concentration Camp: "German Guilt [is] Unnecessary," He Says
March 21, 1985

(After announcing plans to make a state visit to the Federal Republic of Germany [West Germany] to commemorate the end of World War II, President Reagan responded to reporters' questions at a Washington news conference as to why he would not visit a Nazi concentration camp.)

Q: Mr. President, would you tell us why you decided not to visit a Nazi concentration camp when you make your trip to Germany in May commemorating V-E Day?

A: Yes. I'll tell you. I feel very strongly that this time, in commemorating the end of that great war, that instead of reawakening the memories and so forth, and the passions of the time, that maybe we should observe this day as the day when, 40 years ago, peace began and friendship, because we now find ourselves allied and friends of the countries that we once fought against, and that we, it'd be almost a celebration of the end of an era and the coming into what has now been some 40 years of peace for us. And I felt that, since the German people have very few alive that remember even the war, and certainly none of them who were adults and participating in any way, and they do, they have a feeling and a guilt feeling that's been imposed upon them. And I just think it's unnecessary. I think they should be recognized for the democracy that they've created and the democratic principles they now espouse.

Q: If I could just follow that up. Has the West German Government asked you to take one position or another on it?

A: No. But in talking, just informally some time ago with Chancellor Kohl and others, and all felt the same way—that if we could observe this as the beginning of peace and friendship between us. All right.

President Explains Purpose Of West German Visit

The New York Times
April 13, 1986

By Bernard Weinraub

SANTA BARBARA, CALIF. — The White House, facing growing protests about a plan by President Reagan to honor German soldiers killed in World War II, said today that a visit to a military cemetery in West Germany was under review.

The disclosure came as veterans' groups such as the American Legion joined Jewish organizations in protest against Mr. Reagan's plan to recognize the German war dead.

No Allied Cemetery Visit

Mr. Reagan has no similar plans to visit an Allied war cemetery when he goes to Europe next month. What especially stirred anger about the announcement of the visit was that it followed Mr. Reagan's decision several weeks ago not to visit the Nazi concentration camp at Dachau.

Larry Speakes, the White House spokesman, speaking to reporters today in Santa Barbara, noted Mr. Reagan's "long and deeply emotional involvement in the Holocaust remembrances over the years."

Mr. Reagan, who is on vacation near here, issued a statement that said, "While we remember the past with deep sorrow, we must look to the future with a firm resolve that it will never happen again."

Elie Wiesel, chairman of the United States Holocaust Council, said in a statement today that he had called an emergency session for Monday in New York to discuss the President's trip. He said he was convening the meeting as a result of calls from members and others.

Mr. Wiesel, who is to be awarded the Congressional Gold Medal at a White House ceremony next Friday in recognition of his work as a writer and scholar on the Holocaust, said:

"I cannot believe that the President, whom I have seen crying at a Holocaust remembrance ceremony, would visit a German military cemetery and refuse to visit Dachau or any other concentration camp."

"Were it not for the observance of Passover," he added, the council meeting "would take place today."

"I am baffled by this announcement," Mr. Wiesel said of the cemetery visit. "I know that the President is a sensitive man and I do not understand how he could show such insensitivity. Knowing him as a person, I must conclude that the decision was influenced by his advisers. I do not know who they are or what their motives are, but I am sure that it is the wrong advice."

In Washington, James E. Witek, director of the capital office of the American Legion, the nation's largest veterans' organization with 2.6 million members, said in a statement that the group was "disappointed" in the President's plans to visit the cemetery.

"Honoring German war dead, while ignoring the thousands of Allied war dead who fought there and the millions of European Jews who were victims of the Third Reich, has nothing to do with reconciliation," he said.

Mr. Speakes, discussing the President's decision not to go to Dachau, said today that Mr. Reagan thought such a visit would "send the wrong signal" to Germans and that the Presidential trip to Europe in May was designed to emphasize the "spirit of reconciliation" between the United States and Germany.

White House officials indicated that a decision may be made early next week to alter the cemetery visit. Some Administration officials, who themselves voiced dismay about the planned cemetery visit, said the White House would be watching for signs of continuing protests before a decision was made.

In response to questions, Mr. Speakes said: "The President's schedule is, as always, on any trip, under review. It always has been. It will be reviewed periodically."

Another White House official said meetings were held today in Santa Barbara and at the White House to discuss alternatives to the visit, which was announced Thursday.

"We've got some real problems with this one," a White House official said. "It was badly thought out."

Menachem Rosensaft, founding chairman of the International Network of Children of Jewish Holocaust Survivors, representing about 5,000 sons and daughters of survivors, called Mr. Reagan's plans to visit the German cemetery a "calculated insult."

"While he refuses to go to pay homage to the victims of the Holocaust on the site of a Nazi concentration camp," Mr. Rosensaft said, "he now intends to go to a German military cemetery and lay a wreath on a grave of German soldiers who wore a swastika on their uniform and who died preventing Allied forces from liberating the death camps."

Mr. Speakes, in his comments to reporters, emphasized Mr. Reagan's "sensitivity" and "commitment" to the remembrance of the Holocaust.

Mr. Speakes said that Secretary of State George P. Schultz planned to attend Holocaust memorial events in Israel next month, and that the United States Ambassador to Bonn, Arthur F. Burns, would visit the Bergen-Belsen concentration camp in a ceremony on April 21 attended by Chancellor Helmut Kohl.

At the Foreign Ministry in Bonn, officials said Michael K. Deaver, the deputy chief of staff who is in charge of overall planning for the President's trip to Europe, had recently visited the Bitburg cemetery twice with a West German planning group. The cemetery is near the Luxembourg border.

Kenneth J. Bialkin, chairman of the Conference of Presidents of Major American Jewish Organizations, termed the decision to visit the cemetery but not Dachau "deeply offensive."

"A new beginning in our relations with the new Germany is a laudable goal," he said in a statement, "but when the first step of that new beginning is taken in a way that diminishes Hitler's victims, including the millions of American and Allied soldiers who bled and died fighting the Nazi war machine, the result is a deep insult to the soul of remembrance."

In New York, Mayor Koch deplored Mr. Reagan's decision not to visit Dachau, but said it was "perfectly appropriate" for him to visit the German cemetery. If the President of West Germany visited the United States, he "might very well go to Arlington," the mayor said, "and similarly with any other country, whether we were on the same side or not."

"It's simply respect for the fallen dead," said Mr. Koch, who saw combat with the infantry in northern France and in the Rhineland in World War II and served as a denazification specialist in Bavaria after the war.

Bitburg On Reagan's West German Agenda

April 18, 1985

WASHINGTON — *Following is a segment of a question and answer session of broadcasters and editors with President Reagan at the White House today about his German trip, as transcribed by the White House.*

Q: Regarding the upcoming trip to West Germany, 53 Senators have signed a letter requesting that you drop the trip to the cemetery, and in light of this and wave of other opposition, would it damage German-American relations to seek some other gesture of reconciliation and drop the visit and, secondly, would you say that it was a failure of political analysis to realize the fallout that resulted from the itinerary as it was scheduled?

Reagan: The failure that I will admit to, and I realize now I should have listened to you — the failure that I will admit to is in the press conference I didn't completely answer the question as to why I have said no to an invitation to visit Dachau. And I realize now that I'd given those who were questioning me credit for knowing more than they knew about the situation.

Helmut Kohl, sometime ago, back, I guess, when we were celebrating or observing the Normandy landings last June, he and President Mitterand went to a military cemetery together in Verdun. Now, here were the representatives of the two countries that have been at odds in the War of 1870, the First World War, the Second World War. The impact on all of Europe was so great to see them standing together at this ceremony that Helmut Kohl told me about this and told me how deeply he felt about it.

Now, the summit places us in Bonn in Germany close to the time of the anniversary. And he invited me to accept an invitation to be state visitor following the summit meeting. And he suggested to me this visit, as he had done with Mitterrand, to a cemetery there.

'We Have a Base There'

The cemetery that was picked, Bitburg, was picked because at the same time, also, there has been a church service with our military at Bitburg — we have a base there and our Americans — and I'm going there and go to church with them and have lunch with them. And the Kohls will be with us also.

When the invitation to visit a concentration camp was offered, whether it was my confusion or the way in which it was done, I thought that the suggestion had come from an individual and was not a part of the state visit. And I thought there was no way that I, as the guest of the government at that point, could on my own take off and go someplace and, then, run the risk of appearing as if I was trying to say to the Germans, "Look what you did," and all of this when most of the people in Germany today weren't alive or were very small children when this was happening.

And I know the feeling they have. And I know this government that for 40 years — what [Kohl] asked me to do in the cemetery was that we should start this day now, observing this day as the day that 40 years ago the world took a sharp turn, an end to the hatred, an end to the obscenities of the persecution and all that took place.

'Our Staunchest Allies'

And today, after 40 years of peace, here we are, our staunchest Allies in that summit are the countries that were our enemies in World War II. Now, their leaders have come here and visited Arlington. They have — leaders from Germany, from Italy, from Japan. And this cemetery, we only found out later, someone dug up the fact, that there are about 30 graves of SS troops. These were the villains, as we know, that conducted the persecutions and all. But there are 2,000 graves there. And most of those, the average age is about 18. These were those young teenagers that were conscripted, forced into military service in the closing days of the Third Reich, when they were short of manpower, and we're the victor and they're there.

And it seemed to me that this could be symbolic, also, of saying — what I said about the — what this day should be. And let's resolve, in their presence, as well as in the presence of our own troops, that this must never happen again.

'Dachau Was Part of Itinerary'

Well, when the furor erupted and got as far as Germany, Helmut Kohl sent me cable. And the cable informed me that there was a mistake, that the Dachau was a part of the state itinerary, the planned trip. Well, I immediately communicated and said, "Fine, that's fine with me. If it is you, the government, that is inviting me to do this, I am more than happy to do it because I have said repeatedly, and I would like on that occasion to say again, the Holocaust must never be forgotten by any of us. And in not forgetting it, we should make it clear that we're determined the Holocaust must never take place again. And—

Q: Does that mean you're still going to Bitburg?

Reagan: I think that it would be very hurtful and all it would do is leave me looking as if I caved in in the face of some unfavorable attention. I think that there's nothing wrong with visiting that cemetery where those young men are victims of Nazism also, even though they were fighting in the German uniform, drafted into service to carry out the hateful wishes of the Nazis. They were victims, just as surely as the victims in the concentration camps. And I feel that there is much to be gained from this, and, in strengthening our relationship with the German people, who, believe me, live in constant penance, all these who have come along in these later years for what their predecessors did, and for which they're very ashamed.

No, I can't take any more. I'm told that I've run out of time.

Thank you all very much.

Reagan Awards Holocaust Writer Elie Wiesel Congressional Gold Medal

White House
April 19, 1985

(President Reagan presents the Congressional Medal of Achievement to United States Holocaust Memorial Council Chairman Elie Wiesel.)

Jewish people have just finished celebrating Passover, the holiday that marks the exodus from Egypt, the deliverance from slavery. But this week, we commemorate a nondeliverance, a time when exodus was refused, when the doors of refuge were closed and in their place came death. In the Passover narrative, the Haggadah, there is the phrase, "In every generation, they rise up against us to annihilate us." In the generation of the Holocaust, that annihilation nearly succeeded in Europe. Six million murdered, among them over a million children.

How does life continue in the face of this crime against humanity?

The survivors swore their oath, "Never again." And the American people also made that pledge, "Never again," and we've kept it. We kept it when we supported the establishment of the state of Israel, the refuge that the Jewish people lacked during the Holocaust, the dream of generations, the sure sign of God's hand in history. America will never waver in our support for that nation to which our ties of faith are unbreakable. To say "Never again," however, is not enough. When with Israel the United States reached out to help save Ethiopian Jewry we were also fulfilling our pledge. This was truly God's work.

The Future of Soviet Jewry

Today, we work on and on to help Soviet Jewry, which suffers from persecution, intimidations and imprisonment within Soviet borders. We will never relinquish our hope for their freedom and we will never cease to work for it. If the Soviet Union truly wants peace, truly wants friendship, then let them release Anatoly Shcharansky and free Soviet Jewry.

But our pledge was more than "Never again." It was also "Never forget." And we've kept that pledge, too. We kept that pledge when we established the Holocaust Memorial Commission and set the cornerstone for its museum. We keep that pledge when in our colleges and universities we teach each new generation of Americans the story of the Holocaust. And in our lives we keep that pledge when we privately in our own families and in our hearts remember.

From the ashes of the Holocaust emerged the miracle of Israel and another miracle — that the survivors began life again. They came to new lands, many to Israel and many, thank God, to America. They built new families and with each child gave us the greatest symbol of this faith in the future. They brought to us the eloquence of a people who, in surviving such suffering, asked only for the right to remember and be remembered. A people who did not permit themselves to descend into the pits of and quagmires of hatred but lifted themselves instead, and with them all of humankind, out of darkness, up toward a time when hatred is no more and all nations and all people are as one.

A Sharing of Grief

We who had not suffered the tragedy of the Holocaust directly shared their grief and mourned for their victims. We too prayed for a better future and a better world where all peoples and all nations would come together in peace and defense of humanity!

Today, there is a spirit of reconciliation between the peoples of the allied nations and the peoples of Germany and even between the soldiers who fought each other on the battlefields of Europe. That spirit must grow and be strengthened. As the people of Europe rebuilt their shattered lands, the survivors rebuilt their shattered lives, and they did so despite the searing pain. And we who are their fellow citizens have taken up their memories and tried to learn from them what we must do.

No one has taught us more than Elie Wiesel.

His life stands as a symbol. His life is testimony that the human spirit endures and prevails. Memory can fail us, for it can fade as the generations change. But Elie Wiesel has helped make the memory of the Holocaust eternal by preserving the story of the six million Jews in his works. Like the prophets whose words guide us to this day, his works will teach humanity timeless lessons. He teaches about despair, but also about hope. He teaches about our capacity to do evil, but also about the possibility of courage and resistance and about our capacity to sacrifice for a higher good. He teaches about death, but in the end he teaches about life.

Elie, we present you with this medal as an expression of our gratitude for your life's work.

In honoring Elie Wiesel, we thank him for a life that's dedicated to others. We pledge that he will never forget or that we will never forget that in many places in the world the cancer of anti-Semitism still exists. Beyond our fervent hopes and our anguished remembrance we must not forget our duty to those who perished, our duty to bring justice to those who perpetrated unspeakable deeds. And we must take action to root out the vestiges of anti-Semitism in America, to quash the violence-prone or hate groups even before they can spread their venom and destruction.

And let all of us, Jew and non-Jew alike, pledge ourselves today to the life of the Jewish dream, to a time when war is no more, when all nations live in peace, when each man, woman and child lives in the dignity that God intended.

On behalf of your fellow citizens, now let me sign this proclamation commemorating Jewish Heritage Week.

"Your Place Is With The Victims," Wiesel Tells Reagan

White House
April 19, 1985

By Elie Wiesel

(Elie Wiesel responds to President Reagan upon receiving the Congressional Gold Medal of Achievement at the White House.)

Mr. President, speaking of the conciliation, I was very pleased that we met before, so a stage of the conciliation has been set in motion between us. But then, we were never on two sides. We were on the same side. We were always on the side of justice, always on the side of memory, against the SS and against what they represent.

It was good talking to you, and I am grateful to you for the medal. But this medal is not mine alone. It belongs to all those who remember what SS killers have done to their victims.

It was given to me by the American people for my writings, teaching and for my testimony. When I write, I feel my invisible teachers standing over my shoulders, reading my words and judging their veracity. And while I feel responsible for the living, I feel equally responsible to the dead. Their memory dwells in my memory.

Forty years ago, a young man awoke and he found himself an orphan in an orphaned world. What have I learned in the last 40 years? Small things. I learned the perils of language and those of silence. I learned that in extreme situations when human lives and dignity are at stake, neutrality is a sin. It helps the killers, not the victims. I learned the meaning of solitude, Mr. President. We were alone, desperately alone.

Today is April 19, and April 19, 1943, the Warsaw Ghetto rose in arms against the onslaught of the Nazis. They were so few and so young and so helpless. And nobody came to their help. And they had to fight what was then the mightiest legion in Europe. Every underground received help except the Jewish underground. And yet they managed to fight and resist and push back those Nazis and their accomplices for six weeks. And yet the leaders of the free world, Mr. President, knew everything and did so little, or at least nothing specifically, to save Jewish children from death. You spoke of Jewish children, Mr. President. One million Jewish children perished. If I spent my entire life reciting their names, I would die before finishing the task.

Mr. President, I have seen children, I have seen them being thrown in the flames alive. Words, they die on my lips. So I have learned, I have learned, I have learned the fragility of the human condition.

And I am reminded of a great moral essayist. The gentle and forceful Abe Rosenthal, having visited Auschwitz, once wrote an extraordinary reportage about the persecution of Jews, and he called it, "Forgive them not, Father, for they knew what they did."

I have learned that the Holocaust was a unique and uniquely Jewish event, albeit with universal implications. Not all victims were Jews. But all Jews were victims. I have learned the danger of indifference, the crime of indifference. For the opposite of love, I have learned, is not hate, but indifference. Jews were killed by the enemy but betrayed by their so-called allies, who found political reasons to justify their indifference or passivity.

But I have also learned that suffering confers no privileges. It all depends what one does with it. And this is why survivors, of whom you spoke, Mr. President, have tried to teach their contemporaries how to build on ruins, how to invent hope in a world that offers none, how to proclaim faith to a generation that has seen it shamed and mutilated. And I believe, we believe, that memory is the answer, perhaps the only answer.

A few days ago, on the anniversary of the liberation of Buchenwald, all of us, Americans, watched with dismay and anger as the Soviet Union and East Germany distorted both past and present history.

Mr. President, I was there. I was there when American liberators arrived. And they gave us back our lives. And what I felt for them then nourishes me to the end of my days and will do so. If you only knew what we tried to do with them then. We who were so weak that we couldn't carry our own lives, we tried to carry them in triumph.

Mr. President, we are grateful to the American Army for liberating us. We are grateful to this country, the greatest democracy in the world, the freest nation in the world, the moral nation, the authority in the world. And we are grateful, especially, to this country for having offered us haven and refuge, and grateful to its leadership for being so friendly to Israel.

And, Mr. President, do you know that the Ambassador of Israel, who sits next to you, who is my friend, and has been for so many years, is himself a survivor? And if you knew all the causes we fought together for the last 30 years, you should be prouder of him. And we are proud of him.

And we are grateful, of course, to Israel. We are eternally grateful to Israel for existing. We needed Israel in 1948 as we need it now. And we are grateful to Congress for its continuous philosophy of humanism and compassion for the underprivileged.

And as for yourself, Mr. President, we are so grateful to you for being a friend of the Jewish people, for trying to help the oppressed Jews in the Soviet Union. And to do whatever we can to save Shcharansky and Abe Stolar and Iosif Begun and Sakharov and all the dissidents who need freedom. And of course, we thank you for your support of the Jewish state of Israel.

But, Mr. President, I wouldn't be the person I am, and you wouldn't respect me for what I am, if I were not to tell you also of the sadness that is in my heart for what happened during the last week. And I am sure that you, too, are sad for the same reasons.

What can I do? I belong to a traumatized generation. And to us, as to you, symbols are important. And furthermore, following our ancient tradition, and we are speaking about Jewish heritage, our tradition commands us "to speak truth to power."

So may I speak to you, Mr. President, with respect and admiration, of the events that happened?

We have met four or five times. And each time I came away enriched, for I know of your commitment to humanity.

And therefore I am convinced, as you have told us earlier when we spoke, that you were not aware of the presence of SS graves in the Bitburg cemetery. Of course you didn't know. But now we all are aware.

May I, Mr. President, if it's possible at all, implore you to do something else, to find a way, to find another way, another site? That place, Mr. President, is not your place. Your place is with the victims of the SS.

Oh, we know there are political and strategic reasons, but this issue, as all issues related to that awesome event, transcends politics and diplomacy.

The issue here is not politics, but good and evil. And we must never confuse them.

For I have seen the SS at work. And I have seen their victims. They were my friends. They were my parents.

Mr. President, there was a degree of suffering and loneliness in the concentration camps that defies imagination. Cut off from the world with no refuge anywhere, sons watched helplessly their fathers being beaten to death. Mothers watched their children die of hunger. And then there was Mengele and his selections. Terror, fear, isolation, torture, gas chambers, flames, flames rising to the heavens.

But, Mr. President, I know and I understand, we all do, that you seek reconciliation. And so do I, so do we. And I too wish to attain true reconciliation with the German people. I do not believe in collective guilt, nor in collective responsibility. Only the killers were guilty. Their sons and daughters are not.

And I believe, Mr. President, that we can and we must work together with them and with all people. And we must work to bring peace and understanding to a tormented world that, as you know, is still awaiting redemption.

I thank you, Mr. President.

April 15, 1945, Bergen-Belsen is liberated by the British. While this was not normally an ex-termination camp, in the 3 months prior to liberation 40,000 inmates of other camps were force-marched there. Tens of thousand of them died from diseases and epidemics prior to liberation—including Anne Frank; many more thousands died shortly after liberation.

Chapter 2

Political Reaction To The Gathering Storm—U.S.

A Congressman Voices Concern Over West German Visit
Washington, D. C.
April 12, 1985

The President
The White House
Washington, D. C.

Dear Mr. President:

I write out of profound concern for the well-being of our nation. The decision to drop a scheduled visit to a concentration camp and to visit a cemetery where many avowed fighters for the cause of Nazism are buried threatens to polarize citizens around the country.

One of the most noble foreign policy initiatives of our nation has been to build and strengthen an alliance with the Federal Republic of Germany. But a relationship which ignores reality is built on a shaky foundation.

It has been said that a majority of Germans today were not born and do not know the events that occurred on their native soil and neighboring conquered territory 40 years ago, and drawing attention to this tragedy will inflict undue guilt and reopen emotional wounds. However, Mr. President, millions live with a daily memory of horrors past. These include death camp survivors and liberators who share the emblazoned images of crematoriums, suffering, starvation, disease, torture, the stench of death, and the fearful eyes of crippled victims who had not yet been sent to "their final solution". Others, whether they be parents, siblings, children, distant relatives or coreligionists, are scarred and haunted by the grim realization of the planned extermination of their people.

As the elected leader of the most powerful democracy on earth, you have the unique opportunity to make a gesture and take a stand for all humanity. During your visit to Temple Hillel last fall, a synagogue in my district, you told those assembled that the living have a responsibility to keep alive the memory and the fate of those who perished. As you so appropriately noted, it is "the fundamental moral obligation" of those who remember the lessons of the Holocaust "to assure never again".

I respectfully urge you to reconsider this decision. As our moral burden is to bear witness and remember, I am certain you will heed the message of Yom Hashoa, the Day of Remembrance.

Sincerely,

Raymond J. McGrath
United States Representative

Senators Remind President of "Battle of the Bulge"
United States Senate
April 15, 1985

The President
The White House
Washington, D.C.

Dear Mr. President:

We wish to express to you our deep concern about your plan to visit the Bitburg military cemetery during your forthcoming German trip, while foregoing a visit to the site of the Dachau concentration camp.

As you know, the German soldiers interred at Bitburg fell during the 1944 Battle of the Bulge, a German offensive that cost 81,000 U.S. casualties of whom 19,000 were killed in action. The lead German element in that massive attack was the Sixth Panzer Army of the notorious Waffen SS, under the command of SS General Josef "Sepp" Dietrich. General Dietrich was subsequently convicted of war crimes, including responsibility for the massacre by SS troops of American prisoners-of-war at Malmedy, a town approximately thirty miles from Bitburg. According to published reports, at least thirty members of the Waffen SS are buried in the Bitburg cemetery.

Given the bitterness of the Battle of the Bulge, the atrocities it entailed, and the massive participation of the SS, we believe that a visit to Bitburg by an American President would be most unfortunate. We suggest that a more appropriate gesture of reconciliation be found.

In addition, we believe that congratulating our German friends on their great accomplishments of the past forty years does not preclude your memorializing the millions of innocent victims of the Nazi regime who died in the Holocaust. The monstrous crimes of the Nazis are a reality that cannot be forgotten, diminished or denied.

We strongly urge you, therefore, to alter your published itinerary so as to omit the Bitburg visit and to include in your schedule an event commemorating the Holocaust.

Sincerely,

Howard M. Metzenbaum
United States Senator

Co-signed, United States Senators:

Rudy Boschwitz	William Proxmire	Carl Levin
Christopher J. Dodd	Lowell P. Weicker, Jr.	Ernest F. Hollings
Dennis DeConcini	Arlen Specter	Wendell H. Ford
Jim Sasser	Robert C. Byrd	Lawton Chiles
J. Bennett Johnston	Spark M. Matsunaga	George J. Mitchell
John D. Rockefeller IV	Tom Harkin	Albèrt Gore, Jr.
Bill Bradley	Donald W. Riegle, Jr.	Lloyd Bentsen
Paul S. Sarbanes	Frank R. Lautenberg	Howell Heflin
Joseph R. Biden, Jr.	Max Baucus	Daniel K. Inouye
Charles E. Grassley	Gary Hart	David L. Boren
William S. Cohen	David Pryor	Jeff Bingaman
John C. Danforth	John F. Kerry	Alfonse D'Amato
Mark Andrews	John Glenn	Dave Durenberger
Paul Simon	Quentin N. Burdick	Mark O. Hatfield
Alan J. Dixon	John Melcher	Claiborne Pell
Alan Cranston	Edward M. Kennedy	Larry Pressler
Daniel Patrick Moynihan	Partick J. Leahy	J. James Exon
John C. Stennis		

Congressmen Suggest Bitburg Visit Dishonors U.S. Soldiers
Washington, D.C.
April 19, 1985

President Ronald Reagan
The White House
Washington, D.C.

Dear Mr. President:

We are writing with respect to your upcoming visit to Germany from April 30-May 10. Although we recognize your desire to work toward full reconciliation with our German aliies, we believe it is inappropriate to visit the cemetery in Bitburg where soldiers from the elite Nazi guard, the SS, are buried. We believe that a ceremony at this cemetery would be a dishonor to the American soldiers who fought to save the world from Hitler's deadly campaign, as well as for victims of the genocide perpetrated by the Nazis.

We feel that a ceremony to commemorate the death of even one individual who participated in the Nazi war crimes would denigrate the significance of your trip. As you know, many of us would have preferred that your original itinerary include a stop at the Dachau concentration camp, the site where tens of thousands of innocent victims lost their lives to the Nazis. However, a visit to such a site does not obviate the insult of the ceremony at Bitburg.

Reconciliation is a goal which all Americans can support. However, at the same time, we firmly believe that retaining our commitment to remembering the victims of this terrible period in history cannot be overshadowed. We fear that could easily be the result of the planned ceremony at Bitburg. The crimes which took place during the Holocaust are of such great magnitude that the United States, as the leader of the free world, must maintain a vigilant respect for those Americans and Europeans who lost their lives to the Nazis. Therefore, the act of laying a wreath at the tombs of the Waffen SS is a particular affront to countless Americans, and other people throughout the world, whose closest relatives and friends lost their lives during World War II. Therefore, we respectfully urge you to remove the Bitburg ceremony from your itinerary and replace it with a visit to a site which would signify your commitment to remembrance in addition to reconciliation.

Co-signed, United States Congressmen:

Robert A. Borski	Gary L. Ackerman	Anthony Beilenson
Les AuCoin	Edolphus Towns	Mickey Leland
William Lehman	Tom Lantos	Bill Lowery
Robert J. Mrazek	Lawrence J. Smith	Stephen J. Solarz

(see over)

(continued)

Ted Weiss
Cecil Heftel
William D. Ford
Richard A. Gephardt
Henry A. Waxman
Mario Biaggi
Sander M. Levin
Robert A. Roe
Ben Erdreich
Howard L. Berman
Robert A. Young
Bruce A. Morrison
Charles E. Schumer
Joseph P. Addabbo
Sala Burton
Norman F. Lent
Ron Wyden
Robert Garcia
John Bryant
Morris K. Udall
Peter H. Kostmayer
Barbara Boxer
Dan Glickman
Thomas Foglietta
Tony P. Hall
Ronald Coleman
Buddy Roemer

Joseph J. DioGuardi
Harry M. Reid
Joe Moakley
Barney Frank
Barbara A. Mikulski
Michael D. Barnes
Gerald D. Kleczka
Raymond J. MacGrath
Mel Levine
Ed Jenkins
Parren L. Mitchell
James L. Oberstar
Julian C. Dixon
Hamilton Fish
Jim Moody
Walter E. Fauntroy
Vic Fazio
Donald J. Pease
Albert G. Bustamante
Louis Stokes
James J. Howard
Robert G. Torricelli
James J. Florio
Jim Cooper
Howard Wolpe
Gerry Sikorski

Lane Evans
Patricia Schroeder
Sam Gejdenson
Buddy McKay
Bill Richardson
Matthew McHugh
James Scheuer
Edward Feighan
Matthew Martinez
Alan Wheat
Benjamin A. Gilman
Thomas J. Downey
Paul Kanjorski
Don Edwards
Marcy Kaptur
Bob Edgar
Mike Synar
Wyche Fowler
Barbara Kennelly
Henry Gonzalez
Tony Coehlo
John Porter
Tom Manton
Gerry E. Studds
Jim Saxton
Charles Hayes

House of Representatives
Washington, D.C.

"Visit is a Travesty of Reconciliation."
U.S. Senate
April 26, 1985

By Senator Edward M. Kennedy

(Senator Edward Kennedy rises in U.S. Senate to urge President Reagan not to visit Bitburg.)

I join Senator Specter, Senator Metzenbaum, Senator Cranston, and others in asking the Senate to adopt our resolution which urges the President not to visit the German military cemetery in Bitburg. It is now two weeks since the plan to make this visit was announced, and the outcry against it across the country continues unabated—and with good reason.

President Reagan's plan to lay a wreath at the Bitburg military cemetery contradicts the important purpose of his trip to Europe. It makes a travesty of reconciliation. It reopens old wounds, offends American veterans who fought bravely in the war, and dishonors the memory of the millions of victims of the Nazis who died in the Holocaust.

April is a month of anniversaries for the Jewish people. We remember how, in April, 1943 the courageous citizens of the Warsaw Ghetto rose up in defiance of their fate; against all odds, they fought for themselves, for their families already gone, for their dignity as human beings. This April, we also commemorate the liberation of the Nazi concentration camps 40 years ago. And in April we honor not only the martyrdom of the millions of men, women and children who died at the hand of the Nazis, but we celebrate the miracle that emerged from the horror of the Holocaust, the miracle of April, 1948, the birth of the state of Israel.

So sadly, in this month of major anniversaries, we are dismayed by the President's persistent plan to visit the German military cemetery at Bitburg. In the past, the President has demonstrated both understanding and commitment to the Jewish people. Now I hope that, while there is still time, he will heed the eloquent words of Elie Wiesel at the White House last Friday, when he told the President that Bitburg was not his place.

We all know the reasons why Bitburg is not the President's place. In the words of the Passover song, *Dayenu*, any one of these reasons would have been enough. The 19,000 Americans killed and the 77,000 wounded during the Battle of the Bulge would have been enough. Nazi SS graves in the cemetery would have been enough. And Chancellor Kohl's declaration Monday that Germans bear a "never-ending shame" for the Holocaust, the greatest crime in history, would have been enough.

Listen to the names of some of the cities and towns where Jews lived and died during the Holocaust: Warsaw, Kiev, Babi-Yar, Amsterdam, Lublin, Czernowitz, Ponary, Nuremberg, Staragradiska, Riga, Lvov, Bialistok, Vilna, Lodz, Kovno, Minsk, Radom.

And listen to the names of the death camps and the message they send to us across the years: Auschwitz, Buchenwald, Bergen-Belsen, Dachau, Majdanek, Treblinka, Landsberg, Flossenburg, Nordhausen, Torgau, Ohrdruf, Ravensbruck, Sachsenhausen, Lenta, Kaiserwald, Oranienbrug, Neuengamme, Papenburg, Stutthof, Grosfrosen, Mausenhausen, Ebensee, Theresienstadt, Sered, Malines, Westerborg, Drancy, Nantzweiler, Gurs, Jasenovak, Zeman, Plaszou, Chelmno, Sobibor, Belzec.

These are haunting names whose history is forever embedded in the soul of humanity. They are names that will stand for all eternity as symbols of the tyranny and massive cruelty of the Nazis and their systematic and brutal attempt to exterminate the Jewish people and other minorities.

In this time of remembrance, all of us find it difficult to believe that the Bitburg visit would ever have been scheduled in the first place if adequate information about the cemetery had been available. We have seen the press reports, for example, that the SS graves were covered with snow at the time the first preliminary visit to the cemetery was made by the planning team.

Since the outcry about the trip began, we wonder whether other possibilities for the visit have been adequately explored. A number of worthwhile alternatives have been suggested. The President could attend a service in St. Paul's Church in Frankfurt, which President Kennedy visited in 1963, where there is a memorial to anti-Nazi Germans. He could go to the Berlin prison where Hitler brutally executed his German opponents. Or he could lay a wreath on the grave of Konrad Adenauer to recognize the new Germany that arose under the historic postwar leadership of that chancellor.

All Americans applaud the spirit of reconciliation that has flourished over the past four decades between the peoples of the United States and the other Allied nations and the people of West Germany. That spirit must continue to grow and be strengthened; but there is no inconsistency between reconciliation and remembrance, and reconciliation at the expense of remembrance is wrong.

The President made a serious mistake when he scheduled the visit to the military cemetery, and he is making an even worse mistake by refusing to cancel it. I hope that he will heed the resolution we are offering today, and revise his visit in accord with the true purpose of what should be a truly historic trip.

All of us are survivors, and as survivors we understand that there are times when faith and hope are difficult. In the words of the *Kaddish*, the ancient Hebrew prayer of sanctification for the dead:

> May there be abundant peace from Heaven and life, for us and for all Israel. He who creates peace in the High places, may he create peace for us and for all Israel.

In the spirit of these words, it is my sincere hope that the President can find the courage and compassion to comprehend the feelings of all those people who are deeply concerned by his plan to visit Bitburg.

82 Senators Urge Reagan to Cancel His Cemetery Visit

The New York Times
April 27, 1985

Senate Adopts Resolution

WASHINGTON — The Senate overwhelmingly urged President Reagan today to cancel his planned visit to a German military cemetery.

By a voice vote, the senate adopted a resolution co-sponsored by 82 legislators hailing the reconciliation between the United States and West Germany but adding, "The President should reassess his planned itinerary during his forthcoming trip to the Federal Republic of Germany."

Instead of visiting the military cemetery at Bitburg, the resolution said, Mr. Reagan "should visit a symbol of German democracy."

Opposition Has Grown

The unusual Senate resolution came amid a growing chorus of opposition to Mr. Reagan's planned visit on May 5 to the cemetery, where 49 SS soldiers are buried among 2,000 German war dead. The outcry against the cemetery visit has embarrassed the White House, strained relations between the United States and West Germany and stirred protests from Jewish groups, veterans' organizations and others.

The Senate resolution followed by a day a letter signed by 257 of the 435 members of the House of Representatives urging Helmut Kohl, the West German chancellor, to withdraw the cemetery invitation. Mr. Kohl has refused to do so, and Mr. Reagan's aides have said he will not cancel the visit unless Mr. Kohl takes the first step and withdraws the invitation.

In Bonn, the Kohl Government said it would not be swayed by the letter from the House.

Wiesenthal Invitation Reported

Also today, Rabbi Marvin Hier, dean of the Simon Wiesenthal Center in Los Angeles, said the United States embassy in Vienna had invited Mr. Wiesenthal to accompany President Reagan to the concentration camp at Bergen-Belsen and the cemetery at Bitburg. Mr. Wiesenthal, the hunter of Nazi war criminals, turned down the invitation according to Rabbi Hier.

"It makes little difference that the SS soldiers buried at Bitburg were not concentration camp guards," Rabbi Hier said, explaining Mr. Wiesenthal's decision. "They did wear the uniform of the SS. Mr. Wiesenthal did not in any way want to sanction such a visit."

The nonbinding resolution in the Senate included among its co-sponsors the Republican majority leader, Bob Dole of Kansas.

The resolution did not specifically mention the Bitburg cemetery, apparently so as not to embarrass Mr. Reagan and to gather as many Republican signatures as possible among the 100 senators.

"The emphasis has not been any criticism of the President," said Mr. Dole, a World War II veteran, whose right arm was disabled in combat against German soldiers. "It is an expression by the Senate that we should pay tribute to the memories of millions of innocent civilians and Allied soldiers who suffered and died at the hands of the Nazis."

"The record is clear this is not an effort to jump on the President," he added.

Virtually all the debate on the resolution, which was sponsored by Senator Howard M. Metzenbaum, Democrat of Ohio, centered on urging Mr. Kohl to withdraw the invitation. Some senators asked Mr. Kohl "to take our President off the hook."

"The message is to the head of West Germany, Chancellor Kohl," said Senator Alan Cranston, Democrat of California. "The message should be very, very clear now that if we do not get that cooperation, unfortunate damage will be done to the relations of our two countries.

"I don't think the President of the United States should go to a German cemetery to honor German soldiers who died killing American soldiers in the service of the greatest tyrant of our times, Adolf Hitler," Mr. Cranston said. "That there are graves of SS troops in that cemetery makes an unsavory act intolerable."

At one point, Mr. Cranston said: "Are Germany's ties to the United States and the West so weak, so tenuous, so insecure and uncertain that Germany's price for reassurance is the humiliation of our President?

"Chancellor Kohl! Free President Reagan! Let our President go!" he said.

Senator Edward M. Kennedy, Democrat of Massachusetts, intoned the names of concentration camps where Jews and others were killed by the SS and German troops. "President Reagan made a mistake when he scheduled the visit," the senator said, "and he will be making an even bigger mistake by refusing to cancel it.

"The trip to Bitburg cemetery contradicts the important purpose of his visit," Mr. Kennedy said. "It opens old wounds at the expense of reconciliation."

William S. Cohen, Republican of Maine, called the decision "a grievous mistake," adding, "Memories run very deep."

Bergen-Belsen Protest Planned

Meanwhile, Menachem Rosensaft, founding chairman of the International Network of Children of Jewish Holocaust Survivors, comprising more than 5,000 sons and daughters, said plans were under way to stage a protest against the President's visit to the Bergen-Belsen concentration camp, which is planned for the same day as his visit to Bitburg.

"We want to make sure we do not become confused with anti-American demonstrations at Bitburg," said Mr. Rosensaft, who was born in Bergen-Belsen after the war. "If the President pays homage to both the victims of the Holocaust and German soldiers who participated in any way in perpetrating the Holocaust, especially the SS, I believe he will be violating the sanctity of the mass graves of Bergen-Belsen."

Kenneth J. Bialkin, chairman of the Conference of Presidents of Major American Jewish Organizations, an umbrella group of 38 national groups, said in a statement today, "We are dismayed by the statement of Chancellor Kohl yesterday, which can only be interpreted as still another effort to rehabilitate the Waffen SS."

Mr. Bialkin was referring to the fact that Mr. Kohl, a Christian Democrat, quoted Kurt Schumacher, who headed the Social Democratic Party after the war. According to the chancellor, Mr. Schumacher said that of the 900,000 members of the Waffen SS, "hundreds of thousands were, without any effort on their part, conscripted into or transferred to the Waffen SS" and had not committed crimes. Mr. Schumacher had therefore called for rehabilitation of "the vast majority" of them.

Mr. Bialkin said: "We cannot believe that President Reagan's legitimate concern for reconciliation with a new and democratic Germany includes forgiveness of the SS. Chancellor Kohl's latest statement adds fuel to the fire over the Bitburg visit and offers further reason for President Reagan to cancel his appearance there."

Following is a list of the 82 senators who were co-sponsors of a resolution urging President Reagan to reconsider his trip to the Bitburg cemetery.

Democrats

Baucus, Mont.	Dixon, Ill.	Johnston, La.	Nunn, Ga.
Bentsen, Tex.	Dodd, Conn.	Kennedy, Mass.	Pell, R.I.
Biden, Del.	Eagleton, Mo.	Kerry, Mass.	Proxmire, Wis.
Bingaman, N.M.	Exon, Neb.	Lautenberg, N.J.	Pryor, Ark.
Borem, Okla.	Ford, Ky.	Leahy, Vt.	Riegle, Mich.
Bradley, N.J.	Glenn, Ohi	Levin, Mich.	Rockefeller, W.Va.
Bumpers, Ark.	Gore, Tenn.	Long, La.	Sarbanes, Md.
Burdick, N.D.	Harkin, Iowa	Matsunaga, Hawaii	Sasser, Tenn.
Byrd, W. Va.	Hart, Colo.	Melcher, Mont.	Simon, Ill.
Chiles, Fla.	Heflin, Ala.	Metzenbaum, Ohio	Stennis, Miss.
Cranston, Calif.	Hollings, S.C.	Mitchell, Me.	Zorinsky, Neb.
DeConcini, Ariz.	Inouye, Hawaii	Moynihan, N.Y.	

Republicans

Abdnor, S.D.	Domenici, N.M.	Kasten, Wis.	Quayle, Ind.
Andrews, N.D.	Gorton, Wash.	Lugar, Ind.	Roth, Del.
Boschwitz, Minn.	Grassley, Iowa.	Mathias, Md.	Rudman, N.H.
Chafee, R.I.	Hatfield, Ore.	Mattingly, Ga.	Simpson, Wyo.
Cohen, Me.	Hawkins, Fla.	McConnell, Ky.	Spector, Pa.
D'Amato, N.Y.	Hecht, Nev.	Murkowski, Alaska	Warner, Va.
Danforth, Mo.	Heinz, Pa.	Nickles, Okla.	Weicker, Conn.
Denton, Ala.	Humphrey, N.H.	Packwood, Ore.	Wilson, Ca.
Dole, Kan.	Kassebaum, Kan.	Pressler, S.D.	

56

Please Withdraw Invitation, Chancellor Kohl
Washington, DC.
April 27, 1985

His Excellency Helmut Kohl
Chancellor
Federal Republic of Germany
Bonn

Dear Chancellor Kohl,

We are writing in regard to President Ronald Reagan's upcoming trip to West Germany from April 30-May 10. While we share your belief that the U.S. Government should send a signal to the German people of friendship and peace between our two nations, we believe that the President's plan to lay a wreath at Bitburg military cemetery has instead had the unintended effect of reopening painful wounds here in the United States.

The decision to visit Bitburg cemetery has become the most embarrassing incident of President Reagan's four and one half years in office. In the United States, it has awakened deep and bitter emotions among thousands of Holocaust survivors, and has elicited the unqualified condemnation of veterans and Jewish groups. We understand that it has become a highly-charged issue in West Germany as well.

The sentiment felt throughout our nation was eloquently stated by Elie Weisel in his moving statement at the White House last week. We concur with Mr. Weisel's view that the President was unaware of the fact that 47 SS officers were buried at Bitburg when the decision was made to visit the site. Further, we believe that the President would not have made such a decision if he had known this fact. It is clear to us that the major remaining justification for the President's visit to Bitburg is his fear of offending the German people.

Clearly, this a difficult problem which evokes strong emotion from all parties involved. We believe, however, that an opportunity remains to deal with this incident in a manner which will address the needs and aspirations of all involved.

We therefore implore you to intervene in this matter by withdrawing your government's invitation to the President to visit Bitburg cemetery. We ask you instead to extend an invitation to President Reagan to visit some other appropriate site to pay respect to the German people. Such a move would satisfy our collective aim of fostering peace and understanding between our two nations, and will send a strong signal throughout the world that neither the Government of the United

States nor the Government of West Germany intends to condone or forget the barbarity of the Nazi regime.

Sincerely,

Robert J. Mrazek, M.C.
House of Representatives
United States Representative

Co-signed, United States Congressmen:

ALABAMA
Democrats — Erdreich, Shelby.

ALASKA
Republican — Young.

ARIZONA
Democrat — Udall.
Republicans — Kolbe, McCain.

ARKANSAS
Democrats — Alexander, Anthony, Robinson.

CALIFORNIA
Democrats — Bates, Bellenson, Brown, Burton, Coelho, Dixon, Fazio, Hawkins, Lantos, Levine, Martinez, Miller, Mineta, Panetta, Roybal, Stark, Torres, Waxman.
Republicans — Dannemeyer, Dornan, Dreier, Hunter, Lowery, Lungren, Packard, Thomas, Zschau.

COLORADO
Democrats — Schroeder, Wirth.
Republican — Kramer.

CONNECTICUT
Democrats — Geldenson, Kennelly, Morrison.
Republican — Johnson.

DELAWARE
Democrat — Carper.

FLORIDA
Democrats — Fuqua, Hutto, Lehman, MacKay, Mica, Nelson, Smith.
Republicans — Billrakis, Mack, McCollum.

GEORGIA
Democrats — Darden, Hatcher, Jenkins, Rowland, Thomas.
Republican — Gingrich.

GUAM
Republican — Blaz

HAWAII
Democrat — Akaka.

IDAHO
Democrat — Stallings.

ILLINOIS
Democrats — Annunzio, Bruce, Collins, Durbin, Evans, Gray, Libinski, Russo, Savage, Yates.

Republicans — Crane, Hyde, Martin, Porter.

INDIANA
Democrats — Jacobs, Sharp.
Republicans — Burton, Myers.

IOWA
Republicans — Leach, Lightfoot, Tauke.

KANSAS
Democrats — Glickman, Slattery
Republicans — Roberts.

KENTUCKY
Democrats — Hubbard, Mazzoli, Perkins.
Republicans — Hopkins, Rogers.

LOUISIANA
Democrats — Boggs, Breaux, Roemer, Tauzin.
Republican — Livingston.

MAINE
Republicans — McKernan, Snowe.

MARYLAND
Democrats — Dyson, Hoyer, Mikulski, Mitchell.
Republican — Bentley.

MASSACHUSETTS
Democrats — Boland, Donnelly, Early, Frank, Markey, Mavroules, Moakley.
Republican — Conte.

MICHIGAN
Democrats — Bonior, Carr, Conyers, Crockett, Ford, Hertel, Kildee, Levin, Traxler, Wolpe.
Republicans — Broomfield, Davis, Pursell, Sillander, Vander Jagt.

MINNESOTA
Democrats — Sabo, Sikorski.
Republican — Weber.

MISSOURI
Democrats — Clay, Gephardt, Skelton, Volkmer, Wheat, Young.
Republican — Emerson.

MONTANA
Democrat — Williams.
Republican — Marlenee.

NEBRASKA
Republican — Daub.

NEW HAMPSHIRE
Republican — Gregg.

NEW JERSEY
Democrats — Dwyer, Floria, Howard, Torricelli.
Republicans — Courter, Gallo, Rinaldo, Saxton, Smith.

NEW MEXICO
Democrat — Richardson.

NEW YORK
Democrats — Ackerman, Biaggi, Downey, Garcia, LaFaice, Manton, McHugh, Mrazek, Nowak, Owens, Rangel, Scheuer, Schumer, Solarz, Stratton, Towns, Weiss.
Republicans — Boehlert, Carney, DioGuardi, Gilman, Green, Lent, Martin, McGrath, Molinari, Solomon.

NORTH CAROLINA
Democrats — Hefner, Valentine.
Republicans — Cobey, Hendon.

NORTH DAKOTA
Democrat — Dorgan.

OHIO
Democrats — Applegate, Eckart, Feighan, Hall, Oakar, Pease, Stokes, Traficant.
Republicans — DeWine, Kasich, McEwen, Miller, Oxley, Regula.

OKLAHOMA
Democrats — English, Jones, McCurdy, Synar.

OREGON
Democrats — Weaver, Wyden.
Republican — R. Smith.

PENNSYLVANIA
Democrats — Borski, Coyne, Edgar, Gaydos, Gray, Kolter, Kostmayer, Walgren.
Republicans — Clinger, Coughlin, Goodling, McDade, Ridge, Ritter, Walker.

SOUTH CAROLINA
Democrat — Spratt.
Republican — Harinett.

SOUTH DAKOTA
Democrat — Daschle.

(see over)

(continued)

TENNESSEE
Democrats — Boner, Cooper, Jones.

TEXAS
Democrats — Andrews, Bryant, Bustamante, Coleman, Frost, Gonzalez, Leath, Leland, Ortiz, Pickle, Stenholm.
Republican — Boulter.

UTAH
Republican — Nielson.

VERMONT
Republican — Jeffords.

VIRGINIA
Democrats — Boucher, Olin, Sisisky.

VIRGIN ISLANDS
Democrat — deLugo.

WASHINGTON
Democrats — Bonker, Dicks, Foley, Lowry, Swift.

Republicans — Chandler, Miller.

WEST VIRGINIA
Democrats — Mollohan, Rahall, Staggers.

WISCONSIN
Democrats — Aspin, Moody.
Republicans — Gunderson, Sensenbrenner.

Congress Urges President Reagan To Reconsider Bitburg Visit
U.S. Congress
April 29, 1985

(The House of Representatives Resolution 130, the Senate concurring.)

H. CON. RES. 130

Resolved by the House of Representatives (the Senate concurring), It is the sense of the Congress that —

(1) the United States Government should pay honor to the memories of the millions of innocent civilians and hundreds of thousands of American and Allied soldiers who suffered and died at the hands of the Nazis;

(2) on the occasion of the fortieth anniversary of the end of the Second World War it is fitting and appropriate for the President, in a gesture of reconciliation, to visit the Federal Republic of Germany, a country which has taken its place among the community of democratic nations and which is now a friend and ally of the United States;

(3) the President should recognize the importance of the relationship between our Nation and the Federal Republic of Germany by paying tribute to appropriate symbols of that nation's current democracy; and

(4) the President should reconsider the inclusion of the Bitburg Cemetery in his forthcoming trip to the Federal Republic of Germany.

Reagan Understands Lessons of History: Bush
Washington, D.C.
April 29, 1985

(Concluding Remarks of Vice President George Bush to the U.S. Chamber of Commerce Annual Meeting, Washington, D.C., Monday, April 29, 1985)

Now before I leave, let me say a word in support of the President and his forthcoming trip to Germany.

This has been a difficult time for everyone, especially so for the President. But as with any trying experience, I hope that we can learn from it.

This experience has compelled us all in a deeply personal way to face the anguish in Germany's past. The President recognizes, as all of us must, that there are things that can be forgiven and have been reconciled, and things that can never be forgotten, never reconciled.

I call upon all of you to do two things. First, in thinking about the President's decisions in this situation, keep in mind his record — 40 years of deep commitment. Keep in mind also the demands upon him as leader of the Free World and an alliance in Europe that has kept the peace for 40 years.

Over the next two weeks, he will make clear to the world that he understands the lessons of history, that he knows that we can never let time blur our memories, and that we must not be unclear about the deep truths learned during World War II.

Ronald Reagan hasn't changed on his abhorrence of the Holocaust — he never will. But the time has come for understanding and support for the President.

Senator Moynihan Responds to President Reagan
Washington, D. C.
May 2, 1985

By Senator Daniel Patrick Moynihan

(The following radio address was given on Saturday, May 4, 1985 by Senator Daniel Patrick Moynihan [D.-New York] in response to President Reagan. The speech was delivered at 1:06 E. S. T. from the CBS studios in Washington, D. C.)

Good afternoon.

This is Senator Daniel Patrick Moynihan of New York. I have been asked to give the Democratic response to President Reagan's regular weekly broadcast.

I had expected to respond to what the President said today.

Instead, I must respond to what the President, seemingly, will not allow to be said tomorrow. Tomorrow, that is, at the gates of the Nazi concentration camp known as Bergen-Belsen. It is a site sacred to the victims of the Holocaust. Some 50-60,000 human beings are buried in the mass graves there, including young Anne Frank.

There is an organization known as the International Network of Children of Jewish Holocaust Survivors. Its founding chairman is a New York attorney and constituent, Mr. Menachem Z. Rosensaft. Bergen-Belsen is more than sacred ground to him; it happens also to be his birthplace.

As you know, tomorrow morning President Reagan is going to visit Bergen-Belsen in conjunction with his visit to the military cemetery at Bitburg, the site of the graves of SS soldiers, Hitler's elite guard, the men and women who ran Bergen-Belsen, and concentration camps across Europe.

Recall that these are the SS troops who killed Polish priests, Romany Gypsies, American prisoners of war with the same ferocity that they set out to exterminate the Jews.

In this circumstance Mr. Rosensaft and a group of associates went to the Consul General of the Federal Republic of Germany in New York City and asked if a group of them might travel to Bergen-Belsen to be there on the occasion of the President's visit. Their purpose, of course, was to declare their disapproval of the President visiting the sacred site of Bergen-Belsen as some kind of offset to his visit to Bitburg.

Their purpose, open, was to make a statement through non-violent demonstration. They intended no embarrassment to the President. They were exercising a right guaranteed them in the First Amendment to the Constitution of the United States: "the right of the people peaceably to assemble."

The German officials were "highly sympathetic"—I use Mr. Rosensaft's words—and fully cooperative. The group flew off to Hanover.

Two hours ago, I spoke with Mr. Rosensaft, now in Germany. He reported to me the incredible news that despite the full cooperation of the West German government, the American government has denied these American citizens the right to be present at Bergen-Belsen when our President is there, also.

Security for non-Germans is apparently fully under control of our White House. They have told fellow Americans that they may not get closer than one kilometer, which is to say half-a-mile, to their own president.

The mind cracks, the heart breaks. What has possessed the White House?

Was it not bad enough that they insisted on going through with the visit to Bitburg? That violates the rights of the dead. This violates the rights of the living.

In the White House, two weeks ago, Elie Wiesel, a Holocaust survivor, spoke to the President and told of the ancient task of the Jews to "speak truth to power."

In the most urgent, poignant but respectful manner Elie Wiesel said of Bitburg: "Mr. President, that place is not your place."

Might I now say to the same president, or to any of his staff who are now listening, "Mr. President, forty or so survivors of the Holocaust and children of survivors wish to be at Bergen-Belsen when you are there. That place, Mr. President, *is* their place."

It is not only their place, Mr. President, it is their right.

Please, won't you reconsider. It is not like you. It is not like us. We must not let the world see this happen.

"On The Way To Bitburg"

Chapter 3

Veterans' Organizations Respond

VFW Issues A Vote Of Confidence
Veterans of Foreign Wars Resolution No. 303

Resolution No. 303
VOTE OF CONFIDENCE FOR THE COMMANDER-IN-CHIEF IN HIS STAND FOR THE SUPPORT OF PRESIDENT REAGAN'S BITBURG & BELSEN-BERGEN [sic] GERMANY VISITS IN MAY 1985

WHEREAS, the President visited the former WW II Concentration Camp at Belsen-Bergen and the cemetery at Bitburg in the Federal Republic of Germany where some SS Troops are interred in May 1985; and

WHEREAS, both visits were made jointly with the Chancellor of the Federal Republic of Germany and many active and retired officers and soldiers from the United States and the Federal Republic of Germany; and

WHEREAS, both visits were made in an official capacity of the office of the President of the United States at the invitation of the Chancellor of an allied nation, "The Federal Republic of Germany"; and

WHEREAS, the stated purpose of the visits was to promote German-American relations, and to make a gesture of reconciliation of WW II enmities; now, therefore

BE IT RESOLVED, by the 86th National Convention of the Veterans of Foreign Wars of the United States, that we hereby express our wholehearted support in behalf of our Commander-in-Chief for his stand in support of the actions of the President as set forth in this resolution.

Submitted by Department of Germany
To Committee on General Resolutions

Catholic War Veterans
Ask President To Forego Bitburg

The Catholic War Veteran
May-June, 1985

On May 5, the same day as President Reagan's controversial visit to the German military cemetery at Bitburg, a German priest and bishop prevented former SS members from laying a wreath in a Catholic cemetery.

In Nesselwang, a town in the extreme southern part of West Germany, Father Franz Gress barred about 200 former members of the Waffen SS Death's Head Division from laying a wreath at a monument of German war dead. Members of the division held a three-day reunion in the town, about 50 miles southwest of Munich. They made no effort to defy the ban, which had the support of Bishop Josef Stimple of Augsburg, West Germany.

Reagan's visit to the Bitburg cemetery had been protested by National Commander Dave Zielinski in a letter to the President on April 15. He asked President Reagan "to forego any public demonstration on your part to pay homage in honoring the members of the German armed forces who fought to destroy humanity and freedom throughout the world."

Most of the approximately 2000 German soldiers buried at Bitburg, 100 from World War I, 1800 from WW II and 49 SS members, died in the Battle of the Bulge, the most ferocious battle ever fought between Americans and Germans. In six weeks of combat in Belgium and Luxembourg, 19,000 GI's died and about 50,000 were wounded. The Germans suffered 100,000 casualties.

On December 16, 1944, a German counter-offensive began. The attack took the GI's by surprise and the German army advanced rapidly. The "bulge" in the American defenses gave the battle its name, eventually 50 miles deep and 70 miles wide. The Germans' ethos was "take no prisoners." On the second day of fighting near the Belgian town of Malmedy, the First SS Panzer Division overran an American field-artillery battalion.

The American prisoners of war, their hands over their heads, were herded into a snow-packed field where the Germans opened fire — witnesses later said the shooting lasted for 15 minutes — with volleys from mounted machine guns and rifles. There were 86 U.S. soldiers murdered — the worst atrocity against American troops in the European Theatre. For many GI's, the Battle of the Bulge produced the bitterest memories of the war.

The 49 SS graves belong to members of the criminal Schutzstaffel — literally, "protective rank," a quasi-military unit of the Nazi party. Even today, veterans of the SS — whether of the ordinary SS (which ran the concentration and extermination camps) or of the Waffen SS (which was in combat) — are not considered veterans of the German army in West Germany and are not entitled to military pensions.

The entire SS was ruled a criminal organization at the Nuremberg Tribunal on War Crimes.

National Commander Zielinski told President Reagan, "The wounds of World War I and II suffered by this nation's 28 million living veterans and their acts of heroism to preserve a humane world would be placed on a parallel with the inhumane war criminal acts of Nazi Germany. The atrocities and scars of our soldiers who were held prisoners of war by their Nazi captors cannot be eradicated within a short period of 40 years."

In the weeks before the President's visit to Bitburg, American Catholic Church leaders added their voices to the protest of the members of the U.S. House and Senate, Jewish leaders and veterans throughout the U.S.

Newsweek magazine, April 29 issue on page 16, reported: "The Bitburg visit was publicly opposed by the Catholic War Veterans, the Jewish War Veterans and the American Legion."

The May 5 issue of the *New York Times* published an "open letter" directed to President Reagan concerning his visit to Bitburg. National Commander Dave Zielinski was a letter signatory along with Claude L. Callegary and Paul L. Thompson, both Past National Commanders of the Disabled American Veterans (DAV); John Pavlik, National Commander of the Veterans of World War I; American Legion Past National Commanders William J. Rogers and L. Eldon James; National Commander Sam Greenberg of the Jewish War Veterans; retired Army Lt. General James Gavin of the 82nd Airborne Division; and religious, labor and nationality leaders totaling 43 signatures.

Prior to the scheduled visit to the Bitburg cemetery on Sunday, May 5th, President Reagan began his day in Bonn with an unscheduled drive in the hills overlooking the Rhine to place a wreath at the grave of Konrad Adenauer, West Germany's first Chancellor. President Reagan, accompanied by Chancellor Helmut Kohl, flew to Hanover and helicoptered to Bergen-Belsen concentration camp where he placed a wreath of green ferns near an obelisk at the site.

Following their arrival at the gates of the Bitburg cemetery (Kolmeshöhe Military Cemetery), President Reagan and Chancellor Kohl walked slowly past the graves accompanied by General Matthew Ridgeway, who led the 82nd Airborne Division in Europe and later fought in the Battle of the Bulge, and Lt. General Johannes Steinoff, a World War II flying ace who later rose to the highest ranks of the West German Air Force. While they walked to the memorial tower, a somber drum roll was played.

The President and Chancellor briefly arranged two large circular wreaths at the foot of the memorial tower before standing at attention. A trumpeter played a melancholy German soldiers' song, "I Had a Comrade." The simple ceremony took less than 10 minutes.

In the end, the President's mission became far less the buoyant celebration of German-American friendship that Mr. Reagan once envisioned than a delicate balancing act. Only time will tell whether it will bear lasting scars from the Bitburg visit.

Jewish War Veterans Express
Deep Sense Of Indignation
April 11, 1985

President Ronald Reagan
The White House
1600 Pennsylvania Ave.
Washington, DC.

Dear Mr. President:

It is with a deep sense of indignation that I write to you today. As National Commander of the Jewish War Veterans of the U.S.A., I am appalled at your decision to visit a German military cemetery, and pay homage to German soldiers. To memorialize those who killed American soldiers fighting to preserve the world from the onslaught of Nazi madness is an outrage.

I protested your earlier decision not to visit a concentration camp and, in that communique, reminded you that the Germany we defeated — the fascist, totalitarian regime of Hitler — is not the Germany of today. We smashed and destroyed Hitler's Germany with our armed forces — and we have a long list of American war dead by which to remember WWII.

In laying a wreath at the German military cemetery you show, not solidarity, but disdain for the American human sacrifices whose memory it is your duty, as commander-in-chief, to sanctify.

It is not too late to reverse a bad decision. I urge you, in the name of all of our American war dead, not to cheapen their deaths by laying a wreath at the graves of their adversaries. Alliances are not made by denying what was but, rather, by acknowledging the past, learning from it, and dedicating ourselves to a better tomorrow.

Sincerely,

Samuel Greenberg
National Commander
Jewish War Veterans of the United States of America

The American Legion: "Don't Do It"
USA Today
April 15, 1985

By Clarence M. Bacon

American veterans — and not only those who fought during World War II — have spoken with one voice in response to President Reagan's plan to honor German war dead at West Germany's Bitburg military cemetery next month:

Don't do it.

To say the planned visit and wreath-laying would not sit well with American veterans remains an understatement. The men and women represented by The American Legion strongly believe that the President has been ill-advised in his determination to carry on with the visit. Nevertheless, the facts are clear.

Bitburg cemetery contains the remains of not only German soldiers, but also at least 30 elite Waffen SS troops. The cemetery is on the site of a Battle of the Bulge staging area used by the Panzer Army under the command of SS General Josef "Sepp" Dietrich. And, Waffen SS troops were responsible for the summary execution of more than 75 unarmed U.S. prisoners at Malmedy, just 30 miles from Bitburg. Are these the same SS troops buried beneath the stones of Bitburg?

There can be no accommodation with the forces of world conquest, with the troops who died to establish the "Thousand Year Reign" of the Third Reich. There can be no reconciliation with the forces of evil. Our position is not one of recrimination, nor is it an effort to assign collective guilt to the generation of Germans who rebuilt a shattered nation. The President's objectives in traveling to West Germany — the economic summit, furthering U.S. solidarity with the Western Alliance, and underscoring Western unity — are laudable. The American Legion fully supports these goals. But we remain convinced the President could — and should — select a more appropriate place and means to demonstrate reconciliation with post-war Germany.

The President has demonstrated great sensitivity and compassion in scheduling a visit to Bergen-Belsen, to commemorate the horrible suffering and loss of life during the Holocaust. But even in this — a trade-off where no compromise can be accepted — the President continues to slight essential players in this real-life drama: the Allied soldiers who died to stem the tide of tyranny across Europe. They, and they alone, have earned his reverence; they, and they alone, deserve his honor.

The President is doing the wrong thing for the right reasons. No addition to the present plans can change that.

(Clarence M. Bacon, National Commander, The American Legion, wrote this editorial at the invitation of USA Today.)

Veterans of World War I Approve
April 17, 1985

President Ronald Reagan
The White House
1600 Pennsylvania Avenue
Washington, D. C.

Dear Mr. President:

The Veterans of World War I of the U.S.A., Inc., wish to go on record stating that we are pleased with the change in your itinerary for your upcoming trip to Germany. However, we would like to see one other change.

Mr. President, on the morning of November 11, 1921, the 3rd anniversary of the Armistice that ended World War I, the American Unknown Soldier was buried in Arlington National Cemetery.

Four cemeteries near the major fronts on which American troops had fought (Belleau Wood, the Somme, St. Mihiel, and the Meuse-Argonne) randomly chose a coffin of a soldier who had been buried among the unidentified dead in France.

The final selection was made by the dropping of roses on one of the earth-stained coffins. After the trek across the Atlantic on the Cruiser U.S.S. Olympia, the unknown warrior lay in state as a grateful nation paid homage. President Harding headed a cavalcade escorting the casket across the river to the Arlington National Cemetery.

The Veterans of World War I, who now are an average age of 89, would consider it an HONOR to have our President visit a cemetery where many of our American Buddies still sleep beneath the battlefields of France.

We appreciate you giving this suggestion consideration and wish you much success on this timely visit.

Sincerely in Buddyship,

John Pavlik
National Commander
Veterans of World War I of the U.S.A., Inc.

Chapter 4

Jewish Leaders Protest

Reagan Errs on the Holocaust
New York Times
March 30, 1985

By Menachem Z. Rosensaft

President Reagan apparently believes that all Germans alive today are under 60 years old. According to him, "very few" Germans today even remember, let alone took part in, the Second World War, and none of them "were adults and participating in any way" in the events of 40 years ago.

This is his rationale for not going to Dachau next month and not paying homage to the victims of Nazism. He is afraid that the German people's "unnecessary" guilt feelings would be aggravated if the President of the United States were to visit the site of a Nazi concentration camp. It would seem that a brief history lesson is in order.

In 1943, when my parents arrived at Auschwitz, they were in their early 30's. Most of the German guards and doctors who tortured them and sent their families to the gas chambers were their age or younger. Similarly, many of the killers of Treblinka, Bergen-Belsen, Dachau, and all the other death camps were in their 20's and 30's when they participated in the annihilation of six million European Jews. Nazi Germany was, after all, youth-oriented. Relatively few of these mass murderers died in battle, and only a handful of them were executed for their crimes after the war. Thus, many of them are today in their 60's and 70's, still alive and well and living in Germany.

Josef Mengele, the notorious chief doctor of Auschwitz, for example, was two months younger than my father and only a year and a half older than my mother. Mengele is now 74 years old—exactly the same age as President Reagan. Somehow, I think Mengele remembers the Third Reich. So do his high school and university classmates.

Klaus Barbie, a Gestapo chief in Nazi-occupied France, who is now awaiting trial in a French jail, was born in 1915. Seven of the 22 defendants in the 1963 trial in Frankfurt of onetime Auschwitz SS men were also born after Mr. Reagan.

One frequently reads about the reunions that the old SS gangs hold throughout Germany. When they meet, they reminisce about the good old days—when men were men and Jews were subhuman—and proclaim anew their loyalty to the Führer. Today, they must be in great spirits. After 40 years, the President of the United States has finally said that it is all right to forget all about them and their barbarous exploits.

But Nazi war criminals are not the only Germans who were adults between 1940 and 1945. West Germany's president, Richard von Weizsäcker, is 65 years old; the Bavarian Prime Minister, Franz Josef Strauss, is only 70. They, together with all the surviving veterans of Hitler's armed forces and storm troopers, bear at least a share of responsibility—if not personal guilt—for the Holocaust.

I do not mean to imply that all Germans were Nazis, or that any German born after 1945 should be held responsible for the Holocaust. The fact is, however, that Hitler's Final Solution of the "Jewish Question" was planned and implemented by the German government in the name of the German people. Whatever President Reagan thinks, a nation's identity is the totality of its past, the bad as well as the good. Thus, the Holocaust is and must remain forever a part of the German national heritage.

None of this should really surprise President Reagan. He, too, remembers the war. Two years ago, he told a gathering of more than 15,000 Holocaust survivors: "Our most sacred task now is insuring that the memory of this greatest of human tragedies, the Holocaust, never fades—that its lessons are not forgotten."

Why, then, his disingenuous excuse for not going to Dachau? The disturbing answer is that while it is politically advantageous for him to speak about the Holocaust to Jewish audiences in the United States, he does not want to risk offending anyone—even Nazis—in Germany.

President Reagan's refusal to observe the 40th anniversary of the end of the Holocaust is morally offensive. He has made it clear that for him, the dead of Dachau, symbolic of the dead of all the Nazi concentration camps, are less worthy of respect than the fallen soldiers of Normandy or the G.I.'s who lie buried in Arlington National Cemetery. In essence, he is telling the world that he cares more about contemporary German sensibilities than about the memory of Hitler's victims. As a son of Holocaust survivors, I am angry. As an American, I am ashamed.

(Menachem Z. Rosensaft, a lawyer, is founding chairman of the International Network of Children of Jewish Holocaust Survivors.)

Germany: Opening Old Wounds
The MacNeil/Lehrer News Hour
April 12, 1985

(Robert MacNeil conducted this interview with Harris Stone, Executive Director, Jewish War Veterans, and Lothar Griessbach, German-American Chamber of Commerce, shortly after the announcement of the President's proposed visit to Bitburg.)

MacNEIL: Tonight's lead focus, the fuss over the President's visit to Germany next month. As we reported earlier, the American Legion today joined Jewish organizations in protesting the President's plan to honor Nazi dead war soldiers. Mark Talisman, Washington director of the Council of Jewish Federations, called it a tragic error, a historic kind of mistake. Jewish organizations want the President to visit the site of a Nazi concentration camp, but at his last news conference, on March 21st, the President explained why he wouldn't.

"I feel very strongly that this time, in commemorating the end of that great war, that instead of reawakening the memories and so forth and the passions of the time, that maybe we should observe this day as the day when, 40 years ago, peace began and friendship, because we now find ourselves allied and friends of the countries that we once fought against, and that it be almost a celebration of the end of an era and the coming into what has now been some 40 years of peace for us. And I felt that since the German people, and very few alive that remember even the war, and certainly none of them who are adults and participating in any way, and they do — they have a feeling and a guilt feeling that's been imposed on them, and I just think it's unnecessary. I think they should be recognized for the democracy that they've created and the democratic principles they now espouse."

MacNEIL: Despite growing criticism of both decisions, the White House says there's no plan now to change them. Spokesman Larry Speakes said it's only a working itinerary and events can be added or deleted. And he also said the President was disturbed that anybody would question his sensitivity. To take this a little further, we have two different views of the matter. Lothar Griessbach is director of the German-American Chamber of Commerce. Harris Stone is past national commander and current executive director of the Jewish War Veterans of the USA. His organization has sent the President a letter expressing indignation about the decision to visit the cemetery.

MacNEIL: Mr. Stone, what's the basis of your protest?

HARRIS STONE: We have a problem, if you will, when the fact that we're trying to honor the war dead or commemorate and memorialize a situation that has happened in the past and we see the President of the United States, the commander in chief of our armed forces, if you will, going to the gravesite of the enemy at that time. Now, we very well know the difference of Germany today and Germany in the past. But what we're talking about is the Germany that we fought, that our people died for, that our people were wounded for and in VA hospitals today, and the fact that we don't honor their memory. We go to, effectively, the cemetery of the enemy and honor their dead and don't go to honor the dead of the United States or the British or the French or the Belgians, or all of our allies, the Russians included. And then you say, "I am not interested or I don't feel I have to go to Dachau or Bergen-Belsen or any of the other places where there were murders." These were outright murders that occurred. We don't understand that. We don't appreciate it. We think it's wrong. So we've requested the President to reconsider a very, very bad decision and please reconsider and not go and go to the sites where the Allies were.

MacNEIL: Mr. Griessbach, you approve of the way the President's organized this trip, is that correct?

LOTHAR GRIESSBACH: Well, I think it would be inappropriate, really, for any German to question what the American people and its president decide to do. I think the gesture to see the cemetery in Bitburg has been recognized as what it is apparently intended to be, a very gracious and generous gesture of compassion for victims of a war that nobody likes to think too much about.

MacNEIL: Well, what about the point that's just been made, that by not going to a concentration camp, for example, which Jewish organizations wanted him to do, he ignores that side of the war. What do you feel about that?

Mr. GRIESSBACH: I undestand if people in this country and all over the world feel that this originally planned visit would have helped them or would have had some impact on their cause, I would understand. And I don't think that too many people in Germany would object to that visit, either. But I also feel that, again, the President has proven to be very sensitive and very careful about his trip to Germany, and they will respect and honor the decision not to go to Dachau as well as they honor the one to see the war cemetery in Bitburg.

MacNEIL: Mr. Stone, who are the targets of your concern? Who do you think needs to be reminded on a visit like this? Is it the Germans or Americans?

Mr. STONE: I think the world. We've seen even most recently what a holocaust can do and what war can do that's indiscriminate and doesn't make a differentiation between the soldier and the civilian. In Cambodia, for instance, we very much decry what has happened over there in that holocaust. We object to the fact that the world seems to be blinded by the fact that these things happen even today and we can't seem to get people aware of what's stopping them. It's been said many times that if you don't worry about what's happened in the past that you're going to repeat it in the future. Look, even in the United States today the Congress of the United States is the law of the land. We have a Holocaust Memorial Commission headed by Elie Wiesel. It's going to have in the capital of the United States a Holocaust memorial museum. We don't want this forgotten. We don't want it ever forgotten and we don't want it excused, because it's not excused.

MacNEIL: Well, Mr. Griessbach, do you think that it is time for foreign leaders visiting your country to stop going to concentration camp sites, that it's time to let the wounds be healed and forget and stop laying, as the President put it, a burden of guilt on this generation?

Mr. GRIESSBACH: I think it is part of our history as well as it is, unfortunately, part of other people's history, and so long as the memory is there, and I think it will be there for a very, very long time, people will make personal decisions and governments will make decisions to visit places like that. And you have witnessed several years ago visits of German officials to similar memorials in foreign countries. So I don't think there is a time to stop thinking about it, and I can assure you that Germans, although, as the President has mentioned, about two-thirds of the population have absolutely nothing to do with these events because they're just born after the fact, although this is the case, I think you will find very few people in Germany who are not very much aware of what has happened.

MacNEIL: What is the harm being done, Mr. Stone, by the plan as it is at the moment?

Mr. STONE: I think it's an affront to those of us in this country and in our Allied nations who fought the tyranny of Nazism and the terrorism of the Hitler regime. Again, we recognize that there's a different Germany today than in the past. Germany in the past is gone, really, because it's now split in two parts, unfortunately. But the facts are people cannot forget this, and there are even people in this country today who are trying to revise history. They claim the Holocaust never was fought. They want to release Nazi war criminals. They want a statute of limitations on murder. And there are no such things as recognized by our law and most laws of the world. We can't afford to let these things go on. There are people actively lobbying the United States Congress today to get such, what I consider to be, poor things approved and into law.

MacNEIL: What's the right solution for this quandary at the moment? To drop the visit to the German war cemetery or add one to Allied war cemeteries and a concentration camp, or what? What do you think, Mr. Stone?

Mr. STONE: I could readily see the President in trying to promulgate an even-handed and cooperative policy with the Federal Republic of Germany. It's worthwhile. It's a new nation, effectively, with many new people. The point is that I think he must really be even-handed. He cannot at the same time affront his American troops, if you will, his Allied troops, his allies of the past. And I think that he should take a more balanced view, and if he's going to honor the memory of some, he's got to honor the memory of all.

MacNEIL: Mr. Griessbach, because this is becoming an embarrassing issue, what do you think the best way out of it is?

Mr. GRIESSBACH: I really have no recommendation. I can maybe speculate on the feelings of people in Germany, although I am not permanently living there anymore. I think that the younger people get in Germany the more they are worried about the future. They think the future is difficult. And any positive conclusions in that direction which will point out to them how they can resolve their problems or our problems in the future would be the more important thing. That's what they would look for.

MacNEIL: Well, thank you both for joining us, gentlemen.

Stormtroopers Wantonly Killed Gentiles, Jews

New York
April 12, 1985

President Ronald W. Reagan
White House
Washington, D. C.

Dear Mr. President,

I am a survivor of five concentration camps. My parents, my brother, and my little sister were brutally murdered by SS stormtroopers.

These SS stormtroopers were not just following Hitler's orders. All over Europe, wantonly and willingly, they killed innocent children, old and helpless people, the sick, men and women in the prime of their lives, Gentiles as well as Jews. These SS stormtroopers also massacred in cold blood American prisoners of war.

I know about your personal feelings regarding the horrors of the Nazi atrocities. I have watched you speak about them. I saw the tears in your eyes.

I came to live in this great country as a free man. I am, and will forever be, grateful to it for opening its gates to me.

I voted for you in both elections for President. I admire you for inspiring all of us to believe in ourselves and renew our faith in our country.

The news of your planned visit to a German cemetery containing graves of SS stormtroopers came as a shock to me. I was not able to sleep that night. A President of the United States should not be honoring the remains of the butchers of Europe. It would be inconsistent with your record and commitment to freedom. Adding a visit to a former concentration camp site is welcome but does not bear on the visit to the Bitburg cemetery. One cannot memorialize sadistic killers and compensate for it by honoring their victims as well.

I agree with your policy of reconciliation with the Germans. It is important to strengthen our partnership with them in building a stronger defense against the encroachment of communism.

A small and valiant minority of the Germans opposed Hitler and often paid for it with their lives. They are the real heroes of Germany. A young gentile German, we called Willie, was a fellow prisoner of mine in the Ravensbruck concentration camp. He was a brave as anyone I have ever known. I saw him shield, with his own body, his fellow prisoners from the blows inflicted on them by the brutal SS guards.

Mr. President, it is not too late.

Changing your itinerary to honor people like Willie, instead of the SS stormtroopers, would further enhance the respect and admiration you have earned among the nations of the world, including the German people.

Respectfully,

Henry Orenstein

Holocaust Group Bars Trade-Off in Itinerary
The New York Times
April 16, 1985

By Jane Gross

Elie Wiesel, chairman of the United States Holocaust Memorial Council, said yesterday that President Reagan would not assuage Jews by adding a visit to a former concentration camp or a synagogue to his scheduled trip to a West German military cemetery.

"A visit to Dachau or a synagogue is one item and a visit to the Bitburg cemetery is another item," Mr. Wiesel said at a news conference at Hebrew Union College in New York. "We would not want a trade-off."

The news conference followed a meeting of the council, a 65-member group established by Congress in 1980. The council meeting was called to respond to recent decisions by President Reagan regarding his itinerary in Western Europe next month.

Mr. Reagan has decided not to visit the Dachau concentration camp while agreeing to lay a wreath at a cemetery with the graves of 2,800 soldiers of Nazi Germany, among them members of the SS, the Nazi elite guard.

Members of the SS, which fought alongside regular army units in World War II, were regarded as Germany's best combat soldiers. But the SS was adjudged after the war to have been guilty of war crimes, including the mass killing of Jews and the massacre of prisoners of war.

President Reagan's decisions, which are under review, have prompted protests from Jewish and veteran groups.

Mr. Wiesel, who is a survivor of Buchenwald, one of the German camps, said about Mr. Reagan's plan to visit the Bitburg cemetery:

"A visit to this particular cemetery is to us unacceptable. This is not just a cemetery of soldiers. This is tombstones of the SS, which is beyond what we can imagine. These are and were criminals."

The Holocaust council sent a telegram to the White House requesting a meeting between Mr. Reagan and Mr. Wiesel, who is to be honored with the Congressional Gold Medal on Friday for his experiences in Nazi Germany.

In the council meeting, Mr. Wiesel said, "Some voices urged extreme measures, and the only extreme measure we know is resignation."

"Others suggested moderation," he continued. "We all believe that a visit to that cemetery must be eliminated from the calendar. We also all believe the situation can be resolved."

Mr. Wiesel said the telegram was "an act of faith" in Mr. Reagan.

"We meet once a year at the Remembrance Day ceremonies," Mr. Wiesel said, "and he has always responded humanely, warmly, generously to our agony. I think the President really didn't look into the matter. I know how these things work on high-level visits, so I am sure he didn't go through every detail. He didn't know the implications and I think he can withdraw the visit without losing face."

Not all of those in attendance agreed.

"I do not subscribe to the theory that this is something to blame on advisers," said Menachem Z. Rosensaft, chairman of the International Network of Children of Jewish Holocaust Survivors. Mr. Rosensaft, who is an unofficial adviser to the council, said he was in no way speaking for the council.

"It is a tragedy that on the 40th anniversary of the liberation of the camps we are forced to deal with the question of honoring the memory of SS men," he said. "This is so morally repugnant as to defy credibility. We are asking the President, please, not to honor the murderers of six million Jews. Would that have been necessary with any other President, beginning with Harry Truman?"

Later, Mr. Wiesel, speaking at a City Hall ceremony marking the beginning of Jewish Heritage Week, differed with remarks Mayor Koch made last week about President Reagan's plan to visit the German cemetery. The mayor had said that it was "perfectly appropriate" for the President to do so.

Turning to Mr. Koch, Mr. Wiesel said that had the mayor known the cemetery contained the graves of SS men, "I know you wouldn't have said it."

The mayor said he had assumed no SS men were buried at the cemetery.

"It would be an outrage for a President to go to honor in any way those who participated in the barbarism of the Holocaust," he said.

"They Established A School Upon His Grave"
New York
April 17, 1985

By Dr. Norman Lamm

(Yom Hashoah Speech by Dr. Norman Lamm, president of Yeshiva University, on the 40th Anniversary of The Liberation, in Madison Square Garden, New York.)

Arbaim shanah akut be'dor. For forty years our generation struggled to understand the mystery of those fatal years of the Holocaust. Neither our speech nor our silence helped us to uncover the secrets of God or of man. Perhaps we shall have to wait another forty or another four hundred years, or perhaps we shall never be wise enough even to know how to react.

But events march on, and history does not permit us the luxury of contemplation. Hence, some reactions began to emerge fairly quickly. The first and enormously significant response to the Holocaust was the political one: the founding of the state of Israel. Powerlessness would never again be considered a Jewish virtue. The desperate struggles of the heroic Jewish fighters in Warsaw and elsewhere were metamorphosed into the pride of statehood and the military confidence of the Israeli Defense Forces. Today, the future of the Jewish people is unthinkable without the state of Israel.

Another response has been a holy, compulsive drive to record and testify. We do not want to forget, and we do not want the world to forget. We have resolved to keep the memory of our *Kedoshim* alive by demonstrations and by meetings such as this. And many of us have undertaken projects of sculpture and art and museums and exhibits to perpetuate the memory of the Six Million. As the years slip by and memory begins to fade, we desperately want to prevent their anguish and blood and cry from being swallowed up by the misty, gaping hole of eternal silence, banished from the annals of man by the Angel of Forgetfulness.

The efforts at remembering and reminding must continue. As long as so-called "revisionist historians" deny that the Holocaust occurred; as long as Babi Yar and Buchenwald behind the Iron Curtain contain almost no reference to Jews; as long as it is even conceivable that an American administration, which preaches more compassion for the victim than for the criminal on the domestic front, can see nothing wrong in its President honoring dead Waffen SS while pointedly ignoring their Jewish victims in Dachau — there will be a need for Jews to remember and remind, even if we know in our hearts that the world will not long remember or want to be reminded. And let it be said here clearly and unequivocally: A courtesy call at a conveniently located concentration camp cannot compensate for the callous, obscene scandal of honoring dead Nazi killers. Surely the President's aides can arrange a visit by him to the tomb of Konrad Adenauer or some of the decent German anti-Nazis who perished at Hitler's hands for their principles.

Yet — and yet…these responses alone are inadequate. The problem of the Jewish people today is not the state of Israel; it will survive. The problem is not the world's conscience. I have no faith in it, though we must continue to prod and pick and provoke it. The problem of the Jewish people today is — the Jewish people. With a diminishing birth rate, an intermarriage rate exceeding 40%, Jewish illiteracy gaining ascendance daily—who says that the Holocaust is over? President Herzog of Israel estimates that we are losing 250 Jews per day! From the point of view of a massive threat to Jewish continuity, the Holocaust is open-ended.

The monster has assumed a different and more benign form, a different and bloodless shape, but its evil goal remains unchanged: a *Judenrein* world.

The Holocaust is not yet ready to be "remembered"; we are still in the midst of attempting to avoid the *final* Final Solution: a world without Jews.

In the light of this sobering, ominous reality, our responses are open to serious and deep reexamination.

I deeply sympathize with the heartfelt, sincere effort of memorial-building. But is that the Jewish way? No archaeologist has yet found a statue to the memory of

Rabbi Hanina, Rabbi Tradyon or Rabbi Ishmael. No seeker after antiquities has yet unearthed an ancient museum to preserve the story of the victims of Masada or Betar or Rabbi Akiva and his martyred students — or, for that matter, the victims of the Crusades or the Inquisition or Kishinev.

Our people have historically chosen different forms of memorialization. They asked for the academy of Yavneh as a substitute for and in memory of the Holy Temple. They ordained days of fasting and prayer and introspection. They devised ways of expressing *zekher le'mikdash* (Reminder of the Temple) and *zekher le'chur-ban* (Reminder of the Destruction). They created the Talmud. In other words, they remembered the past by ensuring the future.

Museums and art have their place. In the context of an overall Jewish life, they serve as powerful instruments to recall the past for the future. But without that comprehensive wholeness, all our museums are mausoleums, our statues meaningless shards, our literature so much ephemeral gibberish.

We must seek to remember our dead, but not by being obsessed with death. We must be obsessed with life. *Lo ha-metim yehallelu Yah* (Psalm 115, "The dead praise not the Lord"). The dead cannot tell their own story. Only the living can testify to them and perpetuate them: *Va'anachnu nevarekh Yah (Ibid.,* "But we will bless the Lord"). Their deaths make sense — even the sense of unspeakable and outrageous grief — only in the context of their lives. And their lives — their loves and hates, their faith and fears and culture and creativity and traditions and learning and literature and warmth and brightness and Yiddish-keit — are what we are called upon to redeem and to continue in our own lives and those of our children.

We know more or less how the Aztecs and Incas were butchered. But there is no one to mourn them today because there was no one to continue their ways and resume their story. That is bound to happen to our Six Million if we fail to ensure the continuity of our people. An extinct race has no memory. If there are no living Jews left, no one else will care about the Holocaust, and no one but a few cranky antiquarians will bother to view our art or read our literature or visit our museums.

Let me cite an example from the American-Jewish experience. There was a time when most American Jews memorialized their deceased parents by saying Kaddish for them for eleven months and on Yahrzeit and by reciting the Yizkor prayers four times a year; otherwise, their Jewishness became progressively more tenuous as they abandoned their parental lifestyles, values, and faith. What happened when these children died? For the most part *their* children did not do for *them* what they had not done for their parents. For the most part, it was those who continued the whole rubric of Jewish life and living of their parents who also most fully cherished and reverenced their memories.

The reason for this is both profound and simple: Death has no staying power. Only life lives. Death is only past, it is over and done with. Who will remember a parent on Yizkor? Usually one who will be in *shul* as well on Hanukkah and Purim and Shabbat and even during the week. Those who somehow continue their parents' lives in their own lives will be there to note and recall their deaths. In a word: without life, death doesn't have a future.

At the Seder, a little less than two weeks ago, we ate a hard-boiled egg immediately before the meal as a sign of mourning. Jewish tradition teaches that since the first night of Passover always falls on the same night of the week as does Tisha B'Av, the egg is a token of grief for the victims of the destruction of Jerusalem and of pogroms throughout the ages. It occurs to me that not only do we eat an egg at the Seder because no Jewish *simchah* may be conducted or complete without remembering the tragedies of Jewish history, but equally so because there can be no enduring memorial to the fallen martyrs of our people unless it lies in the context of the Seder of Jewish life. Without a child to ask the *Mah Nishtanah*, there will be no adult to tell the story of *avadim hayyinu*. Without *seder* or order; without the holiness of *kadesh* or the purity of *rechatz*—there will be no *maggid* to tell the story of Auschwitz and relate the *marror* of Buchenwald and Belzec. And so the *churban* will remain without a *zekher*. There can be no Tisha B'Av without a Pesach. And there will be no Yom Hashoah without the rest of the Jewish Calendar.

How did Jewish tradition cherish and pay homage to its heroes? We are told of the righteous King Hezekiah that upon his death he was honored greatly by the people of Judah and Jerusalem (II Chronicles 32:33), and the Talmud (*B.K.* 16b) explains that the honor that they accorded him was that *hoshivu yeshivah al kivro*—"they established a school upon his grave."

That is what Jewish history and destiny call upon us to do now—before it is too late. The resources and energies and intellectual power of our best and brightest must be focused on making sure that there will be Jews remaining in the world lest the Holocaust prevail even while it is being denied. And that requires one thing above all else: a fierce, huge effort to expand Jewish education.

Let us resolve to build a school—a yeshiva, a day school, a Hebrew school, an elementary school, a high school, a school for adults, any genuine Jewish school—on the unmarked graves of every one of the million Jewish children done to death by the Nazi *Herrenvolk*. If not a yeshiva on every grave then, for Heaven's sake, at the very least one more Jewish child to learn how to be a Jew for the grave of every one child martyr! A million more Jewish children learning how and what it is to be Jewish will accomplish more for the honor of the Holocaust martyrs than a million books or sculptures or buildings. Teach another million Jewish children over the globe the loveliness and meaningfulness and warmth of Jewishness, and you will have redeemed the million Jewish child-martyrs from the oblivion wished upon them by the Nazis. A million Jewish children to take place of those million who perished—that is a celebration of their lives that will not make a mockery of their deaths and that will be worthy of our most heroic efforts.

Will we have the courage to save our and our children's future from the spiritual Holocaust that threatens us? Will we have the wisdom to reorder our priorities and "establish a yeshiva over the gravesites" of our Kedoshim—before the hearts and minds of the majority of our children themselves turn into private little graves of the Jewish spirit?

That is the fateful question that we are obliged to answer. The future of our people lies in our hands. If we do nothing but utter a sigh and shrug our shoulders with palms extended as a sign of resignation and helplessness—then we will stand accused of being passive onlookers at this bloodless Holocaust, and our guilt will parallel that of the silent spectators of the 1930's and 1940's. But if we resolve to live on despite all, if we stand Jewishly tall and put our shoulders to the wheel and teach and instruct a new generation in the ways of Yiddishkeit, then our hands will grasp the future firmly and surely, and we shall live and the *Kedoshim* will live through us.

Etz chayyim hi la-machazikim bah. Our Torah and our Tradition are a Tree of Life, and by holding on to them we will redeem our past and honor our people by giving them a future.

"Say It Isn't So, Mr. President"

By Abraham H. Foxman

My first reaction was disbelief—it was impossible. No president would honor Nazi SS murderers by placing a wreath on their graves. Not 40 years or 400 years after the Holocaust and Malmedy.

Then shock. How could he do this? What motivated him?

To me it was totally out of character for the man as well as the President.

This cannot be, I thought, the Ronald Reagan who was so eloquent and tearfully moved at the Holocaust remembrance.

I could not square it with the Ronald Reagan who is so staunchly building this nation's alliance with Israel.

And then the news broke that, after all, the President would visit a concentration camp even though he still intended to visit the military cemetery. The rethinking seemed more like the President I admired, I felt.

But then, it was stunning when he equated the fate of young Wehrmacht and SS soldiers with that of the six million Jewish victims of Hitler's Final Solution.

I was appalled at the insensitivity, the mechanical equation of victims and victimizers, murdered and murderers.

Myself a survivor of the Holocaust, I wondered at the mind set of a man who could make such a connection between soldiers who goose stepped off to do their duty in Hitler's mad attempt to conquer and subjugate the world and innocent men , women and children who were slaughtered indiscriminately because of an imagined ancestral taint.

As I wondered, a scene came into mind out of American legend. When the Black Sox scandal broke in 1919, a disillusioned young newsboy is said to have approached Shoeless Joe Jackson, the great natural hitting star, and asked him, "Say it ain't so, Joe."

I wanted to say, "Say it ain't so, Mr. President."

But, unfortunately, it is so.

The President knows that there are some things that it is best never to forget. The great philosopher Santayana pointed that out when he said that "Those who forget history are doomed to repeat it."

Whether or not the President intends it—and I believe that he does not—the effect of his words and his visit to the SS gravesite, if he still persists in that folly, is to demean the Holocaust and diminish it in scale to the level of just another atrocity like the St. Valentine Day's massacre in Chicago.

What is lacking here, it seems, is a sense of history, of perspective. The past is full of massacres, no doubt. No nation on earth is without its share of dark and bloody ground, of actions of which it is ashamed and which it buries in the footnotes of oblivion.

Nevertheless, the Holocaust is unprecedented not only in scale but in conception. This was an endeavor pursued relentlessly even at the cost of the German war effort to obliterate Jews from the race of the earth. As far as Europe was concerned, it almost succeeded. One of every three Jews in existence at the time was killed in every conceivable diabolic manner.

How could an American President, the ultimate symbol of our democracy and values, contemplate honoring men even remotely linked to such a fiendish enterprise.

It is an offense against our tradition and all those who died—in our armed forces and those of our allies — to make certain that such an evil did not reach our shores.

Say it ain't so, Mr. President. Think again!

(Abaham H. Foxman is Associate National Director of the Anti-Defamation League of B'nai B'rith.)

Reagan Cemetery Visit Criticized
At Holocaust Survivors Ceremony
The New York Times
April 21, 1985

By William K. Stevens

PHILADELPHIA — Survivors of the Holocaust cheered loudly and lustily today as one of their most prominent children called for an intensified campaign to persuade President Reagan to cancel a visit to a German cemetery containing the graves of Waffen SS troopers.

"The time for soft-spoken words and appeals is over," said Menachem Z. Rosensaft of New York, a son of concentration-camp victims who is chairman of the International Network of Children of Jewish Holocaust Survivors. "For the sake of history, we must prevent him from going to Bitburg." He argued that the visit next month would be exploited by "revisionist historians, neo-Nazis and their sympathizers."

If Mr. Reagan visits the military cemetery at Bitburg, West Germany, he went on, "we must see to it that survivors, children of survivors and American war veterans will be waiting for him at the gates of that cemetery."

He said that his plea, contained in one of the strongest statements of protest yet made against the proposed visit, was designed to ignite renewed efforts to force Mr. Reagan to cancel the Bitburg visit or substitute another cemetery. There was no immediate indication as to what response it would draw from other Jewish leaders.

But one of them, Benjamin Meed, the president of the American Gathering and Federation of Jewish Holocaust Survivors, the group of survivors now gathered here, told the crowd after Mr. Rosensaft had spoken, "I can feel the heat, your heartbeat, and the emotions, and the message is coming through."

Ceremony at Independence Hall

The speech took place in the shadow of Independence Hall, where, in a moving ceremony minutes before, thousands of Holocaust survivors had laid white carnations beneath the Liberty Bell in a symbolic linking of American freedom and their own liberation from Nazi captivity and torture 40 years ago.

The ceremony opened what is called the Inaugural Ceremony of the American Gathering of Jewish Holocaust Survivors. The group plans to establish a permanent mechanism to perpetuate the memory of the Holocaust. The assembly first met four years ago in Jerusalem, and again two years ago in Washington. Mr. Rosensaft was invited to take part in today's ceremonies.

While many participants in today's prayers, singing, speechmaking and commemorative march through the streets alluded to the controversy generated by Mr. Reagan's plan to visit Birburg, most had been restrained until Mr. Rosensaft spoke.

His talk came last, as the sun sank on a lovely spring afternoon, just before the commemorative ceremony at Independence Hall ended with the pealing of the historic building's tower bell and the ceremonial blowing of the Shofar, or ram's horn.

Mr. Reagan's refusal to change his plan to go to Bitburg after learning that 47 members of the elite Nazi combat organization, are among the 2,000 soldiers buried there, he said, was a "calculated, deliberate insult to the memory of the victims of the Holocaust."

"Now," he said, "is the time for concentrated, immediate action by every American Jew." He called for a broad telegram and telephone campaign directed at the White House.

Senator Arlen Specter, Republican of Pennsylvania, told the crowd at Independence Hall that the issue of the Bitburg visit "is not over with finality," but did not elaborate.

Mr. Rosensaft said his plea was an attempt to ignite new efforts to forestall what he described in his speech as "the image — the photograph — of the President of the United States laying a wreath in the name of the United States at a cemetery where SS men are buried." This, he said, could only lend legitimacy to those who are looking for "proof that the perpetrators of the Holocaust have been forgiven, and that it is now all right to forget."

But if Mr. Reagan was not the most popular person at today's gathering, the country he leads was warmly celebrated.

The observance began this afternoon with prayers and songs at a statue at 16th Street and Benjamin Franklin Parkway in downtown Philadelphia, about 13 blocks away from the Liberty Bell. The statue, which depicts terrified Holocaust victims dying in flames, is Philadelphia's monument to the Holocaust martyrs, the nation's first.

Philadelphia, with what is said to be the third largest Jewish community in the nation, has played a leading role in the Holocaust remembrance, and this is given as one reason why the city was selected for this year's assembly of survivors. A second reason, said a spokesman for the assembly, is that Philadelphia was one of the well-springs of American liberty, a place full of the symbolism of freedom.

At both the Memorial and Independence Hall, some survivors walked about — as they will all through these three days — wearing placards that say things like, "Do you come from Vitebsk?" or "Is anyone here from Krzepice, Poland?" These are parts of continuing attempts, in one of the assembly's main functions, to track down family members separated during the Holocaust.

The estimated 5,000 survivors and children paraded 13 blocks through the streets, led by bearers carrying American and Israeli flags, and another carrying a torch lit from a ceremonial Menorah at the Holocaust memorial. Behind them came young people, each bearing the name of a country or city from which Holocaust victims came.

As the parade moved along Chestnut Street, marchers sang, first, "God Bless America," and then "Hatikvah," the Israeli national anthem. Some in the procession stopped to buy cold drinks, for by midafternoon some of the elderly marchers were finding the heat oppressive.

Finally, each marcher was given a white carnation to deposit in one of three wicker baskets resting on blue satin cloths on the floor underneath the Liberty Bell in its glass-walled pavilion.

The crowd looked much like any Sunday afternoon crowd, with many men, women and children dressed in shorts or slacks. But the mood, enhanced by hymns from the United States Army Band, was partly spiritual. Later, as the ceremonies ended, the band played "The Star-Spangled Banner" and the "Polish Partisans' March," composed in the Vilna ghetto in the 1940's.

Soldiers in dress blues trooped the colors of army divisions that liberated Nazi death camps. And then, with the statue of George Washington looking over their shoulders, the speechmakers began.

Nazi Terror Recalled

"I recalled the other times when we walked together," said Mr. Meed. He talked of those times: death marches, shuffling lines to be selected for death. "Today," he said, "we affirm our love of liberty."

And he cited last week's face-to-face admonition to President Reagan by Elie Wiesel, the Holocaust scholar and writer, that "Bitburg is not your place" as evidence in itself of America's genuine freedoms. "We could never have done that" in Europe, he said.

But Mr. Rosensaft's speech was the most intense moment of the ceremony. Thirty-seven years old, he was born in Bergen-Belsen concentration camp after it was liberated, when it served as a displaced-persons camp for Holocaust victims. Both of his parents, he said, had seen their entire families taken off to the gas chambers of Auschwitz, and he — one of the children born to Holocaust survivors — grew up with its lessons.

When Mr. Reagan announced last week that he would visit Bergen-Belsen, Mr. Rosensaft said in his speech, "the news was shattering."

"President Reagan plans to stand beside the mass graves where Anne Frank and tens of thousands of other Jews lie buried anonymously — only a few hundred yards from where I spent the first two years of my life — and probably intends to deliver a moving speech. How we wish that he could have decided to go to Belsen voluntarily. How we would then have valued his presence at the one place in contemporary history which symbolizes both the Holocaust and the rebirth of the Jewish people. Tragically, we must now reject his gesture as totally inadequate."

The audience applauded vigorously.

"Today," he went on, "let us say to President Reagan clearly and unambiguously that if he insists on going to Bitburg we do not need him and we do not want him in Bergen-Belsen."

If the visit to the military cemetery takes place, he said, survivors should descend on Bergen-Belsen. "Let him pass in front of us there and look into our faces, and perhaps then, at last, he will understand the enormity of the outrage which he is perpetrating."

"For heaven's sake," Mr. Rosensaft said, "let him find another cemetery. There must be at least one in all of Germany which does not contain SS men."

To Be True To Their Cause
Munich, Germany
May 3, 1985

By Henry Siegman

(Remarks by Henry Siegman, Executive Director of the American Jewish Congress, at Commemoration for Sophie and Hans Scholl at Perlacher Cemetery, Munich, Germany.)

For many of us who have come to this solemn commemoration, this is a moment of difficult emotions. You will forgive me if I speak in personal terms and say that this is particularly true in my own case, having been born in Germany and having experienced the Nazi terror — in Belgium and in France — from 1939 to 1942. My immediate family and I managed to escape, miraculously, in 1942 to the U.S. But virtually every other member of my family — aunts, uncles, grandparents, cousins — all perished in the gas chambers and the crematoria.

This is the first time in 43 years that I have returned to German soil.

I am here, on German soil, not because there are yet heroic acts to be performed; there are none, on this continent that has been transformed into a gravesite for my people. I am here, rather, because I wish to be true to the memory of my martyred family, to the memory of the millions of Jews, and Christians, who died at the hands of the Nazis.

To be true to their memory, I must say — respectfully but without equivocation — to you Chancellor Kohl and to you President Reagan, that the symbol of Bitburg, which you are about to visit on Sunday, is a lie. We are here at Perlacher to bear witness to the truth. And the truth is, Mr. Kohl and President Reagan, that Hitler's SS were not victims. They were not soldiers who died honorably in the field of battle. They were killers, who deliberately and systematically and brutally murdered my little cousins, my grandmother, my aunts and uncles, one million Jewish children, and countless others.

Oddly enough, what is most damaging about the lie of Bitburg is the implied suggestion that we, Germans and Americans, need to falsify history in order to find some common ground between us; that only by ghoulishly clasping hands over the graves of the SS will we find that which unites us. But we already possess that common ground, and nothing symbolizes it more eloquently than the heroes of the White Rose — those who paid the supreme sacrifice, and those who somehow survived and are with us today.

Hans and Sophie Scholl, we honor you and your comrades, both martyred and alive. We have come from far distances to pay you this tribute of love, of remembrance, and — above all — of truth, for in that truth lies our hope and our salvation.

Mr. President, Mr. Chancellor, even at this late hour, we address this request to you: We ask you, do not dishonor these martyrs. Do not go to Bitburg. You are driven to Bitburg neither by principle nor by truth. Instead, join us in honoring the heroes of the White Rose. By doing so, you will pay tribute to that which is most noble in our past, and which enables us, together, to look to a better future.

Arlington Address By Holocaust Survivor
Arlington National Cemetery
May 5, 1985

By Benjamin Meed

(While President Reagan was laying a wreath in Bitburg, Benjamin Meed, president of the American Gathering and Federation of Jewish Holocaust Survivors, was addressing a memorial service for American dead.)

We are here today to honor and to remember.

Forty years ago, an awesome world war came to an end. The world's most evil tyranny was defeated by the Allied soldiers, hundreds of thousands of young men and women, American and Russian, British and French, Australian and Canadian, who gave their lives to defeat Nazism.

Each Holocaust survivor can remember the moment of liberation and each liberator will never forget his first encounter with a survivor.

We looked at each other as strangers, afraid of one another. To the survivors, all soldiers represented war and suffering, pain and evil. But here were young men, wearing the uniform of a friendly army, willing to help and offering comfort. Yet, we could not believe the nightmare was over. What a horrifying sight we presented to our liberators: human skeletons — skin and bones, surrounded by death, disease, and the stench of the death camps — enough to frighten even the bravest of soldiers.

Yet, we reached out to each other: the survivor with gratitude and with thanks — gratitude for defeating the enemy and thanks to the soldiers who had made the supreme sacrifice to free us.

Even though the war had ended, neither of us could celebrate. For us, the victory had come too late — far too late. Our suffering had been endless. We Jews had lost more — much more — than our defeated enemies.

These young men — our liberators — could find no words with which to comfort us. Yet, we could read it in their eyes, in their faces and in their tears. They told us again and again, "You are free! You are free!" Words we found so hard to believe.

The liberators in turn were shocked by what they saw. The unthinkable and unspeakable evil of the enemy was more than they were able to comprehend. No one had prepared them for what they were to witness: the open pit of hell.

Now, forty years later, it seems a bit strange that no one had prepared them to see these things, because the Allied governments did indeed know of the existence of the death camps. But these young soldiers were never told what they would find. Therefore, we cannot allow the governments of today to keep our youth and future generations equally in ignorance.

Today, we gather here, on this sacred ground of Arlington Cemetery, to pay tribute at the Shrine of the American Soldier, to remember and honor those heroic young men and women.

Forty years ago, during the darkest moments of our lives, in the death camps, in the ghettos and in the forests, when we felt most alone, we hoped and prayed not to be left abandoned by the world, that somewhere our messages would be received and our voices would be heard. Somehow, we would be saved by men and women of decency and courage. Your presence here today, and that of the distinguished Christian clergy alongside us, demonstrates that today we are not alone.

The Holocaust was the darkest chapter of our century, of all centuries. It is a darkness, an abyss into which we dare not avert our gaze, if future generations shall continue to live in freedom.

We must never forget the lessons of the Holocaust, nor its victims, nor indeed can we forget the *murderers*. Their crimes must never be forgotten.

As Americans and Jews, we seek reconciliation among nations because we know full well the consequences of tyranny, war, hatred and bigotry. But there can be no reconciliation between the murderers and their victims. We must not betray the memory of our martyrs.

Sadly, we live in a world of images. The image of an American President, however well intentioned, at a German cemetery where soldiers are buried, including Nazi SS elite officers and concentration camp guards, sends the wrong signal to the world. It says to future generations: all these men are the same; all were engaged in an honorable struggle.

We have seen our leaders go to great pains to separate the evil of Nazism from the German people as a whole. We must remember that the Nazis did not operate in a vacuum. While there were exceptions, and we acknowledge and honor those exceptions, the German nation was willingly mobilized to carry out the Nazi policies, and therefore shares in the moral responsibility for the destruction they brought.

The reason for the outcry about Bitburg is precisely this: the attempt to obscure and absolve a nation of its moral responsibility, both to the victims and to humanity.

Others, including our friends, may suggest that we forget, or at least minimize, in the name of current realities. But true reconciliation can only be found if we confront this fact of history — as painful and ugly as it was — truthfully and fully.

We believe that the memory of death can serve life, that understanding evil can sustain good, and most of all, we believe that we have survived for a purpose — to bear witness and warn so that another Holocaust shall never happen again.

So, our message to the world today, and for the future of all humanity — let us remember together and not allow history to repeat itself. We will forever honor and remember each soldier who fell in battle to liberate us and who saved an entire world. Let us make sure that their sacrifice was not in vain.

Chapter 5

"Dear Mr. President..." —National Leaders Protest

"Victims of Nazism" Is False Idea: National Leaders
New York
April, 1985

The President
The White House
Washington, D.C.

Dear Mr. President:

We deeply regret your decision to go to the Bitburg cemetery.

All Americans join you in supporting reconciliation with the new and democratic Federal Republic of Germany. But there can be no reconciliation with the evil of Nazism.

At Bitburg lie buried soldiers of the German army and members of the notorious SS — the "elite guard" that Hitler placed in charge of the Nazi death camps, the murderers of the American prisoners in Malmedy.

In the words of William L. Shirer, historian of the Nazi era: "The German soldiers fought for the Führer and the Fatherland . . . with immense enthusiasm and dedication, and very bravely. They appeared to me to believe fanatically in Hitler's cause and in the leader himself. . . . The idea that most German soldiers felt themselves 'victims of Nazism' is false."

To honor the perpetrators of Nazi outrages is to dishonor the sacrifice of millions of American and Allied soldiers who fought and died to liberate Europe from the Nazi death grip. And it mocks the suffering and death of millions of innocents, including six million Jews, who perished at Nazi hands.

We know that is not your purpose, Mr. President. And so we say, your place is not at Bitburg but with the victims, so that—in your own words—never again will the world stand silent before man's inhumanity to man.

Respectfully,

Andrew Athens, Nat. Ch.,
  United Hellenic-American Congress

Rev. Charles V. Bergstrom, Dir., Wash.
  office, Lutheran Council in the U.S.A.*

Kenneth J. Bialkin, Ch., Conference of
  Presidents of Major American Jewish
  Organizations

Rev. Arie R. Brouwer, Gen. Sec.,
  National Council of Churches

John Buchanan, Ch. of the Bd.,
  People for the American Way

Claude L. Callegary,
  Past Nat. Commander,
  Disabled American Veterans*

S. Andrew Chen, Pres.,
  Organization of Chinese Americans*

Prof. Henry Steele Commager

Rev. Jerry Falwell, Pres.,
  The Moral Majority

Anthony J. Fornelli, Past Pres.,
  UNICO National*

Lt. Gen. James Gavin, U.S. Army (ret.)
  Commanding General, 82nd Airborne
  Div.

Sam Greenberg, Nat. Commander,
  Jewish War Veterans of the U.S.A.

Antonio Hernandez, Exec. Vice Pres.,
  MALDEF*

Benjamin Hooks, Exec. Dir., NAACP

Haviland Houston, Gen. Sec.,
  Board of Church and Society,
  United Methodist Church*

Msgr. Daniel Hoye, Gen. Sec.,
  U.S. Catholic Conference

John E. Jacob, Pres.,
  National Urban League

L. Eldon James, Past Nat. Commander,
  American Legion*

Arthur Keys, Exec. Dir.,
  Interfaith Action for Economic Justice*

Le Xuan Khoa, Exec. Dir.,
  Indochina Resource Action Center*

Coretta Scott King

Lane Kirkland, Pres., AFL-CIO

* John Kromkowski, Pres.,
  National Center for Urban Ethnic
  Affairs*

Dr. Myron Kuropas, Sup. Vice Pres.,
  Ukrainian National Association*

Aloysius Mazewski, Pres.,
  Polish American Congress*

Benjamin Meed, Pres.,
  American Gathering and Federation of
  Jewish Holocaust Survivors

Matthew Nizza, Ch., Committee for Social
  Justice, New York Order, Sons of Italy*

Mary Jane Patterson, Dir., Wash. office,
  Presbyterian Church (U.S.A.)*

John Pavlik, Nat. Commander,
  Veterans of World War I

Rev. Eugene Picket, Pres.,
  Unitarian-Universalist Association*

William J. Rogers, Past Nat. Commander,
  American Legion*

Frank S. Sato, Pres.,
  Japanese-American Citizens League*

Connie Seals, Ch.,
  Illinois Consultation on Ethnicity
  and Education*

Paul L. Thompson, Past Nat. Commander
  Disabled American Veterans*

Mary Travers

Joseph M. Trevino, Exec. Dir.,
  League of United Latin American
  Citizens*

Barbara Tuchman

Joseph T. Ventura, Pres.,
  Concerned Italian-Americans for Better
  Governmen*

Leland Wilson, Dir., Wash. office,
  Church of the Brethren*

David S. Wyman, author,
  "The Abandonment of the Jews"

Peter Yarrow

Paul Yzaguirre, Pres.,
  National Council of La Raza*

David J. Zielinski, Nat. Commander,
  Catholic War Veterans

*Organization listed for identification purposes only.

"Please, Find Another Way!"
Requests Ad Hoc Committee of Conscience *
April, 1985

Dear Chancellor Helmut Kohl and President Ronald Reagan:

As Americans of all races, religions and creeds we come together to respect-fully urge that you not visit the cemetery at Bitburg. The wounds of those who suffered and lost loved ones at the hand of the Nazis, of those who paid in the dearest terms for opposing them, of the allied forces who valiantly fought to re-store freedom and democracy, are being reopened. For their sake and your sake, a more suitable site must be found so that this important mission will succeed.

Forty years have passed since the end of World War II. The United States and the Federal Republic of Germany have worked to assure that the carnage, the en-mity and the brutality of that war will never recur. An intrinsic element of this com-pact is a fundamental sense of morality—our nations act to endorse what is right and to eschew what is wrong.

The German people consciously chose to turn in another direction and to build a new system of government. The first chancellor of the Federal Republic of Germany was a hero in the struggle against the Nazi Party. He serves as a genuine symbol of the new era of reconciliation.

The United States and the Federal Republic of Germany have become allies based on a commonality of interests and shared principles. But history cannot be ignored. No matter how many years pass, some crimes are too heinous to be en-titled to forgiveness. They must be inalterably etched in the memory of humankind to assure that they never happen again. It is our duty not to forget.

Please, find another way!

Respectfully,

THE AD HOC COMMITTEE OF CONSCIENCE*

*Committee in Formation

New York, State
Mario Cuomo(*), Governor
Robert Abrams, Attorney General
Edward V. Regan, Comptroller
Daniel P. Moynihan(*), Senator
Alfonse D'Amato, Senator
Herman Badillo, Chairman Mortgage Agency
Douglas H. White, Commissioner of Human Rights
Basil Paterson(*), Former Secretary of State

New York, City
Edward Koch, Mayor
Carol Bellamy, President of the Council
Harrison Goldin, Comptroller
Abraham Beame, Former Mayor, City of New York

New York, City *(Cont'd.)*
Paul O'Dwyer(*), Former President of the Council
David Dinkins, City Clerk
Marcella Maxwell, Chairperson, Commission on Human Rights
Isaiah Robinson, Off. of Univ. & Corp. Affairs
    Board of Education
Basil Paterson (*), Former Secretary of State

Borough Presidents
Howard Golden, Brooklyn
Ralph Lamberti, Staten Island
Donald Mannes, Queens
Stanley Simon, Bronx
Andrew Stein, Manhattan

District Attorneys
Denis Dillon, Nassau
Kenneth Gribetz, Rockland
Elizabeth Holtzman, Brooklyn
Robert Morgenthau, Manhattan

Congress
Joseph DioGuiordi
Hamilton Fish, Jr.(*)
Charles Rangel
Theodore Weiss

State Legislature
Leon Bogues(*)
Herman D.Farrell, Jr.
Angelo Del Toro
Jerrold Nadler

City Council

Jerry L. Crispino	Carol Greitzer
Walter Crowley(*)	Samuel Horowitz
Michael DeMarco	Joseph Lisa(*)
Robert Dryfoos	Ruth Messinger
June Eisland	Stanley E. Michels
Wendell Foster	Mary Pinkett
Miriam Friedlander	

Religious Leaders

Rev. Richard Bratton	Church of God and Christ
Margaret Gilmore	National Conf. of Christians and Jews
Rabbi Paul Hait	New York Board of Rabbis
Rev. N.J. L'Heureux	Queens Federation of Churches
Colette Mahoney, R.S.H.M.(*)	Marymount College
Bro. William Martyn, S.A.	Catholic Archdiocese of New York
Rev. Donald Morlan	American Baptist Churches of Metro. NY
Rev. Robert Polk	New York Council of Churches
Rev. Bruce Salsworth	Community Church
Rev. David Simpson	National Council of Churches
Rev. Chic Strout	Brooklyn Council of Churches
Robert Tembeckjian	Armenian Church of America
Rt. Rev. Stuart Whetmore	Episcopal Diocese of New York

Civic Leaders
Robert Curvin(*), New School for Social Research
Howard Fogel, League of Mutual Taxi Owners
Neil Goldstein, American Jewish Congress
Roy Innes, Congress of Racial Equality
Charles Hughes, Local 372, AFSME
John Kaiteris, Hellenic American Neigh. Action Committee
George Klein, Co-Chair, NY Holocaust Memorial Council
Louis Klein, Jewish War Veterans
Haskel Lazere, American Jewish Committee
Horace Morris(*), Greater New York Fund
Paul Patrick, Council of Belmont Associations
Nancy Rubinger, National Council of Jewish Women
Wilbur Tatum(*), Amsterdam News
Peggy Tishman, Jewish Community Relations Council

Roman Catholic Survivor Of Auschwitz
New York
April 22, 1985

President Ronald Reagan
White House
Washington, 20510

Dear Mr. President:

Polish Americans regret your plans to honor the Nazi dead.

Nowhere else did the Hitlerites unleash the insane fury of their bestial rage and hatred as in Poland. They drenched Polish soil with the blood of innocent people.

We mourn the death of six million Polish citizens, most of whom were mercilessly butchered by the type of primitive barbarians who lie in the graves of the German cemetery you will visit. Their goal was to forever destroy everything Polish, be it Christian or Jewish. In the genocide of Europe's Jews, at least half were Poles.

Measured by numbers who died, Polish Jews and Polish Christians perished almost equally. Measured by percentage, Poland lost more of her population to the Nazis than any other country.

As Christians, we feel compelled to forgive them. As their victims, we find it inconceivable to honor them.

Michael Preisler, President
Polish American Congress
Downstate New York Division
Roman Catholic Survivor of Auschwitz
No. 22213

"The Liberator." Anatoly Rappaport's statue commemorating the U.S. military's release of prisoners from German war camps stands in Liberty Park, New Jersey.

Chapter 6

Bonn Reacts

"Your Attitude Has Not Been Understood By All"
April 19, 1985

His Excellency
Ronald Reagan
President of the United States of America
White House
Washington, D.C.

Excellency,

I wish to thank you for the noble attitude which you have shown towards the German people, an ally of the United States in Europe. I regret that your attitude has not been understood by all, neither in the United States nor in Germany. I hope and trust, however, that in a few years' time it will be understood by all.

Yours very respectfully,

Dr. Alfred Dregger
Chairman of the parliamentary group of the CDU/CSU
in the German Bundestag

Enclosure: Copy of the letter which I have sent to the Members of the U.S. Senate.

"Congressional Letter Fills Me With Dismay"
April 19, 1985

The Honorable
Howard Metzenbaum
United States Senate
Washington, D.C.

Dear Senators:

For those of you who did not know me, let me introduce myself: I am the Chairman of the parliamentary group of the CDU/CSU in the German Bundestag. I consider an intact German-American alliance to be of vital importance for the free world. I have expressed my views on the topical issue of SDI before the German Bundestag in a manner which can be seen from the verbatim record attached.

On the last day of the war, 8 May 1945—I was 24 years old at the time—I defended with my battalion the town of Marklissa in Silesia against attacks by the Red Army.

The contents of your letter to the American President in connection with his visit to the German military cemetery in Bitburg have filled me with dismay. I should not like to conceal from you the feelings which this letter has aroused in me and in many of my fellow countrymen: My only brother, Wolfgang, died in the Kurland pocket on the Eastern front in 1944, I do not know how. He was a decent young man, as were the overwhelming majority of my comrades.

If you call upon your President to refrain from the noble gesture he plans to make at the military cemetery in Bitburg I must consider this to be an insult to my brother and my comrades who were killed in action. Let me ask you whether one may refuse dead soldiers, whose bodies have decayed, the last honors? I ask you whether such an attitude is compatible with our shared ideals of decency, human dignity and respect for the dead? I ask you whether you regard as an ally the German people which was subjected to a fascist dictatorship for twelve years and which has been on the side of the West for forty years?

My sons are serving in the Federal Armed Forces. The younger son stood by my side when at Fort Douaumont near Verdun the French President of state, Francois Mitterand, and the German Federal Chancellor, Helmut Kohl, bowed in honor of the war dead of both parties.

There are forces which would like to abuse the commemoration of 8 May 1945 to undermine the German-American alliance. We should not further their endeavors.

Yours sincerely,

Dr. Alfred Dregger
Chairman of the parliamentary group of the CDU/CSU
in the German Bundestag

"Earth Conceal Not The Blood Shed On Thee": Kohl
Bergen-Belsen, West Germany
April 21, 1985

By Chancellor Helmut Kohl

(Address given during a ceremony marking the 40th anniversary of the liberation of Bergen-Belsen.)

"Earth conceal not the blood shed on thee"

These words, taken from the Book of Job and inscribed on the Jewish memorial over there, have today summoned us here to mourn, to remember, to seek reconciliation. We are gathered here in memory of the many innocent people who were tortured, humiliated and driven to their deaths at Bergen-Belsen, as in other camps. This site's admonition to us must not go unheard or be forgotten. It must be heeded by us as we define our basic political principles and requires each of us to examine his own life and way of thinking in the light of the suffering sustained here. Reconciliation with the survivors and descendants of the victims is only possible if we accept our history as it really was, if we Germans acknowledge our shame and our historical responsibility, and if we perceive the need to act against any efforts aimed at undermining human freedom and dignity.

For twelve years, the light of humanity in Germany and Europe was concealed by ubiquitous violence. Germany under the National Socialist regime filled the world with fear and horror. That era of slaughter, indeed of genocide, is the darkest, most painful chapter in German history. One of our country's paramount tasks is to inform people of those occurrences and keep alive an awareness of the full extent of this historical burden. We must not nor shall we ever forget the atrocities committed under the Hitler regime, the mockery and destruction of all moral precepts, the systematic inhumanity of the Nazi dictatorship. A nation that abandons its history forsakes itself. The presence of history is illustrated in a particularly cogent manner by the survivors of Bergen-Belsen who are here today at the invitation of the Central Jewish Council.

We recall above all the persecution and murder of the Jews, the pitiless war which man, in the final analysis, waged against himself. Bergen-Belsen, a town in the middle of Germany, remains a mark of Cain branded in the minds of our nation, just like Auschwitz and Treblinka, Belzec and Sobibor, Chelmno and Majdanek and the many other sites testifying to that mania for destruction. They epitomize what man can do against his fellow beings out of hatred and blindness. We do not know exactly how many people perished here at Bergen-Belsen. They numbered more than 50,000. But what does this figure tell us about how death befell every individual, his next of kin, his family? Vicariously for them all I name Anne Frank. She was 15 years old when she died here a few days before the liberation of the camp. We do not know exactly how her life was extinguished. But we know what awaited people here, how they were maltreated, what pain they suffered. Their lives, their human dignity were wholly at the mercy of their tormentors.

Despite their own great suffering, many inmates found the strength to stand by others, to turn to their fellow beings and offer them solace and consolation. An old Jewish saying goes: "Whoever saves a human life saves the whole world." A few known and many unknown detainees afforded their fellow beings strength at that time of great agony. We also recall those courageous people who, in their everyday lives under the Nazi dictatorship, gave the persecuted refuge at the risk of their own lives. They all helped to save our conception of man as God's image on earth.

Forty years ago Bergen-Belsen was liberated. But for thousands of people in this camp, salvation came too late: too drained were their bodies, too deeply scarred their souls. The National Socialist despisal of mankind was demonstrated not only in the concentration camps. It was ubiquitous, just as the dictatorship was totalitarian. Violence prevailed everywhere, and everywhere people were shadowed, persecuted and abducted. They were incarcerated, tortured and murdered. They were people from all walks of life, people of many nationalities, faiths and creeds, and with highly different political convictions. From the very outset, the terror of the totalitarian regime was directed against the Jews in particular. Envy and crude prejudice, nurtured over the centuries, culminated in an ideology of manic racism. The mass graves here show us where that led to.

Today, forty years later, it is still our duty to ask ourselves how a culture could disintegrate, to whose development and maturity German Jews in particular made an outstanding contribution. Many of them openly professed their German patriotism. Throughout the world they were representatives and ambassadors of German and Western culture. When the forces of evil seized power in Germany, the Jews were deprived of their rights and driven out of the country. The regime officially declared them "subhumans" and condemned them to the "final solution." The latter became Nazi terms in the German language — in the language of Goethe and Lessing, of Immanuel Kant and Edmund Husserl, of Dietrich Bonhoeffer and Leo Baeck. Hitler's misanthropic regime even sullied our language.

But before that it poisoned the spirit of the nation. The rulers were the henchmen of anarchy. With their arrogant use of power and their unbridled demands, they blinded the nation and then plunged an entire continent into misery. The deepest cause of this destruction was the accelerating disintegration of values and morals. In the final analysis, the totalitarian state was the product of the denial of God. The Nazi regime's hypocritical invocation of "divine providence" merely served to gloss over their own arbitrariness. That was and remains indeed the gravest perversion of religious faith: contempt for the living God professed by the great religions.

This darkest chapter of our history must always serve as a reminder to us, not because of the question of why those who risked their lives in opposing terror ultimately failed in their efforts. The decisive question is, instead, why so many people remained apathetic, did not listen properly, closed their eyes to the realities when the despots-to-be sought support for their inhumane program, first in back rooms and then openly out in the streets. The intentions of the National Socialists were apparent well before November 9, 1938, when 35,000 Jews were abducted to concentration camps.

We ask ourselves today why it was not possible to take action when the signs of National Socialist tyranny could no longer be overlooked—when books regard-ed as great cultural works of this century were burned, when synagogues were set on fire, when Jewish shops were demolished, when Jewish citizens were denied a seat on park benches. Those were warnings. Even though Auschwitz was beyond anything that man could imagine, the pitiless brutality of the Nazis had been clear-ly discernible. At the Barmen Synod in 1934, Hans Asmussen clear-sightedly warned of the designs of the new rulers:

"They claim to be redeemers, but are proving to be the tormentors of an unredeemed world."

The truth of this observation is clear to us today. Millions of Jews fell victim to National Socialist terror. The horror of this occurrence is still with us today. In view of such depravity, one could use the words of St. Augustine who once said: "To myself I have become a land of misery."

Like the Jews, many other innocent people fell victim to persecution. We can-not separate the ashes of the murdered. Let us remember those victims, too. The racial hatred of the National Socialists was also directed against gypsies. In the mass graves before our eyes lie countless Sinti and Romany gypsies. The inscription here at Bergen-Belsen reads: "Their violent death exhorts the living to oppose injustice." We mourn all those who lost their lives under the totalitarian regime because of their unswerving faith—among them many who refused to render military serv-ice on religious grounds.

A totalitarian state claims to possess the absolute truth, to be alone in know-ing what is good and what is bad. It does not respect the individual's conscience. It seeks to provide its own answers not only to the penultimate questions, those of politics, but also to the final questions, those concerning the meaning and value of our lives. Only in this way could there arise the demonic official dogma that cer-tain lives are not worth living. Only in this way could Mengele and others perform horrifying experiments on living people.

We recall the persecution of the mentally handicapped, of those people who were treated as social outcasts, and of the many others who, for very different rea-sons, were slaughtered—some of them simply because they expressed doubts about the so-called "final victory."

When this camp was set up, Russian prisoners-of-war were the first to be brought here. Their accommodation and treatment amounted to no less than tor-ture. Over 50,000 died alone in the region around Bergen. Something we should recall today and in future is the fact that of the almost 6 million Soviet soldiers who were captured by the Germans as prisoners-of-war, far less than half survived. Hence at this hour we also reflect on the suffering inflicted in the name of Ger-many on the peoples of Central and Eastern Europe. We commemorate the 30 mil-lion people from the Soviet Union who died during the war. We remember the crimes perpetrated against the Polish nation. And we also mourn those people who suffered injustices committed in revenge for Nazi injustices, for those Germans who fled their home regions and perished during the flight. But we would not have learned anything from history if we were to want to draw up a balance of atrocities.

Germany bears historical responsibility for the crimes of the Nazi tyranny. This responsibility is reflected not least in never-ending shame.

We will not let anything in this context be falsified or made light of. It is precisely the knowledge of guilty involvement, irresponsibility, cowardice and failure that enables us to perceive depravity and nip it in the bud. The totalitarianism that prevailed in Germany from January 30, 1933 onwards is not an unrepeateable deviation from the straight and narrow, not an "accident of history". An alert and sensitive stance is needed above all towards any views and attitudes that can pave the way for totalitarian rule:

• belief in ideologies which claim to know the goals of history and promise paradise on earth,

• the failure to exercise freedom responsibly, and

• apathy about violations of human dignity, basic rights and the precept of peace.

Peace begins with respect for the unconditional, absolute dignity of the individual in all spheres of life. The suffering and death of people, the victims of inhumanity, urge us to preserve peace and freedom, to promote law and justice, to perceive man's limits and to follow our path in humility before God.

What Konrad Adenauer said here at Bergen-Belsen in February 1960 remains valid:

"I believe we could not choose a better place than this one to give a solemn pledge to do our utmost so that every human being — irrespective of the nation or race to which he belongs — enjoys justice, security and freedom on earth in the future."

The collapse of the Nazi dictatorship on May 8, 1945 was a day of liberation for the Germans. It soon became apparent, however, that it did not mean freedom for everyone.

We in the free part of our nation have, following the experience of Hitler's dictatorship, made it a rule that especially in central political questions each individual must decide for himself. We have established a free republic, a democracy based on the rule of law. The founders of our democratic country perceived and took advantage of the moment which Werner Nachmann [Chairman of the Central Council of Jews in Germany] spoke of. By possessing the strength to face up to the responsibility imposed by history, they restored for us the value and dignity of freedom that is exercised responsibly. For this reason, we have also linked ourselves irrevocably to the community of free Western democracies based on shared values and entered into a permanent alliance with them. This was only possible because those nations — and not least of all former concentration camp inmates and the relatives of victims of the Nazi dictatorship — reached out their hands to us in reconciliation. Many of those nations directly experienced Nazi terror in their own country. There was bitter hatred for those who had subjugated and maltreated them — hatred which ultimately was directed against the entire German nation. We in the free part of Germany realize what it means, following Auschwitz and Treblinka, to have been taken back into the free Western community. Those nations did so with the justified expectation that we will not disown the crimes perpetrated in the name of Germany against the nations of Europe.

Today, 40 years later, we continue to acknowledge that historical liability. Precisely because we Germans must never dismiss from our minds that dark era of our history, I am today addressing you and our fellow countrymen as Chancellor of the Federal Republic of Germany. We have learned the lessons of history, especially the history of this century. Human dignity is inviolable. Peace must emanate from German soil.

Our reconciliation and friendship with France is a boon to the Germans and the French, to Europe and the world as a whole. We wish to attain a similar peace-directed achievement in our relations with our Polish neighbors.

We are grateful that reconciliation was possible with the Jewish people and the State of Israel, that friendship is again growing, particularly among young people. And we respectfully pay tribute to those men and women who, looking to the future, were prepared to surmount the forces of hatred with the strength of humanity. We are especially thankful to eminent representatives of Israel such as Nahum Goldmann and David Ben-Gurion. We are also grateful to Konrad Adenauer. They all sought reconciliation.

Reparations were paid to secure a homeland for the Jews and to assist the survivors of the Holocaust. However, today we know just as we did then: suffering and death, pain and tears are not susceptible to reparations. The only answer can be collective commemoration, collective mourning, and a collective resolve to live together in a peaceful world.

In his memorial address at the Cologne Synagogue on November 9, 1978, Nahum Goldmann recalled the creative mutual influence of Jews and Germans and spoke of a "unique, historical occurrence". This co-existence of Jews and Germans in particular has a long, eventful history. It has been studied very little thus far and is scarcely known to many people. For this reason we intend to promote the establishment of an "Archive for the study of Jewish History in Germany". We want to trace German-Jewish interaction through history. Over many centuries, Jews made decisive contributions to German culture and history. And it is an accomplishment of historical import that, even after 1945, Jewish compatriots were prepared to assist us in building the Federal Republic of Germany. We wish to preserve this memory, too, in order to resolve to live together in a better future. It is therefore essential to make it clear to the up-coming generation that tolerance and an open-minded attitude towards one's fellow beings are irreplaceable virtues without which a polity cannot survive. Emulating each other in the quest for humanity is the most pertinent answer to the failure of an era marked by intolerance and the abuse of power. At Yad Va-Shem, the words of a Jewish mystic of the early 18th century became firmly impressed upon my mind: "Seeking to forget makes exile all the longer; the secret of redemption lies in remembrance." For this reason, the exhortation expressed here at Bergen-Belsen rightly is "Earth conceal not the blood shed on thee".

Letter From a German Correspondent
April 22, 1985

Dr. Alfred Dregger
Chairman, CDU/CSU
German Bundestag
Bonn, West Germany

Dear Mr. Dregger:

Thank you very much for your letter to Senator Metzenbaum.

What you said reflected my and my wife's heartfelt feelings. Both our fathers are, like your brother, buried in places unknown to us.

My father was "reported missing" in March 1945 near Königsberg. I was five years old at the time.

The gravestones in Bitburg on which the words "An unknown German soldier" are inscribed are thus memorials to our fathers as well, which would, incidentally, apply even if they had died in combat against what are our allies today.

(Signed by a German correspondent, born 1940)

(**Editor:** Submitted by Dr. A. Dregger without signature.)

Letter From a Jewish Professor
April 22, 1985

Dr. Alfred Dregger
Chairman, CDU/CSU
German Bundestag
Bonn, West Germany

Dear Dr. Dregger,

I would like to write a few personal lines to you in connection with your letter to 53 American senators, of which I read only an excerpt in the newspaper, and in connection with the current controversy over President Reagan's visit to Germany.

As a Jew who lost nine of his closest relatives in Germany during the Nazi period, I think I can understand the bitter tone of your letter: you speak of the death of your own brother. I think the key to the unfortunate events surrounding President Reagan's visit lies in *one* fact — not in the clumsiness of politicians (which does exist), not in the self-righteousness of the descendants of Jewish victims (which also exists), but in a basic fact to be observed in our time, namely that we have grown used to interpreting all problems from a purely economic or political standpoint (in the narrower sense of the word) and thus forget the purely human factors of whatever kind. I would hope that the current situation will cause everyone involved in this embarrassing controversy to realize that this is not the right approach. Neither repression nor self-righteousness, neither political gestures nor Sunday rhetoric can be a substitute for people from the various camps meeting *as* human beings and quietly helping each other to solve their problems. Drawing up a balance sheet of the victims and the crimes (which none of us can forget) is not enough, indeed, it is totally inappropriate. Nor is it enough to appeal to the unity of mankind. We must struggle on a person-to-person basis (and thus vicariously from nation to nation and culture to culture) not to see who is right or wrong — because we are all wrong — but rather to make sure that humanity still exists. If this is not the case, we do not need to worry about its future, for it would be a mere skeleton.

Let us have the courage and the humility to make a start and meet as human beings, in your living room or in ours, without superficial rhetoric, as persons who doubtless have very divergent views on many, many issues. That is not the point, however. Should not we, you as a Christian and I as a Jew, honour your dead brother and my dead family by — very quietly — making a new start? Let us admit to ourselves that neither you nor I have come to terms with the past. From this joint admission insights and forces may grow that will also help other people to perceive that politics is more than just politics.

With very best wishes and greetings,

(Signed by a Jewish professor)

(**Editor:** Submitted by Dr. A. Dregger without signature.)

Letter From a German War-Widow
April 23, 1985

Dr. Alfred Dregger
Chairman, CDU/CSU
German Bundestag
Bonn, West Germany

Dear Mr. Dregger,

I belong to that group in our population that has never had a lobby in the past and still does not today — I am a *war widow*.

Through more or less qualified commentaries and broadcasts, our radio and television stations see to it that wounds in the process of healing are torn open time and again.

Now even those servicemen who were killed in action, regardless of the branch of the armed forces in which they served (my husband was in the Fourth Cavalry Regiment from Cologne-Kalk), *have become a target of hatred and calumny.*

You have been the only person so far who had defended the war dead in the media. I would like to express my heartfelt thanks to you. I shall never forget this.

(Signed by a German war widow)

(**Editor:** Submitted by Dr. A. Dregger without signature.)

"You Severely Damaged The Image Of The FRG In The American Mind"
April 23, 1985

Dr. Alfred Dregger
Chairman, CDU/CSU
German Bundestag
Bonn, West Germany

Dear Dr. Dregger:

You will know, from those parliamentary debates in which we opposed one another, that I do not depict my political adversaries as evil. In spite of the profound differences of viewpoint between us, that has also included Dr. Alfred Dregger. I have to say about your open letter to Senator Howard Metzenbaum and a number of other members of the American Senate that with this letter you have severely damaged the image of the Federal Republic in the American mind. You have also—in an irresponsible way—overburdened German-American friendship. My objection is not to the American President's visit to the military cemetery. It is certainly right to show respect for the dead of the war, forty years after its end, without going into the convictions of every individual involved. It is an entirely different question as to why, in preparing the visit, the Federal German government stumbled from one embarrassment into another. But that isn't the reason for my letter.

I find it very disturbing that a leading German politician, forty years after Hitler's capitulation, should use the formulation that the German people "was subjugated by a brown dictatorship for twelve years." Do you actually intend to try to obscure the fact that only a small—and terribly decimated—minority of Hitler's opponents was subjugated, while millions of Germans chose Hitler and well into the Second World War accepted him as "Führer?" Is the repression of this fact your way of dealing with the past?

How can our friends in the United States and everywhere else understand your terrible recourse to the distorted idea of the "decent German"—with which you send your brother, killed in action, into battle once more. You insist that he was "a decent young man," and add that so were "most of his fellow soldiers." Isn't precisely that what we have to try to understand—that millions of subjectively "decent" human beings allowed themselves to be misused by a criminal regime in an aggressive war? Until now I did not believe that we would encounter another West German politician who would so thoughtlessly proclaim the fable of a small minority of deceivers and a large majority of decent Germans. You present our history to the younger generation as if it were impersonal fate. With polished simplicity, you repeat the tones and words of the nationalists who destroyed the Weimar Republic. It is shocking how you reject all the knowledge we won so painfully in the forty years since Hitler's death.

What is equally shocking is the unconcealed undertone of blackmail in your letter. What is the intention of your menacing question as to whether the Americans see in the German people, after it has stood on the side of the West for forty years, an ally? And what is the meaning of your reference to a parliamentary speech in which you enthusiastically endorsed the President's SDI? What do these things have to do with one another? Should the President visit a cemetery in Bitburg because the Germans declare themselves in favor of arms in space? And should he refrain from making the visit in case the Germans (as did the Norwegians under a conservative government) declare themselves against the militarization of space? You write in your letter that you "fought against attacks by the Red Army with your battalion" in Marklissa in Silesia. Between the lines of your letter it is easy to read that you are still fighting there. You still conjure up that terrible error of the "decent Germans"—the mute reproach of the Americans that were allied to the Soviet Union. Your letter is infused by the idea that the Americans would do well to forget the past, because we are now allies and support the arms policies of the present American administration. That idea is morally corrupt.

The Federal German Republic found its way back to the community of free peoples, when Konrad Adenauer clasped hands with Charles de Gaulle in the Reims Cathedral, and when Willi Brandt kneeled in respect in the Warsaw Ghetto. Our moral capital is being squandered by a government whose foreign ministry recently recommended to the American President that, during an official visit forty years after the war's end, he should avoid a concentration camp. In your effort to please a small minority of incorrigible and unteachable voters, you and the government you support endangers the good name of German democracy. You say that your sons are serving in the Federal German Army. I fervently hope that they do so in another spirit than their father's.

Respectfully,
Peter Glotz

(Professor Peter Glotz is a member of the Federal German Parliament and General Secretary of the Social Democratic Party.)

"A Contribution To Peace And Reconciliation Among Nations"
Bundestag, West Germany
April 25, 1985

By Chancellor Helmut Kohl

(Statement in the Bundestag concerning preparations for President Reagan's visit.)

Mr. President [West German President von Weizsäcker], ladies and gentlemen.

Anyone who is at present confronted with Germany's recent history is well advised to approach with circumspection and a sense of concern the matters that we have to discuss in connection with the forthcoming state visit of the President of the United States of America. This is what I feel very strongly because my intention was and continues to be that of achieving on the occasion of this visit a contribution to peace and reconciliation among nations. That was also the purpose of the many talks which have been held to prepare the visit.

Early in the spring of 1984, President Mitterand of France informed me of the plans for the celebrations marking the 40th anniversary of D-Day in Normandy. I wish to state this here because a great deal of false information has been propagated on this subject. In that conversation I immediately pointed out that as German Chancellor and head of government I was not interested in being invited to and attending the celebrations. This met with considerable understanding. We also discussed on that occasion the possibility of documenting in a gesture of reconciliation over the graves—40 years after D-Day, at the time 39 years after the end of World War II and about 70 years after the end of World War I—what had been possible after the war as a result of many fortunate circumstances and vigorous efforts on the part of many important democratic statesmen in France and Germany: to become allies, to bury past animosity, to bring the younger generations closer together—in short, one of the greatest achievements of modern times.

The suggestion was then made of doing so last autumn at Douaumont in Verdun. You all remember those scenes—90-year-old veterans of World War I, participants in World War II and several tens of thousands of German and French school children who in their youthful innocence did not realize what it all meant, namely that a seal was placed by a few people for entire nations on the fact that we have overcome our animosity and become friends and that fratricidal wars in Europe have been relegated to the past. Last November, I then discussed in detail with President Reagan that event and the talks leading up to it. I know that he is a friend of our people. I have experienced this time and again in the past few years. On the basis of the model of Franco-German cooperation I just described, we discussed the possibility of attempting—on the occasion of his visit on the eve of the 40th anniversary of Germany's capitulation—to achieve peace and reconciliation across the graves.

We agreed that it was desirable for the President to address young Germans 40 years later on the future, on the world of tomorrow, and to commemorate at a suitable site the victims of the National Socialist regime in view of the dreadful occurrences in Germany at the time. I proposed this from the very outset. I also proposed, if possible, to commemorate at a military cemetery the dead of all nations—not only the dead of our nation and the young Americans killed in the war, but also all the dead of World War II. Ronald Reagan immediately took up the idea of this very noble gesture and understood it to be a gesture of friendship. We started the preparations for his visit in this spirit. I find it most regrettable that this great man, who is a friend of the Germans, has encountered considerable domestic difficulties because of this envisaged noble gesture. Let me state this as a German and as the German chancellor: I am grateful to him for the attitude that he has once again demonstrated.

During the detailed preparations for his visit, various sites for the gesture were then discussed in numerous talks. I suggested that he should meet with young Germans in Hambach, the site of German democracy, the site of European solidarity, the site which so strongly recalls German-American traditions going back to the 18th and 19th centuries. We also discussed at length the possibility of a meeting with young soldiers, soldiers of the U.S. Army and of the Bundeswehr—not for the purpose of holding large parades, but of having private conversations with soldiers insofar as the circumstances permit, with young Americans vicariously for all the hundreds of thousands of American soldiers who have constantly maintained peace and freedom for our country over the last 30 years, and with young German soldiers—19, 20, 21-year-old conscripts.

In our discussion I repeatedly presented a powerful argument: that I consider it important that the President of the United States, our most important ally, should meet with young German soldiers, with the grandchildren of those who died during the war, whom we also wish to commemorate at the cemetery, with this young generation who must see the point of their service in the cause of defending freedom and peace.

The idea thus arose of going to Bitburg, a little town in Germany which, more than others, lives in a symbiosis with the American garrison. Well over 100,000 U.S. soldiers have rendered their military service there over the decades. The town and the garrison are of such a size that close ties have arisen between them. They do not speak of partnership, they experience it at first hand in their everyday lives. Well over 5,000 marriages have come about there between Germans and Americans, many thousands of children have been born of German-American marriages. If there is anywhere in Germany where one can make clear that Germans and Americans can live together as a matter of course, then Bitburg best illustrates this. I suggested that town because I believe that it is right for tribute to be paid in a special manner—vicariously for the entire Federal Republic Germany—to those people who are exposed to strains owing to the presence of military installations.

In view of the time for the visit, it was only natural to consider the military cemetery on the immediate outskirts of Bitburg. It is a soldiers' cemetery set up in 1959, with the graves of over 2,000 soldiers—some of them from World War I, but the majority from World War II. They are soldiers who fell in combat during the last few days of the war and who were transferred there after 1959 from cemeteries in nearby towns and villages. Former members of the Waffen-SS were also buried at the cemetery in Bitburg, as in almost all of the cemeteries that are looked after by the Association for the Maintenance of War Graves. Anyone who discusses the subject of SS soldiers buried in military cemeteries, of SS combat troops buried there, must now, 40 years later, also live up to the obligation of adopting a differentiated approach towards historical occurrences. Many of those very young soldiers did not have a chance to evade conscription by the Waffen-SS.

During the past few days I have asked for the names and dates inscribed on the tombstones there to be presented to me. Of the 49 SS soldiers named there, 32 were younger than 25 when they died. We are today speaking of soldiers who died at the age of 17, 18, or 19. Their lives were much shorter than the space of time that has elapsed since their deaths. They lived but a short life in a barbaric war. Even those who lived through the war find it difficult to understand what happened, and this is even more difficult for the present generation, and it cannot be understood by those who have not lived here but have grown up on a different continent. I do not venture to judge those who experienced all the horror and barbarity of the Third Reich at Auschwitz, Treblinka and Bergen-Belsen, who are unable to forget those occurrences, what they suffered and their next of kin suffered, and who are unable to forgive.

I believe that we are not entitled to judge or condemn such an attitude. It is a magnificent achievement if someone who experienced all that—as we witnessed at Bergen-Belsen last Sunday—is able to express liberating words of forgiveness.

But we have neither a moral nor a legal claim to such an attitude. In view of the undifferentiated judgments, in some cases the unacceptable collective accusations and some instances unacceptable distortion of historical facts during the past few days, I consider it important to quote an impartial witness to those times, whose life and activities as a German patriot are beyond question in this House, namely Kurt Schumacher. In the autumn of 1951 he expressed certain ideas which are almost of a visionary nature in view of today's debate here.

I quote:

"Over 900,000 members of the former Waffen-SS returned from World War II. This Waffen-SS is not equivalent to either the general SS or the organizations specializing in the liquidation of people. It was set up for the purposes of the war. Many of the young people were undoubtedly imbued with specifically Hitlerian ideology, but their political objectives did not include crime as perpetrated by the twelve-year dictatorship. Hundreds of thousands were, without any effort on their part, conscripted into or transferred to the Waffen-SS from the Wehrmacht.

Most of those 900,000 people have become downright social outcasts. They are held jointly liable for the crimes of the Security Service (SD) and the liquidation campaigns, although, as members of the Waffen-SS, they hardly had any more to do with that than other sections of the Wehrmacht. Every totalitarian system seeks, by creating involvement in every way possible, to generate a sense of total complicity. In the case of the Waffen-SS, the world was successfully convinced of their total complicity. We believe it is necessary for humanitarian and civic reasons to dispel this belief and to clear the way for the vast majority of former members of the Waffen-SS so that they can live their lives as individuals and citizens."

I believe that one cannot more cogently underscore the dilemma and the duty to differentiate than Kurt Schumacher did then as a result of his own personal experience. That statement by Schumacher was an appeal to the living, to the generation of former SS members who had survived the war. Today we are discussing on both sides of the Atlantic the fate of SS soldiers who died 40 years ago. Last Sunday I clearly stated at Bergen-Belsen that we Germans must keep alive an awareness of the full extent of the burden and responsibility imposed by history. Anyone who was unable to evade the ubiquitous violence of the National Socialist regime became involved in its injustice in one way or another as members of the Hitler Youth Organization, as soldiers, frequently as civil servants, and many in other fashions. Let me state this to our friends abroad and to our many young compatriots: the extent of such involvement was in many cases determined solely by one's age, by one's personal circumstances or by arbitrary decisions by the rulers.

Does it truly fall to us to judge people who were involved in that injustice and lost their lives, while we respect the others who were perhaps no less involved but survived and have since then rightly made use of the opportunities that life has afforded them, who have served the cause of freedom and our republic by participating in the political parties.

The idea underlying our discussions and the visit was and continues to be that President Reagan, our friend, and I will jointly commemorate the victims of the war and pay reverence to the soldiers' graves. I am grateful to the American President for this noble gesture. I am grateful that he will visit, together with me and others, Bergen-Belsen, one of the sites of Germany's shame, but I am also thankful to him for visiting the cemetery. I believe that I am expressing what millions of people feel who lost relatives during the war. If one looks around this chamber, one will discover many members on all benches who lost their fathers, brothers or—in the case of older members—even their sons and who feel that this noble gesture is directed towards them. The gesture also has another meaning: that of being a sign for young people serving in the Bundeswehr, indicating that we have learned the lesson of history.

In their Pastoral Letter on the occasion of May 8, 1985, the Catholic Bishops state the following: We must pray the Lord's Prayer for and with those people against whom the German nation committed wrongs. The link between bitter animosity and war remains a link of fate pointing towards the path of reconciliation.

At the cemetery in Bitburg we intend to commemorate those who died in the war, those who had to die in the war started by Hitler in Europe and overseas, those Germans who were forced into the war by Hitler and perished in it. Reconciliation will be achieved between erstwhile adversaries if we are capable of mourning people irrespective of the nationality of those who were murdered, who fell or died. This we demonstrated at Douaumont in Verdun, and we intend to do so at Bitburg. Commemoration of the victims always keeps alive an awareness of the guilt of the perpetrators. War graves are always a reminder to those who assisted and committed the crimes of the war and the tyranny.

Werner Nachmann, Chairman of the Central Jewish Council in Germany, stated at Bergen-Belsen, a place where Jews sustained untold suffering in the name of Germany, that he returned to his former home country, like many others, in order to dispel mistrust and to build bridges. He also said that most people considered his action impossible and many regarded it as inappropriate. Who, if not we Germans, appreciates the feelings of those who survived the Nazi atrocities and cannot forget or forgive. We must accept that attitude, respect it and live with it. We ask our friends, especially our American friends, to consider the reconciliation across the graves as a desire that is rooted in our hearts and minds because our meeting at the graves—those of the victims of the tyranny located in a concentration camp and those on a military cemetery—will be above all a common pledge that our nations must never again be exposed to such barbarity, that war and violence are not a means of pursuing political goals, and that we are committed to the principle that peace must emanate from German soil.

For a Free Germany in a Free Europe
Bonn, West Germany
April 28, 1985

By Dr. Alfred Dregger

(Chairman of the parliamentary group of the CDU/CSU in the German Bundestag, Dr. Alfred Dregger, addressed the Federation of German Expellees in Beethovenhalle, in Bonn.)

A week ago I attended a commemorative ceremony held by the Council of Jews in Germany at the site of the former Bergen-Belsen concentration camp. We commemorated the victims of the National Socialist tyranny, in particular the Jews, primarily German Jews, who, at that time, were humiliated, tortured, murdered or driven from their German homeland. With no other European nation had these Jews entered into a closer symbiosis than with the German nation. They had made unique contributions to German culture. In the First World War they distinguished themselves as German soldiers.

Today, survivors of the Jewish Holocaust are among the most brilliant minds in the Western world. The wounds that blind racial hatred have caused to the Jewish people and thus also to the German people surpass human comprehension. We are grateful to those who have returned to Germany for making a renewed attempt to form a German-Jewish symbiosis.

Here among German patriots in particular I would like to say to Werner Nachmann, to the Central Council of Jews and to the Jewish communities in Germany that we extend our hand to those who seek reconciliation with us, that we stand by their side and that we would like to make a contribution towards ensuring that the evil that was done to them can finally be overcome.

Today, a week after the commemorative ceremony at Bergen-Belsen, we recall what befell the people at the end of the Second World War who, for centuries, had lived in East and West Prussia, Pomerania, Silesia, the Sudetenland, Transylvania, Banat, and other areas of German settlement in Eastern and Southeastern Europe.

Without Hitler, the man who brought ruin upon Germany, there would have been no crimes of expulsion and no murder of Jews. It is only today that many people are beginning to grasp what a great moral deed the uprising of 20 July 1944 against Hitler was. I say moral deed, because the men and women of the German resistance movement were completely on their own. The Allies, including our allies today, rejected any contact with them. After the Conference of Casablanca in 1943 Roosevelt and Churchill had only one answer: unconditional surrender not of Hitler, but of Germany. They did not envision a future for a Germany freed from Hitler. The alternative which the German resistance movement faced together with the German people was either to defend Germany along with Hitler, who

had destroyed it, or to deliver Germany, along with Hitler, into the hands of its enemies. At the mercy not only of those who occupied the Western part of Germany,
but also of Stalin, who, in millions of murders in his own country, had already
proved what human rights and human life were worth to him. The men and wom-
en of the resistance movement did not want to destroy the Reich; they wanted to
save it and restore the honour of the German people. When this proved to be impossible in a merciless war that was filled with hatred and fiercely fought by both
sides, they decided in favour of the second alternative. This involved more than just
enormous courage, which was also displayed by the soldiers on the front and by
the people at home, it also involved the ability to grasp the overall situation and
to make judgements. That, under the artillery and propaganda barrages, most people no longer had this ability, the ordinary soldiers on the front and the old men,
women and children plagued by constant bomb attacks at home, who could criticize them for this?

Today we must express our thanks to Colonel Count Stauffenberg, to the lawyer Joseph Wirmer, and to the trade unionist Julius Leber—I could name many
others—for what they did. They form part of the foundations without which a
democratic Germany could not have been built. In 1984, we, the CDU/CSU,
honoured the memory of these men and women at the site where they were executed in Berlin-Plötzensee. Many of the founders of the CDU/CSU were companions of theirs who survived.

Let me repeat: without Hitler the catastrophes of the concentration camps
and the expulsion could not have taken place. It is also true, however, that Hitler's
crimes can serve neither as a justification nor as an excuse for the crimes of others.
Crimes are crimes, whoever they are committed against and whoever they are committed by. Equality before the law is one of the most elementary legal principles
of Western civilization. Monetary claims can be offset against each other, but this
does not apply to crimes. Every crime affects an individual human being and violates human dignity; only because it violates the dignity of the individual, every
crime also represents an offence against mankind as a whole. This applies to
crimes against Jews and Germans alike; it applies to both the victors and the vanquished.

Just as I have thanked the Jews who have made a new start in Germany since
1945, I wish to thank you, who were expelled from your homes, for the contribution you have rendered since 1945 to building up the Federal Republic of Germany
and to peace in the world. To the frightful experiences to which you were exposed
you responded with the Charter of German Expellees, a document reflecting humanity and a love of peace; representing all those who shared your fate, you made
a symbolic gesture pointing to a common future of the free peoples on the European continent.

You wanted to help close the deep rifts that had opened up between the peoples of Europe. You wanted to help give moral strength and moral courage for the
future back to your own people, since you knew that a people can do justice to its
historical responsibility only if it lives in peace with itself.

You have proved for decades now that all this has not merely been lip service. I know no expellees in the world whose actions have been freer from hatred, more desirous of peace and more aware of their political responsibility than those of the German expellees. Neither in the past nor in the present are there other examples of this approach, be it in Palestine, in Indochina or anywhere else.

As with the Jews and the other victims of the National Socialist tyranny, I therefore express my solidarity also with you, the expellees. With two million of your fellow countrymen who lost their lives while fleeing or being driven out of their homes, and with 12 million who, at the end of the Second World War, lost nearly everything but their lives—their homes, their property, their families and their honour—I do not wish to describe what was done to women.

Let me say expressly that this solidarity also includes the German expellee organizations and those bearing responsibility in them. Without you, without your humanity, without your sense of responsibility, without your personal integrity and credibility, Herr Czaja, Herr Hupka and all of you, ladies and gentlemen, some expellees would perhaps already have become what Stalin intended them to be: a source of explosive social unrest and opponents of the democratic state which we newly established in 1949.

Let me add: one cannot simply ignore more than 14 million people. It is highly immoral to pay attention to those who resort to acts of terror to oppose the injustice that has been done to them, such as the Palestinians, and to disregard or even despise those who, for the sake of peace and reconciliation, renounce revenge and retaliation, such as the German expellees. Reconciliation presupposes respect for one another. The least that the expellees can expect is renunciation of the attempt to deprive them of their identity. Silesia, East Prussia and the other areas of German settlement in the East were not conquered by Hitler. They, like the other German regions, had for centuries been the home of Germans, who made them flourish culturally and who were driven from them by force in 1945. Even if they and their descendants should never again set eyes on these regions, no one may dispute the fact that they were their homelands.

In this respect the Russians are more honest than many others. They have never claimed that they "returned" to Königsberg, the city of Immanuel Kant. The Russians no more returned to East Prussia than the East Poles who were resettled in the other parts of East Prussia. The Russians speak of the "results of the Second World War". During his recent visit to Bonn I told Mr. Simyanin, the secretary of the Soviet Central Committee, that every war has results and that it would be foolish to ignore them. However, the results of a war do not mean the end, but rather the starting point of politics. In spite of everything that separates us from Soviet imperialism and its totalitarian practices—the people, the Russians, have one thing in common with us. They did not merely watch the war on television; like us, they experienced it in their own country. This trauma is shared by both peoples. The purpose of a constructive Ostpolitik by the free Europeans and the free West cannot be to legitimize the rape and division of Europe. Its purpose can only be to overcome the division of Germany and Europe in a long and peaceful process, in which our neighbours as well as the superpowers must be involved. Only if, in the shaping of future policy in East and West, everyone follows the example set by the German expellees, only if everyone pursues a policy based on reconciliation and a desire for peace will it be possible to prevent another disaster.

Let me say a few words about the campaigns accusing you of "revanchism", with which you have been afflicted repeatedly for decades now. It is dreadful when a desire for reconciliation is responded to with ideological hatred or chauvinistic nationalism.

You know that I have always stood at your side in fending off these campaigns and will continue to do so in the future. I consider this my duty. I am an elected representative of the German people and, in the words of our former colleague Reichsfreiherr von Guttenberg, an elected representative of the entire German people, and thus also of the expellees. I can well imagine what I would feel if I and my family had been forcefully driven from Westphalia, where my family has lived for centuries, or from Hesse, which has become my second home. And what I would feel if, in addition to the violation of my human rights, decades of constant abuse and unjustified attacks were added as a response to my desire for reconciliation.

Early this year Cardinal Höffner said that love of one's country was based on dedication to those to whom we owe our existence — that is God, our parents, and the land of our fathers, to which we are attached by destiny through a common homeland, common descent, a common history, a common culture, and a common language. For this reason — he said — the love of our country is not a mere feeling, but also a moral duty.

The land of your forefathers is Pomerania, or West Prussia, or Transylvania, or the Sudetenland. I do not wish to enumerate all the regions. People are shaped by their homeland, which remains alive in them forever. Love of one's homeland, as Konrad Adenauer said, has an "ethical basis".

A policy seeking to deny us Germans what is granted to all other peoples — love of one's homeland and one's country — the right to self-determination and national dignity — such a policy aimed at denying and destroying our identity would contain the seeds of a new catastrophe.

Law is the basis of peace. "Opus justitiae pax" is the motto of a great pope. Indeed, peace is the work of justice, not the work of oppression.

We have all suffered injustice, Germans, Czechs and Poles. Not a few of us continue to suffer injustice today. If we do not turn against one another, but overcome injustice together, the way will be paved for solutions that will stand the test of time.

8 May 1945 did not mark the end of the German question. The division of our country — and thus of Europe — is not the result of the Second World War, as has been repeatedly claimed by the Soviet Union. The German Reich in its borders of 31 December 1937 was not dissolved under international law and obliterated. True, plans to divide Germany did exist during the war. However, they all remained in desk drawers.

Michael Stürmer, a historian from Erlangen, rightly wrote: "The division of

Germany after 1945 was not caused by Hitler, but made possible by him." The form which it then took was not what had been originally planned. The division into zones was not intended to become a division of the world. It was meant to be only provisional.

Neither in Yalta nor in Potsdam was a treaty concluded which provided for the permanent division of Europe into two blocs and stipulated that Germany cease to exist. Ronald Reagan, the American President, Francois Mitterrand, the French President, and Margaret Thatcher, the British prime minister, have confirmed this on several occasions.

For 35 years now the Soviet Union has endeavored to push aside or make people forget this clear fact. It wants the division of Berlin, Germany and Europe to be retroactively sanctioned under international law and to attain legal validity. However, power must not go before the law.

- We uphold the right of the German people to free self-determination.
- We uphold the mandate of our constitution to achieve the unity and freedom of Germany in free self-determination. This is a historical not a transient mandate.
- We know that the law is the weapon of the weaker side; we will not throw this weapon away.
- The mere insistence on legal positions is of course no substitute for a policy. However, legal positions are indispensable instruments of a liberal policy oriented toward peace and accommodation.

What Herbert Wehner said in a television interview in 1968 has lost none of its significance today. In response to the question whether we Germans would not do better to renounce the right to self-determination for our people, Wehner replied, and I quote:

> No, we would not have the right to do that. We would be scoundrels. Whether I am able to enforce a right or whether I keep alive a right which cannot be enforced are two different matters. If it cannot be done, then it cannot be done for a longer or shorter period of time, then this question will remain open between the countries in question until it can be solved. However, in giving up a right, we would be sinning against our neighbour and would be causing serious damage to ourselves.

Indeed, we would be committing a sin — not only against the Germans but also against the Poles and the other peoples of Eastern Central Europe; their future in freedom also remains open only as long as the German question remains open.

Some of those who, with inconceivable superficiality and thoughtlessness, state that the German question is "no longer open" obviously do not know what they are saying. The reservation concerning the conclusion of a peace treaty, the fact that the German question is open — this is the most important operative approach to overcoming the division of Germany and Europe. If the reservation concerning the conclusion of a peace treaty were abandoned

- then the division of Berlin, Germany and Europe would be final; the GDR would become a foreign country for us;
- then a single German nationality, the legal band holding together the German nation, could no longer be maintained;
- then the Germans in the free part of Berlin would be without a nationality; they would be nationals neither of the Federal Republic of Germany nor of the GDR;

then the basis of the Four Power status for the whole of Berlin would be lost — as a result of which the free part of Berlin would no longer be protected by our Western allies;

- Poland, Czechoslovakia and Hungary would disappear behind the Iron Curtain for good.

Those who say that the German question is no longer open, those who give up the reservation that the final decision on Germany as a whole can only be made in a peace treaty

- are undermining not only the foundations on which the free part of Berlin is based,
- they also adopt a position which clearly contradicts the law in force, and our constitution, the Basic Law and — let me add — the will of the German people.

The awareness of being one nation has not been broken — neither West nor East of the border dividing us.

German history has always also been European history. The German question was and is a European question. The border that divides our country also divides Europe into two blocs.

It was Konrad Adenauer's great historical achievement to make the unresolved German question a matter of the entire West and in this way firmly to connect the free part of Germany and the West.

In a few days' time, on 5 May, it will have been 30 years since the Bonn Convention concluded between the Federal Republic of Germany and its Western allies, the prerequisite for our accession to NATO, entered into force.

Article 7 of this Convention continues to apply unchanged:

1. The signatory states are agreed that an essential aim of their common policy is a peace settlement for the whole of Germany, freely negotiated between Germany and her former ene-

mies, which should lay the foundation for a lasting peace. They further agree that the final determination of the boundaries of Germany must await such a settlement.

2. Pending the peace settlement, the signatory states will co-operate to achieve, by peaceful means, their common aim of a reunified Germany enjoying a liberal-democratic constitution, like that of the Federal Republic, and integrated within the European Community.

These provision are still valid today. The treaties concluded with a number of Eastern countries have not changed this is any way.

In the "joint resolution" passed by the German Bundestag in connection with the treaties concluded with a number of Eastern countries reference is made to the "continued and unrestricted validity of the Bonn Convention." In the "Letter on German Unity," which is part of the treaties concluded with the U.S.SR, Poland and the GDR, it is stated that the treaties do not "conflict with the political objective of the Federal Republic of Germany to work for a state of peace in Europe in which the German nation will recover its unity in free self-determination." The "Letter on German Unity" was accepted by the Soviet Union without objections at the conclusion of the treaties with the above-mentioned countries. What was "revanchist" then cannot be so today either.

Those who denounce adherence to the historical mandate of the Basic Law as "revanchism" insult the German people and, in addition, the Western Alliance, which has made our cause its own.

A look at history teaches us that the Germans in the East lived in harmony with their neighbours for many generations. We wish to resume this tradition.

In a few days we will be commemorating the 40th anniversary of the day on which the Second World War ended with the surrender of the German armed forces. In the weeks leading up to this event I said what I considered necessary from my standpoint and would like to repeat it briefly here: Every European and every democrat can rejoice at the fact that the Nazi dictatorship was eliminated forever on 8 May 1945. However, no one can rejoice at the victory of communist dictatorship, at Stalin's triumph. The end of the Second World War marked a European catastrophe, the greatest in the history of our continent.

- It included the subjugation of the whole of Eastern Central Europe under a communist dictatorship, the cadres of which moved in with the Red Army.

- It included the division of Berlin, Germany and Europe into two antagonistic halves, a division that still persists.

- And it included the expulsion of 14 million Germans, of whom 2 million died.

The Soviet Union will celebrate the victory of 8 May 1945, as a result of which it achieved domination over half of Europe, with great pomp. The peoples and countries of Eastern Central Europe that have been incorporated into the Soviet empire will be forced to join in the celebrations. Our fellow countrymen in the GDR will also have to celebrate 8 May. No one can expect that of us who live in freedom.

For us Germans 8 May is a day of remembrance, a day on which we commemorate our dead and the dead of all nations.

In Bitburg President Reagan and Chancellor Kohl want to seal what President Mitterrand and Chancellor Kohl sealed for their peoples at Douaumont near Verdun. Douaumont was more than an expression of reconciliation. It was the sealing of an alliance that defends human rights and freedoms in Europe and the world. It was the sealing of friendship between two peoples who for centuries tried their strength on the battlefield but who have now understood that, if they have any future at all, it can only be in common.

Before Mitterrand another great Frenchman referred to the moral legacy deriving from Europe's Christian civilization. President de Gaulle called out to us, his former adversaries:

"Even though a bad policy led to crime and oppression, the respect of the courageous for one another still forms part of the moral legacy of mankind."

Are the Americans and Germans too capable of such a human, Christian and chivalrous gesture? Ultimately it is not the power of weapons but rather the power of hearts which will determine the viability and value of an alliance. I do not want to injure the feelings of those who oppose the visit to Bitburg.

Everyone will have to answer this and answer for this. Let me merely make one remark: The dead are beyond earthly justice. They can no longer defend themselves. They are judged by a different and higher authority applying its own standards and ours. It will probably not ask what army we belonged to, but rather what we did. Be this as it may; the living can only bow before the dead and their judge. Hatred must end at the grave.

What has become a matter of course among the peoples of Western Europe has long been a matter of course also between Germans and Americans. Honour guards of the American armed forces have always taken part in our commemorative ceremonies in the Federal Republic of Germany each November in honour of those killed in action. This applies to Bitburg, Fulda and elsewhere.

What is a reality in the West must also be achieved in the East, vis-à-vis the Soviet Union and especially vis-à-vis our immediate neighbours to the East, the Poles and the Czechs. I do not give up my vision that Germany and Poland will one day make peace with one another as sovereign states, a peace based on reconciliation and on the insight that our peoples belong to the same Christian and Western civilization and that they will regain their freedom and unity only if they do not stand against each other but together. This also includes the insight on the Polish and Czech sides that the German expellees cannot be excluded from a peace based on reconciliation; on the contrary: they must be the foundation on which this peace is built.

Let me quote merely one of them, a letter from a Jewish fellow citizen from

Munich. He writes: "As a Jew who lost nine of his closest relatives in Germany during the Nazi period, I think I can understand the bitter tone of your letter: you speak of the death of your own brother. I think the key to the unfortunate events surrounding President Reagan's visit lies in *one* fact … and that we thus forget the purely human factors of whatever kind … we must struggle on a person-to-person basis (and thus vicariously from nation to nation and culture to culture) — not to see who is right or wrong, because we are all wrong — but rather to make sure that humanity still exists . . . Should not we, you as a Christian and I as a Jew, honour your dead brother and my dead family by — very quietly — making a new start? Let us admit to ourselves that neither you nor I have come to terms with the past. From this joint admission insights and forces may grow that will also help other people to perceive that politics is more than just politics. With very best wishes and greetings." My response to this letter is respect and gratitude.

8 May has predictably been used to sow new enmity and new hatred. Not everyone involved has had sufficient stature to counteract this. They revel in alleged "mishaps" and "embarrassing incidents". The only embarrassing thing, however, is the malicious laughter of the self-righteous. What particularly burdens us and the Americans is not mishaps, the reasons lie deeper. Our Jewish fellow citizen from Munich rightly said so. We have not yet come to terms with the past. This also applies to the Americans. I say this without any arrogance: American television films that make German and Japanese soldiers objects of ridicule are not a historical source; they serve neither the truth nor reconciliation. Unless appearances deceive, the Japanese bear this with composure. We are affected more deeply.

The public debate in the last few weeks has not only opened up old wounds, it has exposed hypocrisy and self-righteousness. After 40 years it should at long last be possible to face the past truthfully. It is not lies but the truth that makes us free. Truth must also be the guiding principle when the fate of German expellees and the fate of German soldiers is described and honoured.

We must understand that Hitler's and Stalin's concentration camps, that the expulsion of the Germans in the Eastern territories and of the East Poles, that the death of millions of German soldiers and their adversaries were part of one and the same catastrophe that destroyed Europe, devastated the hearts and minds of the Europeans and divided the old continent.

We must master the future, the future of Germany and the future of Europe, on the basis of historical truth and on the basis of lessons to be learned from it. Let us work towards ensuring a free Germany in a free Europe and, let me add, a reconciled Germany in a reconciled Europe.

Western Europe Forty Years After World War II
New York
May 2, 1985

By Dr. Alois Mertes

(Speech by Dr. Alois Mertes, Minister of State in the Foreign Office of the Federal Republic of Germany, at the American Jewish Committee's 79th Annual Meeting.)

Mr. President,

Distinguished officers and leaders of the American Jewish Committee, ladies and gentlemen,

Allow me first of all to thank you for having invited me, as a German and European, to speak at the 1985 meeting of the American Jewish Committee on the subject of "Western Europe forty years after World War II." I am greatly honored by your kind invitation to speak on this important subject.

I take pleasure in accepting your invitation for two reasons. First, because you are a highly regarded organization in the United States, a country with which the Federal Republic of Germany is linked in close friendship. Second, because you are a Jewish-American community of great merit which has been fostering mutual understanding between young American Jews and young Germans for many years.

On behalf of the Government of the Federal Republic of Germany, I should like to thank sincerely, the American Jewish Committee for your unique contribution to the German-Jewish dialogue, strengthening the understanding of our common values and our common destiny. I am doing so as a German who was 11 years old in 1933, 23 years old in 1945 and who is now 69 years old and shares with the overwhelming majority of Germans in East and West the profound conviction that after the crimes committed by Germans and in Germany's name during the dictatorship of Hitler and his underlings, German patriotism can no longer be separated from dedication to human rights and democracy, which the American Jewish Committee has held as its objective since 1906. This is the message we wish to transmit to our children and grandchildren.

When you invited me, neither you nor I ever dreamt that a cemetery near the centre of my electoral district would become the subject of strong emotions and intense discussions in the United States and in Europe. I cannot and will not remain silent on the historical and moral background of these emotions, discussions and misunderstandings. Let me begin with two facts which are not sufficiently known.

In the Bitburg electoral district which I have the honor to represent in the German Bundestag, only a small minority of 17.4% voted for Hitler in the last free national elections held on 6 November 1932, before Hitler seized power. If voters in all electoral districts at the time had cast their ballots this way, the Nazis would never have come to power. In the most recent elections to the Bundestag on March

5, 1983, the three traditional democratic parties (CDU, SPD, and FDP) received 95.9%, of which the CDU alone under Chancellor Kohl received 65.4%. I am therefore proud of my electoral district and of my native Eifel region because the overwhelming majority of the population is democratic, patriotic and pro-Western. They maintain excellent relations with the many American soldiers stationed at the two U.S. Air Force bases there. More than ten thousand American children have been born in Bitburg.

We Germans will never forget the most infamous moment of German history. Hitler misused our own people, in particular the loyalty of German soldiers towards their country. Officers of the Wehrmacht such as Richard von Weizsäcker, Helmut Schmidt, Franz Josef Strauss and Walter Scheel served together with the vast majority of Germans, including myself, in the belief that they were serving their country and not its ruthless leadership. Many German soldiers, especially those on the Western front, felt a growing conflict of loyalties in the last years of the war between patriotic duty and Christian ethics, a conflict which was expressed tragically in the revolt of 20 July 1944.

Such a conflict does not exist for today's German soldier. Together with his American, British and French counterparts, he is serving an alliance defending our countries as well as individual human dignity and personal freedom. Life in a totalitarian dictatorship which my generation experienced caused us in 1945 to swear; never again dictatorship on German soil and never again war from German soil!

These are the words of Kurt Schumacher, the first chairman of the Social Democratic Party of Germany, who himself spent ten years in concentration camps. Today, in New York, I would like to express on behalf of the Government of the Federal Republic of Germany our appreciation for the far-sightedness and steadfastness of all U.S. presidents since 1945 in all questions pertaining to Germany as a whole, and, in particular, to the security of West Germany and Berlin. I also do this as a former German soldier, who became a prisoner of war of the U.S. Army on this day 40 years ago and thereby escaped Soviet captivity and was able to return home 4 months later.

The subject you have given me should serve to enable us to see the dangers threatening Europe today, and therefore the United States and Canada as well, and indeed international peace. In particular, to see the opportunities at our disposal to preserve peace, and what is more, to foster a peace which alleviates injustice and eliminates oppression and persecution. For peace is not only a state of non-war; it is the work of righteousness, to quote the prophet Isaiah.

Our experience during the 12 years of National Socialist dictatorship and during the subsequent forty years belong together. It has molded the judgments of my generation up to the present day. Over the last forty years, the western part of Germany has been able to reconstruct a politically and economically viable democracy, based on the rule of law, whereas the eastern part of Germany and our eastern neighbours have been prevented by force from doing so. It is only possible to talk in an adequate manner about the 8th of May 1945, and about the development of Western Europe, if one is aware of the origins and consequences of the 12 years of Hitler's rule. The 8th of May 1945 for us Germans meant more than the end of a totalitarian regime which brought suffering, death and destruction to every corner of Europe, and which burdened Germany's name by planned genocide. For my generation, the 8th of May was above all the beginning of an historic opportunity to design a future of freedom, justice, and peace. Human rights and the renunciation of force were henceforth to determine German policies.

These have been years of democratic stability, years of reconciliation with our neighbours and years of identification of our security interests with those of the peoples of the Atlantic Alliance. These have been years in which we tried to restore Germany's good name by our resolute will to make amends to the survivors of Nazi terror, by our solidarity with Israel's right to exist within secure borders, by our desire for genuine detente and balanced disarmament, by successfully defending ourselves against anti-democratic temptations from within and totalitarian pressures from without, and by our development assistance to the Third World which today is greater and more efficient than that of all the Warsaw Pact countries. We want our grandchildren and their grandchildren to accept gladly being part of the German nation into which we were born and to which we shall remain faithful in good times and in bad.

We do not want to forget the villainy of the National-Socialist dictatorship. This is especially true of the genocide of the Jews which was obviously beyond the rationale of war, victory or defeat. It constituted in itself an exclusively criminal proclivity for annihilation. This genocide cannot be compared with any other event between 1942 and 1945. And this I state as someone who served his country in good faith at the time and who rejects any collective accusations against Germany since they would correspond neither to historical reality nor to Biblical ethics. But we Germans must also recall all the great things our people have given humanity. U.S. Ambassador Arthur Burns, who is now leaving Bonn, recently appealed to German teachers, politicians and churches to do more in propagating this aspect of political education. He has encouraged us Germans to take more pride in our country and its history. In addition to the dark years of National-Socialist, which we should not forget, Ambassador Burns also pointed to the great achievements of our nation. I find it imperative at this point to recall with national gratitude, the inestimable contribution made to Germany and its culture by its Jewish citizens.

When they were free to choose after 1945, the German people decided for Western democracy because there can now no longer be anything of national interest to Germany which is separable from justice and freedom. This will demand political steadfastness on the part of the Federal Republic of Germany and of its major allies. Hitler's 1939 "recipe," in all its possible variants, including the threat and use of force, and collusion with Russia to the disadvantage of Poland and the West, is forever banned from German foreign policy.

Now let me turn to the situation of Europe forty years after the war. When the armed forces of Germany surrendered unconditionally in 1945, large expanses of

Europe, and especially all of Germany, lay in physical and moral ruins. The victorious Western Allies, in particular the United States, believed in the possibility of creating a worldwide order for peace on the basis of the UN Charter. But it was soon to be seen that the Soviet Union, as today, both in theory and in practice, interpreted almost all the principles of post-war policies which it had agreed to with the Western powers, in a manner which remains incompatible with freedom and democracy, self-determination and independence, peace, security and disarmament. The Soviet Union exploited its military victory over Germany in order to create by force a buffer zone in Eastern Europe and its occupation zone in Germany, from 1945 to 1948, which led to the division of Europe. And Germany is still known as the open European question and the open German question.

At the Conference on Confidence and Security-building Measures and Disarmament in Stockholm on 18 January 1984, Secretary of State George Schultz said:

"Since 1945, Western Europe has seen a great reconciliation of old enemies and a great resurgence of freedom, prosperity, unity, and security. It is a crowning achievement of the European tradition in which the United States has been proud to play a part. But throughout the same period, an artificial barrier has cruelly divided this continent—and indeed heartlessly divided one of its great nations.

This barrier was not placed there by the West. It is not maintained by the West. It is not the West that prevents its citizens' free movement, or cuts them off from competing ideas.

Let me be very clear: The United States does not recognize the legitimacy of the artificially imposed division of Europe. This division is the essence of Europe's security and human rights problem, and we all know it."

On the same subject, President Reagan stated on 5 February 1985:

"There is one boundary which Yalta symbolizes that can never be made legitimate, and that is the dividing line between freedom and repression. I do not hesitate to say that we wish to undo this boundary. In so doing, we seek no military advantage for ourselves or for the Western Alliance. We do not deny any nation's legitimate interest in security. But protecting the security of one nation by robbing another of its national independence, and national traditions, is not legitimate. In the long run, it is not even secure."

This is the best possible description of the reality and the consequences of the division of Europe. The determination of the United States to defend its rights, responsibilities and interest in all the East-West crises since 1945 against all pressure, threats and blackmail is, in addition to its military presence in Western Europe, the most visible political incarnation of the credibility of the American position in Europe. The Western powers are defending not only the freedom of West Berlin, they are also defending the claim of the German people and of the Eastern Europeans to a just peace based on individual and national human rights.

The security of Europe and of the United States are inseparably linked since the political objectives and the military potential of the Soviet threat are directed against both Europe and America.

I would ask you to take the following into consideration in all questions related to Germany and Europe. The risk of war in Europe is almost zero. But, as Chancellor Kohl stated, the Soviet Union wants a political victory in Europe in a military peace. Its will for expansion westward, as former chancellor Schmidt put it recently, is unbroken. It does not wish to conquer the territory of the Federal Republic of Germany, but rather win over the minds and hearts of the German people, especially of young Germans. Trying to drive a wedge between Germans and Americans is the logical consequence of Soviet foreign policy, which is characterized by exceptional perseverance and which no doubt will continue for quite some time. Any division between the American people and Germany or between the German people and America serves, as a result, only Moscow's interests. I cannot conceive of how such a division could possibly benefit the United States or Europe. On the contrary, such a division places us all in danger. I am afraid that the Bitburg controversy has *ipso facto* only raised Moscow's chances of influencing young people psychologically. I regard it as our duty, in public discussion on the past, not to forget the needs of the present and the future vital interests of Europe and America. Any selective or partial attitude towards complex historical or political situations is simply irresponsible if we are really convinced that Europe and America need one another.

If today we want to describe the present conditions and prospects for European policy, we first have to refer, as I did, to the basic facts which emerged from the Second World War.

Germany and Europe were divided into an area of democracy and self-determination and one of totalitarianism and foreign domination. The splitting of Europe into two halves has become a major factor determining European and above all German policy. Relations between the two superpowers, which since the Second World War have gone through different phases, have a decisive bearing on the policies pursued by the Europeans.

But important developments have also taken place in Europe itself. We have seen the establishment and growth of the European Community and the relative increase in the importance of the Europeans within the Atlantic Alliance, whilst on the other hand there have been very slow yet noticeable evolutionary trends within the Warsaw Pact.

When I speak of "Europe" I mean the whole of Europe. The nations of Eastern Europe, Poland, Czechoslovakia and Hungary are, according to their own self-perception, also nations of Central Europe; the other members of the Warsaw Pact are a part of Europe. (The Soviet Union, too, is of course partly a European country, but it is first and foremost a global or superpower. Russia, by the way, has never belonged to that part of Europe, which was shaped by Western Christianity and Judaism, by the era of enlightenment and democracy.)

In this Europe the two most heavily armed military alliances in the world stand face to face. Germany lies on the border between the totalitarian East and the democratic West: The dividing line passes right through Germany. That is why the effect of the division of Europe is more intensely felt in my country than anywhere else. The Federal Republic of Germany is firmly integrated into the European Community and the Western Alliance of free and democratic countries. This integration is based on a deep conviction and not on opportunist considerations. Our political priority has been and remains: freedom before unity.

That is why our policy in the short term must aim at mitigating the effects of the division of the country and of Europe and, in the long term, at reaching a state of peace in Europe in which the German people will recover its unity through free self-determination. We are fostering with the United States and other allies a peaceful, evolutionary process as a result of which all Europeans can live freely and in peace. Thus, we keep the national interests of the Germans strictly in harmony with the interests of the West, in general, and of Europe, in particular, in seeking a favourable development of relations with the East. We have linked our destiny to that of our neighbours.

When we speak of the two most heavily armed military alliances standing face to face in Europe, however, we must not forget that Europe has lived in peace since the end of World War II. During this period military force in Europe has been used only within the Soviet sphere of influence—East Berlin in 1953, Hungary in 1956, and Czechoslovakia in 1968. We must bear this basic fact in mind when we speak of the relationship between the two superpowers and its impact on Europe. The long period of stability in Europe would have been hard to imagine without the preventive influence of a balance of military power. For Western Europe the nuclear protection, which only the United States can provide, will remain essential for maintaining this balance in the foreseeable future.

There are, of course, fundamental, indeed decisive differences between Soviet and American policy.

We Germans know which power since the Second World War has twice tried to strangle the freedom of West Berlin and which power twice saved this freedom. We know which power suppresses human rights and the trade unions in one part of Europe and which power guarantees these fundamental rights in our part of Europe. There are two ethnic minorities in the Soviet Union who suffer particularly under discrimination and the lack of freedom: the Jews and the Germans.

The Soviet Union has traditionally seized every opportunity to exert influence on the West European members of NATO so as to counteract the joint plans of the Alliance and split it. This is, and will probably remain, a fundamental objective of Soviet policy towards West Europe. In pursuing this aim, Moscow, through excessive use of political pressure and propaganda designed to intimidate the public, has achieved the opposite to what it wanted in that it has caused the West European allies to strengthen their ties with the United States.

We have noticed too that the Soviets have adopted a varied approach to the Western European members of NATO. Of late, the Federal Republic of Germany has been the main target of Soviet propaganda, in which attacks on NATO's arms modernization plans have been intermingled with denunciations of an alleged revanchist attitude on our part.

"Playing the European card" will certainly remain a prominent feature of the Soviet Union's policy towards the Western Alliance. Even now Moscow is trying to exert political pressure on European countries whom it accuses today of giving un-qualified support to the American Strategic Defense Initiative.

Although the period of low profiled relations between the superpowers, has placed a strain on East-West relations as a whole, it has at the same time shown that the Europeans were able on their own initiative to help bridge tension during that spell. The dialogue between the Europeans in East and West was not cut off. The Europeans on both sides of the dividing line in Europe have played their part in bringing the superpowers back to the conference table in Geneva. They will now have to ensure that their viewpoints are brought to bear in the negotiations. They will have to remind the superpowers that the results they seek can only lead to a more stable security in Europe if determined efforts are also made to achieve great-er stability in the balance of conventional forces in Europe. This is a question of growing importance.

As the negotiations get under way, the Europeans in East and West will not content themselves with the role of spectators. They shouuld not regard the emerg-ing tendency of the United States and the Soviet Union to adopt a more bilateral approach to international problems as a threat to their interests but as an improve-ment in the general conditions for their own involvement in the process. The CSCE [Conference on Security and Cooperation in Europe] is the principal framework within which to seek improvements in the overall relationship between East and West. Such improvements include progress in economic cooperation where, on account of the complementary nature of the economic potentials in Western and Eastern Europe (including the Soviet Union itself), considerable possibilities remain untapped. That is also true for environmental protection, scientific and technological cooperation, and culture.

In the development of bilateral relations as well, the Europeans are rendering their own special contribution. Contacts between the populations of Eastern and Western Europe have been intensified in recent years. In this context I need only mention as examples the visit by the British Prime Minister Mrs. Thatcher to Budapest, the visits of the German Foreign Minister Genscher to Warsaw, Moscow and Sofia, and the recent visit of the British Foreign Secretary Sir Geof-frey Howe to East Berlin, Prague and Warsaw.

We believe that in many respects there exist favorable conditions for a start of a realistic policy in the direction of genuine detente. For this, we need a clear vision of what is necessary and what is possible.

As a guest of the American Jewish Committee, I would like in particular to comment on the obvious importance of the Middle East for the geopolitical in-terests of Western Europe. Although much more time would be needed, let me mention a couple of things at least: We in the European Community wish to make a contribution to a lasting peace in this region. But this must not block American endeavors toward an alleviation of, or solution to, the Arab-Israeli conflict. It must support them. For this reason, dialogue and consultations between the United States and Europe are particularly essential with regard to the Middle East.

As a German, nevertheless, I would like to stress that it is essential for us in East and West, never to forget that Germany's special responsibility for Israel is an element of credibility and ethics in any good German foreign policy. The remarks of the federal chancellor in his Government Statement of 4 May 1983 remain just as valid as they were during his visit to Israel where I accompanied him.

"Our policy on the Middle East" he said, "is founded on respect for the legitimate interests of all peoples and States—some of them mutually opposed—in that region. In addition, we are particularly attached to Israel, and we stand up for Israel's right to live in freedom and security. This attitude denotes every aspect of our Middle East policy which hopes to contribute to a lasting peace in the region. This does not preclude, however, that there may be individual political questions between the Federal Republic of Germany and the State of Israel on which we disagree."

In conclusion I would like to bring up a matter before this distinguished audience, which occurred to me as a result of my years of discussions with young Germans. The peace question must be repoliticized, it must not be allowed to degenerate into military and technical details.

It is not weapons and soldiers as such which are a threat to peace; they are the instruments of political will. Unless the debate on peace and security is brought back into the arena of political discussion, it will degenerate into the technical jargon of military strategy and disarmament diplomacy. I once said in the German Bundestag that some of the supporters of armaments and some of the supporters of disarmament had one thing in common; they talked only of weapons, no longer discussing the underlying political issues. In the Atlantic Alliance, we secure peace in freedom vis-a-vis the Soviet Union—that is the purpose of NATO. Parallel to this, we try to build peace with the Soviet Union and its allies—that is the purpose of dialogue, arms control, co-operation and confidence-building measures.

Moscow's political objectives and the military potential available for achieving them represent, in themselves, a serious threat to the security of the West and justify the existence of the Atlantic Alliance, with all the burdens we carry for assuring security: the deployment of a sufficient defensive potential, the sharing of calculated risks, demanding both personal sacrifices and financial expenditures.

Internally, the Soviet Union acts repressively. Externally, it acts expansively on a global scale. Both internally and externally, the Soviet Union aims run counter to elementary tenets of the liberal democracies of the West. Its long-term goal of expansion, so contrary to the vital security interests of the West, is not based on a master plan deposited in a Kremlin safe. It can rather be clearly observed, being based in the first instance on the Soviet Union's imperial concept of security, and secondly on Lenin's foreign policy openly subscribed to by the Soviet leadership, which claims to world hegemony. As far as the Soviet security concept is concerned, an insatiable quest for absolute security, it aims logically at a constant "peaceful" extension of influence in Western Europe and the Third World.

It is of interest to note that in the West people often shy away from squarely facing these facts. I am in favor of taking seriously what Eastern leaders say: Why is it that we do not want to listen? Do they not state their aims clearly? Indeed, the Soviet Union may be accused of many things, but it cannot be accused of concealing its political principles and objectives. For reasons of self-interest, Moscow cannot run the risk of attacking any member country of the Alliance. Instead, Moscow tries to induce us to adopt presumptive "good behavior" and to submit increasingly to its wishes. In other words, the Soviet leaders are counting on our willingness to appease through what may be called anticipatory compliance. Moscow wants to achieve superiority in Europe by gradually decoupling the Federal Republic of Germany, first psychologically, then politically from the West, and Europe from the United States, to split up the Atlantic Alliance into zones of American security and European insecurity with the aim of gaining controlling access to Europe's resources and inventiveness.

The motto of the Atlantic Alliance is: *Vigilia precium libertatis* — vigilance is the price of freedom. Americans and Europeans are paying this price. And I believe, Mr. President, ladies and gentlemen, this motto is the best yardstick for preserving the right proportions in discussing controversial subjects between Americans and Europeans, be they of an historical, political, economic or military nature. My beloved parents who were practising Christians and good Germans, and my older brother who was a Catholic priest and taught me to respect Jewish piety and Jewish faithfulness to the Law.

I am aware of how righteousness, i.e., fairness, determines Jewish ethics. It is expressed in the sayings of old which Rabbi Natan Levinson of the Institute of Jewish Studies in Heidelberg pointed out to me: "Do not judge your neighbour for you do not know what you would have done in his place." Jesus of Nazareth also lived in this spirit when he said in the Sermon on the Mount: "Judge not, and ye shall not be judged."

With its fairness, its far-sightedness and its will to build bridges, the American Jewish Committee embodies the best traditions of American and Jewish humanism. Ladies and gentlemen, Mr. President, the thanks of the German people, which I express here once again in all sincerity, go to you all.

Part II

Reagan Proceeds With German Visit

This section deals with the visit by President Reagan to the former concentration camp in Bergen-Belsen and the military cemetery in Bitburg. Despite the clamor for President Reagan to change his agenda, he held fast to his plans. The official speeches of the president and Chancellor Kohl at the sites are printed in full in Chapters 7 and 9. So, too, are those of protesters in Chapter 8. The reaction after the two ceremonies appears in Chapter 11.

Included in this section are a speech and an article by Menachem Z. Rosensaft, founder of the International Network of Children of Jewish Holocaust Survivors. His group chose to stage their protest at Bergen-Belsen rather than at Bitburg for two reasons: (1) they regarded Bergen-Belsen as a holy place that had been desecrated by politics and politicians, and wished to reconsecrate and restore holiness to the site; and (2) they did not want to participate in protests at Bitburg because those planned were anti-American in nature led by various left-wing groups and the Green Party, and the Children of Holocaust Survivors had no ax to grind with America in general.

Appearing in Chapter 10 are three additional speeches of the president and others during his tour.

Chapter 7

May 5th At Bergen-Belsen —Reagan And Kohl

"We Bow in Sorrow..."
Bergen-Belsen
May 5, 1985

By Chancellor Helmut Kohl
(Speech at the former concentration camp in Bergen-Belsen.)

Mr. President:

You have come here to pay homage to the victims of National Socialist tyranny. Bergen-Belsen was a place of unimaginable atrocities. It was only one of the many sites testifying to a demonic will to destroy.

At a ceremony here two weeks ago, I, in my capacity as chancellor of the Federal Republic of Germany, professed our historical responsibility.

You, Mr. President, represent a country which played a decisive part in liberating Europe and ultimately the Germans, too, from Hitler's tyranny. We Germans reverently commemorate the soldiers of your nation who lost their lives in that act of liberation.

We bow in sorrow before the victims of murder and genocide.

The supreme goal of our political efforts is to render impossible any repetition of that systematic destruction of human life and dignity. With their partners and friends, the Americans and Germans therefore stand together as allies in the community of shared values and in the defense alliance in order to safeguard man's absolute and inviolable dignity in conditions of freedom and peace.

Israeli Ambassador Yitzhak Ben Ari and U.S. Ambassador Arthur Burns, the only Jewish dignitaries present, together with President Ronald Reagan and his wife Nancy, listen intently as Chancellor Helmut Kohl recites "We Bow in Sorrow," at ceremony commemorating the liberation of the Jewish and other prisoners at Bergen-Belsen camp.

"Never Again . . ."
Bergen-Belsen
May 5, 1985

By President Ronald Reagan
(Speech at the former concentration camp in Bergen-Belsen.)

This painful walk into the past has done much more than remind us of the war that consumed the European continent. What we have seen makes unforgettably clear that no one of the rest of us can fully understand the enormity of the feelings carried by the victims of these camps.

The survivors carry a memory beyond anything that we can comprehend. The awful evil started by one man—an evil that victimized all the world with its destruction—was uniquely destructive to the millions forced into the grim abyss of these camps.

Here lie people—Jews—whose death was inflicted for no reason other than their very existence. Their pain was borne only because of who they were and because of the God in their prayers. Alongside them lie many Christians—Catholics and Protestants.

For year after year, until that man and his evil were destroyed, hell yawned forth its awful contents. People were brought here for no other purpose but to suffer and die. To go unfed when hungry—and left to have misery consume them when all there was around them was misery.

Nancy Reagan and Hannelore Kohl place wreaths on the graves of Dr. Konrad Adenauer, the first chancellor of the Federal Republic of Germany, en route to Bergen-Belsen. Their husbands look on.

I'm sure we all share similar first thoughts. And that is: what of the youngsters who died at this dark Stalag? All was gone for them — forever. Not to feel again the warmth of life's sunshine and promise, not the laughter and splendid ache of growing up, nor the consoling embrace of a family. Try to think of being young and never having a day without searing emotional and physical pain — desolate, unrelieved pain.

Today, we have been grimly reminded why the commandant of this camp was named, "The Beast of Belsen". Above all, we are struck by the horrors of it all — the monstrous, incomprehensible horror. That is what we have seen — but is what we can never understand as the victims did. Nor with all our compassion can we feel what the survivors feel to this day and what they will feel as long as they live.

What we have felt and are expressing with words cannot convey the suffering that they endured. That is why history will forever brand what happened as the Holocaust.

Here, death ruled. But we have learned something, as well. Because of what happened, we found that death cannot rule forever. And that is why we are here today.

We are here because humanity refuses to accept that freedom or the spirit of man can ever be extinguished. We are here to commemorate that life triumphed over the tragedy and the death of the Holocaust — overcame the suffering, the sickness, the testing, and, yes, the gassings.

President Reagan stands before wreath in Bergen-Belsen.

We are here today to confirm that the horror cannot outlast the hope — and that even from the worst of all things, the best may come forth. Therefore, even out of this overwhelming sadness, there must be some purpose. And there is. It comes to us through the transforming love of God.

We learn from the Talmud that, "it was only through suffering that the children of Israel obtained three priceless and coveted gifts: the Torah, the land of Israel, and the World To Come." Yes, out of this sickness — as crushing and cruel as it was — there was hope for the world as well as for the World To Come. Out of the ashes — hope. From all the pain — promise.

So much of this is symbolized today by the fact that most of the leadership of free Germany is represented here today. Chancellor Kohl, you and our countrymen have made real the renewal that had to happen. Your nation and the German people have been strong and resolute in your willingness to confront and condemn the acts of a hated regime of the past. This reflects the courage of your people and their devotion to freedom and justice since the war. Think how far we have come from that time when despair made these tragic victims wonder if anything could survive.

Surely we can understand that, when we see what is around us — all these children of God, under bleak and lifeless mounds, the plainness of which does not even hint at the unspeakable acts that created them. Here they lie. Never to hope. Never to pray. Never to love. Never to kneel. Never to laugh. Never to cry.

President Reagan and his wife Nancy are shocked at the horror graphically depicted on the walls of the Bergen-Belsen Museum.

And too many of them knew that this was their fate. But that was not the end. Through it all was their faith and a spirit that moved their faith.

Nothing illustrates this better than the story of a young girl who died here at Bergen-Belsen. For more than two years, Anne Frank and her family had hidden from the Nazis in a confined annex in Holland, where she kept a remarkably profound diary. Betrayed by an informant, Anne and her family were sent by freight car to Auschwitz and finally here to Bergen-Belsen.

Just three weeks before her capture, young Anne wrote these words: "It's really a wonder that I haven't dropped all my ideals, because they seem so absurd and impossible to carry out. Yet I keep them, because in spite of everything I still believe that people are really good at heart. I simply can't build up my hopes on a foundation consisting of confusion, misery and death. I see the world gradually being turned into a wilderness, I hear the ever approaching thunder, which will destroy us too, I can feel the sufferings of millions, and yet, if I look up into the heavens, I think that it will all come right, that this cruelty, too, will end, and that peace and tranquility will return again."

Eight months later, this sparkling young life ended at Bergen-Belsen.

Somewhere here lies Anne Frank. Everywhere here are memories—pulling us, touching us, making us understand that they can never be erased. Such memories take us where God intended his children to go—toward learning, toward healing, and, above all, toward redemption. They beckon us through the endless stretch of our heart to the knowing commitment that the life of each individual can change the world and make it better.

We are all witnesses. We share the glistening hope that rests in every human soul. Hope leads us—if we are prepared to trust it—toward what our President Lincoln called, "the better angels of our nature". And then, rising above all this cruelty—out of this tragic and nightmarish time—beyond the anguish, the pain, and the suffering and for all time, we can and must pledge ... never again.

A memorial to the Jews who died in Bergen-Belsen

Chapter 8

May 5th At Bergen-Belsen —Protest

A Jew At Bergen-Belsen
Bergen-Belsen, West Germany
May 5, 1985

By Menachem Z. Rosensaft

(Speech by Menachem Z. Rosensaft, founding Chairman of the International Network of Children of Jewish Holocaust Survivors, at Bergen-Belsen.)

We are standing here today at one of the holiest sites in the world—the mass graves of Bergen-Belsen. Around us, covered by grass and marked by stark stones, are the remains of fifty thousand European Jews who were brutally and deliberately murdered by the willing and enthusiastic servants of Nazi Germany. We are surrounded by the images, the eyes, the final words and thoughts, of Anne Frank and of the thousands of others whom the SS doctors, officers and guards annihilated only and exclusively because they were Jews.

I speak today on behalf of the dead. As the son of two survivors of Auschwitz and Bergen-Belsen who suffered here and were liberated here, I speak on behalf of all the survivors and of thousands of sons and daughters of survivors. I speak as a Jew, and as an American. But above all, today, I speak on behalf of all those who lie buried here in these mass graves, and whose memory has now been desecrated by the President of the United States and the Chancellor of the German Federal Republic.

Menachem Z. Rosensaft, addressing the demonstration at Bergen-Belsen on May 5, 1985.

In stark contrast with the words that have been spoken here today, Bergen-Belsen has today been exploited for the political interests of these two men, and the sanctity of this place has been violated.

For forty years, no one has dared to stand here for any reason except to mourn, to commemorate, to remember, and to vow that the horrors of Nazism, of the Third Reich, will never be repeated, and that the murderers will never be forgiven.

Never, until today, has anyone dared to use these graves as part of an attempt to rehabilitate the SS.

Never, until today, has anyone dared to come here and act in total and deliberate disregard of the sensitivities and moral demands of the survivors and the entire Jewish community.

Never, until today, has anyone dared to prevent survivors and children of survivors from standing beside these mass graves and this monument while two politicians violate their sanctity and every principle of decency by coming here on their way to honoring the memory of the SS.

During the past seven weeks, President Ronald Reagan and Chancellor Helmut Kohl have created and aggravated a moral crisis of unprecedented proportions. As part of an appalling effort to achieve a reconciliation with the ghosts of Nazi Germany, President Reagan is now on his way to the Bitburg Cemetery where some 47 SS men are buried.

President Reagan and Chancellor Kohl know very well that the SS were the ultimate personification of Hitler's nightmarish regime, the ultimate embodiment of evil, and still they insist on honoring their memory.

President Reagan and Chancellor Kohl have heard the anguished outcry of the survivors, and the outrage expressed by virtually the entire civilized world, and still they insist on desecrating the memory of the Six Million Jewish victims of the Holocaust, and of all the other victims of Nazism.

Today we say to Chancellor Kohl that his attempt to describe the Waffen SS as simple soldiers is a perverse rewriting of history, and we say to President Reagan that his comparison of the SS or any German soldiers to the victims of the Holocaust is morally repugnant.

President Reagan and Chancellor Kohl have embarked on a macabre tour, an obscene package deal, of Bergen-Belsen and Bitburg. Today we say to them that they can either honor the memory of the victims of Belsen, or they can honor the SS. They cannot do both. And by entering Bitburg, they desecrate the memory of all those who were murdered by the SS, and of all those whom they pretended to commemorate here at Belsen.

President Reagan and Chancellor Kohl should understand that we are committed to genuine reconciliation and friendship with the new Germany of the past 40 years, but we shall never accept or acquiesce in any reconciliation with the Third Reich. We shall never allow any rehabilitation of the SS. And despite their efforts, we shall never tolerate any compromise with evil.

Today, the survivors of the Holocaust and their children have been deeply and permanently offended by two politicians who fail to understand the moral imperatives of Belsen. The entire Jewish community has been insulted by the total lack of sensitivity demonstrated by these two men. And all decent human beings everywhere are outraged by President Reagan's and Chancellor Kohl's exploitation and desecration of the mass graves of Belsen for their selfish political purposes.

I hope that as they enter Bitburg, both President Reagan and Chancellor Kohl will realize that the only ones who applaud their actions are the bands of SS men meeting this weekend at Nesselwang, and all other Nazis, neo-Nazis and their sympathizers throughout the world.

We demand that Belsen be restored to its place as a sacred shrine under the moral authority—the moral jurisdiction—of those whose families lie buried here. We demand that no politician shall ever again be allowed to come here for impermissible purposes. And we hope that our presence here today will in some small way compensate for the pain and anguish which President Reagan and Chancellor Kohl have caused the survivors of the Holocaust during the past seven weeks.

Our moral obligation is clear. For us, it is a matter of conscience. And we swear today to the tens of thousands buried here, and to all the other victims of the Holocaust, that *we* shall forever protect and defend their memory, that *we* shall never abandon them.

The Two Ceremonies at Bergen-Belsen

The New York Times
May 6, 1985

By John Tagliabue

BELSEN, WEST GERMANY — There were two ceremonies at the Bergen-Belsen memorial today.

The first ended when President Reagan's helicopter lifted out of a sea of West German policemen. Rows of invited guests, shaking hands and chatting, then filed out and climbed into the Mercedes-Benz limousines of postwar West German prosperity.

The second ceremony began 20 minutes later, when 50 or so Jews, some former inmates and some the children of victims, entered the concentration camp in a somber procession, each bearing a rose and many in tears. They attended a brief commemorative service that one of their leaders, Menachem Rosensaft, said was to "reconsecrate" the memorial.

Says It Was "Desecrated"

Mr. Rosensaft said the memorial had been "desecrated" by the visit of President Reagan and West Germany's Chancellor, Helmut Kohl.

"Never, until today, has anyone dared to prevent survivors and children of survivors from standing beside these mass graves and this monument," Mr. Rosensaft told a gathering at the squat, gray memorial to the more than 50,000 people who died in the camp, "while two politicians violate their sanctity and every principle of decency by coming here on their way to honoring the memory of the SS."

Mr. Rosensaft, the founding chairman of the International Network of Children of Jewish Holocaust Survivors, was born at Bergen-Belsen in 1948, when it served as a camp for displaced persons.

Camp Is Sealed Off

Hundreds of West German policemen, with American Secret Service agents at their side, sealed off the camp for all but the 400 or so invited guests while President Reagan and Mr. Kohl visited the memorial and laid a wreath to its dead.

"Here lie people — Jews — whose death was inflicted for no reason other than their very existence," Mr. Reagan said in his address.

Chancellor Kohl, in his brief remarks, said, "We bow in sorrow before the victims of murder and genocide."

Jewish leaders in the United States, Israel and elsewhere refused to send representatives to the service because of President Reagan's decision to go from the camp to the Bitburg cemetery, where SS soldiers are buried.

On Saturday night, West German policemen removed a group of about a dozen Jews from the camp's document center, where they intended to remain to protest the President's visit. At 5 A.M. today, the West German police carried off about 35 French Jews, some of them former camp inmates, who refused to leave the parking lot where Mr. Reagan's helicopter later landed.

United States Secret Service agents were with the West German police patrols that blocked two forest roads leading to the camp memorial.

The roadblocks infuriated Jewish leaders, like Rabbi Avraham Weiss of the Hebrew Institute of Riverdale, the Bronx, who accused the White House of having ordered the West German police to seal the camp and bar Jews from protesting.

"They Cannot Do Both"

Speaking later by the camp memorial, Mr. Rosensaft said of the President and Chancellor Kohl: "Today, we say to them that they can either honor the memory of the victims of Belsen, or they can honor the SS. They cannot do both."

The absence of Jews at Mr. Reagan's service troubled some official guests, like Friedrich Wöbbeking, Belsen's village pastor, who expressed "distress" and said he had considered staying away. By contrast, Norbert Blüm, Bonn's Minister for Social Affairs, approved the removal of the protesters. "Quiet is important," he said. "Dignity must prevail."

One who remembered less dignified times was Dimitri Pluchator, 71 years old, a Galician Jew and survivor of Auschwitz, Birkenau and Bergen-Belsen, who said he had visited the memorial almost every Sunday since British soldiers liberated him and other survivors in April 1945.

"For 14 days we wandered through here, stepping over corpses like wood in the forest," he said. "And now, I cannot enter, though I come every Sunday."

Wrapped in a trench coat against a chill wind, he shook his head and repeated, "Sad, sad."

Protesters in Bergen-Belsen:
More Than Just Grandstanding

Long Island Jewish World
May 24-30, 1985

By Walter Ruby

May 3, 1985, 6:30 p.m., in a Kennedy Airport lounge. The International Network of Children of Jewish Holocaust Survivors was holding a press conference to explain why they had chosen to send a delegation of 40 odd people to Bergen-Belsen to protest the upcoming visit of President Reagan and German Chancellor Helmut Kohl to that former concentration camp, preceding their visit to a military cemetery in Bitburg which contained the graves of 49 Waffen SS soldiers.

As earnest rhetoric flowed from five members of the delegation, I found myself wondering why I myself had chosen to disrupt my already too busy schedule to fly to Germany for three days to cover the goings-on at Bergen-Belsen.

Some Jewish leaders had condemned the decision of a number of small Jewish contingents to go to Bergen-Belsen and Bitburg, hinting that such actions amounted to "grandstanding"—jumping at a chance to get one's name in the international press, while at the same time causing further damage to the Jewish community's already frayed relations with the Reagan administration.

As I listened to the speeches, I asked myself whether I was guilty of journalistic grandstanding. Was I, in effect, chasing a flashy story to Europe, when the more significant Jewish community response to Reagan's Bitburg visit would be in the streets of New York and other U.S. cities?

Abraham Foxman, the influential international affairs director of the Anti-Defamation League of B'nai B'rith, had said that of the various Jewish groups planning protests in Germany during Reagan's visit, the children of the survivors groups had the most legitimacy because of their direct familial connection to the full brunt of the Holocaust.

Recognition for Group

While listening to the speech of Jerzy Warman, who is president of the International Network (but definitely the number two man to Menachem Rosensaft, the founding chairman of the organization, who would fly from Israel to meet the group in Germany the next day), I reflected that the explosion of the Bitburg controversy over the past month had given this group an increased recognition and moral authority that is turning it into a force that will have to be reckoned with in Jewish communal affairs in the years ahead.

According to Warman, "As sons and daughters of Jews who were miraculously saved from the Nazi genocide "...we want to demonstrate our outrage against equating the killers with their victims. The combination of the killers with their victims constitutes a morally repugnant package deal that would violate the sanctity of the mass graves . . ."

Warman remarked, "We hope that this gesture will in some measure compensate for the shame the President is going to inflict on our country by rehabilitating the murderers. He will be giving a signal to all neo-fascists, racists, anti-Semites, and revisionists that it is all right to incite hatred and violence again."

Stating succinctly the reasoning behind a decision that had agonized the organization the week before, Warman commented, "We are going to Bergen-Belsen and not to Bitburg, because neither we, nor the President, belong anywhere near the graves of the SS."

Noting that the children of the survivors had passed up Bitburg in part in order to avoid being confused with or used by anti-Reagan demonstrators, Warman stated, "Our demonstration is neither political nor partisan, and our protest is not aimed against the government of the United States, the government of Germany, or the alliance between our countries. We will be there to make a moral statement...to declare as forcefully as we can that we shall never forget and that we shall never let the world forget."

Survivors' Children

After the take off from Kennedy, I moved around the plane talking to the children of the Holocaust survivors. They are an intriguing bunch, combining an all-American, rather yuppieish aura with an intense personal connection and identification with a cataclysm that took place 40 years ago which they did not themselves experience.

The group seems to consist predominantly of upwardly mobile professionals in their 30's—lawyers, academics, and business people. Some of them come from parents who were already quite well to do. An impressive number of survivors of places like Auschwitz and Treblinka seem to have had the capacity, after surviving the most hellish conditions endured in our era, to come to a new country with no money or prospects and by sheer force of will to attain material security for themselves and their children.

The offspring of the survivors seem to be motivated by something of the same instinct—to build a strong castle and surround it with moats against the day that a Hitlerian madness might return and again sweep the Jewish people into the cauldron.

Interestingly, most of the children of the survivors seem to be of secular or Reform background and to have relatively little connection to Yiddishkeit. It is as though many of the survivors, in seeking to protect their children from direct contact with horrible memories of the conflagration they endured, also muted that aspect of themselves—their Jewishness—that was the direct contributing factor that motivated their tormentors to try to destroy them.

Personal Echoes

In the personal accounts of the children of the survivors, I heard echoes of my own life. My mother was born in Berlin and managed to flee Germany with her mother literally in the nick of time—two months before Kristallnacht in November, 1938. Then came three years of nightmarish fleeing across Belgium, France and Portugal, as the Nazis pressed westward in pursuit.

My mother reached the safety of the New York harbor in 1941, and thus, unlike the parents of these people, never experienced the mind-shattering horror of Auschwitz or Bergen-Belsen. Yet in the broader sense, she too is surely a survivor. Like many of the survivors, she had made a total break with her past and embraced America fully and without reservations.

I was brought up in non-Jewish suburbs of cities like Pittsburgh and Chicago, without a bar mitzvah and without much of a sense of positive Jewish identity. As an adult I have been inching skittishly back to Judaism like a hermit crab in search of a permanent home. I have grown into a close identification with Israel, with the Hebrew language, and with various Jewish cultural norms, while continuing to manifest a profound ignorance of, and something of a resistance to, most forms of Jewish religious observance.

One of the most personally compelling of the children of the survivors with whom I spoke was Charlie Silow, 35, a psychologist from Detroit. Silow's mother had survived Auschwitz and Bergen-Belsen, from which she had been liberated by the British from the Nazis as she lay near death from typhus. Silow's father was, like his wife, originally from Lodz, Poland, and had fled to Russia at the time of the Nazi invasion, spending the war years working in Siberian salt mines.

According to Silow, "I am embarked on this trip—my first ever to Germany—not only because I feel a protest is necessary, but for my own personal needs as well. I want to visit the places where my mother suffered—not only Bergen-Belsen, but if possible, the labor camp outside Hamburg about which she told such vivid stories of being practically naked and wearing wire shoes—of the cold, the mud, and the misery."

More Than History

Silow was asked why he wanted to visit those places. "To understand that, you have to comprehend that for me the Holocaust is more than history. It is living in me and in other children of survivors. It is something we never experienced directly, but it is something we know…because we incorporated our parents' pain and suffering into ourselves. Stated simply, I want to go to Bergen-Belsen because I want to experience my roots."

Silow said that his mother had been extremely agitated by his announcement that he intended to take part in the protest at Bergen-Belsen. Silow said "My mother pleaded with me, 'Don't go. Please don't go. That is not a place for you. You don't have to expose yourself to that.'"

Silow said he replied, "No, I do need to go and see it first hand. I have only artifacts of that experience. I need to go to Germany to understand better what you endured…to get a better perspective and to continue the healing process, so that perhaps in time we can begin to put this pain to rest."

Silow remarked, "The world has never dealt with the Holocaust, and Reagan's gesture is part of that refusal to look at reality. The fact that we stand at the edge of nuclear annihilation proves we have learned nothing. If one nation can turn into savages, it can happen to any nation. I hope that I personally, and this organization as an entity, can play a role in bringing insight into the process that allows a holocaust to develop, and also to have an impact in terms of trying to prevent a recurrence."

Shielded from Pain

Rebecca Knaster, 34, a New York City fashion designer, said that her parents, both the sole survivors of their families, had told her very little about their Holocaust related experiences when she was growing up.

"Looking back, I assume they wanted to shield me from the pain," Knaster recalled. "Whenever they did talk about any aspect of their experience, it was always so painful for me that I had to close my ears and block it out."

According to Knaster, "I got involved with the Second Generation movement about five years ago. I suddenly felt a need to see what other survivors' children felt and experienced . . . It was difficult for me at first but I hung in, and soon I felt my involvement snowballing. Now this is a terribly important part of my life. This group feels like family to me."

Knaster said that her mother, too, pleaded with her not to make the trip. "I told my mother that I understood her fear, but that I could not be afraid, and was determined to go to Bergen-Belsen for her and for my father . . . I asked my mother, 'How can you ask me not to do this?' and she replied, 'Don't you think I'm not proud of you?'"

Knaster added, "I believe that all of our parents are deeply moved and proud that we are standing up for them when they couldn't stand up for themselves, no matter how hard they tried. Everyone has heard that disgusting line about how the Jews went like sheep to the slaughter. Part of our purpose is to make sure everyone understands how untrue and misguided that is."

Arrival in Germany

The arrival at Hamburg Airport and the passage through customs was normal and routine—eerily normal for many members of the delegation.

Silow explained, "I had all sorts of paranoid feelings about coming to Germany. I was somehow not prepared for this to be a regular airport where everything is bright and efficient. I don't feel anything sinister here."

After riding with the delegation in a plush bus down the autobahn to the Intercontinental Hotel in the city of Hanover, I caught a ride with Jerzy Warman to Bergen-Belsen, located in the countryside about 40 miles away. The small towns and farming villages we passed through appeared prosperous, clean and charming, and the countryside, with its dairy farms, evoked memories of Wisconsin. Any connection with Hitler and the Holocaust seemed tenuous and deeply buried.

On the way to Bergen-Belsen, I talked to Warman and found him a complex and fascinating individual. The child of parents who took part in the Warsaw Ghetto uprising, Warman was raised in Warsaw in a very Polish, non-Jewish milieu. However, Warman (now in his late 30's) and his parents pulled up roots and headed for the U.S. in 1969, after his mother was fired from a high level government job during a wave of officially sanctioned anti-Semitism.

A bright and ambitious individual, who today holds a high level job with the City of New York, Warman had decided to check out the physical layout of Bergen-Belsen in order to bring back a recommendation to the delegation in Hanover as to what strategy the International Network should follow during the Reagan visit the following day.

Sought to Dissuade Weiss

Warman also wanted to see if it was still possible to head off a rumored civil disobedience action by Rabbi Avi Weiss of Riverdale and a group of followers who were said to be planning to refuse a police order that they vacate the small museum at Bergen-Belsen where they had been sitting in for nearly 24 hours — since just before the start of the Sabbath.

Warman, like virtually every other member of the International Network, strongly disagreed with Weiss' tack and appeared concerned that screaming headlines about the arrest of Weiss' group would submerge media coverage of the activities of the International Network.

According to Warman, "I don't believe that civil disobedience is appropriate in this situation, and I feel strongly that such action does not square with the sanctity of the mass graves of Bergen Belsen. We do not believe that one can engage in an effective moral statement in this situation by using those kinds of tactics."

It took only a few moments inside the Documentation Center at Bergen-Belsen to see that Weiss had a very different perception of the correct course of action. An Orthodox rabbi in his late 30's who was heavily impacted by both Jewish and secular protest movements of the late 1960's Weiss has held high the torch of Jewish activism because many former comrades have drifted into the establishment.

Unique Philosophy

Weiss' philosophy is a strange amalgam of humanism and intense Jewish nationalism. Among his heroes are Martin Luther King and Anatoly Shcharansky — as well as members of the Jewish underground in Israel who were tried and convicted last year for planting the bombs that blew the legs off two West Bank Arab mayors.

Weiss had arrived in Frankfurt several days before, together with a small delegation from his Riverdale synagogue (including his associate rabbi), and had convinced several young German Jews to join his group in spending the Sabbath in the Documentation Center. Later, sometime after the group had arrived at the camp late Friday, three non-Jewish Germans who were visiting the camp spent several hours talking to Weiss and his people—and then donned yarmulkas and expressed a commitment to stay with the group to the end.

When Weiss saw me walk into the museum, he immediately enveloped me in a warm bear hug of greeting. Weiss' followers were seated around a wooden table clad in tallisim, and were immersed in prayer and study beneath huge graphic black and white photographic blow-ups of thousands of naked Jewish corpses stacked in open pits. The symbolism of Jewish survival and strength manifested by Weiss' group in this setting of Jewish humiliation and destruction was powerful and compelling.

Weiss forcefully and uncategorically dismissed Warman's plea that he and his followers reconsider their plan to court arrest by the German police. Weiss said that he and the others had carefully considered the implications of their action and decided that because Kohl had insisted that Reagan go to Bitburg, an action of civil disobedience, and not simply a symbolic protest, was needed to drive home to the German people what Weiss termed "the obscenity of this effort to rehabilitate Nazism."

Minyan at Bergen-Belsen

Weiss then dramatically informed Warman and me that our arrival had raised the number of Jews at Bergen-Belsen to ten and made possible the first minyan at the camp in 40 years.

I accepted the invitation to step out of my journalistic observer role and participate in the minyan with a muddled feeling combining a sense of spiritual uplift with a counterveiling feeling of embarrassment that with my minimal knowledge of Judaism, I would make a fool of myself in the middle of this prayer service, which Weiss had elevated to a level of almost cosmic import.

I felt like I had stepped out onto the stage at a highly significant moment of the 4,000-year-old Jewish drama—and, grotesquely, I did not know my lines.

Then Weiss asked me if I would like to carry the Torah and I assented. As I firmly grasped the scrolls and gazed out the window of the museum across the bleak and empty fields where thousands of Jews had suffered and died, I felt my own concerns and neuroses quickly drop away, to be replaced by a sense of peace and contentment.

I felt for a timeless split second a sense of oneness with the voiceless thousands who were sacrificed here. I lowered my eyes as kaddish was recited.

Journalists Gathered

The sense of Jewish unity powerfully manifested during the minyan quickly dissolved as the light of that special Shabbat at Bergen-Belsen faded into dusk.

As an ever growing flock of German and American journalists gathered in the one room museum impatiently anticipating the promised confrontation between Weiss' group and the police, Michael Furst, head of the Jewish community of Lower Saxony, arrived to attempt a last ditch effort to head off the confrontation.

Addressing Weiss, Furst argued forcefully that the German Jewish community, traditionally a rather low profile group, has already taken the unprecedented step of declining an official invitation to take part in the upcoming ceremonies at Bergen-Belsen. For Weiss' group to compel the police to arrest them, Furst asserted, "could cause great problems for the Jews of Germany."

Weiss responded with praise for the German Jews' refusal to take part in the ceremony, but firmly refused to call off the civil disobedience, arguing, "You are standing up as proud Jews in your own way, and we are doing the same thing in our own way." When Furst argued that the two actions could not be equated, Weiss responded, "Don't be afraid. Don't be afraid."

Group Members Have Doubts

By then, however, Weiss' own group had begun to fray around the edges. Aryeh Steinman, 27, one of the several young German Jews who had joined Weiss' group, announced to the assembled company, including the journalists, that he had reconsidered his position and now agreed with Furst's analysis that the sight of a Jewish group refusing to obey the German police could lead to a German backlash, which could endanger German Jews. Weiss' response was to cut off all communication with Steinman, despite an appeal by the anguished young man that they discuss the situation reasonably.

Weiss' behavior toward Steinman seemed rather callous at the time, but may, in fact, have saved the group from total disintegration. George Horny, another young German who had also expressed agreement with Furst and Steinman, now decided to stay with the group and go through with the civil disobedience, as did Weiss' associate rabbi, Rabbi Ronald Schwarzberg, who also said he had misgivings about the confrontational tactics.

Weiss seemed to win over the remaining waverers when he made clear that he was ready to agree that instead of forcing police to carry the protesters out, the delegation members would instead get up and walk out peacefully as soon as they had been officially 'apprehended' by the police.

The standoff between police and protesters, which came sometime after 9:30 p.m. on what had become a cold, rainy night, had elements of the absurd, with the local police militia, led by Commander Johannes Thecke, seemingly trying to smother the protest with kindness and compassion.

Thecke and about 30 officers surrounded the nine protesters, and stood gravely and deferentially by as they completed a havdalah service that ended with the protesters locking arms and singing "Am Yisrael Chai." Thecke then gave the protesters three widely spaced warnings to disperse , each time allowing them to vent their feelings in songs and speeches.

Jewish Journalist's Pain

If the minyan had been the high point of the day for me, the singing of "Am Yisrael Chai" was surely the most painful. As the protesters sang, rocked, and swayed together as a unit of Jewish commitment, I felt miserably inadequate as a Jew, standing outside the circle, snapping photographs and playing the role of 'journalist' along with gentile colleagues from the *New York Times,* NBC Radio and German papers.

How I envied those reporters, their professional non-involvement and their sense that this was just another story. For one of the first times in my career as a 'Jewish journalist', the contradictions inherent in that term seemed to be pressing in on me and demanding resolution. By standing outside the circle and furiously taking notes as the police circled the protesters, I knew that I was saying that my priorities were first and foremost as an unbiased reporter and not an involved Jew.

In an effort to rationalize the situation, I told myself that I had serious doubts that Weiss' tactic of compelling the German police to escort his people out of Bergen-Belsen represented the most thoughtful and effective response to Reagan's visit.

Yet as I stood outside the circle of Jewish activism and watched the police prepare to close in, I recalled a long forgotten incident when I was about 11 years old and staying at a YMCA sleepaway camp. Deeply confused about my Jewish identity in that overwhelmingly Christian milieu, I replied 'Catholic' when another camper asked me what religion I was.

Now my religion was 'journalist' instead of Catholic, but I felt like it came down to the same kind of denial. I was still choosing not to enter the circle.

Sense of Satisfaction

After Thecke and his police had finally evacuated Weiss and his followers, there appeared to be a sense of general satisfaction. The police and German officials were obviously pleased that they had brought the protesters out without violence or untoward incident, whereas Weiss and his people seemed exhausted but exultant that they had stayed the course and played out heroic roles before the assembled world media.

In fact, the very peacefulness of the evacuation seemed to somehow confirm Weiss in his assumption that German police could evacuate Jewish protesters from a concentration camp without the sky falling in.

Nevertheless, a German journalist, Ulricke Sudmeyer, told me that the day's events left her "shaken and angry." She stated, "The last thing those police wanted to do was to have to bring those people out, but Weiss forced them to do it. He wanted pictures that would make it appear that Germans are still brutalizing Jews, and that is completely untrue. I can appreciate the anger of Jews at Kohl and Reagan, but it really wasn't fair to try to make our police look like the SS."

I woke the next morning in a non-descript hotel room in the nearby village of Bergen, frustrated by the realization that I had not secured the proper press credentials the day before for the Reagan-Kohl visit to Bergen-Belsen. In the cold light of morning, I realized that without the necessary press card, I was unlikely to get within a mile of the concentration camp, given the overwhelming security precautions being taken by the German government and the White House.

Melted Into 'Photo Pool'

But then a strange series of events began to occur. I managed to bluff my way through two security check-points by claiming that a State Department man was waiting for me at the gate of Bergen-Belsen with the proper credentials.

Arriving there, I found myself momentarily stymied in my efforts to get into the camp itself. But as helicopters full of White House advance men began landing on the parking lot in front of the entrance, security seemed to break down for a moment. Acting on impulse, I climbed over a flimsy barrier and into the proscribed area.

Feeling vulnerable without the proper credentials, I slipped into the Documentation Center, where I tried to melt into a knot of very professional looking photographers, who turned out to be the 'photo pool,' who had been assigned to photograph the President's five minute tour of the tiny museum. Before anyone had a chance to ask me what I was doing there, Reagan, Kohl and their wives entered the building.

Reagan, standing about five yards from me, listened intently as a guide pointed out to him the grim photographic tableau on the walls of the museum. Reagan looked stiff (maybe it was the protruding bullet-proof vest) and wary, as though he was still afraid that despite all the security, an angry demonstrator might jump out and confront him in this uncongenial place.

Chance for Confrontation

It occurred to me that if Avi Weiss were in my place, he would use this precious opportunity to effect exactly such a confrontation. Why had fate or God arranged for me to pass undetected through all the security barriers and to get so close to Reagan, except to give me a chance to atone for my non-involvement the day before and to express the outraged feelings of world Jewry face to face to the most powerful man in the world?

I considered the option briefly and quickly rejected it. To start shouting slogans now would not stop Reagan from his appointed rounds at Bitburg and would forever discredit me as a professional journalist. My role, I told myself, was not to be an activist in the Avi Weiss mold, but rather someone who serves the Jewish people by trying to discern and articulate meaning and truth. Enough with the guilt trips, I told myself—it's okay to be a Jewish journalist.

As the Reagans left the museum, I was rushed, together with my 'colleagues' in the photo pool, across the great green lawns of Bergen-Belsen to a modest stone memorial with Hebrew inscriptions known as the "Jewish memorial." Moments later Reagan pulled up in his limousine and emerged to briefly pay his respects at the monument. We were then trotted briskly to a reviewing stand in front of a memorial obelisk at the very center of Bergen-Belsen where Reagan would shortly make his speech.

Looking over Bergen-Belsen from the vantage point of the reviewing stand, it was hard to conceive that this had once been one of Europe's most horrific killing grounds. The prisoners' barracks and the rest of the buildings from the 1940's had long since been demolished, leaving only a grassy plain, with gentle rolling hillocks to mark the location of the mass graves.

The overall impression of Bergen-Belsen was one of silent desolation, of blankness. Rather than bringing grief and anger to the fore, the place had a rather tranquilizing, numbing effect. One felt moved to profound melancholy, but not to action or revelation.

Reagan's speech seemed to echo the emptiness around him. Speaking in an expressionless monotone that was often difficult to hear, Reagan appeared like a wax figure, devoid of his usual Hollywood radiance. He avoided any mention of the roiling Bitburg controversy which had forced him to change his earlier decision not to go to a concentration camp. Under other circumstances, Reagan's speech, with its explicit recognition that the victims of Bergen-Belsen died solely because they were Jews, might have had resonance in the Jewish community. In this situation, with the SS graves of Bitburg the next stop on the presidential itinerary, the speech at Bergen-Belsen seemed a vain and morally vacuous attempt to rhetorically square a circle.

Survivors' Children Entered

Ten minutes after Reagan's helicopter had lifted off, the International Network group entered the grounds of Bergen-Belsen with a police escort. Marching as a unit, each person carrying a rose, they crossed the grassy plain and gathered in front of the Jewish memorial, erected by Menachem Rosensaft's late father in 1946 while he was still a resident at the Bergen-Belsen displaced persons' camp and maintained by him until his death many years later.

Upon his birth at Bergen-Belsen in 1948, Menachem Rosensaft became known to many of the refugees in the camp as 'the Prince,' because his birth seemed to symbolize the triumph of life after the long dance of death. In recent years, the younger Rosensaft, today a New York corporate lawyer, has created a new role for himself as a prince of the children of the survivors movement, which he had been instrumental in creating.

As he spoke, Rosensaft seemed to radiate a sense of mission.

Terming the mass graves of Bergen-Belsen "one of the holiest sites in the world," Rosensaft stated, "For 40 years no one has dared to come here for any reason except to mourn, to commemorate, to remember, and to vow that the horrors of Nazism, of the Third Reich, will never be repeated and the murderers will never be forgiven. Never until today has anyone used these graves as part of an attempt to rehabilitate the SS.

"President Reagan and Chancellor Kohl have embarked on a macabre tour, an obscene package deal, of Bergen-Belsen and Bitburg. Today we say to them that they can either honor the memory of the victims or they can honor the SS. They cannot do both. And by entering Bitburg, they desecrate the memory of all those who they pretend to commemorate here at Belsen." '

After the speech, the children of the survivors recited kaddish, and in a moving gesture, sang in Yiddish the hymn of the Jewish partisans who fought the Nazis in the forests of Poland.

Delivered on Promise

Rosensaft and the International Network of Children of Jewish Holocaust Survivors had, it seemed to me, more than delivered on their promise of a dignified ceremony to express the Jewish community's deep hurt and anger at the Reagan visit. If Weiss and his followers had raised the flag of renascent Jewish activism at this shrine of Jewish destruction, Rosensaft and his followers seemed to speak as the voices of the mass graves themselves.

Despite their evident conflict in style and tactics, Rosensaft and Weiss seemed finally to complement each other. Both groups, I decided, deserved the gratitude of the entire Jewish world for having come here to make the world aware of the unacceptability of Reagan's gesture of reconciliation.

As the government of Israel and the American Jewish leadership had scrambled to come up with the right equation of condemnation of Reagan and accommodation with the administration for the future. Weiss and Rosensaft had understood that it was vital that there be a Jewish protest at Bergen-Belsen on May 5.

The effect of Jewish protest at Bergen-Belsen, it seemed to me, had been somehow to exorcise much of the poison of Bitburg. In 1945, the British liberated Bergen-Belsen and helped to ensure the physical survival of the remnants of European Jewry. In 1985, the Jewish return to Bergen-Belsen symbolized a self-liberation, a casting off of fear and dependence.

I had not taken part directly in those efforts, but as I left the one-time death camp, I felt strengthened as a Jew by having been in a position to communicate to others something of the complexities and emotions of a moment in Jewish history that is likely to resonate for a long time to come.

A Journey to Bergen-Belsen
Special Contribution

By Menachem Z. Rosensaft

The Jewish monument of Bergen-Belsen is one of the most somber memorials in the world. Standing alone in the midst of mass graves, it was erected by the Central Committee of Liberated Jews in the British Zone of Germany in April 1946, on the first anniversary of the liberation of the concentration camp. The text inscribed on this grey slab of stone in Hebrew and English is poetic in its stark simplicity:

> "Israel and the World shall remember thirty thousand Jews ex-
> terminated in the concentration camp of Bergen-Belsen at the
> hands of the murderous Nazis. Earth conceal not their blood shed
> on thee!"

On Sunday, May 5, 1985, a group of some fifty American Jews — most of them sons and daughters of Holocaust survivors — stood beside this monument. We had come to Belsen not to mourn, but to express our anger. We had come to Belsen because on that day, in another part of Germany, the President of the United States was about to lay his wreath at the German military cemetery at Bitburg. Less than an hour after President Reagan and West German Chancellor Helmut Kohl had stood at Belsen in an attempt to neutralize the negative impact of their visit to Bitburg, we had come to tell the dead that we had not abandoned them and that we would not permit their murderers to be rehabilitated. We had come to Belsen because, on that day, it was the only place for us to be.

* * * * *

On April 19, 1985, immediately following Elie Wiesel's impassioned, nationally televised appeal to President Reagan that he not go to Bitburg, the White House announced that while the Bitburg trip would take place as planned, the President had now decided to add a visit to the Memorial Site of Bergen-Belsen to his itinerary. This announcement was perceived by many leaders of the American Jewish community as a positive development in the on-going crisis. On the whole, the news of President Reagan's planned trip to Bergen-Belsen — in contrast to his projected wreath-laying at Bitburg — did not invoke a great deal of controversy.

In reality, there were two separate issues. The first was whether or not the President of the United States should lay a wreath at a cemetery were SS men and officers lie buried. The second was whether or not this same President of the United States should also be allowed to exploit the mass-graves of a Nazi concentration camp, and the memory of those who had perished there, in order somehow to off-set his paying tribute to the soldiers of Nazi Germany. By and large, the American-Jewish community and its leaders reacted strongly against the Bitburg trip. For the most part, however, the implications of President Reagan's decision to go to Bergen-Belsen were completely ignored.

As far as I was concerned, the Bergen-Belsen visit was nothing more than political damage control. Moreover, both Ronald Reagan and Helmut Kohl utterly failed to comprehend the grotesque nature of the pairing of Bitburg and Bergen-Belsen.

Not only did President Reagan not want to pay tribute to the victims of Nazism during his May 1985 trip to West Germany, but he had even gone so far as to describe the German soldiers at Bitburg as "victims of Nazism." "They were victims," he had said at the White House on April 18, "just as surely as the victims in the concentration camps." There seemed to be little difference in his mind between the murderers and the murdered. Accordingly, consistent with such a perverse view of history, he was also able to equate a perfunctory appearance and speech at Bergen-Belsen with his wreath-laying at Bitburg.

It was evident that Ronald Reagan was setting his schedule for May 5 in the manner of an experienced vote-seeking politician. It included something for everyone: He was going to Bergen-Belsen in order to appease the Jews and other anti-Nazis, and to Bitburg to please the Germans, including all those who looked back on the Third Reich with undisguised nostalgia. That is why I felt compelled to declare in an address to some 5,000 survivors and children of survivors in Philadelphia on April 21, 1985, that if Ronald Reagan refused to cancel his visit to Bitburg, his very presence at the mass-graves of Bergen-Belsen would violate their sanctity. "If he insists on going to Bitburg," I said, "we do not need him and we do not want him at Bergen-Belsen."

* * * * *

Long before anyone realized that there would be a Bitburg crisis, I was invited to participate in the Inaugural Assembly of the American Gathering and Federation of Jewish Holocaust Survivors at Philadelphia in April of 1985. The purpose of this event was the formal establishment of a national organization of survivors, and I was asked to represent the Second Generation, that is, the sons and daughters of the survivors. Initially, I was going to speak about our generation's obligation to keep alive our parents' legacy of remembrance, and our role in the struggle against anti-Semitism and all other forms of racial and religious hatred.

By the end of the third week of April 1985, however, I had become known, for better or worse, as one of the most vocal critics of President Reagan's visit to Bitburg. During the week following the initial disclosure of the scheduled wreath-laying at the German cemetery, I had spoken out sharply against the President at various Holocaust commemorations in New York, New Jersey and Texas, and my remarks had been widely quoted in the media. Thus, the organizers of the Philadelphia gathering had good reason to suspect that I would once again address the Bitburg issue in my April 21 speech to the survivors.

Even though I knew that several of the leaders of the survivors believed that I was too extreme in my opposition to President Reagan, I did not anticipate the extent of the pressure to which I was going to be subjected. On numerous occasions, I was told by some of them that my speech should not be inflammatory, and I was asked to adhere to my original theme. Each time, I replied that I would say what I believed to be appropriate and necessary under the circumstances. However, I did not hide the fact that I would continue to criticize the President's offensive agenda, and I refused to submit an advance copy of my remarks.

On April 21, shortly before 7:00 a.m., I was woken up by a telephone call from Ernest Michel, the Honorary Chairman of the Board of the American Gathering, who had been the principal organizer of the historic 1981 World Gathering of Jewish Holocaust Survivors in Jerusalem. Michel told me that he "and others" in the leadership of the survivor organization wanted to discuss the content of my speech with me within the hour. Of course, I understood precisely what Michel had in mind. Although he supported what he considered to be "respectful" criticism of the Bitburg visit, Michel had never hidden the fact that he opposed any direct confrontation with the President. Thus, it seemed that he had undertaken to try to dissuade me from castigating President Reagan that afternoon. Apparently, Michel and the unnamed "others" were afraid that I might turn the Philadelphia event into an anti-Reagan manifestation.

I was angered by Michel's peremptory summons, and at first declined to meet with him. However, he implied that unless I agreed to conform my remarks to his directives, I might be prevented from speaking altogether. I then called up Sam Bloch and Norbert Wollheim, respectively the senior vice president and treasurer of the American Gathering, who told me that Michel had spoken to me without their knowledge or support. Thereupon, I called Michel back and agreed to get together with him on condition that Bloch and Wollheim, as well as several members of the Second Generation, would be there as well.

Immediately after hanging up with Michel, I asked four of the senior leaders of the International Network of Children of Jewish Holocaust Survivors—Jerzy Warman, Rositta Kenigsberg, Michael Korenblit and Stephen Tencer—to accompany me. Warman had succeeded me as president of the International Network, and the two of us had represented the Second Generation on the steering committee of the American Gathering; Kenigsberg, the head of Miami's Second Generation organization, and Korenblit, who had written a moving book about his parents' wartime experiences, were the vice presidents of our organization; and Tencer who, like myself, had been born in the Displaced Persons camp of Bergen-Belsen after the war, was the chairman of the Second Generation Council of New Jersey. All four were well known to, and respected by, Michel, and I hoped that they might convey to him and the other survivors that I was not alone in my views.

About half an hour later, we met in the coffee shop of the hotel where we were all staying. On the way down from my room, I ran into Joseph Tekulsky, one of the founders and a former president of New York's Warsaw Ghetto Resistance Organization, and asked him to join us as well. Michel said that while he respected my right to my opinions, he considered any highlighting of the Bitburg issue to be detrimental to the American Gathering and inappropriate. Accordingly, he demanded that I refrain from attacking the President. Moreover, he added, if I insisted on referring to Bitburg in my speech, my remarks should not be belligerent or offensive.

Except to say that I would not submit to censorship, I listened quietly throughout most of the meeting. However, Warman, Kenigsberg, Korenblit and Tencer told Michel that they disagreed adamantly with him and expressed confidence in my judgment, as did Bloch, Wollheim and Tekulsky. They argued that I had the absolute right to speak freely, and that explicit criticism of the President over Bitburg was perfectly justified. That afternoon, I said precisely what I had intended to say.

* * * * *

In my Philadelphia speech, I called for an intensified public campaign to try to persuade Ronald Reagan to cancel the Bitburg visit, and, if such protests turned out not to have the desired result, for demonstrations in Germany during the course of the President's trip. It was clear from the enthusiastic response of the assembled crowd of survivors and children of survivors that they agreed wholeheartedly. Their anger at President Reagan was deep, and many felt frustrated at the absence of any real outlet for their emotions.

There was no question in my mind that it was too late for soft-spoken, deferential appeals and supplications. Even Elie Wiesel's moving plea at the White House had fallen on deaf ears. The President had already demonstrated his disregard for moral principles, and he was by nature not disposed to respond to intellectual arguments. Thus, the only thing left that might have averted his going to Bitburg was a show of strength.

As one who remembered the dramatic and effective mass demonstrations for civil rights and against the Viet Nam war during the 1960's and early 1970's, I believed that if even a few thousand American Jews—especially Holocaust survivors—would demonstrate in Lafayette Park outside the White House during the week before his departure for Germany, Ronald Reagan might well be embarrassed into changing his mind about Bitburg at the last minute. Accordingly, on April 21 and 22, the leadership of the Second Generation tried to generate a grassroot reaction to Bitburg among the survivors who had come to Philadelphia. Overnight, we placed signs throughout the Civic Center urging them to flood the White House with telephone calls and telegrams, and we were hoping that they might become the nucleus of a genuine protest movement.

Unfortunately, however, while the survivors themselves were willing to take a strong stand against the President, many of their leaders discouraged any type of active anti-Reagan sentiments. Indeed, several of the principal organizers of the Philadelphia gathering, including a Republican *apparatchik* who was a veteran of both Richard Nixon's Committee to Re-Elect the President and the 1980 Reagan-Bush campaign, explicitly distanced themselves from us and our efforts. Thus, on April 22, Benjamin Meed, the President of the American Gathering who had publicly embraced me after my speech the day before, told a reporter for *The Washington Post,* "I personally am not going to lead this organization to threaten anybody." According to Meed, "The young are more radical — not in the political sense, but in that they feel the pain of their parents." He said that if the survivors "would have to react" to the Bitburg controversy, "we would react against Germany, not America."

To his credit, even though Meed may have disagreed with the vehemence of our protest, he did not try to prevent me from speaking out against the President. As a matter of fact, Meed actually vetoed a last-minute demand by Ernest Michel that I preface my speech to the survivors by stating that I represented only the Second Generation. Late in the morning on April 21, Meed told me in Michel's presence that I should speak in the name of the American Gathering as a whole. At the same time, however, Meed and a number of others in the American Gathering leadership did not want to antagonize the Reagan Administration, and consequently, they were anxious to de-emphasize the Bitburg issue as much as possible at the Philadelphia assembly.

Consistent with this overcautious attitude, a mild, inoffensive resolution deploring the Bitburg visit was proposed and adopted by the survivors at a plenary session of the American Gathering on April 22 together with another resolution thanking the President for his and the administration's role in evacuating Ethiopian Jews to Israel. The message to Washington was clear: a few hotheads might make noise, but there would be no mass protest. And if the survivors of the Holocaust were not going to engage in any serious anti-Bitburg demonstrations, the rest of the American Jewish community was not likely to do so either. In other words, Ronald Reagan had no reason to be unduly concerned. His trip to Bitburg could proceed as planned.

At this point, the other leaders of the International Network of Children of Jewish Holocaust Survivors and I decided that we would go to Germany on our own. We were convinced that it would be a betrayal of our responsibilities to our murdered families if our opposition to the wreath-laying at Bitburg were limited to mere lip service.

After some discussion, it became clear to us that the proper place for us on May 5 was not Bitburg, but Bergen-Belsen. To begin with, we did not want to be part of, or somehow to be confused with, the various anti-American demonstrations that we knew were going to occur at Bitburg on that day. Rather, we wanted our protest to reflect our repugnance at President Reagan's perverse package tour of Bergen-Belsen and Bitburg, and our objection to his very presence at Bergen-Belsen on that day. Accordingly, we concluded that we could make our point most effectively by being at Bergen-Belsen and compelling President Reagan and Chancellor Kohl to pass in front of us and to look at us as they entered the Memorial Site of the concentration camp.

Moreover, we believed that we could not allow the dead of Bergen-Belsen to be overlooked or forgotten. Our answer to the survivor leader who opposed our demonstration on the ground that "Our place is not in Germany" was to remind him that the victims of the Holocaust are buried there and in other parts of Europe, not in the United States. While we, of course, supported the various memorial services for American servicemen, including one at Arlington National Cemetery, that were being planned for May 5, we did not agree that such commemorations constituted the only appropriate response to Bitburg. The Memorial Site of Bergen-Belsen, which includes the mass-graves, is a sacred shrine that belongs to the entire Jewish people. We felt, therefore, that we had an absolute obligation to go there in order to defend both the sanctity of the Bergen-Belsen soil and the memory of its dead.

For more than thirty years—from the liberation of Bergen-Belsen on April 15, 1945 until his untimely death on September 10, 1975—my father, Josef Rosensaft, had been the leader of the survivors of Bergen-Belsen and the fierce advocate for its victims. Throughout those years, he had kept a watchful eye over the mass-graves, returning periodically with other Belsen survivors from around the world to say *Kaddish*, the Jewish prayer of mourning, and to ensure that the grounds of the Memorial Site were being properly maintained. I was certain that if my father were alive, he would have confronted President Reagan and Chancellor Kohl at Bergen-Belsen on May 5. With him gone, I believed that I, at least, had to be there. My friends of the International Network agreed.

On Friday, April 26, we publicly announced our intention to hold our demonstration at Bergen-Belsen. This was widely reported in the press the following day. We planned to arrive in the nearby city of Hanover on May 4, and to proceed to the Memorial Site early the following morning.

At first, we thought that only about a dozen of us would travel to Germany. However, there turned out to be a great deal of interest in our trip throughout the United States. For the next several days, my telephone did not stop ringing. Many who had heard about our planned demonstration wanted to know if they could join us. They, too, wanted the opportunity to express their anger at the President. In the end, our delegation consisted of some 50 Americans, including leaders of the International Network* and children of survivors as well as other American Jews of the post-Holocaust generation, American war veterans who had liberated a number of concentration camps, and several Christians.

In addition, it was particularly meaningful that several Holocaust survivors went with us to Germany as well. Among them were Berlin-born historian, Henry Friedlander, a professor at Brooklyn College whose guidance throughout the trip proved to be invaluable; Jack Eisner, founder and President of the Holocaust Survivors Memorial Foundation; and Dr. Yehuda Nir, a noted New York psychiatrist. On May 5, we were also joined at our demonstration at Bergen-Belsen by Kalman Sultanik, vice president of the World Jewish Congress and a member of the Executive of the World Zionist Organization. The presence of these survivors added a unique dimension to our group.

* * * * *

Among the International Network leaders who went to Germany were President Jerzy Warman, Vice Presidents Rositta Kenigsberg of Miami, Florida, and Michael Korenblit of Washington, D.C., Secretary Sarah Ducorsky of Long Island, Rebecca Knaster, Joyce Celnik, Eva Fogelman, Tom Teicholz, and Ritalynne Brechner of New York City, Stephen Tencer and Jeanette Friedman-Sieradski of New Jersey, Esther Fink of Chicago, Charles Silow and Bernard Kent of Detroit, and Lee Kagan of Los Angeles.

Once we had decided to go to Bergen-Belsen, we set out to make the necessary logistical arrangements. On Wednesday, April 24, Jerzy Warman and I met with Dr. Peter Sympher, the Consul General of the Federal Republic of Germany in New York, and we asked his assistance in obtaining permission from the West German authorities for us to hold our protest demonstration on May 5. We had no idea how he would react to our request. We anticipated a cool reception from the German diplomat: he was, after all, a representative of the Kohl government which was directly responsible for the entire Bitburg fiasco, and we could hardly expect him to be more positively disposed toward us than the officials of our government.

To our surprise, we found Dr. Sympher to be extremely cordial. He and Dr. Eckart Herold of the Consulate listened attentively while we explained that we did not intend to attack the German people of today, or to criticize the relationship that exists between the United States and West Germany, or between Israel and West Germany. Rather, we said that as the sons and daughters of Jews who had been liberated at Bergen-Belsen, and as the grandchildren and relatives of those buried there, we believed that we had an absolute right to express our protest at Bergen-Belsen against what we believed to be a desecration of its mass-graves.

We further assured Dr. Sympher that we were in no way opposed to reconciliation with present-day Germany. However, we would never agree to any rehabilitation of the murderers of millions of Jews as well as millions of non-Jews during the period of the Nazi regime. As far as we were concerned, true reconciliation with Germany on the part of the Jewish people or the United States had to be predicated on the absolute repudiation of Nazism, Fascism, Hitlerism, and all that epitomizes these noxious evils of the Twentieth Century. Thus, we could not acquiesce in a public tribute by President Reagan and Chancellor Kohl to the memory of members of the SS who had carried out the policies of the Third Reich in the name of the German nation and of the German people.

Dr. Sympher told us that he understood our position, but that he had no control over the situation. Nonetheless, he promised to help as best he could. He intervened with the West German Foreign Office on our behalf, and he put me in contact with the local authorities in Lower Saxony where Bergen-Belsen is located. I then had several long telephone conversations with officials in the district of Lüneberg who have direct responsibility for the Memorial Site of Bergen-Belsen. During the course of these discussions, I emphasized that we did not want in any way endanger the safety of President Reagan or Chancellor Kohl, and that we were therefore ready to comply with all appropriate security precautions. These German officials, too, assured me that they were prepared to cooperate with us, but explained that they would have to receive approval for our demonstration from the Federal Government in Bonn.

At precisely this time, I was scheduled to attend an international conference of Holocaust survivors in Israel. On May 2, upon my arrival in Tel Aviv, I called Dr. Klaus Becker, the head of the district government of Luneburg, who informed me that we would not be allowed to go to Bergen-Belsen on May 5. The West German authorities had agreed to clear all security arrangements for the Reagan trip with what had become known as the "Bonn White House", that is, the entourage of President Reagan which was head-quartered at the United States Embassy in Bonn. Accordingly, Dr. Becker told me, his office had forwarded our request to Bonn, and our demonstration had been vetoed by the American authorities.

I tried repeatedly but in vain to obtain permission from the "Bonn White House" for us to hold our demonstrations. On May 2 and 3, I placed four separate, lengthy calls from Tel Aviv to Bonn, and spoke to different White House and State Department officials at the United States Embassy. On each occasion, I was told that no one was available to even discuss the issue. On each occasion, I explained in detail what we wanted to do, our reasons for wanting to do so, and our readiness to comply with the necessary security measures. I also told them that we, the sons and daughters of the survivors, had at least as much of a right to be at Bergen-Belsen on May 5 as President Reagan and Chancellor Kohl. These lower-level American officials heard me out but did not react in any manner. At the conclusion of each of these telephone conversations, I was told that someone would call me back. No one ever did. Meanwhile, in New York, Jerzy Warman was equally unsuccessful in reaching anyone in authority at the State Department. We were being stonewalled by experts.

On May 3, after it had become evident that we would be prevented from holding the kind of demonstration we planned, I called Dr. Becker again. Unlike the American officials with whom I had spoken, he seemed genuinely apologetic about his inability to comply with our request, and together we tried to find a solution. Ultimately, he and I reached what I considered to be a less than ideal but tolerable compromise. Dr. Becker offered to provide us with a police escort which would take our group from Hanover past the police barricades that would be surrounding Bergen-Belsen on May 5, to a spot a kilometer or two away from the Memorial Site. He explained that we would then have to wait there until after the conclusion of the official ceremony, but that we would be allowed to enter Bergen-Belsen as soon as President Reagan and Chancellor Kohl had left by helicopter. This appeared to be the best that he could do for us, and the most that we were likely to obtain.

However, we were determined to publicize the Reagan Administration's refusal to let us demonstrate at Belsen in the vicinity, if not the presence, of the President. On May 3, at a press conference in Jerusalem, I expressed our anger at the treatment we were receiving from our own government, and pointed out that it would have been unconstitutional for President Reagan and his minions to prohibit us from holding a peaceful, non-violent demonstration in a public place in the United States. In other words, I said, they were accomplishing in Germany that which they would not have been able to do in their own country. In response to questions, I stressed that it was indeed the American and not the German authorities who were preventing us from holding our demonstration. Later that weekend, a police spokesman in Lower Saxony confirmed to the *Los Angeles Times* that, indeed, the refusal for permission to carry out our protest "was made at the political level, from the American side."

* * * * *

During the ten days following my speech in Philadelphia quite a few leaders of the American Jewish community, including several prominent Holocaust survivors, told me that they considered my criticism of President Reagan to be too sharp and too extreme. They were afraid that a confrontation over Bitburg could jeopardize the positive attitude of the Reagan Administration with respect to such non-Holocaust related issues as United States support for Israel and for Soviet Jewry. Accordingly, they said that I had made my point, and I was asked to tone down my public statements.

On the other hand, there were those who agreed with our stance and said so. We received strong encouragement and support from the leaders of the World Federation of Bergen-Belsen Associations, in particular, Sam Bloch, Hadassah Rosensaft, Norbert Wollheim and Mannes Schwarz, as well as from Israel Singer and Elan Steinberg, respectively the Secretary-General and the Executive Director of the World Jewish Congress. In fact, these two organizations were the only ones to publicly endorse our decision to go to Belsen. and Sam Bloch, the President of the Bergen-Belsen survivors, reiterated his full backing for our demonstration at the May 3 press conference in Jerusalem. In addition, William Lowenberg, one of the most prominent leaders of the San Francisco Jewish community, a member of the Board of Governors of the Jewish Agency for Israel and a senior vice-president of the American Gathering of Jewish Holocaust Survivors, told me on several occasions that he stood fully behind and with us.

The attorneys at my law firm, Kaye, Scholer, Fierman, Hays & Handler, were not only extremely supportive, but allowed me to devote a considerable amount of time to the Bitburg controversy. Steven Glassman, a partner with whom I was working closely during that period, told me after my return from Philadelphia that, "So long as you don't moderate your position, you can take off all the time you need."

I was gratified when Abraham Feinberg, a long-time American Zionist leader and a prominent figure in the Democratic party, wrote to me on April 23, "I applaud your more assertive approach, as evidenced in Philadelphia, and I hope that you can carry out your planned demonstration at the cemetery so that the world can see how blatantly [President Reagan] will have disregarded the will of all his people, Jewish and non-Jewish." Similarly, some five weeks later at the end of May, I was deeply moved to receive a letter from author Cynthia Ozick in which she wrote, "As you can imagine, we followed (my husband and I) every moment of your harrowing and courageous Representation: you were truly an Ambassador for the Jewish People. Elie [Wiesel] went to the King's Court, and you went out to the killing fields. Those of us who watched from home felt our voices rise from your throats."

Furthermore, several American Jewish leaders defended the legitimacy of our demonstration even though they disagreed with our approach. Kenneth Bialkin, the Chairman of the Conference of Presidents of Major Jewish Organizations, said in an interview with the *Associated Press* on April 22 that he had "no quarrel with confronting Reagan with demonstrations" in Germany of the type I had proposed, adding that "I think people have got to be guided by their consciences." And Abraham Foxman, the Associate National Director of the Anti-Defamation League of B'nai B'rith said publicly that of the various Jewish groups planning protests in Germany during President Reagan's trip, our group had the most legitimacy because of our direct familial connection to the Holocaust.

In contrast, Ernest Michel went out of his way to disparage our protest. After our return from Germany, we were unpleasantly surprised to discover that Michel, who had himself participated in anti-Bitburg ceremonies at Dachau and Munich only a few days before our demonstration, had said in an interview with the *Long Island Jewish World* that while his going to Germany had been legitimate, "I think it was wrong to go to Belsen to oppose your President while he's there."

* * * * *

One of the more serious unresolved issues during the last week of April and the first three days of May, 1985 was whether or not the leaders of West Germany's Jewish community would accompany President Reagan and Chancellor Kohl to Bergen-Belsen on May 5 as they had been asked to do by the West German Government. Any formal Jewish participation in either one of that day's scheduled ceremonies would have been construed as a sign that there existed at least some difference of opinion within the international Jewish community regarding the pairing of tributes to Nazi soldiers and to the victims of Nazism. Thus, a general Jewish boycott of the official visits to both Bergen-Belsen and Bitburg was a prerequisite to an effective repudiation of the wreath-laying at Bitburg.

In the United States, every American Jewish leader who had been approached by the White House turned down the invitation to go with the President to Bergen-Belsen so long as Bitburg remained on his itinerary. However, even though Werner Nachmann, the chairman of the *Zentralrat der Juden in Deutschland*, the Central Council of Jews in Germany, had voiced some restrained criticism of the decision to visit Bitburg, he was close to both Chancellor Kohl and West German Foreign Minister Hans-Dietrich Genscher, and he had never been known to turn down any request of the Bonn government.

On the afternoon of Friday, May 3, I telephoned Michael Fürst, the head of the Jewish Community of Lower Saxony. Since we were about to hold a protest demonstration in what was essentially his territory, it seemed appropriate that he should be told of our plans.

Fürst, a Hanover attorney born in Germany after the war, informed me of the most recent developments. Had I heard, he asked, that the *Zentralrat* would not be sending a delegation to Bergen-Belsen that Sunday? I had not. Fürst proceeded to tell me that earlier the same day, the members of the *Zentralrat* had met in an emergency session near the Frankfurt Airport with World Jewish Congress Vice President Kalman Sultanik. Sultanik, who had taken as uncompromising a position as I throughout the entire Bitburg controversy, had warned the West German Jewish leaders that any participation on their part in the government-sponsored ceremony at Belsen on May 5 would be considered an act of treason by the rest of world Jewry. A few hours later, Fürst said, after a heated discussion the *Zentralrat* had decided to decline Chancellor Kohl's invitation.

However, Fürst added, there remained one last problem. The *Zentralrat* had asked him to send a *minyan*, the quorum of ten adult males required by Jewish law for the holding of a public religious service, to Bergen-Belsen on May 5. I asked him whether he intended to honor this request. Fürst replied that he would prefer not to, but that he needed a valid excuse. I then suggested a possible ground for not sending a *minyan*. Neither Reagan nor Kohl, I reminded Fürst, was Jewish. Why, Fürst asked, was that important or relevant? I explained that if a Jew wants to go to a cemetery to say *Kaddish*, the local Jewish community might have a moral obligation to provide him with a *minyan*. However, I said, the presence of a *minyan* at Bergen-Belsen during the May 5 ceremony would have no religious significance whatsoever since no Jew would be trying to hold a memorial service there at that time. Fürst expressed interest in this approach and said that he would discuss it with his colleagues. The following evening, when I met with him and Sultanik in Hanover, Fürst told me that no representative of the Jewish community of Lower Saxony would be at Bergen-Belsen on May 5 in any capacity.

*   *   *   *   *

Shortly after arriving in Hanover on May 4, we learned that two non-Jewish United States senators were attempting to get the Reagan administration to reverse its position and permit us to hold our demonstration at Bergen-Belsen. Still on Friday, in New York, my wife, Jean Bloch Rosensaft, and Dr. Bonnie Maslin, whose husband, Yehuda Nir, was a member of our delegation, enlisted the assistance of two prominent Jewish communal leaders, Nina Rosenwald and Aaron Ziegelman. Jean, our American spokesperson while we were in Germany and a leader in her own right of both the International Network and the New York Second Generation organization, told Rosenwald and Ziegelman of our predicament, and they, in turn, alerted New York Senator Daniel Patrick Moynihan.

That same evening, Ziegelman also called Joel Boyarsky, one of the most influential figures of New York's United Jewish Appeal and a friend of Senator Joseph Biden of Delaware. Boyarsky had just returned from Germany where he had attended commemorative ceremonies opposing the President's Bitburg visit, organized and led by Henry Siegman of the American Jewish Congress, at Dachau and at the Munich graves of a small number of young anti-Nazi Germans, known as the "White Rose" group who had been executed in 1943. Shocked at what Ziegelman told him, Boyarsky woke Senator Biden up at 1:00 a.m. on Saturday and asked for his help on our behalf. Thereupon, the senator and members of his staff spent the better part of that night and the following day trying to persuade State Department officials to allow our demonstration to take place as planned.

Early in the morning on Saturday, May 4, Senator Moynihan, who that day was scheduled to give the Democratic party's response to Ronald Reagan's weekly radio talk, called Jean at our home, and she provided him with the necessary details.

The senator then called me in Hanover to confirm the information which he had received from Jean and to express his total support for us. Shortly thereafter, at 1:06 p.m. Washington time, Senator Moynihan went on the air *(see page 60)* and proceeded to devote his entire radio broadcast to the "incredible" fact "that despite the full cooperation of the West German government, the American government has denied these American citizens the right to be present at Bergen-Belsen when our President is there, also."

Senator Moynihan explained to his national audience that the purpose of our going to Germany was to declare our "disapproval of the President visiting the sacred site of Bergen-Belsen as some kind of offset to his visit to Bitburg." The senator continued: "Their purpose, open, was to make a statement through non-violent demonstration. They intended no embarrassment to the President. They were exercising a right guaranteed them in the First Amendment to the Constitution of the United States: the right of the people peaceably to assemble."

Senator Moynihan then put into words the bewilderment and anger which we—several thousand miles away in Germany—were experiencing. "The mind cracks, the heart breaks," he said. "What had possessed the White House? Was it not bad enough that they insisted on going through with the visit to Bitburg? That violates the rights of the dead. This violates the rights of the living." And, addressing himself directly to President Reagan "or to any of his staff who are now listening," Senator Moynihan concluded: "Mr. President, forty or so survivors of the Holocaust and children of survivors wish to be at Bergen-Belsen when you are there. That place, Mr. President, *is* their place. It is not only their place, Mr. President, it is their right. Please, won't you reconsider. It is not like you. It is not like us. We must not let the world see this happen."

Unfortunately, neither Senator Moynihan's appeal nor Senator Biden's intervention made any impact on the Reagan administration. However, the knowledge that they, and individuals such as Nina Rosenwald, Aaron Ziegelman and Joel Boyarsky, were making efforts and speaking out on our behalf reassured us, in Germany, that we were not completely alone.

* * * * *

On the eve of our demonstration, there was a heated debate among the members of our group in Hanover. Quite a few urged that we try to force our way through to Bergen-Belsen early the next day. They did not think that the German authorities would carry out their part of my agreement with Dr. Becker of the Lüneburg government. How, I was asked, did I know that they were not going to renege at the last moment, leaving us far away even from the police barricades?

I could not give any guarantees since I had no way of knowing whether Dr. Becker would in fact keep his word. I, too, did not feel altogether comfortable about our improbable alliance with the German officials. Nonetheless, I was convinced that we had no alternative but to gamble on their good faith. The other leaders of the International Network and I believed that we should not give up the possibility, however uncertain, of holding a dignified, meaningful protest demonstration at Bergen-Belsen immediately after the departure of President Reagan and Chancellor Kohl. That, after all, was the reason for our being in Germany. In any event, we were determined to avoid any violent confrontation with the German police.

Late that night, I called Dr. Becker at his home, and he assured me that everything was arranged along the lines we had discussed. On Sunday morning, we assembled outside our hotel and waited. Around 10:30, a small police car pulled up. The promised escort had arrived. We all breathed a silent sigh of relief and boarded our bus. About two hours later, we arrived at Bergen-Belsen.

* * * * *

It took us only a few minutes to walk from our bus to the Jewish Monument, but they were among the most intense I have ever experienced. Each of us carrying a rose, the sons and daughters of survivors leading the way, we entered the desolation that is Belsen.

Belsen. My father once wrote that, "The lives of Jewish children, fathers, mothers, grandparents consecrated this ground." It is estimated that some 53,000 human beings perished here—between 80 and 90 percent of them Jews. When the concentration camp was liberated by British troops on April 15, 1945, more than 10,000 unburied corpses were strewn inside and outside the barracks. During the weeks following the liberation, approximately 14,000 more inmates died of starvation, typhus, typhoid, fever, tuberculosis, and a host of other epidemics that were raging throughout the camp. Unable to conduct individual burials, British soldiers had to put the dead into huge mass-graves, often with the use of bulldozers.

Belsen. In order to contain the spread of disease, the survivors were transferred to nearby Germany Army barracks within a few weeks after the liberation, and on May 21, 1945, the British burned the concentration camp of Bergen-Belsen. Now only the graves and monuments remain as a reminder that this had once been a center of pain and suffering. Covered by grass and surrounded by trees, Belsen has become a park, a park where death has dominion.

Belsen. We walked where Ronald Reagan and Helmut Kohl had not wanted us to walk that day. My parents had met here after the liberation, and had stayed on in the Displaced Persons camp of Bergen-Belsen for five years. This was my birthplace, my first home. Before leaving Belsen in 1950, my father had sworn to the dead that they would not be abandoned.

Belsen. In the distance, beyond the graves, a tall obelisk looms in front of the long wall containing inscriptions in fourteen languages. The International Monument was erected by the British authorities in 1952, as a memorial to all the victims of Belsen, Jews as well as non-Jews. When the wall of languages was first put up, my father discovered that Yiddish and Hebrew had been omitted. All the other languages—French, Russian, Italian, English, Norwegian, Polish, German, etc.— were there, but not the two languages of European Jewry. At my father's insistence, a section of the wall was taken down, and separate inscriptions in both Yiddish and Hebrew were added.

Belsen. In April 1958, my father learned that French officials were about to open one of the mass-graves. In accordance with a 1954 Franco-German Convention, the French government wanted to exhume, attempt to identify and return to France the remains of some 139 French nationals who had been buried there. My father then began a formidable eleven-year long political and legal struggle to prevent such a desecration from taking place. In response to the protest of the Belsen survivors, the West German government, citing "reasons of extraordinary importance," reversed its position and refused to allow the exhumations to proceed, but the French authorities remained intransigent. In 1966, after years of unproductive discussions and negotiations, the two governments placed the dispute over the Belsen graves before the Arbitral Commission on Property, Rights and Interests in Germany.

Belsen. As we approached the Jewish Monument, I realized that sixteen years before, almost to the day, on May 6, 1969, my father had walked on the same path with the nine members of the Arbitral Commission who had come to see Belsen for themselves before reaching a decision. "In 1945, we couldn't tell a dead man from a dead woman, so many bodies were bulldozed into the graves," he had explained to them. "Now they're going to try and tell French bones from the others? It's a macabre fantasy." Asked by one of the jurists whether he had made a special trip from New York in order to accompany them on their visit to Belsen, my father had replied, "How could I not come?" Several months later, on October 30, 1969, the Arbitral Commission had ruled that the mass-graves were not to be opened.

Belsen. After taking part in a pilgrimage to Belsen in 1965, Elie Wiesel noted that there had been no speeches or eulogies. "All were silent," he wrote, "and it seemed that the silence would never be broken, that no one would dare remind the dead that some have remained alive." On May 5, 1985, we could not remain silent. In his speech at Belsen, Ronald Reagan had ascribed its horrors to "that man and his evil," thereby absolving the rest of the German people of responsibility for the carnage. President Reagan and Chancellor Kohl had exploited the mass-graves as a political platform, and now the dead were waiting for our answer.

Belsen. We walked, through time and beyond time, until we reached the Jewish Monument. I stood where my father had stood when, on April 15, 1946, as chairman of the Central Committee of Liberated Jews in the British Zone of Germany, he had dedicated this monument. We sang the same prayer, *Ani Ma'amin*, "I Believe," that Jews had sung in the ghettos and camps, on their way to death and upon their return to life. Around us were the graves, and the grass, and the trees, and the wind, and thousands of invisible, faceless shadows. I thought of my father and what he would have said, what he would have wanted me to say. And then, I addressed the only audience that mattered on this Sunday in May of 1985. I spoke to the dead, and I tried to speak on their behalf as well.

Chapter 9

May 5th At Bitburg

"Thank you, Mr. President For Visiting The Graves With Me"

Bitburg, West Germany
May 5, 1985

Retired U.S. Gen. Mathew B. Ridgeway (center left) and German Gen. Johannes Steinhoff shake hands in reconciliation at wreath laying before Bitburg memorial. President Reagan (left) and Chancellor Kohl (right) did not shake hands during the ceremony.

By Chancellor Helmut Kohl

(Speech addressed to German and American soldiers and their families at Bitburg.)

Mr. President, Members of the U.S. Armed Forces, Members of the Bundeswehr, Excellencies, Ladies and Gentlemen, Dear American Friends, Fellow Countrymen:

It is not often that the link between the past, present and future of our country reaches us as vividly as during these hours at Bitburg.

A few minutes ago, the President of the United States of America and I paid homage at the military cemetery to the dead buried there and thus to all victims of war and tyranny, to the dead and persecuted of all nations.

Our visit to the soldiers' graves here in Bitburg was not an easy one. It could not but arouse deep feelings. For me it meant first and foremost deep sorrow and grief at the infinite suffering that the war and totalitarianism inflicted on nations, sorrow and grief that will never cease.

Stemming from them is our commitment to peace and freedom as the supreme goal of our political actions. And the visit to the graves in Bitburg is also a reaffirmation of a widely visible and widely felt gesture of reconciliation between our peoples, the people of the United States of America and us Germans, reconciliation which does not dismiss the past but enables us to overcome it by acting together.

Finally, our presence here testifies to our friendship, which has proved to be steadfast and reliable and is based on our belief in shared values.

I thank you, Mr. President, both on behalf of the whole German people, and I thank you very personally as a friend, for visiting the graves with me. I believe that many of our German people understand this expression of deep friendship, and that it presages a good future for our nations.

The town of Bitburg witnessed at first hand the collapse of the Third Reich. It suffered the year 1945. It was part of the reconstruction in the year of reconciliation. For 25 years now, Bitburg has been the site of joint ceremonies in which American, French and German soldiers and citizens of this town and region commemorate the victims of the war and time and again affirm their friendship and their determination to preserve peace jointly. Here close and friendly relations have evolved in a special way in these years between the U.S. Forces and the German population.

Bitburg can be regarded as a symbol of reconciliation and of German-American friendship.

Members of the Bundeswehr, most of you have been born since May 8, 1945, you have not yourselves experienced the war and tyranny in this country, you grew up in the years in which we built our republic, at a time when friendship re-emerged and developed between us and the American nation. You got to know our American friends as helpers, as partners and allies.

Days like this are a suitable way of reminding our people's young generation in particular that this development—so favorable for us—was not a matter of course and that the preservation of peace and freedom requires our very personal dedication.

You, the members of the U.S. forces in the Federal Republic of Germany, serve your country, the United States of America, and our republic alike.

The security of the Federal Republic of Germany is closely linked to the partnership and friendship of the United States of America. We know what we owe you and your families. We also know that serving overseas means sacrifice for many of you. Let me assure you that you are welcome guests in our country, in the Federal Republic of Germany. Do not let a small and insignificant minority give you a different impression. We sincerely welcome you here as friends, as allies, as guarantors of our security.

Relations have developed over many years between the U.S. armed forces and the Bundeswehr and are closer than ever before. I should like to thank you, the American and German soldiers, for this partnership we now almost take for granted. It strengthens our joint determination to defend the peace and freedom of our nations, and this partnership—as I wish expressly to state here at Bitburg—thus is a source of mutual understanding of our peoples, generating many personal friendships.

I wish the members of the U.S. forces, I wish our soldiers of the Federal Armed Forces, I wish for us all that together we make our contribution to the peace and freedom of our country and of the world,—and may God's blessing be with us.

"We Do Not Believe in Collective Guilt"
Bitburg, West Germany
May 5, 1985

By President Ronald Reagan

(Speech at the American Air Force base in Bitburg.)

I have just come from the cemetery where German war dead lay at rest. No one could visit there without deep and conflicting emotions. I felt great sadness that history could be filled with such waste, destruction, and evil. But my heart was also lifted by the knowledge that from the ashes has come hope, and that from the terrors of the past we have built 40 years of peace and freedom — and reconciliation among our nations.

This visit has stirred many emotions in the American and German people, too. I have received many letters since first deciding to come to Bitburg Cemetery, some supportive, others deeply concerned and questioning, others opposed. Some old wounds have been reopened, and this I regret very much, because this should be a time of healing. To the veterans and families of American servicemen who still carry the scars and feel the painful losses of that war, our gesture of reconciliation with the German people today in no way minimizes our love and honor for those who fought and died for our country. They gave their lives to rescue freedom in its darkest hour. The alliance of democratic nations that guards the freedom of millions in Europe and America today stands as living testimony that their noble sacrifice was not in vain.

To the survivors of the Holocaust: your terrible suffering has made you ever vigilant against evil. Many of you are worried that reconciliation means forgetting. I promise you, we will never forget. I have just come from Bergen-Belsen where the horror of that terrible crime, the Holocaust, was forever burned upon my memory. No, we will never forget, and we say with the victims of that Holocaust: "never again".

The war against one man's totalitarian dictatorship was not like other wars. The evil world of Nazism turned all values upside down. Nevertheless, we can mourn the German war dead today as human beings, crushed by a vicious ideology.

There are over 2,000 buried in Bitburg cemetery. Among them are 48 members of the SS. The crimes of the SS must rank among the most heinous in human history. But others buried there were simply soldiers in the German army. How many were fanatical followers of a dictator and willfully carried out his cruel order? And how many were conscripts, forced into service during the death throes of the Nazi war machine? We do not know. Many however, we know from the dates on their tombstones, were only teenagers at the time. There is one boy buried there who died a week before his 16th birthday.

There were thousands of such soldiers to whom Nazism meant no more than a brutal end to a short life. We do not believe in collective guilt. Only God can look into the human heart. All these men have now met their Supreme Judge, and they have been judged by Him, as we shall all be judged.

Our duty today is to mourn the human wreckage of totalitarianism, and today, in Bitburg Cemetery, we commemorated the potential good and humanity that was consumed back then, 40 years ago. Perhaps if that 15 year old soldier had lived, he would have joined his fellow countrymen in building the new democratic Federal Republic of Germany devoted to human dignity and the defense of freedom that we celebrate today. Or perhaps his children or grandchildren might be among you here today at Bitburg Air Base, where new generations of Germans and Americans join together in friendship and common cause, dedicating their lives to preserving peace and guarding the security of the Free World.

Too often in the past, each war only planted the seeds of the next. We celebrated today the reconciliation between our two nations that has liberated us from that cycle of destruction. Look at what together we have accomplished, we who were enemies are now friends. We who were bitter adversaries are now the strongest of allies. In the place of fear we have sown trust, and out of the ruins of war has blossomed an enduring peace. Tens of thousands of Americans have served in this town over the years. As the Mayor of Bitburg has said, in that time there have been some 6,000 marriages between Germans and Americans, and many thousands of children have come from these unions. This is the real symbol of our future together, a future to be filled with hope, friendship, and freedom.

The hope we see now could sometimes even be glimpsed in the darkest days of the war. I'm thinking of one special story— that of a mother and her young son living alone in a modest cottage in the middle of the woods. One night as the Battle of the Bulge exploded not far away, three young American soldiers arrived at their door— standing in the snow, lost behind enemy lines. All were frostbitten and one badly wounded. Even though sheltering the enemy was punishable by death, she took them in and made them a supper with some of her last food.

Soon, they heard another knock at the door. This time four German soldiers stood there. The woman was afraid, but she quickly said with a firm voice "...there will be no shooting here". She made all the soldiers lay down their weapons, and they all joined in the makeshift meal. Heinz and Willi, it turned out, were only 16. The corporal was the oldest at 23. Their natural suspicion dissolved in the warmth and comfort of the cottage. One of the Germans, a former medical student, tended the wounded American.

Now, listen to the story through the eyes of one who was there. "Then mother said grace," remembered the boy. "I noticed that there were tears in her eyes as she said the old, familiar words, 'Komm, Herr Jesus. Be our guest.' And as I looked around the table, I saw tears, too, in the eyes of the battle-weary soldiers, boys again, some from America, some from Germany, all far from home."

That night— as the storm of war tossed the world— they had their own private armistice. The next morning the German corporal showed the Americans how to get back behind their own lines. They all shook hands and went their separate ways. That was Christmas Day, 40 years ago.

Those boys were reconciled briefly in the midst of war. Surely, we allies in peacetime should honor the reconciliation of the last 40 years.

To the people of Bitburg, our hosts and the hosts of our servicemen, like that generous woman 40 years ago, you make us feel very welcome.

And to the men and women of Bitburg Air Base, I just want to say that we know that, even with such wonderful hosts, your job is not an easy one. You serve around the clock, far from home, always ready to defend freedom. We are grateful, and very proud of you.

Four decades ago, we waged a great war to lift the darkness of evil from the world, to let men and women in this country and in every country live in the sunshine of liberty. Our victory was great, and the Federal Republic, Italy, and Japan are now in the community of free nations. But the struggle for freedom is not complete, for today much of the world is still cast in totalitarian darkness.

Twenty-two years ago, President John F. Kennedy went to the Berlin Wall and proclaimed that he, too, was a Berliner. Today, freedom-loving people around the world must say, I am a Berliner, I am a Jew in a world still threatened by anti-Semitism, I am an Afghan, and I am a prisoner of the Gulag, I am a refugee in a crowded boat foundering off the coast of Vietnam, I am a Laotian, a Cambodian, a Cuban, and a Miskito Indian in Nicaragua. I, too, am a potential victim of totalitarianism.

The one lesson of World War Two, the one lesson of Nazism, is that freedom must always be stronger than totalitarianism, that good must always be stronger than evil. The moral measure of our two nations will be found in the resolve we show to preserve liberty, to protect life, and to honor and cherish all God's children.

That is why the free, democratic Federal Republic of Germany is such a profound and hopeful testament to the human spirit. We cannot undo the crimes and wars of yesterday, nor call the millions back to life. But we can give meaning to the past by learning its lessons and making a better future. We can let our pain drive us to greater efforts to heal humanity's suffering.

With the lessons of the past firmly in our minds, we have turned a new, brighter page in history. One of the many who wrote about this visit was a young woman who had recently been bar [sic] mitzvahed. She urged me to lay the wreath at Bitburg cemetery in honor of the future of Germany, and that is what we have done. On this 40th anniversary of World War Two, we mark the day when the hate, the evil, and the obscenities ended and we commemorate the rekindling of the democratic spirit in Germany.

There is much to make us hopeful on this historical anniversary. While much of the world still huddles in the darkness of oppression, we can see a new dawn of freedom sweeping the globe. And we can see—in the new democracies of Latin America, in the new economic freedoms and prosperity in Asia, in the slow movement toward peace in the Middle East, and in the strengthening alliance of democratic nations in Europe and America—that the light from that dawn is growing stronger.

Together let us gather in that light, and walk out of the shadow, and let us live in peace.

Delicate Reagan Path
New York Times
May 6, 1985

By Hedrick Smith

BITBURG, WEST GERMANY—On this mournful pilgrimage to the gravesites of the Holocaust and World War II, President Reagan walked a careful path today, hoping finally to disentangle himself from the most wrenching political episode of his presidency without abandoning Chancellor Helmut Kohl.

As he promised the West German leader, the President preached reconciliation with the German people and their past. But he also tried to halt the political damage of nearly a month of protests from Jewish groups and veterans' organizations and majorities in both houses of Congress, outraged by the symbol he accepted for that reconciliation: a visit to the German military cemetery here with its 49 SS graves.

Both by what he did and what he did not do, Mr. Reagan tried to soften the blow and perhaps close that book.

At the last minute, he added a tribute at the grave of Konrad Adenauer, the postwar chancellor, and arranged for Matthew B. Ridgway, the 90-year-old retired general and World War II hero, to be his escort in the Bitburg ceremony.

No Symbolic Handclasp

Always sensitive to lasting visual images, the President avoided a symbolic handclasp over the German military graves with Chancellor Kohl, denying Mr. Kohl the kind photograph that he so deeply cherished from his ceremony with President Francois Mitterand at the German-French military cemetery in Verdun last year.

To the critics of his Bitburg visit Mr. Reagan offered his solemn homage to "the human wreckage" of Nazi concentration camps and offered an open apology for having bared the emotional scars of the Holocaust once again.

"Some old wounds have been reopened, and this I regret very much, because this should be a time of healing," the President said at an American air base at Bitburg after visiting the site of the Bergen-Belsen concentration camp and then the Bitburg cemetery. "Many of you are worried that reconciliation means forgetting. I promise you, we will never forget."

In the end, his mission became far less the buoyant celebration of German-American friendship that he once envisioned than a delicate balancing act. Only time will tell whether his gestures and concessions have halted the political damage to his presidency or whether it will bear lasting scars from the Bitburg visit.

Reactions of some leading American Jews suggested Mr. Reagan had eased but not ended the controversy.

"That couple of minutes in Bitburg poisoned what could have been a glorious day," said Representative James H. Scheuer, a Queens Democrat.

"The President's gentle eloquence at Bergen-Belsen will resonate for a long time," added Nathan Perlmutter, national director of the Anti-Defamation League. "Not so his discomforting walk at Bitburg. The President has a new debit in his ledger: Bitburg."

The climax today, as Mr. Kohl observed at one ceremony, "was not an easy walk for Ronald Reagan." Not everything went his way. West German and American Jews refused invitations to visit Bergen-Belsen with him. Some prominent German anti-Nazi heroes declined to come to Bitburg.

Not surprisingly for a leader known for the politics of cheerful optimism, the President seemed burdened today by his grim incantations of horror.

Passed Through in Silence

His somber path through the Koimeshöhe cemetery took him within three feet of some SS graves, but he did not glance at them. Rather stiffly, he passed through the grove in silence.

When the moment came for some mutual German-American recognition, it was General Ridgway, the paratroop commander in the Battle of the Bulge where many of these German dead had perished, who solemnly shook hands with a German air ace in the war, Lieut. Gen. Johannes Steinhoff.

In all, the President spent only eight minutes at the cemetery. Earlier in the day, he spent 50 minutes touring the desolate remains of Bergen-Belsen and gave a speech that evoked both the "grim abyss" of the Nazi concentration camps and his vision of postwar Germany: "Out of ashes, hope."

Other little distinctions were made. The wreath presented by Mr. Reagan at Bergen-Belsen bore the legend that it was from the "people of the United States," while the wreath he offered here said it was from "the President of the United States."

Speaking to an audience of Americans and West Germans at the American Air Base, the President noted the presence of SS graves at Bitburg and added, in a gesture to his critics, that "the crimes of the SS must rank among the most heinous in human history."

Then, in a balancing gesture to his German hosts, Mr. Reagan said that many in the cemetery were "simply soldiers in the German army" and that "we do not know" whether still others were merely "conscripts" or "fanatical followers of a dictator."

Several times, he narrowly laid responsibility for the "awful evil" perpetrated by Nazism to "one man," Hitler, whom he did not name. Americans, he suggested, could mourn the German military dead "as human beings, crushed by a vicious ideology," a gentler version of his earlier comments that German soldiers, like concentration camp inmates, were victims of Nazism.

The duality in Mr. Reagan's speeches today mirrored the ambiguity of his visit to the cemetery, in which some Americans fear he has granted a form of symbolic absolution to elements in the German past they find unforgivable.

Come to Terms With Ambiguity

Many Germans have to come to terms with that ambiguity in their past, and some, like Mr. Kohl and Mayor Theo Hallet of Bitburg, felt it was vital to proceed with the visit to the cemetery.

A few days ago, Mayor Hallet acknowledged that there was another German military cemetery about five miles from Bitburg that had no SS graves. Some people, he said, suggested it would have been better for Mr. Reagan to visit that cemetery.

But the Mayor considered the local cemetery a truer reflection of Germany and therefore a more symbol of reconciliation. "Here German history is clear," he said. "There's nothing hidden. There are no secrets."

Chapter 10

Reaction After Bitburg

"Our Countries Have Linked Their Fates," Says President von Weizsäcker
Bruehl, West Germany
May, 5, 1985

By President Richard von Weizsäcker

(Speech by the President of the Federal Republic of Germany, Richard Von Weizsäcker, at a dinner in honor of their Excellencies The President of the United States of America and Mrs. Reagan, at Augustusburg Castle, Bruehl.)

Mr. President, Madam, Ladies and Gentlemen:

It is a great pleasure for me to welcome you, Mr. President, and you, Madam, to the Federal Republic of Germany. In you I greet the first citizen of a country with whom we share a warm friendship.

The Federal Republic of Germany and the United States of America have a common, unshakeable foundation, a foundation consisting of our common convictions of the dignity and freedom of every individual, and of the rule of law and justice for the protection of less fortunate members of the community. Those are the ideals that have characterized the evolution of the United States of America. They remain binding for us today.

Tomorrow, Mr. President, you will be meeting with young Germans at Hambach castle. When Germany's youth made their historic commitment to liberty there in the year 1832 they were fired by the ideas that shone from the American Declaration of Independence and the Constitution of the United States. These ideas have retained their binding force over two centuries. John Quincy Adams put it most charmingly when, in describing the responsibilities of the American nation, he said that it would support the universal cause of freedom by raising its voice and by the sympathetic influence of its example. In many parts of the world America's example is an inspiration to people to develop their own culture and way of life in a free society. For freedom in democracy is also the best compass in stormy periods.

At this time many nations look back on the year 1945. We Germans know what untold suffering was brought upon nations and individual citizens by the Nazi barbarism and the war which originated in Germany. The suffering caused to our Jewish fellow men in the name of Germany, epitomized by the Holocaust, to the Russians, the Poles and nearly all our neighbors, but also the suffering of countless Germans as a result of persecution, death and the loss of their homeland—none of this will ever be erased from memory. In the meantime young Germans have grown up who had no part in all this. They themselves certainly bear none of the blame, but they cannot cast off a heavy legacy. All of us in Germany, whether old or young, face up to this dark chapter in our history. We all bear responsibility for its consequences.

We are well aware of what the victorious powers felt when they came to Germany in 1945. Since then 40 years have passed. The change from the sentiments of then to those of today is hard to believe. In that period our countries have linked their relations and bound their fates together as at no other time in their history. As the defender of freedom America was an enemy of the National Socialists in Germany. As a friend of freedom America became a friend of the democratic Germany.

The meaning which you, Mr. President, have given to your visit to our country is that of making this transformation visible and of reinforcing it. Precisely for this reason you have today visited sites which remind us of the horror and death. You have done so not as a victor but in order to commemorate the injustice and human suffering, to recall liberty regained, and to mark the reconciliation of nations.

You embark on your journey against a background of serious and at the same time painful controversy. No one wanted it, but no one could try to evade the issue. The deep emotions aroused by this are only too easy to understand considering the grave injustice and untold suffering. We respect those emotions and face them with an open heart. But we are also confident that no one will call into question what has been achieved in recent decades. You, Mr. President, have remained faithful to the notion of partnership, a partnership that has stood many a test, precisely where this has imposed a painful burden on you. You have acted responsibly and magnanimously towards us. That we shall never forget, and on behalf of the German people I wish to thank you for your far-sightedness and your friendship.

Your sentiments are in the best tradition of the American people, which those of my generation vividly experienced immediately after the war. In those years countless American citizens, through their private means, helped us Germans, the vanquished, to heal the wounds of war. We have not forgotten the CARE parcels and the Quaker food supplies. Through the Marshall Plan America played a crucial part in the rebuilding of Germany as well.

At the time when the free part of Berlin was to be starved and blackmailed, the Americans, together with the British and French, protected the lives and the freedom of courageous Berliners. It is above all in Berlin that the mutual respect has been nurtured which made friends out of enemies.

Americans in positions of responsibility found that the Germans had the mental and moral strength to create a democratic society. They placed their faith in that democratic society and we, acting of our own free will, pledged ourselves to it. Only a few weeks ago, Mr. President, you and I met in the White House to honor John McCloy, who deserves much of the credit for the change to democracy in Germany. I am pleased to welcome his son, John McCloy II, here this evening. And I also greet Miss Eleanor Dulles, who has just been made an Honorary Professor of the Free University of Berlin. This morning, in Wiesbaden, she was awarded the Lucius D. Clay Medal of the German-American clubs for her services in promoting German-American friendship. My warm congratulations on both these honors. We shall always be grateful to these and many other men and women for their trust and for their assistance.

So we also have reason to recall that 30 years ago today the Federal Republic of Germany gained full sovereignty. The next day, the 6th of May 1955, we became a member of the Atlantic alliance. In the preamble to the North Atlantic Treaty, the members pledged "to safeguard the freedom, common heritage and civilization of their peoples, founded on the principles of democracy, individual liberty and the rule of law."

Our commitment to these values is irrevocable. Our alliance serves the cause of freedom and peace. We will not and cannot allow our freedom to be restricted. Consequently we must be ready and able to safeguard it. No one should be left in doubt as to our determination and ability to do so. It is this clarity which also helps to maintain peace. And on the basis of that clarity we strive for detente, dialog and cooperation. At the beginning of this year you, Mr. President, expressed the hope that 1985 would become a year of dialog and cooperation. We support you in this hope and link with it the expectation that every effort will be made to achieve progress in the current negotiations aimed at the control and reduction of armaments. The aim of German policy will always be to keep freedom and peace linked together. We must never allow a situation to arise in which we have to make a choice between the two. In this spirit we are working for a state of peace in the whole of Europe which will overcome the division and give all nations, including the Germans, the freedom to decide their own future. Our aim is not to change boundaries but to remove their divisive character.

In the meantime a new generation has grown up which did not live through the developments of the postwar era but regards them as a matter of fact. Let us be grateful that it is and will remain a matter of fact. But this requires us to be constantly giving new life to our mutual trust, that it may prove itself reciprocally. Your visit, Mr. President, is an important and welcome opportunity to make young people on both sides of the Atlantic aware of those developments once more.

You, Mr. President, have earnestly and convincingly called for more exchanges among the young people in our countries. We are grateful to you for this. Already the first postwar generation, thanks to the generosity of the exchange programs organized by the American Field Service, as well as to the Fulbright scholarships and other endowments, has been able to gain deep impressions of America and establish lifelong friendships. There have since been fresh initiatives. Members of the United States Congress and the German Bundestag now personally play host to young people from the other country. In this way not only do the young people gain lasting impressions but the legislators themselves are in a better position to assess and do justice to their hopes. Youth exchange programs are most likely to achieve their objective when young people have confidence in today's generation of political leaders.

Europeans and Americans, as members of an alliance of free nations, contribute to common security. We Europeans remain dependent on the United States for that security. No one in our country should think that America's commitment in Europe is a matter of course. Many thousands of American soldiers and their families are living here, a long way from home, in order to maintain our security. In our country, together with us, they are serving to protect our common ideals. I am glad, Mr. President, that I shall have an opportunity to tell them this personally and to thank them and their families when I visit them in a few weeks' time.

The weight of the two transatlantic partners differs. On the one hand we have the United States, a world power, on the other its European partners, who still have not reached their goal of unification. But Europe will continue along this road and will make progress. Far-sighted Americans have always advocated and appreciated this. Soon Spain and Portugal will be members of the European Community. Your visit to the European Parliament in Strasbourg, Mr. President, demonstrates, as you yourself put it, that the United States has a 40-year pledge to the goal of a restored community of free European nations.

Our common responsibility must also stand the test in regard to transatlantic economic relations. National egoisms and vested interests still threaten to block the path to genuinely free world trade. In everybody's long-term interest, however, we need a system which leaves no room for protectionism, closed markets, restrictions on the transfer of technology, or subsidies which distort competition. Otherwise we shall be acting against the spirit of our time.

The Americans have made great strides in the field of modern technology, progress which symbolizes their impressive dynamism, vitality and confidence. But Europe, too, in spite of the doubts we hear from across the Atlantic, will again increase its capabilities. We will learn how to improve cooperation across national boundaries. We will acquire a greater flexibility without abandoning our well-

West German President von Weizsäcker (R) presents outgoing U.S. Ambassador Arthur Burns with the Federal Republic of Germany's Grand Cross for Distinguished Service at Villa Hammerschmidt on May 10, 1985.

established social system.

It remains a crucial task to remove the impression on both sides of the Atlantic that national economic and trading interests can be asserted unilaterally at the expense of others. Anyone who attempts to do so is only hurting himself in the long run. Our conviction of the need for a free world economy forces us as industrial nations to act responsibly. This applies as regards employment and social harmony at home, and no less as regards our task of helping to ensure a fair distribution of goods and opportunities throughout the world.

Everyone who visits America is always impressed by how sincerely its citizens regard freedom as an obligation to help their neighbors and join in community work in order to provide effective assistance to those in great need. In this field you, Madam, have dedicated yourself to the task of fighting the dangers inherent in drugs. We greatly admire you for the help you are thus giving to parents and families, and above all to young people who are suffering from the consequences of drug use. On behalf of my wife and many German families who are devoted to the same task, I wish to thank you for the encouragement and the example you have given.

Mr. President, the world is faced with tremendous problems. Winston Churchill once said that the price of greatness is responsibility. We know how great is the burden of responsibility borne by America, the leading nation of the Western world, and by you personally. The Federal Republic of Germany will continue to share that responsibility as best it can and without reserve. We will jointly have to harness all our energies to protect and strengthen freedom, to maintain peace, and to serve the cause of social justice.

The selfless assistance afforded by the United States in past decades fills us with confidence, as do the strength and dynamism that the American people have developed anew under your leadership.

I now raise my glass to you, Mr. President, to you, Madam, to the members of your delegation who are our guests this evening, to all Americans who are living with us in our community, and to friendship with the great American nation.

Though there is a great geographical distance between Germany and America, the cultural, political and human relations linking us together are very close and friendly. Tracing the historical roots of those relations and imparting knowledge of their present-day significance will be the task of an Institute for German History to be set up in the United States. My Government regards this project, too, as a contribution to greater understanding between Americans and Germans.

The partnership between our countries thrives on the dialogue between our peoples and on the dialogue between generations. We are pleased that you, Mr. President, will now address the young German generation. You come as the leader of a democracy rich in tradition, of a dynamic country whose citizens are fully confident of their own potential and of their prospects for the future. And you are addressing young Germans who feel at home in Europe and in the free world, who want to play a vigorous part in shaping this world—out of love for life and freedom.

President Ronald Reagan, accompanied by his wife Nancy and Chancellor Kohl, spoke on the future of Europe at the conclusion of his official visit to the Federal Republic of Germany to a crowd of thousands of young Germans in front of historic Hambach Castle.

The Spirit of West Germany's Future
Hambach Castle
May 6, 1985

By President Ronald Reagan

(Speech to German Youth at Hambach Castle.)

Chancellor Kohl, honored guests, and my young friends of Germany and Europe: Thank you. Nancy and I are very happy to be with you and to see that the ideals of the first Hambach Fest live on today. To join you at this site so rich in history makes this a very special day.

Already, you have given us a gift of hope and beauty from the sight of this sturdy, old castle, from the spirit of your youth—the spirit of Germany's future—and, yes, from the warmth we feel in German hearts.

In welcoming us, you honor the 237 million Americans I am privileged to represent. I might add that more Americans trace their roots to this land, these towns, and your families than to almost any other place or people in the world.

It is fitting that we meet where so much that is good and worthy of our two nations began. From here in the Rhineland-Palatinate, thousands left to cross a mighty ocean, to push back America's frontiers and to help us win a great struggle for independence. One regiment came from Zweibrücken, led by Count Christian and Viscount Wilhelm von Forbach. They fought by our side. They were with us that day we won the historic battle of Yorktown, the day the American Revolution triumphed.

And it was from this hill, on this good soil, that freedom was proclaimed and the dream of democracy and national unity came alive in the German soul. I am only a visitor to your country, but I am proud to stand with you today by these walls of "Schloss Hambach". They are walls of time that cradle a glorious past, and that reach toward the promise of a future written for eternity across this wide-open sky.

Think back to that first festival of freedom held here in 1832. What noble vision was it that inspired and emboldened your first patriots? Not violence, not destruction of society, and not some far-flung utopian scheme.

No, their vision and cry were revolutionary in the truest sense of that word. Those first patriots cried out for a free, democratic, and united Germany—we do so again today. They cried out for friendship and cooperation within a free, democratic, and united Europe—we do so again today. They cried out for solidarity with freedom fighters in Poland—we do so again today. The dream was voiced by many who came here. But there was one student—I am told his name was Karl Heinrich Brüggemann—whose passion and eloquence echo with us still: "All Germanic peoples," Karl said, "will and must acquire greater dignity, the times of tyranny have passed ... free states will flourish ... patriotic nations will in future celebrate the new Europe".

The new Europe. One hundred fifty-three years have come and gone, bring-ing great change and progress. But the New Europe is yet to be complete. Why is this so? We know the answer. It is not that freedom has not worked for the Euro-pean people, but that too many Europeans have been forbidden to work for free-dom. It is not that democracy was tried and found wanting, but that some forbid democracy to be tried because they know it would succeed.

Europe today— divided by concrete walls, by electrified barbed wire, and by mined and manicured fields, killing fields— is a living portrait of the most com-pelling truth of our time: the future belong to the free.

You are living in the springtime of your lives. The world needs your idealism, your courage, and your good works. From one whose own life spans many years permit me to offer you some observations about the future, about the creative fu-ture that can be ours if only we apply our wisdom and will to heed the lessons of history. Let me speak to you a moment about your responsibilities and your op-portunities.

In many ways, the challenges of 1832—when thousands of young Germans came here to protest repression—were similar to those you face today. By that year of 1832, Germany was changing rapidly; the industrial revolution was sweeping across Europe. But in dealing with these new problems, strong forces inside and outside Germany resisted democracy and national unity. The great hopes that arose in 1832 and again in 1848 were set back. But despite the difficulties of democratic movements, we know for sure that totalitarianism, by whatever name, will never fulfill German aspirations within a united Europe. The cause of German unity is bound up with the cause of democracy. As Chancellor Kohl said in his State of the Nation Address last February: "Europe is divided because part of Europe is not free; Germany is divided because part of Germany is not free". And democracy will only be complete, Europe will only be united, when all Germans and all Eu-ropeans are finally free.

But even if national unity cannot be achieved immediately, you, the youth of Germany, you who are Germany's future, can show the power of democratic ideals by committing yourselves to the cause of freedom here in Europe and everywhere.

History is not on the side of those who manipulate the meaning of words like revolution, freedom, and peace. History is on the side of those struggling for a true revolution of peace with freedom all across the world.

Nothing could make our hearts more glad than to see the day when there will be no more walls, no more guns to keep loved ones apart. Nothing could bring greater happiness than to reach an agreement that will rid the earth of nuclear weapons forever— and we will never stop praying, never stop working, never stop striving one moment to bring that blessed day closer.

But my young friends, I must also plead for realism. For unless and until there is a changing by the other side, the United States must fulfill a commitment of its own— to the survival of liberty. The first frontier of European liberty begins in Ber-lin, and I assure you that America will stand by you in Europe, and America will stand by you in Berlin.

Understanding the true nature of totalitarianism will be worth as much to us as any weapons system in preserving peace. Realism is the beginning of wisdom, and where there is wisdom and courage, there will be safety and security—they will be yours.

Your future awaits you; so, take up your responsibilities and embrace your opportunities with enthusiasm and pride in Germany's strength. Understand that there are no limits to how high each of you can climb. Unlike our cousins on the other side of the wall, your future is in your hands—you are free to follow your dreams to the stars. You know, we have something so precious if we'll just remember: the eternal youngness of freedom makes it irresistible to people everywhere.

And we who live in this great cathedral of freedom need to remind ourselves: we can see our future shining, we can see new freedom spires rising, and, yes, we can see the times of tyranny passing, if we will just believe in our own greatest strengths—our courage, our worthiness, our unlimited capacity for love.

Let us ask ourselves, what is the heart of freedom? In the answer lies the deepest hope for the future of mankind, and the reason there can be no walls around those determined to be free. Each of us, each of you, is made in the most enduring, powerful image of Western civilization. We are made in the image of God—made in the image of God the Creator.

This is our power. This is our freedom. This is our future. And through this power, not drugs, not materialism, nor any other-ism, we can find brotherhood; and you can create the New Europe—a Europe democratic; a Europe united East with West; a Europe, at long last, completely free.

Now, we hear it said by some that Europe may be glum about her future, that Europe dares no more. Well, forgive me, but I think this kind of talk is nonsense, and I hope you think it's nonsense, too. It is you, Germany, and you, Europe, that gave the values and vitality of Judeo-Christian civilization to America, and the world. It is Europe that has known more tragedy and triumph than anyplace else in history. Each time you suffered, you sprang back, led by giants—Adenauer and Schuman, Churchill and Monnet.

Today, only 40 years after the most devastating war known to man, Western Europe has risen in glory from its ruins. Today, Europe stands, like "Schloss Hambach", a magnificent monument to the indomitable spirit of free people.

No country in the world has been more creative than Germany. And, no other can better help create our future. We have already seen one miracle, your "Wirtschaftswunder". The experts expected it would be decades before Germany's economy regained its prewar level. You did it in less than one. The experts said the Federal Republic could not absorb millions of refugees, establish a democracy on the ashes of Nazism and be reconciled with your neighbors. You did all three.

Germany's success showed that our future must not depend on experts or on government plans, but on the treasures of the human mind and spirit—imagination, intellect, courage and faith. We remember Ludwig Erhard's secret; how he blazed Germany's path with freedom by creating opportunity and lowering tax rates, to reward every man and woman who dared to dream and to create the future—your farmers, labor leaders, carpenters, and engineers—every German hero who helped to put the pieces of a broken society back together.

I want to encourage you today to consider joining with your friends now or in the future, to start up your own business and become part of a great new movement for progress—The Age of the Entrepreneur. Small businesses will be the biggest job creators for the future.

Human faith and skill discovered oil, where once there was only sand. Today we are discovering a new world of computers, microchips, and biotechnology. The new technologies can bring opportunities, create more jobs, produce medical breakthroughs, make our world cleaner and more humane, and provide better means of communication to bring the people of the world closer together. One top American computer firm was started by two college students in a garage behind their house.

Technology developed in the Federal Republic can make your air and water more pure and preserve the environment for your children. And because you are free, because you live in a democracy, you can help make all these things happen. You can make your voices heard so that technology works for us, not against us. My young friends, you can not only control your lives, you can help invent the future.

New technologies may someday enable us to develop far safer defenses—a non-nuclear defense not to harm people, but to prevent missiles from reaching our soil; a non-nuclear defense not to militarize space, but to demilitarize the arsenals of Earth. For now, we must rely on a system based on the threat of nuclear retaliation call Mutual Assured Destruction. But some day, your children may be protected, and war could be avoided, by a system we could called Mutual Assured Survival; some day, technology developed by your generation could render nuclear weapons obsolete.

Working together in space—as we have done with your fine astronaut, Ulf Merbold—we can create the future together. We have learned enough from our Shuttle flights to believe we will be able to manufacture in space rare crystals and medicines in far greater quantities, medicines to treat diseases that afflict millions of us. In the zero-gravity of space, we could make medicines to treat victims of heart attack and manufacture factor 8, a rare and expensive medicine used to treat hemophiliacs. We could study the beta cell, which produces insulin and which could give us mankind's first permanent cure for diabetes. In your lifetime, men and women will be living and working in space.

We are going to make the extraordinary commonplace—this is freedom's way. And these secrets for our future belong not just to us in Europe and America, but to all people, in all places, for all time. Look at Singapore, Hong Kong, and Taiwan—tiny specks on the globe, densely populated and with few natural resources. But, today, they are stunning success stories—mighty little engines of growth and progress, pulling the world forward, thanks to their dynamic policies of incentives that reward innovation, risk-taking and hard work.

The future awaits your creation. From your ranks can come a new Bach, Beethoven, Goethe and Otto Hahn for Germany's future. Your future will be a way station further along that same journey in time begun by the great patriots here at Hambach 153 years ago—a journey that began in a dream of the human heart; a journey that will not be complete until the dream is real; until the times of tyranny have passed; until the fear of political torture is no more; until the pain of poverty has been lifted from every person in the world forever. This is freedom's vision; and it is good; and you must go out from here and help to make it come true.

My young friends, this is a wonderful time to be alive and to be free. Remember that in your hearts are the stars of your fate; remember that everything depends on you; and, remember not to let one moment slip away, for, as Schiller told us, "He who has done his best for his own time has lived for all times".

Thank you for welcoming me; thank you for your warmth and your kindness; thank you for this wonderful day. I will always remember it, and I will always remember you.

"When They Turned The Lights On, It Was Like Being Reborn"
Strasbourg, France
May 8, 1985

By President Ronald Reagan

(Speech to the European Parliament in Strasbourg. It was repeatedly interrupted by hecklers.)

We mark today the anniversary of the liberation of Europe from tyrants who had seized this continent and plunged it into a terrible war. Forty years ago today, the guns were stilled and peace began—a peace that has become the longest of this century.

On this day 40 years ago, they swarmed onto the boulevards of Paris, rallied under the Arc de Triomphe, and sang the "Marseillaise" in the free and open air. On this day 40 years ago, Winston Churchill walked out onto a balcony in Whitehall and said to the people of Britain, "This is your victory." And the crowd yelled back, in an unforgettable moment of love and gratitude, "No—it is yours." Londoners tore the blackout curtains from their windows, and put floodlights on the great symbols of English history. And for the first time in nearly six years, Big Ben,

Buckingham Palace, and St. Paul's Cathedral were illuminated against the sky.

Across the ocean, a half million New Yorkers flooded Times Square and laughed and posed for the cameras. In Washington, our new President, Harry Truman, called reporters into his office and said, "The flags of freedom fly all over Europe."

On that day 40 years ago, I was at my post at an Army Air Corps installation in Culver City, California. Passing a radio, I heard the words, "Ladies and gentlemen, the war in Europe is over." I felt a chill, as if a gust of cold wind had just swept past, and — even though, for America, there was still a war on the Pacific front — I realized: I will never forget this moment.

This day can't help but be emotional, for in it we feel the long tug of memory; we are reminded of shared joy and shared pain. A few weeks ago, an old soldier with tears in his eyes said, "It was such a different world then. It's almost impossible to describe it to someone who wasn't there, but when they finally turned the lights on in the cities again it was like being reborn."

If it is hard to communicate the happiness of those days, it is even harder to communicate, to those who did not share it, the depth of Europe's agony. So much of it lay in ruins. Whole cities had been destroyed. Children played in the rubble and begged for food.

By this day 40 years ago, over 40 million lay dead, and the survivors, they composed a continent of victims. And to this day, we wonder: How did this happen? How did civilization take such a terrible turn? After all the books and the documentaries, after all the histories, and studies, we still wonder: How?

Hannah Arendt spoke of "the banality of evil"— the banality of the little men who did the terrible deeds. We know they were totalitarians who used the state, which they had elevated to the level of a "God," to inflict war on peaceful nations and genocide on innocent peoples.

We know of the existence of evil in the human heart, and we know that in Nazi Germany that evil was institutionalized — given power and direction by the state and those who did its bidding. And we also know that early attempts to placate the totalitarians did not save us from war. They didn't save us from war, in fact, they guaranteed it. There are lessons to be learned in this and never forgotten.

But there is a lesson, too, in another thing we saw in those days and perhaps we can call it "the commonness of virtue." The common men and women who somehow dug greatness from within their souls, the people who sang to the children during the Blitz, who joined the resistance and said "no" to tyranny, the people who had the courage to hide and save the Jews and the dissidents — the people who became, for a moment, the repositories of all the courage of the West, from a child named Anne Frank to a hero named Raoul Wallenberg. These names shine. They give us heart forever. The glow of their memories lit Europe in her darkest days.

Who can forget the hard days after the war? We can't help but look back and think: Life was so vivid then. There was the sense of purpose, the joy of shared effort, and, later, the impossible joy of our triumph. Those were the days when the West rolled up its sleeves and repaired the damage that had been done, the days when Europe rose in glory from the ruins. Old enemies were reconciled with the European family. Together, America and Western Europe created and put into place the Marshall Plan to rebuild from the rubble. Together, we created an Atlantic Alliance, which proceeded not from transient interests of State, but from shared ideals. Together, we created the North Atlantic Treaty Organization, a partnership aimed at seeing that the kind of tyrants who tormented Europe would never torment her again.

NATO was a triumph of organization and effort, but it was also something very new and very different. For NATO derived its strength directly from the moral values of the people it represented, from their ideals, their love of liberty, their commitment to peace.

But perhaps the greatest triumph of all was not in the realm of a sound defense or material achievement. No, the greatest triumph after the war is that in spite of all the chaos, poverty, sickness, and misfortune that plagued this continent, the people of Western Europe resisted the call of new tyrants and the lure of their seductive ideologies. Your nations did not become the breeding ground for new extremist philosophies. You resisted the totalitarian temptation. Your people embraced democracy, the dream the fascists could not kill. They chose freedom.

Today, we celebrate the leaders who led the way—Churchill and Monnet, Adenauer and Schuman, De Gasperi and Spaak, Truman and Marshall. And we celebrate, too, the free political parties that contributed their share of greatness: the liberals and the Christian Democrats, the Social Democrats and labor and the conservatives. Together, they tugged at the same oar, and the great and mighty ship of Europe moved on.

If any doubt their success, let them look at you. In this room are those who fought on opposite sides 40 years ago, and their sons and daughters. Now you work together to lead Europe democratically. You buried animosity and hatred in the rubble. There is no greater testament to reconciliation and to the peaceful unity of Europe than the men and women in this chamber.

In the decades after the war, Europe knew great growth and power, amazing vitality in every area of life, from fine arts to fashion, from manufacturing to science to the world of ideas. Europe was robust and alive, and none of this was an accident. It was the natural result of freedom, the natural fruit of the democratic ideal. We in America looked at Europe and called her what she was: an economic miracle.

And we could hardly be surprised. When we Americans think about our European heritage, we tend to think of your cultural influences and the rich ethnic heritage you gave us. But the industrial revolution that transformed the American economy came from Europe. The guiding intellectual lights of our democratic system—Locke, Montesquieu, and Adam Smith—came from Europe. And the geniuses who ushered in the modern industrial-technological age came from—well, I think you know, but two examples will suffice. Alexander Graham Bell, whose great invention maddens every American parent whose child insists on phoning his European pen pal rather than writing to him—was a Scotsman. And

Guglielmo Marconi, who invented the radio—thereby providing a living for a young man from Dixon, Illinois, who later went into politics—I guess I should explain that's me—so blame Marconi. Marconi, as you know was born in Italy.

Tomorrow will mark the 35th anniversary of the Schuman Plan, which led to the European Coal and Steel Community, the first block in the creation of a United Europe. The purpose was to tie French and German—and European—industrial production so tightly together that war between them "becomes not merely unthinkable but materially impossible." Those are the words of Robert Schuman. The coal and steel community was the child of his genius. And if he were here today, I believe he would say: "We have only just begun."

I am here to tell you America remains, as she was 40 years ago, dedicated to the unity of Europe. We continue to see a strong and unified Europe not as a rival but as an even stronger partner. Indeed, John F. Kennedy, in his ringing "declaration of interdependence" in the Freedom Bell city of Philadelphia 23 years ago, explicitly made this objective a key tenet of postwar American policy. That policy saw the New World and the Old as twin pillars of a larger democratic community. We Americans still see European unity as a vital force in that historic process. We favor the expansion of the European Community. We welcome the entrance of Spain and Portugal into that community, for their presence makes for a stronger Europe, and a stronger Europe is a stronger West.

Yet despite Europe's economic miracle, which brought so much prosperity to so many, despite the visionary ideas of the European leaders, despite the enlargement of democracy's frontiers within the European Community itself, I am told that a more doubting mood is upon Europe today. I hear words like "Europessimism" and "Europaralysis." I am told that Europe seems to have lost the sense of confidence that dominated that postwar era. If there is something of a "lost" quality these days, is it connected to the fact that some, in the past few years, have begun to question the ideals and philosophies that have guided the West for centuries? That some have even come to question the moral and intellectual worth of the West?

I wish to speak, in part, to that questioning today. And there is no better place to do it than Strasbourg—where Goethe studied, where Pasteur taught, where Hugo knew inspiration. This has been a lucky city for questioning and finding valid answers.

It is also a city for which some of us feel a very sweet affection. You know that our Statue of Liberty was a gift from France, and its sculptor, Auguste Bartholdi, was a son of France. I don't know if you have ever studied the face of the statue, but immigrants entering New York Harbor used to strain to see it, as if it would tell them something about their new world. It is a strong, kind face. It is the face of Bartholdi's mother, a woman of Alsace. And so, among the many things we Americans thank you for, we thank you for her.

The Statue of Liberty—made in Europe, erected in America—helps remind us not only of past ties but present realities. It is to those realities we must look in order to dispel whatever doubts may exist about the course of history and the place of free men and women within it. We live in a complex, dangerous, divided world, yet a world which can provide all of the good things we require, spiritual and material, if we but have the confidence and courage to face history's challenge.

We in the West have much to be thankful for—peace, prosperity, and freedom. If we are to preserve these for our children, and for theirs, today's leaders must demonstrate the same resolve and sense of vision which inspired Churchill, Adenauer, De Gasperi, and Schuman. Their challenge was to rebuild a democratic Europe under the shadow of Soviet power. Our task, in some ways even more daunting, is to keep the peace with an ever more powerful Soviet Union, to introduce greater stability in our relationship with it, and to live together in a world in which our values can prosper.

The leaders and people of postwar Europe had learned the lessons of their history from the failures of their predecessors. They learned that aggression feeds on appeasement and that weakness itself can be provocative. We, for our part, can learn from the success of our predecessor. We know that both conflict and aggression can be deterred, that democratic nations are capable of the resolve, the sacrifices, and the consistency of policy needed to sustain such deterrence.

From the creation of NATO in 1949 through the early 1970s, Soviet aggression was effectively deterred. The strength of Western economies, the vitality of our societies, the wisdom of our diplomacy, all contributed to Soviet restraint. But certainly the decisive factor must have been the countervailing power—ultimately, military, and, above all, nuclear power—which the West was capable of bringing to bear in the defense of its interests.

It was in the early 1970's that the United States lost that superiority over the Soviet Union in strategic nuclear weapons which had characterized the postwar era. In Europe, the effect of this loss was not quickly perceptible. But seen globally, Soviet conduct changed markedly and dangerously. First in Angola in 1975, then, when the West failed to respond in Ethiopia, in South Yemen, in Kampuchea, and ultimately in Afghanistan, the Soviet Union began courting more risks, and expanding its influence through the indirect and direct application of military power. Today, we see similar Soviet efforts to profit from and stimulate regional conflicts in Central America.

The ineffectual Western response to Soviet adventurism of the late 1970's had many roots, not least the crisis of self-confidence within the American body politic wrought by the Vietnam experience. But just as Soviet decision-making in the earlier postwar era had taken place against a background of overwhelming American strategic power, so the decisions of the late 1970's were taken in Moscow, as in Washington and throughout Europe, against a background of growing Soviet and stagnating Western nuclear strength.

One might draw the conclusion from these events that the West should reassert that nuclear superiority over the Soviet Union upon which our security and our strategy rested through the postwar era. That is not my view. We cannot and should not seek to build our peace and freedom perpetually upon the basis of expanding nuclear arsenals.

In the short run, we have no alternative but to compete with the Soviet Union in this field, not in the pursuit of superiority, but merely of balance. It is thus essential that the United States maintain a modern and survivable nuclear capability in each leg of the strategic triad—sea, land, and air-based. It is similarly important that France and Britain maintain and modernize their independent strategic capabilities.

The Soviet Union, however, does not share our view of what constitutes a stable nuclear balance. It has chosen, instead, to build nuclear forces clearly designed to strike first, and thus to disarm their adversary. The Soviet Union is now moving toward deployment of new mobile MIRVed missiles which have these capabilities, plus the potential to avoid detection, monitoring or arms control verification. In doing this, the Soviet Union is undermining stability and the basis for mutual deterrence.

One can imagine several possible responses to the continued Soviet build-up of nuclear forces. On the one hand, we can ask the Soviet Union to reduce its offensive systems through equitable, verifiable arms control measures. We are pressing that case in Geneva. Thus far, however, we have heard nothing new from the other side.

A second possibility would be for the West to step up our current modernization effort to keep up with constantly accelerating Soviet deployments. But is this really an acceptable alternative? Even if this course could be sustained by the West, it would produce a less stable strategic balance than the one we have today. Must we accept an endless process of nuclear arms competition? I don't think so. We need a better guarantee of peace than that.

Fortunately, there is a third possibility. It is to offset the continued Soviet offensive build-up in destabilizing weapons by developing defenses against these weapons. In 1983, I launched a new research program—the Strategic Defense Initiative.

The state of modern technology may soon make possible for the first time the ability to use non-nuclear systems to defeat ballistic missiles. The Soviets themselves have long recognized the value of defensive systems and have invested heavily in them. Indeed, they have spent as much on defensive systems as they have on offensive systems for more than 20 years.

This research program will take time. As we proceed with it, we will remain within existing treaty constraints. We will also consult in the closest possible fashion with our allies. And when the time for decisions on the possible production and deployment of such systems comes, we must and will discuss and negotiate these issues with the Soviet Union.

Both for the short and long term, I am confident that the West can maintain effective military deterrence. But surely we can aspire to more than maintaining a state of highly-armed truce in international politics.

During the 1970's we went to great lengths to restrain unilaterally our strategic weapons programs out of the conviction that the Soviet Union would adhere to certain rules in its conduct—rules such as neither side seeking to gain unilateral advantage at the expense of the other. Those efforts of the early 1970s resulted in some improvements in Europe, the Berlin Quadripartite Agreement being the best example. But the hopes for a broader and lasting moderation of the East-West competition foundered in Angola, Ethiopia, Afghanistan and Nicaragua.

The question before us today is whether we have learned from those mistakes and can we undertake a stable and peaceful relationship with the Soviet Union based upon effective deterrence and the reduction of tensions. I believe we can. I believe we have learned that fruitful cooperation with the Soviet Union must be accompanied by successful competition in areas—particularly Third World areas—where the Soviets are not yet prepared to act with restraint.

(Hecklers walk out, accompanied by applause and foot pounding.)

You know, I've learned something useful. Maybe if I talk long enough in my own Congress, some of those will walk out.

But let me talk about the reflections which have molded our policy toward the Soviet Union. That policy embodies the following basic elements:

While we maintain deterrence to preserve the peace, the United States will make a steady, sustained effort to reduce tensions and solve problems in its relations with the Soviet Union.

The United States is prepared to conclude fair, equitable, verifiable agreements for arms reduction, above all with regard to offensive nuclear weapons.

The United States will insist upon compliance with past agreements both for their own sake and to strengthen confidence in the possibilty of future accords.

The United States seeks no unilateral advantages, and, of course, can accept none on the Soviet side.

The United States will proceed in full consultation with its allies, recognizing that our fates are intertwined, and we must act in unity.

The United States does not seek to undermine or change the Soviet system nor to impinge upon the security of the Soviet Union. At the same time it will resist attempts by the Soviet Union to use or threaten force against others, or to impose its system on others by force.

Ultimately, I hope the leaders of the Soviet Union will come to understand that they have nothing to gain from attempts to achieve military superiority or to spread their dominance by force, but have much to gain from joining the West in mutual arms reduction and expanding cooperation.

I have directed the Secretary of State to engage with the Soviet Union on an extended agenda of problem solving. Yet even as we embark upon new efforts to sustain a productive dialogue with the Soviet Union, we are reminded of the obstacles posed by our so fundamentally different concepts of humanity, of human rights, of the value of a human life. The murder of Major Nicholson by a Soviet soldier in East Germany, and the Soviet Union's refusal to accept responsibility for this act, is only the latest reminder.

If we are to succeed in reducing East-West tensions, we must find means to ensure against the arbitrary use of lethal force in the future—whether against individuals like Major Nicholson, or against groups, such as the passengers on a jumbo jet.

It is for that reason that I would like to outline for you today what I believe would be a useful way to proceed. I propose that the United States and the Soviet Union take four practical steps.

First that our two countries make a regular practice of exchanging military observers at military exercises and locations. We now follow this practice with many other nations, to the equal benefit of all parties.

Second, as I believe it is desirable for the leaders of the United States and the Soviet Union to meet and tackle problems, I am also convinced that the military leaders of our nations could benefit from more contact. I therefore propose that we institute regular, high-level contacts between Soviet and American military leaders, to develop better understanding and to prevent potential tragedies from occurring.

Third, I urge that the conference on disarmament in Europe act promptly and agree on the concrete confidence-building measures proposed by the NATO counties. The United States is prepared to discuss the Soviet proposal on non-use of force in the context of Soviet agreement to concrete confidence-building measures.

Fourth, I believe a permanent military-to-military communications link could serve a useful purpose in this important area of our relationship. It could be the channel for exchanging notifications and other information regarding routine military activities, thereby reducing the chances of misunderstanding and misinterpretation. Over time, it might evolve into a "risk-reduction" mechanism for rapid communication and exchange of data in times of crisis.

These proposals are not cure-alls for our current problems, and will not compensate for the deaths which have occurred. But as terrible as past events have been, it would be more tragic if we were to make no attempt to prevent even larger tragedies from occurring through lack of contact and communication.

We in the West have much to do—and we must do it together. We must remain unified in the face of attempts to divide us and strong in spite of attempts to weaken us. And we must remember that our unity and strength are not a mere impulse of like-minded allies, but the natural result of our shared love for liberty.

Surely we have no illusions that convergence of the communist system and the free societies of the West is likely. We are in for an extended period of competition of ideas. It is up to us in the West to answer whether or not we will make available the resources, ideas and assistance necessary to compete with the Soviet Union in the Third World. We have much in our favor, not least the experience of those states which have tried Marxism and are looking for an alternative.

We do not aspire to impose our system on anyone, nor do we have pat answers for all the world's ills. But our ideals of freedom and democracy—(shouts of 'Nicaragua, Nicaragua')—Is there an echo here? Our ideals of democracy and freedom and our economic systems have proven their ability to meet the needs of our people. Our adversaries can offer their people only economic stagnation and the corrupt hand of a state and party bureaucracy which ultimately satisfy neither material nor spiritual needs.

I want to reaffirm to the people of Europe the constancy of the American purpose. We were at your side through two great wars. We have been at your side through 40 years of a sometimes painful peace. We are at your side today because, like you, we have not veered from the ideals of the West—the ideals of freedom, liberty, and peace. Let no one—no one—doubt our purpose.

The United States is committed not only to the security of Europe—we are committed to the re-creation of a larger and more genuinely European Europe. The United States is committed not only to a partnership with Europe—the United States is committed to an end to the artificial division of Europe.

We do not deny any nation's legitimate interest in security. We share the basic aspirations of all of the peoples of Europe—freedom, prosperity and peace. But when families are divided, and people are not allowed to maintain normal human and cultural contacts, this creates international tension. Only in a system in which all feel secure, and sovereign, can there be a lasting and secure peace.

For this reason we support and will encourage movement toward the social, humanitarian and democratic ideals shared in Europe. This issue is not one of state boundaries, but of insuring the right of all nations to conduct their affairs as their peoples desire. The problem of a divided Europe, like others, must be solved by peaceful means. Let us rededicate ourselves to the full implementation of the Helsinki Final Act in all its aspects.

As we seek to encourage democracy, we must remember that each country must struggle for democracy within its own culture. Emerging democracies have special problems and require special help. Those nations whose democratic institutions are newly emerged and whose confidence in the process is not yet deeply rooted need our help. They should have an established community of their peers, other democratic countries to whom they can turn for support or just advice.

In my address to the British parliament in 1982, I spoke of the need for democratic governments to spread the message of democracy throughout the world. I expressed my support for the Council of Europe's effort to bring together delegates from many nations for this purpose. I am encouraged by the product of that conference, the "Strasbourg Initiative."

We in our country have launched a major effort to strengthen and promote democratic ideals and institutions. Following a pattern first started in the Federal Republic of Germany, the United States Congress approved the National Endowment for Democracy. This organization subsequently established institutes of labor, business and political parties dedicated to programs of cooperation with democratic forces around the world. I hope other democracies will join in this effort and contribute their wisdom and talents to this cause.

Here in Western Europe, you have created a multi-national democratic community in which there is a free flow of people, of information, of goods and of culture. West Europeans move frequently and freely in all directions, sharing and partaking of each other's ideas and culture. It is my hope that in the 21st century—

which is only 15 years away—all Europeans, from Moscow to Lisbon, will be able to travel without a passport and the free flow of people and ideas will include the other half of Europe. It is my fervent wish that in the next century there will be one free Europe.

I do not believe those who say the people of Europe today are paralyzed and pessimistic. And I would say to those who think this: Europe, beloved Europe, you are greater than you know. You are the treasury of centuries of Western thought and Western culture; you are the father of Western ideals and the mother of Western faith.

Europe, you have been the power and the glory of the West, and you are a moral success. In the horrors after World War II, you rejected totalitarianism, you rejected the lure of a new "superman" and a "new communist man." You proved that you were—and are—a moral triumph. You in the West are a Europe without illusions, a Europe firmly grounded in the ideals and traditions that made her greatness, a Europe unbound and unfettered by a bankrupt ideology. You are, today, a new Europe on the brink of a new century—a democratic community with much to be proud of.

We have so much to do. The work ahead is not unlike the building of a great cathedral. The work is slow, complicated and painstaking. It is passed on with pride from generation to generation. It is the work not only of leaders but of ordinary people. The cathedral evolves as it is created, with each generation adding its own vision—but the initial ideal remains constant, and the faith that drives the vision persists. The results may be slow to see, but our children and their children will trace in the air the emerging arches and spires and know the faith and dedication and love that produced them. My friends, Europe is the cathedral, and it is illuminated still.

And if you doubt your will, and your spirit, and your strength to stand for something, think of those people 40 years ago—who wept in the rubble, who laughed in the streets, who paraded across Europe, who cheered Churchill with love and devotion and who sang the "Marseillaise" down the boulevards. Spirit like that does not disappear. It cannot perish; it will not go away. There's too much left unsung within it.

I would just like to conclude with one line, if I could, and say we've seen evidence here of your faith in democracy, in the ability of some to speak up freely, as they preferred to speak. And yet I can't help but remind all of us that some who take advantage of that right of democracy seem unaware that if the government that they would advocate became reality, no one would have that freedom to speak up again.

Thank you for all your graciousness on this great day. Thank you and God bless you all.

"Germans Who Recognize Their Responsibility"
Nuremberg, West Germany
May 7, 1985

By Willi Brandt

(Excerpts from a speech given by former Chancellor Willi Brandt at a Peace Conference in Nuremberg's "Meistersingerhalle".)

We have come together here to reflect on the military capitulation of Nazi Germany 40 years ago. I am grateful for the fact that we are not meeting alone here, i.e., that there are guests among us. Our guests are both from the East and the West. Hopefully they will be able to report at home that Germans met here who recognize their responsibility.

I welcome the representatives of Auschwitz (West Germany), Lidice (Czechoslovakia), Villenneuve d'Ascq (France), Coventry (England), Minsk (U.S.S.R.), Rotterdam (The Netherlands), Warsaw (Poland), Leningrad and Volgograd (U.S.S.R.), Dresden (East Germany) and Cologne (West Germany), In them we welcome at the same time many other cities on our continent that suffered heavily in the war, cities in Yugoslavia, Greece, Norway and Italy.

We consider it a special honor that the Jewish Labor Committee in the United States is represented here. To all of you we extend a cordial welcome. Let us jointly mobilize all those forces capable of making it impossible for anything of this kind ever to happen again.

The military capitulation of Nazi Germany 40 years ago was preceded 12 years earlier by Germany's moral and cultural capitulation. As such, it can be said that the actual defeat was at the beginning of the Nazi period and not when it ended. The unleashing of a total and insane war as well as the destruction of freedom brought shame on the name of Germany.

On May 8th let us strengthen our determination to recognize reality and bear the responsibility that derives from it. We want to face the tasks of the future and make it clear to everyone inside and outside of our borders that we are doing so.

We have come together today to reflect on what the month of May 40 years ago was and what it signifies for us. Was it a liberation?

For many it was the gradual transition to a state of non-war and a situation in which it was once again possible to continue living. It was felt to be a liberation most strongly by those for whom the Allies unlocked the gates behind which they had been forced to await their "extermination," the insidious term that was used. People were tormented and maltreated millions of times over for their convictions, their origins or simply for being different. Those who survived were marred for life by this experience.

Liberation in those spring days 40 years ago was a moral event that outweighed everything else. It freed Germany from adding more guilt to what it had already accumulated.

Servicemen and civilians were liberated from the hell of an insane "total war." People were freed from a constant fear for the safety of their loved ones.

This is the basic situation. I am not forgetting the victims of war and postwar internment. They followed the millions of POWs who had died before them in German camps. We speak openly of the suffering undergone by refugees and expellees.

Many at that time, and I was among them, hoped that the historic and symbolic handshake between Americans and Russians on the Elbe River 40 years ago would have a greater effect than it did. It would not have been easy for us.

The handshake with which Americans and Russians met on the Elbe River did not conclude European history. Some people act as if Europe were nothing more than a pawn in the hand of the superpowers. It has long been evident that what Europe is, achieves and becomes depends on us in Europe, even under the conditions that have been created by the war and the cold war.

Our task must be to exert peace-provoking influences. This means that, wherever possible, we must help reduce tensions and, in the process, direct energies from the senseless arms race to human purposes. This means we must seek to have a reconciling influence. . . .

Since 1945 the two superpowers—and they alone—have acquired the ability to extinguish life on this planet. This is a new quality. As such, there will not be a second attempt to bring the nations of the world together. As a German, particularly on a day like this one, I don't hesitate to say that the United States and the Soviet Union have shown sufficient farsightedness in the past 40 years to avoid the extreme case. That is a not inconsiderable fact, even though at times they came close and even though we might have expected the situation to be different after the end of Nazi Germany and the war it caused.

We are committed to our responsibility.

We want to keep the horrors of the extermination camps from spreading and keep the world from traveling the route of self-destruction.

Let me conclude by expressing that it is my commitment and my hope that May 1985 will be commemorated with a view to the future.

In 1970 the then-Chancellor Willi Brandt kneels before monument to Warsaw's ghetto in a gesture of reconciliation.

"We Must Look Truth Straight In The Eye"
May 8, 1985

By President Richard von Weizsäcker

(Speech during a commemorative ceremony in the Plenary Room of the German Bundestag.)

Many nations are today commemorating the date on which World War II ended in Europe. Every nation is doing so with different feelings, depending on its fate. This may have involved victory or defeat; liberation from injustice and alien rule or transition to new dependence; division; new alliances and vast shifts of power. May, 1945 is in any event a date of decisive historical importance for Europe.

We Germans are commemorating that date among ourselves, as is indeed necessary. We must find our own standards. We are not assisted in this task if we or others spare our feelings. We need and we have the strength to look truth straight in the eye—without embellishment and without distortion.

For us, the 8th of May is above all a date to remember what people had to suffer. It is also a date to reflect on the course taken by our history. The greater honesty we show in commemorating this day, the freer we are to face the consequences with due responsibility. For us Germans, May 8th is not a day of celebration. Those who actually witnessed that day in 1945 think back on highly personal and hence highly different experiences. Some returned home, others lost their homes. Some were liberated, while for others it was the start of captivity. Many were simply grateful that night bombings and fear had passed and that they had survived. Others felt first and foremost grief at the complete defeat suffered by their country. Some Germans felt bitterness about their shattered illusions, while others were grateful for the gift of a new start.

It was difficult to find one's bearings right away. Uncertainty prevailed throughout the country. The military capitulation was unconditional, placing our destiny in the hands of our enemies. The past had been terrible for many of those enemies, too. Would they not make us pay many times over for what we had done to them? Most Germans had believed that they were fighting and suffering for the good of their country. Now it turned out that their efforts had not only been in vain, but had served the inhuman goals of a criminal regime. The feelings of most people were those of exhaustion, despair and new anxiety. Had one's next of kin survived? Did a new start from those ruins make sense at all? Looking back, they saw the dark abyss of the past and, looking forward, they saw an uncertain, dark future.

Yet every passing day made something clearer, and this must be stated on behalf of all of us today: May 8, 1945 was a day of liberation. It liberated all of us from the inhumanity and tyranny of the National Socialist regime.

Nobody will, because of that liberation, forget the suffering that only started for many people on May 8th. But we must not regard the end of the war as the cause of flight, expulsion and deprivation of freedom. The cause goes back to the start of the tyranny that brought about war.

End of an Aberration

We must not separate May 8, 1945 from January 30, 1933.

There is truly no reason for us today to participate in victory celebrations. But there is every reason for us to perceive May 8, 1945 as the end of an aberration in German history, an end bearing the seeds of hope for a better future.

May 8th is a day of remembrance. Remembering means recalling an occurrence honestly and undistortedly so that it becomes a part of our very beings. This places high demands on our truthfulness.

Today we mourn all the dead of the war and tyranny. In particular we commemorate the six million Jews who were murdered in German concentration camps. We commemorate all nations who suffered in the war, especially the countless citizens of the Soviet Union and Poland who lost their lives. As Germans, we mourn our own compatriots who perished as soldiers, during air raids at home, in captivity or during expulsion. We commemorate the Sinti and Romany gypsies, the homosexuals and the mentally ill who were killed, as well as the people who had to die for their religious or political beliefs. We commemorate the hostages who were executed. We recall the victims of the resistance movements in all the countries occupied by us. As Germans, we pay homage to the victims of the German resistance movements in the military, the churches, and trade unions, among others, communists and the public at large. We commemorate those who did not actively resist, but preferred to die instead of going against their consciences.

Alongside the endless hosts of dead, there were huge mountains of human suffering—grief caused by death, suffering caused by injury, crippling or barbarous compulsory sterilization, suffering during the air raids, during flight and expulsion, suffering because of rape and pillage, forced labor, injustice and torture, hunger and hardship, suffering because of fear of arrest and death, grief at the loss of everything which one had wrongly believed in and worked for. Today we sorrowfully recall all this human suffering.

Perhaps the greatest burden was borne by the women of all nations. Their suffering, renunciation and silent strength are all too easily forgotten by history. Filled with fear, they worked, bore human life and protected it. They mourned their fallen fathers and sons, husbands, brothers and friends. In the years of darkness, they ensured that the light of humanity was not extinguished. After the war, with no prospect of a secure future, women everywhere were the first to set about building homes again, the "rubble women" in Berlin and elsewhere. When the men who had survived returned, women had to take a back seat again. Because of war, many women were left alone and spent their lives in solitude. Yet it is first and foremost thanks to the women that nations did not disintegrate spiritually on account of the destruction, devastation, atrocities and inhumanity and that they gradually regained their foothold after the war.

At the root of the tyranny was Hitler's immeasurable hatred of our Jewish compatriots. Hitler had never concealed this hatred from the public, and made the entire nation a tool of it. Only a day before his death, on April 30, 1945, he concluded his so-called "will" with the words: *Above all, I call upon the leaders of the nation and their followers to observe painstakingly the race laws and to oppose ruthlessly the poisoners of all nations: international Jewry.* Hardly any country has in its history always remained free from blame for war or violence. The genocide of the Jews is, however, unparalleled in history.

The perpetration of this crime was in the hands of a few people. It was concealed from the eyes of the public, but every German was able to experience what his Jewish compatriots had to suffer, ranging from plain apathy and hidden intolerance to outright hatred. Who could remain unsuspecting after the burning of the synagogues, the plundering, the stigmatization with the Star of David, the deprivation of rights, the ceaseless violation of human dignity? Whoever opened his eyes and ears and sought information could not fail to notice that Jews were being deported. The nature and scope of the destruction may have exceeded human imagination, but in reality there was, apart from the crime itself, the attempt by too many people, including those of my generation, who were young and were not involved in planning the events and carrying them out, not to take note of what was happening. There were many ways of not burdening one's conscience, of shunning responsibility, looking away, keeping mum. When the unspeakable truth of the Holocaust then became known at the end of the war, all too many of us claimed that they had not known anything about it or even suspected anything.

There is no such thing as the guilt or innocence of an entire nation. Guilt is, like innocence, not collective, but personal. There is discovered or concealed individual guilt. There is guilt which people acknowledge or deny. Everyone who directly experienced that era should today quietly ask himself about his involvement then.

The vast majority of today's population were either children then or had not been born. They cannot profess a guilt of their own for crimes that they did not commit. No discerning person can expect them to wear a penitential robe simply because they are Germans. But their forefathers have left them a grave legacy. All of us, whether guilty or not, whether old or young, must accept the past. We are all affected by its consequences and liable for it. The young and old generations must and can help each other to understand why it is vital to keep alive the memories. It is not a case of coming to terms with the past. That is not possible. It cannot be subsequently modified or made undone. However, anyone who closes his eyes to the past is blind to the present. Whoever refuses to remember the inhumanity is prone to new risks of infection.

The Jewish nation remembers and will always remember. We seek reconciliation. Precisely for this reason we must understand that there can be no reconciliation without remembrance. The experience of millionfold death is part of the very being of every Jew in the world, not only because people cannot forget such atrocities, but also because remembrance is part of the Jewish faith.

"Seeking to forget makes exile all the longer; the secret of redemption lies in remembrance." This oft quoted Jewish adage surely expresses the idea that faith in God is faith in the work of God in history. Remembrance is experience of the work of God in history. It is the source of faith in redemption. This experience creates hope, creates faith in redemption, in reunification of the divided, in reconciliation. Whoever forgets this experience loses his faith.

If we for our part sought to forget what has occurred, instead of remembering it, this would not only be inhuman. We would also impinge upon the faith of the Jews who survived and destroy the basis of reconciliation. We must erect a memorial to thoughts and feelings in our own hearts.

Hitler's Aim: Domination of Europe

The 8th of May marks a turning point not only in German history but in the history of Europe as a whole. The European civil war had come to an end. The old world of Europe lay in ruins. "Europe had fought itself to a standstill" (M. Stürmer). The meeting of American and Soviet Russian soldiers on the Elbe became a symbol for the temporary end of a European era.

True, all this was deeply rooted in history. For a century Europe had suffered under the clash of extreme nationalistic aspirations. At the end of the First World War peace treaties were signed but they lacked the power to foster peace. Once more nationalistic passions flared up and were fanned by the distress of the people at that time.

Along the road to disaster Hitler became the driving force. He whipped up and exploited mass hysteria. A weak democracy was incapable of stopping him. And even the powers of Western Europe—in Churchill's judgement unsuspecting but not without guilt—contributed through their weakness to this fateful trend. After the First World War America had withdrawn and in the Thirties had no influence on Europe.

Hitler wanted to dominate Europe and to do so through war. He looked for and found an excuse in Poland. On May 23, 1939 he told the German generals: "No further successes can be gained without bloodshed ... Danzig is not the objective. Our aim is to extend our 'Lebensraum' in the East and safeguard food supplies ... So there is no question of sparing Poland; and there remains the decision to attack Poland at the first suitable opportunity ... The object is to deliver the enemy a blow, or the annihilating blow, at the start. In this, law, injustice or treaties do not matter."

On August 23, 1939 Germany and the Soviet Union signed a non-aggression pact. The secret supplementary protocol made provision for the impending partition of Poland. That pace was made to give Hitler an opportunity to invade Poland. The Soviet leaders at the time were fully aware of this. And all who understood politics realized that the implications of the German-Soviet pact were Hitler's invasion of Poland and hence the Second World War.

That does not mitigate Germany's responsibility for the outbreak of the Second World War. The Soviet Union was prepared to allow other nations to fight one another so that it could have a share of the spoils. The initiative for the war, however, came from Germany, not from the Soviet Union. It was Hitler who resorted to the use of force. The outbreak of the Second World War remains linked with the name of Germany.

In the course of the war the Nazi regime tormented and defiled many nations. At the end of it all only one nation remained to be tormented, enslaved and defiled: the German nation. Time and again Hitler had declared that if the German nation was not capable of winning the war it should be left to perish. The other nations first became victims of a war started by Germany before we became the victims of our own war.

Division of Europe

The end of the war was followed by the division of Germany into the zones previously agreed upon by the Allied Powers. In the meantime the Soviet Union had taken control in all the countries of Eastern and Southeastern Europe that had been occupied by Germany during the war. All of them, with the exception of Greece, became socialist states. The division of Europe into two different political systems took its course. True, it was the post-war developments which cemented that division, but without the war started by Hitler it would not have happened at all. That is what first comes to the minds of the nations concerned when they recall the war unleashed by the German leaders. And we think of that, too, when we ponder the division of our own country and the loss of huge sections of German territory. In a sermon in East Berlin commemorating the 8th of May, Cardinal Meissner said: "The pathetic result of sin is always division."

The arbitrariness of destruction continued to be felt in the arbitrary distribution of burdens. There were innocent people who were persecuted and guilty ones who got away. Some were lucky to be able to begin life all over again at home in familiar surroundings. Others were expelled from the lands of their fathers. We, in what was to become the Federal Republic of Germany, were given the priceless opportunity to live in freedom. Many millions of our countrymen have been denied that opportunity to this day.

Learning to accept mentally this arbitrary allocation of fate was the first task, alongside the material task of rebuilding the country. That had to be the test of the human strength to recognize the burdens of others, to help bear them over time, not to forget them. It had to be the test of our ability to work for peace, of our willingness to foster the spirit of reconciliation both at home and in our external relations, an ability and a readiness which not only others expected of us but which we most of all demanded of ourselves.

We cannot commemorate the 8th of May without being conscious of the great

effort required on the part of our former enemies to set out on the road of reconciliation with us. Can we really place ourselves in the position of relatives of the
victims of the Warsaw ghetto or of the Lidice massacre? And how hard must it have
been for the citizens of Rotterdam or London to support the rebuilding of our
country from where the bombs came which not long before had been dropped
on their cities? To be able to do so they had gradually to gain the assurance that
the Germans would not again try to make good their defeat by use of force.

In our country the biggest sacrifice was demanded of those who had been
driven out of their homeland. They were to experience suffering and injustice long
after the 8th of May. Those of us who were born here often do not have the imagination or the open heart with which to grasp the real meaning of their harsh fate.

But soon there were great signs of readiness to help. Many millions of refugees and expellees were taken in who over the years were able to establish new
roots. Their children and grandchildren have in many different ways formed a loving attachment to the culture and the homeland of their ancestors. That is a great
treasure in their lives. But they themselves have found a new home where they are
growing up and integrating with the local people of the same age, sharing their
dialect and their customs. Their young life is proof of their ability to be at peace
with themselves. Their grandparents or parents were once driven out. They themselves, however, are now at home.

Compulsory Migration

Very soon and in exemplary fashion the expellees identified themselves with
the renunciation of force. That was no passing declaration in the early stages of
helplessness, but a commitment which has retained its validity. Renouncing the
use of force means allowing trust to grow on all sides. It means that a Germany that
has regained its strength remains bound by it. The expellees' own homeland has
meanwhile become a homeland for others. In many of the old cemeteries in Eastern Europe you will today find more Polish than German graves. The compulsory
migration of millions of Germans to the West was followed by the migration of
millions of Poles and, in their wake, millions of Russians. These are all people who
were not asked, people who suffered injustice, people who became defenseless objects of political events and to whom no compensation for those injustices and no
offsetting of claims can make up for what has been done to them.

Renouncing force today means giving them lasting security, unchallenged on
political grounds, for their future in the place where fate drove them after the 8th
of May and where they have been living in the decades since. It means placing the
dictate of understanding above conflicting legal claims. That is the true human
contribution to a peaceful order in Europe which we can provide.

The new beginning in Europe after 1945 has brought both victory and defeat
for the notion of freedom and self-determination. Our aim is to seize the opportunity to draw a line under a long period of European history in which to every
country peace seemed conceivable and safe only as a result of its own supremacy,

and in which peace meant a period of preparation for the next war.

The nations of Europe love their homeland. The Germans are no different. Who could trust a nation's love of peace if it were capable of forgetting its homeland? No, love of peace manifests itself precisely in the fact that one does not forget one's homeland and is for that very reason resolved to do everything in one's power to live together with others in lasting peace. An expellee's love for his homeland is in no way revanchism.

The last war has aroused a stronger desire for peace in the hearts of men than in times past. The work of the churches in promoting reconciliation met with a tremendous response. The "Aktion Sühnezeichen", a campaign in which young people carry out atonement activity in Poland and Israel, is one example of such practical efforts to promote understanding Recently, the town of Kleve on the lower Rhine received loaves of bread from Polish towns as a token of reconciliation and fellowship. The town council sent one of those loaves to a teacher in England because he had discarded his anonymity and written to say that as a member of a bomber crew during the war he had destroyed the church and houses in Kleve and wanted to take part in some gesture of reconciliation. In seeking peace it is a tremendous help if, instead of waiting for the other to come to us, we go towards him, as this man did.

In the wake of the war, old enemies were brought closer together. As early as 1946, the American secretary of state, James F. Byrnes, called in his memorable Stuttgart address for understanding in Europe and for assistance to the German nation on its way to a free and peaceable future. Innumerable Americans assisted us Germans, who had lost the war, with their own private means so as to heal the wounds of war. Thanks to the vision of the Frenchmen Jean Monnet and Robert Schuman and their cooperation with Konrad Adenauer, the traditional enmity between the French and Germans was buried forever.

A new will and energy to reconstruct Germany surged through the country. Many an old trench was filled in, religious differences and social strains were defused. People set to work in a spirit of partnership.

Opportunity for a Fresh Start

There was no "zero hour", but we had the opportunity to make a fresh start. We have used this opportunity as well as we could.

We have put democratic freedom in the place of oppression. Four years after the end of the war, on this 8th of May in 1949, the Parliamentary Council adopted our Basic Law. Transcending party differences, the democrats on the Council gave their answer to war and tyranny in Article 1 of our constitution: "The German people acknowledge inviolable and inalienable human rights as the basis of any community, of peace and of justice in the world." This further significance of May 8th should also be remembered today.

The Federal Republic of Germany has become an internationally respected country. It is one of the most highly developed industrial countries in the world.

It knows that its economic strength commits it to share responsibility for the struggle against hunger and need in the world and for social adjustment between nations. For 40 years we have been living in peace and freedom, to which we, through our policy in union with the free nations of the Atlantic Alliance and the European Community, have ourselves rendered a major contribution. The freedom of the individual has never received better protection in Germany than it does today. A comprehensive system of social welfare that can stand comparison with any other ensures the subsistence of the population. Whereas at the end of the war many Germans tried to hide their passports or exchange them for another one, German natonality today is highly valued.

We certainly have no reason to be arrogant and self-righteous. But we may look back with gratitude on our development over these 40 years, if we use the memory of our own history as a guideline for our future behavior.

- If we remember that mentally disturbed persons were put to death in the Third Reich, we will see care of people with psychiatric disorders as own responsibility.

- If we remember how people, persecuted on grounds of race, religion and politics and threatened with certain death, often stood before the closed borders with other countries, we will not close the door today on those who are genuinely persecuted and seek protection with us.

- If we reflect on the penalties for free thinking under dictatorship, we will protect the freedom of every idea and every criticism, however much it may be directed against ourselves.

- Whoever criticizes the situation in the Middle East should think of the fate to which Germans condemned their Jewish fellow human beings, a fate that led to the establishment of the State of Israel under conditions which continue to burden people in that region even today.

- If we think of what our Eastern neighbors had to suffer during the war, we will find it easier to understand that accommodation and peaceful neighborly relations with these countries remain central tasks of German foreign policy. It is important that both sides remember and that both sides respect each other. Mikhail Gorbachev, General Secretary of the Soviet Communist party, declared that it was not the intention of the Soviet leaders at the 40th anniversary of the end of the war to stir up anti-German feelings. The Soviet Union, he said, was committed to friendship between nations. If we have doubts about Soviet contributions to understanding between East and West and about respect for human rights in all parts of Europe, we must not ignore this signal from Moscow. We seek friendship with the peoples of the Soviet Union.

Germans — One Nation

Forty years after the end of the war the German nation remains divided.

At a commemorative service in the Church of the Holy Cross in Dresden held in February of this year, Bishop Hempel said: "It is a burden and a scourge that two German states have emerged with their harsh border. The very multitude of borders is a burden and a scourge. Weapons are a burden."

Recently in Baltimore in the United States, an exhibition on "Jews in Germany" was opened. The Ambassadors of both German states accepted the invitation to attend. The host, the president of Johns Hopkins University welcomed them together. He stated that all Germans share the same historical development. Their joint past is a bond that links them. Such a bond, he said, could be a blessing or a problem, but was always a source of hope.

We Germans are one people and one nation. We feel that we belong together because we have lived through the same past. We also experienced the 8th of May 1945 as part of the common fate of our nation that unites us. We feel bound together in our desire for peace. Peace and good-neighborly relations with all countries should radiate from the German soil in both states. And no other states should let that soil become a source of danger to peace either. The people of Germany are united in desiring a peace that encompasses justice and human rights for all peoples, including our own. Reconciliation that transcends boundaries cannot be provided by a walled Europe but only by a continent that removes the divisive elements from its borders. That is the exhortation given us by the end of the Second World War. We are confident that the 8th of May is not the last date in the common history of all Germans.

Many young people have in recent months asked themselves and us why such animated discussions about the past have arisen 40 years after the end of the war. Why are they more animated than after 25 or 30 years? What is the inherent necessity of this development?

It is not easy to answer such questions. But we should not seek the reasons primarily in external influences. In the life-span of men and in the destiny of nations, 40 years play a great role. Permit me at this point to return again to the Old Testament, which contains deep insights for every person, irrespective of his own faith. There, 40 years frequently play a vital part. The Israelites were to remain in the desert for 40 years before a new stage in their history began with their arrival in the promised land. Forty years were required for a complete transfer of responsibility from the generation of the fathers.

Elsewhere too (in the Book of Judges), it is described how often the memory of experienced assistance and rescue lasted only for 40 years. When memory faded, tranquility was at an end. Forty years invariably constitute a significant time span. Man perceives them as the end of a dark age bringing hope for a new and prosperous future, or as the onset of danger that the past might be forgotten and a warning of the consequences. It is worth reflecting on both of these perceptions.

In our country, a new generation has grown up to assume political responsibility. Our young peole are not responsible for what happened over 40 years ago. But they are responsible for the historical consequences.

We of the older generation owe to young people not the fulfilment of dreams but honesty. We must help younger people to understand why it is vital to keep memories alive. We want to help them to accept historical truth soberly, not one-sidedly, without taking refuge in utopian doctrines, but also without moral arrogance. From our own history we learn what man is capable of. For that reason we must not imagine that we are quite different and have become better. There is no ultimately achievable moral perfection. We have learned as human beings, and as human beings we remain in danger. But we have the strength to overcome such danger again and again.

Hitler's constant approach was to stir up prejudices, enmity and hatred. What is asked of young people today is this: do not let yourselves be forced into enmity and hatred of other people, of Russians or Americans, Jews or Turks, of alternatives or conservatives, blacks or whites.

Let us honor freedom.

Let us work for peace.

Let us respect the rule of law.

Let us be true to our own conception of justice.

On this 8th of May, let us face up to the truth as well as we can.

(Official translation)

Chapter 11

The Participants' Retrospective

"My Objective Was Reconciliation": Kohl
Time Magazine
May 6, 1985

Chancellor Helmut Kohl

(In a moving 90-minute meeting with Time *Bonn Bureau Chief William McWhirter, West German Chancellor Helmut Kohl replied to criticisms of the Bitburg visit with an emotional assessment of his country and its relations with the U.S. The Chancellor, in his only formal interview on the subject with the U.S. press [prior to Bitburg], was firm and assertive as he explained why the ceremony must take place.)*

Q: Mr. Chancellor, why Bitburg? Why is it important to you and to the German people?

A: In these days and hours I have suffered as I have rarely suffered before in my life. Ronald Reagan is a friend. He is a man for whom I would like to do only good. When the President is in Bitburg, he will encounter a wave of sympathy such as he has rarely experienced in his life. This may be more important than the occasional editorial he has to read these days.

If we don't go to Bitburg, if we don't do what we jointly planned, we will deeply offend the feelings of our people. There are letters on my desk that are heartrending outcries. A woman wrote how her 17-year-old brother was picked up and taken away with his classmates by military authorities and put into an SS uniform in which he was later killed. The Germans consist of more than minds.

They also have hearts and souls.

I too have asked myself whether the alliance of the past 30 years has been without consequence. This has nothing to do with a glorification of the Nazis. I have no need for anything of that kind. At the end of the war, I was 15 years old. Thank God, I was not involved in any guilt. Thus I can speak openly. My brother was killed at the end of the war at the age of 18. My own sons are now soldiers. We have a conscript army. What are our young servicemen to think if our remembrance of the dead 40 years later is distorted in a way that does not do justice to the dead at all? Around 2,000 former servicemen are buried at Bitburg. Included among them are 49 members of the Waffen SS. Of these 49 more than half were under the age of 20. If these young people had survived, they would have been amnestied under Allied regulations.

My objective was reconciliation over the graves of the past. We have never forgotten what the Marshall Plan did here. The Germans experienced the Americans as their friends. In 1946, as half-starved schoolchildren, we saw American trucks drive onto our school playground at 11 o'clock every morning with food. I met my wife at a dancing class where I wore a suit that was a Quaker donation. My wife wore a dress that was much too big for her and also an American donation. And now it was in November 40 years later that I was at the White House. I told [President Reagan] this May 8 would be a very difficult time for us, when we would look back to our own liberation from the Nazis, but also to a day that was the revelation of national shame. I said we wanted to commemorate the day as one of remembrance, and far from denying the horrible acts perpetrated by Nazism, to do everything to see that they may never occur again.

Q: Your critics here and in the U.S. say that the time may not be right for this kind of symbolism, that such intended reconciliation will only reopen old wounds.

A: You may very well be right. A part of the American public, in contrast to the German public, feels the time is not right. I would like to ask a question in return. American freedom, not just German freedom, is now being defended in this country. In a few weeks we will even extend the compulsory military service of our own youth from 15 to 18 months. Can you tell me what I am supposed to say to our soldiers when they ask why they are supposed to make this personal sacrifice? Many of my fellow citizens have told me recently that it was right for us to have supported the U.S. over its missile deployment. However, they also ask me if it is also right for us to be actually alone when it comes to our feelings.

Q: Yet are you concerned that the controversy could have a detrimental effect on the upcoming summit and even on personal relations between Germans and Americans?

A: I hope not. If you are right, then we would have to ask ourselves whether or not we have been building on sand these past decades. I don't think so. When a hurricane suddenly comes up and threatens to destroy the landscape, I am not willing to accept the idea that what I have been doing and believed in for decades is wrong. What I have to do is everything necessary to contain the storm and protect myself. I know this is a difficult situation, but I am sure of myself.

Q: Do you recall a time when German-American relations have been so tested?

A: No. What is involved affects more than just a rational argument. The debate over deployment also had its strong emotional elements. I remember a Saturday when I flew in a helicopter away from the Chancellery grounds over 300,000 people who were demonstrating against my decision to deploy the Pershings. Like anyone in politics, you must always ask youself whether you have acted correctly. But you can't govern by the numbers. Otherwise, we could replace a Chancellor with a polling institute. I consider the most important task I have is to contribute toward making the ties between the Federal Republic and the Western community irreversible and part of our basic political philosophy. This is, if you will, a declaration of love for the Americans. The only thing is that, as we see in everyday life, declarations of love that are only unilateral can cause feelings of frustration.

Q: You have referred to yourself as the first West German Chancellor of the postwar generation. Can this be perceived as an attempt to escape from history?

A: Why do I mention this? In order to signal that there has been a change of generations in our country. Two-thirds of our people did not experience May 1945 and this has to have consequences. Even as a young boy, I heard and saw horrible things. As was customary at the time, I was in one of those groups that put out fires after bombing raids. I can still show you the house where at the age of 13 I had to dig bodies out from under the rubble. The house has been rebuilt, but I still think of that day whenever I drive past it. At the age of 15, only 18 days before Germany surrendered, I was asked if I wanted to join the SS. I could refuse because of my age. But they hanged a boy from a tree who was perhaps only two years older with a sign saying TRAITOR because he had run away. I can still see it now.

Q: The U.S. has seen moods of penitence and humility from postwar Germany. Now it seems to be hearing from you a tone that is more aggressive and insistent on Germany's right to be accepted and forgiven.

A: You are quite right. Isn't that actually a perfectly natural process, particularly among friends? More important, is this not proof that we are coming out of the dark ages of the Nazi era?

Q: What issues will be most important for your government at the summit?

A: We should all be aware of the supreme importance of free world trade. It is not a specific German-American problem. It is the Japanese who should open their market. I have suggested to my friend [Japanese Prime Minister Yasuhiro] Nakasone that we engage in genuine competition. I am not afraid of the Japanese. They don't have any more gray cells than we do. A return to protectionism would have disastrous consequences.

With reference to SDI [Reagan's Strategic Defense Initiative, popularly called Star Wars], I strongly support the idea. In this, I would like to insist on two

basic conditions: that it should not be a one-way street and that what we do together should be for our common benefit. The research carried out will not only
be of military value, three-fourths of the research will have civilian applications.
We can add a lot to this effort, in sophisticated optics, for example, I would like
other Europeans to cooperate with us in this effort, like the French, British and
Italians.

Q: If there is a slowing of the U.S. economy, how should Europe respond?

A: Of course, there is concern over the irregular pace of the American
economy. You need only to look at the dollar exchange rate. We must continue to
steer the course we are now on: consolidation of public finances and bringing interest rates under control to achieve a lower inflation rate and freedom for the
economy to move away from governmental restrictions. We are cutting taxes by
20 billion marks [$6.4 billion] as part of the recovery process.

Q: Finally, do you think there is anything more you can do personally to
ease the controversy over the ceremony at Bitburg?

A: No. I will not give up the idea. I suggested it. I stick to it.

"Let Us Seek And Never Turn From the Truth": Shultz
Jerusalem, Israel
May 10, 1985

By George P. Shultz

*(Speech made by The Honorable George P. Shultz, U.S. Secretary of State, at The Yad Vashem
Holocaust Memorial, Jerusalem, Israel.)*

The Yad Vashem memorial poses a question that has haunted mankind since
the beginning of time, and never more so than after the Holocaust. Can one stand
amidst the proof of human suffering and human evil in this place, and still hope?
Can one look at the sea of faces—faces of children, of mothers, fathers, and grandparents, faces without hope, faces that were destroyed, faces that are no more—
can one look into the eyes of the victims of a hell made on earth by men and still
have the will and the courage to look ahead to mankind's future?

Four decades have passed since the horror of the Holocaust ended with the
defeat of the Nazis. For four decades the world has worked to restore itself, to begin again. Nations have made war, and made peace. Efforts to build a better world
have gone forward, sometimes successfully, sometimes not. Older generations have
passed on; new generations have grown up; and for those new generations living
so far from this place forty years after the fact, the memory of the evils recorded
here may be distant—perhaps fading.

But here, time has not passed—and never will. The evil remembered here at Yad Vashem might as well have been committed just a moment ago.

Forty years, or four hundred years, are but an instant in this place. For here, as nowhere else, the evil in man has been recorded in excruciating fullness. Here, time has no meaning because time cannot wash that evil away. Men and women may lead their lives elsewhere and avert their eyes from this cold and awful reality. But no one can walk through this memorial and harbor the slightest doubt that mankind's capacity for evil is unbounded. Here we must look evil in the face. How, then, do we go on?

Miraculously, here there is also hope. For who has erected this memorial? Not the perpetrators of evil, but the conquerors of evil. Who preserves the memory? Not the enemies of the human spirit, but its defenders. Not the enemies of the Jews, but the Jews.

Yes, Yad Vashem stands in remembrance of suffering, of death, of evil. But Yad Vashem also commemorates a great victory. Yes, here we know, we can *see*, mankind's shameful capacity for inhumanity. Yet here we also see that when men and women refuse to accept and acquiesce in evil—when men and women struggle and sacrifice for the higher good—then evil can be defeated, and justice restored.

The very fact that the memorial to the Holocaust victims stands here in Israel is a symbol of hope. It reminds us that from the abyss of Jewish suffering at Nazi hands re-emerged the Jewish state—a haven, finally, after centuries of anti-Semitic persecution. The birth of Israel was a rebirth of hope, and not only for Jews, but for peoples everywhere. That the Jewish people could not be vanquished even by so vicious a tyrant as Hitler is testimony to the indomitable human spirit. It showed that right will prevail, even against the greatest odds. It is an inspiration for all. This memorial is in Israel because Israel is the true witness to the Holocaust, and the truest symbol of the victory of good over evil. That is why Israel must endure, and that is why the American people are forever committed to Israel's security.

After the Holocaust, the American people, and decent men and women around the world, made a solemn pledge: Never again. Never again would we fail to confront evil. Never again would we appease the aggressor. Never again would we let the Jewish people stand alone against persecution and oppression. Today we honor the pledge by standing beside the state of Israel. We honor the pledge when we, with the people of Israel, reach out to help save Ethiopian Jewry. We honor the pledge when we work tirelessly to help Soviet Jewry—and other minorities—against the Soviet regime's systematic persecution. We honor the pledge when we pursue and prosecute Nazi war criminals, and when we commit ourselves to bring them to justice no matter how long it takes.

But above all we honor our pledge by remembering, by teaching our children the story of the six million Jews, by establishing the Holocaust Memorial Commission in the United States, and by coming here to Yad Vashem. Every year thousands of Americans come here—to remember, to see and to feel the evil in its immediacy. The images of Jewish suffering still burn in our minds and our hearts. We must make sure those images never fade. For only by seeing and knowing that the capacity for evil exists in mankind can we do what we must to see to it that our humanity prevails.

We do not avert our eyes. We do not forget. But neither do we despair. Let us be guided by both memory and hope. The prophet Isaiah teaches us: "For the Lord shall comfort Zion; He will comfort all her waste places; and He will make her wilderness like Eden, and her desert like the garden of the Lord. Joy and gladness shall be found therein, thanksgiving and the voice of melody."

It is Judaism that has taught us that the human being not only has the capacity for evil, but also the capacity for hope. It is Judaism that has taught us that we are made in God's image and, therefore, have the capacity to grow to greatness and to nobility of spirit. It is that faith which is the essence of the democratic philosophy — a philosophy based on the principles of human dignity and human brotherhood — that binds Israel and America together.

That is our joint commitment to humanity. May we always have the courage to recognize and confront evil whenever we see it. May we always have the vision and the strength to shape and build the better world we seek. Let us seek and never turn from the truth.

U.S. Will Always Oppose Nazism
New York
June 5, 1985

By Vice President George Bush

(Speech by Vice President George Bush to The 30th Anniversary Convocation of Bar-Ilan University.)

It's a pleasure and honor to be here.

Today we observe the 30th anniversary of Bar-Ilan University. One of the world's great universities, Bar-Ilan is testimony to the dedication of Israel, of the Israeli people and of you — Bar-Ilan's supporters in America — to education. Israel has one of the finest education systems in the world. Bar-Ilan is one of the finest institutions in Israel.

But to me, Bar-Ilan is more than a university. It is a statement of faith.

Faith in the importance of the sacred in a secular world, of tradition in a world of innovation. I'm impressed that Bar-Ilan's students master both the most modern, secular arts and sciences and their enduring Jewish heritage.

Faith in the enduring bond between Israel and the United States. Many of Bar-Ilan's secular schools—for example, its business and law schools—are patterned after American models. And Bar-Ilan is the only Israeli university chartered by the New York State Board of Regents.

And, finally, faith in life and in the capacity of man to repair a broken world. Born only ten years after the end of the Holocaust, Bar-Ilan stands, with Israel itself, as testimony to the ultimate triumph of freedom over oppression, life over death, good over evil.

And, let me add, no man better embodies the spirit of Bar-Ilan than Dr. Emanuel Rackman, whose 75th birthday we also celebrate today. In mastery of both secular and sacred traditions, in embodiment of the bond between America and Israel, in building for the future good of man—Dr. Rackman *is* the spirit of Bar-Ilan today, and I know that everyone here admires and respects him as much as I do.

Tonight I want to talk, in a broader context, about each of the articles of faiths that Bar-Ilan represents—about faith in values, in the bond between Israel and America and in man's ability to improve the world.

Forty years ago the world was in desperate need of improvement. The most destructive of history's wars had just ended.

I fought in that war, in the Pacific. I saw terrible things. But it wasn't until I got home, and talked with friends who'd fought in Europe and helped liberate some of the concentration camps, that I realized that as horrible as combat was, there was something yet more horrible still.

World War II was a struggle of good against evil—evil of a sort the world had never before seen.

Yes, the world had known aggression. It had known brutality.

But never before had there been an ideology that—like the Nazi ideology—was dedicated to the destruction of entire peoples because of their religion or race.

Never before had there been death camps and gas chambers that claimed lives by the millions.

Never before had mankind known the horror the Jews of Europe knew during the Holocaust.

Never before ... and when allied troops liberated the concentration camps, decent people everywhere vowed never again.

This vow—never again—was the genesis of the American bond with Israel. It sustained and nurtured that bond, until over the years, the relationship became broader and more mutual.

It is not just that millions of American families now claim sons, daughters, brothers, sisters or even parents in Israel and feel deep affection and admiration for that nation—although that's important.

No, it's also that America and Israel share common values. We are both democracies dedicated to common concepts of freedom and justice.

Over the years common values have made our common bond stronger—and so has common need. Israel and America share broad strategic concerns. As the area's one true democracy, Israel is America's foremost strategic friend in the Middle East.

This aspect of the relationship — strategic friendship — has come to full maturity only in the last few years.

In 1983, President Reagan and then-Prime Minister Shamir recognized it when they announced a strategic cooperation agreement between the U.S. and Israel.

As a result of that agreement, the United States and Israel now engage in regular, detailed discussions regarding how to cooperate to defend shared interests. Joint military exercises have been held and prepositioning of equipment is under discussion.

We are helping to fund the development of the LAVI fighter and are sharing critical technologies for use in the fighter. We're purchasing Israeli made weapons. We've announced that Israel and the U.S. will together build missiles, submarines and reconnaissance drones. And we have invited Israel to participate in research related to the Strategic Defense Initiative.

President Reagan and I are committed to maintaining Israel's qualitative edge over any potential combination of adversaries.

We've also taken a strong interest in helping Israel improve its economy.

Last year we changed the military aid package from loans to grants. Economic and military aid in 1984 totaled $2.6 billion and this year may be more.

This year we signed a U.S.-Israeli free trade agreement. It's good for both American and Israeli business to have full access to each other's markets, and we believe it will help strengthen both the U.S. and Israeli economies.

And we've established a Joint Economic Development Group, which includes several of our nation's most distinguished economists to help improve Israel's economy.

All this is why just a few months ago Mr. Shamir said Israeli "relations with the U.S. are better than ever before," and Mr. Peres echoed that judgment, saying they "have reached a new level of harmony and understanding." That's what strategic cooperation has meant for U.S.-Israeli relations — a strong friendship based on common values and shared interests.

Ultimately, the President and I would like — as Israel would like — to see the day when Israel and its neighbors live at peace. We remain committed to the President's peace initiative.

Last week, Jordan's King Hussein visited Washington to discuss his thoughts on this search for peace. With the developments in the last few months between Egypt and Israel and Egypt and Jordan, we may have an opportunity now to take strides towards peace.

But there has been a great deal of anxious speculation about what was said and not said in the meetings with the King. So let me repeat here pledges that have been and remain the foundation of our policy on negotiations.

First pledge: Regarding the PLO, until the PLO explicitly accepts Security

Council Resolutions 242 and 338 and recognizes Israel's right to exist, the United States will neither recognize nor negotiate with the PLO.

Second pledge: The United States will try to facilitate negotiations, but we will never attempt to impose a settlement.

We have — as Israel has — real problems with the concept of an international conference. We believe that negotiations must be between the parties themselves. But we recognize the value of proceeding to direct negotiations within a supportive international context, and we will work with Israel to find one we, Israel and Jordan can support.

And while we're on pledges and international conferences, let me repeat one last pledge, now law, about the most prominent international conference, the UN itself. And that's, very simply, if Israel is ever voted out of the UN, the U.S. will go out with it.

The Talmud teaches that, "It was only through suffering that the children of Israel obtained three priceless and coveted gifts: The Torah, the Land of Israel, and the World to Come."

Although the death and suffering of the Holocaust led to the birth of Israel, there are still many Jews who have not known deliverance, who still suffer. And wherever, on whatever continent, there is such suffering—whether suffering of the body or more subtle forms—I am committed, as this Administration is committed, to helping. Never again will the cries of abandoned Jews go unheard by the United States government.

I am particularly concerned about the plight of Soviet Jewry—about Shcharansky, Nudel, now Edelstein and so many others. I was the first American to meet with each of the past three Soviet leaders. And in each of those meetings, I told them how strongly we feel on this. If the Soviet leaders want to signal a sincere desire for improved relations, they know where to start—let the refuseniks go.

If the United States should last a million years or a million million years, this country will still remain the enemy of anti-Semitism, of Nazism, of all such oppression. It is our obligation as a free people.

We Americans must never forget those who suffered and died in the Holocaust. We must remember so that if something like Nazism should return to the earth, we recognize what is happening and we act. That's why the Administration hasn't taken lightly the threat of neo-Nazi groups in this country.

We Americans have a responsibility to those who died in the Holocaust. Part of that responsibility in our time is to capture the killers who survive. In the last four years the U.S. has initiated legal action against 400 of these, and we are hunting others. Josef Mengele is at the top of the list. Time cannot redeem such monsters or reconcile us to their deeds.

Another part of that responsibility is to resolve our problems with the genocide treaty ... and to ratify it.

We Americans have a responsibility to the victims of the Holocaust, and Americans related by blood or faith have, perhaps, a special responsibility.

I've heard some people criticize the Jewish community for its vocalness on issues it believes in. Well, I don't go along with that. I believe that citizen advocacy is the greatness of America. It's what strengthens and gives vitality to our country. Let no one tell you that support for Israel and efforts on behalf of Soviet Jews is "special interest politics." It is your right and duty as Americans to advocate causes important to you.

Our heritage as Americans requires that we remember the Holocaust.

Our heritage as Americans requires that we remember those who suffer anti-Semitism today—whether in Africa, the Soviet Union or Nicaragua.

Our heritage as Americans requires that we remember those in our time who face genocidal threats—whether they are Cambodian, Afghan or Miskito Indians.

Our heritage as Americans requires that we remember the obligation of great democracies, like the United States, to support small ones, like Israel.

But all I am saying is that our heritage as Americans requires that we remember our values, our faiths, our traditions and let them guide us in making our nation and our world a better place.

Kohl Says He Has No Regrets About Bitburg
Los Angeles Times
July 28, 1985

By Lally Weymouth

In his first interview with an American reporter since President Reagan's visit to Bitburg, German Chancellor Helmut Kohl said that despite the uproar in the United States, he would have Reagan go to the cemetery all over again.

He also called Germany's alliances with France and the United States the pillars of his country's foreign policy and promised to support the Strategic Defense Initiative, or "Star Wars," at least through its research phase.

Kohl opened the interview by describing ties between Germany and the United States as "close, old and long standing." He pointed to the number of Americans with German ancestry, the haven provided by the United States for Jewish emigres fleeing from Nazi terrorism and the Marshall Plan's major role in rebuilding a Germany shattered by World War II.

Today's best symbol of "German-U.S. ties" he said, is the German commitment to the North Atlantic Treaty Organization of 500,000 soldiers, "the biggest commitment apart from the Americans."

Reagan's visit to Bitburg was as vigorously opposed in the United States, because it contained graves of Waffen SS troops, as it was popular in Germany. Would he do it again? "I'd do it exactly as I did it," Kohl said vehemently, staring straight ahead. "It was bitterly needed. I think there was no generalized outcry in the U.S. There was an outcry from a group of people which influenced public opinion," he said, in an obvious reference to the U.S. Jewish community.

Somewhat defensively, the chancellor added: "I told my fellow countrymen that we Germans would have to bear the whole burden of German history. I said we would have to accept all those shameful crimes committed by the Nazis because this is part of our history. As a Christian and a German, I can ask the victims of that persecution and their relatives to forgive. And I can repeat that we have not forgotten what happened. But I think we can say we also learned a lesson from history."

If Americans could put themselves in German shoes, he said, they would see Bitburg in this way: "If one thinks of war, one also has to think of those who were killed in the course of the war and I think respect for the dead is also part of the civilization and culture of a nation. Among the more than 2,000 soldiers who are buried there, there are some 40 soldiers who belonged to the Waffen SS.

"The Waffen SS was made up of groups who committed crimes at concentration camps. But the major part of the Waffen SS was ordinary soldiers who were fighting battles at the front line and the greater part of these soldiers did not join the Waffen SS voluntarily. They were drafted. More than 50% of the people buried in Bitburg are below 25 years of age. And these young people haven't done anything—they just served and were killed in action."

As for Reagan, whom he calls a friend, Kohl praised the President for acting as he did, adding: "Furthermore, I say it didn't do him any harm in the U.S." In the end, he said, Reagan's gesture in going to Bitburg—seen as damaging in the United States—was to Kohl "confirmation that as friends we may trust each other," something Germans have doubted at times in the past.

Kohl's view of Bitburg as "the strongest blow against anti-Americanism," is not shared by opposition leaders in Germany. Egon Bahr, a leading spokesman of the left, said of Bitburg, "It was terrible theater. The chancellor shouldn't have forced the American President to go there. We didn't need it to become friends. We are friends."

Kohl demonstrated his friendship the hard way when he ignored popular protests and allowed deployment of U.S. cruise and Pershing missiles. His predecessor, Chancellor Helmut Schmidt, also wanted to deploy the missiles but couldn't overcome opposition within his own party and the conflict brought down his government.

"I told my people, we have got to deploy the missiles," Kohl recalled. "We've got to do it because our friends must be able to rely on us."

As he did often during the interview, Kohl returned to the subject of Bitburg, saying that the deployment of U.S. missiles was "another reason why it was important for our people to see in Bitburg that we can rely on our American friends" just as the Americans were able to rely on him.

Many Germans complain that the United States talks tough to the Soviet Union but doesn't act tough, citing its reaction to the Berlin Wall, the uprising in Hungary and the fatal shooting of Maj. Arthur D. Nicholson, Jr. earlier this year in East Germany. These incidents are a factor in the advocacy by opposition SPD politicians of German neutralism.

Kohl dismissed the idea of neutrality. "Since Stalin the Russians have tried again and again to convince the Germans that neutrality would be the price of unity," he said. "But this is not a genuine offer. What it would mean is that we would get unity but lose freedom." Oskar Lafontaine, a left-wing member of the SPD, proposes nuclear-free zones in Germany and even the conservative Kohl doesn't take as hard a line toward the Soviet Union as the U.S. Administration.

One of Kohl's major foreign-policy battles is over the Strategic Defense Initiative. Among U.S. European allies, Germany has proved the strongest supporter of SDI research.

"I think both in political and moral terms, the American efforts in connection with SDI are justified," Kohl said.

As to U.S.-Soviet arms-control talks in Geneva, Kohl said that "without the missile deployment the negotiations would not have resumed." He cautioned against giving in on SDI, noting that the Soviets are "realistic people. They respect acts. They want to blackmail people. This has been our experience with the missiles and now we have the same experience with SDI. They will be ready for talks, provided the West will be united and is also ready for talks."

In announcing his intention to sell German arms to so-called moderate Arab countries, Kohl defended this controversial action. "It's not my intention to become the biggest arms exporter in the world," he said, "but nor are we ready to say we will export none at all. We have to take into account two points. After the terrible things we have gone through under the Nazi regime, we have now friendly relations with Israel. We must cultivate them. We also have good relations with the Arab world, and I think the moderate Arab world is of the greatest importance for the future of the world."

Knowing that King Hussein could be shot or the Saudi regime overthrown and German tanks turned on Israel, is the sale appropriate in light of German history? Kohl responded angrily, "Here again, that brings us back to Bitburg. I'm familiar with the history of my country, and I will never forget it. But I have to take decisions which will affect the future."

Hard decision in tense times make for interesting politics and Germany is no exception. The opposition SPD is stronger than expected—actually running neck-and-neck with Kohl in present polls. Kohl's Christian Democratic Union has been wracked by financial scandals, forcing the chancellor to testify under oath about campaign contributions. His former finance minister will go on trial later this month for mishandling campaign funds and avoiding taxes. Unemployment has increased, evoking for older Germans memories of the Weimar Republic.

Yet German political analysts warn against underestimating Kohl's political skills. He may be provincial, they say, but he knows how to win party elections. The chancellor himself remains confident about the 1987 elections. "I am going to win," he said.

I Took The Journey The President Should Have Taken," Says Senator
Special Contribution

By Senator Frank R. Lautenberg

The President's visit to Bitburg may have faded from public memory. But this book is proof that this sad episode still reverberates among many who believe the wreath laying ceremony at the once obscure German cemetery was a mistake.

On April 11, 1985, the White House announced President Reagan would visit Bitburg. He would do so to make a gesture of reconciliation on the 40th anniversary of World War II's end. In the days that followed, the American public learned that 49 Waffen SS, Hitler's elite purveyors of terror, were buried there.

I reacted to the President's decision on many levels, and on many levels opposed it. As a Jew, I felt that the trip was insulting to those who died in the Holocaust, and to those who survived. As a veteran, I believed the President's decision to visit the grave site of those who died defending facism was a blasphemous affront to those who gave their lives trying to crush that hateful evil. And, as a senator, I felt that the President of the United States had an obligation to understand the difference between German war dead, whom he labeled "victims of the Nazis" and the real victims.

From the global outcry that followed, I realized my feelings were shared by many.

Neither continuing public protests nor nearly unanimous resolutions passed by both Houses of Congress deterred the President from making his mistaken visit. Even the impassioned pleas of Holocaust survivor and author Elie Wiesel, present at the White House to receive the Congressional Gold Medal, failed to move the President. In the midst of the escalating world debate over the President's pending Bitburg visit, Wiesel's plea turned into an extraordinary confrontation.

On national television, just feet from the President of the United States, stood Elie Wiesel, survivor of Auschwitz, voice of a generation of survivors. He was there to accept an award expressing the American people's appreciation of his life's work in chronicling the ghastly tragedy of the Holocaust. The long planned ceremony had been conceived as a fitting culmination of Holocaust memorial week.

Now, instead of capstoning the week of Holocaust remembrance, Wiesel's acceptance of a Congressional Gold Medal provided a climax of sorts to the mounting controversy over Bitburg.

In a voice that was both soft yet dramatic, in a tone that was simultaneously anxious yet sure, deferential yet uncompromising, the sallow-eyed scholar of the Holocaust delivered his plea.

"That place, Mr. President, is not your place. Your place is with the victims of the SS"

Inevitably, unavoidably, the Roosevelt Room ceremony was a fiasco of unforeseen proportions for the beleaguered White House. Elie Wiesel had prudently rejected the option of publicly declining the award. Instead, he spoke eloquently and directly to the President in a way that is so typical of Elie. For the millions of Americans who opposed the Bitburg visit, we could have had no finer spokesperson.

The evening before he made his remarks at the White House, Elie and I sat together. Friends for many years, we talked about the next day's ceremony. The substance of Elie's remarks was already determined. But the issue of tone and directness needed to be settled. Senator Howard Metzenbaum (D-Ohio) and Congressman Sidney Yates participated in the discussion.

There was no question that Elie would speak his mind. Despite considerable pressure from the White House to reserve his criticism for a private meeting with the President, there was never any doubt that Bitburg would be the focal point of Elie's public remarks.

Wiesel faced a dilemma. While the Bitburg trip was unpopular with the American people, the President had just won re-election by a stunning margin. So the question was how to persuade without rebuking. How to persuade without appearing strident. How to communicate the offensiveness of the Bitburg visit without closing off a last chance for the President to reverse himself gracefully. We all held out hope that the President might reconsider.

Reviewing a draft of Elie's remarks, one phrase struck me as uncharacteristically sharp. I offered as much. We discussed it. I think my recommendation was accepted. I'm not certain. Elie Wiesel, a writer of Nobel prize stature, was quite cious about the modest advice my congressional colleagues and I had to offer.

As I watched the ceremony the next day on television, it was clear Elie had found a voice loyal to his moral argument yet still appropriate to the occasion. That was not surprising. What was surprising was a call I received at 10:30 a.m., just ninety minutes before the networks began their live broadcast from the Roosevelt Room in the White House.

The call was from Marshall Breger, Special Assistant to the President for Public Liason.

I had known Marshall for several years in his role as liaison to the Jewish community. I respected his loyal service to the President, his country and the interests of the Jewish-American community. I knew this could not be an easy phone call for him.

Breger informed me that Chief of Staff Donald Regan and others had seen an advance copy of Wiesel's speech. Breger told me the White House was distressed. At best, the White House had hoped Wiesel would confine his discussion of Bitburg to a private meeting with the President. I already knew this. At worst, the White House hoped that Elie would moderate and shorten his public criticism.

Breger inquired if I would intercede with Wiesel.

The request was peculiar. By inclination and personal history, I was the most unlikely and unwilling of candidates for this assignment. I told Breger as much. Even if I had disagreed with the substance of what Elie intended to say, neither I nor even the President had the right to try to quiet him. But the point was, I agreed with Wiesel.

Bitburg was a mistake. The President's mistake. And Elie was the best person to tell the President so. Directly. Personally. In public.

It was now nearly 11:00 a.m. In less than forty-five minutes Wiesel would be sitting with the President. He needed to know of my conversation with Breger. Breger's request revealed the state of mind of the President's closest advisors, if not the President's. Breger also wanted Wiesel to know of his conversation with me.

I reached Elie just as he was leaving for the White House. My account of Breger's call seemed to mean little, if anything, to him. I was pleased.

Unfortunately, the President turned a deaf ear to the entreaties of Wiesel and others. The President called his decision "morally right." A visit to a concentration camp was added to his itinerary, as if the offer of a side-trip to a death camp could diminish the indignity of the Presidential visit to Bitburg.

I was very disturbed by the President's persistent failure to appreciate the feelings and memories that were being trampled on by his determination to visit the Bitburg cemetery. Reconciliation is a laudable goal. But it is a process. A process that is taking place over the years since those dreadfilled days. West Germany is one of our most important allies. It cannot be compressed into a day, or through one ceremony.

The alliance with West Germany is important to this country. But the President made a grievous error in thinking he could improve relations by paying tribute to those who systematically murdered the Jews of Europe. We must not only remember the Holocaust, but act in accordance with that memory. There can be no reconciliation with the evil that the Nazis represented.

That's why I decided to go to Germany the same weekend as the President. That's why I took the journey I believe President Reagan should have taken. My trip coincided exactly with the President's. My itinerary included two stops—Dachau and an American war cemetery in Belgium.

I stood quietly in that American military cemetery on an unlikely Sunday morning. The cemetery was near the small Belgian village of Henri-Chapelle.

Seven thousand nine hundred and eighty four Americans lay in that Belgian field. Most gave their lives repelling the Nazi counter offensive at the Battle of the Bulge. A few had died just days before the Reich's ultimate capitulation, even as the back of the Nazi Army was broken.

Though I had not known those buried before me, each one was my comrade. I served in Belgium at the time of the Nazi "breakthrough." Many of the men buried at the Henri-Chapelle would be my age today. The dates of their death, marked on each headstone, reminded me how young we were. Eighteen. Nineteen.

The variety of names provided showed we were truly an "American" army. Two hundred and ninety-seven of those buried at Henri-Chapelle called New Jersey their home. That Sunday, in front of each New Jerseyan's grave, the Army had placed a small American flag.

In one section of the cemetery, three brothers were buried side by side. Ninety-four of the headstones at Henri-Chapelle are marked "unknown." Thirty two pairs of brothers lay beside each other in that same field.

That Sunday I was alone at Henri-Chapelle. Just one hour later, only 70 miles away, the President visited Bitburg. In time and mileage, the President and I were only a small distance apart but in purpose and commitment we were on different planets. We were both there to commemorate the end of the World War II and the release of mankind from Satan's grip but how differently we viewed the way to accomplish it. Although the President could turn his back on 49 SS graves at Bitburg, he could not turn his back on history. My trip—a visit of personal remembrance—was intended to remind all who would know that political winds may change but they should wash away the demonic legacy of man's bestiality. That's why the day before the President went to Bitburg—and I to Henri-Chapelle—I went to Dachau to bear witness.

More than 30,000 perished at Dachau from starvation, illness, arbitrary executions and macabre "scientific" experiments. While the President's visit signified his desire to put these horrors behind him, I visited Dachau with three who could not.

Morris Glass, Polish born survivor of Dachau and Auschwitz, now a resident of my home state of New Jersey, travelled with me on the day before Bitburg. Mrs. Martin Neimoller, whose late husband, a Lutheran pastor, spent most of the war in Dachau for his outspoken resistance to the Nazis, met with us at the site. Since his liberation, he lived in the community adjacent to the death camp to serve "as a living reminder of what once happened here." And an old friend, Dr. Franklin Littell, a Temple University professor of religion whose specialty is the history of the church's behavior to the Nazis, also join us. The eves of those dark days is forever etched in his mind.

As I walked to one of the side gates, Morris Glass, now a 57-year-old clothing manufacturer was taken back in time to the day he entered Dachau as a terrified 17 year old. He had already lost his mother and two sisters in Auschwitz. Dachau would later claim his father.

"I never thought I'd leave this place alive," he told me as we walked through the gate. "You could smell the human flesh burning as you entered the gate. There's no mistaking that smell."

"There is no way in hell that a civilized human being can comprehend what it was like in these camps," Morris said.

But he tried to make me comprehend. He tried to make me see it through his eyes.

We looked at the cruel joke of a wrought iron sign above the gate, "Work makes you free." Nearby were the gallows where prisoners were hanged for the slightest infractions or whim of the jailers.

We paused to look up at the towers.

"It's hard to believe there are no guards in those towers. You got so used to that. They were there every minute, every hour. I can almost see them as I speak," Morris said.

We walked the paths for long periods without talking. Only our footsteps on the crushed gravel broke the silence. Occasionally, he'd stop and stare for a long moment. Near a barbed wire fence. By a small footbridge across a moat. By a woods. I left him to his own thoughts, though I felt dread at what they might have been.

We spent a large part of the day at Dachau, often walking past individuals and small groups from all over the world. Some would look up with tears, others would simply nod. No words were needed.

Toward the end of the day, I walked by myself into one of the standing barracks. Row after row of bunks atop bunks were in the rooms. I recalled Morris' descriptions of life inside these rooms. The dead being brought outside in the morning roll call so the living got an extra food ration that day. You dared not resist the beating because it would incite the guards to greater violence and certain death.

Death and brutality every day and night. Hell on earth. Here at Dachau. In this room. As I look down the hall of the room, I noticed a large group of school children, and I walked up to them to listen. They were German schoolchildren. While I couldn't understand the language of their teacher, I saw the students were comprehending the horror of the site.

I was saddened by the thought that while this handful of German schoolchildren were seeing this lesson in history, millions of their classmates across the country would see only President Reagan's visit to Bitburg.

Which lesson would be remembered?

(Frank Lautenberg is U.S. Senator from New Jersey.)

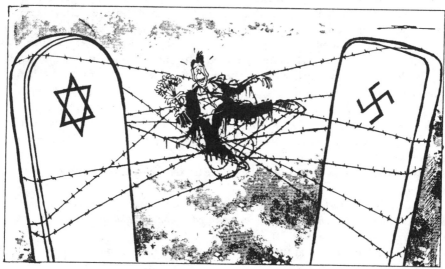

The Bitburg Affair
Special Contribution

By Arthur F. Burns

(At the time of the wreath-laying ceremony, Arthur F. Burns was United States Ambassador to the Federal Republic of Germany.)

The Bitburg affair came toward the end of my sojourn in Germany.

May 8 marked the 40th anniversary of the end of World War II in Europe. To Americans it was a time for commemorating the victory of the Allies, the end of Nazi tyranny, and the rebirth of freedom in Western Europe. The citizens of West Germany, however, inevitably had ambivalent feelings about the occasion. The end of bombings and the restoration of their freedom were indeed cause for rejoicing; but May 8 also evoked memories of the defeat of their country, its dismemberment, and the replacement of Nazi tyranny by Soviet tyranny for many millions of their brethren in the Russian zone. This was a time when the spiritual need of the German people was to be by themselves; it was a time to recall and come to terms with the past, a time for meditation, a time for prayer, a time for rededication to democracy, tolerance, and international good will. Eager though the German people might be for a visit by the American President, early May was hardly the best time for it. But it so happened that the German government had invited President Reagan; he had graciously accepted, and the German Chancellery and the White House were proceeding with plans for the visit.

Despite the sensitivity of the season, everything would probably have gone smoothly had it not been for the fact that soon after parts of the President's itinerary had become public, the discovery was made that some members of the Waffen-SS were buried at a military cemetery in Bitburg which the President was scheduled to visit. A violent storm of protest immediately broke out in our country and in much of the Western world against the President's participating in a ceremony that could be interpreted as honoring Hitler's elite troops—soldiers who had led the atrocities against the millions of Jews as well as others whom the Nazis marked for extermination. Here at home, war veterans of every faith, leaders of the Jewish community, members of Congress, journalists—all joined in urgent, at times tearful, appeals that the President drop the Bitburg visit.

In view of my responsibilities in Bonn, I of necessity had a part in this unfolding drama. It was as clear to me as to many others that the original decision to go to Bitburg was ill-conceived. I thoroughly understood and respected the feelings of moral outrage of the distinguished citizens who pleaded with the President to reconsider. But I also knew what some critics either did not know or did not understand sufficiently.

The German chancellor, Helmut Kohl, is among the staunchest friends the

United States has anywhere in the world. He was the architect as well as the manager of the President's visit. His political prestige was committed to it. Had he relieved the President of the commitment to go to Bitburg, his power to govern would certainly have been weakened and could have been destroyed. His political opponents were already charging him with bungling and being an American lackey. Moreover, while there were many Germans who doubted the wisdom of the Bitburg visit, there were many more who were puzzled or resentful of the pressure being put on the President not to go there. They did not feel about the Bitburg cemetery as did the more violent critics of the President outside their country. To be sure, the Germans of today generally despise Hitler's storm troopers; nevertheless, many could not overlook the fact that those buried at Bitburg were among their kith and kin, and that they died in defense of their country along with ordinary soldiers. Some who felt that way began to murmur that American Jews were exercising undue influence on world affairs, and a widely read German periodical actually published an unabashed antisemitic article on "Die Macht der Juden" (The Power of the Jews).

In these circumstances, it became clear to me that the American-German relationship would be seriously damaged if the President refrained from going to Bitburg, and that anti-semitism might well be reawakened here and there. On the positive side, I felt that America's reputation in Germany as well as elsewhere in the world required that our President remain true to his pledged word, and that it served American interests to have the Germans as well as other peoples abroad accept President Reagan as a steadfast leader whose devotion to international harmony was strong enough to overcome massive domestic pressure. I therefore never wavered in supporting the President's decision to go to Bitburg. The soundness of this judgment was later confirmed by the upsurge of good will among the German people towards the United States that was released by the President's visit. And in our country and elsewhere the furor about Bitburg soon died down — in part, I like to think, because of calmer understanding of the circumstances surrounding the President's visit.

The Bitburg affair contains an important lesson for all of us. What I learned from it, and what I believe everyone should learn from it, is that reconciliation between the German public and other peoples of the world is less complete than was generally supposed. Unhealed wounds remain a painful legacy of the Nazi era. "Shadows of the evil past"—as Helmut Schmidt put it—are still haunting us, and many years of sensitive moral and political education will be required before we Americans, the Germans, and other peoples reach the mutual understanding and the indestructible friendship to which a troubled world aspires. We cannot expect our German friends, especially those born during the past half century, to live with a sense of personal guilt on account of the Nazi crimes; and we certainly should avoid subjecting every German action to a special test of moral purity. Nevertheless, there is no way for the German nation to escape the historical burden of responsibility for the Holocaust. The German people cannot be proud of Beethoven and forget Hitler's crimes against humanity.

Part III

The Issues

While a conflict between absolute morality and political compromise may be the most important underlying theme in the planning of President Reagan's state visit to the Federal Republic of Germany in 1985, three other issues emerged as well in the seemingly endless round of speeches, debates, and articles:

1. Questions about the nature of the Waffen SS.
2. The state of American-German relations.
3. The nature of German relations both to Jews and to Israel.

Heinz Hohne, a German authority on the Waffen SS, reminds us that the Waffen SS was the military vanguard of the Nazi party, notorious of its vicious fighting that often bordered on the suicidal. As he leads us through the structure of this elite corps, he shows that in its conflict with the Wehrmacht — the German army, which controlled supply of men and equipment — the Waffen SS initiated a drafting policy that enabled it to enlist the Volksdeutsche members of the German nation, those of German descent that lived outside the Reich in places such as Czechoslovakia and the Balkans. Once that supply of thoroughly ideologically indoctrinated men was exhausted, it tapped into a reservoir of Belgian, Norwegian, Baltic, Ukrainian, and finally Russian natives willing to don the black uniforms with the lightning bars.

At issue, in honoring the military graves — which included those of Waffen SS members — was not the guilt of these particular soldiers, but the legitimization of the symbol of Nazism.

Young soldiers of the Waffen SS are the subject of the letter of Mr. Sattler. He describes his encounters with the young SS members during and after the war. The debate concerning the nature of this notorious band of killers is also dealt with in the pages of *Army: the Magazine of Landpower.* In its June 1985 issue one supporter suggested that the Waffen SS was but a mere military unit; the editor, however responds differently.

The rehabiltation of the 47 or 49 members in the Waffen SS graves in Bitburg also received the full attention of West Germany's right-wing press. Many took the opportunity to rewrite German history. For example, the weekly *Deutsche National Zeitung,* in a series of articles under the collective title of "The Lies of Bitburg," attempted to exonerate not only the soldiers buried in Bitburg, but the SS and the German Army as a whole.

Although it was not President Reagan's intention, his visit gave indirect encouragement to former Waffen SS members. While the West German and United States teams were skirting the issue of the Waffen SS graves, some former members of the division were scurrying around putting together reunions. (They could do this legally because they had been decriminilized in 1982.) In the first two weeks of May, several took place in the small town of Nesselwang, in the Hotel Krone, whose owner Rolf Bucheiser had served in the Waffen SS.

As the reunions were taking place, it was learned that Bucheiser was a member of the CDU — the party of Chancellor Kohl. This embarrassment prompted CDU State Chairman Edmund Stoiber to state, "Like other parties, we still have some weirdos in our ranks, and we openly regret this." The party decided to expel Bucheiser, but he didn't wait for them to act and promptly resigned.

Embarrassing discoveries became the theme of the entire Bitburg Affair. At the time the West German press was reporting the Waffen SS reunions, it was learned in the United

States that for ten years the U.S. 70th Infantry Division had been exchanging visits with the troops they had battled 40 years earlier. Once Bitburg appeared as an ugly word in the U.S. media, the U.S. soldiers' reunion was cancelled. (It has not been determined if this was a decision made on principle, or only for the year 1985).

The second issue, the nature of American-German relations as perceived by a conservative West German, is outlined in contributions by Dr. Alfred Dregger, chairman of the parliamentary group CDU/CSU. He is also the author of a letter to Senator Howard Metzenbaum and 53 other senators, included in this chapter as well, in which he responds to the Senate resolution discouraging the President from visiting Bitburg.

As he sees it, ideal relations would be characterized by two loyal respectful, receptive partners who consult each other on matters of common concern. In this regard, Dr. Dregger supported the recent U.S. initiative of stationing chemical weapons in West Germany and advocated the participation of West Germany in the Strategic Defense Initiative ("Star Wars"). In his letter to the senators supporting the Bitburg visit, he voices the opinion of an injured friend.

A problem of West German foreign policy toward the United States is balancing friendly alliance and loyalty with the growing demand for self-assertiveness and national identity. Then, too, West Germany has to maintain its own delicate internal balance. There is always a danger of West Germany appearing to certain political constituent, such as the Greens and the Communists, as a satellite of the United States.

The last chapter in this section deals with the intricate web of German-Jewish-Israeli relations as they were perceived by the leading participants at the two ceremonies. The issue of these relations, of course, is beyond the scope of this book, but its core elements can be touched upon.

An embracing of things Jewish can be observed in West German culture. For example, Israeli Ephraim Kishon is West Germany's leading humorist. His books, plays and movies depicting the life in Israel have become extremely popular. Also in the forefront of West German culture are such Israelis as Esther Opharim and Daliah Lavi, two top popular singers. Israeli theater, too, has recently taken hold in West Germany. One such play by Joshua Sobel, called *The Ghetto.* which is playing in Berlin and Duesseldorf, strikes right at the heart of a crucial dilemma of some Jews during the Holocaust; whether to die in a concentration camp, or face the compromising reality of working for Germans during World War II in order to survive.

The popularity of cultural things Jewish would suggest an end to anti-Semitism, but recently there has been a rise of political and traditional anti-Semitism in West Germany. Political anti-Semitism emanates from the extreme right and left wing of the West German political spectrum, while traitional anti-Semitism is just part of the mythology of the German middle class.

The Nazis developed the technique of controlling how people think and act not only by force but also by manipulating words and ideas. Some phrases of Nazi propaganda were totally dropped from usage after World War II; therefore, it was a shock when the German liberal and left-wing press in describing the June 1982 invasion of Lebanon used some of the old phrases for the first time since the Third Reich era: the Final Solution *(Endloesung)*, murder of nations *(Voelkermord)*, war of annihilation *(Vernichtungskrieg)*, Holocaust, genocide and other terms.

If this weren't enough of a reminder of the days of the Holocaust, it was compounded by Rudolf Augstein, the long-time editor of the influential weekly *Der Spiegel*, who wrote, "Just as Jews were victims of the Nazis, so the Arabs are now victims of the Israelis."

Continuing with this stirring up of dormant feelings, the same weekly later produced a photograph caption about bombings in Beirut: "Victims of massacre in Beirut: The German guards in Buchenwald and Treblinka also did not want to know what was going on!"

As if this weren't enough of a warning of a return to past sentiments, the Social Democratic Party's weekly, *Vorwaerts,* reported that " . . . now that the taboo period has ended, we Germans for the first time for several decades, can express our criticism of Israel." It was a not too subtle hint that former attitudes were once again acceptable. These waves of anti-Semitic rhetoric reached such a degree that former Chancellor Willy Brandt felt the need to express the warning "We shall carry our responsibility for Auschwitz not by pointing a finger at Beirut."

Another important word from the past was resurrected in the debate over Bitburg. The opponents of the critics of the visit stated that a process of *selektion* (selection) was being conducted in the examination of the contents of the graves in the military cemetery. This word had dropped out of usage after the Nuremburg trials, because it was the expression used during the Third Reich to describe the process of separating people fit for work in the crematoriums of the death camps.

A recent development in the German approach to the past was the passage of a law which prohibits the denial of the Holocaust. Initiated in 1982 by the SPD, this law was later broadened to include prohibiting denial of atrocities committed against Germans: the Soviet expulsion of 12 million Germans and the victimization of Germans who opposed Hitler. While these additions appear on the face of it to be well-reasoned in an antidefamation law, it should be noted that they were added to what had been a special law concerning Jews solely because of political pressure from the right.

The net result was to equate crimes of the Holocaust with other crimes. In this way, the history of the specific, legal, racial persecution of Jews in Nazi Germany is diluted. While this law has not yet been tested in the courts, it did bring out a general awareness of anti-Semitism in West Germany because debate over this issue in the Bundestag received wide press coverage.

Werner Nachmann, chairman of the Central Council of German Jews (see his story in Chapter 8), disagrees that there is a growing anti-Semitism in the Federal Republic. He calls attention to the fact that a German-Jewish commission was set up for the sole purpose of recommending new textbooks specifically concerning Jewish history. The toal of the commission is to place in the schools textbooks that emphasize Jews as having a history of their own.

The Jewish community does enjoy a close relationship with the leaders of the three major parties. Nachmann, for example, on August 12, 1985, received written congratulations on his 60th birthday and for his 16 years as chairman of the council, from President Richard von

Weizsacker; Chancellor Helmut Kohl; Foreign Minister Dietrich Genscher; the Minister of Justice Hans Engelhard; and Hans-Jochen Vogel, the parliamentary leader of the SPD.

However, there is a persistent traditional perception of Jews embedded in the West German culture. This comes up strikingly in the least expected places. For example, in January 1986 Count Wilderich von Spee, the mayor of the small town of Korschenbroich, said that "a few rich Jews should be slaughtered to balance the budget of this town." Initially, the townspeople were jubilant. Then, after the words of von Spee, the descendant of a German naval hero, sank in, a protest erupted and he was forced to resign. A civil case against him was dropped, with the approval of the small Jewish community, after he had donated 100,000 deutsche marks to a cancer hospital for children.

Yet in this discussion of Jews in Germany, one stark fact should be noted: In 1933 the ratio between Jews in Germany (in the area now defined as East and West) and Germans was 1:100. Today, there are 28,000 Jews only in West Germany, with a ratio of 1:2000!

Mr. Broder's thorough anlaysis illustrates the underpinnings of the middle-class culture that keeps medieval anti-Semitic notions alive about this miniscule group in West Germany.

"The Auschwitz Lie"

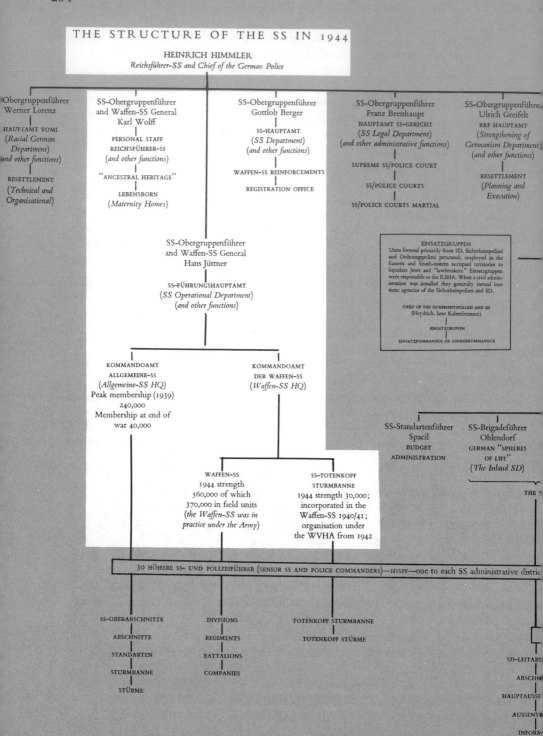

THE STRUCTURE OF THE SS IN 1944

HEINRICH HIMMLER
Reichsführer-SS and Chief of the German Police

Obergruppenführer
Werner Lorenz

HAUPTAMT VOMI
(Racial German Department)
(and other functions)

RESETTLEMENT
(Technical and Organisational)

SS–Obergruppenführer
and Waffen-SS General
Karl Wolff

PERSONAL STAFF
REICHSFÜHRER-SS
(and other functions)

"ANCESTRAL HERITAGE"

LEBENSBORN
(Maternity Homes)

SS–Obergruppenführer
Gottlob Berger

SS–HAUPTAMT
(SS Department)
(and other functions)

WAFFEN-SS REINFORCEMENTS

REGISTRATION OFFICE

SS–Obergruppenführer
Franz Breithaupt

HAUPTAMT SS-GERICHT
(SS Legal Department)
(and other administrative functions)

SUPREME SS/POLICE COURT

SS/POLICE COURTS

SS/POLICE COURTS MARTIAL

SS–Obergruppenführer
Ulrich Greifelt

RKF HAUPTAMT
(Strengthening of Germanism Department)
(and other functions)

RESETTLEMENT
(Planning and Execution)

SS–Obergruppenführer
and Waffen-SS General
Hans Jüttner

SS–FÜHRUNGSHAUPTAMT
(SS Operational Department)
(and other functions)

EINSATZGRUPPEN
Units formed primarily from SD, Sicherheitspolizei and Ordnungspolizei personnel; employed in the Eastern and South-eastern occupied territories to liquidate Jews and "lawbreakers." Einsatzgruppen were responsible to the RSHA. When a civil administration was installed they generally turned into static agencies of the Sicherheitspolizei and SD.

CHIEF OF THE SICHERHEITSPOLIZEI AND SD
(Heydrich, later Kaltenbrunner)

EINSATZGRUPPEN

EINSATZKOMMANDOS OR SONDERKOMMANDOS

KOMMANDOAMT
ALLGEMEINE-SS
(Allgemeine-SS HQ)
Peak membership (1939)
240,000
Membership at end of war 40,000

KOMMANDOAMT
DER WAFFEN-SS
(Waffen-SS HQ)

SS–Standartenführer
Spacil
BUDGET
ADMINISTRATION

SS–Brigadeführer
Ohlendorf
GERMAN "SPHERES OF LIFE"
(The Inland SD)

WAFFEN-SS
1944 strength
560,000 of which
370,000 in field units
(the Waffen-SS was in practice under the Army)

SS–TOTENKOPF
STURMBANNE
1944 strength 30,000;
incorporated in the
Waffen-SS 1940/41;
organisation under
the WVHA from 1942

THE S

30 HÖHERE SS- UND POLIZEIFÜHRER (SENIOR SS AND POLICE COMMANDERS)—HSSPF—one to each SS administrative distric

SS–OBERABSCHNITTE

ABSCHNITTE

STANDARTEN

STURMBANNE

STÜRME

DIVISIONS

REGIMENTS

BATTALIONS

COMPANIES

TOTENKOPF STURMBANNE

TOTENKOPF STÜRME

SD–LEITABS

ABSCHN

HAUPTAUSS

AUSSENS

INFORM

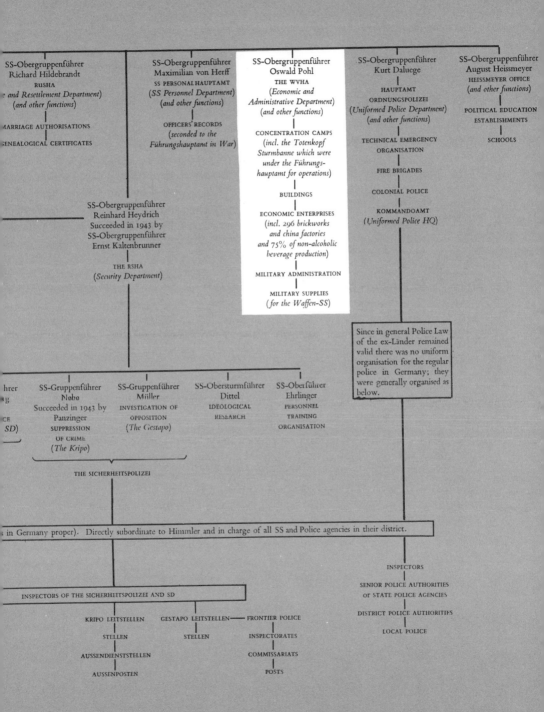

SS-Obergruppenführer
Richard Hildebrandt
RUSHA
e and Resettlement Department)
(and other functions)
|
MARRIAGE AUTHORISATIONS
|
GENEALOGICAL CERTIFICATES

SS-Obergruppenführer
Maximilian von Herff
SS PERSONAL HAUPTAMT
(SS Personnel Department)
(and other functions)
|
OFFICERS' RECORDS
*(seconded to the
Führungshauptamt in War)*

SS-Obergruppenführer
Oswald Pohl
THE WVHA
*(Economic and
Administrative Department)*
(and other functions)
|
CONCENTRATION CAMPS
*(incl. the Totenkopf
Sturmbanne which were
under the Führungs-
hauptamt for operations)*
|
BUILDINGS
|
ECONOMIC ENTERPRISES
*(incl. 296 brickworks
and china factories
and 75% of non-alcoholic
beverage production)*
|
MILITARY ADMINISTRATION
|
MILITARY SUPPLIES
(for the Waffen-SS)

SS-Obergruppenführer
Kurt Daluege
HAUPTAMT
ORDNUNGSPOLIZEI
(Uniformed Police Department)
(and other functions)
|
TECHNICAL EMERGENCY
ORGANISATION
|
FIRE BRIGADES
|
COLONIAL POLICE
|
KOMMANDOAMT
(Uniformed Police HQ)

SS-Obergruppenführer
August Heissmeyer
HEISSMEYER OFFICE
(and other functions)
|
POLITICAL EDUCATION
ESTABLISHMENTS
|
SCHOOLS

SS-Obergruppenführer
Reinhard Heydrich
Succeeded in 1943 by
SS-Obergruppenführer
Ernst Kaltenbrunner
|
THE RSHA
(Security Department)

Since in general Police Law
of the ex-Länder remained
valid there was no uniform
organisation for the regular
police in Germany; they
were generally organised as
below.

hrer
g
CE
SD)

SS-Gruppenführer
Nebe
Succeeded in 1943 by
Panzinger
SUPPRESSION
OF CRIME
(The Kripo)

SS-Gruppenführer
Müller
INVESTIGATION OF
OPPOSITION
(The Gestapo)

SS-Obersturmführer
Dittel
IDEOLOGICAL
RESEARCH

SS-Oberführer
Ehrlinger
PERSONNEL
TRAINING
ORGANISATION

THE SICHERHEITSPOLIZEI

s in Germany proper). Directly subordinate to Himmler and in charge of all SS and Police agencies in their district.

INSPECTORS
SENIOR POLICE AUTHORITIES
or STATE POLICE AGENCIES
DISTRICT POLICE AUTHORITIES
LOCAL POLICE

INSPECTORS OF THE SICHERHEITSPOLIZEI AND SD

KRIPO LEITSTELLEN
GESTAPO LEITSTELLEN — FRONTIER POLICE
STELLEN
STELLEN
INSPECTORATES
AUSSENDIENSTSTELLEN
COMMISSARIATS
AUSSENPOSTEN
POSTS

Chapter 12

The SS

There's Butcher Mentality
Der Spiegel, West Germany
April 29, 1985

By Heinz Höhne

To Rabbi Norman Lamm they are nothing but "Killer-Nazis", a visit to their graves is an "obscene scandal"; to Ronald Reagan, on the other hand, they are "teenagers who were drafted for military service", even victims of the Nazi dictatorship: 49 dead soldiers of the Waffen SS, buried in the military cemetery in Bitburg are upsetting the U.S. like no other issue of the German-American past.

"Waffen SS" became a verbal provocation to America's World War II veterans, Jews and politicians, since the American President took it into his mind to lay a wreath in Bitburg on the occasion of the 40th anniversary of Germany's capitulation — and of all places, he planned on doing so in the vicinity of those ominous 49 Nazi graves *(Newsweek)*.

Ever since then, no day goes by without the U.S. media enlightening the President in their own way on what kind of an infamous troop he intends to "honor" there. In the course of their campaign, the enlighteners tend to mix things up. They can hardly tell the difference between the SS and Waffen SS; the structures and tasks of the military SS are obviously an enigma to them.

Irony has it that it was mainly American historians who had started in the Sixties to revise the image of the murdering, berserk Waffen SS. It was not the least a result of the Nuremberg Crime-of-War trials, during which, in 1946, nearly all SS divisions, among them the Waffen SS, had been declared criminal organizations.

U.S. historians like George H. Stein and Robert Authur Gelwick would no longer accept the "prevailing myths about the Waffen SS", which to Gelwick, were a "bunch of onesided, highly selective facts, semi-facts, omissions, and deliberate distortions." The young scholars had, as Gelwick mockingly put it, "the interest or boldness" to do research on the actual life of the Waffen SS beyond all the attempts for justification made by their former relatives and the legends created by the Allied war propaganda.

Each of them did research on one section of the Waffen SS: Gelwick on the troops' personnel and organizational structure, his colleague James J. Weingartner on the operation of the *Leibstandarte-SS* Adolf Hitler (Lifeguards-SS Adolf Hitler), Charles W. Snyder on the Skull SS division, and Basil Dymytryshin on the Ukrainian SS troops.

Meanwhile, Professor Stein, an emigrant from Vienna, took to writing a history of the Waffen SS. His resume: "Without wanting to diminish the extent of the atrocious crimes committed by Himmler's followers, recent research brought to light that the SS was actually far more differentiated and complex than the monolithic organization of criminals who stood trial at the International Military Tribunal."

This is by no means to exonerate the Waffen SS of the war crimes committed (Stein: "Harsh, tough, ruthless, and capable of the most atrocious crimes"), but it illuminates that there existed more distinct differences between the troops and other SS organizations than has been previously assumed.

It was the only SS organization the leadership of which Himmler had to share right from the start with a non-SS institution, the army. In all basic questions concerning reserve troops and equipment, the Waffen SS depended on the army; only the army generals could decide on the troops' actions at the front, and they consolidated them so strongly that in the end, the Waffen SS seemed nothing but a fourth section of the army (which *de jure* they were not, however).

Already the data compiled by Stein and Gelwick make it evident that the Waffen SS differed from the rest of the SS. Of the 1.1. million men who went through the Waffen SS during World War II, only 300,000 were members of the Common SS (*Allgemeine* SS), the political core-organization of Himmler's SS empire.

There is also statistical evidence that Reagan's idea of "drafted" SS teenagers was, after all, not as unreasonable as it had seemed to the critics, because: most of the soldiers had become members of the Waffen SS in a most involuntary way — by draft notice or by orders of the army supreme command. The data:

- In 1942, a quarter of the men entering the Waffen SS consisted of drafted men,
- in 1943, they already made half of those who had entered,
- in 1944, more than sixty percent.

In addition, mass assignment of individual members of whole army units to the Waffen SS were made during the last two years of the war: 50,000 Air Force men, 5,000 Navy men, 10,000 men from the former Sevastopol Army, an additional 125,000 army and police men. Who was still a volunteer there?

This alone gives an idea of how this troop evades simple explanations. Too many factors going against the grain were involved: a troop, which was part of the SS, but not entirely; a national guard (*Staatstruppenpolizei*), trained for the racial and ideological war and yet longing to be a troop "like any other."

And then there were those many politically oscillating members of this troop: *Obersturmführer* Kurt Gerstein, who later informed the world of the Jews being murdered by the millions, *Sturmbannführer* Graf von Salviati, whom Himmler had shot on account of his participation in the conspiracy against Hitler, and the three Waffen SS generals who together with Rommel, refused to obey Hitler in the summer of 1944, and had wanted to abandon France with their troops without asking Hitler's permission.

This all had started after the Nazis' assumption of power in Germay, in spring 1933, when subaltern leaders of Himmler's Protection Squadron (*Schutzstaffel-SS*), thirsty for power, started forming combat troops equipped with small arms to terrorize political opponents, but also as a warning to NS internal competitors like the SA.

In the divisions and sub-divisions of the Common SS, so-called staff guards (*Stabswachen*) or special detachments were formed, each consisting of about 100 armed men. They assumed police functions and soon became the most brutal executors of the Nazi terror in eliminating political opponents (*Gleichschaltungsterror*).

Whenever a special detachment reached a certain number of members they called themselves Political Alert (*Politische Bereitschaft*). In most cases in their leaders, almost always former army officers, military ambitions were aroused then. The consequences: The Alerts were organized like regiments.

The most spectacular Alert was a unit formed by a shrewd-clever Bavarian by the name of Joseph ("Sepp") Dietrich, a former tank gunner, service-station attendant and factory steward, for Hitler's protection. He gathered 120 people around him and, on March 17, 1933, the "SS-Guard Berlin (*SS-Stabswache* Berlin) came into existence. Half a year later, they carried their master's name: "SS-Lifeguard Adolf Hitler" (*Leibstandarte — SS Adolf Hitler*).

On Bloody Sunday, June 30, 1934, the day when the SA-commander Ernst Röhm was shot, a squad of Dietrich's lifeguards shot six prominent SA leaders in the courtyard of the Munich-Stadelheim prison; in Berlin, lifeguard raiding squads chased NS opponents and executed them on the grounds of the Lichterfelde barracks.

The increasing influence of the Alerts — not least also the seizure of vast SA-ammunition depots — inspired Himmler to the plan of creating his own strike force, a rear-guard of an SS-controlled state security corps with whose help the SS-Reich's leader hoped to turn his organization into the true center of power of the NS-regime. Apart from the army, Himmler already had his hands in all important executive and repression organs: he was in control of the Gestapo, the criminal and regular police, he was the sole commander of the concentration camps, he had his own intelligence service at his disposal by means of the *SD-Sicherheitsdienst* (secret service).

Hitler was not happy with the military ambitions of his *Reichsheini,* even more so, as he was running risk of getting into trouble with the army generals who immediately sensed competition. Therefore, he approved of the formation of three armed SS regiments, on the one hand, while objecting to their formation into a division on the other.

All the same, this was the Waffen SS hour of birth, which was then called Reserve Troop (RT) (*Verfügungstruppe, VT*). Himmler avoided everything, however, which might raise the suspicion of wanting to create a second army. This he did not intend, anyhow: Each of Himmler's new orders underlined that the RT was merely in existence for the internal protection of the regime.

The RT was to be prepared for military action solely in case of a war. For this purpose Himmler, however, needed experienced professional soldiers, if the troop wanted to be taken seriously. The RT did not have them, so Himmler had to recruit them.

And many came: The retired General Paul Hausser, the former Major Felix Steiner, the Air Force Officer Wilhelm Bittrich — all of them deemed the Führer's Guard to offer them and their ideas career opportunities like no other troop. Hausser, and even more so Steiner, created a troop as never seen in Germany before. The privileges of birth and education had been done away with (also non-high school graduates could become officers), the mechanical drill of the parade ground was abolished, the training was reduced to small, mobile assault detachments equipped with battle dresses that were to be introduced to all armies later on.

This promoted an elite consciousness which was in stark contrast with the "reactionary" army and attracted a new stratum of young RT leaders: the young Nazis who had been pre-conditioned in the Hitler Youth movement and had been ideologically trained in the Junkerschools, were driven by an aimlessly dynamic "political soldiership", to whom the rationality of military pros of Haussner's and Steiner's kind was alien.

The changing of the troop with Nazi and SS-own ideology could not cover up the fact that two radically different leadership groups had come into being: on the one side, the elder, superior leaders, coming from the upper-middle class, sociologically nearly identical with the army generals, on the other, the younger leaders, lower in rank, members of the petty-bourgeoisie, whose entry into the officers' ranks had only just been opened to them by modernization propagated by National Socialism.

There was, however, a minimal consensus uniting both groups on the surface: the ambitious desire to turn the RT into an unsurpassable guard and elite troop. None of them was content with Himmler's ideas focusing still on being a state security corps. They wanted more: a status comparable to that of the army and to be recognized as an autonomous army. Himmler, weak in dealing with energetic subleaders, was increasingly pressured by his military men demanding of him not to put up any longer with the clandestine boycott policies of the army. It reduced any major RT recruitment and opposed better SS equipment.

When Himmler hesitated, the RT leaders took things into their own hands and adapted their troops' outfit to the army. Instead of the black uniforms, the RT introduced the grey one worn by the army troopers, in the summer of 1938, and also started wearing the epaulettes and stripes customary in the army. Earlier already, the troops' leaders had succeeded in having RT-service acknowledged as regular army service.

The attempt, however, to do away also with the SS-own unit concept and the serviced ranks failed on Himmler's veto. To the SS boss this was an alarming sign: Leading RT men obviously harbored the idea of drifting away from the rest of the SS. Hitler's war ruined Himmler's concept for good, the RT was now needed as a military troop, only. The RT troops, meanwhile grown into four regiments with 18,000 men, were put into action as early as the invasion of Poland: In the battle of Bzura and in the thrusts on Modlin and Lemberg (Lodz).

The army, to be sure, was not impressed by their activities. The RT had heavier losses than similar units in the army, their officers had not matched for the demands of complicated troop leadership.

The RT leaders saw only one alternative: The troop was to form into a division with heavier arms and more troops. This, however, was counteracted by the army, which still hampered RT recruitment of volunteers and released only as many army inductees as they deemed necessary for the 18,000 men troop. But where to get new men from?

Just then, a cleaver Swabian by the name of Gottlob Berger, SS headquarter superior, had a seemingly brilliant idea. If the Führer , suggested Berger, should agree on the Skull Division's and the police's change of assignment to the RT— as had been contemplated earlier— Himmler would have four divisions in no time. The RT leaders agreed enthusiastically.

This was the fatal step throwing the RT in with the world of political crime. Because: The Skull Divisions under the leadership of the Röhm-murderer Theodor Eycke, serving as concentration camp guards which had trained them into systematic dehumanization after years of service in the camps, introduced the poison of barbarian prisoners' mistreatment into the troop, which it would never quite be able to free itself from.

It went almost unnoticed, when 100,000 men of the Waffen SS, as it was called now, set out on their West campaign of 1940 and stormed through Holland, Belgium, and France—fanatical, irresistible and without any concern for their own losses and driven by an aggressiveness, which set Himmler's divisions apart from all other units of the Germany army. Now the results of what they had learned at the Junkerschools took effect: that to inflict death and to take death was the chief command in battle.

In horror, the conservative military men watched this total "disintegration of emotional and rational restraints of action" (as the scholar of contemporary history, Bernd Wegner put it) take place. When Eycke reported to General Hoepner that the attack commands had been carried out and human lives had not been spared, the general broke out saying, "That is a butcher's mentality!"

And the "butcher's" men acted accordingly: On May 27, 1940, Obersturmführer Fritz Knochlein, commander-in-chief of the Skull Division, had 100 British prisoners shot near Le Paradis at the La-Bassee Canal, as revenge for their persistent resistance they had put up previously—the first major crime committed by the Waffen SS, which was to be followed by many others.

The battle-happy SS generals had no eye for such things (they obstructed the court-martial investigations against Knochlein), their fixation was on the expansion and strengthening of their divisions. Again and again, they urged the recruiting officer Berger to supply the Waffen SS with new men. The latter incessantly chased for SS recruits: He enlisted in West and North Europe, where many were eager not to miss their connection with the new masters, he secured ways to recruit the hundreds of thousands of Germans on the Balkan (*Volksdeutsche*—ethnic Germans), later, he even recruited Slavs, defamed by Himmler's "sub-human" agitation.

In the end, they turned out to be "Europe's largest multinational army ever to fight under any flag," as Stein put it. It was the first German army with an overwhelming majority of foreign citizens: 400,000 Reich's Germans stood side by side with 410,000 aliens and 310,00 ethnic Germans who were not citizens.

The Waffen SS generals were so immersed in expanding their troops that they hardly noticed how deeply Himmler kept entangling them in the murderous underworld of his empire. With a seemingly insignificant decree, he turned the Waffen SS into involuntary accomplices of the concentration camp guards.

On April 22, 1941, Himmler had the SS headquarters enlist 179 SS units and departments, which, from then on, were to be integral parts of the Waffen SS, among them also the concentration camps, their administrations and guards. From then on, the concentration camp guards were also regarded as Waffen SS members.

They had the same paybooks and uniforms as the Waffen SS soldiers proper.

The headquarters were in charge of the concentration camp guards' equipment with arms and their military training; for a short period of time even the concentration camp inspection was part of it, if only formally.

The leaders of the Waffen SS may have believed that the troop's discipline and ethnics would be strong enough to keep a distance from Himmler's destruction apparatus. They never succeeded, however, in dissociating from it clearly: The Waffen SS had to turn over units to the murdering strike forces and some of their reserve units participated in the most atrocious SS activities, such as the oppression of the Warsaw ghetto uprising.

Not before the Waffen SS became the German infantry's fire-brigade in the East during the crises of war with Russia coming to the rescue of the German army at bay, did their senior leaders achieve to win a certain distance from the SS, even more so, because their bravura was now even admiringly acknowledged by the in-fantry's generals. General Wöhler fell into raptures, "Like a rock in the infantry." The Waffen SS stood up against the enemy with "unswerving combat power."

This encouraged the SS generals to oppose Himmler and his policies more and more frequently. Some of them were declared opponents of the "subhuman-race" ideology and showed complete discontentment when Hitler did not grant the West European SS legionnaire more autonomy in their occupied countries.

Nobody articulated this discontentment more distinctly than General Haus-ser, who refused to comply to Hitler's command to hold out during the battles at Kharkov, in February 1943. Instead of defending the city "to the last bullet", he retreated with his tank corps and then coolly reported his disobedience to the "Führer's headquarters, prompting many army officers to scold him for his boldness."

Felix Steiner also criticized the Führer. One of the most resolute anti-Hitler conspirators, Fritz-Dietlof von der Schulenberg, initiated the SS general in the *coup d'etat* planned by his friends, upon which Steiner had a map exercise in the staff of his III (Teutonic) Tank Division as to how the Führer's headquarters could be raided. Himmler had known all along, "Steiner, you are my most disobedient general!"

However brave the troop, or self-confident their generals—the barbarian methods employed by "a minority in the Waffen SS" (according to Stein) in treat-ing their prisoners of war and civilians, spoiled any of their chances to become soldiers 'like any others.' The traces of offenses and atrocities the Waffen SS left be-hind on all battlefields were much too obvious. Any "national comrade" knew that in 1942. A secret service report noted the public opinion, "The Waffen SS was the most radical troop, which did not even take prisoners, but eliminated every oppo-nent completely."

Certainly, crimes of war were committed on all sides, not least in the ranks of the Red Army, which on occasions murdered captured Germans by the dozens. It remains remarkable, however, that those crimes the Waffen SS has been justly charged with were practically unknown in the German army.

In most cases they were committed by fanaticized young officers, who went berserk in situations of crises and did not have the control mechanism that de terred the senior officers. Knochlein, the executor of Le Paradis, was one of them and also *Sturmbannführer* Dickmann, the man who commanded one of the most horrid crimes: the murder of the entire population of the French village Oradour-sur-Glane, in June 1944.

The gunners of the SS Tank-Division Hitler Youth were also young, those who mowed down 64 allied prisoners of war in Normandy, and the executors, whom 71 captured Americans fell prey to in the Ardennes Battle were just slightly older—a long shadow falling on the graves at Bitburg.

(Translated by Renate Steinchen)

(Heinz Höhne is the editor of Der Spiegel, *a leading West German weekly magazine, and the author of the definitive work* The Order of the SS Death's Heads: The Story of Hitler's SS.)

SS Veterans Feel 'Rehabilitated' by Reagan Visit

The New York Times
May 3, 1985

By John Tagliabue

NESSELWANG, WEST GERMANY — They stood relaxed, shaking hands, introducing wives, these men of Germany's dark past, looking forward to a three-day meeting that began here today.

The Hotel Krone, in this Swabian ski resort, where about 250 veterans of the Waffen SS Death's Head Division have gathered, is closed to outsiders. But the veterans, in the loden coats of postwar German prosperity, are more relaxed, less defensive.

Long the pariahs of West German society, for their record of atrocity and brutality during the Third Reich, this year they are returning reporters' telephone calls, and talking, quietly, assuredly, over beer, in the bars of the Nesselwang hotels where they flee unusual May snowfalls.

Conversations with the veterans leave no doubt that President Reagan's insistence on going to Bitburg, despite an outcry from American veterans' groups and Jewish organizations, has made them feel better about their role in history.

'A Real Straight Guy'

"We were soldiers like all the soldiers in the war, and I think that's what the President is trying to say," said Gerd Höfer, a 77-year-old SS veteran and a native of Gratz in Austria. "You have to congratulate your President. When he says yes, he means yes."

In response to a reporters' question about whether he felt rehabilitated by the President's gesture, Johan Rosenberg, a 63-year-old Death's Head veteran, said, "I can only say he is a real straight guy."

"It took a long time," he went on, "but this shows we were soldiers, just like the others. I never committed a war crime, and I don't know anyone who did. We didn't have time for that sort of thing. Our guys were disciplined, and we were too busy fighting."

Officials with the Reagan party in Bonn, asked to respond to the SS veterans' remarks, did not return telephone calls from reporters.

The veterans insist the units of the Waffen SS were fighting units, distinct from the uniformed bands that ran Nazi Germany's extermination camps.

According to George H. Stein, an American historian and author of the book *The Waffen SS: Hitler's Elite Guard at War,* the Death's Head Division was set up as a combat force in 1939 around a group of about 6,500 former concentration camp guards. Its commander until his death in 1943 was Theodor Eicke, who headed the entire concentration camp system starting in 1934.

Besides their fierce fighting at the front, Death's head soldiers were particularly involved in hunting partisans in Eastern Europe, in campaigns that often led to the killing of large numbers of civilians.

Asked about these charges, Mr. Rosenberg replied: "Sure, there was maybe one in a thousand guys who did something wrong. But show me the army where that doesn't happen. Show me the division records of the Americans, the French or the Russians — and I mean the real records. No one ever said war was nice."

Hitler set up the SS — for *Schutzstaffel,* or guard unit — in the 1920's as a ragtag bodyguard to protect Nazi leaders in secret marches and sometimes turbulent demonstrations. Its real importance, however, began in 1929 with the appointment of Heinrich Himmler, then 28 years old, as its leader.

Under Himmler the SS grew rapidly, assuming many police functions and gaining a reputation for ruthlessness. With the outbreak of World War II, its combat arm, the Waffen SS, was forged into crack tank and infantry divisions.

Trained More Intensely

Though the Waffen SS was subject to the Wehrmacht command, making it a de facto unit of the army, its soldiers were trained more intensely, had superior equipment, including the most modern tanks and other vehicles, and were subjected to more intense political and ideological indoctrination. Until 1943 its divisions consisted only of volunteers. After that, because of the high attrition rate, its members were conscripted.

The West German Government pays the SS veterans the pensions due their ranks, and took many of their number into the armed forces when West Germany rearmed in the 1950's. Veterans' contributions to the Federal Association of Former Soldiers of the Waffen SS, which was founded in 1966 as an umbrella organization, are tax deductible.

But civil rights groups and Jewish organization, citing both the Nuremberg war crimes tribunal, which branded the SS a "criminal organization," and subsequent West German legislation banning the use of signs and symbols relating to Nazism, have hounded the veterans, making their annual gatherings the targets of violent demonstrations in recent years.

The meeting of the Death's Head Division, which ends on Sunday, the day Mr. Reagan visits Bitburg, will be followed by a comparable gathering of veterans from the First SS Panzers Corps, consisting of the Adolf Hitler Bodyguard and the 12th SS Panzer Division, the Hitler Youth, on May 11-12.

Condemned by Catholic Pastor

The town council of Nesselwang, population 3,000, has distanced itself from the meetings; the town's Catholic priest has condemned them and refused to allow the veterans to lay a wreath at a local cemetery. A local political action group has sprung up to oppose the gatherings, and labor unions, with the support of several political groupings, plan a protest rally in the town.

This enraged the men from the old soldiers' organization, who sipped their beers and accused the same circles who create resistance in Nesselwang of seeking to prevent the Bitburg ceremony.

"The Zionists stop at nothing," Mr. Höfer said, "But the President is an honest man. He made his decision, and he sticks to it."

There were anecdotes about the Führer, usually in a tone of subdued reverence. "My proudest moment as an SS man," Mr. Höfer related, "was when I stood guard outside his hotel room in Leipzig in 1941."

"He was such a modest man," he said, with a slight, fleeting modulation in tone. "There were six of us. He would come out, take you by the arm, chat with you."

'It Was an Honor'

By contrast the veterans bitterly deny and feel mildly insulted by the contention of the Bonn Government that, although the Waffen SS was a volunteer unit until 1943, many young men, including perhaps those SS soldiers buried in Bitburg, were later conscripted against their will.

According to Mr. Rosenberg, who said he enlisted right after high school, "That is nonsense, pure nonsense. No one was forced into the SS. Kids were proud to get in, it was an honor."

In the living room of his home in Kaufbeuren, a 20-minute drive from Nesselwang, where he has begun receiving American reporters and television teams, Maj. Gen. Otto Ernst Remer, a 73-year-old former Waffen SS officer who is not attending the Nesselwang gatherings, agreed with his comrades. "It was high time," he said, referring to the President's visit to Bitburg. "After all we are sitting in one boat, in NATO."

General Remer was highly decorated for his role as a commander of the Berlin guard regiment that held to Hitler and rounded up the disgruntled Wehrmacht officers who staged an unsuccessful bomb attempt on Hitler's life on July 20, 1944.

"It's hardly to the President's merit" he went on, inserting a note of mild criticism. "For us, this was the most natural thing in the world."

Copyright © 1985 by The New York Times Company. Reprinted by permission.

The 'Cowardly' Executioner: On Disobedience in the SS
Patterns of Prejudice
May 6, 1985

By Daniel Goldhagen

The systematic extermination of European Jewry began in June 1941 with the German onslaught against the Soviet Union. The agents of destruction were the Einsatzgruppen — mobile killing squads commissioned specifically for the task. The Einsatzgruppen, consisting of only 3,000 men, killed approximately one million Jews, dispatching most of them by machine-gun fire into mass graves.[1] Some of the killers were SS men. The majority, however, were not.[2] Many were regular policemen, who had been drafted into the Einsatzgruppen without special training or indoctrination, ignorant of the task before them.[3] Nevertheless, when ordered to shoot defenseless, unarmed people *en masse*, they complied.

Many theories and numerous volumes have tried to explain what could have impelled men to slaughter thousands of harmless people. Though this question is urgent, I will not address it here directly. Instead, I wish to focus on the neglected attendant question of what happened to those who decided not to participate in mass murder, and to tell the story of one man who was unwilling to continue killing Jews. An understanding of the circumstances in which SS men could avoid killing, and of the men who actually did so, might provide some insight into the minds that made such slaughter possible.

There is a popular misconception that if an SS man refused to carry out an order to kill Jews, he would himself be killed. There are three reasons for this widespread belief. First, defendants in postwar trials contended repeatedly and emphatically that to assert one's unwillingness to comply with an order to kill Jews was to pronounce one's own death sentence. Second, a belief in the severity, brutality and fanaticism of the SS has now become part of our lore. It is thus axiomatic to us that the punishment for a recalcitrant SS man would have been harsh and merciless.[4] Third, we do not want to accept that so many men could have participated in mass murder unless forced to do so. For, though the killers are considered to have been cruel and unfeeling, we find it hard to believe that every killer was a moral beast, and we cling to the hope that only the evil power of the Nazi regime could have forced innocent subjects to perpetrate such crimes.

But such beliefs are mistaken. In light of the assertions of postwar trial defendants, it is in itself telling that there are only 14 cases when it has been claimed that the punishment for refusing to carry out an execution order (not only of Jews) was either death (9 cases), imprisonment in a concentration camp (4 cases) or transfer to a military penal unit (1 case). Moreover, not one of these cases has been able to withstand systematic scrutiny. Two separate comprehensive studies of the possibility of an SS man refusing execution orders have each demonstrated these claims to be false.[5] Herbert Jäger, the author of one of the studies, states unequivocally: 'In no case could it be proven that the refusal to kill resulted in an injury to life and limb'.[6]

This conclusion is all the more noteworthy because of the pains taken to unearth such cases. The defense attorneys at the Nuremberg trials were allowed into the Allied internment camps to question SS prisoners so that they would have every opportunity to substantiate their defense claims. Had any German been so punished for disobeying an order to kill Jews, then the SS would have publicized his fate among the killers as an example of what would befall others who disobeyed orders. After the war, any interned SS man knowing of such a case would naturally have come forth at Nuremberg because his knowledge would have helped defend his comrades and, potentially, himself. Despite the defense attorneys' strenuous efforts, they emerged empty-handed, unable to produce even one example of a man executed or sent to a concentration camp for not obeying an order to kill Jews.[7] The captured records of the SS and police courts also show no record of this ever happening, or even the slightest hint that such punishment was possible.[8]

It is also unlikely that SS field commanders ordered on-the-spot executions of disobedient subordinates. Himmler himself demanded that he review every death sentence passed by the SS and police courts because he was hesitant to kill SS men and wanted to ensure that those condemned to death had committed sufficiently serious crimes; it is therefore improbable that he would have authorized field commanders to order summary executions unless extraordinary conditions existed. Without Himmler's approval, a commander's execution of a soldier for disobedience would in itself have constituted an act of insubordination. There is no evidence that such executions ever occurred.[9]

Because the records of the SS and police courts show that no one was ever executed or sent to a concentration camp for refusing to kill Jews, because Himmler's personal role in confirming death sentences for SS men precluded the possibility of summary executions and, most of all, because no one has ever produced even one verified case of a man being killed or sent to a concentration camp for not carrying out an execution order, we can only conclude that the likelihood of any SS man ever having suffered such punishment for refusing to kill Jews is small. The abundance and strength of the evidence, in fact, justify the belief that it never happened.

Unable to produce for the courts even one example to substantiate their assertions, many of the killers resorted to the argument that, regardless of the true state of affairs, they had sincerely believed that refusing to carry out an execution order was suicidal, and that they had simply acted on this belief; if their knowledge had been faulty, they were not to blame.[10]

This postwar assertion is also false because it was well-known among the executioners that they were permitted to transfer from their killing units—that they could stop killing. There was a written order by Himmler which allowed all members of the Einsatzgruppen who so wished to transfer to the front. Himmler issued this order on the request of the Einsatzgruppen officers, who presumably believed that only those who were dedicated to the task should be killing Jews.[11]

There were, moreover, instances when people requested transfers from the Einsatzgruppen so that they would not have to continue killing and lived on to tell the story. Franz Six, the leader of Einsatzgruppen B's Advance Commando Moscow, described such instances while testifying at Eichmann's trial:[12]

During the war one could at least attempt to be transferred from an Einsatzgruppe. . . . There were certainly instances, in which the transfer from an Einsatzgruppe brought with it disadvantages. I cannot now, however, remember any individual instances. In any case no one was on such an account shot, as far as I know.

According to a lieutenant, attached to Einsatzgruppe D as an adjutant, transfers arising from the refusal to carry out orders to kill Jews occurred frequently in the Einsatzgruppen. He stated 'that repeatedly within Einsatzgruppe D people refused to participate in executions, because they were incapable of doing so. . . .' The lieutenant further indicated that the executioners knew they could transfer because the 'commanding officer himself announced to the Gruppe that particular individuals were unfit for the performance of such tasks and therefore were to be released.'[13]

The commander of Einsatzgruppe D, Colonel Otto Ohlendorf, substantiated this during his trial at Nuremberg in 1947. When Ohlendorf discerned that one of his men opposed the order to kill Jews, he did not force the man to act against his conscience: 'I had sufficient occasion to see how many men of my Gruppe did not agree to this order in their inner opinion. Thus, I forbade the participation in these executions on the part of some of these men and I sent some back to Germany.'[14] One man who obtained such a transfer from Ohlendorf was a technical sergeant named Martin Mundschütz.[15]

The case of Martin Mundschütz

Mundschütz was born on 9 November 1909 near Innsbruck in a small town named Guttaring. He moved to Innsbruck, where he passed his adolescence and became a mechanic. After spending two years as a railway construction worker, he lost his job during the depression in 1929. As Mundschütz put it, he had the good luck to enter the police force in 1930, serving as a patrolman for four years. In 1934 he was transferred to the criminal police, where he remained until he joined the Einsatzgruppen in 1941 at the age of thirty-one. He was never active politically because he thought politics inappropriate for a policeman. It is likely that Mundschütz was among the many who were drafted into the Einsatzgruppen. Though clothed in an SS uniform and carrying an SS rank, he never truly became an SS man; his status and that of all draftees as members of the SS was temporary, lasting only for the duration of their duty in the Soviet Union. Upon completion of their task, their membership came to an end. Mundschütz had, however, applied to the SS on his own in 1940. When he entered the Einsatzgruppen his application had not yet been acted upon; Mundschütz was still an ordinary policeman.

Less than three months after their killing operation began, Mundschütz wrote to Ohlendorf to explain his embarrassing behaviour during the recent meeting between them. He described the effect that the killings had on him, and he requested a transfer. Mundschütz's letter, the letter of a whimpering SS man, is such a rare document that it deserves to be quoted in full:

What I am unable to say in words, because my voice failed me, I now want to convey to you by these lines, Herr Standartenführer [Colonel].

Standartenführer, you are under the assumption that I have succumbed to a spell of weakness which will pass again without injury. Weakness was not the cause of my regrettably unmanly behaviour towards you on the occasion of our discussion, rather my nerves snapped. They snapped only as a result of the nervous breakdown of three weeks ago, as a result of which visions have haunted me day and night, driving me to the verge of madness. I have partly overcome these visions, but I find that they had bereft me totally of all my energy and that I can no longer control my will. I am no longer able to contain my tears; I flee into doorways when I am in the street and I slip under the covers when I am in my room.

I am supposed to drive out to the villages as a buyer. Please, spare me, so that before my travelling companions and before other people I should not present the unsightly spectacle of a whining soldier.

Until now I have been able to conceal my condition from my room-mates. But since the crying fits recur with increasing frequency, I fear for a new nervous breakdown.

Standartenführer, if you consider it absolutely necessary to send me from here only when my condition becomes so obvious that my name is on everyone's lips, then please at least put me in a room where I can be alone or, still better, send me to the military hospital.

If you, Herr Standartenführer, however, have an understanding and a heart for one of your subordinates, who wants to sacrifice himself to the very last for the cause of Germany, but who does not want to present the spectacle of one who is said to have succumbed to cowardice, then please remove me from this environment. I will thankfully return when recovered, but please allow me to leave before I succumb to the same melancholia that afflicts my mother.

According to his letter Mundschütz asked for a transfer not only for his sake but also for comrades and for Germany. He did not want to shame his fellow killers or disgrace Germany's image, and he declared his willingness to do anything his country required of him. His incapacity to continue killing resulted, as he portrayed it, not from principled disapproval, but from an emotional reaction to the act that rendered him psychologically unfit for further duty. He closed his letter with the plea that Ohlendorf grant him a transfer, lest he fall victim to the hereditary condition that afflicted his mother. Mundschütz, shamed, had to flee the duty he wished he were strong enough to perform.

Mundschütz also communicated his troubles to his immediate superior, Gustav Nosske, the leader of Einsatzkommando 12, which was one of the four commando units composing Einsatzgruppe D under Ohlendorf's command. Nosske, convinced that Mundschütz affliction was real and serious, wrote to Ohlendorf describing Mundschütz's ordeal and suggesting that he be transferred:

Einsatzkommando 12 member, SS Technical Sergeant Martin Mundschütz, born, 9 November 1909, home station — the office of the criminal police in Innsbruck, is not fit for further action. Mundschütz has recently taken part in various executions, which had the effect of producing in him hallucinations. At night he has left his quarters, wandered around for a long time, and then announced to his group leader that he could not find the people who had allegedly escaped him during the execution. Although he is no longer assigned to executions and is employed in a way that appears more suitable, his hysterical attacks, which are not infrequently accompanied by crying fits, recur constantly. A thorough examination by the Einsatzgruppe's physician has confirmed his unfitness for action. Mundschütz's heredity is deeply marred by a streak of illness [*erblich schwer belastet*]. According to expert medical opinion there exists the danger that without the proper measures he will share in the fate of his deranged mother [*in Schwermut umnachteten Mutter*].

I request, therefore, that Mundschütz be discharged from the Einsatzgruppe and transferred to the RSHA for further determination.

Nosske described Mundschütz's mother's illness in more severe terms than Mundschütz had to Ohlendorf. While in Mundschütz's letter she merely suffered from depression, Nosske was conveying the belief, certainly originating with Mundschütz, that she was also deranged. Nosske believed that unless Ohlendorf granted Mundschütz a transfer, Mundschütz might well fall prey to his diseased inheritance.

After receiving these two letters Ohlendorf wrote to the RSHA, informing it of Mundschütz's transfer and recommending for him a stay in an SS nerve sanatorium:

I have spoken with M. myself and tried to straighten him out. As an answer, I have received from him the enclosed letter, whose original I am submitting with the personnel file. According to it, it seems all in all that a hereditary disposition of Mundschütz has asserted itself. Mundschütz is no longer fit for action. I therefore have transferred him to the rear and request that all formalities necessary for his return be completed. According to the opinion of the unit's doctor, a transfer to the SS sanatorium for the mentally ill in Munich appears necessary.

This series of letters is truly remarkable. A member of the infamous mobile killing squads, the Einsatzgruppen, appealed to the compassion of SS officers by asking that the be permitted to forsake his duty because he was a coward. The SS officers did not shoot or start proceedings against the coward who disgraced Germany's name. Instead, solicitous of their subordinate's health, they decided to relive him of his burden. The man who would not, or could not continue killing was sent back to Germany for rest and recuperation.

When asked to discuss this incident at a trial of some Einsatzgruppen officers in 1970, Mundschütz stated in documents submitted to the court[16] that he had only simulated a nervous breakdown in order to acquire a transfer from the Einsatzgruppen. He also said that the story of his mother's depression was an embellishment upon the truth:[17] 'My mother was somewhat depressed. I used this circumstance to corroborate my simulation. In my family there is, however, no indication of the existence of mental illness. If I did maintain it at the time, it was only to secure the desired discharge from the commando.'

In light of Mundschütz's postwar testimony, his appeal to be transferred could be read as shrewd stratagem designed in full awareness of the Nazis' and, in particular, Ohlendorf's racial-biological deterministic beliefs. Mundschütz knew that, by citing a hereditary infirmity, he could convince Ohlendorf both that his incapacitation was real and enduring, and that it was beyond his control, thereby absolving him of culpability.

The contents of Mundschütz's SS personnel file suggest that he probably did exaggerate the nature of his mother's illness. The SS application questionnaire, which Mundschütz completed in 1940, asked only two questions about the applicant's mother if she were alive: what her age was and whether she had survived any sicknesses. Replying to the latter question in 1940 Mundschütz neglected to mention his mother's 'derangement and depression.' Although this in itself hardly proves that Mundschütz later fabricated his mother's illness, findings of the State Health Office support the notion that it was invented. In response to an SS Race and Resettlement Office inquiry in 1943 about genetic defects of Mundschütz and his family, the State Health Office wrote, 'In regard to his heredity and health nothing unfavourable has hitherto become known.'

Mundschütz's contention that he simulated a nervous breakdown is also consistent with the swiftness of his recovery from what was supposed to be a deeply distressed condition. A Dr. Gasser of the State Criminal Police in Innsbruck wrote to the RSHA on 7 November 1941 that Mundschütz's physician, Dr. Finger, had declared him capable of resuming work on 28 October, only eighteen days after his return to Innsbruck. Pronounced fit by this recommendation, Mundschütz resumed his post in the criminal police on the following day, 29 October. Gasser further stated that Mundschütz's resumption of his post seemed to have facilitated his recovery. Based on his own observations and on Dr. Finger's counsel that Mundschütz would do well under ambulatory care, Gasser recommended that Mundschütz not be sent to the SS nerve-sanatorium as Ohlendorf had suggested. The next day, 8 November 1941, Dr. Finger declared Mundschütz fully recovered: 'Herr Mundschütz was today examined anew and is entirely fit for work. A commitment for the purpose of treatment and observation is no longer necessary, however, it is still necessary that he remain to serve in his home town for a long time.'

Despite such evidence to support Mundschütz's postwar declarations, we should still be suspicious of them. By maintaining that he purposely extricated himself from the Einsatzgruppen, he portrayed himself in the light of an opponent of the killings, and thus lent himself a moral aura. He said that, as a Catholic, he was revolted by what he saw.[18] This contradicts his claim to Ohlendorf, that he was simply too cowardly to perform his duty, that he had to ask reluctantly for his own removal not because of moral conviction, but in spite of it. Because Mundschütz's postwar statements exculpate him and depict him in a vastly more favourable light than does his explanation to Ohlendorf, we should view his postwar assertions with circumspection and consider a possible alternative interpretation of the events.

Mundschütz may have lied to Nosske and Ohlendorf in claiming that his mother's supposed derangement was the origin of his reactions to the killings and that his own derangement was its likely consequence. Nevertheless, he still might have had a nervous breakdown. Mundschütz's statements to the court demonstrate that he would be a crafty strategist in pursuit of his goal; they illustrate that his declaration to his superiors about his mother's health was a cleverly composed half-truth. In the same way, his appeal to be transferred might have been a mixture of truth and conscious, purposeful prevarication. Contrary to his postwar statements, Mundschütz may have actually had a nervous breakdown and then portrayed it in the way most propitious to obtaining a transfer.

In a sense, however, it is immaterial whether Mundschütz feigned a nervous breakdown because of a moral opposition to the extermination of the Jews, or whether he really had one. In either case, there is no doubt that he suffered deep mental and emotional anguish over the killings, and that he put on a charade in order to extricate himself from an operation he could no longer genuinely endure. With regard to the question of whether the killers could influence their own fate, what matters is that when Mundschütz expressed his unwillingness to continue killing, he did escape his appointed duty.

But that is not all that matters. Mundschütz's motives are important. Our understanding of his act and, in the end, our judgement of it, will differ if he feigned a nervous breakdown because he opposed the extermination of the Jews out of principle, or if he simply found the strain of killing too great to bear. Why was Mundschütz unwilling to continue killing? And how did he view his task and Nazism? An analysis of how the SS treated his membership application after he had managed to secure a transfer from the Einsatzgruppen, and of his attempt in 1944 to strengthen the application might help us answer these questions.

Membership in the SS

Mundschütz applied to the SS in 1940, before he had become a member of the Einsatzgruppen. Upon his release from the Einsatzgruppen, his application had still not been acted upon. On 9 April 1943, more than three years after the application was filed and a year and a half after Mundschütz returned from the Soviet Union, the RSHA Personnel Department notified the SS Main Office of Mundschütz's nervous breakdown and submitted the relevant documents for consideration in the evaluation of Mundschütz's fitness for the SS. On 20 April, the SS Main Office sent the documents along to the Race and Resettlement Office, making a point to request 'that the documents enclosed in the folder be carefully considered in the decision about his SS suitability'. Although the State Health Office informed the Race and Resettlement Office that Mundschütz suffered from no genetic infirmities to disqualify him from the SS membership, there remained the disquieting question of his Aryan heritage, his racial wholesomeness. For among the racial criteria for admittance to the SS was an iron rule: the applicant had to prove that he had no Jewish ancestors as far back as 1750.[19] Because Mundschütz did not know the full name or identity of his mother's father, he stood little chance of gaining admission to the SS.[20]

To address this problem, Mundschütz submitted an affidavit from his mother on 4 February 1944. In it, Mundschütz's mother related that she had asked her mother about Mundschütz's grandfather and learned the following: Mundschütz's grandmother did not know her lover's last name, only that he went by the name 'Nandi' (Ferdinand). She and he were employed on the same estate in 1888. He left his position the following year, never to be seen again. Mundschütz's mother said that his grandfather had been an agricultural worker and of Aryan birth. Subsequent inquiries had uncovered various tidbits about Nandi, but nothing of substance about his identity.[21]

Mundschütz's mother's assertion that his grandfather was Aryan was not a sufficient substitute for a birth certificate. On 15 June 1944 the decision on Mundschütz's application was disclosed. He was 'unqualified because the grandfather on the mother's side (section 6 of the ancestral tree) of SS-candidate Martin Mundschütz is unknown.'

Considering Mundschütz's unwillingness to continue killing, the course of his SS application is extraordinary. One might think that if not put to death for his recalcitrance, Mundschütz would have at least been disqualified immediately and automatically from admittance to the SS. This was not the case. His application to this most severe and fanatical organization remained under consideration for almost three years after his return from the Soviet Union. To be sure, special attention was drawn to the circumstances of his transfer, but they seem not to have contributed to Mundschütz's rejection. The SS refused to accept Mundschütz not because of his unwillingness to continue killing Germany's eternal enemies, the Jews, but because he could not prove the purity of his Aryan heritage.

Even more noteworthy than the course of Mundschütz's application is his enduring desire to become an SS man. Despite having killed defenseless people, and subsequently having the wherewithal to arrange a transfer from his unendurably gruesome task, Mundschütz still wanted to join the organization responsible for the extermination. One might think that this man, having suffered such distress, would have withdrawn his application upon his return home. Or, if he believed that this entailed some sort of danger, then he could have let the application run its natural course, which he knew would have resulted in rejection. But he did neither. Instead, Mundschütz tried to strengthen his application. In submitting his mother's affidavit in 1944, he attempted to overcome the main obstacle to his admittance to the SS.

How could a man who suffered a nervous breakdown as a result of his participation in mass killings, or who feigned one in order to obtain a transfer, still want to join the highest order of the regime that had put the rifle into his hands and told him to shoot?

One possibility is that Mundschütz believed the extermination of the Jews to be morally wrong but was possessed by an incurable opportunism. Though unwilling and unable to partake in the killings, he might still have wanted to join the

SS in order to further his career and to reap the rewards of Nazism's victory.

This interpretation is unlikely to be valid. If Mundschütz had disapproved of the killings out of principle, then an immense cynicism must have been at the root of his desire to become an SS man. And had his cynicism and ambition been so overwhelming and his compassion so paltry that upon his return home he could have ignored his belief in the immorality and inhumanity of Nazi policy towards the Jews, then it is hard to believe that he would have been unwilling to continue killing in the first place. Moreover, had Mundschütz truly held the killings to be unjust, then the merest prospect of once again donning an SS uniform, especially if his nervous breakdown had been genuine, would have sent shudders through him; the notion that he could have later wanted to become an SS man is psychologically implausible. If we assume that Mundschütz disapproved in principle of the extermination of the Jews, as he suggested after the war by saying that the killings sickened his Catholic beliefs, then we are at a loss to explain his enduring desire to-become an SS man.

Mundschütz's seemingly unfathomable ambition to join the SS is, nonetheless, consistent with a different interpretation of his attitude towards his tenure in the Einsatzgruppen. At the beginning, Mundschütz killed. However, he found that he could not endure it, so he then performed other support duties. When he reached the point when he could no longer accommodate himself to participating in the extermination in any way, he had to transfer. Mundschütz first approached Ohlendorf and then wrote to him. In his letter, Mundschütz himself supplied the only plausible explanation for his initial endurance in the Einsatzgruppen, for his eventual unwillingness to remain, and for his persistent wish to join the SS: 'If you, Herr Standartenführer, however, have an understanding and a heart for one of your subordinates, who wants to sacrifice himself to the very last for the cause of Germany, but who does not want to present the spectacle of an alleged coward, then please remove me from this environment.' Although Mundschütz composed these words for instrumental purposes, they nevertheless contained the truth: he wanted to sacrifice himself for the cause of Germany, which was the cause of Nazism, but he was too weak to accomplish this most difficult task.

A powerful conflict raged within Mundschütz. He believed in the justice of the Einsatzgruppen's task, yet he could not endure it emotionally. At first his commitment to the extermination of the Jews was stronger than his elemental revulsion of the deed, so he remained in the Einsatzgruppen. In the end, the strain became too great and, his beliefs notwithstanding, he had to get out. Just as many people favour the death penalty without relishing the hangman's role or, perhaps, without being capable of carrying it out, Mundschütz did not in principle oppose the extermination of the Jews—he simply could not bring himself to partake in it.

That Mundschütz believed the killings to be just provides the only plausible explanation for how he could come away from the slaughter of defenseless civilians without hatred or enmity for Nazism and for why the extermination of the Jews did not in his mind discredit Nazism or even the directly responsible institution, the SS. Mundschütz's ideological fealty to Nazism is the only plausible explanation for his persistent desire to join the SS. From the Nazi point of view, Mundschütz, though ideologically attuned, was not made of the appropriate mettle. Therein lay his failure.

Killing—the supreme calling of the elite

Martin Mundschütz was but one of many who succeeded in being transferred from killing operations. Many others could have done the same without fear or serious retribution. It is indisputable that no SS man was ever killed or sent to a concentration camp for seeking such a transfer. But why? The Nazis conceived of the Jews as Germany's and humanity's greatest foe, as a malignant race determined to destroy all other races. The struggle with the Jews was eternal and to the death. It was therefore of the highest priority and demanded a herculean effort if Germany were to emerge victorious. It seems odd, then, that the refusal to kill this apocalyptic enemy was not met with severe punishment. If a soldier in the German army refused an order, he could have been executed, and many were. But an SS man's refusal to kill Germany's deadliest foe, the Jews, was met at most with shame and disgrace.

The probable explanation for this state of affairs is to be found in Himmler's own words, uttered on 26 May 1944 in Sonthofen to a political-ideological course of instruction:[22]

Now you will realize one thing. Within the Reich these measures [the extermination of the Jews] could not be carried out by a police force consisting simply of officials. A body which had merely sworn the normal official oath would not have the necessary strength. These measures could only be tolerable to and could only be carried out by an organization consisting of the staunchest individuals, of fanatical, deeply-committed National Socialists. The SS believes that it is such an organization, considers that it is fitted for this task, and so has assumed this responsibility.

Himmler said that only the most fervent Nazis could carry out this essential yet difficult task. It followed from this that an individual's failure excluded him in the eyes of the Nazis from belonging to this exalted group. It did not, however, make him a criminal.[23] Therefore, the consequent punishment was not the concentration camp or the firing squad. It was no more than the disgrace and shame of failing one's calling, of not measuring up to the forbidding ideal of the Nazi superman.

Still, an SS man's refusal could not take any form. Himmler addressed this issue in his famous speech of 4 October 1943 in Posen to the SS Group Leaders. What he said was already familiar to them, that the punishment for refusing to obey an order was imprisonment—except in one case:[24]

Thus if a man thinks that he cannot be answerable for obeying an order, then he should say quite honestly: I cannot be answerable for it. I beg you to excuse me from it. Then the order will usually be: You must still carry it out. Or you think: his nerve has gone, he's weak. Then you can say: Good, retire on a pension.

As Mundschütz demonstrated and Himmler confirmed, an SS man's failure to perform his duty because of cowardice or weakness was permissible; however, ideological opposition would not have been tolerated. One former SS judge addressed this point, saying that if an SS man[25]

had skillfully managed to explain that he was physically or spiritually unable to carry out such executions, then certainly little would have happened to him. He would have been relieved of his post and replaced by other suitable men. Only in one case would the man certainly have been shot, namely, if he had declared he could not carry out such executions on the grounds of his sympathy for the Jews or on the grounds of his opposition to the SS. Such a case has never become known to me.

There is no doubt that an SS man's expression of solidarity with the Jews would have doomed him to a concentration camp or to death, for this fate befell many other Germans. Since no person was so punished for failing to carry out an order to kill Jews, we can conclude that no one ever uttered such sentiments. Perhaps those who refused to kill were astute, practical men who knew what to say and, out of necessity, disguised their disapproval and hid their belief that the killings were immoral. Or perhaps they really thought the killings to be just, but simply could not themselves bear killing defenseless people. Let us hope that the majority of those who refused to kill belonged in the first category, believing the extermination of the Jews to be immoral. It is unfortunate that this cannot be said of Martin Mundschütz.

The knowledge that the executioners could transfer from the Einsatzgruppen and the case of Mundschütz should lay to rest any arguments that the executioners were coerced into killing — that they either had to kill or be killed. By not applying for a transfer from the Einsatzgruppen, the overwhelming majority of the executioners, in effect, *chose* to continue killing Jews. Why would men want to kill defenseless people, unless they believed that those people deserved to die? If they had not been animated by such a belief, the psychic burden of having to kill thousands of weeping people and of routinely becoming splattered with the victims' blood would have been enormous. Mundschütz believed in the justice of the Einsatzgruppen's enterprise, and yet, even he had a nervous breakdown.

The difference between Mundschütz and his compatriots in the Einsatzgruppen was that the belief system which he and they had together imbibed, whose central tenet was the congenital malignancy of the Jews, had not hardened Mundütz as it had others. Nazi ideology provided them all, Mundschütz included, with the justification to partake in mass murder. It also steeled the majority of men in the Einsatzgruppen — but not Mundschütz — with the heartlessness and the will necessary to perform its inhuman dictates. Perhaps, Mundschütz's incapacity to endure this task betrayed some unconscious vestiges of decency, making Mundschütz a bit better than the others. Mundschütz, however, considered himself less good. If motives and intentions are what matter to us, then Mundschütz was as criminal as the other members of the Einsatzgruppen. That he would not continue to kill makes no difference.

Notes

1 Raul Hilberg, *The Destruction of the European Jews* (New York 1973), 767.
2 Although not all men in the Einsatzgruppen were members of the SS, I will refer to them as SS men because their behaviour was governed by the codes of the SS and in cases of disciplinary or criminal charges they fell under the jurisdiction of the SS and police courts.
3 Hilberg, 189.
4 Herbert Jäger in *Verbrechen unter Totalitärer Herrschaft* (Crimes under Totalitarian Rule) (Olten 1967) echoes Hans Bucheim (see Helmut Krausnick, *Anatomy of the SS State* (London 1968), 381-2) when he writes that it is a mistake to assume that the well-known ferocity of the SS would also be unleashed on one of its own: 'It must above all be considered as an "error in reasoning" (*Denkfehler*) to identify the "terror directed externally" *Terrors nach außen*) and the generalized menace issuing from the SS, with the internal organizational conditions, that is, with the internal disciplinary rigours' (p. 159). In 1948 Karl Hauptman, describing his experience while in an SS tank corps, said that internal discipline in the SS was not an iron discipline, enforced by the threat of punishment: 'There were no pedantic forms, which were anxiously observed. This did not lead to indiscipline, but to a voluntary discipline, as I have seldom experienced. Here was no coercion and, even more, no terror . . . One felt oneself completely free in this corps' (quoted in Felix Steiner, *Die Freiwilligen: Idee und Opfergang* (The Volunteers: Idea and Self-Sacrifice) (Göttingen 1958), 376).
5 Jäger and Kurt Hinrichsen, 'Befehlsnotstand' ('Acting under Coercive Superior Orders') in Adalbert Rückerl, *NS-Prozesse* (NS Trials) (Karlsruhe 1971), 131-61. Hinrichsen's article is based on an unpublished, more comprehensive study he did under the auspices of Zentrale Stelle der Landesjustizverwaltungen Ludwigsburg, *Zum Problem des sog. Befehlsnotstandes in NSG-Verfahrens* (On the Problem of Acting under the So-called 'Coercive Superior Orders' in NSG Trials) (1964).
6 Jäger, 120.
7 Hinrichsen, 156-7.
8 Ibid., 143-6. The SS and police courts convicted 77 people of disobedience, 42 of whom were convicted of other charges at the same time. A total of 6 were put to death: 3 had been convicted of race-defilement (*Rassenschande*), 2 of military corruption (*Militärische Bestechlichkeit*) and 1 had killed another SS man. Of the 35 men convicted only of disobedience, most were given very light sentences (under a year of imprisonment) and 1 was simply fined. Not 1 of the 77 cases involved the refusal to carry out an order to kill Jews (ibid., 145). Moreover, not one SS judge has ever been found who adjudicated a case in which the accused was charged with refusing to kill Jews (ibid., 145).
9 For a more detailed discussion of this issue, see ibid., 149-53.
10 This defense argument was known as 'putative coercion by superior orders' (*putaiver Befehlsnotstand*).
11 According to State's Attorney Kurt Hinrichsen, the author of the previously mentioned study, who discussed this order at Siegfried Severing's trial in Munich on 9 July 1970, a voluntary transfer was to be recorded in the man's personnel file. Rudolf Aschenauer, Severing's defense lawyer, explained the history of this order. Apparently, volunteering to the front was at first forbidden. The officers of the Einsatzgruppen complained and Himmler changed the order.
11 Quoted in Robert M.W. Kempner, *SS im Kreuzverhör* (SS under Cross-Examination) (Munich 1964), 284-5. Six also claimed that he transferred because of his opposition to the killings. Though he was transferred after only a few weeks in the Einsatzgruppen, it is unlikely that he sought the transfer, or if he did, that he did so for the reason he stated. Shortly after his transfer from the Einsatzgruppen, Himmler himself commended Six for his outstanding service in the Einsatzgruppen and promoted him to Senior Colonel (*Oberführer*). Moreover, in a speech delivered at a conference in April 1944, Six spoke of the extermination of the Jews with

approval: 'The physical elimination of Eastern Jewry would deprive Jewry of its bio-logical reserves . . . The Jewish question must be solved not only in Germany but also internationally' (see *Trials of War Criminals before the Nüremberg Military Tribunals, VOL. IV: Nüremberg, October 1946-49* (Washington: U.S. Government Print-ing Office, n.d.), 525-6). That Six lied about his own actions does not mean we should disbelieve Six's testimony that others transferred from the Einsatzgruppen without being shot or, to his recollection, punished. Six had no motive to fabricate these statements.

13   Jäger, 147. In Einsatzgruppe C a similar situation prevailed. A witness at the Ein-satzgruppen trial said that SS General Max Thomas, the head of Einsatzgruppe C, had explained to his men that he would send back to Germany or assign to other work anyone who did not agree with the order to exterminate the Jews. And, in fact, he did send a number of people home (Kempner, 82).

14   *Official Transcript of the American Military Tribunal N 2-A in the Matter of the United States of America against Otto Ohlendorf et al., Defendants Sitting at Nüremberg Germany on 15 September 1947*, 593.

15   The main source for the material on Mundschütz is his SS personnel file (Docu-ment Centre, West Berlin). Unless otherwise indicated, all statements of fact about Mundschütz are drawn from this source. In 1970 he refused an interview request, saying that he had nothing to add to the contents of the documents he submitted to the court (referred to below).

16   Mundschütz's affidavit had been given on 3 August 1965 and submitted by the prosecution in a trial against Paul Zapp and three other Einsatzgruppen officers in Munich in 1970. Along with the affidavit the prosecution submitted an accom-panying deposition given by Mundschütz on 23 January 1970, in which he af-firmed the statements made in the earlier affidavit. In both documents Mundschütz stated that he faked his nervous breakdown in order to obtain a trans-fer from the Einsatzgruppen. Unfortunately, the affidavit of 3 August 1965 seems to have been lost. Thus, the only record of the affidavit available to me is the notes of Erich Goldhagen, taken at the trial.

17   Martin Mundschütz, 'Deposition', 23 January 1970.

18   Erich Goldhagen's notes of Martin Mundschütz, 'Affidavit', 3 August 1965.

19   On 17 December 1943 Himmler wrote to Richard Hildebrandt, Chief of the Race and Resettlement Office, discussing the desirability of requiring all future SS men to demonstrate the racial purity of their still more distant ancestors. According to Himmler, the date should be pushed back first to 1700 and then to 1650. See Hel-mut Heibert (ed.), *Briege an und von Himmler* (Letters to and from Himmler) (Stutt-gart 1968), 247.

20   On the SS application Mundschütz wrote that his maternal grandfather was 'unknown'.

21   On 30 December 1940 Mundschütz described his grandfather as 'tall, thin, having blonde hair' and thus lent him the physiognomy of the Nazi Nordic ideal.

22   Quoted in Buchheim, 366.

23   This point is also made in Hinrichen, 161.

24   1919-PS. Quoted in Office of United States Chief Counsel for Prosecution of Axis Criminality, *Nazi Conspiracy and Aggression, Vol. 4* (Washington: United States Government Printing Office, 1946). 567.

25   Jäger, 150-1.

(Patterns of Prejudice *is published by the World Jewish Congress.*)
(*Daniel Goldhagen is a graduate student in the Government Department of Harvard University, specializing in European politics.*)

American Dead Were Young, Too, Mr. President
April 19, 1985

The President of the United States
1600 Pennsylvania Avenue, N. W.
Washington, D. C.

Dear Mr. President:

Having had four definite contacts with the Waffen SS (that I can remember) in WW II, I thought — perhaps presumptuously — that you might be interested in my observations concerning your visiting a German cemetery. Although near the end of the war many of the Waffen SS were young, believe me, Mr. President, one ages very quickly in combat. Having enlisted at seventeen and having received my orders on my eighteenth birthday, I was just past my nineteenth birthday when my outfit was committed (C Company, 410th Infantry Regiment, 103rd Infantry Division). For the most part (while I was in combat) we fought in Alsace, Lorraine and in the Schwartzwald (Black Forest).

Having had a smattering of both German and French in school, I was the main unofficial company interpreter. My first encounter — face to face — with a Waffen SS soldier was early one morning in the fall of 1944. It was a beautiful and sunny, albeit chilly, day. If it weren't for the constant sounds of war and dead and wounded all around (theirs and ours), it would have been a perfect day for a walk in the surrounding woods. My task was to interrogate the young soldier. In answer to my first question, "How old are you," he spat directly into my face and would have been killed on the spot by my buddies had I not interceded. I wiped my face, reluctantly he answered a few questions and he was taken away. He was eighteen years of age and Hitler would have been proud of him.

The next encounter with the Waffen SS was when one of their units — young soldiers — wiped out half of our company in a ferocious tank, infantry and artillery attack. I can still hear Lew June, a very young Chinese American screaming as they killed him after having captured him and I can still see a very young lieutenant, an Italian American from the Bronx, die in Captain Neely's arms. The Germans were very young and so were we! Having spent three months in Army hospitals (from just behind the lines, through evacuation hospitals, with a week or so in a former German Army hospital in Paris, where all the signs were still in German, and, finally, in an American Army hospital near Cambridge, England), I can assure you, Mr. President, we Americans were also very young. Young, honorable, dedicated Americans, fighting in foreign lands for freedom and decency for our allies and for ourselves and, as it turned out, even for the Germans as well!

There were other wartime encounters with Waffen SS, but the last two that I distinctly remember were after the war. The first was in the spring of 1945, immediately following the end of the war. It was in Höchst am Main, just outside of Frankfurt. I was "running" a Red Cross Club (under the supervision of two Red Cross ladies). One of my young employees had just been released from the Waffen SS, because of his age (as dim memory serves). He had just turned seventeen. He was strong, proud and arrogant and he made it very clear that the only reason for his being in my employ was that we were victors and they the vanquished. He also made it clear that on a man-to-man basis we were no match for them! My last close encounter with a former SS trooper was in Berlin in the fall of 1945. By then, I was working in "The American Little Theatre of Berlin," along with other Special Service duties. Another German youngster was assigned to my office. During the first few days, we became friendly and I performed some personal favors for him. However, when he described to me in detail how his outfit had inflicted heavy casualties on what turned out to be my outfit, I asked to have him transferred immediately and I never saw him again.

To make a long story less long, suffice it to say, Mr. President, that you make a big mistake when you talk about young SS troopers being victims of Nazism. They were part of it. They were proud of it. They provided the leaders for the other armed forces and for the Gestapo. And when you talk about visiting a Nazi death camp where innocent people were put to death without rhyme or reason as balancing your visiting a German cemetery where SS troops are buried, you demean yourself, your high office and all Americans. You even demean the decent Germans who cannot understand why an American president would even consider visiting the graves of those who have helped to curse Germany with a permanent history of what the Nazis wrought.

Mr. President, I implore you to rethink your position and to change your itinerary. A leader as great as you have been should have little trouble in realizing what pain you will inflict upon your people, the German people and our WW II allies were you to do otherwise.

With best wishes to you and yours, I remain

Respectfully yours,
Leonard S. Sattler

(Leonard Sattler is a member of the Disabled American Veterans and of the Jewish War Veterans of America.)

Chapter 13

German-American Relations

What The Bitburg Episode Means For An Alliance
Die Zeit, Hamburg, West Germany
May 3, 1985

By Christoph Bertram

What ever has happened? Is the entire Western alliance on the brink of break-up? Does German-American cooperation no longer count for anything?

Commentaries on President Reagan's visit to Germany almost make it seem as if, under pressure of public criticism of the President's visit to the German war cemetery in Bitburg, the German-American alliance was in danger of collapse.

Nothing could be further from the truth. The Bitburg dispute will remain a mere intermezzo.

Yet both in America and in Germany it has brought to light currents that in the long term could well wash away the very foundations of cooperation.

What has happened? The President's visit was planned as a gesture of reconciliation — as if, after such fine cooperation for so long, any such gesture were still needed!

But it was transformed by a succession of clumsy moves into its very opposite — regardless what course the visit took.

The spirit of ill-will, not partnership, was conjured, with U.S. newspapers, Congress, Jewish organizations and the influential veterans' lobby calling on the President to cancel the Bitburg ceremony.

President Reagan may not have yielded to this pressure but many people in

Germany feel most uneasy and Chancellor Kohl has visions of a storm that could devastate the landscape.

The leader of the CDU/CSU parliamentary party, Alfred Dregger, warned of an "unholy alliance between left-and extreme right-wing anti-American sentiment in Germany and anti-German sentiment in America." He even talked in terms of difficulty in ensuring that the alliance survived the anniversary of VE Day in a reasonable state of repair.

The *Frankfurter Allgemeine*, not usually a newspaper given to excitement, almost lost control over itself.

"In their unthinking self-assurance many Americans," its leader-writer wrote, "are deluding themselves on the extent to which anti-Americanism is gaining ground worldwide.

"They feel they can work themselves up into a Pearl Harbour mood in the Pacific on account of economic rivalry while at the same time treating one of their most loyal allies like a vassal."

The intensity of the American debate on Bitburg and Germany's past has clearly caused annoyance in this country.

The U.S. Senate may not have been alone in criticizing Bitburg. So have Mrs. Thatcher and leading political parties in the Netherlands. But German opinion is still riled first and foremost by the American reaction.

The question is, as so often when Germans are upset, how deep-seated is the sense of outrage and what consequences will it have?

Will everything be back to clover when Air Force One takes off again on 7 May and President Reagan leaves Germany?

Will it just have been a storm in a teacup? Or have German-America relations taken a knock for good?

The answer is that they will take a fair amount of "punishment." Statesmen and journalists may be fond of describing world affairs in terms of human relations, but in reality "friendship" is not a category into which relations between countries fit.

An alliance is a community of interests based on the conviction that one's own well-being and security are best served by joining forces with others.

This is a fact that remains unchanged by the Bitburg controversy. Besides, Bitburg is by no means the first crisis in German-American relations.

The relationship has survived much more serious crises: over nuclear armament and Vietnam, detente and oil pipelines, money and missiles.

Any alliance worth its salt ought to be able to take a disagreement like the one over Bitburg in its stride. Yet Bitburg must nonetheless be taken more seriously.

It isn't that the upset has shaken the foundations of German-American relations — over and above the annoyance and shame we all feel about how the affair has developed.

What matters is that the mistrust and sensitivity shown on both sides of the Atlantic could well lead to a long-term deterioration in German-American trust. They testify to and intensify lines of development that have long been in the offing.

On the American side there is a growing inclination to mistake ideology for politics, as evidenced by both President Carter's human rights offensive and President Reagan's crusade ideology.

"Americans," historian Gordon A. Craig recently wrote, "have always felt obliged to regard their policies not only as effective and to the point but as good in the moral sense, and to believe that their foreign policy behaviour is based on idealistic rather than mere *Realpolitik* motives."

This tradition was suppressed in America's heyday as a world power. It is now recurring.

America is increasingly showing signs of lacking the generosity with which it used imperturbably to pursue its own interests jointly with those of its smaller partners and to take their sensitivities into account.

The Bitburg debate has supplied fresh instances of both moral self-righteousness and an uninhibited striving to look after U.S. interests.

It is a little ironic that Ronald Reagan of all people, a President who has furthered the present trend, has been hoist by his own petard.

Much like his predecessors in the 1950's and 1960's, he has refused to yield to pressure and taken a political knock as a result.

On the German side there is a growing inclination to allow doubts as to our own identity to affect German policy toward the United States.

What lies behind left-wing criticism of President Reagan's ideology of dividing the world into good and bad is, at least in part, a hope that divided Germany might at long last be able to find a place for itself in a united Europe free from superpower rivalries.

Right-wingers may never have felt President Reagan's ideology to be suspect, but the same cannot be said for what was imagined to be a refusal on his part to reward the Federal Republic of Germany for its loyalty.

The vehemence of the missile deployment debate has left behind traces.

Left-wing polemics against Germany being a vassal have their counterpart in right-wing rancour about American technological and economic self-interest.

There was full agreement on both sides of the political spectrum when it came to the latest upset in Bonn over the Nato friend-foe recognition system which is now to be made in America rather than in Germany.

This may be one reason for German upset over Bitburg. To be annoyed about being constantly reminded by other countries of Germany's past is not to deny the desire for a normal, undisputed German identity.

It is no coincidence that Germans who have made such heavy weather of the Bitburg dispute are the ones who are keen at all costs to keep the German Question open.

Bitburg and the problems it has created for President Reagan's visit to Germany need not have long-term consequences.

That is more than can be said for currents in both America and Germany to which recent excitement over and above the immediate issue have borne witness.

German policymakers face a tough twofold assignment:

- In an America that has grown narrower and more emotional in outlook they must maintain the impression of staunch and unswerving friendship.
- At the same time they must foster at home a sense of self-confidence that encourages a spirit of partnership rather than fuelling anti-American sentiment.

Under Chancellor Kohl the Bonn government has consistently sought to achieve the one ambition. In the other it has not always been successful—apart from its amazingly uncompromising stand on Bitburg.

In the March 1983 general election the SPD made very little mileage out of its slogan "In Germany's Interest."

But if what has lately so upset German sentiment and opinion continues to have an effect, others might one day prove more successful with this appeal to national instincts.

Even so, what has happened? Two politicians have made a mistake: not for lack of good will but for lack of historical tact and intuition.

It has been a serious mistake, but not a catastrophe. It could only be that if the emotions the Bitburg debacle has brought to the fore on both sides of the Atlantic were simply to be ignored as soon as the show is over.

(Die Zeit is a leading West German newspaper.)

Bitburg and the Strengthening of German-American Relations
Special Contribution

By Dr. Alfred Dregger

I

1985 saw May 8th for the 40th time since World War II came to an end in Europe. As this event approached, I said that every European and every democrat can rejoice that on May 8, 1945, the National Socialist dictatorship was eradicated for all time. On the other hand, however, the victory of the red dictatorship, Stalin's victory, can please no democrat. The end of the Second World War left a catastrophe, the greatest in the history of this continent:

- all of Eastern and Central Europe lay under the subjugation of communist dictatorship;
- Berlin, Germany and Europe are partitioned;
- over 14 million eastern Germans were expulsed from their homelands, costing the lives of more than two million of them.

In the Soviet Union, where the victory of May 8, 1945, brought with it the domination of half of Europe, the day was remembered with splendid display. The peoples and states of Eastern and Central Europe, incorporated into the Soviet empire, were forced to celebrate alongside them. Our countrymen in the GDR had to celebrate it as well. No one would expect such behavior from those of us living in freedom. For us Germans, May 8th, is a day of mourning—a day to remember our dead and the dead of all nations.

II

On May 5th and 6th of this year, the president of the United States and the chancellor of the Federal Republic bridged May 8, 1945, with the day when, 30 years ago, this republic became an integral part of the western world, aligning itself alongside those nations for which the values of freedom, democracy, rule of law and human rights have the same meaning.

During their visits to the Bergen-Belsen concentration camp, the military cemetery in Bitburg and Hambacher Castle, Ronald Reagan and Helmut Kohl set a touching example of the reconciliation between Americans and Germans: one which, as the chancellor said in Bitburg, "does not ignore the past, but rather through cooperation overcomes it." Ronald Reagan replied that in this manner, the past is "given significance,…that we may learn from it and create a better future." On the 40th anniversary of the end of the Second World War, according to the American president, "we celebrate that day when hate, evil and despicable events ceased, and we joyfully commemorate the rebirth of the democratic spirit in Germany."

III

In Bitburg, Ronald Reagan and Helmut Kohl wanted a reaffirmation of the goals set by the president of France and the German chancellor for their countries at Douaumont, near Verdun, in Autumn of 1984. Douaumont sealed an alliance to defend human and democratic rights in Europe and the world—an alliance of friendship between two peoples who, over the centuries, have tested each other on the fields of battle, and who have now just learned that if they are to have a future at all, it can only be together.

In Bitburg, it was seen that Americans and Germans are also capable of such human and Christian gestures. The plan to lay a wreath at the military cemetery ignited such a controversy that it threatened to tear open old wounds, and to cast ominous shadows on the German-American alliance. However, the American President and the German chancellor held firm.

Respect for the dead is part of the ethical heritage of humanity. The dead are removed from earthly justice. Over them, a higher authority passes judgement— that of the Lord. He will measure them against His, not our standards.

IV

In his address at Hambacher Castle, Ronald Reagan called upon the young people of Germany to participate in the great spiritual and cultural accomplishments of the German people, to take advantage of the opportunities of freedom and lead all of Germany and all of Europe towards a better future. Indeed, a future of freedom, democracy and human rights for all Germans and for all of Europe is our goal.

We can only achieve this together. The U.S.A and Germany have depended upon each other ever since the Soviet Union assumed control over the greater part of Europe. On the dividing line of Europe, we Germans would not be able to defend ourselves without the U.S.A. Without us, the U.S.A would lose the western part of Europe to the Soviet Union as well, thus making it the greatest power in the world.

It is time for Germans and Americans to devote themselves more to their future than before. In an alliance based upon common values, common interests, and mutual respect, the U.S.A and we would be insurmountable by any power on earth.

(Translated by Ilya I. Levkov.)

(Dr. Dregger is majority leader of the Bundestag of the Federal Republic of West Germany.)

Treacherous Signposts:
The Perils of Misreading Germany's Past
The American Spectator
November, 1985

By Franz M. Oppenheimer

There is another world for the expiation of guilt; but the wages of folly are payable here below.
— Lord Acton

Hitler's seizure of Germany was a historical fluke. As Golo Mann has put it: "The entire 'Third Reich' was a shamefully stupid episode of German history, in no way the inevitable result of what went before, but the result of a chain of accidents, errors and avoidable bungles."

At the beginning of January 1933 Hitler was on the ropes. The high tide of his party in free parliamentary elections had come on July 31, 1932, when the Nazi Party obtained 37.2 percent of the vote. Three months later, in what were to be the last free elections for the Reichstag, the Nazi Party lost two million votes and reduced its percentage to 33.1 — 5 percent less than McGovern's in 1972. Shortly thereafter the party lost 40 percent of its prior votes in the Thuringia state elections. The party was bankrupt; it had debts of 12 million marks and no visible means of prospective financial support. Henry Ashby Turner tells us that the "relations between the NSDAP and the business community," which, contrary to Marxist folklore, had never been amicable, "seemed to have reached an all-time low." At the beginning of January 1933 even the Social Democratic party newspaper, *Vorwärts,* had to conclude that "Hitlerism has long since lost all credit with high finance, heavy industry and the large landowners." One of the reasons for the disenchantment was the Nazis' alliance with the Communists in a wildcat strike of transportation workers in Berlin, which caused widespread violence and paralyzed the capital for five days.

At about that time Gregor Strasser, the head of the party bureaucracy and after Hitler the party's strongest personality, resigned from the party. His resignation caused fear of a more general revolt against Hitler by other Nazi leaders. At least for a while, Hitler seems to have been in a deep depression, and talked of ending it all with his pistol.

Moreover, the economic misery that had propelled his party towards power had also begun to recede in the summer of 1932. Decline in employment had come to a halt; the output of producers' goods had turned up in the second quarter of 1932 and that of consumer durables in the third quarter. Profits had begun to rise as a proportion of industrial income and costs had begun to fall enough to restore some measure of business confidence. This was reflected in the rising of shares on the stock markets and the rising prices of raw materials. Workers were given new confidence when Chancellor Schleicher restored the inviolability of wage contracts, which Chancellor Franz von Papen had abolished.

During the same period, Germany's political humiliations by the Allies of World War I, which had been almost as useful a propellant for Hitler as the economic Depression, had come to an end. The reparation payments imposed by the Dawes and Young Plans were virtually abolished by the Lausanne Conference in June 1932. And during the first few days of Schleicher's chancellorship, in December 1932, a treaty between the United States, Great Britain, France, Italy, and Germany lifted the limitations on Germany's armaments imposed by the Versailles treaty in order to make possible, as the treaty had humorously put it, "the beginning of a general limitation of the armaments of all nations." Thus the Weimar Republic had finally achieved international equal rights; it was a pariah no longer. In the light of those developments, it was not surprising that the *Frankfurter Zeitung* summed up a widespread general consensus on January 1, 1933: "The mighty National Socialist assault on the democratic state has been repulsed."

The best account I have found of the "accidents, errors, and avoidable bungles" that caused Hitler to be appointed chancellor thirty days after that obituary is given in a recent biography of the last chancellor of the Weimar Republic, Reichskanzler Kurt von Schleicher, by Friedrich-Karl von Plehwe. The destructive system of proportional representation in the Reichstag made it impossible for Schleicher, as it had made it impossible for Brüning, to obtain a majority from the representatives of the two-thirds of German voters who did not want Hitler. Franz von Papen, Schleicher's immediate predecessor, held Schleicher responsible for losing the chancellorship and used his influence with his next door neighbor and friend, President Hindenburg, to prevent Schleicher from obtaining the authority to dissolve parliament. New elections would have spelled the demise of Hitler, for, as we have seen, the party had no funds for another campaign. Probably Schleicher's crucial error, which permitted Papen to turn Hindenburg against Schleicher, came in his first speech as chancellor, which endorsed the resettlement of unemployed people from the West to Prussia east of the Elbe, on the large bankrupt estates of noblemen—estates that had been kept going only by enormous governmental subsidies. Hindenburg was himself the owner of one of those estates, and his closest friends were fellow East Prussian noblemen and landowners.

Obviously, Papen could have found no better ammunition against Schleicher than a plan to convert the property of Hindenburg and his closest friends into small family farms. And revelations by a committee of the Reichstag of numerous instances of landowners' misuse of governmental subsidies had made Hindenburg and his friends especially sensitive to plans of east-Elbian agrarian reform. In short, Papen succeeded in overcoming Hindenburg's aversion to Hitler by touching the old man's rawest self-interest. In Alan Bullock's words, "Hitler did not seize power, he was jobbed into office by a backstairs intrigue." Von Papen, the principal intriguer, stupidly believed that he had hired a pilot; instead he had placed a highjacker in the nation's cockpit.

Be that as it may, so the conventional view of German history goes, some thirteen million Germans, one out of three, voted for Hitler, a big enough minority to indicate the climate of a country and only that climate could have produced the gas chambers. Such reasoning, however, must be predicated on the assumption that those thirteen million Germans knew and desired what they were voting for. When that assumption is examined it must be found faulty. What those voters wanted in the first place was an out from the economic misery of the Depression. The existing political system seemed unable to help them—and only the Communists and the Nazis promised a break with the system. To find a particular culpability in Germany—because it was the only industrial country in which so many voted for so evil a party, although other countries, like the United States, had been hit equally or worse by the Depression—is to forget that in Germany, the misery of the Depression had come as a last straw. In the twelve years before the Depression, Germany had lost a war, had been dismembered, had been stamped a pariah for its supposedly exclusive responsibility for starting the war it lost, and had the savings of its people wiped out by inflation. The victors of World War I suffered no comparable series of disasters.

That the Nazi voters' hope for something new had nothing to do with Hitler's crimes to come, must be concluded from a recent scholarly work by Sarah Gordon, *Hitler, Germans and the "Jewish Question."* Since the murder of six million Jews is generally considered the result, if not of the anti-Semitism of Germans as a whole, then at least of that of the German Nazis, determining the prevalence and kind of anti-Semitism among Nazis is crucial to the issue of culpability, an issue that, as we have just seen again in the Bitburg controversy, continues to bedevil the Federal Republic of Germany's relations with the United States. Professor Gordon's data on anti-Semitism should lay to rest the conventional wisdom. She shows that, even among the committed core of Nazi Party members before Hitler's seizure of power, rabid anti-Semites were a small minority of 12.5 percent, and even that minority of card-carrying Nazi Party members "did not appear to have envisioned the expulsion of Jews from Germany, much less genocide or extermination." One-third of those early Nazis were not anti-Semites at all; and the remaining majority were either mild anti-Semites or indifferent to the "Jewish question."

To gain perspective on the meaning of these percentages, it is useful to compare them with public opinion polls taken in the United States from 1938 to 1946, presented in David S. Wyman's chilling description of American anti-Semitism during the period: "From 15 to 24 percent...looked on Jews as a 'menace to America.'" Fifteen percent "would have supported an anti-Jewish campaign, and another 20 to 25 percent would have sympathized with such a movement. Approximately 30 percent...would have actively opposed it. In sum...as much as 35 percent to 40 percent of the population was prepared to approve an anti-Jewish campaign, some 30 percent would have stood up against it, and the rest would have remained indifferent." We do not know how many Americans among those 15 percent of active anti-Semites nurtured genocide in their hearts—probably a statistically insignificant minority* — but the same can be said of the 12.5 percent of rabidly anti-Semitic Nazi Party members — murder or expulsion of the Jews was not on their agenda either.

Given these statistics, and the fact that even the hard core of card-carrying Nazi Party members in the Weimar Republic contained only a small rabidly anti-Semitic minority, I find it difficult to attribute any culpability (beyond original sin) to the *average* Nazi *voter.*

Hitler's election tactics from 1928 to his seizure of power in 1933 can be explained only by his knowledge of the lack of appeal anti-Semitism had for the German voters. According to several historians cited by Sarah Gordon, anti-Semitism was not a major campaign theme during that period, and, in particular, Hitler himself toned down his anti-Semitism to win votes after 1928. During the critical campaign for the elections in the first Depression year of 1930, elections in which the Nazi vote jumped from 2.6 percent to 18.3 percent of total votes, "Hitler even proclaimed that he had nothing against 'decent' Jews and discountenanced violent anti-Semitism. He particularly avoided any discussion of future measures against Jews. His speech before major industrialists in Düsseldorf during 1932 also omitted

---

* In *Diary of a Nightmare: Berlin, 1942-1945,* Ursula von Kardorff, a young Prussian anti-Nazi journalist, notes how an American consular official rebuked a German "Aryan" colleague of hers for attempting to help a Jewish girl obtain a visa: How could a German woman "intervene on behalf of a Jewess, 'because after all that is forbidden, isn't it?'" Miss von Kardorff's dismay would have been even greater had she known that just before the War the American ambassador in London, Joe Kennedy, had advised the Nazi ambassador to be less noisy about the Jews, adding that "he himself understood...(Hitlerian) policy on Jews completely."

anti-Semitic references."

The reactions of Germans to the anti-Semitic realities that prevailed after Hitler's seizure of power are consistent with this analysis. Before the start of World War II, the regime staged two spectacular anti-Semitic outrages by which it could test popular reactions. The first of these was a boycott against Jewish businesses, doctors, and lawyers in April 1933 that was abandoned after four days "when it failed to receive domestic or foreign support." Gordon's analysis of available data reveals a conflicting pattern of reactions. "Hardly anyone spoke up publicly in protest." Moreover, in a few limited geographic regions like Middle Franconia and Munich, the boycott seems to have been partially successful; i.e., some people did stay away from Jewish shops. On the other hand, "many people bought deliberately from Jews. In some parts of Germany, they tried to force their way into Jewish shops (picketed by Storm Troopers) and even generals in uniform bought in Jewish stores."

Somewhat surprisingly the second spectacular anti-Semitic outrage before World War II, the pogrom known as *Kristallnacht,* launched by the regime in November 1938 after more than five years of constant, virulent anti-Semitic propaganda, aroused more widespread dismay among Germans than the boycott of April 1933, launched after only two months of totalitarian propaganda. Prior to the pogrom, the socialist underground's *Deutschland-Berichte,* which "made a fetish of trying to report objectively," reported that "anti-Semitism was slowly taking root among the German people. It was more kindly anti-Semitism than that preached by the Nazis, but anti-Semitism nevertheless." By contrast there was a "torrent of reports"indicating public disapproval of *Kristallnacht.* For example, the British consul general in Frankfurt reported: "I am persuaded that, if the government of Germany depended on the suffrage of the people, those in power and responsible for these outrages would be swept away by a storm of indignation if not put up against a wall and shot." The U.S. ambassador filed a similar report: "In view of this being a totalitarian state, a surprising characteristic of the situation here is the intensity and scope among German citizens of a condemnation of the recent happenings against Jews."

The most persuasive evidence of the extent Germans disapproved of *Kristallnacht* is found in the Propaganda Ministry's directive to the press. "The extensiveness of murder and property destruction...was never reported. All newspapers were ordered to describe general events at local levels only, not at regional or national levels. Pictures and reports of individual burnings and lootings were prohibited, and articles were to appear on the second or third, rather than first, page."

After the *Kristallnacht,* besides trying to hush up the scope of the outrages, Nazi rulers reacted to their failure to arouse anti-Semitic popular feelings by starting a great "hunt for state enemies." The *Deutschland-Berichte* reported that "people were arrested while traveling in the train and taken to Dachau." On the other hand, Hitler must have concluded that he could not succeed in reaching his objective of murdering all Jews in peace time. Indeed in his profound and brilliant book on Hitler, Sebastian Haffner argues persuasively that Hitler gave the order for "the final solution of the Jewish question" only after he was convinced that his war was lost—because of the Russian offensive in December 1941, and his declaration of war against the United States. For Hitler, killing Jews was more important than winning the war.

There has been much controversy about how much "the Germans" knew about the ultimate horror of the gas chambers. Those directly involved knew, killed, and tortured. A significant minority could have known but willfully shut their eyes and ears. Even more people had seen the deportation of Jews with their own eyes but chose to believe that they would "merely" be "resettled." But it is equally true, as Sarah Gordon discusses, that the Nazi regime went to great lengths in attempting to conceal its crimes. Jews were deported at night in a variety of public and private vehicles, including furniture vans. Soldiers who had witnessed the shooting of Jews and Poles in the East were threatened with execution for revealing what they had seen. The extermination camps in the East "were in most cases out of view of soldiers and were kept strictly secret. Knowledge about them was very limited except among top officials, the resistance, and church leaders."

Information that eventually did seep through was widely disbelieved by Germans, just as it was by the British, American, and Vatican authorities. Nor was that disbelief surprising, as Sarah Gordon says:

> Since what they heard was on the surface incredible by normal standards of common sense and past experience, this is not shocking; no human beings had ever had to contemplate premeditated carnage on quite so vast a scale... Even so prominent a Jewish leader as Leo Baeck, the head of the Berlin Jewish community, said that he did not know of Auschwitz and the systematic murder of Jews until 1943, by which time millions had already been murdered.

It is instructive to contemplate how an especially well-informed young woman, Ursula von Kardorff, heard for the first time of Auschwitz. She was a journalist in Berlin, a hater of the Nazis and everything they stood for, and a close friend of many of the participants in the plot against Hitler of July 20, 1944. She adored Fritz von der Schulenburg, one of the leaders in that plot. This is her diary entry for December 27, 1944:

> I read surreptitiously in the lavatory at the Kochstrassse a copy of the *Journal de Geneve*, which Barchen slipped to me. There was a horrifying article by two Czechs, who escaped from a concentration camp in the East. They say the Jews there are systematically gassed. They are taken into a big washroom, ostensibly to have a bath, and gas is then pumped in through hidden valves, until they are all dead. The corpses are burned. The article was seriously written and did not sound like atrocity propaganda. Is one bound to believe such a ghastly story? It simply cannot be true! Surely

even the most brutal fanatics could not be so absolutely bestial! Barchen and I could talk of nothing else all evening.

It said the camp is at a place called Auschwitz. If what was in the paper is really true there is only one prayer left for us, "Lord deliver us from the evildoers who besmirch our name by their shame."

The Ardennes offensive has bogged down. The objective was to reach the Channel coast in order to get better launching sites for the V-2s. In the east, ominous quiet.

When she made that entry, Schulenburg and many others among her friends had been hanged. Her fiance was missing on the Eastern front. Her favorite brother had been killed there. Her apartment had been bombed out; she had lost all her possessions. Who would be willing to criticize her for simply noting in her diary the horror she had learned and going on to other things? She had already risked her life by helping Schulenburg.

Under conditions of total war and total terror, it is more than doubtful, in any event, whether effective popular resistance to the extermination would have been possible, even if the facts had been widely known. By 1942, the brave and vigorous were themselves being killed at the Russian front; and the kind of remark that might have led to arrest and temporary incarceration in 1938 would have led to swift execution in 1942. Only an army of saints and martyrs would have been capable of a giant spontaneous uprising "*pour ecraser l'infame.*" But lack of sainthood and of readiness for martyrdom are not unique to Germans, nor have other peoples been subject to continuing reprobation for such deficiencies. Stalin and his successors have by now starved, tortured, and murdered more innocent people than even Hitler, yet we never hear the aspersions that are routinely cast on the Germans cast on the Russians. And rightly so. Just as the Russians were unable to stop the crimes of Stalin, and are unable to stop the crimes in the Gulag, Afghanistan, and elsewhere, so the Germans were unable to stop the crimes of Hitler.

One great merit of Sarah Gordon's study is its emphasis on Hitler's overwhelming responsibility for the deportations and exterminations between 1940 and 1944. "The average American," she says, "or even the typical present day German who did not experience Hitler's tyranny, has little conception of the magnitude and functions of power in a non-democratic state." Hitler was virtually alone, even among the Nazi hierarchy, in being possessed by the psychotic conviction that "Jews were not merely inferior and despicable subhumans…(but) were the embodiment of an absolute immutable evil…parasites…poison…an abscess, virus, or contagion."

Hitler's obsession was not rooted in, nor comparable with, the marginal strains of anti-Semitism that had their ups and downs in nineteenth-century and Wilhelminian Germany. Quite to the contrary, old time German anti-Semites, of whom "the Court Chaplain," Pastor Adolf Stocker, is a prominent example, far from wanting to kill the Jews, wanted them to abandon their separate ways and become fully assimilated into German life and culture. The Vienna of Hitler's youth contained a few closer models, although the most successful Viennese politician who made anti-Semitism a major issue, Mayor Karl Lueger, enforced scrupulous fairness toward Jews in his city administration. Still, there were Austrian anti-Semites in parliament who, according to Karl Bracher, asked "that a reward be paid to anyone who murdered a Jew and that the property of the victim be awarded to the murderer." I do not believe that these parliamentarians were more than freaks and outsiders, nor do I agree with Sebastian Haffner that Hitler's anti-Semitism bent on extermination existed "only in Eastern Europe from where he copied it." Moreover, pogroms, however beastly, committed by primitive peasants against mysterious strangers, cannot have been the inspiration for Hitler's technology of murder, nor did those murderous peasants have the commensurate ideology.

As far as I know, only Hannah Arendt in *The Origins of Totalitarianism* recognized France of the turn of the century as a main inspiration for Hitler's psychotic anti-Semitism. In fact, the only Western country in which anti-Semitism in the Hitlerian mode ever became a popular movement is France, and if the source of Hitler's dementia can be traced to any country it is to France. Jean Denis Bredin's masterful book on the Dreyfus case, *L'Affaire* (1983), brings the passionate intensity of that popular movement alive. The Dreyfus case was not the cause but only a symptom of anti-Semitic paranoia, of which a high point was a public campaign, launched by Drumont's virulently anti-Semitic newspaper *La Libre Parole*, to permit the widow and orphan of Commandant Henry to sue one of his accusers — after Commandant Henry had cut his own throat, when it had been established beyond any reasonable doubt that he had forged one of the crucial documents on which the case against Dreyfus was founded.

"The subscription," wrote *La Libre Parole*, is "to defend the honor of a French officer, killed, assassinated by the Jews." The response to that appeal became a triumph. The high and the low, workers, artisans, generals, students, doctors, lawyers, and, alas, many priests rushed to the defense of the forger and false witness's honor. The letters sending contributions bore signature lines such as "one of the Vende who would be happy to take up the gun of his ancestors of 1793 to shoot the Yids who poison France" and "for God, my country, and the extermination of the Jews...." The contents of those letters were even worse: "A Jew is a 'stinking and malignant beast,'" "vermin," "pest," "a centipede," "a microbe," "a tick," "a cancer," "a hideous spider," and "a flea of the synagogue." An army doctor proposed "to use the Jews for vivisection rather than inoffensive rabbits." A cook sends his subscription "to roast the Jews." A group of officers suggests that their contribution be used to buy nails to "crucify the Jews." A reserve officer wants "to massacre the dirty Yids." Someone from Baccarat would like to see "all the Yids...of his town in big ovens of the Glass Works." Bredin concludes: "At least a latent justification, if not the expectation, of genocide permeates the subscription in memory of Commandant Henry."

The sentiments brought to light by the responses to the campaign of *La Libre Parole* did not grow independently in individual backyards, but had been nourished by a massive campaign carried on primarily by Drumont and Catholic clergy. The quotes just cited could be duplicated by quotes from the newspaper of the Assumptionist Fathers, *La Croix,* which had a circulation of more than 70,000, in addition to the circulation of about 100 papers of the same name and inspiration. While *La Croix* was not the authorized official organ of the French Catholic Church, many of the faithful treated it as such, and the Church did nothing to change their belief. Many issues of *La Croix* incited to murder.

Anti-Semitic violence in France during the 1880s and 90s did not remain verbal only. Street violence broke out with particular vehemence throughout France after the publication of Zola's *J'accuse.* In countless cities mobs of thousands took to the streets crying death to the Jews. They smashed shop windows, looted and attacked synagogues. In many cities this violence raged for several days. These events were spontaneous and not organized by a totalitarian government.

There were no comparable events in Germany until they were arranged by the Hitler regime. Nor did the kind of virulent anti-Semitism that was embraced by much of the French literary elite — from Celine and Jules Romains on the left, to Drieu la Rochelle, Jouhandeau, and Brasillach on the right — throughout the 1930s and the occupation have any counterpart among German writers of comparable distinction, not even during the Hitler regime.

It is not an idle exercise to rehearse these historical facts. The myths that Hitler and his crimes were the result of "the German character" inevitably following Hegel, Bismarck, the Kaiser, Richard Wagner, Nietzsche, if not Emperor Frederick Barbarossa, that Germany was the nursery of genocidal anti-Semitism, and that the ordinary German shared a heavy responsibility for Hitler's crimes, bedevil our foreign policy here and now. These are myths that are constantly reiterated as the gospel truth. For instance in the *New York Times* of August 22, Herbert Mitgang, in a review of *Hitler: Memoirs of a Confidant,* quotes the following from William Shirer's simplistic history of the Third Reich, in the manner of one proclaiming an unquestionable fact:

> Germany was ready for its Führer. He gave the masses and the centers of power . . . what they wanted: militarism and defense contracts, promises of prosperity and linguistic conquest, racial theories about their own superiority, a scapegoat in the Jews.

Without historical illiteracy the extravagant uproar about President Reagan's visit to the Bitburg cemetery would have been impossible. I am convinced that that uproar came close to wrecking NATO and Germany's place in it.

These myths also play a malignant role in Germany itself. Two books, just published, *Germany Today* by Walter Laqueur* in this country, and *Le Vertige Allemand* by Brigitte Sauzay in France, permit us to trace the connection between mistaken assumptions about German collective guilt and the prevalence of irrational anti-Americanism, pacifism, and other peculiarities among the German young.

The two books run remarkably parallel in their diagnoses of the Federal Republic today; Laqueur is an optimist and Sauzay a pessimist. Both make much

---

* **Editor:** See Epilogue for an excerpt from *Germany Today.*

of the German need for ideological certainty and perfection, both describe the young's delusion about the moral equivalence of the Soviet Union and the United States and the resulting neutralism and agitation for unilateral disarmament, and both stress the need and search for a sense of national identity.

The misreading of German history, with its attribution of a measure of collective culpability to the Germans, amplifies and perverts that search for national identity. The Greens revel in the horror of the twelve Hitler years. Since the passivity of their parents and grandparents made that horror possible, the young Greens and their fellow-travelers glorify resistance against *any* authority, *any* government, *any* military establishment. Thus, in Brigitte Sauzay's phrase, "the Peace Movement constantly fuses Pershing and Hitler.... Having been repressed, the past has become omnipresent. Some Germans want to resurrect it at all costs to make 'reparation' for the derelictions.... German Protestants have never been able to accommodate themselves to the human condition. They want to look directly at the sun without blinking." It is no accident that Heinrich Boll and Gunter Grass, the most visible postwar German writers, who were overwhelmed by the Nazi past and did more than any historians to resurrect it, have also been major advocates of crippling NATO.

The Marxists, who according to Laqueur have had a belated renaissance in the Federal Republic, also exploit the feelings of collective guilt for their purposes. They dwell on the Nazi crimes, but trivialize them at the same time. "Marxism," says Laqueur, "ought to prove that Hitler and his party had not been free agents, but merely running dogs of monopoly capitalism. It had to show that Hitler's personal role...was of little consequence, but that the money he received for Emil Kirdorf and other industrialists was all important... that National Socialism was not a phenomenon *sui generis,* but broadly speaking the same as fascist and reactionary parties elsewhere...the same as capitalism, a right-wing, conservative political party." As for resemblances between the Nazi and Communist regimes, they are merely coincidental and at any rate vastly exaggerated by cold warriors.

It is sad to report that the third column attacking NATO's battle for the survival of decency in the world is the German Protestant Church. The wallowing of Protestant clerics in guilt is a bit more understandable than that of other groups, for if any calling can be expected to respond to the challenge of martyrdom it is the priesthood. Yet with heroic exceptions, the Protestant, and only to a somewhat lesser extent the Catholic, clergy were as passive in the face of evil as the laity; and resistance heroes like Martin Niemöller and Dietrich Bonhöffer were matched by some Protestant "German Christian" bishops and other clergy who were vociferous Nazis. In all charity, however, it is difficult to sympathize with German clergy who somehow manage to confuse their hang-ups over the past of their Church and their willful blindness to the exploding toys given by the Soviets to children in Afghanistan.

Not that there are no lessons to be drawn from the past. They are to be found in the human penchant for making use of abstractions in order to be able to ignore the uncomfortable and to pursue the questionable. Thus the German Protestant clergy, like many American liberals, use the abstraction of a past collective German responsibility in their arguments justifying surrender to totalitarianism by unilateral disarmament now. At the same time they manage to convert the concrete crimes of the Soviet government into an abstraction that can be kept in a desk drawer while pursuing the lofty goals of peace and brotherhood. The chief preachers and practitioners of "constructive dialogue" with the Soviets usually do not deny Soviet crimes; they simply choose not to dwell on them. The stench and gore of the Gulag, the deaths of slave laborers during the construction of the Siberian pipeline, are not permitted to intrude into discussions with civilized Soviet economists of the benefits of liberalizing trade.

We should realize that the willingness of so many "good" and anti-Nazi Germans to participate in Hitler's economy and in Hitler's war, even to the point of doing heroic deeds, is not a different phenomenon from that of the willingness of so many well-meaning Americans to participate in Pugwash and countless other conferences, meetings, and seminars with supposedly Russian "opposite numbers" that are carefully selected by the KGB. As those Americans manage to put aside their knowledge of Soviet crimes, so those Germans managed to put aside their knowledge of Hitler's crimes while fighting for the abstractions of "doing their duty," "not letting their comrades down," and a "legitimate" German government.

I know that by spelling out the proposition that the vast majority of Germans, "the Germans" in common parlance, carried no greater guilt for Hitler's crimes than others did for those of Stalin yesterday and of dear Mr. Gorbachev today, I am leaving myself open to violent accusations. It will be said that I am belittling the Holocaust, whitewashing its perpetrators, and displaying "insensitivity" to the ordeal of the victims—including presumably that of my aunt, uncle, and grandmother. But I hope a few readers will understand: While we must at all times and in all places be conscious of the burden of original sin and the role of the Devil in the human condition, we must also know that though we sin every day *cogitatione, verbo, opere et omissione,* we cannot do the Lord's work when obsessed by guilt for past and repented sins. This truth applies equally to the way a country must live with its history and the way nations must deal with one another. Only the Devil can have been amused during the recent Bitburg circus of the American media: He wants us to let the murdered victims of the past make us forget the murdered and tortured slaves of an empire that is still with us.

(Franz M. Oppenheimer, a frequent contributor to The American Spectator's *Book Review Section, is a Washington lawyer.)*

At a mass Nazi rally in Berlin (August 15, 1935) the Germans discussed what to do about their plight (slogan on banner): "The Jews Are Our Misfortune."

Ledger Sheet of Jews To Be Killed Worldwide

Seven years after Germans discuss their problem of what to do with the Jews, a secret Nazi committee arrives at "The Final solution" at the Wannsee Conference, January 20, 1942.

L a n d	Zahl
A. Altreich	131.800
Ostmark	43.700
Ostgebiete	420.000
Generalgouvernement	2.284.000
Białystok	400.000
Protektorat Böhmen und Mähren	74.200
Estland – judenfrei –	
Lettland	3.500
Litauen	34.000
Belgien	43.000
Dänemark	5.600
Frankreich / Besetztes Gebiet	165.000
Unbesetztes Gebiet	700.000
Griechenland	69.600
Niederlande	160.800
Norwegen	1.300
B. Bulgarien	48.000
England	330.000
Finnland	2.300
Irland	4.000
Italien einschl. Sardinien	58.000
Albanien	200
Kroati_n	40.000
Portugal	3.000
Rumänien einschl. Bessarabien	342.000
Schweden	8.000
Schweiz	18.000
Serbien	10.000
Slowakei	88.000
Spanien	6.000
Türkei (europ. Teil)	55.500
Ungarn	742.800
UdSSR	5.000.000
Ukraine 2.994.684	
Weißrußland aus-	
schl. Bialystok 446.484	
Zusammen: über	**11.000.000**

In the late 1930s a wave of anti-Semistism swept over Europe. Jews were herded into ghettos and later forced to wear giant-sized stars on their clothing. These actions were designed to isolate Jews; later Jews were humiliated by the Nazi and SS. Not atypical was that of forcing Jews to get down on hands and knees to scrub streets while non-Jews look on. The photograph above was taken in Vienna, Austria, shortly before the start of World War II.

This Nuremburg synagogue was burned down in a move "to turn this city into a truly German city once again," according to that city's mayor.

In January 1986, one-time inmate of Auschwitz concentration camp, Elie Wiesel (left), chairman of the U.S. Holocaust Memorial Council, when meeting with a U.S.-German committee, presented a wreath at the Jewish parish hall in Berlin with the words, "We must not forget the horror of the past."

Chapter 14

German-Jewish/Israeli Relations

Twenty Years of German-Israeli Relations
Deutschlands-Berichte
June, 1985

By Yitzhak Ben Ari

(Yitzhak Ben Ari is Israeli ambassador to West Germany.)

In January 1963, the Jerusalem correspondent of the German Press Agency reported, "Government circles in Jerusalem understood that the establishment of diplomatic relations between the Federal Republic of Germany and Israel had failed so far on account of the Hallstein Doctrine. Also, it was assumed in Israel that the Federal Republic of Germany had vital interests in the Arab countries that she did not want to jeopardize unnecessarily.

"It was not denied in Jerusalem either that the actual relations between Israel and the Federal Republic were good and could hardly be improved by the establishment of formal diplomatic relations."—Rudolf Küstermeier, a German journalist much respected and appreciated in Israel.

This is an example of public opinion concerning the ways of political actions between peoples and countries, international relations and the diplomatic representatives' loss of influence.

Certainly, international relations have undergone a profound change since World War II.

Who, for instance, knew about "economical co-operation," or "summit meetings," or "Cold War" a generation ago? Today, we have the dubious pleasure of being able to participate in all atrocities and wars via the TV set in our living rooms. What used to be a "closed business" of the diplomats turned into an arena of public concern.

Despite this popularization of relations and manifold contacts between our countries, I believe that the establishment of diplomatic relations between our countries was a milestone and a new starting point of significance. The establishment of these relations did not fall like manna from heaven.

The German Social Democrat Party, for example, had been advocating normal diplomatic relations for years, but the majority of the German Parliament held a different view on this question. For the sake of fairness it should be pointed out here that a political opposition party has an easier stand pleading for moral and ideological ideals than a ruling party which, after all, has to take practical and pragmatic considerations into account. Surely, all of them were in favor of good and friendly relations, but were afraid that a formal establishment might have consequences concerning the Arab countries and might change their relations toward what was then called the zonal regime (Hallstein Doctrine).

During World War II, the large majority of Arabs emotionally took sides with Nazi Germany. Their hatred of England and France made them sympathizers of Hitler's actions and the rabid policies of Germany's rulers against the Jews invited the radical National Socialist forces (e.g., the Mufti of Jerusalem) to cooperate with the SS and other organizations of the Nazi tyranny.

Therefore, the relations between the new Germany and the independent Arab states were largely based on this Arab way of thinking, and for that reason the Arab rulers spoke of "traditional friendship" with Germany. Soon after negotiations were taken up between Jewish organizations and Israeli state representatives and the Federal Republic of Germany, during the early '50s, the Arabs started to exert pressure and attempted to influence German-Israeli relations negatively.

On January 13, 1965, Klaus Bölling [spokesman of the government — Ed.] said in *Kommentar* (*Commentary*, a political German TV program), "The friendship with the Arab peoples and states, dear spectators, should be precious to us and I believe that the Arabs' feelings of friendship are not solely based on their memory of Generalissimo Rommel's military activities against the British during the last war."

"But the friendship has been severely put to the test these days. The point of view expressed to us was that the Arab states would consider recognizing, or even positively decide on recognizing East Berlin, if the Federal Republic should decide to establish diplomatic relations with Israel.

"Now, the Arabs went one step further and said they might even take into consideration recognizing communist Germany, if the government does not dispense with military aid to Israel, and if this aid will not be ceased. I think the Federal Republic ought to say loud and clearly that she can hardly give in to duress. In recent years, we spent a lot of money on developing aid to the Arab world. Now, we ought to make it clear to the Arab governments — this seems the Federal Republic's inevitable duty — that free Germany and communist-ruled Germany are not two competing companies which may be bidded up against one another. It must be asked what they hope to achieve with this kind of duress, or, one may well say, policies of blackmailing Bonn."

The Ministry of Foreign Affairs, headed by Secretary Gerhard Schröder, declared repeatedly "that the establishment of diplomatic relations may not be treated separately, but in view of foreign political concerns, which is why this question ought to be deferred." In other words, the Ministry of Foreign Affairs gave in to the duress for the longest time.

I cite this development mentioned above because it has been symptomatic of the attitude of Arab countries until today. It would go too far, however, to go into details as to what led to the establishment of relations on May 12, 1965. The representatives of all democratic parties, Dr. Kurt Birrenbach, Dr. Rainer Barzel, Prof. Böhm, Theodor Heuss, Carlo Schmid, Erich Ollenhauer, Franz Josef Strauss, 430 professors, trade-union representatives—just to name a few—advocated the establishment of diplomatic relations.

Konrad Adenauer repeatedly wrote and declared that it was one of his main concerns, which had to be solved politically and from a human point of view, when he was elected the first chancellor in September 1948—to create a new relationship between Germans and Jews. The atrocities committed in the name of the Germans and by the Germans during the National Socialist tyranny overshadowed—as Adenauer put it—like a heavy burden all other political issues to be dealt with by the new German government. Adenauer considered it—apart from reconstructing the new democratic state and creating friendly relations with other nations—the most crucial political task for the government and the people of Germany to find a way to reach out to Israel, which takes a central place in the religious beliefs and in the history of the Jewish people.

On May 12, 1965, Bonn and Jerusalem declared, after very difficult but open negotiations: "The government of the Federal Republic of Germany—according to an authorization given to it by the President—and the Israeli government agreed on establishing diplomatic relations between the two countries."

It is in the nature of our complicated relations that attempts are being made at categorizing them and finding terminological denominations. Thus, Willy Brandt spoke of "normal relations with a particular background" on the occasion of his official visit to Israel in 1973. Similar and other definitions have been used on various occasions—and have in most cases been received in Israel and in Jewish circles at large with more or less criticism. This semantic discussion shows that something very *special* or even *extraordinary* exists in our relations, as there is no comparable historical burden like the one between Germans and Jews, Germans and Israel.

Let us be open and honest about it—there have been, and there are still, circles in Germany that would like to see a *"formalization of relations"* as tantamount to *"normalization."* If normalization is to mean that there should be diplomatic, cultural, economic and human cooperation between Germans and Israelis no objections are to be raised. If *normalization* is to mean, however, that the Nazi tyranny was nothing but a *road accident* of history and does not obligate this country to anything, that the murdering of a third of the Jewish people was an atrocity like *any other,* if Germans think that forty years after the end of World War II they may supply overt enemies of the state of Israel with massive, highly developed weapons systems, or may rape the deplorable historical truth (key word: Auschwitz lie), then the existing bridge between Germany and the Jews which connects us beyond the dark past only becomes unpassable and the memory of all the atrocities only the more vivid.

Twenty years, the period since the establishment of diplomatic relations, is the timespan of nearly a generation. Controversies loaded with emotions exist in this country concerning not only Israel — but nothing is as burdened and as delicate as the issue of German-Israeli relations.

Despite this burden, our relations are good, if not excellent. Our relationship is characterized by a growing sense of trust in one another, both because of the changing situation in the Middle East and a lively dialogue on various levels.

The Federal Republic is one of Israel's most important partners in trade. Concerning cultural exchange (theater, music, dance, film or literature), concerning the city partnerships and the youth exchange, in the fields of vocational training and scientific research, agricultural cooperation and the partnership between our befriended trade unions, we have better relations with Germany than with most other countries in the world.

The Arab countries keep on trying to put pressure on German-Israeli relations, just as they did twenty years ago. When the German Chancellor planned a visit to Israel, my Arab colleagues deemed it correct to interfere and to make critical remarks.

This is not the Israelis' way. When the German President and the Chancellor went to Jordan and Egypt, I publicly wished them a good journey and success — as *we* are of the opinion that it is possible for democratic statesmen to exert a positive influence on our less democratic neighbors and thus help establish peace. For that reason, we are in favor of this country having friendly relations with the Arab world — as long as they are not counter-productive to Israel.

The visit of the German Chancellor to Israel, visits of politicians of democratic parties to Israel and of Israeli politicians to the Federal Republic of Germany are examples of a productive and rational dialogue which promotes understanding and rapprochement.

But some of these visits have brought to light animosities still existing. Many examples of secondary importance, but also many painful and concrete examples of these still existing sensibilities, could be listed here, which agitated the public opinion in Israel as well as Jews the world over. Probably it is a matter of human weakness for the memories of the relatives of those who harmed others to be less developed and long-term than the memories of those who were harmed. This also applies to the relations between people and countries.

I do not want to conceal here that this also concerns a possible development — i.e., the supply of arms to countries which are at war with Israel.

This country, Germany, supports disarmament, arms limitation and arms control. What Germany claims for Europe is even more significant in the Middle East and may well make the difference between war and peace in this region. More people with fewer and fewer weapons is appropriate for all parts of the world. Not only the historical past — the geopolitical location, too, burdens the Germans with a special responsibility for preventing any war ever from being started again from this country and to promote peace initiatives.

Modern weapon systems, however, are no peace doves!

I refer to the erosion of diplomats' tasks. Still, I think that the activities of the German ambassadors in Israel and the Israeli diplomats in Bonn have been decisive for the good and meaningful relations we have achieved during these past twenty years. The tasks — to supply the government with a balanced and fair opinion from the abundance of information available, to smooth conflicts and misunderstandings, to calm waves of mutual lack of understanding with much tact — those were but a few of the obligations and tasks of this profession. If I may put it casually and in musical terms: we diplomats try to transform politics' drum beats into the gentle sound of a flute.

I am one of those in Israel who already believed in establishing relations with Germany 35 years ago and moderately contributed to them. There are very few people, both in Israel and in Germany, who doubt the reason and wisdom of the establishment of diplomatic relations. The "moral and historical background" exists and will continue to exist for a long time. Taking into consideration what has been done to Jews by Germans in our generation or in our fathers' generation, it is almost a miracle that we may speak of friendly relations today. On both sides, we ought to behave in such a way as to prevent anything from jeopardizing this new and fragile friendship!

Some Germans believe that 40 years after the "final solution" of the Jews all has been forgotten while some of us Israelis tend to be extremely optimistic or pessimistic as to what we may expect of the Germans — both are wrong. There is nothing to be afraid of in responsibly looking for ways of mutual co-existence. Even today, Germany is still judged partly by her relationship with the Jewish state — even today, there are still Jews trying to regain their faith in humankind through the Germans. From the diplomat's desk one may contribute to such an enterprise in the future by giving positive impulses, such as suggesting combining German innovation with Israeli experience in cultivating the desert or inventing new irrigation systems. The utilization of highly developed technologies in agriculture may open a new way here for Jewish-German cooperation — to the benefit of millions of people in the Third World suffering and dying of starvation in this world.

It was not long ago, 25 years, since Konrad Adenauer and Ben-Gurion met in New York on March 14, 1960. Both gentlemen admitted to each other that their knowledge of economics was limited and, therefore, decided that Mr. Abs should take care of that. But they considered the necessity of cultivating Israel's Negev, which was still a desert then, as a living example to the developing worlds of Africa and Asia. And Ben-Gurion also realized that the coming generation would repress what happened during the Nazi tyranny. He believed, however, that there would be young people in Germany who would keep asking themselves, "How was this possible?" And, therefore, both visionaries thought, why should this coming generation not have a reason to be proud of something commonly achieved — the cultivation of the desert, and providing the starving world with bread through their joint efforts?

Much was said about a German-Jewish symbiosis. Gershom Sholem expressed his point of view of the situation of German Jewry in his analysis, stating that this symbiosis had been invented on the Jewish side, while the great majority of the Germans rejected this symbiosis.

Particularly because there was a radical rupture of German politics and intellectual history in 1945, and because there is a Jewish state today which hence became the center for Jewish culture and scholarship, I believe in a possible symbiosis.

Whatever people think, they can also act out. Without our willingness to change things, the differences between North and South cannot be changed and millions of people will go on starving! The cooperation in this field may still be a vision — but haven't we made visions come true together in the postwar era?

(Translated by Renate Steinchen.)

Bitburg Is A Blow To Jewish-German Relations
The Canadian Jewish News
May 16, 1985

Jewish Tombstones Damaged In West Germany

By Sheldon Kirshner

FRANKFURT, WEST GERMANY— Forty years ago Frankfurt, West Germany, was in ruins, a city without Jews, in a country all but shorn of morality and conscience.

When Nazi Germany surrendered to the Allies on May 8, 1945 — VE Day — the darkest chapter in Jewish history was closed. Six million Jews lay dead, the victims of racist madness, and Germany itself was prostrate.

It would have been foolhardy to predict, in May 1945, that Germany would emerge from the devastation and that Jews would return to Germany.

Now, as Europe marks the 40th anniversary of Nazi Germany's downfall, the unimaginable has happened. Germany, having humiliated, thrown out and murdered its Jews, is once again home to a Jewish community. The overwhelming majority live in West Germany, an immensely rich capitalistic state, while a handful reside in Marxist East Germany.

The 30,000 Jews of West Germany, of whom 5,000 reside in Frankfurt — a mix of Germans, Russians, East Europeans and Israelis — live in a country that in all respects is democratic, liberal and part and parcel of mainstream Western civilization.

The Germans have jettisoned the sins of their past — never again dictatorship in Germany, never again war emanating from German soil — declared Kurt Schumacher, a Social Democratic politician who, having spent 10 years in a Nazi concentration camp, went on to become a prominent postwar leader.

"The Germans have opted for Western democracy because there is no longer a national German interest that can be detached from law and liberty," noted Alois Mertes, the Minister of State for Foreign Affairs.

"To my generation, May 8, 1945, meant. . . first and foremost the beginning of a great historical opportunity to build a future of freedom and justice, of reconciliation and peace."

West Germany has indeed made a clean break with the Nazi past — not only by embracing democracy, but by treating its Jewish citizens humanely and by maintaining good ties with Israel.

How, given West Germany's emergence as a modern, progressive nation, could it have blundered into the sorrowful, tragic Bitburg affair?

For Jews here, Bitburg appears to have been more than a grievous insensitive affront to their dignity. More important, it represented something of a blow to the gradual, delicate process of reconciliation between Jews and Germans.

"Bitburg was a step backwards," said Ignatz Bubis, a member of the executive of the Central Council of Jews in Germany. He, together with German Jewry, boycotted a memorial service in Bergen-Belsen which preceded the brief, embarrassing ceremony at the Bitburg war cemetery containing the graves of some 49 members of the dreaded SS. "Bitburg has set back reconciliation," he added.

Stefan Szajak, the director of Frankfurt's Jewish Community Centre, also believes that Bitburg damaged, if only temporarily, Jewish-German relations.

Szajak, 37, thinks that Bitburg has aroused latent anti-Semitic feelings prevalent among some Germans: "They are saying that Jews are trying to create a wedge between West Germany and the United States."

Recently, *Quick,* the mass-circulation weekly magazine, ran a cover story entitled: "Reagan visit in Germany: The power of the Jews." Heiner Emde, the writer of the story, posed the question whether the "legendary Jewish power has once again influenced the course of Washington and its President."

Such innuendos aside, Bitburg created more than just coarse yellow journalism. As this reporter was interviewing Szajak, the police department phoned to inform him that 35 tombstones had been overturned — and four seriously damaged — in the Jewish cemetery by vandals. Szajak was told, as well, that anti-Jewish calls had been recorded by the police.

Szajak is not overly concerned by these incidents, since he is confident they are isolated and are basically insignificant to the community's future.

What seems to concern him particularly is that Germans, although deluged by a flood of books, newspaper stories and TV programs on the Hitler era, want to dispense with their history.

"A lot of Germans want to forget, it's a human reaction, but the Jews can't forget."

Wolfgang Günther Lerch, the Middle East editor of the *Frankfurter Allgemeine,* one of West Germany's leading dailies, said most of his fellow Germans are "very tired of hearing about the Holocaust," and supported in principle President Reagan's decision to go to Bitburg.

In general, he said, Germans are not well informed of the Third Reich and the Holocaust. He blames the educational system, and the attitude of old Germans. Still, he pointed out, the majority of Germans share Chancellor Kohl's expression of shame of the Holocaust.

Jochen Siemens, who writes on current political affairs for the *Frankfurte Rundschau,* said Germans are no different than anyone with an unsavory past. As he put it, "The French want to forget Vichy, the Americans want to forget Vietnam."

Ignatz Bubis, a 58-year-old Polish Jew who settled in Germany a few years after World War II, disagrees with this assessment. "You can't live for the future if you forget the past," he said.

This, probably more than any other sentiment, summarizes the mood of hurt which has enveloped German Jews in the wake of Bitburg and the 40th anniversary of the end of Nazi tyranny.

German-Jewish Relationship After Bitburg
Washington, D.C.
May 21, 1985

By Ambassador Günther Van Well

(Speech by Gunther Van Well, Ambassador of The Federal Republic of Germany in Washington at the Annual Board of Governors Meeting of B'nai B'rith International.)

I have gratefully accepted your invitation because I was and I am deeply appreciative of its motive, namely to be helpful in the search for mutual understanding and in strengthening our common cause, which is to serve and promote human rights, democratic freedoms, peace and international cooperation, and — above all — to prevent the scourge of intolerance, racism and hatred ever from getting the upper hand again, leading to the abyss of genocide and holocaust.

B'nai B'rith International and the Federal Republic of Germany are on the same side of the struggle for human dignity and a better world. Your organization and the new Germany of the Basic Law have joined forces — always keeping very much in mind the terrible experience of Nazism.

We are committed never to forget Dr. Leo Baeck, your courageous last president in Germany before and during the Hitler regime and the first to call for the reinstitution of European B'nai B'rith after his return from the Theresienstadt concentration camp. We will gratefully remember the visit to the Federal Republic of Germany of your first official delegation under the leadership of Honorary President David Blumberg in 1983. We recognize another token of your organization's solidarity with the new Germany in the bestowing of the distinguished award for humanitarianism on our former chancellor Willy Brandt. My Government has asked me to extend today an invitation to President Kraft and Executive Vice-President Thursz to visit the Federal Republic of Germany as our official guests. We welcome the BBYO-German Youth Exchange, which will be implemented this summer to further what B'nai B'rith has always stood for: sound intercultural and interfaith relations. This first exchange of 30 American Jewish and German youth should be the beginning of a determined effort to get our young people together in defining a common purpose for the future. After the experiences of the last weeks, there seems to be a new urgency to have our young people know each other better. Hambach as a symbol for the mission of European youth in shaping a free and democratic Europe should be made better known also to American Jewish youth.

The future of Europe, which is tightly connected with the future of Germany, is of vital importance for America and for Israel. The Soviet Union has moved its power into the center of Europe and further into the Middle East. A new totalitarian ideology is challenging our common Western culture and civilization rooted in Judaeo-Christian values. Let the terrible past and the dangers of the present guide us towards recognizing our common goals and interests. Let us help each other and strengthen each other. Let us build a solid, long-term basis for our relationship so that sudden eruptions, like the painful debate of the last few weeks, can be avoided.

Forty years have passed since the end of World War II. But that war and the twelve years of Nazi dictatorship are not only a part of German history. They have taught us a lesson like no other lesson a nation can be taught. Federal President von Weizsäcker said in his speech before the German Parliament on May 8, 1985: "All of us, whether guilty or not, whether old or young, must accept the past. We are all affected by its consequences and liable for it. The young and old generations must and can help each other to understand why it is vital to keep alive the memories. It is not a case of coming to terms with the past. That is impossible. It cannot be subsequently modified or made not to have happened. However, anyone who closes his eyes to the past is blind to the present. Whoever refuses to remember the inhumanity is prone to new risks of infection." In his speech President von Weizsäcker also referred to the fact that the historical burden and responsibility of all Germans as a nation lies upon both German states. He said: "Recently in Baltimore in the United States, an exhibition on 'Jews in Germany' was opened. The ambassadors of both German states accepted the invitation to attend. The host, the President of the Johns Hopkins University, welcomed them together. He stated that all Germans share the same historical development. Their joint past is a bond that links them. Such a bond, he said, could be a blessing or a problem, but was always a source of hope."

The traumatic lesson of our past determined one of the fundamental elements of the policy of the Federal Republic of Germany. We have accepted a responsibility which we share with the other Western democracies and which is the basis also of the work of B'nai B'rith: The protection and promotion of human rights. In his address commemorating the 40th anniversary of the liberation of the Bergen-Belsen concentration camp Chancellor Kohl said: "The suffering of people, the victims of inhumanity, urge us to preserve peace and freedom, to promote law and justice."

The Jewish community has always been in the forefront of those who fight for human rights. There are many reasons why we should stand together in particular in this area.

For most of us in this room, whose memories span more than the last four decades, 1945 was truly a watershed year, marking in many significant ways the end of an era. 1945 saw the defeat of a tyranny previously unmatched in the historical record; it saw a catastrophe for the Jewish people unequaled in Jewish history. It saw the physical and spiritual collapse of Germany, unprecedented in German history.

Beyond all the grief and desperation, we saw the beginning of a new era. Out of the cataclysm of the Jews and out of the physical and moral ruins of a criminal regime in Germany we saw arise two miraculous achievements in history and in the struggle of human beings to establish free societies — the establishment of both

Israel and the Federal Republic of Germany.

We know that the foundations of these two countries are anchored to the foundations of European and American culture. We know that they are inconceivable without the Jewish and Christian tradition, which holds that the dignity of each individual and his creation in the image of God cannot be called into question, and that they constitute the standard on which our order is based.

German-Jewish relations will retain the mark of the Holocaust. But let's not forget the times when German-Jewish relations were close and fruitful.

We know that the steadfast commitment of Leo Baeck, Nahum Goldmann, Ben Gurion, Konrad Adenauer to the rebuilding of German-Jewish relations after May 8, 1945, drew strength from the Judaeo-Christian roots of our culture. Their objectives and standards remain valid for us. They knew that it was not possible simply to carry on where the past left off. But this did not prevent them, on the basis of a shared cultural heritage, from talking to each other, from establishing German-Jewish relations in a slow process of getting closer to each other. This process has been more intensive with Israel than with American Jewry. We would wish that the troubling, painful discussion of the last few weeks leads American Jews to join us in new determined efforts to establish closer links also between the Federal Republic of Germany and American Jewish communities. We Germans wish to make our contribution to it. B'nai B'rith — in inviting me today — gives me the opportunity, on behalf of my Government, to say this before a most legitimate representative of Jewish international responsibilities and leadership. The development of a reciprocal relationship of my country with B'nai B'rith is extremely important for two reasons:

Since the days of the Mendelssohnian Enlightenment one of the most creative, dynamic and vibrant centers of Jewish economic and cultural life had developed in Germany. In fact, the most important in the pre-Hitler era had been that of Germany. At its apogee in 1925, it comprised 564,000 individuals. The history of B'nai B'rith-Germany, which began in Berlin in 1881 and saw its peak in 1924, when district 8 (Germany) with over 15,000 members was the most populous district of the Order, surpassing even the largest American district, speaks for itself.

During the first six years of Nazi rule, 350,000 Jews fled Germany, among them almost every German Jew of intellectual, scientific, or academic stature; 180,000 more perished in the concentration camps. With their exodus and death a magnificent era of German-Jewish culture came to an end. The great majority of my people has, therefore, up to this day never been exposed to what the older generation referred to as the Ashkenazim culture. All Germans of today are in many ways still its heirs without knowing their spiritual fathers.

There are at present 73 Jewish communities in the Federal Republic of Germany with altogether some 30,000 members. These are very few to keep the torch of the Ashkenazim heritage burning. It is American Jewry which has become the main torch bearer.

In Germany, in Israel and in the United States, we are witnessing a transition from the generation who lived through the war and Holocaust to the generation which was born after this inferno. This change cannot but affect German-Jewish relations. The new generation in Germany, too, views its relationship with Jews in the light of moral criteria. But the young people regard the forming of these relations as a matter of a free political decision, not as an expression of a feeling of guilt.

On the other side there is a new generation of self-confident Israeli citizens emerging who lack the traditional ties with Europe and the United States.

In the United States a generation is coming to adulthood whose knowledge and attachment to European and Middle East history is less profound and intensive.

The facts and developments I have just mentioned may contribute to more dispassionate relations among these three countries, but they can also lead to alienation.

In order to prevent this, the American-Jewish organizations could play a vital role. Because of the past, our solidarity with the Jewish people and with the state of Israel is an integral part of the ethics of our republic and our policy. Federal President von Weizsäcker has accepted the invitation to pay a state visit to Israel in October, the first visit to Israel by a Federal President ever. This will be a suitable occasion to solemnly restate our commitment to the Jewish people and to the state of Israel.

Germans and Jews — 40 years after the end of World War II — should strive to achieve what Moses Mendelssohn wanted to achieve:

Nach Wahrheit forschen,
Schönheitlieben,
Gutes wollen,
Das Beste tun.

To seek after truth
to love what is beautiful
to wish for good
To do the best.

"It Thinks Inside Me...":
Fassbinder, Germans & Jews
Encounter Magazine

By Henryk M. Broder

Ever hear the one about the Jew in the German railway station? This poor Jew arrives at a station in Germany, carrying everything he owns in one battered old suitcase. Spotting an elderly gentleman studying the timetables, the Jew goes up to him and asks, "Excuse me, sir, are you an anti-Semite?"

The man is shocked. "How dare you ask me such a question?" he indignantly replies.

"No hard feelings," says the Jew and moves on to a woman standing nearby. "Excuse me, madam, are you an anti-Semite?" Her reaction is the same.

The scene repeats itself several times before the Jew finally meets up with a pleasant-looking, respectable couple and asks them the same question, "Pardon me, are you by any chance anti-Semites?"

"We certainly are," says the man. "We detest the Jews, the whole stinking lot of them."

"Ah," replies the Jew, "what a pleasure to meet such honest people. Would you mind keeping an eye on my suitcase for me?"

It would be interesting to try a similar experiment in a German theatre or concert hall. Just before the performance begins, I would like to come on stage and ask everyone who does not like Jews to raise his right hand. I am quite certain not a single hand would go up. You might just as well ask wife-beaters and child-abusers to raise their hands.

The real problem with anti-Semitism in Germany is not that it exists, but that nobody is willing to own up to it. It is not the open anti-Semite who is perverse, but the society he lives in, a society which believes it can do away with a phenomenon simply by claiming it does not exist.

In his *Reflections on the Jewish Question,* Sartre claimed that anti-Semitism was a "passion." The early Zionist Leo Pinsker, on the other hand, wrote in his 1882 essay "Auto-Emancipation" that "Judophobia" was a "disease" which had been passed on for over 2,000 years and was, as such, "incurable." Whether one views it as a passion or as an hereditary cultural disease, in the long run the suppression of so vital an urge and the refusal to allow it any free form of expression is bound to lead to serious neuroses or perversions, or both. And if the urge is unable to achieve satisfaction along a direct path, it will be forced to seek relief in an indirect manner.

Just as dirty jokes are always indicative of some repressed desire, so it is no coincidence that in Germany, where anti-Semitism "officially" does not exist, the joke about how to fit 20 Jews into a VW Beetle is part of the standard repertoire of every elementary school student. Their teachers are always "deeply dismayed" at hearing such things, at a loss to understand "where they pick them up." Where indeed?

The classic trinity of Jews, anti-Semitism, and anti-Semites would appear to have vanished from Germany. Not only have the Jews, with the exception of a token remainder, disappeared from German society, but, with them, the anti-Semites. All that is left is a floating anti-Semitic potential, a kind of platonic hate affair, with neither Jews nor anti-Semites to breathe life into it.

So it would appear. But the appearance is a deceptive one, the result of a mutual misunderstanding.

The Jews labor under the belief that anti-Semitism must not and, therefore, cannot exist after Auschwitz; that the anti-Semites themselves would have to be too exhausted, or, at least, too ashamed of themselves, to muster the necessary forces for new endeavor. And the officially non-existent anti-Semites, on the other hand, believe that a condemnation of Auschwitz and the systematic murder of Jews would have to be sufficient evidence of their good will to place them beyond even the slightest suspicion.

What the Jews have failed to realize is that anti-Semitism in Germany today does not exist *in spite of* Auschwitz, but, much rather, *because of it,* because it serves as a constant reminder to people of their own misdeeds and failings. The anti-Semites, on the other hand, tend to forget that Auschwitz was an atypically excessive outburst in the history of anti-Semitism, and that it cannot be taken as a standard. It is quite possible, in other words, to be opposed to Auschwitz and still be anti-Semitic. In fact, a condemnation of Nazi anti-Semitism is a necessary pre-condition for any viable new form of anti-Semitism which does not wish to discredit itself from the outset.

This misunderstanding was a cooperative effort on the part of Jews and Germans alike. Both sides had an equal interest in side-stepping the reality, neither wished to see the post-War "rehabilitation" of Germany (not mere *Wiedergutmachung* but also *Wiedergutwerden*) threatened by unpleasant insights into the true situation.

The level of anti-Semitism at any given time was measured by the success or failure of radical nationalist parties at the ballot box, while studies documenting intent or manifest anti-Semitism in other sectors were categorically dismissed as "unfounded." And by none were such studies considered more "questionable" than by the official representatives of the Jewish community, who, as the author of one study put it, seemed to think everything was fine as long as leading politicians continued making solemn speeches at the opening of "Brotherhood Week" each year.

And now it turns out that there is a spot of trouble in paradise. Things are not quite what they ought to be. Jewish community leaders, who showed no hesitation in calling the police when their own buildings were being occupied by squatters, are now going around trying to take public theatres by force. And Germany's leading liberal newspapers, unflagging in their sympathy for the squatters, describe the stopping of a single theatre performance as an "intolerable breach of law." The "Frankfurt Follies" — a political farce in several acts, performances in the main lobby — compliments of Rainer Werner Fassbinder.

I do not know whether Fassbinder himself was anti-Semitic, but it is not very likely. The fact that he allows anti-Semitic characters a place in his play *Der Müll, die Stadt und der Tod (Garbage, the City and Death)*, says nothing about his own feelings.

Und Schuld hat der Jud, weil er uns schuldig macht, denn er ist da. Wär er geblieben, wo er herkam, oder hätten sie ihn vergast, ich könnte heute besser schlafen. Sie haben vergessen, ihn zu vergasen. Das ist kein Witz, so denkt es in mir. . . .

It's the Jew's fault, since he makes me feel guilty, just being there [one character says]. If he had stayed where he came from, or if they'd gassed him, I'd be able to sleep better tonight. I'm not joking. That's the way it thinks inside me.

It would be difficult to find a better, more pointed expression of the persecutor's rage at the sight of the victims who survived, whose very existence is a constant, barely tolerable provocation for him. Here in Fassbinder's play, the authentic voice of anti-Semitism *because* of Auschwitz can be heard.

The play itself can only be considered anti-Semitic in the sense that it has served as a catalyst to anti-Semitic reactions. It wakes sleeping dogs and, in that sense, is both instructive and confusing. We have taken a giant step towards recognizing reality.

Consider the Director of the Frankfurt Theatre where *Garbage* was to have been performed, Günther Rühle. In his former capacity as *feuilleton* editor of one of Germany's most respected newspapers, the *Frankfurter Allgemeine Zeitung,* Rühle was active for many years in the effort to prevent Fassbinder's play from being performed. In his new job, Rühle now considers the very same play's performance virtually indispensable for Frankfurt's cultural advancement. This is not to be construed as opportunism, however, it is merely an instance of unswerving loyalty towards any given employer at any given time — a much-sought and highly-admired virtue in the world of commerce.

The fact that Rühle also announced that the days of "restraint" towards the Jews had "come to an end" (*"das Ende der Schonzeit"*) received only marginal attention in the heat of the debate. But what exactly does the end of "restraint" mean? What else can it mean but that the hunting season can now resume?

Rühle would, naturally, be the first to say that that is not what he meant. Maybe he does not think that way. But that is the way "it thinks inside" him, just as "it thinks inside (*so denkt es in ihm*)" Fassbinder's hero, Hans von Gluck.

When Rühle, in proclaiming the end of "restraint," also announces a return to "normality" in German-Jewish relations, he is merely offering a socially acceptable version of the same demands the neo-Nazi newspapers have been printing for years. "It's time to draw the line — enough is enough." One of Germany's most prominent theatre critics, Peter Iden, noted in a television discussion that the Germans were "no longer prepared to let themselves be humiliated by the Jews." It would appear to be thinking inside Mr. Iden, too: *"Deutsche, wehrt Euch . . . !* (Germans, defend yourselves!)"

For the sake of clarity, it should be pointed out that a return to a state of "normality" cannot be proclaimed quite as one-sidedly as its end was announced in 1933. And, just for the record, it is also extremely difficult to imagine that anybody would be calling for "normalization" today if six million Germans had been killed by Jews as recently as 40 or 50 years ago — particularly when one considers the trouble we have had being forgiven for a single, unproved murder some 2,000 years ago.

Or take Heiko Holefleisch, for another example. Heiko Holefleisch was in charge of production of the Fassbinder play in Frankfurt. In an interview with a *Ma'ariv* correspondent, he spoke out against making a taboo of anti-Semitism:

> What I mean by making a taboo of anti-Semitism [he explained] I will try to answer in a very personal way. I was born in 1949, I'm the same age as this Republic. I was born into a non-Jewish, German family. My father was a member of the Nazi Party.
>
> While I was growing up, it was a constant problem for me to try and comprehend the discrepancy between the way I saw my father — whom I loved very much, and who seemed very humane to me — and his political convictions, his former political convictions.
>
> The picture I got in school was of this monster, this demon Hitler and his loyal followers, and there was a lot about that which I didn't understand. I knew I would have to learn to comprehend this if I was ever going to be able to grow up, as a German, after the War.

What Heiko Holefleisch is concerned with, in his touchingly awkward statement, has been nicely expressed by the critic Eike Geisel as "family reconciliation (*Familienzusammenführung*)." It has been thinking inside Heiko Holefleisch, too.

The sons cannot be expected to live their whole lives with a demonic image of their fathers in their hearts. They want to rehabilitate their fathers, "de-monsterfy" or "de-demonize" them, so to speak. That is why the taboo on anti-Semitism has to be lifted — for their fathers' sakes, so they will finally be able to "grow up as a German after the War." Happy graduation, you're a grown boy now.

It would seem the children of the persecutors do not have it any easier than the children of the concentration-camp survivors. I suppose I ought to be grateful my parents ended up on the right side of the barbed wire. That is the way it sometimes "thinks" inside me.

Or take the *Vorwärts,* the official newspaper of the Social Democratic Party and traditional vanguard of the labor movement in Germany. One month before

the scheduled premiere of the Fassbinder play, the *Vorwärts* ran a background article, entitled "Can Jews Never Be Evil? (*Sind Juden niemals böse?*)." In that article the
"rich Jew" is removed from the cover of anonymity and put on full display. The
"rich Jew" of Frankfurt, unnamed in Fassbinder's play, truly exists, we are told.
"Half of Frankfurt" belongs to him and he is "considered one of the richest men in
Germany." The article then proceeds to record the "fact" that "the land speculation business in Frankfurt is mainly in Jewish hands."

Interested as I was in learning who the other half of Frankfurt belongs to, I
asked the *Vorwärts* to supply me with more detailed information regarding these
apparently well-known facts. I also wanted to know exactly where the "rich Jew"
fits in among the Flicks, Thyssens, Fuggers, Henkels, Reemtsmas, and other
landed and industrial aristocrats whose names actually make up the list of the
richest men in Germany.

And I was particularly interested in seeing the statistical basis for the statement that the Frankfurt land speculation business is "mainly in Jewish hands." Is
there a special office where land speculators are registered on the basis of their
religious and cultural backgrounds? Surely no responsible democratic journalist
would make a statement like that without being able to back it up.

I am still waiting for a reply.

In a society not contaminated with anti-Semitism there would be no reason
not to put on a play in which the leading character is a nasty, despicable Jew. The
innocent, playfully teasing question posed by the *Vorwärts* article "Can Jews
Never be Evil?" is not really a question, and it is not looking for an answer. What
the article does is to offer a socially acceptable form for expressing a resentment
which has been lying dormant for too long, and for once again enjoying the thrill
of seeing the words "speculation," "business," and "Jewish hands" side by side in
the same sentence. Wouldn't it be simpler, and healthier, for them to simply
pound the table with their fists and shout, "*Sau-juden!*" with all their hearts? That
might at least have some therapeutic value.

Instead of carrying on endless and fruitless debates about the "freedom of the
arts" and the "inadmissibility of censorship," it would be far more satisfying, and
more honest, to simply admit that Fassbinder's play states loudly and clearly exactly the way "it thinks" inside many people in Germany. Much like a porno-
graphic movie, the main attraction of the play lies in its allowing the audience to
hear their own thoughts spoken out loud without having to stand up for them.

All these strange comments, responses, self-portrayals and self-exposures
are owed to a single play, written on a flight to New York (or Los Angeles or
Dakar or wherever), and about whose real artistic value critics are anything but
unanimous. And now, before receiving a single proper performance, it has been
cancelled in Frankfurt (although rushed hastily into a performance in Kassel).

The Jewish community of Frankfurt can chalk up a victory and everyone
who always knew about "the power of the Jews" has been given new fuel for his
thoughts.

I am not certain whether the performance of the play would have been a lesser evil than its cancellation; but I am fairly certain that the anti-Fassbinder front is celebrating a victory which will soon be proving itself highly Pyrrhic in nature. Last November, German Television's prime-time schedule included the film Shadow of the Future (*Schatten der Zukunft*), by Wolfgang Bergmann.

The film was originally scheduled to be shown on 13 November, until at the last moment it occurred to someone in the programming department that the date was embarrassingly close to the anniversary of *Kristallnacht,* that notorious day of the 1938 pogrom. For reasons of piety, it was rescheduled for two weeks later.

The film's subject is a question, namely, "What do we Germans have to do with the Israel/Palestine conflict?" Here, again, we are dealing with a tactical question, and in a press release, the young film-maker gives us his answer:

> Due to our historic experiences, we Germans have a special responsibility toward peace and international understanding in the world. The First World War and the expulsion and extermination of Europe's Jews by National Socialism created many problems, a number of which remain unsolved to this day. . . . Today, we Germans still have a cramped relationship toward Jews, as can be seen in the rising trend of animosity toward foreigners.

Bergmann, a progressive among film-makers, with a marked preference for referring to himself in public as "We Germans," wants to help loosen up his cramped relationship. He does this by asking further questions bearing on the subject of his film: the special German responsibility toward peace and international understanding:

> Can I, as a German, criticize Israel without becoming anti-Semitic, and do I have the right to be concerned about the future of the Jews in Israel? Are the bombing attacks on Jewish restaurants and travel agencies spontaneous anti-Israel protests or a renewal of the old anti-Semitism? Or is it even possible that Israel's politics are provoking new animosity towards Jews!

By posing the question as to whether the attacks on Jewish restaurants are spontaneous anti-Israel protests or revivals of the old anti-Semitism, the film-maker gives us strong reasons to suspect that his problems are not merely of a political, but also of a mental nature.

At the start of his film, Bergmann reveals a further dilemma. As photographs showing the mountains of dead bodies in a concentration camp are shown, the narrative voice tells us:

> My father took me to see a film which was supposed to explain what had happened in the Second World War. He had been forced to be a part of it, too, hadn't had any choice, he said.

Some of those pictures I still cannot forget. How was it possible? Why hadn't my parents known? Why hadn't they offered any resistance?

Like Holefleisch, Bergmann has a family problem. He asks why his parents hadn't known what was being done, implicitly accepting as a fact the idea that they really hadn't known. Presumably, his father went to a film explaining the War so that he, too, could find out what had happened in that War he had been forced to be a part of.

Rather than confronting his parents and asking whether it was truly possible that they did not have *any* idea about what was happening all around them, Bergmann prefers to show his "concern about the future of the Jews in Israel." Bergmann shows footage of Jewish children standing behind the fences of Auschwitz, their shirt-sleeves rolled up, exposing the numbers tattooed on their arms; the narrator speaks:

These are the liberated children of Auschwitz. They are a warning to us all. What has come of their longing for a more human future and a more secure home in Israel?

For a brief moment the viewer is left to believe he will be seeing a film about these survivors. Then, suddenly, it becomes clear what the liberated children of Auschwitz are being used for.

A low whistling sound grows louder, draws nearer. It is the sound of a falling bomb. At the very moment it is heard exploding, the faces on the screen change. The children of Auschwitz are gone and now we see the war-torn city of Beirut, the Palestinian refugee camps Sabra and Shatilla, and the war's victims — the children. In his commentary, the film-maker tells us that "a Jewish man living in Germany" had been reminded of Babi Yar, where the SS had had Jews slaughtered by the native Ukrainians, and even Bergmann himself said he had been unable to keep himself from "drawing comparisons with National Socialism."

The message is clear. The Israelis are doing to the Palestinians what the Nazis did to the Jews. This is Bergmann's contribution to what the philosopher Jürgen Habermas calls "*die Entsorgung der Vergangenheit* (the de-problematization of the past"), the next step after successful "family reconciliation." The Jews take on the roles of the Nazis, the Palestinians take on the role of the Jews — and Wolfgang Bergmann is there to stand up for the persecuted and fight the persecutors who, in this case, conveniently happen to be Jewish Nazis. Bergmann now has the chance to make up for the resistance his parents neglected to offer — and, killing a second bird with the same stone, to eliminate any residual guilt he may have felt toward his parents' victims. It all works out very nicely.

"How is it possible," asks Bergmann, "that the Jews, who had suffered so much themselves, could wage such a brutal war in Lebanon?" Ironic, isn't it? After all, weren't the concentration camps primarily concerned with rehabilitation? And wasn't the purpose of submitting the inmates to such severe trials solely to make better persons of them?

The closet anti-Semites, as Sartre might have put it, can only be enjoying their secret lust behind disguises. They clothe their passion in "the garb of theoretical proposals." They speak of the need to do away with taboos, of the end of restraint, and the start of normalization. They want to know whether bombing Jewish restaurants might not be a form of spontaneous anti-Israel protest, and complain about their cramped relationship with the Jews. But whatever garb they clothe it in, what they mean is always the same: after 40 years of restraint, when the whole nation was required to love them, it ought finally to be allowed again for Germans not to like Jews.

It is not the characters in Fassbinder's play who behave like anti-Semites, but the people in the theatre audience who shout to the Jewish demonstrators occupying the stage:

Kommen Sie nicht immer wieder mit ihrem Auschwitz! (Leave us alone with your Auschwitz!)

Your Auschwitz? *Whose* Auschwitz?

"Without Auschwitz, no Israel," says Bergmann, citing Nahum Goldmann, and he then expands the thought to "Without Auschwitz, no expulsions of the Palestinians." That may or may not be correct, but Bergmann would do far better to concern himself with a slightly different problem: *Without anti-Semitism in Germany, no Auschwitz.* But that would entail focusing his attention on his own parents again, and the whole projection of both his problems and those of German history on to the Judean desert would be spoiled and German television audiences would be robbed of a chance to see one more pretentious and superfluous contribution to their evening entertainment.

Oy gevalt! What complicated maneuvers, what amazing feats of emotional acrobatics, just to express a feeling of distaste which the honest anti-Semite Wagner described without the slightest embarrassment: "Whenever one sees a Jew, one immediately senses a feeling of revulsion . . . ."

It may be a long time before a Jew in Germany is able to find an anti-Semite he can trust to watch his suitcase.

(Mr. Henryk M. Broder, a prominent journalist, lives in Israel.)

Germany and Israel —
The Road to Trust Without Forgetting

By Johannes Rau

Our Federal Republic is a young state.

Yet, there are many times that the citizens of this state come to feel the burdens of a history, without which our democratic polity would certainly not have developed in such a way.

We had that in mind when we commemorated the fiftieth anniversary of the so-called National Socialists' assumption of power, two years ago.

Several weeks from now, we shall be confronted again with this history, which to call our "own" we should and must avoid.

Concerning that, we are advised in many different ways: Whether we had not better be quiet as to whether we consider the end of the war a liberation or a catastrophe or both, whether we want to stand by our friends or how we could avoid giving offense or exposing ourselves.

In such a way, our view is sometimes obstructed from seeing historical connections; even on commemoration and anniversary days still ahead of us — in the Eighties and Nineties — this may happen, when we will look back on things past, on the deeds and atrocities committed, or on the omissions made fifty years ago.

We're hearing that many older citizens do not want to be reminded of German participation in those acts committed between 1933 and 1945 while curiosity, questions related to that era and the need for more and more detailed information are increasing among the younger generation.

I think, when our Center for Political Education (Landeszentrale für politische Bildung) sent out invitations to think and talk about Israel and our relations to this country of Israel for two days, commemorating twenty years of German-Israeli diplomatic relations, reference to past history — both to the more recent one starting in 1933, and the older one encompassing centuries should not be omitted.

An analysis of this past history, I cannot impart here today.

But I can ask you and the participants in this seminar to combine the understandable desire for an objective assessment of German-Israeli relations with the insight that looking at the present and future relations, there will hardly be ever an open dialogue without embarrassment on the German side.

We cannot set out and walk on the road leading to new trust, while hoping to obliterate the past at the same time.

It is and will be a stony road.

The certainties of German wrong-doing and of National Socialist crimes will be lying like heavy rocks blocking the way and there may be stumbling-blocks of new misunderstandings obstructing our way as we go along.

Even today it will not always be easier for us than twenty years ago, when on May 13, after long negotiations, it was mutually agreed upon to establish diplomatic relations between Israel and the Federal Republic, when we were able to welcome Asher Ben Nathan as ambassador and could give our hopes to Rolf Pauls to take with him on his way to Tel Aviv.

Let us remember: Then, many Arab states, even those that were on friendly terms with us, broke off diplomatic relations with the Federal Republic.

Arrangements were made then in German politics to somehow make up for this disruption in German-Arab friendship—which had often been of long standing—by discontinuing military aid to Israel and by ascribing to her a "normal" rather than a privileged status in our developing aid policies.

It took a long time until normal relations between the Federal Republic and the Arab countries were restored.

And whoever still remembers the year 1952, when on September 10, the Restitution Agreement was signed by the Federal Republic and Israel, will not have forgotten that the payment of DM 3 billion—payable over a period of twelve years—was, more often than not, regarded by Israel's enemies as a complication in their relations with us.

This was a matter of German obligation after 12 years of National Socialism and the crimes against the Jews: never to help any other friends against the interests of this one friend Israel.

That we cannot—on the other hand—assist Israel in her struggles and efforts in the same way as the U.S.A for reasons of self-interest and for the sake of peace, many Israeli friends have understood and accepted.

Who says something like that with the welfare of both countries in mind, has also to consider Israel's and her citizens' expectation that Germany will not export weapons to Israel's neighbors, even if they are not at war with Israel and have not been involved in the Middle East conflict so far.

It can and must not be possible to German politics to contribute, even indirectly, to aggravating Israel's situation, not to speak of assisting what may have become a threat to her.

Even economic interests have to be second in such considerations. And all interests concerning potential working places through the armament industry have proved pseudo-arguments a long time ago in this case.

Also this: to abstain from all actions which could distress Israel is the unrenounceable part of the process which will foster trust between Israel and us.

There are other things as well that we do not want to cover up, looking at German-Israeli relations:

This refers to both the unnatural euphoric mood of some German media and in some German households during the Six-Day War in 1967 and the overt partisanship of left-wing student groups with Israel's enemies in the past.

I think, in the meantime, both moods have given way to what we may call disillusionment, which I think is good.

Sobriety can, indeed, be an indicator for both partners. On such a foundation, trust and critical partnership can flourish.

Not the least because it allows us to keep a distance from such instances when Israeli politics are not accepted unequivocally in Israel, either. This holds true of the settlement policies of the former government, this may hold true of the occupation of vast parts of the Lebanon and maybe also for the acceptance of the right to self-determination for the Palestinians.

Concerning the latter we should, however, try to understand the Israelis' attitude, who, after all their experiences, have problems reconciling themselves with the concept presented by the ECC.

It would be asking too much of us if we were to try taking the role of the mediator in this conflict area. Israeli politics knows how to assess that.

But, especially during these economically hard times, expectations are expressed in Israel which are related to Israel's economic and social situation, i.e., to her concern that, as a result of the Common Market's negotiations about accepting Spain and Portugal, Israel's export interests will not be damaged in the long run.

I think that we as Germans, knowing about Israel's dependence on her export of goods to West Europe, are called upon to look for ways to keep Europe open to further imports of Israeli goods.

After all, we cannot seek partnership by imposing unbearable sacrifices on other partners.

Both attitudes characterizing our way to trust *and* sobriety with Israel must include our absolute commitment to Israel's right to exist and to pursue Middle East policies, in the spirit of critical partnership, which are moderate, aiming at attaining mutual understanding and will not support or encourage Israel's and the Jews' enemies, and they must also include our willingness not to forget.

That is to say, not to forget that it was the inexorable persecution of the Jews by National Socialist Germany which ultimately led to the strengthening of the "love of Zion" and the enormous Jewish immigration to the former British mandate territory and brought about the UN agreement of November 29, 1947, which then led to the founding of the state of Israel.

In our Federal state of Northrhine-Westphalia not only the politicians of all parties, but also many citizens, old and young, participated actively in finding and walking on this road toward trust, to support and to strengthen the ties between Israel and Northrhine-Westphalia.

Here, I can report on these activities only in a fragmentary way:

I do so with joy and satisfaction.

To begin with, I would like to mention the youth-exchange, which was started about 25 years ago, and in those days still operated without the support of funds from the Federal State County Youth Programs (Bundes-und Landesjugendplan).

In the beginning, our state was the only one to have a German-Israeli support program.

First, young people from our country went to Israel and worked in the kibutzim and moshavim, participated in vocational training seminars, and regarded that as a kind of symbolic restitution. Since 1966, Israeli youth groups have come to us as well; in the last year, 11 came from Israel and 15 went from here to Israel. In the most affluent years, the county contributed between DM 200,000 and 300,000 for this purpose. The Federation gives as many subsidies as possible, particularly to the supporting agencies of private youth aid.

We wish to continue this youth-exchange and, I believe, Israel, her government and citizens wish to do the same as well.

Therefore, it would be helpful if those in charge of the program in Israel would decide soon not to impose the common special taxes for travel abroad on officially supported youth travel. At the current exchange rate of the dollar, this is clearly a great hardship.

Apart from the youth-exchange, the city partnerships are particularly important to us.

Among the numerous city partnerships, I only mention here those between Cologne and Tel Aviv, between Düsseldorf and Haifa, between Dortmund and Nethanya, Münster and Rishon, Wuppertal and Beer Sheva.

Also the partnerships between universities ought to be appreciated, such as the ones between the TH Aachen and Haifa University, between the Gesamthochschule Wuppertal and Ben-Gurion University of the Negev.

The nuclear research plant Jülich cooperates with the Haifa Technion under the so-called umbrella agreement, which is still expendable. On both sides, high hopes are set on these scientific projects.

In my files I also have a long list of a great number of scholarly contracts between university institutes and faculties.

In our county such contacts are maintained by nine universities, according to my impression they are particularly close and diversified at the universities of Bochum, Bielefeld, and Bonn.

On the Israeli side, the universities of Jerusalem, Tel Aviv, Beer Sheva, the Weizmann-Institute, and the Wingate-Institute partake of contacts.

Apart from that, Northrhine-Westphalia is also rather proud of the Josef-Neuberger scholarship.

The economical exchange, which is presently beset by difficulties, due to the inflationary developments in Israel, has improved during the 80's all the same.

In 1983, goods worth DM 637 million were exported from Northrhine-Westphalia to Israel. Our imports from Israel amounted to DM 324 million.

The flower growers on both sides set good examples for a co-operation which is complimentary to each other — and this is for as long as ten years.

The exhibition of our County Center (Landeszentrale) illustrates also the kind of institutional interrelations existing between Israel and Northrhine-Westphalia.

The County Working Circle (Landesarbeitsgemeinschaft) "Work and Life" has been particularly active in this respect since 1964. But I would also like to mention the Karl-Arnold Foundation, the Friedrich-Ebert Foundation, the distinguished Rheinisch-Westfälische Auslandsgesellschaft (Rhine-Westphalia Foreign Society), the committed Socialist Educational Associations (Sozialistische Bildungsgemeschaften), the Federal Center for Political Education, our Cultural Affairs Department, the Ministry of Labor, Health, and Social Affairs, the German-Israeli Society, and the political parties as well.

I think all this demonstrates that in the past two decades (and in some cases even three decades, or longer) a mutual relationship of trust developed, which may well put us in a hopeful and optimistic mood.

Germans and Jews—this did not only seem to Leo Baeck a relationship destroyed once and for all through German crimes committed during twelve years of National Socialist rule, both in peace and during the war.

I said "in peace" and I have to correct myself there: it may be said that the National Socialist war against the Jews started as early as in 1933 and concerning the para-military organization it was even started ten years earlier, on the day when the party was founded, calling itself "national" and "socialist", and "labor party".

The stages of this war, first against the German Jews and then against European Jewry at large, can be looked up in every book on modern history, specifically in a book by Günther Bernd Ginzel entitled, "Jewish Everyday Life in Germany between 1933 and 1945" (Jüdischer Alltag in Deutschland 1933 bis 1945), which was published only recently.

And not to forget: when speaking of our "mission", a look at history, at legal decrees and organized so-called "anger of the masses" will suffice to know why.

Only those who seriously cope with the suffering of Jews among us, or living in the days of our fathers and grandfathers will be able to think about and anticipate the problems and aspirations of German-Israeli relations.

And they will find out the following: Young people on both sides have been working to overcome feelings of guilt and shame, of sadness and disappointment, of mistrust and memories of Jewish suffering during these past decades.

I was particularly moved, however, to be able to witness in recent years—and presumably many of you present here, too—that many of the Jews who were still able to escape, who survived—occasionally with the help of Germans—started reaching out their hands and looked at the second German Republic and at German democrats with some hope.

There will be the time of new generations, a time when the eyewitnesses of the crimes committed during those twelve years will not be with us anymore, to speak to us. There will be a time when all those marked by suffering and all those who were themselves blindly involved in the work of destruction will not be here to speak to us.

Maybe, some will say then with relief: now, normality will start.

I want to contradict those, because I believe that history, the history of war and suffering in this century and its impact on other nations, particularly on the Jewish people, will stay alive in the memories of our youths.

The dialogue between Germans and Jews may eventually be more free, but it will not be conducted without the awareness of the historical burden.

A common road of trust will lead to those times, that is what I hope together with everybody of good will.

But we should not have any illusions: We will not be spared trials.

World politics will always remain related to the difficult questions of life and peace in the Middle East.

Whoever knows this country of Israel, a small country, which was cultivated with unspeakable hardship and great commitment in the midst of the desert wastelands and which, now, is the most modern and "Westernized" state in a large region, knows that she needs partners, not only in Europe and the U.S., but also needs neighbors as partners.

It is unthinkable to fight two, three, or more wars for survival in every generation.

We know: Today, tomorrow, and in the future it is and will be a difficult task for Israel not to cease trying to find a way out of an imposed siege mentality after decade-long wars and, at the same time, to negotiate detente and partnership with fierce opponents, who are, after all, neighbors.

Egypt was a promising starting point, which, however, did not develop into a snowball system which affected the other Arab states.

We noticed, and Israel does, too, yet without deriving any hope from that so far, changes in the so-called "Arab camp" and among the Palestinians as well.

It seems that Israel's right to exist is no longer a question of principle as it was ten or twenty years ago, but rather a question of an autonomous Palestinian state. And of course, the problem concerning Israel's protective and vital borders remains a matter of dispute.

It is not up to us to give Israel advice concerning her policies.

At the same time, we may not turn away indifferently.

The recent history of European Jewry and our part in it are too closely tied up to Israel's establishment and development, to her threat and survival to leave us cold and indifferent to the present and future life perspectives of the Jews in their new state.

And speaking of "us", I do not only refer to the older generation, but also to their children and the generation to come.

New ties between Israel and the Federal Republic were made, a long time ago, particularly in Northrhine-Westphalia.

We are not only aware of these ties today, tomorrow and in the future, here in Cologne, but nearly each and every day, many times at least every year: in and at our schools, in associations, in societies, in the fractions of our parties, in the unions, in cities and in villages.

With gratitude and delight we accepted offers for discussions, we sit together again, either over there in Israel or here; gaps have not remained unbridged, the word "Shalom" can be said with laughter—all this after all the pain, the horror, and despite wounds that will take a long time to heal.

The trials I referred to, we are aware of. But I hope we do not just remember them on the occasion of commemorations, anniversaries of our "numerous Societies for Christian-Jewish Cooperation."

But in political and social everyday life. On May 8, yes, and also when we commemorate the end of National Socialist rule, without forgetting how it started.

During retrospectives, which are due, of the Nuremberg laws, of the destruction of the synagogues in 1938, of the outlawing of Jews for many years, of the "integration" of Austria, which hit the Jews badly, and, finally, of the "final solution".

And it may well be that questions will not only be raised concerning our new legal actions against new signs of anti-Semitism, which is often combined with national chauvinism.

And it may also be that our anger ought to become more fierce and overt in view of those allegations still going strong that Auschwitz and other places of destruction were nothing but lies.

At present Bonn is contending for a law concerning this matter.

After long and irritating debates, the government coalition agreed on having any insult or defamation of victims of the NS regime or other despotic regimes or tyrannies punished by law through the public prosecutor.

The Social Democrats will look into this suggestion. It will be crucial to them, however, that the uniqueness of the National socialist genocide not be doubted.

I admit openly that I would feel much better if we were not forced to protect this historical truth, which has been proven as evident many times.

But I understand the anguish and the deep injuries of our Jewish fellow-citizens and of many Jews the world over.

And therefore—and also because of the endangering of new trust between Germans and Jews—we have to find means and ways—and if all else fails, even legal measures—to order the new agitators and those who will take no advice to be quiet.

We owe this to the dignity of the survivors and to the dignity of our democracy and constitutional state.

Let us be steadfast democrats in such trials beyond all party lines and not budge an inch from the road of trust, so we may look into each other's eyes also in the future, whether here in Cologne or in Münster, whether in Haifa or in Tel Aviv. Jews and Germans live in two states that are very different, in which democracy and human freedom, however, are deeply rooted.

Let us be steadfast and in solidarity, so "Shalom Aleichem" will not be a hollow form of salutation, but a reality that may actually be experienced, both in Israel and here with us, and so "Shalom" will remain a reality between us.

(Translated by Renate Steinchen.)

(Johannes Rau is Prime Minister of North Rhineland—Westphalia, where Bitburg is located, and whose re-election campaign was a factor in prompting Chancellor Kohl to schedule the Bitburg visit. Rau opposed Kohl's candidate. After the Bitburg visit, Rau was re-elected.)

Part IV

The American Response

This section documents the wide involvement of various political, ethnic, religious, and veterans' groups in the effort to change the president's itinerary. The most directly offended were the veterans' and Jewish organizations and their constituents. Their concerted involvement in this conflict was without parallel in its timing, scope, intensity, and perseverance. This, however, did not preclude dissension within these two broad groups, whose reponses ranged from vehement criticism on the one hand to outright support of the president's decision, in the case of the Veterans of Foreign Wars.

The response of the Jewish establishment differed as well in its methods, and the results sought. The conventional machinery of conveying the interests of the Jewish community to the president via Marshall Breger, special assistant to the president for public liason, was notably stilled during the initial stages of this affair.

Breger was on a personal visit to Israel when the announcement of the visit took place; thus, the essential administration Jewish input was missing during the time when an essentially Jewish affair was being discussed. Neither was he active in the consultations between the White House and the American Jewish Committee (see the essay by Mark Tanenbaum). What he was noted for was his effort to tone down the remarks Elie Wiesel planned to made to the president at the White House on April 19. He tried to cut them to three minutes (see the detailed description by Senator Frank Lautenberg). It is possible that Breger was locked out of the process by White House chief of staff Donald Regan; yet he neither protested nor resigned as one of his precedessors, Mark Siegel, had done over a different issue during the Carter administration.

The American and Jewish organizations directly concerned with the Holocaust, such as the United States Holocaust Memorial Council, American Gathering and Federation of Jewish Holocaust Survivors, and the International Network of Children of Jewish Holocaust Survivors publicly voiced their objections. (See "Reagan Errs on the Holocaust" by Menachem Rosensaft.) There was a strong possibility that the entire U.S. Holocaust Memorial Council would resign over the issue of Bitburg until its chairman, Elie Wiesel, delivered his moving speech at the White House in which he reminded the president that his place was with the victims, not with the perpetrators of crimes.

This encounter between Wiesel and Reagan prompted Charles Silberman to declare it one of the most remarkable in the annals of American Jewry. On the other hand, there were those who felt that Wiesel should have been more confrontational.

The leaders of the national Jewish organizations openly registered their protests. Kenneth Bialkin, chairman of the Conference of Presidents of Major Jewish Organizations, for example, stated that the decision to visit Bitburg but not Dachau was "deeply offensive." This is not the type of language normally associated with Jewish leaders when dealing with the administration. The official and public protests of such leaders as Abraham Foxman, Nathan Perlmutter, Howard Friedman, Marc Tanenbaum, David Gordis, Henry Siegman, and Norman Lamm were offered in the traditional vein — all of them couched their protests in such a manner as not to decrease their effectiveness in future dealings with the president.

It should be made clear that the Jewish organizations were not opposed to a reconciliation with West Germany. On the contrary, many of them had long been advocates of the normalization of relations with a new-style Germany, and it was Nahum Goldman, president of the World Jewish Congress, who had initiated and conducted the first steps that lead to the reconciliation between Israel and the FRG. The efforts of the American Jewish Committee in this regard date back to 1960 when they implemented a special project to bring West German high-school teachers to the United States. The object was to allow the West Germans to experience democracy at work and to translate this into the German experience when the teachers returned to their native schools.

In 1966 Jacob Blaustein, president of the AJC, explained that the aim of his organization was to support a "pragmatic" position toward postwar Germany, and insisted on behalf of the AJC that 60 million Germans could not be kept forever beyond the pale of world society. The AJC continues the German-American Jewish Exchange Program in cooperation with the Konrad Adenauer Foundation and the Friedrich Ebert Foundation.

Howard Friedman, president of the AJC, spoke of "the new Germany and its commitment to upholding the sanctity of human life and defending constitutional democracy" in Berlin in July 1984 when addressing a commemorative gathering of the 40th anniversary of the attempt to assassinate Hitler and overthrow the Nazi regime. Thus, while it may have surprised many people when Friedman's April 1985 statement about Bitburg referred to Germany as a democratic state, it is consistent with the AJC's view of modern Germany. Numerous Jewish critics of the AJC, however, perceived its stand as irrelevant, and even apologetic.

In contrast, Henry Siegman of the American Jewish Congress noted that German-Jewish reconciliation could not take place at the expense of remembering the past. Thus, he wrote that the "most damaging lie of Bitburg is the implied suggestion that we, Germans and Americans, need to falsify history in order to find some common ground."

WJC President Edgar Bronfman went so far as to contact the leaders in Jewish communities in 70 countries — from Argentina to Zimbabwe — to request that each one contact the U.S. ambassador in that country and demand that President Reagan not visit Bitburg. WJC leaders Israel Singer and Elan Steinberg met with the German Ambassador Gunter van Well at his home in Washington, D.C. However, the ambassador informed them that there was no cemetery in Germany that would not contain graves of Waffen SS members. (While this information was incorrect, it did have an effect on the WJC. The news took Chancellor Kohl off the hook, so future protests were focused on President Reagan.)

The WJC leadership traveled to Germany in order to convince Chancellor Kohl that he should urge Reagan to drop the idea of a Bitburg visit, laboring under the impression that Reagan had the exclusive control over the itinerary. Although they were not successful in this goal, they did convince the West German Jewish community not to participate at the ceremonies at Bergen-Belsen and Bitburg.

Yet, the executive director of the WJC, Israel Singer, criticized the Jewish leadership, stating, "I find it shocking that Jewish defense organizations have not found Reagan shocking. The leaders of the Jewish community have been entirely too acquiescent."

This criticism was openly supported by Menachem Rosensaft as well as by Jack Eisner, president of the Holocaust Survivors Memorial Foundation, and other leaders of the Holocaust survivors.

Indeed, the loudest voices of the protest against Bitburg came from outside the Jewish establishment: Elie Wiesel, as the spiritual voice, and Rosensaft, the radical who called for action and who led the demonstrations on April 21 in Philadelphia and at Bergen-Belsen on May 5.

This was true because both men saw the issue in terms of morality and historical justice without the burden of political obligation. This conclusion is supported by the criticism of the May 5 demonstration at Bergen-Belsen voiced by some Jewish establishment leaders, who said of the protestors: "they are grandstanding"; "[these are] people who want to have their names in the papers;" "this action is causing further damage to the American Jewish community's relations with the President."

Making a complete break with its past policy of working primarily behind the scenes, the WJC took off after leading Jewish organizations after the visit, referring to "the whitewash being undertaken by organizations like the ADL and the AJC on behalf of Reagan's Administration." They are acting like the Neville Chamberlains of the Bitburg Affair. This harsh accusation made by WJC Executive Director Israel Singer is based on the premise that the prophet traditionally speaks Truth to Power. The question that should be kept in mind in such a dilemma is: Does such a leader (or prophet) have a responsibility to his his constituency to protect his future effectiveness?

It would be erroneous to expect Jewish leaders in today's political milieu in the United States to lambast the president in the tradition of Jeremiah and Ezekiel. However, if "outsiders" such as Wiesel and Rosensaft held establishment posts, they would be more likely to follow that tradition, thus moving — when required — into positions of uncompromising opposition.

The intellectuals and Jewish leaders discussed the merits of the intended visit on the lines of politics or morality. The press, on the other hand, had a field day in covering the three-week long development of the Bitburg affair. They honed in on and sharpened their pencils (or plunged down on their word processors) on three major issues:

1. The presidents's refusal to drop Bitburg from the itinerary after it was determined that Waffen SS members were buried there.
2. The president's statement on April 18, 1985, that German soldiers buried at Bitburg were victims of the Nazi regime "just as surely as" the victims of the Holocaust.
3. The president's initial decision not to visit a Nazi concentration camp and his subsequent decision to include the death camp of Bergen-Belsen in his itinerary.

Analysis: Bitburg

All the 50 largest U.S. daily newspapers devoted considerable editorial reaction to the president's trip to West Germany. Most of them editorialized more than once in the three-week span from the announcement of the visit to Bitburg and the actual visit.

Forty-three (86 percent) were opposed to the president's visit. Four of them were in favor of the president visiting Bitburg so long as he also visited Dachau, until they learned about the Waffen SS graves. Then they joined the list of dissenters.

Two (4 percent) felt the president should have planned his trip better and should have turned down Chancellor Kohl's invitation to visit Bitburg. They also editorialized that once the president announced his visit, he should not back down.

Four (8 percent) were in favor of the president visiting Bitburg.

One (2 percent) did not voice an opinion about the Bitburg visit, but concerned itself with other issues surrounding the state trip.

Sixteen newspapers (32 percent) commented on the statement President Reagan made concerning the Waffen SS buried there being victims of the Nazis. Fifteen (30 percent of the total or 93.8 percent of those who commented) disagreed strongly with Reagan's statement. One newspaper (2 percent of the total or 6.25 percent of those who commented) agreed with the president. The remaining 34 did not comment!

Analysis: Dachau

Twenty-nine newspapers (58 percent) editorialized about the omission of Dachau from President Reagan's original announced itinerary. Fourteen (48.3 percent of the 29) were disturbed that the president was planning to visit a German World War II military cemetery while he had previously rejected an invitation to visit Dachau, a former concentration camp (this was prior to the announcement that he would visit Bergen-Belsen). Four of these latter newspapers editorialized that they had no objection to the president's itinerary providing he also visit Dachau. All four changed their positions when they learned of the Waffen SS graves. One newspaper was not disturbed by the omission of a concentration camp — and wrote as much.

The other 15 newspapers (51.7 percent) editorialized about the omission of Dachau from the original itinerary only after it was announced that Reagan would visit Bergen-Belsen.

The remaining 21 papers had no comment on Dachau.

Should Not Go To Bitburg

As noted, 43 newspapers stated that the president should not go to Bitburg. Their major points were:

1. Honoring Nazi Germany's dead soldiers was not the ideal way to reconcile with modern Germany.

2. Because of the presence of SS graves, it would appear that Reagan was honoring Hitler's brutal elite.

3. Reconciliation with the Germany of today — the U.S.'s friend and ally — is fine, yet one should not forget the evils of Nazi Germany in general and the Holocaust — the mass murder of European Jewry and others — in particular.

4. The last-minute addition of Bergen-Belsen to the planned itinerary could not symbolically counterbalance the visit to Bitburg, where SS murderers were buried.

Many of these newspapers maintained that the itinerary was insensitive, unwise, and badly planned. Many urged that the visit to Bitburg be canceled regardless of West German feelings, and that a less sensitive site be chosen.

Several commented after the president's visit. They stated, however, that while he had acquitted himself well in his ten-minute stay in Bitburg, he should not have gone there in the first place.

(This analysis is based on data furnished by the Anti-Defamation League of the B'nai B'rith.)

It was tempting to arrange this section on the media in a pro and con fashion. But, while this approach would have presented the argument in a logical manner, it would not have accurately reflected the day-by-day direction of the editorials. Thus, all the stories reprinted here follow on a specific dateline order.

Religious and political leaders called on President Reagan to cancel his scheduled visit to the Bitburg cemetery during a rally in New York at the Isaiah Wall across from the United Nations. This rally was sponsored by the Jewish Community Relations Council of New York.

From the left: Rabbi Moshe Birnbaum, New York Board of Rabbis; Rev. Stuart Whetmore, suffragan Episcopal bishop of New York; Kenneth Gribetz, Rockland County district attorney, Brooklyn Borough President Howard Golden; Donna Shalala, Hunter College president; Peggy Tishman, JCRC president; former Mayor Abraham Beame; Rep. Ted Weiss; Assemblyman Angelo Del Toro; City Clerk David Dinkins; State Controller Edward Regan; Malcom Hoenlein, JCRC executive director; Sen. Alfonse D'Amato; Councilwoman Carol Greitzer; Attorney General Robert Abrams; City Comptroller Harrison Goldin; Assemblyman Herman Farrell, Bronx Borough President Stanley Simon; Mayor Edward Koch, Assemblyman Jerry Nadler.

Chapter 15

Leaders And Intellectuals

Bitburg: Who Forgot What
Commentary
August, 1985

By Midge Decter

It hardly seems possible that in the year 1985, with a number of grave decisions and responsibilities facing him, the President of the United States would permit himself to get embroiled in a debate about so unquestionably settled an issue as the nature of Nazism. What seems even less likely is that of all presidents, the author of this imbroglio should have been Ronald Reagan, a man who has paid a price in derision for his undeviating— or as his opponents like to call it, "simpleminded"— hatred of totalitarianism. Yet that is exactly what happened during the month of April past, and in a manner calculated to stir deep resentment and disaffection on all sides, not least his own.

Anyone who reads newspapers or watches television hardly needs to be reminded of the circumstances in which this improbable brouhaha took place. Mr. Reagan was going to Germany for an economic summit conference. His visit there was to coincide, or very nearly, with the fortieth anniversary of V-E Day. Chancellor Helmut Kohl requested that as a visible acknowledgment of the deep postwar friendship between the United States and the Federal Republic of Germany, Mr. Reagan accompany him to the military cemetery at Bitburg, a site conveniently located in the immediate vicinity of an American air base, and there lay a wreath in honor of the German war dead.

Mr. Reagan had also been invited, by whom it is not clear, to visit Dachau. He accepted the first invitation and declined the second, on the grounds, he said, that a concentration camp would introduce the wrong symbolism into what was supposed to be a celebration of the birth of the new democratic Germany.

Whether Mr. Reagan's going so far toward settling the account of World War II as a visit to any German military cemetery would by itself have stirred much strong opposition is at this point difficult to say. Certainly many American veterans of that war would have found reason to be unhappy with a ceremonial display of retroactive homage to the German army, as, no doubt, would the Jewish community. In any case, it was soon revealed that along with those of some two thousand ordinary soldiers, the cemetery at Bitburg also contained the graves of forty-eight (some said forty-seven, some forty-nine) members of the SS. This for large sectors of American public opinion entirely altered the nature of the occasion: honoring soldiers was one thing, however debatable, but including the SS, Hitler's special corps of genocidal murderers, was quite another, particularly in view of the President's refusal at the same time to visit a concentration camp.

Washington gossip had it that the ensuing embarrassment to the President, an embarrassment that was to plague him up to and through the actual ceremony on Sunday, May 5, was owing to the sloppy advance work of the team he had sent to Germany to fix the arrangements for his visit. Snow had covered the graves at Bitburg when they inspected the place, the explanation ran, and they had been unable to see the SS markings on the headstones. Some people laid the blame instead at the feet of Helmut Kohl, who, in his insistence that Mr. Reagan go to Bitburg of all places, had led his good friend up, so to speak, the graveyard path. But whoever was responsible for so needlessly troublesome an obligation, Mr. Reagan announced that he was determined to fulfill it. He had given his word, and he was not a man to go back on that.

Washington gossip also had it that the President was surprised, as well as deeply dismayed, by the explosion that followed. Helmut Kohl had after all been at some political risk in accepting deployment of U.S. intermediate-range missiles. The Soviets were using the forthcoming anniversary to make propaganda hay with Nazism. The real politics of the occasion, that is, were to be found elsewhere, and it was in the direction of these that the President felt his primary duty lay. People in the United States might have been expected to understand.

Nevertheless, the American Legion, normally among his staunchest supporters, strongly protested his plan to go to Bitburg. Editorialists and columnists across the land, and far from only the unfriendly ones, took up the cry. As did Congress. Even a group of conservative loyalists joined the congressional majority and made urgent representations to Mr. Reagan. The main thrust of all the criticism and pleading that burst upon the President in those last painful days of April was that there were other ways, other gestures to make, other gravesites to visit, that would more appropriately signify forgiveness and reconciliation.

It was widely agreed, for example, that he should at the very least add Dachau or some other concentration camp to his itinerary. "If anything," said the *Christian*

Science Monitor, "to visit a concentration camp in the company of a President's West German hosts...can be an affirmation that the future of better conduct, of repentance and forgiveness and the healing of enmity, is already under way." Others made further suggestions, the *New York Post* and a dozen other newspapers that he visit the grave of Konrad Adenauer, *U.S.A Today* that he go to the cathedral in Cologne or the bridge at Remagen, where U.S. troops first crossed the Rhine. It was even suggested that he pay homage to the late Pastor Martin Niemoeller — a man whose subsequent winning of the Lenin Peace Prize might be thought to have cast a certain backward shadow on the anti-totalitarian bona fides of his criticism of Hitler. Alternatives aside, Mr. Reagan was above all urged not to go to Bitburg. With the rather surprising exception of Jody Powell, once press secretary in the Carter White House and now a syndicated columnist, and to some extent also George F. Will in *Newsweek,* no one, not even those who supported the President's decision, defended it on its merits.

And then, of course, there were the Jews. Perhaps most notable among them was Elie Wiesel, who spoke not only for Jews in general but more particularly for survivors of the Holocaust. By chance in the White House to receive a congressional medal, Mr. Wiesel stood face to face with the President in the full view of the television cameras and eloquently instructed him that his place was not with the SS but with its victims. There was no question, then or later, that with but few exceptions Elie Wiesel was expressing the sentiment of the Jewish community.

If Mr. Reagan had been taken by surprise to find himself in what was to prove a major confrontation with that community, the Jews for their part had also been taken by surprise: would they really, after forty years, be forced to explain to the President of the United States the significance of the Holocaust and the reasons for their passion about it? Hitler's systematic slaughter of the six million was still officially much on their lips — after all, Elie Wiesel himself was chairman of a presidentially-appointed Holocaust commission — but certainly with no expectation that its meaning would once again be subject to public argument.

To complicate these difficult matters still further, it was no secret to the world that Mr. Reagan's relations with the American Jewish community were somewhat touchy. Though in 1984 the Democratic party had knuckled under to a known and identified anti-Semite, the Jews had continued to vote Democratic. Though Mr. Reagan's policy was no less supportive of Israel than any other president's, and more than many, and though he was far more supportive of the views of most Jews on affirmative action, they had continued by a healthy margin to reject him.

In this case, however, he would be making his gesture toward Germany not as a politician but as the spokesman for, the embodiment of, the American people. The Jews, it seems no exaggeration to say, were up in arms. They began relentlessly to pressure him both in public and in private to cancel his visit to Bitburg. Protest meetings were organized. A group of Holocaust survivors called for a demonstration against him at Bitburg itself. The American Jewish Congress announced that on the day of the Bitburg ceremony, it was taking a delegation to Munich to honor the graves of anti-Nazi martyrs.

There is little doubt that when Ronald Reagan first announced his German itinerary, he did not imagine that he was putting himself in the position of having to discourse on questions of German collective guilt and responsibility. His mind had clearly been elsewhere, on the budget, on the crisis in international trade, on his battle to secure even token congressional support for the *contras* in Nicaragua. But hit, as it were, from the blind side, he marched himself exactly into the moral minefield, it had been the purpose of his day with Helmut Kohl to avoid. Challenged where challenge had obviously neither been expected nor prepared for, he responded again and again with the nearest defense to hand — each dragging him closer to a place he could not possibly have wanted to get to.

First he said that Bitburg had been chosen because Americans as well as Germans were buried there, which happened simply not to be true. At another time he said that there were hardly any Germans left alive who had gone through the Nazi era, which was not, like his first statement, a plain error, but a piece of self-evident foolishness. These miscarried efforts to defend himself might have been forgotten but for the most tangled and sensitive, and costly, piece of defensive reaching of all: against the immediate violent reaction to the news that his wreath was to be laid in the presence of SS graves, he declared that the SS men buried in those graves were not men at all but mere boys, and as much victims of the Nazis as those who perished in the camps.

All this from the man who has by foe as well as friend, *ad nauseam* in fact, been acknowledged to be the Great Communicator. But what people actually mean by this is that Mr. Reagan is gifted with certain compellingly attractive qualities not often seen among our political leaders: genuine modesty and simplicity, humor, and an unmistakably easy relation to himself. These are what he "communicates," and the public believes him. More than that, it *likes* him. Communicating in the strict sense of the term, however, he does hardly well at all. He so often says things not meant to be taken in quite the way he puts them, and his remark about the members of the SS being victims was surely one of these. Probably what he meant was that the SS men buried at Bitburg were only young conscripts and hence had served their monstrous masters against their will. Even that was something neither he nor anyone else could any longer know. Moreover, his remark among other questionable ideas presupposed that same dangerous lack of distinction between being conscripted to fight for one's country and relief from all responsibility for one's behavior that constituted the defense of so many war criminals at the Nuremberg trials. Thus for many days running Mr. Reagan was treated to stern lectures from the press about the several ways in which one might distinguish between the SS and unarmed murdered innocents. As for the Jews, they did not know how to express the full measure of their outrage at such a statement.

Still, once he had made the decision to go to Bitburg at all, a decision whose initial incaution was further compounded by an evident failure to predict just what it might lead him into, some such misspeaking was almost inevitable. What really was there to defend it with but gaucherie piled upon Gaucherie? Be that as it may, he had succeeded precisely in drawing attention away from the achievements of West German democracy and focusing it in the exactly opposite direction. He plunged the public, as it had for some years not been plunged, into a fresh consideration of the Holocaust.

For let us face it: the word "Holocaust," even for Jews, induces by now a mostly dead sensation. The fact that there is a Holocaust commission empowered to erect monuments and create museums dedicated to that which "must not be forgotten"; the fact that a piece of sentimental grossness on television called *Holocaust* kept tens of millions of people glued to their sets; the fact that there are professors of the Holocaust and textbooks of the Holocaust; the fact that all those classic photographs of victims, most of them produced by camera-crazy Germans bent on recording their proud deeds for posterity, have become the picture postcards of a ritual tour into lost lands of suffering—all this means precisely that the Holocaust is no longer a living memory. The very word, as Raul Hilberg, himself a leading historian of the Holocaust, recently pointed out, has lost its meaning. It may now be applied anywhere and everywhere, to whichever kind of violence people currently find appalling.

But dead or alive, the Holocaust continues to sit there, athwart the history of the modern Western world. No matter how calcified and ritualistic the public response, as a historical fact this primary accomplishment of Nazism will not recede. For what remains unique about the genocidal slaughter of the Jews of Europe in the years 1939 to 1945 is not its revelation of the human capacity for mass murder—the world had often enough been presented with ample evidence of that—nor even the magnitude of the numbers involved. What makes it incomparable and incommensurable experience is that it was an eruption of evil that could be given steady, efficient, institutionalized expression within our own, as we thought, superior civilization.

Anti-Semitism had down through the ages been a morally acceptable, in some cases even a morally requisite, feature of Christendom. But by the time of Hitler, the Western world had come to believe of itself that it had been advancing to ever higher levels of enlightenment. Nazism came to full fruition, and with very little in the way of resistance, in the very midst of that enlightened civilization. The spiritual and intellectual jolt administered by the Holocaust was in some way definitive. Anti-Semitism stood exposed as something a conscious, decent man could no longer take for granted within himself. And the Jews themselves were left with a taste of the kind of desperate strength that comes to people to whom the worst that can happen has already happened.

The Holocaust, then, was pretty heavy stuff for a President of the United States, especially when he had so many other things on his mind, to get mixed up in.

It was also heavy stuff to be weighing upon the customarily fleeting attention span of the media. If there was wide agreement among them that the President should cancel his visit to Bitburg, and nearly universal agreement that he would change his mind and visit a concentration camp, there was, too, a fairly speedy surrender to the idea that Bitburg was fundamentally and in the main a Jewish issue.

The broader reaches of general principle can sustain the media only so far; the Jewish angle, much easier and more convenient to handle, was now to take over. News stories tended more and more to focus on Jewish reactions and on White House reactions, in turn, to these. Jewish leaders were called upon to make comments in the press and — that most significant barometer of the state of play with regard to any controversy — sought out for television discussions. For their part, people purporting to speak in the name of the Jewish community as a whole declined no opportunity to declare themselves singularly affronted.

The idea that there, at bottom, was an "ethnic" issue, involving pressure for the interests of a particular segment of the population, was a convenient one not only for the media but for the White House and its defenders as well. Henceforth, instead of walking some fine and eternally problematical line between German guilt and German innocence, the President could be seen to be treating with merely another difficult and unpleasant instance of pressure politics. The pressure, at that, was coming from a group to whom as a politician he owed little. Richard Nixon and Henry Kissinger had called him to say he must not back down, lest the Europeans get the impression that he was a man who caved in to such pressure. Thus to himself, and to those on his side in this matter, he could now go to Bitburg and be justified doing it.

He could also, and not without justification, view the media' assault upon him as politically motivated. True, among those who joined the opposition were editorial-page editors who could usually be counted on to support him; but a good deal of the flak had come from sources barely able to conceal their pleasure at having caught him out once more. "Be careful what you pray for, it is said, for your prayer might be granted," wrote *Washington Post* columnist Lou Cannon on April 22 in a leading example of the phenomenon. "Reagan is now being Reagan, and the true believers are learning more than they ever wanted to know about the perils of unleashing him." In much the same spirit, Anthony Lewis of the *New York Times* wrote on April 21 that Mr. Reagan's handling of his planned visit to Germany was an extraordinary exercise in self-revelation of a man with "no sense of history" and of "shattering insensitivity." Key to this revelation in Mr. Lewis' view was that "he sees no difference between war and genocide."*

Ultimately, however, it all came back to the Jews, as both actors and audience. Their insistence on "ethnicizing" the issue of Bitburg, coupled with an inclination to question Mr. Reagan's policies anyway, was spelled out by an editorial in the *Wall Street Journal* on April 19:

> But if Mr. Reagan can be accused of insensitivity, some of his critics might be equally guilty of political cynicism. . . . Some of his attackers are a great deal less concerned about the Holocaust than about exploiting any weak spot they can find in Mr. Reagan's political armor. The

---

*Those familiar with Mr. Lewis' writings on Vietnam might be somewhat taken aback by the passion with which he is now prepared to insist on this distinction.

primary audience for this endeavor is American Jews, torn between their predominantly liberal politics of the past and the modern appeal of hawkish neoconservatism.

This kind of identification of the Jewish community with the questionable political motives of many of the President's attackers was to lead to great irritation with the Jews on the part of many of the President's supporters. No matter how mistaken Mr. Reagan had originally been, the Jewish community, they complained, was going out of bounds.

Next, inevitably, came an older complaint, a complaint that in former days had been heard almost exclusively among Communists and their well-wishers but was now ironically issuing from such voices of the Right as Joseph Sobran's. After all, said Mr. Sobran in a syndicated column—repeating an idea whose leftist provenience, had he known enough of the history to be aware of it, might have given him pause—Jews are not the only people who have suffered. By what right to they claim special consideration?

In the span of less than a month, then, the Jews had progressed from being seen as people whose overweening sensitivity sometimes got in the way of necessary policy to being seen as no more than a self-serving pressure group, like the oil or farm lobby.

One of the least noted consequences of the view of Bitburg as a "narrow" Jewish issue is the way it deflected attention from a truly interesting question—the question of Helmut Kohl and *his* relation to Bitburg. Possibly Mr. Kohl, like Mr. Reagan, was not entirely aware of the implication of what he was asking. In 1984, it was said, he had been offended by his exclusion from the commemoration of D-Day. If "offended" is the right word—or if a more strictly political one would serve—there is something to be seen about the political predicament of present-day Germany in the fact that it should even have crossed his mind to take part in that occasion. The celebration of D-Day was after all a celebration of the invasion that led to the overwhelming defeat of his country's army. If President Reagan was caught in a confusion about the relation between wartime and postwar Germany, what shall we say of Mr. Kohl? Paradoxically, of course, the West Germans did and do have much to celebrate in the triumph of the Allied armies. Their defeat achieved for the Germans that which they had to the bitter end been unable to do for themselves: namely, to rid them of the Nazis. For their celebration to have taken the form of joining in a ceremony at Normandy would nevertheless have been, to say the least, strange, giving rise as it must logically have done to some expression of satisfaction at the death of multitudes of German soldiers. Stranger still would it have been for Mr. Kohl to imagine that the American veterans gathered on the beach in Normandy could have felt anything but the deepest embarrassment, and probably worse, to find him in their midst. He had reason to be grateful, rather than offended, to have been spared from acting on his own folly.

V-E Day, on the other hand, can in a sense be thought of as German liberation day—although from another point of view, it was also the day that sealed the partition of Germany and in the Eastern part substituted one form of totalitarian rule for another. All in all, the chancellor's desperate need to take part in some joint U.S.-German ceremony connected with the war, the need to which Mr. Reagan was responding, is not without its curious side.

The Bitburg wreath-laying was to be a symbol of—the word was used over and over—"reconciliation." Why reconciliation? After forty years of American protection, alliance, and other forms of friendship, what was there to reconcile? A possible answer, though an unpleasant one, is that consciously or unconsciously the Germans are seeking forgiveness not for their conduct in the past but for what they sense will be their increasingly neutralist conduct in the future. More likely the answer is a simpler one, that they have grown bored and restless and impatient under their burden of penitence for Nazism and wish for the world, particularly the United States, to relive them of it. Why otherwise of all possible places should the chancellor have picked Bitburg? And why else otherwise did he, as he claimed, need to fear for his political future should Mr. Reagan refuse to appear there with him?

German restlessness and impatience one can understand: so many crimes have been committed since 1945 without much visible atonement. Above all, there, just nearby, is the Soviet Union, still going strong and without apology. But the choice of Bitburg willy-nilly betrays an impulse quite contrary to the one that had been officially articulated. To insist upon hallowing the earth that contains SS bodies is not an act that in any way serves to relieve one of penitence. Rather, it is an act that retroactively denies the need to have repented in the first place. In taking so little care for what he was inviting Mr. Reagan to do, Mr. Kohl was in effect expressing a belief that the Nazis had in the end been just plain Germans like everyone else. This happened to have been the case, we know, but surely not the case Mr. Kohl would admit to making. Thus even for a successful and punctilious statesman does the repressed sometimes, all unbidden, return.

That no one in all the hundreds of thousands of words devoted to the controversy in the press and on the air saw fit to question the curious role of Helmut Kohl and what it might mean is a tribute to the massive moral and political confusion engendered by Bitburg. The confusion was a confusion of ideas as well as attitudes, and it overtook just about everybody.

The original confusion, Chancellor Kohl's —or perhaps Germany's—lay in the hope that Ronald Reagan could in some small degree help to redo or undo Germany history. The Germans are a people boxed in. They have grown somewhat skittish (and not without reason) about their particular place in the Western alliance. Before them stand the Soviets. Behind them, eternally, stand the Nazis: only forty years of an available national experience stretching backward, and then . . . a black hole. The ceremony at Bitburg was implicitly to be an attempt to convert World War II into an ordinary war and so, even if only briefly, relieve the backward pressure. But neither Ronald Reagan nor God Himself has the power to do that. Had there been no ruckus in the United States, and had Mr. Reagan marched through Bitburg as planned and made a stirring and unambiguous speech, the undeniable awkwardness of the occasion would have remained. World War II was not an ordinary war, the Germans and Allied powers were not merely conventional combatants, and every German schoolchild, impatient or not, knows it. The black hole that yawns in the German consciousness when it travels back beyond 1945 cannot be filled and cannot be traversed, it can only somehow be accommodated. The intervention of outsiders can make no difference to the unspoken dialogue between the German young and the German old, not even politically. If German democracy is to survive, it will have to survive despite that dialogue, or perhaps because of it, but the dialogue itself is a strictly German affair.

Ronald Reagan's confusion, though far more innocent than Helmut Kohl's, is no less interesting. It was first revealed in the offending remark about the victimization of the SS. Here again, in all the uproar about his alleged insensitivity and obtuseness, the most significant point was missed—that he had been driven to trade positions with his fiercest opponents, the pious liberals. What he said about those members of the SS in effect was that they had been made to commit crimes by the conditions of their society. To deem an armed man who is committing a murderous assault no less a victim than the unarmed innocent he murders—a victim, as they say, of his environment—is to maintain the very same view of criminal behavior that Mr. Reagan's bitterest enemies have been promulgating since time out of mind (and to which his election to the presidency was itself a public act of resistance).

This much the pressure on him achieved: along with Bitburg, he went to Bergen-Belsen. Within an afternoon, he made two speeches, one at each place, speeches declared by many to be the most moving and effective of a career that had produced not a few. In view of all the turmoil that had preceded them, one may suppose that these speeches were crafted with extreme care. The cameras were in full array at their delivery, and the whole world was watching. So intent was everyone on the question of how he would make his way rhetorically through all the perils lying in wait for him, there seemed to be little notice of the actual intellectual and political ground on which he decided to stand.

Exactly how he had arrived at the choice of Bergen-Belsen we do not know. Dachau had made the day's travels, strenuous enough as they were, a feat of endurance. Moreover, Dachau had been turned down; going there would have suggested not compromise but surrender. However he made the choice, Bergen-Belsen was, if such a term may be used in this connection, a happy one. Both Dachau and Bergen-Belsen were long ago cleaned up and converted to museums. But the Bergen-Belsen site consists only of plaques, monuments, and memorial displays. Dachau would have been another matter. There he would have had a view of something that might have made his message of brotherhood falter on his tongue. That something is the ovens. The ovens bear a secret better left unrevealed to someone who means to speak as the President did. The secret of the ovens—which in our own time leaves only those wild-eyed Cambodian adolescents of the Khmer Rouge humanly comparable to the Germans who designed, staffed, and operated the camps—is their size.

The word Holocaust, among its other inadequacies, conjures a vision of a vast fiery pit or furnace. It is possible to imagine almost anyone in a mere fit of temporary insanity having a hand in throwing bodies into such a mythic conflagration. But the main instruments of the real Holocaust, gas chamber and oven, were not vast at all. They were shockingly, and instructively, small. They were, that is, man-sized, requiring the constant, competent, daily attentions of reliable workmen. The gas chambers at Dachau are the size of, say, an ordinary living room—why waste space when the job of killing by gas is so quickly done? And the ovens are just that, ovens, small chambers into which bodies had to be deposited one by one from a kind of barrow loaded and lifted by two men. The job of overseeing the incineration of human corpses was, in other words, a *personal* one. The murder of millions was a work accomplished by ordinary, everyday fiends. They are the ghosts that Germany to this day struggles to lay, and no outsider can contribute to the exorcism.

So in going to Bergen-Belsen instead of Dachau Mr. Reagan had made a good choice. Unfair as it may be to the new and free and democratic West Germany of today, it is better not to visit Dachau on a day one intends to embrace the Germans. Simply not enough years have yet gone by.

Bergen-Belsen made him sufficiently uncomfortable. He stumbled in his speech there a couple of times, and in the course of his tour of the place looked like nothing so much as a man whose privacy was being invaded by the cameras. No one as clearly genial and affable as Ronald Reagan, experienced actor though he be, can look at such mementos as the stones marking mass graves, or photographs of starved, naked corpses lying in carefully arranged heaps, and figure out something graceful to do with his face and hands and shoulders.

At the Bitburg cemetery he was, for obvious reasons, positively stiff with expressionlessness. Not until he reached the air base did he commence to look like the figure the American public recognizes as its Great Communicator.

He did, however, as might have been expected, have a number of graceful things to say. His words were aimed at striking just the right note of balanced acknowledgment of the hopelessness and hopefulness of which the day was to be a reminder—of the utter and total despair that had been the lot of millions under the Nazis and the promise signaled the reclamation of Germany. But if graceful, these speeches nevertheless revealed something rather odd in the way of underlying attitude. Odd, that is, for Ronald Reagan in particular. For at every point where it was possible to do so, he eschewed the concrete nature of the reality to which he was addressing himself and took refuge instead in the vague and general.

Recourse to generality in the face of the concrete is, morally speaking, the rankest of the rank habits of present-day liberalism. "The brotherhood of man," a liberal favorite, is an attitude of mind that liberates one precisely from the need to regard specific men as one's brothers. "Peace on earth," another, involves one in none of the difficult and sometimes dirty details of how to respond to this or that specific aggression. And so it goes, upward and downward through the whole range of human experiences. It is a basic principle of progressive liberal thought that when confronted with the reality that is under your nose, you must raise your eyes heavenward and refrain above all from giving that reality its own individual name. People become "classes" and the complex network of their relations to one another become "social problems." Evasion of the concrete is ultimately the evasion of any and every single persons' responsibility to the truth. At the moment, the use of the generalized terms "racism" and "sexism" constitutes just such an evasion.

And refrain from giving the reality under his nose its own exact name is precisely what Ronald Reagan did on that Sunday afternoon in Germany. At Bergen-Belsen, for instance, he mentioned the word "Jews" once, and made haste to include "many Christians—Catholics and Protestants" among those who perished there, lumping the Final Solution together with the political persecution of individuals into one undifferentiated mass of brutality. He spoke of suffering, of hunger, of consuming misery, and of death. But he omitted mention of the policy, thought out and fully articulated, of the organized, systematic, scientific murder of the entire Jewish population, left incomplete only by circumstance and not by intention, and he omitted mention of the impressive fact that this policy was given top priority even when it was militarily counterproductive to pursue it.

At the Bitburg air base he spoke the passage, perhaps aimed at the kind of permanent fame achieved by the remark of John F. Kennedy on which it was based: ". . . I am a Berliner, I am a Jew in a world still threatened by anti-Semitism, I am an Afghan, and I am a prisoner of the Gulag, I am a refugee in a crowded boat foundering off the coast of Vietnam, I am a Laotian, a Cambodian, a Cuban, and a Miskito Indian in Nicaragua." It may seem ungracious to point out that John F. Kennedy's declaration of oneness with the citizens of Berlin was made as he stood at the wall dividing their hapless city, the very wall whose construction he had not lifted a finger to stop. And it will no doubt seem positively cantankerous to point out that the groups listed by Mr. Reagan are not all the same as one another, nor have they all equally been the beneficiaries of American (not to say German) solidarity. One thing they do have in common: it is the Soviets and their surrogates who are mainly responsible for their condition. This is a fact it is certainly appropriate to bring home on every occasion, and never more so than in the presence of the Germans. But only someone caught up in the old liberal urge to speak of suffering in the large so as to make all suffering equal would have seen fit to express the idea in quite this way on just this occasion.

In addressing the German question as such, Mr. Reagan barely ventured beyond the war, and treated that as if it were not a war but a war movie. Nazism he referred to as "one man's totalitarian dictatorship" without either naming the man or offering the slightest suggestion of something made perfectly obvious at Bergen-Belsen, even among the neat and abstract memorials: that this one man needed and received a fair amount of cooperation from others.

For him to have spoken with the required precision might not have been fully satisfactory to Mr. Reagan's hosts. But who can say for sure? There is that in people who are being forgiven which yearns to know just what they are being forgiven for. In any case, Nazism, which had once, in Mr. Reagan's words, "turned the world upside down," and in this odd and entirely unnoticed way turned him upside down as well.

As for American Jews, forgiving the Germans is not and has not for a very long time now been much of a problem. It is the forgetting—their own as well as others' —that troubles them. A basic article of faith with them is that the world must remember what happened to the Jews. Even more, they wish for the world to be guided by that memory in its dealings with them. Such a wish, however, has created confusions of its own; and these confusions, too, along with Helmut Kohl's and Ronald Reagan's, played a role in the Bitburg controversy.

First, there is the confusion, so harshly and so grossly responded to by certain of Mr. Reagan's defenders, between the Jews' claim of unique title to the Holocaust and their insistence at the same time that the Holocaust be understood as a universal issue of good and evil. Are they, in other words, a holy witness or a special pressure group? The answer, nearly as difficult for the Jews as for others to keep clearly in mind, is that by virtue of their peculiar history they are both. While they were by no means the only victims of the Nazis, they were a special kind of victim. On the other hand, the nature and the scope of the cataclysm that was theirs was also, in the deepest spiritual as well as moral sense, the West's. Thus they lobby in their own interest and yet are not in the ordinary sense a lobby.

But people, and especially, it would seem, Jews, do not always know where their true interest lies. And here is buried another, and far more significant, confusion. The Jewish expression of determination never to forget does in some cases appear to mask a considerable degree of forgetfulness.

What does it mean to "remember" the Holocaust? If it means anything serious, anything beyond mere ritual, it requires a continuing alertness to certain political and social lessons. There is, for instance, the lesson of Weimar, which is a lesson about how fragile and in need of constant loving protection are the institutions of a decent civilization. Any Jew who permits himself, as so many Jews nowadays do, to grow careless with these institutions, to demand of them more than they can perform while simultaneously becoming ever more tolerant of the kinds of decadence that destroy them, has forgotten the Holocaust. There is the lesson of Munich, which is a lesson about the need to resist totalitarianism early and with strength. Any Jew who decrees, as many Jews nowadays do, that the democracies should divest themselves of the power to threaten and discipline intransigent totalitarianism, especially of the Soviet variety, has forgotten the Holocaust. Any Jew who believes, as many Jews nowadays do, that Israel must extend a hand of appeasing friendship to those who have sworn to destroy it, or who indulges himself in the luxury of waiting until the very survival of Israel is threatened before he makes his commitment to that survival clear, has forgotten the Holocaust—and forgotten himself as well.

The special role that the Jews, justly, would claim for themselves in the history of the Nazi era involves them, whether they acknowledge it or not, in a special obligation: not, as so many like to say, an obligation to be more "compassionate" than others but to be even more clear-eyed than others about the dangers to democracy in our own age.

If Bitburg was a political embarrassment to Ronald Reagan, and far from a triumph for Helmut Kohl, for Jews it was an opportunity—for many too many a lost one—to make it clear to themselves just how stern and relentless is the real task of remembering the Holocaust and keeping faith with their dead.

Copyright © 1985 Commentary. Reprinted with permission.

(Midge Decter is executive director of the Committee for the Free World.)

The American Jewish Committee At The White House
Special Contribution

By Rabbi Marc H. Tanenbaum

(Rabbi Tanenbaum is the Director of the Department of International Relations of the American Jewish Committee.)

On May 5, 1985, President Ronald Reagan, in keeping with a promise he made to West German Chancellor Helmut Kohl in November 1984, joined the Chancellor in a formal wreath-laying visit to the German military cemetery at Bitburg. The 10-minute silent stop, far less elaborate than the ceremonies originally planned, was carried out despite ever-widening dismay, in the U.S. and abroad, over the planned Bitburg visit. The criticism, which began when the White House announced that the President would not stop at the Dachau concentration camp during his German trip, exploded into a firestorm when it was revealed that the Bitburg cemetery included the graves of some four dozen members of the Waffen SS—the Nazi elite guard implicated in wanton atrocities against U.S. prisoners of war and innocent civilians in Nazi-occupied countries, and directly involved in carrying out Hitler's "final solution" for European Jewry.

Jewish and veterans' groups were understandably the first to raise objections to the President's itinerary. The AJC's Washington representative, Hyman Bookbinder, protested to the White House immediately after the plans were officially announced on April 10. But it did not take long for Americans of every religion and background to grasp and express how insensitive and inappropriate to the intended theme of reconciliation they felt the Bitburg visit to be.

How that broadened understanding evolved, and how the White House was ultimately persuaded — when all efforts to convince the President to cancel his visit to Bitburg had failed — to reduce the significance of that stop, must remain largely untold. But I do want to share with you, to the extent possible, the AJC's role in these momentous events.

Our earliest efforts, both public and private, concentrated on education and interpretation. As the only American Jewish organization that has been engaged in fruitful dialogue and educational programs with West Germany for years, we were in a unique position to explain — in dozens of newspaper stories and on countless radio and television programs in the days that followed — why the Bitburg visit was not an acceptable signal of reconciliation.

Our emphasis on the importance of remembering the horrors committed by the Nazis, even as we extended the hand of friendship to the democratic Germany that has grown out of the ashes of World War II, found echoes in the statements of prestigious Americans in every walk of life. Indeed, many religious, black and ethnic leaders with whom we have worked closely over the years called to ask how they could help make the issues clear to the President and to America as a whole. Our Washington office was inundated by calls from political leaders and other public figures, and similar calls also came in to our area offices. Seldom have our efforts to rally public support been more enthusiastically received.

As early as April 12, the General Secretary of the National Council of Churches, the Executive Secretary for Catholic-Jewish Relations of the National Conference of Catholic Bishops, and the pastor of one of America's leading black congregations had categorically condemned the plans for the Presidential visit to Bitburg. In the days that followed, other Christian leaders, representing the widest possible religious and political spectrum, spoke out with equal clarity, both in individual statements and in newspaper ads in *The New York Times,* and other major papers across the country. The same gratifying response came from the black and ethnic communities. A letter to President Reagan urging him to cancel the Bitburg visit was signed by the heads of organizations representing Polish, Ukranian, Hispanic, Italian, Hellenic, Chinese and Japanese Americans, as well as the head of the National Association for the Advancement of Colored People (NAACP); and statements and newspaper ads featuring these and other ethnic and black leaders appeared in Chicago, Los Angeles, Pittsburgh, Philadelphia, Atlanta, Seattle, and other cities.

Because the AJC's Annual Meeting took place during the weekend of the President's Bitburg visit, and because one of the featured speakers of our meeting was Dr. Alois Mertes, Minister of State in West Germany's Foreign Office, the AJC's views got even wider coverage than they might have received otherwise. Dr. Mertes' speech was heavily covered by the media; there was an impromptu press conference with him immediately afterwards.

In addition to these broad-based programs of clarification and consciousness-raising, there was another element of our involvement in the Bitburg affair which has not been publicized until now.

Dr. Billy Graham first telephoned me from his home in Montreal, North Carolina, on Friday morning, April 19th. He told me that he had just spoken to President Reagan and to Nancy Reagan, and they were deeply upset over the furor unleashed in response to that news. Graham said that he had told the Reagans that he thought it was a mistake for the President to have acceded to Kohl's request to honor the SS soldiers, among the other German soldiers. He said he was concerned over this tragic episode's contributing to the undermining of the President's moral authority.

I told him that I shared his concerns. He then asked me if I might be able to help relieve this crisis in some way (as I had tried to help him in the past during his missions to the Soviet Union and other East European countries). I said that, of course, I was prepared to help. He then said he would speak again with the President and Nancy to offer my help, and he would call me back.

The next morning Graham called me at my home and informed me that he had spoken with the President and Nancy. He said they were both grateful for my offer to be of help, and they asked if I would talk with Michael Deaver, who was organizing the President's visit. I said I would. Ten minutes later, Deaver called me and we talked for nearly an hour. I told him that the AJC and I personally believed the proposed visit to the Bitburg cemetery was a "major mistake," that it ought to be dropped. Deaver said that they would like to do that, but that he had spoken with Kohl last week in Germany, and Kohl was very emotional and adamant. I then said that I thought the trip had to be fundamentally reconceptualized. If the intention was to dramatize reconciliation, the place to do that was at the gravesite of Chancellor Konrad Adenauer, the architect of modern German democracy and a foe of Nazi tyranny and totalitarianism. He said the Adenauer idea was floating around, but now maybe they ought to consider making a decision about including that. He wanted to know why Adenauer was important, and I spelled out his record, including his role in establishing German-U.S. reconciliation, Franco-German reconciliation, Germany's entry into the European community, Adenauer's establishing a special relationship with Israel and the Jewish people.

Deaver said he had not been aware of "all that," but that information was certainly persuasive for including a visit to Adenauer's grave. We then discussed plans for the Bergen-Belsen visit and talk, and also the visit to the Bitburg U.S. military base and what the President might say there.

We also discussed the idea of possibly including a visit to the Remagen Bridge as a symbol of German-American reconciliation.

During the week of April 22, Billy Graham and Michael Deaver and I spoke a half-dozen times. On Friday, April 26, Deaver suggested that it might be useful if we met at the White House on the following Monday, the eve of his departure for Bonn. The President was scheduled to leave the next day for the European summit.

A meeting was set in the White House on Monday, April 29, at 11 a.m.

Our delegation was headed by President Howard Friedman, and included David Gordis, Bill Trosten, Hy Bookbinder and myself. Howard and Bill reported on their trip to Bonn, their meetings with Dr. Alois Mertes, Wolf Calibau, and Chancellor Kohl's representatives. They reported on the fact that Dr. Mertes said that the Bitburg cemetery visit could not be changed, but that the schedule could be changed to provide opportunities for emphasizing democracy and anti-Nazi commitments of modern Germany as the basis for reconciliation. They reported that Chancellor Kohl had agreed to these reformulations based on the memorandum that Dr. Mertes had drafted in the presence of Howard and Bill and had sent by messenger to Kohl.

Deaver expressed appreciation for that helpfulness which he said made it easier for him now to make adjustments in the President's schedule. He said he would go to Bonn and try to work in the Adenauer visit, probably as an unannounced surprise. He assured us that in light of our earlier conversations, the President had agreed to a plan to reduce the visit to the Bitburg cemetery to a minimum, "perfunctory ceremony," with General Ridgeway and anti-Nazi General von Stauffenberg laying the wreath. The President would make no statement at the cemetery in order to minimize its importance.

We said it was important to emphasize certain themes in the President's scheduled speeches. Among them, the repudiation of the SS's horrendous crimes against the Jews and others. At that point, Deaver called in the President's speech writer, Mr. Kachigian, and we made a number of points about Adenauer, Democracy, totalitarianism, the importance of remembering the horrors of the Holocaust and rejecting denial and evasion. The speech-writer took detailed notes of our conversation. As it turned out, almost all the themes we proposed were incorporated in the President's speeches at Bergen-Belsen and at the U.S. military base in Bitburg. They also included the visit to Adenauer's grave.

At Deaver's request, I sent him by diplomatic pouch through the White House the next day a proposed text for the President on the moral and political legacy of Adenauer for modern Germany. The President visited the grave but apparently made no statement, although a brief background statement was issued to the press in Germany on the importance of the Adenauer visit along the lines that we suggested.

Deaver expressed gratitude for our helpfulness both in the U.S. and through the German visit.

He then walked out of the room and returned with President Reagan and Donald Regan, White House Chief of Staff. The President thanked us for our cooperation which he said he deeply appreciated. He then said that he was appalled by the horrors of the Nazi Holocaust and wanted us to understand how he felt. He then tried out on us a line about how the dead, all the dead, in the Bitburg cemetery were being judged by the Supreme Judge. We were tempted to respond but did not because it would have meant a long metaphysical polemic. We decided to leave well enough alone.

Donald Regan and Deaver again thanked us. As we left, Deaver said he would be glad to meet with us when the President returned from Germany. We wrote to the President, expressing our views, and asking for a meeting with him as soon as he returned.

Howard and David discussed our work with the White House with Max Fisher who was grateful for our helpfulness. He said he would arrange a meeting for all of us with the President on his return. Billy Graham called me on Monday, May 6, to say that the President and Nancy were deeply appreciative of our constructive efforts.

I alluded earlier to our long-standing relationships with the West German Government. One of the principal architects of that relationship, both with the present government and its Social Democratic predecessor, is AJC's Associate Director, William Trosten. On April 24, Bill Trosten and Howard Friedman flew over to Bonn to meet with Alois Mertes and others close to him. There, too, we urged, most strongly, cancellation of the Bitburg visit; but we also stressed that regardless of that decision it was essential to add symbols that would underscore the new Germany's rejection of Nazi totalitarianism and commitment to democratic values and human rights. Konrad Adenauer, we pointed out, was the first postwar leader of a democratic Germany, and a visit to his gravesite might be one such symbol. A ceremony at the Remagen Bridge, with American and German troops meeting where Americans and Germans had killed one another 40 years earlier, might be another way to stress reconciliation. We also urged that both Chancellor Kohl and President Reagan underscore, at their visit to the concentration camp at Bergen-Belsen, that the Holocaust must be a lesson for the ages for all who cherish human liberty. Before we left Dr. Mertes' office, he dictated a letter to the Chancellor repeating and endorsing our recommendations. And before we left Germany for the States we got word that our suggestions had been well received by the Chancellor himself.

This, in essence, summarizes our Bitburg-related activities. We did not succeed in convincing Bonn or Washington to cancel the ceremony at Bitburg (the President and the Chancellor did go to the Adenauer gravesite). But I am convinced we played an important role in helping to contain the damage, and in setting the stage for the ongoing process of education, here and in Germany, that must be pursued.

Paradoxically, there has been some positive fallout from this event. The entire world has been reminded of the unremitting Jewish anguish over the Holocaust; and we have seen a heightened recognition that the lessons of that horror are universal. This education-in-depth is certainly welcome. The rallying of our friends, Christians, blacks, ethnics; the unprecedented resolution adopted by the U.S. Senate (see Chapter 2) and the unequivocal letter signed by a majority of the House of Representatives (see Chapter 2); the outpouring of statements and letters challenging the most important leader of the world's most important nation on a moral issue of such importance to us are also important pluses. And the sensitization of the Administration, the Federal Republic and of the media will, I think, stand us in good stead in the future.

Does Incessant Recollection of Nazi Past Denigrate Germany of Today?
May 4, 1985

Dr. Alois Mertes, Minister of State
Bundeshaus, Foreign Office
5300 Bonn
West Germany

Dear Dr. Mertes:

Since the beginning of the agitation around Reagan's visit to Bitburg I have thought several times of writing to you, but could not find the time during the busy last weeks of the semester. Now that the semester is over, I shall set forth my thoughts as they occur to me without attempting to arrange them in any order. I shall be utterly candid, not shrinking from expressing my thoughts and feelings even when I know that they diverge sharply from yours.

There is no objective ground for a major conflict of interest between the loose entity called "World Jewry" and Germany. Jews, for all their feelings towards Germany, have no interest in harming her. For example, unlike other nations that dread the very thought of German reunification, Jews qua Jews should have no rational interest in opposing the reunion of Germany under a democratic dispensation.

In dwelling on the Holocaust, in having contributed to its becoming a prominent theme of contemporary culture, the organized Jewish world has been moved by a number of impulses and considerations from which the intention of causing any harm to contemporary Germany is entirely absent.

Before Bitburg the sense of conflict derived from a misapprehension. German politicians and those concerned with promoting the reputation of The Federal Republic abroad hold it as an axiomatic truth that the incessant recollection of the Nazi past denigrates Germany of today and produces ill will towards it. It is my impression that this belief is false. For the American public, and especially the educated part of it, has learned to regard present-day Germany as a world which has increasingly and radically departed from the Third Reich. It is even probable that within the University the study of Nazi Germany and the Holocaust has a therapeutic effect diminishing anti-German stereotypes. I speak from my experience as a teacher of literally thousands of students. I have not taken a scientific poll among my students; but a few days ago I asked my class on the Holocaust at Harvard (170 students) how the course affected their feelings towards Germany. Students who confessed to having had anti-German prejudices said that by the end of the course these prejudices were diluted or dissolved.

The present dispute disclosed the clashing contrast between the conception of Nazism dominant in the Western World and the conception common in Germany. The vast majority of Germans, to be sure, regard Nazism as a bad regime, an evil, *ein Unrechsstaat* [an unjust state] *eine Gewaltherrschaft* [a dominion of violence], etc. But they do not feel towards it the same utter horror harbored by the rest of the Western world. In the eyes of the educated public of that world Nazism is the quintessence of barbarism, an evil of almost cosmic dimensions, without peer in the history of mankind. This image of Nazism is not a *Verteufelung* [demonization], but a studied rendition of the truth. In describing Nazism any hyperbole of evil one uses is an understatement.

A brief exercise of the imagination will show the truth of the above description. Let us imagine the fate of Europe after a Nazi victory: The Jewish people would have been annihilated utterly; the Slavic nations would have been decimated, helotized, decapitated of their leadership and their identities extinguished forever; the intelligentsias of most European nations murdered; the Christian churches gradually dismantled and destroyed. Forty years after Nazi rule the Christians of Bitburg who still dared to worship could probably only do so only in catacombs.

The SS'was the chief instrument of this apocalyptic program. Every SS man was objectively and the vast majority were subjectively Horsemen of the Apocalypse. In the lexicon of the SS the word *Soldat* [soldier], or as they call it *Nur Soldat* [mere soldier], had a pejorative connation. They were *Weltanchauungesskrieger* [ideological warriors] boasting of being capable of performing deeds of destruction from which *Nur Soldaten* recoil. Their spirit is well preserved in their songs. Here is an example:

> *"Wetzt die langen Messer auf dem Buergersteig dass sie*
> *Besser passen in des Pfaffen Leib,*
> *Und kommt die Stunde der Vergeltung*
> *Sind wir zu jedem Massenmord bereit. "*

> "Sharpen the long knives on the sidewalk
> So that they may better fit in the parson's belly,
> And when the hour of revenge has struck
> We will be ready for any mass murder."

The Mayor of Bitburg declared that he was distressed at the 'defamation' of the SS men who lie in the cemetery at Bitburg. If the above portrait of the SS is a defamation, I would respectfully ask the Mayor to enlighten us, to teach us the true character of the Black Order.

The Mayor is evidently gravely deficient in historical understanding. How glaringly his ignorance contrasts with the tragic wisdom of an obscure theology student, Michael Kitzelmann, who in June 1942 wrote in his diary *Wenn diese Verbrecher siegen, mag ich nicht mehr leben.* [If these criminals will win the war, I do not wish to live any longer.] That summer the student was executed for *Wehkraftzersetzung* [demoralization of the troops].

To lay a wreath at the graves of SS men, whether of the Allgemeine SS or Waffen SS, is to honor members of a *Völkermordskohorte* [genocidal cohort]. To forgive mass murderers may be a supreme act of religiosity. But to honor them is to perform an act for which it would be impossible to find a name more fitting than the word "sacrilege".

What about the Wehrmacht? This is a painful subject. I was born into an East European Jewish family in Northern Rumania which had nourished an admiration for German culture, cultivated German literature, had me tutored in German from the age of 5 onwards and considered the German army an institution, which compared with the pogrom-prone East European Soldateskas, was a model of chivalry and decency. I find it therefore painful to speak of the part played by the Wehrmacht in the mass murder of East European Jewry. Let the record speak for itself:

- The Wehrmacht signed an agreement with the SS by which it undertook to support logistically the units charged with the task of killing Soviet Jewry, and it fulfilled the agreement faithfully.

- It delivered all Jewish prisoners of the Red Army to the SS for the purpose of having them killed.

- Army commander after army commander issued orders of the day justifying the extermination of the Jews.

- From 1943 onwards German commanders on the Eastern Front became more active participants in the murder of the Jews, urging the SS to make haste, lending them soldiers for the task.

- General von Leeb, who enjoyed a reputation for decency, on hearing of the murder of Jews in his domain, was distressed. He would have preferred an unbloody method — the sterilization of all Jewish males.

This is but a small fraction of a long and inglorious record. When I unfolded this record in a public lecture before the Bundeswehrhochschule in Munich, my Koreferent Professor Krausnick, the doyen of German historians of Nazism, criticized me for being too objective, too indulgent towards the German officer corps in the East, too anxious to find bright spots in its record. When I think of the Wehrmacht in the East I am invariably reminded of Stefan George's poem "Anti-Christ" which Stauffenberg would recite again and again to express his contempt for his fellow officers who had succumbed to the moral and intellectual corruption of the regime they served.

> *Der Fürst des Geziefers verbreitet sein reich.*
> *Kein schatz der ihm mangelt; kein glück das ihm weicht.*
> *Zu grund mit dem rest der empoerer!*
>
> *Ihr jauchzet, entzückt von dem teuflischen schein,*
> *Verprasset was blieb von dem früheren sein*
> *Und fühlt erst die not vor dem ende.*
>
> *Dann hängt ihr die zunge am trochenden trog,*
> *Irrt ratlos wie vieh durch den brennenden hof . . .*
> *Und schrecklich erschallt die posaune.*

The Master of Vermin far stretches his realm;
No treasure that fails him, no luck that forsakes . . .
Destruction take all other rebels!

You clamor, enticed by the devilish show,
Lay waste what remains of the sap of the spring
And feel your need first when the end comes.

Then you hang out your tongues o'er the emptying trough,
Stray like herds without aim through the courtyard in flames,
And fearfully rings out the trumpet.

(This translation by Sir Maurice Bowra is taken from Wheeler-Bennett, The Nemesis of Power, The German Army in Politics, 1918-1945, *London, 1954, p. 580.)*

Tears come to my eyes when I recite this poem in my mind.

"Innocence is no earthly weapon", writes a contemporary English poet. There is no army and no state on earth whose record is not stained with the blood of the innocent. But Nazism stands apart. It was as if in it Evil strained to surpass itself. Its crimes are inscribed in indelible blood in the annals of human kind, and the SS, its Apocalyptic Horsemen, will be remembered forever with horror and abomination.

The Bitburg episode has left in the minds of many here puzzling and troubling questions. Why were those who opposed the honoring of members of a Völkermordskohorte, who opposed the honoring of men whose objective vocation was the destruction of Judeo-Christian civilization, why were the members of the United States Senate, of the House of Representatives, the vast majority of American intellectuals, Jews and non-Jews alike, the Veterans, accused of insulting the German nation, of preaching collective guilt, when most of them seek amity and concord with present-day Germany? Why is the honoring of SS men a *sine qua non* of friendship with Germany? Why does not the German government join the rest of civilized mankind in treating everything connected with the SS as inimical to Germany and to human kind? We can pity and lament individual members of the SS. But why must one insist on bestowing military honors on them? As you know, Senator Cranston gave an alarming answer to these questions. His answer is manifestly absurd. And the questions remain.

I have suffered immeasurably at the hands of Germans. In the summer of 1941, then a boy of 10, I stood before a firing squad of a subunit of SS Einsatzgruppe D. The commander of the subunit was Heinz Schubert, a descendant of the famous composer. In the eyes of the SS I and the younger children with me were *lebensunwerte* [unworthy of life], squirming vermin to be crushed underfoot. I escaped that day by a miraculous accident. During the next four years of horror and death I ceased to speak German, the language I had been taught since the age of 5, and bore a burning hatred for all things German. Yet ever since I have embarked on a scholarly career and specialized on the history of Modern Germany, I have endeavored to be scrupulously objective in my writings and teaching. I have rejected all Germanophobic interpretations of the Nazi era. My inclination towards the *Betriebsunfallstheorie* [the theory which explains the emergence of

Nazism as a fortuitous concentration of events] has even drawn upon me the criticism of German leftists and liberals, who accuse me of being, in my historiography, akin to the writers of the Bayernkurier.

But the Bitburg episode leaves me saddened, embittered and troubled.

Sincerely,

Erich Goldhagen

(Erich Goldhagen teaches at Harvard University. He is the Director of the Jack Eisner Program on Christian-Jewish Relations at The Harvard Divinity School.)

Interview with Stuart Eizenstat

(Stuart Eizenstat, Chief Domestic Affairs Adviser to President Carter, was interviewed by Ilya Levkov.)

Q: The issue in the American culture of confronting the Holocaust was raised during the Carter Administration when a special commission was established to report on how it should be commemorated. The report established a national monument and the U.S. Holocaust Memorial Council. Could you elaborate?

Eizenstat: A staff member of mine on the Domestic Policy of the White House staff which I headed, Ellen Goldstein, mentioned that we were one of the few Western countries that had no formal government-endorsed monument or memorial to the Holocaust victims. She suggested that this was something that our Administration, the Carter Administration, should consider. Ellen and I sent a memorandum to the President a few weeks thereafter. We suggested that with so many of the Holocaust victims who had survived reaching their sixties and seventies, it would be an appropriate and fitting time this long after the war to memorialize for all time the Holocaust and what meaning and relevance it had not only for the Jewish people but for the world. Because it wasn't clear what type it should be — a statue, a living memorial of some kind, a museum or a library — we suggested the President appoint a council or commission to look into this issue and report back to him. President Carter agreed with our recommendation on the condition that there would be no taxpayer dollars spent. He responded that the memorial would agree to a system in which the Interior Department would manage the facility but that any monies raised would be private monies. He asked me who I thought should head up such a commission. I said there really was only one person who has the stature and who really has become the worldwide spokesman for the Holocaust survivors, and indeed for the victims, and that's Elie Wiesel. As I recollect, Elie was out of the country — I believe he was in

Israel. I called him and asked if, in principle, he would be willing to serve on such a commission.

Q: Was there any pressure?

Eizenstat: No.

Q: I'm trying to dissect this general political and cultural awareness of Carter's Administration and to what extent such a unique event was introduced and actually went through smooth sailing without any objections and without any mobilization of interest groups?

Eizenstat: This was done without any mobilization of interest groups. It was an idea that my staff had, and that I had, and that we got the President to accept.

Q: When you reached Wiesel, did he know about the plans?

Eizenstat: No, not before the President had made the decision. As soon as the President made the decision, agreement had to be reached on who the members of the commission should be. There were disagreements between Elie and, I think, Ann Wechsler, but there were no pressures that I'm aware of.

Q: Before we close this topic on interest groups, how does the role of liaison to the Jewish community within the Administration work?

Eizenstat: First of all, in recent times it has existed in each Administration. Sometimes it's formally designated, at other times less formally. But it's always there. I think it's important but it's importance is exaggerated. It's important because there is a need for different groups, whether Hispanic, Black, Jewish or any other constituency in the country to feel that they have access to the White House — that there's someone there that has their particular concerns and interests in mind and to whom they can go if they have a concern. The problem is that although the people who have served in that role have been highly qualified and very eminent people in virtually every Administration, they are not normally in the policy loop; they're not the decision makers themselves; thus, there's the problem that they're viewed as special pleaders and advocates for the community rather than more neutral decision makers, so that it's important but they rarely are involved in the actual making of decisions. Breger is a good example. He obviously wasn't involved in the decision to go to Bitburg. He had to bear the scars from it, but he was not directly involved any more than Al Moses or Ed Sanders were involved in making our Middle East policy.

Q: In any case, those liaison people have the input . . . ?

Eizenstat: Yes, they have input to all the staff of the White House.

Q: How do you view the argument that President Reagan undertook this decision to visit Bitburg and was not able to maneuver and/or to change his mind?

Eizenstat: It's a good example of policy being made without thinking through the consequences. It apparently was initiated by a meeting between Kohl and Reagan in November. Privately, Kohl asked him to do such a cemetery visit and he personally committed himself. Presidents don't like to reverse themselves when they've personally committed themselves to another head of state because it undercuts their credibility on other issues. That decision was made by Reagan off the top of his head without staff input. That [decision] was compounded by very faulty staff work — Michael Deaver did not thoroughly check out the cemetery to find out if there were SS graves. I'm sure that if they had known that they would have asked for another cemetery. Once that decision was compounded on top of the first decision and was publicly announced, they were into a situation where it was a no-win one for Reagan. If he had asked Kohl to change or rearrange the visit, it would have looked from his perspective as if he were bowing to pressure and that his personal word had been broken. On the other hand, if he didn't and went forward with it he would bear the liabilities, particularly in the Jewish community, that have accrued.

Q: So in a way he had very little space in which to maneuver.

Eizenstat: This often is the case with presidents when they back into a decision without having thought through the consequences or commit themselves prematurely to something without giving people the chance to study it, and it was compounded, again, by sloppy staff work.

Q: Concerning those advisers, to the best of my knowledge, and I think it comes from some German sources, there are practically no so-called clean military cemeteries in Germany.

Eizenstat: Well, I don't know any more than I have read, but there were some statements about the fact that within a mile there was another one. I'm not an expert on military cemeteries so I can't tell you who were buried there.

Q: But from the point of of view of an expert, you think it was really presidential advisers that were in error?

Eizenstat: It was a gross error that was compounded, by the way, by a third decision which I should mention: that was the initial decision not to go to a concentration camp. All this together created the impression that the President was more interested in honoring the perpetrators than the victims. I don't think that was the case. In fact, I'm sure that was not his intent. I think that would be contrary to his whole background and make-up. But that's the impression that was left and unfortunately perceptions sometimes become reality in politics.

Q: From your vantage point as a domestic adviser, how did you analyze the mounting popular uproar?

Eizenstat: Well, I think it was a good example of the degree to which public opinion works on presidential decisions. There was a mounting uproar, but the uproar was mainly from the Jewish community — although there was some protest from the veterans' groups. It was the Jewish community which unfortunately bore the brunt of this. It was unfortunate that a wider range of people didn't take this up — it was mainly perceived as a Jewish issue. The veterans didn't do too much. The Congressional resolution that was passed was perceived as coming from Jewish pressure.

Q: How was this perceived by the White House?

Eizenstat: Unfortunately the results thereafter basically underscored the Jewish pressure — the poll results indicated that to the average American this was a non-issue. It's only in the Jewish community that it remains an issue.

Q: Could you — again to the degree that you can be specific — elaborate on the Jewish leadership in this crisis?

Eizenstat: By and large, the matter was handled appropriately by the Jewish leadership. That is, the issue was raised and raised forcefully, but the Jewish leadership didn't allow the issue to soar or cloud their relationship with the Administration so as to preclude their future dealings with it. That's always a danger. There's a question of how far you can go. You try to influence a decision, you try to do everything legitimately to change it, if you think it's going in the wrong direction. But once it's made and it's in concrete then if you belabor it you can create a rift between the community and the White House which will prevent you from having influence on other issues which will inevitably come up.

Q: To what degree was there pressure on the Holocaust Memorial Committee and even on Wiesel himself to make a stronger statement and even to resign?

Eizenstat: I think that Elie acted in an entirely appropriate way. He made it clear, in eloquent terms, why there was such a furor in the Jewish community about the decision, but at the same time did not cut his bridges by resigning. You can have much more influence when you disagree with a decision by disagreeing with it, trying to change it, and then staying and fighting the next battle.

Q: This actually brings us to the apex of the entire issue: how was this a clash of absolute morality with politics?

Eizenstat: Anyone who wants to go into government service in a serious way has to recognize that there are no such things as absolutes. There are no absolute rights and absolute wrongs. There are gradations of rights and wrongs, at least in the American political system, and the political system works only through compromises and half measures and accommodations. That's what makes the whole system function. We don't have a dictatorial system, and it can only work when people compromise their strongly-held views.

Q: One of the reasons for lack of maneuverability by the President was that the Germans were once so-called betrayed by the Carter Administration on the issue of the neutron bomb.

Eizenstat: Or they *felt* that they had been betrayed. President Carter felt the same about them.

Q: Well, Schmidt put himself on the line and mobilized the party, and then the Administration decided to drop it. Do you see any comparison?

Eizenstat: There's a direct parallel between the perception of the West German reaction to the neutron bomb decision and Reagan's decision. In fact, I think it's one of the factors that led him not to try to change because having made a commitment he did not want to have the same reaction in West Germany as occurred after President Carter's neutron bomb decision. So no decision occurs in a vacuum. It always occurs in the context of previous relationships, even with previous presidents and previous chancellors. But another factor was Reagan's carefully cultivated image as a leader who doesn't bow to pressure and who has a clear-cut course, and that sort of thing.

Q: Could you elaborate on this political framework of President Reagan...?

Eizenstat: Well, I think the President has tried in a very calculated way to create an image of a forceful, decisive and strong leader. And I think it was perceived both by him and his lieutenants at the White House that if they had changed their opinion on a decision that had been so publicly announced, that it would cause a chink in the armor of that image. I'm hypothesizing, but I think that that was a factor.

Q: Somebody has stated that the President has an inability to see the political, historical processes of one unit because he comes from the school of Hollywood and knows only the cue card. Do you think that this pattern of education had anything to do with his decision?

Eizenstat: Well, although I don't think Reagan has any deep knowledge of history, he has a good instinct for the linkage of issues. He has — certainly when Jim Baker was at the White House — a very good strategic sense of how one decision relates to other decisions. On this one the antennae were faulty, because there was not somehow the perception of the historical importance of the Holocaust and how this would be perceived as having not appropriately dealt with the whole history of the Holocaust at the time of the 40th anniversary of the end of the war, and how deep-seated those feelings and memories were. So this is one case where his normally sensitive antennae I think were faulty, and I think that had Jim Baker been at the White House during this whole period it's unlikely that this decision would have been made, or [on the other hand] they would have found some way out of it. But you had a new team coming in and they came in and sort of missed this because they didn't really have their feet on the ground.

Q: What do you think the impact of this affair will have on the historical perception of the Jewish community?

Eizenstat: I think that Bitburg will always be a significant part of the Reagan Administration for the Jewish community but not for the non-Jewish community. I think, at least from their prespective, it's a footnote. From the Jewish community's standpoint it's a major incident. In terms of how the Holocaust will be remembered, perhaps there's a silver lining. The whole debate that was engendered by the Bitburg incident tended to elevate the historical significance of the Holocaust to a level that it would not have had in terms of general consciousness were it not for the incident. It caused more debate, more focus, more attention, more scrutiny than would have been the case without it. To that extent, it could even have led to a greater sensitivity by a greater number of people to the tragedy of the Holocaust.

Speaking Truth To Power
Book Excerpt

By Charles E. Silberman

In one of the most widely reproduced photographs of the Holocaust, taken the day the slave labor camp at Buchenwald was liberated in 1945, twenty-four skeletal figures, lying in cage-like bunks, stare at the camera. Forty years later, in a White House ceremony carried live by every TV network, the President of the United States presented the Congressional Gold Medal of Achievement, the highest honor the American government can give a civilian, to one of the survivors in that photograph, the writer/lecturer/teacher Elie Wiesel. When he came to the podium to accept, the still-gaunt Wiesel, now fifty-seven, did somethig virtually unheard of in American life: he "spoke truth to power," as Jewish tradition demands, firmly but respectfully chiding the president for his planned trip to the military cemetery in Bitburg, Germany, which contains the graves of forty-seven members of the Waffen SS. "That place, Mr. President, is not your place. Your place is with the victims of the SS," Wiesel told the president, urging him "to do something else, to find another way, another site." As *Newsweek* commented, it "was surely one of the more remarkable moments in the annals of the White House."

It was surely the most remarkable moment in the annals of American Jewry — so much so that I felt impelled to add this epilogue after the rest of the book (*A Certain People*) had gone to press. "Think of the cabinet members over the decades who — after resigning over a policy dispute — have stood before the cameras and announced that they were leaving government because of their health or their desire to practice law," the journalist M. J. Rosenberg suggested, delineating what it was that made the moment unique. "Think of all the people who, determined to address a president on a moral issue, backed off as the aura of the White House stifled their protest." Because of that aura, some of the most prominent Jewish political and communal leaders pressured Wiesel to back off. "Never criticize the *poritz* [czar]," some told him, in the traditional Eastern European Jewish formulation. Others urged silence on political grounds: "We have a long agenda," they explained. Important items on it — in particular, an additional $1.5 billion in U.S. aid to Israel — might be jeopardized. "And besides," they added, the old fear showing, "we have to live with Reagan for another three and a half years."

Wiesel held firm. "I understood that we would have to mend fences after the Bitburg visit," he told me three weeks later. "But not before. Compromise was impossible; Jewish dignity was at stake." At stake too was the meaning — indeed, the very memory — of the Holocaust, to which Wiesel devoted his adult life. Nor could a confrontation with the president himself be avoided: this was no decision made by others, to which he had passively consented. On the contrary, Mr. Reagan's explanations of his itinerary had been more offensive than the trip itself.

ITEM: The German people have "a guilt feeling that's been imposed on them, and I think it's unnecessary," Reagan told his March 21 press conference, in defense of his decision not to visit the Dachau concentration camp as expected. He went on to say that he was not interested in "reawakening the memories and so forth."

ITEM: On April 18, Holocause Remembrance Day, the president defended his trip to Bitburg by arguing that the soldiers who died serving the Nazi regime "were victims, just as surely as the victims in the concentration camps," an argument he repeated to a second audience. Twelve days later he insisted that "it is morally right to do what I am doing."

Not since the Six-Day War have American Jews felt so assaulted — or so determined to speak out. Even those leaders who had urged silence on Wiesel felt obliged to criticize the president, and some of Reagan's most ardent supporters made passionate public attacks. At a luncheon meeting of the Conference of Presidents of Major Jewish Organizations, at which its chairman, Kenneth Bialkin, explained that his criticism of the president was made more in sorrow than in anger, the principal speaker, *Commentary* editor Norman Podhoretz, began by saying that he spoke in anger, *not* in sorrow, for this was no casual or minor error on the president's part. "What makes the Bitburg incident so serious," Podhoretz later wrote in his syndicated newspaper column, "is that it undermines the very foundation on which Mr. Reagan's foreign policy . . . has hitherto stood; the idea that there is something special, something unique, about totalitarian states. . . . By proposing to lay a wreath at a military cemetery in which Nazi stormtroopers lie buried, Mr. Reagan is for all practical purposes treating Nazi Germany as though it had indeed been just one ordinary nation at war with other ordinary nations."

Jewish dignity was upheld. After the White House ceremony, in fact, almost every reporter and editorial writer commented on Wiesel's respectful tone and gentle manner and the graciousness with which, in *Time's* phrase, he "lectured [the president] on morality while a national television audience looked on." Wiesel expressed his gratitude to the United Sttes, "for having offered us haven and refuge" and paid tribute to "the freest nation in the world, the moral nation." He expressed admiration for the president, as well, and thanked him for his support of Israel and his efforts on behalf of imprisoned Soviet Jews. Wiesel continued: "But, Mr. President, I wouldn't be the person I am, and you wouldn't respect me for what I am, if I were not to tell you also of the sadness that is in my heart. . . . The issue here is not politics, but good and evil. And we must never confuse them."

Ironically, the Reagan administration's inability to understand that distinction led it into what Representative Vin Weber, a leading congressional conservative, called "an obvious political disaster — The Watergate of symbolism." Although Reagan's own aides defended him and insisted that the Teflon surrounding the president had not been penetrated, those more concerned about the future of the Republican party worried that the party had been tarred with the brush of anti-Semitism and that it might forfeit any chance of gaining Jewish votes in 1988. Weber explained his concern:

> We have had a tremendous chance to move the Jewish community. The Jews had provided most of the talent, brainpower and money for the Democratic party. Many Jews were prepared to vote for Reagan. . . . But the Democrats succeeded [in 1984] in making Jerry Falwell and the religious right a centerpiece issue. A lot of Jewish voters got the uneasy feeling that there is a growing anti-Semitic force within the Republic party. I don't believe that's true, but I understand that concern. Then comes Bitburg, many candlepower greater than the Falwell issue.

Presidential polster Richard Wirthlin expressed the same fear. Mr. Reagan's visit to Bitburg had evoked emotions "stronger than we are able to measure in survey research," he remarked a few days after the president's return — emotions that "go far beyond [questions of] simple political support. I think it has created an emotional tearing that will have some consequences . . . the Jewish community has been strongly alienated. . . ." So much so, in fact, that some Republicans worried that their party might abandon any effort to woo the Jews, considering it a lost cause. After Bitburg it may well be.

To their credit, a great many politicians were concerned with more than just the political fallout. "It was a moral disaster," Representative Weber said. "We were shocked that that was not the feeling at the White House." The "we" was more than editorial: in the House of Representatives 84 Republicans, many of them closely aligned with the president, joined 173 Democrats in a letter urging West German Chancellor Helmut Kohl to give the president a graceful way out by withdrawing his invitation to visit Bitburg. Even more striking, 82 of the 100 members of the Senate, including Republican Majority Leader Robert Dole, voted for a resolution urging the president to bypass Bitburg and "visit a symbol of German democracy" instead.

It was a classic example of American pluralism at work, for members of Congress were not the only ones to respond in this way; there was a similar reaction from the press, the American Legion, and leaders of some religious and ethnic groups. True, at least one Jewish communal leader who actively protested the Bitburg visit was troubled that many Christian leaders did not respond until they were asked; in lending their names to a protest, he told me, the Christians in question seemed to feel that "they were paying off a debt, not addressing a moral issue of concern to them." But as David Gordis, executive vice president of the American Jewish Committee, observed, "Having insisted that the Holocaust was a uniquely Jewish event, we should not be surprised when others do not see it as their issue." And if the church response was not all that Jews might have wished, the congressional and mass media response was. Indeed, the press was almost unanimous in condemning Reagan's moral obtuseness and the shallowness of his view of history, as well as of morality.

In short, the Reagan administration discovered that even an inadvertent display of insensitivity to Jewish sensibilities carried a heavy price. And it *was* inadvertent; Reagan's intention was not to slight Jews but to pay off a political debt to Chancellor Kohl by helping him with conservative elements in his own party. Neither the president nor his aides had any conception of the anger — and anguish — their decision would cause American Jews in general, and survivors of the Holocaust in particular.

The White House fell into a trap of its own devising because it is out of touch with the changes of the past few decades, whereby the United States has become a genuinely multi-ethnic, multi-racial, and multi-religious society. Indeed, Ronald Reagan is the first president since Herbert Hoover who has not had a Jew as a member of his inner circle, either as a friend and/or political confidant or as a ranking member of the White House staff. Since the day Reagan took office, in fact, no Jew — none, that is to say, who acknowledges his Jewishness (or as an old Washington hand puts it, "no one who would show up at Bill Safire's annual Yom Kippur 'break the fast' party") — has had direct access to the president on matters of this sort. Not even the frustrated leaders of the Jewish Republican Caucus have been able to establish any direct relation with him.

It is not because of anti-Semitism. On the contrary, the administration has been unusually responsive to Jewish concerns, not out of benevolence, to be sure, but because such responsiveness serves its own anti-Soviet stance. Whatever the reasons, however, the administration has provided more aid to Israel than any of its predecessors and has formally acknowledged that that aid stems not from Jewish political power but from Israel's strategic importance to the United States; and it has brought considerable pressure on the Soviet Union to release Jewish "prisoners of conscience" and permit the emigration of Russian Jews. (The administration also played a key role in the rescue of Ethiopian Jewry, but the unsung hero of that episode would appear to be Secretary of State George Shultz.) Nor are Jews absent from other government agencies; both Alexander Haig and George Shultz appointed Jews to high State Department posts. The fact remains that, except in minor posts, there are no Jews in the White House. Nor are there any non-Jewish advisers — men such as Joseph Califano or LBJ adviser John Roche — who are attuned to Jewish sensibilities. "The people around Reagan simply do not know many Jews and they seem to be uncomfortable when Jews are around," a prominent Jewish Republican told me. "I think they are as uncomfortable with me as I am with them," the head of a major Jewish organization told me.

The result was that no one was in a position to counsel the president against the Bitburg visit before he had put his prestige on the line, as Stuart Eizenstat would have done during the Carter administration, Leonard Garment under Nixon, or any of a number of people who were close to Gerald Ford and Lyndon Johnson. Nor was there anyone who could interpret the Jewish reaction and help White House officials understand why it was so intense; hence the administration violated what one Democrat called the first rule of politics: when you find yourself in a hole, stop digging. As an administration official from elsewhere in the government observed, there was a complete "lack of understanding about what this cemetery visit really means to Jews."

For the same reason, there was no one to advise the administration against compounding the problem by adding a visit to Bergen-Belsen to the president's schedule, as if the decision to go to Bitburg, and thus to honor Nazi criminals, was simply an awkward bit of scheduling whose harm could be undone by a political balancing act. As *Washington Post* columnist Richard Cohen wrote:

> The issue then became not one of justice or morality, of remembering history and learning from it, of honoring the survivors and their constant pain, but of numbers and alliances — NATO and Star Wars and Pershing missiles. In a way, this was an echo of the very mentality that is associated with the Holocaust itself — a hierarchy of heartless priorities where always there was something more important than the fate of Jews being killed by Nazis, something, that is, more important than morality itself.

In Germany, the consequences appeared to be everything that Jews had feared; former Nazis, at any rate, took the president's visit to Bitburg as a signal that they had been rehabilitated.

ITEM: (From a *New York Times* dispatch, published three days before the Reagan visit): "They stood relaxed, shaking hands, introducing wives, these men of Germany's dark past, looking forward to a three-day meeting that began here today.

"The Hotel Krone . . . where about 250 veterans of the Waffen SS Death's Head Division have gathered, is closed to outsiders. But the veterans, in the loden coats of postwar German prosperity, are more relaxed, less defensive.

"Long the pariahs of West German society for their record of atrocity and brutality during the Third Reich, this year they are returning reporters' telephone calls, and talking, quietly, assuredly. . . . Conversations with the veterans leave no doubt that President Reagan's insistence on going to Bitburg . . . has made them feel better about their role in history. . . . 'It took a long time,' an SS veteran said, 'but this shows we were soldiers, just like the others.'"

ITEM: Visiting the Bitburg cemetery the day after the President and Chancellor Kohl had placed wreaths of reconciliation in front of its chapel, Marvin Kalb reported this scene:

> Six feet to the left of the President's wreath stood an equally impressive one. Across its banner: "To the Waffen SS who fell at Leningrad." No more than a foot to the right of the Chancellor's was another wreath: "For the fallen comrades of the Waffen SS." These two wreaths had been placed in the chapel, out of sight, hours before the president arrived. They were restored to their original places of honor only hours after he left.

Nor were the wreaths the only signs Kalb found that the old Germany was alive and well. "We Germans had been cooperating very well," one Bitburg resident told Kalb, "until the Jews began to make trouble." And his was not an isolated voice. "A number of leading West German politicians and professors — several close to Kohl — think anti-Semitism was on the rise even before Bitburg," Kalb wrote. "'The Jews were getting too impertinent,' one politician said. . . . 'We've listened to them much too long. It's enough.'"

The reaction in the United States was something else again. True, Elie Wiesel received some virulent hate mail, as did Henry Siegman, executive director of the American Jewish Congress, who led a group to Munich to pay tribute to the graves of the heroes of the anti-Nazi White Rose movement. But a certain amount of hate mail was to be expected, since, as we have seen, there is a residue of anti-Semitism in the United States. "We get that kind of mail every time we burp," an executive of the Anti-Defamation League told me—that is, every time Jews (or the ADL) occupy a prominent place in the news. During and after Bitburg, however, the volume of such mail was no larger and its tone no worse than the norm, nor was there any increase in anti-Semitic incidents or acts of vandalism. "I expected a lot of anti-Semitism," the official told me, "but we're not seeing it." Indeed, reports from the League's thirty offices showed "nothing significant."

In fact, nothing could be more significant than the absence of any significant upturn in anti-Semitism. Not that Bitburg was entirely free of cost; if nothing else, it revealed how vast a gulf still separates the Jewish and non-Jewish world views. But if Gentiles did not always understand why Jews reacted with such intensity—as we have seen, memory plays a different role in Judaism than in Christianity—a large majority supported their right to protest, and roughly half the population opposed the president's visit. For all the pain it brought, therefore, the Bitburg incident demonstrated that for American Jews, the United States is now home as well as haven; once characterized as "eternal strangers," Jews are now natives, free to assert their pain and anger—able and willing to "speak truth to power."

(This essay appeared originally in A Certain People *by Charles E. Silberman [Simon & Schuster· New York, 1985]. Reprinted with permission.)*

The Lesson of Bitburg
Special Contribution

By U.S. Representative Sam Gejdenson

When Arthur Godfrey came on, the television went off. Arthur Godfrey, as any Jewish boy growing up in Connecticut in the early 1950s could tell you, owned a hotel in Florida that didn't admit Jews.

The Liberty Lobby, as any Jewish Congressman could tell you 30 years later, is openly anti-Semitic. So when President Reagan nominated former Liberty Lobby executive Warren Richardson to a high post at the Department of Health and Human Services in 1981, my opposition was not only reflexive but quickly successful in getting the nomination withdrawn.

These examples occurred to me recently as I reflected on the significance for America's Jewish community of President Reagan's visit to the Bitburg cemetery. For I think the insensitivity shown by the President and his advisors in planning this visit is more of a threat to Jews than the ones we traditionally recognize.

Open discrimination is no longer much of a problem for Jews in the United States. Thanks to civil rights laws, to changing attitudes and to the increased political prominence we have developed, no longer are there hotels which don't cater to Jews. The Liberty Lobby's anti-black, anti-Semitic extremism is as out of place in mainstream Protestant America (in rural Connecticut, at least) as a Jewish Congressman would have been 30 years ago.

But despite these gains, much of the energy of the American Jewish community is directed against the right-wing crazy groups. We tend to focus our domestic political efforts on those issues we see directly affecting us.

Those issues, though, like Arthur Godfrey's hotel, are not the real problem. What Jews had to fight then was second-class citizenship; what we have to fight now is the attempt by fundamentalist Christians to re-institutionalize this status by gaining acceptance, through school prayer and other seemingly innocuous measures, of America as a Christian nation where those of other faiths can legitimately be excluded.

The greatest challenge facing Jews in America, then, as the Bitburg affair showed, is not opposing the extremists but educating the general public. The President is not anti-Semitic; neither, I am sure, are the advisers who scheduled his trip to Europe observing the 40th anniversary of the end of World War II. But by refusing the invitation to visit Dachau, scheduling the ceremony at Bitburg and then adamantly refusing to change it, the President showed an insensitivity that should not be possible in our top elected official.

When the President first refused the invitation to Dachau, in January of 1985, I wrote a letter asking him to reconsider and released it to the press. The response, from the Administration and from the press, was negligible. Later, when details of the Bitburg visit became known, I joined my Jewish colleagues in an early call for him to reconsider. Again no one was listening. Only when a number of non-Jewish groups, including the American Legion and Veterans of Foreign Wars became involved, and when the entire Jewish community threw its weight into the protest, did the press and public start to pay attention.

The reason? Again, I don't believe it is anti-Semitism on the part of the press or the public. It is indifference. A contributing factor to that indifference is that Jewish groups have for so long focused on attacking the obvious that we have neglected to educate the public about the subtle danger of insensitivity.

By visiting Bitburg, President Reagan degraded the distinction between soldiers fighting for their country and cogs in a killing machine designed to destroy an entire race. He showed that America has not yet learned the lesson of the Holocaust. Elie Wiesel says it simply: Indifference to evil is evil. The lesson of Bitburg to American Jews is to spend more time attacking the indifference of the American public.

(Representative Sam Gejdenson was born in Eschwege, Germany, on May 20, 1948, in an American displaced persons camp, and is the first child of survivors of the Holocaust to serve in Congress. His parents fled Poland after World War II and emigrated to the United States in 1950, settling on a small dairy farm in Bozrah, Connecticut. Sam Gejdenson represents Connecticut.)

On Being Indignant About Bitburg
A Play

By Hans Sahl

(Hans Sahl wrote this play during World War II. He is a renowned writer and translator of American Drama into German.)

Something must be wrong with me, I need help. I cannot bring myself to be indignant about Bitburg.

Oh, yes, I know about the 49 graves of the Waffen-SS, 49 dead human monsters, buried among 2,000 ordinary soldiers of the Wehrmacht. But can you select corpses in the cemetery, can you distinguish between bad and good bodies? Are there graves to be avoided like the remainders of a cholera stricken city?

There was much outrage when President Reagan said that among the 2,000 buried at Bitburg not a few were as much Hitler's victims as were the inmates of Auschwitz.

In 1942, when I arrived in New York from occupied France after having been liberated by the Americans I wrote a radio play, "Furlough from Death", for the Treasury Star Parade which was broadcast by all America radio stations. It was the story of a dead German soldier coming back from the Russian front to accuse his parents for having sacrificed him for the glory of the Hitler inferno.

FURLOUGH FROM DEATH

Martin:
I was only twelve. I didn't know. I just did what everybody did. But you—you were my father…! You knew it! You must have known!—known what they intended to do with us.

Father:
Martin, you must understand, I couldn't do anything about it. I too did what the others did. I couldn't keep out.

Martin:
And I? I had to finish what you began. I had to go through it alone. You haven't seen the gallows that mark our roads. The mountains of corpses we left behind. Women and children mowed down by our machine guns. Towns and cities exterminated like rat's nests. Is that what the "Great Man", the Führer, promised you? My congratulations, father!

Father:
He promised us the whole world!

Martin:
But a world the way *we* are?

(Sudden rap on the door)

Father:
Yes?—Who is it?

(Enter Dr. Seyfritz)

Seyfritz:
Heil Hitler! It is a great pleasure to me, Herr Müller. To shake the hand of a German front line soldier! The eyes of the nation are on you, Herr Martin! Heil to our Führer! Heil to his unconquerable legions! Let me shake your hand!

Martin:
There are some hands that aren't hands anymore, Herr Doctor! Do you know what kind of hand mine is? It's a frozen hand. Better not touch it. It could happen that some of my fingers would remain in your hand, Herr Dr. Seyfritz!

Seyfritz:
What? I don't understand, Herr Müller.

Martin:

Those men out there understand. They're all looking in the snow for their lost fingers. Go and tell your party members that, Herr Doctor — go and tell them that you have seen a soldier who came from the front who didn't have any fingers, or any nose or ears! — Go tell them that!

Father:

Martin, please! — You get us all in trouble.

Seyfritz:

I will not listen to such talk! This is treason. The Gestapo must know about this!

(Fading)

Heil Hitler!

(Seyfritz leaves)

Martin:

It's too bad he had to go. There were some things I wanted to say to him.

Mother:

What sort of things, my son?

Martin:

I wanted to tell him about the voices I heard — Norwegian voices, Dutch voices, Danish voices, Belgian, French, Czech, and Greek and Polish voices...the voices of hatred and cold, relentless fury — the voices which our guns and our Gestapo cannot still — the voices which in the ultimate end will have their say — !

Father:

Yes, I know. They hate us. Perhaps you are right, my son. Perhaps in the end, they will have the final word. But don't you see, we can't turn back. We're all of us accomplices in this rape of the world. Every one of us has his own part to carry. Every one of us has done something which he shouldn't have done and every one of us knows it about everyone else. Each one of us is in the other's power. That's what holds us together — whether we like it or not. That's what makes us a group — a group of murderers and victims. There's no turning back now — there's only victory — or death! They turned our sons into killers and those of our sons who haven't been killed must keep on killing to save themselves. It's all lies and treachery and falsehood. We were promised freedom and we got slavery. We're all of us prisoners here — Germany is just one big concentration camp!

Martin:

And so we have reached the ultimate end. Not even you have any belief anymore.

There has been an end to all belief. Every meaning has been distorted into its opposite. And we've reached *nothing*! Soon there won't be a single home that hasn't lost at least one son. Soon there won't be any more men for the army. Already they are digging up the dead from their graves to send them to the front—but the dead make bad soldiers! They haven't anything to look forward to—no victories, no conquests, nothing.

(Very sadly)

Goodby. Keep well, both of you. I must go now. My furlough is over—they're calling me—

Mother:
You're going back?

Martin:
I'm going back. But I will return. We'll all return. When the first flowers bloom on our graves out there, then all of us are going to be joined together—millions of us.

(With fury)

And then there is going to be a revolution in Germany the like of which the world has never seen.

(Off)

Mother:
Martin! Martin!

Father:
He's gone—you can't call him back. He is dead.

Mother:
I don't understand anymore. Martin dead? But why? When did they kill him? Can you explain it all to me?

Father:
Martin was already dead when he was born.

Mother:
But he was right here—he spoke to us! If it wasn't Martin, who was it?

Father:

A dead German soldier — on leave!

END

"Furlough from Death" was my contribution to the war effort. Much of it still seems to be valid except the hope for a German revolution which unfortunately did not take place. I fought the Nazis ever since I began to become a writer, long before they came to power in Germany. I was indignant about Hitler and Stalin and I intend to be so whenever required. In short, my capacity for indignation is not limitless and I am trying to preserve it for occasions that deserve its application to the utmost.

Reagan's Contempt for History
Dissent Magazine
Summer, 1985

By David Bromwich

Bitburg, Germany, 1945; Managua, Nicaragua, 1985. The two appear to be so far apart that no occurrence could possibly bring them together. But in March and April, 1985, Ronald Reagan asked himself a question, *Whom shall I honor?* And his answers showed that Bitburg and Managua were closer to each other than anyone had supposed.

It began with Michael Deaver's trip to Germany, in search of "photo opportunities" for the President's visit. Deaver used his ingenuity along the way to purchase BMW automobiles for himself, his friends and connections, with a discount reserved for diplomats. This swindle made the news, and President Reagan said of it genially: "People in his position have always done things like that." By people in his position the President seemed to mean: officials who have the honor of serving the American people. Behind such a judgment lies an unusual conception of public virtue. Till now, American democracy had found one of its vindications in the idea that service to the republic could form the highest aspiration of a citizen. The people to whom this honor was given, it followed, would be people above any suspicion of chicanery. And yet, President Reagan's feelings about public service have always been equivocal. He is fond of boasting that his Administration recruits men so successful that "it is a step down for them to serve in government." How a step down? In yearly financial earnings—the President's calculus of distinction. By comparison, the momentous significance of occupying high office in a democracy has remained to him an abstraction. What he understands vividly are the ceremonial aspects of public life.

Late in March, the President's German itinerary was announced. He would lay a wreath in Bitburg Cemetery, where 49 SS men were buried, but he would not visit Dachau. "We don't want to reawaken old memories." In an April 18 *New York Times* article by Bernard Weinraub, an official told of another reason for the choice: "The President was not hot to go to the camp. You know, he is a cheerful politician. He does not like to grovel in a grisly scene like Dachau. He was reluctant to go. I am not saying opposed, but there was a coolness."

A general protest followed, but it was kept urgent by two groups particularly—war veterans and Jews: people with memories. The President's aides soon announced that his schedule was under reconsideration; and eventually a concentration camp opportunity was found. But in the meantime, the President had offered a remarkable apology. The soldiers in Bitburg, he said—among them, men of the Second Panzer Division, which carried out the Oradour massacre—were victims of the Nazis, just as surely as the Jews who perished in the Holocaust. With this analogy it became clear (though reporters understandably found it hard to put into words) that something new to our nation's politics had taken place. Here was a President at the height of his power and in the maturity of life, speaking of the formative event of his generation, in a language that showed he had never learned the first thing about the history of which he was a part.

For him, there were no memories to reawaken, except in connection with the strength or weakness of the "image" he would "project" on a foreign tour. The rest of us, whether we like it or not, are the captives of certain memories. But it has taken us this long to learn what we should have known from the start: that the way a man remembers has something to do with the respect he accords to facts. Mediating between memory and fact, the rest of us are conscious of a third term: history. But again, in Ronald Reagan's mind, history is infinitely malleable, like a soft substance that can be shaped to fit the political need of the moment. Any publicized event may call forth, therefore, the imaginary details of a provisional mythology, with instant data suited to the occasion. In the Bitburg apology, the improvisation was a number: the average age of the soldiers buried there, he decided, was eighteen. A little before, in a speech on Nicaragua, the improvisation had been a name: the Contra rebels were "the moral equivalent of our Founding Fathers." On inspection, this too could be seen as a number, a piece of disguised arithmetic; and, in turn, the renaming of the German soldiers as "victims" was itself a moral judgment. These soldiers, the President was saying, were the moral equivalent of all soldiers, and so an adequate symbol for all victims of war.

It is a lesson our pure ideologues cannot master, that *nothing is ever the moral equivalent of anything else.* In the past several weeks, senators and representatives in the Congress, together with many citizens, have begun to use a special word about these equivalencies. They speak of feeling insulted; and the word is exactly right.

The sense of insult does not come from their disagreement with the policies in question, for often they have no opinion about the policies. Rather they see that the President and his court are trying to obliterate history. To obliterate: that is, to rub out the letters of a name, a thing, an event; so that it no longer matters what gravestone one lays a wreath beside, all the gravestones everywhere having been effaced. Our contest in the next few years will be against those who believe that American democracy rests on a gradual perfecting of masterful performances that enthrall and obliterate. The President and his staff are wagering their second term and, with it, something of our country's fate, on the premise that their contempt for fact and memory will not be thrown back at them in disgust, by a people whose common history begins before 1980.

A visitor to America said: "Reagan doesn't have the emotional range I expected. Instead of joy or grief, he only passes from pleasure to vexation." This was well observed, and it explains a puzzle about his conduct. Why, for example, he is untouchable by the suffering that his policies impose; why, in meeting the objections of his opponents, he falls back petulantly on a questioning of motives; why, as he moves from topic to topic or from day to day, he says the most incompatible things, and then is surprised to find them compared with each other. It is for this reason that most people feel reluctant to describe his false sayings as lies. They seem merely the accidental hostages of *our* unhappy memories—unlooked-for deposits, from the episodic recitals he is called on to perform.

What fault, then, if the demands of a new moment pull our President in a new direction? Three years ago (it is already hard to remember), the Contras were 500 men, who existed solely to interdict the flow of arms to El Salvador. Now they are 15,000, who burn crops, blow up bridges and tear up roads, commit acts of violence and casual plunder that stagger the imagination of an American. Two years from now, they are intended to be 25,000: sufficient to bring chaos to the farthest reaches of the countryside, and to install a regime answerable to American interests. It is easy enough to confront these founding fathers—paternal adepts of rape and murder, loyalists to the old brutality of privilege—with a single staring fact about themselves. A lot of today's fighters for freedom were yesterday's hirelings of tyranny. The connection between past and present, however, held no interest to the President when he talked of continuing the wreck of Nicaragua until its government "cries uncle" (a phrase that is as low as the dirt). Nor had he read any report from Nicaragua, when he decided that a majority of its people think the present government "worse than Somoza's." He was free to talk in this style because he is a man to whom the past is a dead letter. Indeed, a capacity for lying would be an unnecessary addition to his equipment. It would make him less cheerful.

But his henchmen are made of different stuff. Expert at the manipulation of opinion, they have taken courage from the election results, and given up all pretense. They now disregard the truth quite openly. In recent congressional hearings on Nicaragua, Jeane Kirkpatrick was asked by Congressman Kostmayer why she had pressed for military action instead of assisting the Contadora negotiations. Her

answer? She was a steady friend to the Contadora process; it had no more reliable well-wisher than herself. Who can believe this? Once again, when Kostmayer
alluded to the proportion of the Contra leadership and field commanders known
to have come from the ranks of the Somocistas, and regretted he could not read
out the classified figure, Mrs. Kirkpatrick dared to join him in criticizing the restrictions on public knowledge: nobody, she said, had worked harder than she herself to have just such materials declassified. And again, who can believe this?

Something unexpected came out of the exchange, nevertheless. Mrs. Kirkpatrick admitted that, though the classified figures were available to her, she had
never looked to see how many of the rebels *were* former Somocistas. This concession was too embarrassing to have been a deliberate falsehood; and what it suggests
is that President Reagan's short way with history is catching on.

He was, of course, himself a rigid enthusiast for Somoza in 1978, and every
statement he or his advisers now make is predicated on a denial of the memory
of that fact. One can hardly lament the fate of a revolution, on the ground that it
failed to keep its promises, if one first opposed the revolution itself, on the ground
that its promises were not worth keeping. This piece of duplicity is at the very heart
of the Reagan administration's reasoning about Nicaragua. Its policy, the only policy it has ever held in earnest, is aimed at negotiating the surrender of the Nicaraguan government by any means necessary. The current instrument of policy is the
FDN ultimatum, which demands, as a condition for opening discussions, the nul-
lification of the Nicaraguan elections. By most foreign observers, these elections
were judged to stand up favorably beside the American-supervised elections in El
Salvador, and some cogent reasons for supporting the judgment were advanced
by Abraham Brumberg in the last *Dissent.* Thus the Nicaraguan ambassador spoke
with accuracy and restraint when he nicknamed the ultimatum: Drop-dead-or-we'll-
kill-you.

What many Americans instinctively feel about Nicaragua is that the government includes both more repressive and less repressive elements, and what we
want to do somehow is to encourage the latter. How can this be done? By following the diplomatic course proper to a nation that believes in freedom. This means:
by a reversal of the present strategy, which strengthens those in Nicaragua who favor one-party dictatorship, military control, and state surveillance *in any case,* but
whom our policy enables to argue for all of these things as an unfortunate necessity of war. As for the Contras, whom we have created as an active force, the best
we can do for their future is to create no more of them. It is sometimes said, by half-
hearted defenders of the present strategy, that the Contras include many good people. Perhaps so. They certainly include many hungry people, for whom an American rifle, three American meals a day, and the promise of American prosperity
look a great deal better than the filth and strife to which we have condemned their
country. Doubtless also, there are some idealists among them.

Before pursuing this train of thought further, however, democrats ought to
try an experiment. Think what it would mean to become a rebel in Nicaragua today. Who would you be? By what motives, ambitions, resentments would you have

been guided into that path? For you are not only taking up arms against a government that (though committing many wrongs, some of them inseparable from U.S. policy) performed the deed of your lifetime (an achievement so cherished that nobody claims not to have been part of it), by throwing out Somoza. At the same time you are consenting to act in conspiracy with a foreign power—a power famous in your region chiefly for economic exploitation and the rigging of military coups. Finally, you act at the instruction of a government led by Ronald Reagan, the apologist for dictatorship. Granted one may follow this experiment the whole length, and emerge with a picture of a Contra volunteer who finds the position of his commanders at once plausible and sympathetic. But to have come so far, the volunteer must believe that in Latin America the need to fight against Soviet influence outweighs all other considerations—moral and historical considerations, in the light of which the CIA may appear a far from desirable accomplice.

By agreeing to become the noncombatant spokesman for the rebels, Arturo Cruz has turned into something more than a Contra commandant, and something less than a Nicaraguan citizen. It seems right to deplore his choice of ultimate opposition and exile, since, while he worked in Nicaragua, he spoke for a democratic cause. As a collaborator with the U.S. State Department, he can no longer carry conviction with Nicaraguan democrats who wish to retain their independence from the U.S. as well as from the U.S.S.R. The real heroes of the struggle, if they are allowed to survive, will be those who hold out for some such independence. Cruz wishes to be counted among them. But he took a gamble and, as it has turned out, a deeply misguided one, when he abstained from his country's election at the prompting of our war-diplomats. He was ambivalent in Nicaragua, when he needed to be forthright; compliant in America, when he needed to be firm; a weak man, in an unhappy time, whom one would like to have seen strong. As it is, he has attached himself to a different history. His new patrons look back fondly on Somoza as a good friend who never did much harm to anyone they know. In the name of the memories we are being asked to forget, let us remind them again and again that the truth was otherwise.

A Footnote on Bitburg

Dissent Magazine
Summer 1985

By Irving Howe

Let me add a brief note to David Bromwich's trenchant article.

The more public tumult about the Holocaust, the less likelihood that the memory of its terribleness will become a serious part of human consciousness. What has been happening with the Holocaust is what seems all-but-inevitably to happen with everything in our culture— its appropriation by publicity, the vast machine of public relations and manufactured images that spreads like a thick oil across genuine thought and perception. By now, the Holocaust has barely any autonomous reality; it has become a calculation of image, a corrupting photo opportunity. Even the eloquence it can sometimes evoke has a streak of falsity and aggrandizement.

For the people around President Reagan, the Bitburg affair was, as one of them put it, a "public relations fiasco." Not a moral betrayal, not a sign of shameful ignorance, but a failure in mass manipulation. It was a *tactical* mistake for the President to visit a cemetery that harbors the graves of SS men, since the visit would make political trouble at home and perhaps— could anything be worse?—lower the President's rating in the polls. *Nothing seems to matter any more in its own right—* not even the most terrible event of our time.

I suppose most of the people around the President are not evil. Nor are they anti-Semitic, though it's not hard to imagine some of them grumbling about "those Jews who always complain." But the people who control the United States government today are of small imagination, small ethics, small consciousness, small memory. They serve their boss. Suddenly, after many successes, they found themselves— *but how the hell did this happen?*, they must have wondered—entrapped in moral complications beyond their interest or grasp. They could respond only as they have always responded. They did not stop honestly to admit error or confusion; they looked for devices of publicity, in this case, "a concentration-camp opportunity" and a speech that the Great Communicator recited dutifully.

An impudent question: Given what the President had already revealed about his sentiments toward and understanding of the Holocaust, why was it so urgent for Jewish institutional leaders to plead that he do "the right thing"? If someone, even the President, cannot spontaneously do "the right thing" regarding a matter of such elementary moral character as to avoid a cemetery with SS men, might it not be more dignified and, finally, perhaps more effective simply to say—oh, as politely as you wish—Keep your medal, go your way, we will express our disapproval and disgust, and will mourn our dead in our own way?

Or as our friend Abraham Brumberg wrote in a letter to the *Washington Post:*

Only one proper course of action remains: to make it crystal clear that neither the President nor his fellow politician, Chancellor Helmut Kohl, is the proper symbol of historical justice; to end the demeaning supplications; to let Reagan go to Germany and do what he damn well pleases; and to treat the whole indecent spectacle with the only response it deserves—contemptuous silence.

The uncorrupted memory of the Holocaust survives through the voices of some men and women. It survives in the books of the Italian writer Primo Levi, who simply remembers—quietly, modestly, without a touch of self aggrandizement--what happened to him and the others. It survives in the recently published *Chronicles of the Lodz Ghetto, 1941-1944*, edited by Lucjan Dobrowszycki, a record of the destruction of a major Jewish community in eastern Europe compiled by some of its members, a record all the more moving because of the dry factuality and restraint with which it was written. And the memory survives, we may be sure, among people who remember and mourn without so much as issuing a press release.

An Overview of "Bitburg"
Midstream
October, 1985

By Kalman Sultanik

In the wake of the disaster summed up in the very word "Bitburg" it seems more necessary than ever before to clarify its background.

The facts themselves are simple:

On April 11, the White House announced that President Reagan would lay a wreath at a military cemetery for German soldiers who had died in World War II; he wanted to emphasize "reconciliation"; he did not want to reawaken war-time passions.

The visit to Bitburg was suggested by Chancellor Helmut Kohl of Germany when he was in Washington last November; he was upset over the omission of West Germany from the commemoration of the 40th anniversary of D-Day; a Presidential visit to Bitburg would repair that omission. There would be no visit to a death camp, the President said, because there were "very few" Germans alive "that remember even the war, and certainly none of them who were adults and participating in any way."

A defense of the President's itinerary was put forward — he was being a good Christian. Just as he had forgiven Hinckley for that almost-successful assassination attempt, the President was now "forgiving" the Germans.

There were Jews, too, who in Letters to the Editor in many newspapers informed the public that Jewish tradition provides for forgiveness when the sinner repents.

Then, when it was learned there were 49 SS graves at Bitburg, came the President's comment that the German soldiers buried in the cemetery (though not SS) were victims of the Nazis "just as surely" as those who died in the concentration camps were victims. They were all victims of "one man."

Such are the facts.

But the fact — that is, for me, the *fundamental* fact — is that "Bitburg" was a major event in recent Jewish history. It was not in any sense a mere incident: it has affected not only the survivors of the Holocaust and not only the Jewish community as a whole, but a vast number of Americans and the international community as well.

When the President finally decided to visit a concentration-camp site, he did so only under pressure from Jewish leaders, and in order to counterbalance his visit to Bitburg. He did not seem to realize that by visiting Bergen-Belsen at the same time as Bitburg he made the situation even worse — he was desecrating the memory of the martyrs.

When I heard the President's announcement that he was going to Bitburg to lay a wreath at the cemetery of German soldiers I was appalled. The President was making an equation of two things that any moral person must surely consider diametrically opposed—murderers and victims. He was saying that the six million men, women, and children wantonly tortured and slaughtered by the Nazis were on the same moral footing as their torturers and murderers.

I was gripped by the feeling that the martyrs must have someone to speak for them, to keep alive their memory, the memory of their torture and murder.

It was on behalf of those martyrs that I had a feeling of profound outrage. It is I and others who have survived those horrors who must speak. We must speak for the succeeding generations who will have lost contact with the immediate events. We must speak because the martyrs buried in Bergen-Belsen cannot speak.

It was said, at the time, that the President must not be criticized while on a national mission abroad. But I saw no reason for that:

The President, after all, was elected by the people: he must be alive to what is happening everywhere. For that reason it must be we who let him know when, perhaps inadvertently, he is committing a titanic blunder.

How can we react to the behavior of a President of the United States, known for his goodwill, who seems to be incapable of grasping the nature of the Holocaust?

Questions are raised as to the propriety of staging a demonstration against a popular President and a staunch friend of Israel, such as Reagan is, on foreign soil. But surely no demonstration would have left any effect either on the present or on posterity unless it was staged where the horrors had been perpetrated and where President Reagan wished to change the course of history! The event was after all not one of purely European significance; it has global and historical implications. It wasn't confined to Germany alone. Those who had reservations about my going to Bergen-Belsen apparently did not view the visit from the same perspective as I. My going to Bergen-Belsen to demonstrate was an educational and moral act and not, as Kohl and Reagan wished to see it, a purely political step. There are no boundaries on moral issues.

It was precisely because of the President's goodwill, coupled with his manifest unawareness of the enormity of his behavior, that I went to Bergen-Belsen. It was an act of peaceful protest against that unawareness, which the President's position made portentous. I felt I *had* to go to Bergen-Belsen—otherwise I would not have been able to live with myself.

My visit, and the visit of others, including a group of children of Jewish Holocaust survivors from the United States, to Bergen-Belsen itself acquires importance: we were allowed onto the site only after the President had left Bergen-Belsen for Bitburg. Had I been allowed physically onto the site, I had intended to speak to the President directly, as spokesman for the Jews whose corpses were in Bergen-Belsen, and to say: "Mr. President, if you go to Bitburg, you are not wanted here—in Bergen-Belsen."

There are many veterans of that war still living today—both American and German veterans. There are many concentration camp survivors living today in the United States and in Israel, still grieving over the brutal murder of their relatives and friends. There are still widows and children of U.S. servicemen who were killed in battle, possibly by the very German soldiers President Reagan honored at Bitburg. And there are still perpetrators of those heinous crimes living in the United States and West Germany, men 61 years and older, who were legally adult, could have served in the army or SS, today vote, and presumably participate in the world around them. They would like to forget, and would like the world to forget, what they did.

And do the American families who lost brothers, sons, and fathers in the war against the Nazis not remember? Were they not profoundly shocked by President Reagan's equation of the SS murderers with the men they murdered and with the American prisoners who were massacred in cold blood?

Forgiveness can come only from the victim, not from some third party. The President could forgive Hinckley—he cannot forgive the murderers of other people's kith and kin.

It is alleged that the German people neither knew nor approved of what "one man" did, and had no choice but to go along with him. But as far back as 1934, the *Black Book of German Jewry* documented the rapidly deteriorating situation: ". . .over thirty anti-Semitic laws and regulations invalidating Jewish rights. . .were enacted between April and July of 1933. . . . The public cooperated in making the laws effective."

From the very beginning, then, that "one man" was not violating the wishes of the German people.

On May 8, the 40th anniversary of Nazi Germany's unconditional surrender, President Richard von Weizsäcker accepted the guilt of his people. In a speech to the West German Parliament, he insisted that the German people *knew* of the Nazis' extermination of the Jews.

"All of us, whether guilty or not, whether old or young, must accept the past... We are all affected by its consequences and liable for it." And he took issue with those—"all too many of us"—who claimed that they had not known anything about it or even suspected anything.

"Who could remain unsuspecting after the burning of the synagogues, the plundering, the stigmatization with the Star of David, the deprivation of rights, the ceaseless violation of human dignity?" he asked. "Whoever opened his eyes and ears and sought information could not fail to notice that Jews were being deported."

Then why did the President of the United States feel it necessary to keep silence—to grant absolution, even when none was asked?

The soldiers of Bitburg were said to be draftees, rather than enthusiastic Nazis. And the chorus rose, distinguishing between the different kinds of SS, between the SS and the Wehrmacht—the regular army, which was presumably free of Nazi crimes. Yet it was the commander in chief of the Wehrmacht, General Keitel, who ordered the shooting of General Giraud and General Weygand, (it was General Canaris who refused to execute) and it was Keitel, at the Nuremberg Trials, who admitted that the army, too, was "covered with shame." He said: "It is dishonorable, horrible." And Warsaw was not the only place where the Wehrmacht distinguished itself in the slaughter of civilians and the carrying out of the Nazi mandate.

Youth was not immune to the Nazi virus. The young soldiers buried at Bitburg were no different from other German youth at that time. I saw them herd my own family into cattle-trains bound for Treblinka, and I was in the death march from Dresden to Theresienstadt, where I was fortunately liberated before these fanatical young Nazis managed to find a crematorium that was still functioning. The war was lost, the German army was in disarray, but these young Nazis were unrelenting in their zeal to fulfill their murderous duties. Had the Third Reich won the war these so-called unwilling draftees would have happily accepted their Nazi decorations as heroes, and not a Jew would have survived in Europe.

To compare these killers with the innocent victims, among them one and a half million infants and children, is simply immoral.

When Elie Wiesel accepted the Congressional Medal of Achievement from President Reagan at the White House, he appealed to the president not to go to Bitburg. "That place is not your place," he said. "Your place is with the victims of the SS."

Words—particularly the words of the President—are primordial: they go into the record and become part of history, working on the future generations even more invidiously than they do on ours, because there will be no rebuttal in future generations.

Words do inestimable damage: witness the vicious UN resolution that slandered a whole people by equating Zionism with racism. Those words poisoned the atmosphere at the United Nations and made possible the rebirth of vicious anti-Semitic statements and charges in the world forum, and the attempted delegitimation of Israel. Are we to witness the reverse process for Germany—the legitimation of German history and the excusing of Nazism as the excess perpetrated by "one man"?

The very least we owe the six million Jews and the countless other millions of victims of Nazism is a proper memorial: not monuments, not statues, but truth—the truth of how and why they died, and who was responsible for killing them.

The very fact that 40 years after the Holocaust the "Bitburg affair" could even occur, the very fact that in the U.S. and in Israel the Jewish people have so much confidence in the President of the United States and in the American people's friendship for Israel and for Jews generally tells us that any complacency about this matter is fundamentally a delusion.

If it is true that Chancellor Kohl knew what he was doing, he was responsible for a travesty of history.

How could any democratic leader, and *especially* the German chancellor, conceive of a ceremony of commemoration of the 40th anniversary of the defeat of the Nazi regime with the omission of a visit to a death camp and confining this event solely to visiting a German military cemetery, even if one accepts at face value that he was unaware that Nazis of the SS are buried there? It was only after an outcry throughout the Jewish and non-Jewish world that he agreed to add Bergen-Belsen as an afterthought to the Bitburg program. How can such insensitivity be explained?

It is obvious, of course, that the President's advisors, in the wake, no doubt, of Chancellor Kohl's insistence, "botched" things. No doubt the President's advisors had to accommodate Kohl's request that the President go to Bitburg, expecting to balance that, if necessary, against the White House's pro-Israel actions in other respects, its support for Ethiopian Jewry, etc., in the hope that any repercussions would be relatively trivial.

Yet this view, natural, perhaps, for political operations, has proved to be a boomerang. It boomeranged not only among the grassroot Americans and the media but also among 83 members of the Republican-dominated Senate who cosponsored a resolution opposing Reagan's plans.

It was not only that the President made the mistake, after showing reluctance to visit a death-camp site, of visiting the Bitburg cemetery where there were some 49 graves of the SS, one of the chief arms of fanatic Nazi anti-Semitism. On the very Day of Remembrance itself — Yom Hashoah — after I had participated in the candle-lighting ceremony in the Rotunda of the Capitol, I was on my way to the airport to fly to Bergen-Belsen to take part on behalf of the World Jewish Congress in ceremonies there. It was then that I heard on the radio the President *explicitly* equate the victims of the Holocaust with their murderers. I felt as though I were choking with rage.

Never before, in the 40 years since the end of World War II, has any head of state exploited the Holocaust for political purposes. The enormity of the Nazi crimes cannot be obliterated by the dictates of political suppositions.

The Holocaust of European Jewry was made possible by advanced German technology and efficiency. Unless scientific and technological advancement is controlled by deep moral considerations, it could very well lead again to the wholesale slaughter of dissidents, minorities, and even of entire nations.

Reconciliation with the new Germany cannot take place over the graves of murderers. Reconciliation requires full acceptance of the need to transmit the truth of these crimes of the Third Reich to succeeding generations.

Forty years after Auschwitz the world remains ambivalent about the Holocaust. It is incontestable that six million Jews — one third of the Jewish populations of the world — were wiped out because the Jews, unlike all other victims of the Nazi regime, had been uniquely marked for total destruction. Thus the uniqueness of the Holocaust arises not because the Jews stood in the way of Nazi rule — but because they were born Jews.

It is true that the Nazis also killed, through starvation and brutality, no fewer than two and a half million Soviet prisoners of war, and over a million of the Polish intelligentsia, and other Poles as real or alleged resisters. They also destroyed thousands of Russians and Ukrainian peasants during the Germany occupation of those areas. Yet there was never a Nazi policy applying the measures used against the Jews to other national communities.

The term "Holocaust" began to be used in English sometime between 1957 and 1959, in order to express the then widespread feeling that what happened to the

Jews during the Second World War was unprecedented — as indeed it was. The terrible fate that had befallen the Jews of Europe was unique: they had become the first, and so far the only, people to be singled out for complete physical annihilation.

The uniqueness of Jewish suffering and of Jewish catastrophe during the Second World War had no sooner been defined than it was called into question by a great many so-called "universalists," who stubbornly rejected the notion of a distinctively Jewish catastrophe. They believed that the enormity of the Holocaust could be recognized by the world at large only if it were universalized — if its victims were recast as "human beings" rather than Jews. All of them failed to realize that this was a distortion — historically, ideologically, and factually — of what had really happened.

It cannot be denied that Nazi policy was the direct result of the ideology of anti-Semitism, an ideology rooted in the endless variety of books, lectures, pamphlets, all preaching the same bizarre theme — that Jews are not ordinary human beings, but are bearers of a unique kind of Evil that somehow made it seem reasonable to destroy them, even if it meant injuring oneself, as the Nazis did.

It is apparent that throughout the world people in the grip of a "double standard" with respect to the Jews persist in misunderstanding the Holocaust — in blunting, downgrading, and distorting it.

But the penalty of belittling and distorting the meaning of the Holocaust goes far beyond the fate of the Jews. The Holocaust, merely by proving to be *possible* among the most civilized nations of the world, has established the further possibility of being extended far beyond the Jewish people.

"Bitburg" is all the more disturbing because it reminds us of the American reaction to the Holocaust when it was taking place. Against a background of Jewish confusion the highest strata of the U.S. government slighted and falsified the Nazi atrocities, and barred any attempts to mitigate their effects.

For this reason it has been to the highest degree distressing that the Reagan administration, 40 years later, has learned nothing from the failures of the Roosevelt administration. It should be plain to fair-minded people that the past half-century must be thought through once again, and its lessons properly assessed.

The magnitude of the issues that led to "Bitburg" far transcend personal feelings — including our feelings of respect for the President. We can only hope that his fundamental integrity will in time enable him to share our view of "Bitburg" and all it stands for.

(Kalman Sultanik is Vice President of the World Jewish Congress and a member of the U.S. Holocaust Memorial Council.)

Betrayal of Memory
Special Contribution

By Martin Mendelsohn

The President's visit to the Bitburg cemetery was a monumental act of insensitivity to all the living victims of the Holocaust and the Nazis' assault on Europe, a betrayal of the memory of those who perished at the hands of the Nazis and a display of historical indifference and ignorance unmatched in this century.

And yet despite all of these dreadful consequences there was one good omen: the American Jewish community was united and vocal in its outrage. For them to be loud and upset is not news; but it usually occurs when external events force responses, i.e., Jews in the Soviet Union, aid to Israel, etc. This reaction was unique. American Jews were protesting as Americans and as Jews over an issue that offended them both as Americans and as Jews. There was no question of dual loyalty or of ambiguity; the protest was made because the action offended sensibilities of Americans and Jews and Jewish Americans. The President of the American Legion said it for all when he said there could be no reconciliation with the SS.

It strains credibility that an American President alive and in the uniform of our armed forces during World War II would forget that it was the SS that slaughtered American soldiers at Malmedy. After the war the Nuremberg Trials were held and the SS was condemned by the Tribunal as a criminal organization. Not only did the U.S. participate in the hearing but Robert Jackson, a Justice of the United States Supreme Court, was the Chief Allied prosecutor at these proceedings. How could the President not remember? He either did not remember or did not care. It is hard to conclude which is worse — not remembering or not caring — but those are the only conclusions that come to mind.

If it is conceivable that he did not remember (and it may be) then why did he not care? The President is not an evil man and neither is he careless. But the unanswerable question lingers. Chancellor Kohl is available as a villain; he was the one who used President Reagan for Kohl's own domestic needs, but that explanation is simply too simple. The President of the United States of America is rightly considered the most powerful person in the Western world. He can do whatever he wants to. And that includes being too busy or unavailable or unwilling to honor SS dead by going to the Bitburg cemetery.

But he was willing and his willingness became fantasy as he transformed SS members, all of whom were volunteers, into unwilling victims of the Nazis. As he played his fantasy, the world writhed in an agony that he could not see or feel. His staff insulated and misled him. There was the immaturity of school yard toughness: "Let's not give in to those Jews." History was discarded and perspective vanished. The issue came to be viewed as a special interest fight and humanity — the quality of humaneness — was lost.

The President must know better. As awful as the event was, it was mercifully swift. The President attempted to soothe the wounds he could not heal with stirring and comforting words but it was not enough.

Elie Wiesel spoke of the agony and did it with courage and dignity. Wiesel understands the long road of history and attempted to teach that lesson to the President. But he failed. We all failed. The President went to Bitburg.

By going to Bitburg seeking reconciliation, the President produced recriminations. Old memories became vivid realities. There were anti-Semitic mutterings in the United States and Germany. The President accomplished none of his stated objectives and instead seemed to nurture the growth of the kinds of things he considers abhorrent. But why? We will never know.

Months after Bitburg the immediacy of the event recedes but the rancid ugliness remains. Bitburg must be kept in perspective. It was not a significant event or any kind of watershed. It was a tiny blip in history, but one so unnerving and disquieting that we all hope it is an aberration and not a portent of future events.

Weakness was revealed, but every event that exposes weakness must, by definition, show strength. The President was weak in not having the courage to tell Kohl that the American body politic had enough of Kohl's manipulations. Kohl showed he was so self-centered, egotistical and panicked that he was willing to let Ronald Reagan take abuse; it is doubtful that President Reagan will forget the way he was treated by Helmut Kohl. By standing firm the two proved nothing other than their loyalty to one another. The strength of their bond cannot endure past their respective government service.

The Jewish community was united but could not stop the President. The strength of that unity should not be viewed as ephemeral, however. It must be built upon, and we have to go back to the kind of coalition building that enabled Jewish aspirations to become part of the mainstream of American political life. That should be the lesson of Bitburg, but it is doubtful if it has been learned.

All Americans, unfortunately, seem to have both short and selective political memories. Jews have not, despite endless repetition, always been Democrats. It was Al Smith who first brought Jews into the Democratic party and Franklin Roosevelt who solidified that relationship. But it was Theodore Roosevelt who issued the first call for the freedom of Russian Jews, and thereby recognized, legitimized and nurtured Jewish political dreams.

Bipartisan participation makes for bipartisan strength. Eight Jews now serve in the U.S. Senate; four are Democrats and four are Republicans.* This is striking evidence of Jewish activity in the mainstream of American political life and yet we are still left pondering. With all of this power why was the President so insistent?

---

* Howard Metzenbaum (D-Ohio), Carl Levin (D-Michigan), Frank Lautenberg (D-New Jersey), Edward Lorinsky (D-Nebraska), Arlen Specter (R-Pennsylvania), Chic Hecht (R-Nevada), Rudy Boschwitz (R-Minnesota), Warren Rudman (R-New Hampshire)

There are no answers, only questions piled upon questions. As we grope for answers we begin to confront the reality of weakness which is in sharp and hard contrast to the myths of Jewish power. Post hoc rationalizations that Bitburg was not an issue central to Jewish survival are as valid as they are vacuous. Bitburg was a searing flash point in Jewish psyche and nothing happened. Public anguish and private persuasion fell on the same deaf ears and closed minds. The decision was final: *Damn the Torpedoes (or the Jews); full speed ahead.*

The good news is the lack of lasting damage. The President is still generally supportive and the Jewish community relatively comfortable with his positions. There will certainly be another blip and then we will see if there is bad news. Bad news means not understanding the consequences of the failure to convince the President to cancel the Bitburg visit. Bad news means once again screaming in the wilderness with no one willing to acknowledge the agony and anguish. Bad news means being alone.

Are Jews alone? No, clearly Jews are not alone but neither are they together, and that lack of togetherness means that their power is diffuse and unharnassed. It means they are not taken seriously as power brokers. How many votes can they deliver? No one knows. The 1984 election results are a matter of conflict in the nation and in the Jewish community. The Democrats claim most Jews voted for Walter Mondale; most, but not all, Jewish leaders clearly favored the President's re-election. And everyone agrees that their adversary's conclusions are based on erroneous polling techniques. But it is this lack of focus which calls the myth of Jewish monolithic power into question.

People who preach power as Jews are not being realistic. Power as Jews can never really be achieved except perhaps in Israel (but what kind of power do Peres or Shamir really have?). But as long as Jews preach power on the one hand and practice weakness on the other we will never be taken seriously or accorded the kind of respect that some leaders seem to seek.

While one can joke about the contentiousness of the Jews, that condition is more a reflection of the powerlessness than the powerful. To achieve power one must achieve unity. Lacking unity a group dissolves into the powerlessness of anarchy. A thousand flowers can bloom and a thousand voices can be heard, but not if people are serious about the exercise of power. Then there can be only one voice speaking for a united group. But Jews are not normally united and they are not a single group. The proliferation of so many organizations with similar goals is a sign of serious community weakness. An organization is neither created, nor does it succeed if existing organizations are meeting needs of the community. In Jewish religious life the rise of Chasidism and Reform Judaism in the same century is the best illustration of groups filling need. Here two movements, of opposite polarity, continue to attract diverse followers seeking different solutions to different yearnings.

So, too, in America. Different yearnings produce different solutions. But these different solutions should be recognized as luxuries of a ghetto mentality: lacking power, it doesn't matter what solution is proposed because nothing will come of it anyway.

But things do happen here. Jews can be powerful and listened to if they come from strength and unity. We need not come begging in despair; we can come pridefully seeking our rights as Americans, but only if we know what we want, how we want it and the price we are willing to pay. If we do not have a clear idea of what we want, then why should we be taken seriously?

To be taken seriously, of course, is the ultimate compliment in American society. Not to be dismissed as *lightweight, frivolous* or as a *special interest,* means that in political terms one has arrived. In some cases Jewish issues, e.g., Israel, are taken very seriously indeed and command widespread respect and success. But most issues are multi-faceted and the number of *Jewish positions* seem to be a geometric progression related to the number of Jewish organizations. If the community is fuzzy and unfocused, then all who seek its support have to appear similarly fuzzy and unfocused. Thus our relative powerlessness is merely a reflection of our internal weakness. The more we boast of our power, the less we really have. It is axiomatic in American politics that if you have it you don't flaunt it. We can relax in our *power positions* when others seriously approach us for advice and seek our counsel. If we are nothing but self-promoters then we have nothing to offer. If we are available for any *worthy cause* then we have neither principles nor courage; we are for sale. We must learn to pick and choose our fights and our allies. We must exercise judgment and learn, on occasion, to say no to our friends if it is in our self interest to do so; similarly there can be times when we will want to stake a position of principle, but at all times it must be with our community's self interest and well being in mind. There must be a rational basis for what is done, not merely a Dr. Panglossian *feel good.*

To avoid another Bitburg, to learn from history and not merely say we are learning, is difficult. We learn so little. But we must learn and understand. Bitburg was not, in retrospect, as serious as it was symbolic. But that symbolism was wrong and it exposed glaring weaknesses in the supposed power and influence of the Jewish community. We must learn from that exposure and turn that weakness to strength. Enough of hand wringing and teeth gnashing. Both political parties must be taught in serious and consequential ways of the things truly important to the Jews of America and Americans. Unless this is done soon, the next Bitburg will not pass so easily and we could begin to see the fragmenting of Jews from American society and further erosion of the cherished pluralism that has made our country so great.

(An attorney practicing in Washington, Martin Mendelsohn is also counsel to Simon Wiesenthal and was the first Deputy Director of the Office of Special Investigation, Department of Justice, which deals with the prosecution of former Nazis and their collaborators.)

The Worst Effect of Bitburg Visit
New York Post
April 23, 1985

By Norman Podhoretz

Conceivably Ronald Reagan may yet change his mind about visiting the military cemetery in the West German town of Bitburg where, among 2000 ordinary German soldiers, some 50 Nazi stormtroopers lie buried. Conceivably: but the indications are that he will refuse to cancel the visit.

This intransigence is very hard to understand. Only last week, when the uproar against Bitburg was at its height, Mr. Reagan was also fighting for the life of his Central American policy. Yet on aid to the Contras, this President (who has time and again made nonsense of his reputation as an ideologue through spectacular displays of the born politician's instinct for graceful retreat under pressure) announced that his feet were not "in concrete."

Nor were his feet in concrete when it came to resuming arms control negotiations with the Soviet Union, even though his own frequently stated condition (that military balance be restored) had not yet been met.

Nor were his feet in concrete when he quietly forgot his promise to retaliate against Syria for instigating the murderous attack on our troops in Lebanon.

Only in Bitburg, it seems, are his feet in concrete.

Mayor Koch thinks that in refusing to cancel the Bitburg visit, Mr. Reagan is making the worst mistake of his presidency. It may well be. But if so, the reason is not that Mr. Reagan has mortally offended the Jewish community. Nor is it even that he has forced survivors of the Holocaust to endure two gratuitous showers of salt on wounds that remain unhealed, first in deciding to visit Bitburg and then in defending the decision by saying that the soldiers buried there were "just as surely victims of Nazism as the victims in the concentration camps."

Bad as all this is, it still speaks mainly to the past and to the relatively unimportant question of the President's sensitivity" to the concerns of a particular constituency. No; what makes the Bitburg incident so serious is that it undermines the very foundation on which Mr. Reagan's foreign policy in the present has heretofore stood: the idea that there is something special, something unique, about totalitarian states.

It was because Jeane Kirkpatrick had brought this idea back into currency that Mr. Reagan first noticed and then sent her to the United Nations. For in reviving the theory of totalitarianism originally developed by political philosophers like Hannah Arendt, Mrs. Kirkpatrick reminded the world that Russia under communism and Germany under Nazism were variants of the same totalitarian species. She also reminded us all that totalitarianism, whether in its Nazi or its communist form, was both more evil and more dangerous than any authoritarian regime.

In doing all this, Mrs. Kirkpatrick not only shored up the eroding conceptual basis for resisting communism in Central America; she also provided the Reagan administration with the best possible case for putting the Soviet threat at the moral and political center of its foreign policy.

Appeasers and isolationists, both past and present, have tried desperately to discredit the theory of totalitarianism. In the 1930's, unwilling to build the military forces that might have deterred Hitler, they deluded themselves into believing that Nazi Germany was a nation like any other, with ordinary grievances that could be "appeased" and ordinary ambitions for power that could be negotiated.

Today, in an uncannily analogous attempt to rationalize their reluctance to maintain an adequate military deterrent, the political descendants of the old appeasers say the same thing about the Soviet Union as their forbearers said about Nazi Germany. Just as the old appeasers insisted there was no essential difference between Germany under Nazism and Germany under the Kaiser, so the new appeasers tell us that Russia under communism is nothing more than an extension of Russia under the Czars.

Little, to put it mildly, could these people have expected support from Ronald Reagan, a President who has built his entire foreign policy on the view that totalitarian states are not ordinary nations with ordinary fears and ambitions. Yet by proposing to lay a wreath at a military cemetery in which Nazi stormtroopers lie buried, Mr. Reagan is for all practical purposes treating Nazi Germany as though it had indeed been just one ordinary nation at war with other ordinary nations.

In thus offering retroactive vindication to the appeasers and isolationists of the 1930's, Mr. Reagan is by the same logic unavoidably giving aid and comfort to their political descendents who make the same argument with respect to the Soviet Union today.

That is why, if he persists in his decision to visit the Bitburg cemetery, another grave may well have to be dug there: the grave of the great idea that has given political life and moral purpose to Mr. Reagan's foreign policy.

(Mr. Norman Podhoretz is the editor of Commentary *magazine.)*

Reagan Isn't Indifferent To Jews
The New York Times
May 10, 1985

By Morris B. Abram

Before agreeing to lay a wreath at the Bitburg cemetery, President Reagan should have asked himself whether it was right for the leader of the free world to pay his respects at a graveyard that contained the remains of nearly 2,000 Nazi soldiers, including 49 SS troops. But now, those of us who urged him not to go, and who protested his visit, must ask ourselves whether the visit has revealed indifference on his part to the plight of the Jewish people. I think it has not.

On innumerable occasions, Ronald Reagan has given eloquent expression to the American people's revulsion at the Nazis' war crimes.

The writer Elie Wiesel, chairman of the United States Holocaust Memorial Council, reports, for example, that only days before the President's departure for West Germany and Bitburg, remembrance of Nazi atrocities against the Jews brought tears to the President's eyes. His grief, which Mr. Wiesel assures us was genuine, tells us much that we need to know and must acknowledge about the President's attitude.

Of course, tears cannot undo the tragedy of the Holocaust; they cannot bring back to life the six million Jews and millions of others who died. As President Reagan said, at Bergen-Belsen, of those destroyed there: "Here they lie. Never to hope. Never to pray. Never to love. Never to heal. Never to laugh. Never to cry."

To give meaning to their deaths and content to our mourning, we must commit ourselves as Mr. Reagan did on Sunday to the moral commandment "Never again." And, further, we must realize that wherever anti-Semitism has threatened Jews, the Reagan Administration has come to their defense.

The Administration has strengthened our ties to Israel, whose creation and continued existence represents the redemption of the victims of the Holocaust.

America supports Israel, as it always has and should, because it is the only real outpost of Western values in the Middle East. But the Reagan policy of "strategic cooperation" further explains why Israel is now in the front rank of America's allies. The new military relationship is responsible for the already long and continually lengthening list of joint ventures in military planning.

Thus, for the first time ever, the United States and Israel are developing coördinated responses to potential threats to the security of the region. For the first time ever, the United States is prepositioning nonlethal, mostly medical, equipment in Israel, and there is ongoing discussion of prepositioning military equipment as well. And, for the first time ever, the United States and Israel are participating in joint military exercises.

Economic relations between Israel and the United States are also being restructured, to Israel's benefit. Israel has become the first United States trading partner to be given fully free access to American markets. In addition, in the future economic aid to Israel will be in the form of grants so that Israel will not be burdened with additional, economically sapping loan repayments.

In Africa, where the remnants of the Ethiopian Jews are being starved to death, the Reagan Administration has done much that cannot yet be reported. We already know, though, of its extraordinary action in sending United States Air Force planes to the Sudan for the sole purpose of rescuing fleeing Ethiopian Jews and flying them to Israel.

Also, at every high-level encounter with the Soviet Government, the Reagan Administration has demanded that Soviet Jews be allowed to emigrate. By all accounts that I have heard — and I have been privy to many, here and in Israel — no previous Administration has been as steadfast or as forceful as this one in supporting the cause of Soviet Jews.

I believe these to be the policies of a President who indeed remembers the six million and who acts accordingly.

That does not change my view that it was wrong for him to visit Bitburg. But it is vitally important for us to understand that Bitburg was the mistake of a friend — not the sin of an enemy.

(Morris B. Abram, a lawyer, is a member of the United States Civil Rights Commission and has served as president of the American Jewish Committee, and on the staff of Justice Robert H. Jackson, the American prosecutor at the International War Crimes Tribunal, in Nuremberg. He is now Chairman of the Conference of Presidents of Major American Jewish Organizations.)

Jews Did Not Vote for Reagan
Special Contribution

By Mark A. Siegel

The announcement of President Reagan's decision to visit a Nazi cemetery at Bitburg coinciding with the 40th anniversary of the liberation of Buchenwald, represented a phenomenon far more serious than bad scheduling by White House staffers. The White House announcement of the Bitburg visit, juxtaposed on national television with the horrific scenes of the surviving inmates of Buchenwald, and the bones of those murdered, caused damage to the President's image, and certainly seemed to put an end to the aura of brilliance and invincibility of the White House public relations experts, in particular Michael Deaver.

But the issue is far greater than the insensitivity of announcing the visit. We need not dwell on the political wisdom of the decision. We should question, however, the more important issue: the set of values that appear to guide the decision-makers, and particularly the moral sensitivity and standards of basic decency that shape and direct the actions of those around Ronald Reagan, and those who have now unquestionably taken control of the Republican party of the United States. Beyond Bitburg, the future of American politics may have been revealed. The decision of the President and his advisors parallels the ethos of the last Republican convention.

When Walter Mondale, in his concession speech, said, "In each victory lie the seeds of defeat, and in defeat lie the seeds of victory," he may have touched on the hidden theme of the 1984 election result, one which is manifest in the intriguing vote of American Jews. With an exquisite sensitivity to long-term moral, social and political values based on a tragic history of isolation and persecution, the American Jewish constituency may have unknowingly acted as a barometer for the future of American politics as America prepares for the 21st Century.

It is often difficult to use empirical data to explain the voting behavior of American Jewry because of the relatively small Jewish samples generally involved in national surveys and polls. Fortunately, the recent trend by the three major American television networks to conduct massive election day exit polling across the nation generates sufficient Jewish data from which we may learn a great deal more about Jewish behavior and attitudes than ever before, and make comparisons to other ethnic groups in the United States which raise significant questions and issues for the future.

Using data from the New York Times-CBS News exit poll taken November 6, 1984, with a statistically significant Jewish sample, some valid conclusions may be drawn.

On the question of political history, Jews are twice as likely to perceive themselves as liberal than non-Jewish white Americans. Conversely, American Jews by their own self-perception are less than half as likely to consider themselves polit-ical conservatives as other white Americans. On the question of party identifica-tion, Jews are only 16 percent Republican, 60 percent Democratic and 24 percent Independent. Other American whites, by contrast, are 40 percent Republican, 33 percent Democratic, and 27 percent Independent.

In voting behavior, the contrast between Jews and other white voters is even more dramatic. Jews voted 67 percent for Mondale and 31 percent for Reagan. In terms of Congressional voting, Jews voted 68 percent Democratic and 26 percent Republican, while other American whites voted only 39 percent Democratic and 53 percent Republican. This remarkable difference in political ideology and po-litical voting may reflect the first public disquiet with the emerging right-wing domination of the Republican party of the 1980's.

Anthony Downs, a British sociologist, developed an "economic theory of democracy" that suggests that the voting decision is basically an economic deter-mination made by individuals about their futures. In short, Downs suggests that when people vote they are determining what is good for them, what will be eco-nomically beneficial to them. Except for American Jews, all other groups in Ameri-can society—black and white, rich and poor—conformed perfectly to the Downs model in 1984.

The affluent and middle class, doing well under Reaganomics, voted heavily Republican. The poor, blacks, Hispanics and city dwellers also voted their self-interest and their pocketbooks in supporting Mondale. Jews, however, can be seen to have voted directly counter to their own self-interest, measured by standard and traditional economic variables.

For in terms of socioeconomic status, American Jews not only are as well off as other American whites, but often considerably better off. Indeed, data suggest that Jewish incomes, years of education and professional status far exceed those of the general white public. One would have expected, therefore, that the "econom-ic theory of democracy" would have had Jews voting even more Republican and conservative than non-Jewish votes. But that certainly was not the case, and thus we ask why.

Jewish voting behavior does not inherently belie Downs' theory; in fact, Jew-ish voting behavior amends and modifies the Downs dictum by the introduction of non-economic variables into the explanatory model. It would seem that, at least for American Jews, factors other than economics alone are the key determinants to the individual voting decision on what is "good" for them. I would suggest that for American Jews the Downs economic model is modified by moral, social, cul-tural and philosophical variables inherent in Jewish values and history, and may in fact shed some light on the development of these variables as voting deter-minants for the general American public for the next political cycle.

When Jews voted in 1984, they were not suggesting that things were econom-ically bad for them. Indeed, economically, conditions were and continue to remain generally good for American Jewry. I do not believe that anyone can suggest with reasonable credibility that the Jewish vote for Mondale in 1984 was based on a decision that President Reagan was not a good or decent man. Nor can one suggest that President Reagan's attitudes toward the policies concerning Israel and the Middle East could possibly have explained the significant Jewish swing to the Democrats in 1984. Indeed, from 1981 to 1984 under Ronald Reagan, especially contrasted with the 1977-1981 period under Jimmy Carter, conditions with the state of Israel, and relations with the American Jewish community on a political level were smooth and cooperative. The erratic Carter performance in Israel, with overt pressure, unfriendly statements and votes in the United Nations, endorsements for the Palestinian homeland concept, which caused Jewish support for the Democratic candidate for President to drop to a remarkable 40 percent in 1980, was replaced with a stable and friendly working relationship between Israel and the United States under President Reagan, and an open and unthreatening working relationship between the American Jewish community and the Reagan White House from 1981 to 1984. Then what could possibly have caused American Jewry to abandon Ronald Reagan in the 1984 election?

I believe that the Jewish vote in 1984 was based on a determination that something had gone awry in American politics and that the American Jewish constituency was making a far more serious judgement on the future of American politics than a one-shot bread-and-butter reaction to our nation's economic recovery. The Jewish political periscope detected forces that were seen as unsettling, disturbing and threatening, and this perception overrode Jewish voters' economic well-being and triggered a vote for change.

The image of the Republican party presented in Dallas, the direct association of the Republican party with Jerry Falwell and the most strident and doctrinaire elements of Christian fundamentalism, references to "Christian values and the Christianization of America," a direct and unequivocal assault on the principles of separation of church and state in American schools and society, all obviously took their toll on Jewish perceptions of the new Republican party. In addition, a platform insensitive to minority views and minority needs, insensitive to traditional American values of tolerance, the endorsement of economic and social policies which could be seen to promote disparity in society at the expense of the cherished values of American community and pluralism, all may have contributed to reordering Jewish electoral priorities in the 1984 presidential and congressional elections, and may have had a lasting impact on the development of Jewish political values and ideology in the United States for decades to come.

Much of Jewish history is a litany of oppression and persecution. Historically, the most severe problems for Jews arose at times of economic instability, economic polarization and/or political isolation. For a group always in the minority, always "different," economic disparities in society and isolation of any demographic or cultural group soon correlated with scapegoating and persecution. Jews could never historically feel secure in a society when poverty was rampant, injustice was unchecked, and a political underclass seethed with resentment and bitterness. Traditionally, these conditions erupted in either violence or political change, and all too often Jews were somehow singled out for special blame.

So complementing the traditional Talmudic concerns for the well-being of society and the state, traditional Jewish commitment to charity and care for the less fortunate, is straight political self-interest predicated on a rather predictable pattern of persecution. The fear of societal instability, as well as the traditional Jewish commitments to the state and to community make Jewry an interesting case study in voting behavior and may indicate future political patterns transcending the Jewish community.

I believe there are lessons in the American Jewish political behavior and electoral behavior of 1984 that can be directed to both major political parties in this country.

The great political party that had always tolerated pluralism within its ranks, with significant moderate and conservative wings seeking consensus on issues and candidates, was seen in Dallas in 1984 to be a rouge elephant being goaded by extremists, with dissenting voices shut out. It was not a picture well-reviewed by a political community that has been the target of extremists repeatedly in its past, that has been singled out because of its lack of conformity to prevailing religious and cultural norms and one often scapegoated when groups in society have been deprived of economic justice or equality of opportunity. Jews may perceive this first because of their unique history of persecution. Shortly, other groups can be expected to catch on to the implications of the undermining of American pluralism and tolerance.

In her speech at the Republican convention, Jeanne Kirkpatrick made fiery rhetoric over "San Francisco Democrats." In the long term, "Dallas Republicans" may prove to be a major impediment to the political realignment that the GOP has aimed for since 1980. Those "Dallas Republicans" whose insensitivity and arrogance caused them to schedule the President of the United States to honor Nazis while only reluctantly and after-the-fact agreeing to honor their victims, may not seem to be the political opiate to the American people that it was on November 6, 1984.

Let us recall that in the 1920's, at a time of great Republican prosperity and rapid economic growth in the United States, Jews in America shifted dramatically to the Democratic party, fully a decade before the national realignment of 1933-36. If the Democratic party can once again convince the American people that it is capable of governing effectively, that it is broad-based, moderate and forward thinking, with vigorous leaders not afraid of innovation, not dominated by narrow interests and committed to pluralistic community and tolerance in America, the young people who deserted the Democrats in 1984 may comfortably come home. And if that is the case, the Jewish constituency's prescient periscope of 1984 may have accurately foretold a much different America than the 49 state Republican triumph of election night.

Mark A. Siegel is a Washington, DC., government affairs consultant. He holds a doctorate in Political Science from Northwestern University. Currently a member of the Democratic National Committee, he has served as legislative assistant to the late Senator Hubert H. Humphrey, Executive Director of the Democratic National Committee, and Deputy Assistant to President Jimmy Carter.

Thoughts After Bitburg

By Abraham H. Foxman

Bitburg is no longer inconspicuous. It has entered into the long memory of our people.

It was a classic case of the road to Hell being paved with good intentions.

Selecting Bitburg cemetery as the site for reconciliation between the adversaries of World War II was thoughtless, insensitive and an unintended affront to the memory of all those murdered by the SS in the death camps and on the battlefields of the Bulge.

It called for protest and we were not silent.

Our protests were heard. Of that there is no doubt. Yet in a tragicomic sequence of misunderstandings, miscalculations, mistakes, misstatements and missed opportuinities, they were not heeded.

And so the time has come to look back with the 20/20 vision of hindsight to see what went wrong and why, to assess the damage and to learn from the experience.

No one opposed and practically everyone favored the concept of reconciliation four decades after the guns were stilled but it was fatally flawed by the poor staff work that went into the site selection.

That original error was compounded when those involved viewed the prospect of any shift as a threat to face, as surrender to pressure and, most far fetched of all, as an implication of collective guilt for the generation of West Germans with no connection to the Third Reich.

The issue somehow was turned into a test of will as the head of state of each country felt that it put his reputation in jeopardy. Although President Reagan openly apologized for reopening painful wounds, neither he nor Chancellor Kohl was able to acknowledge error but, in different ways, plunged deeper and deeper into quicksand with their efforts to explain the unexplainable.

As polls revealed, Americans were divided into those who supported the presidential wreath laying among SS graves and those who saw it as a rehabilitation of the Nazi enemy. For some, it became just another Jewish issue. They said it was time to let bygones be bygones and they diminished the Holocaust into just another wartime atrocity. They did not walk in Jewish shoes or see it with Jewish eyes as a unique historic expression of governmental malevolence directed at an entire people because of their faith. On the other hand, Jews, veterans and other protesters could not understand why their fellow Americans could not see it as a gesture toward forgiveness of the Nazis and a repudiation of American ethics. It indicated that memory of the genocide had dimmed and that the resonance of its moral lesson had faded.

Inevitably, Bitburg damaged a well meaning American President who had demonstrated his sympathy with the Jewish people by his support of Israel, his dramatic use of the Air Force to rescue Ethiopian Jews and his outspoken support of Soviet Jewry.

Across the ocean, the incident stirred up the stench of anti-Semitism. It became clear that West Germany was not completely purged, that while desirable, reconciliation papered over a poisonous problem that still persists in pockets of the population.

Nevertheless, the situation provided some credits along with the debits. The Jewish community spoke in one clear voice. While not changing the site, the Administration attempted a measure of atonement by visiting Bergen-Belsen where President Reagan spoke with eloquent sincerity. Once again, the Holocaust was exposed to the conscience of mankind as at no time since the mass graves were exposed at the liberation of the concentration camps. No doubt, there is greater understanding of its unique horror and greater appreciation of why we Jews have vowed, "Never again."

For us at the Anti-Defamation League, Bitburg directs us to strive with greater intensity and effectiveness in our Holocaust educational programs.

Like the Holocaust, one Bitburg is too many.

(Abraham H. Foxman is Associate National Director of the Anti-Defamation League of B'nai B'rith.)

Interview With Elie Wiesel
Der Spiegel — West Germany
April 29, 1985

(The following is an interview by the editor of Der Spiegel, *a leading West German weekly, and Elie Wiesel immediately after he met with President Reagan.)*

Bitburg has caused Serious Damage

Elie Wiesel is a professor of humanities at Boston University. He is originally from Rumania and survived imprisonment in the Auschwitz and Buchenwald concentration camps, where his parents died. As chairman of the American "Holocaust Council," Wiesel has in the past few weeks become the sharpest critic of President Reagan's intentions to include a visit to the soldiers' cemetery in Bitburg in his trip to Germany. When Wiesel, 56, received the Congressional Gold Medal the week before last, he used his speech of thanks for an appeal to the President to change the program of the visit.

SPIEGEL: Professor Wiesel, you openly stated to your President that he had no reason to go to Bitburg. Do you believe that Reagan was affronted by that?

WIESEL: No, he told me that later himself. He was deeply affected. His whole staff was affected. They were very grateful. The people on the staff had feared that the President might misunderstand what I would to say.

SPIEGEL: Did you have to submit your address to the staff?

WIESEL: I didn't have to, but out of politeness and decency, I gave my text to White House Chief of Staff Donald Regan and to his staffers one day in advance. They had no objections.

SPIEGEL: Did you stick to your text?

WIESEL: Not entirely, because in the meantime, the President had said that the German SS soldiers buried in Bitburg were victims of fascism just as much as the prisoners who died in the concentration camps. That was a very serious statement that goes against everything that we stand for. I do not believe in hatred; even after the war, I never hated the Germans. It would be foolish and ridiculous to confront the tragedy of the Holocaust with the simple act of hatred. But I think that we should not try to trivialize history by making everyone a victim. Because then, no one is a victim. To say that SS men were victims is an affront to history.

SPIEGEL: Under what circumstances would you recognize the President's claim that young German soldiers could also be considered "victims of fascism?"

WIESEL: Under no circumstances, never, and even the exceptions, which there certainly were, do not change that. This is not a matter of individuals. In general, we should not go so far as to label SS men as victims. They were the oppressors; they were the killers.

SPIEGEL: Would you have had no objection to the wreath-laying by the President at Bitburg if no soldiers of the Waffen-SS had been buried there?

WIESEL: It would certainly have been less injurious. But I would not have scheduled any cemetery, but rather I would have sent the President to universities — maybe to Heidelberg or Freiburg — so that he would talk to young people.

SPIEGEL: Those present — and millions of American TV viewers had a similar impression — described the reaction of the President to your entreaty as one of contained anger. Didn't anyone let you know afterwards that they considered at least the form of your appeal to be inappropriate?

WIESEL: On the contrary. Immediately after the conclusion of my speech, one of Reagan's highest-ranking staffers invited me to fly to Germany in the Presidential airplane and to make a speech at Bergen-Belsen.

SPIEGEL: Did you accept?

WIESEL: Not yet; it depends on Bitburg.

SPIEGEL: If it's not cancelled…

WIESEL: …I won't go.

SPIEGEL: Didn't the original decision of Chancellor Kohl and President Reagan to visit a soldiers' cemetery instead of a concentration camp, and the ensuing bitter discussion, cause a chance to deal conclusively with the trauma of the World War to be missed?

WIESEL: Of course. The two of them got everything mixed up and achieved exactly the opposite of what they actually wanted to achieve.

SPIEGEL: You repeatedly emphasized that there is no collective guilt, that only the murderers of those days and their accomplices are guilty, but not their children and grandchildren. Do you think that an act of reconciliation such as Kohl and Reagan evidently envisioned it — to stand hand in hand at German soldiers' graves, for instance — could change people's consciousness? Or is such symbolism only a hollow media event?

WIESEL: I don't know the motivation of political leaders, but as far as I know, they always are on the look-out for opportunities to be photographed favorably, and I only hope that they really mean what they say and do there. Symbols are important. Bitburg is a symbol, too. It has become a negative symbol, which is causing serious damage.

SPIEGEL: As a victim of the Holocaust, didn't it irritate you that advisors of the U.S. President travelled through the Federal Republic and sought out concentration camps from the point of view of how each would appear most favorably on TV?

WIESEL: It hurt me very much. If people are looking for "pretty" concentration camps, this is hardly the right way to develop normal relations.

SPIEGEL: How do you explain that the President of the U.S. and his staff so wrongly estimated the reaction of large groups of people in America to the Bitburg visit?

WIESEL: It is indeed particularly disquieting that neither on the American or German side did anyone ever think that graves of Waffen-SS might ever become a problem. Instead, the planners seem to have thought the chapter was closed, a page had been turned, and a new era could begin.

SPIECEL: But President Reagan is famous for being a good PR man.

WIESEL: He was; that's why I can't understand that this could happen to him.

SPIEGEL: In your opinion, will the Bitburg affair permanently damage the President?

WIESEL: Probably not, but since we deal with morals, and since Reagan puts great store in a moral image, the equalization of victims with their violators will diminish his reputation.

SPIEGEL: If Reagan does cancel the side-trip to Bitburg after all, or if Kohl, in response to calls for help from the White House, does propose a change of program—would it still be disturbing to you that this change of mind only came about under pressure of public opinion?

WIESEL: That isn't really the question any more. If Reagan were to find a way to cancel Bitburg, we would all know anyway that he had really wanted to go. But for the sake of history, a U.S. President should not bow down before SS graves.

(Translated by Renate Steinchen.)

Reagan Did Better Than Wiesel
Jewish Post and Opinion

By Professor Jacob Neusner

If Elie Wiesel had asked me my advice about what to say to President Reagan and how to say it, I would have told him this:

Remember, not everyone in the world is Jewish.

By that I mean, remember that there are many people in the world who do not see things our way and who do not understand how we see things. To them, as to us all, the President is President. Treat him with respect, with dignity owing to his office, even with tact.

Above all, remember that he is a person of enormous good will for the Jewish people. He has done more for the State of Israel than any president before him (and many have written enviable records).

So do not lecture him, condescend to him, treat him as though he does not feel the things we feel or understand us. He is a man of enormous good will, and especially for us Jews.

He is a friend, not an enemy.

When the whole world condemned Israel for its invasion of Lebanon in 1982, the President defended the State of Israel and its actions. He lost political capital by doing so. He has paid his dues, he owes us no apologies.

He is sympathetic to our feelings and concerns, not hostile.

Friends are permitted to disagree. So, as the Israeli position wisely stated matters: Friends are friends, and mistakes are mistakes. Now let's get on with life.

Now that Bitburg is behind us, we can look back with some regret at the needlessly emotional atmosphere in which our tragedy, which was the tragedy of humanity, reached public consciousness. Things were altogether too contentious.

Our people appeared—as Mr. Wiesel showed the country in his rather discourteous lecture to the President—less concerned for the standing and feeling of our friends than we might have shown. The President, for his part, did all that was humanly possible to express for the world the depth of the tragedy of the Shoah. What more could we have hoped in the cause of remembering the Shoah than what President Reagan accomplished for us and for all humanity?

The President did not gain, and we lost. So we felt self-righteous, but it was the President who went on, at Bergen Belsen, to give one of the great speeches of our time on the subject beyond all speech.

Who taught the world about the Shoah, if not President Reagan in his profound and moving address? I do not think that Mr. Wiesel did so well as did Mr. Reagan.

We have to remember that we are not the only ones who live in America. We do have many friends and allies, people who not only believe in the same things but also respect us. Their good will is worth nurturing.

(Prof. Jacob Neusner is a prominent scholar of Jewish history and lectures at Brown University.)

On Surprises, Linkages and Separations
Special Contribution

By Fred E. Katz

I.

First came the announcement that during his official visit to West Germany in 1985 President Reagan would visit the German military cemetery at Bitburg. It was to be part of the process of further cementing relations between the United States and modern West Germany, a solid ally of the West in its political struggle against the Communist world. Within days of the announcement it became public knowledge that the Bitburg cemetery contained not only graves of regular German soldiers but also graves of a number of SS men — the notorious enforcers of the most gruesome elements of Nazi ideology. There followed gasps of surprise, followed by a wave of shock that was deep, widespread and profound.

American veterans were greatly offended — especially when President Reagan clumsily tried to defuse the issue by saying that all Germans who took part in the war, soldiers and SS alike, did so pretty much against their own will; that these individuals, just as American soldiers, were themselves innocent victims. The President's statement only made matters worse.

Those who really knew World War II were not assuaged by this sort of reasoning. They remembered the mass murder of captured American soldiers by the SS in that very area of Germany the President was planning to visit. Perhaps the murderers themselves now rested in the Bitburg cemetery.

The greatest shock of all came from American Jews. They saw a most odious sign in the indiscriminate honoring of SS men alongside ordinary German soldiers, to be undertaken by the American President at the request of the West German Chancellor, Helmut Kohl. Here all of a sudden, they said, was an effort to whitewash the Nazi past. Here, they said, the Holocaust's perpetrators — of whom the SS were the core — were being forgiven, even honored. Here

Germany's ghoulish war against the Jews was being side-stepped in favor of modern *realpolitik,* where today's friends are prepared to ignore yesterday's deeds, however horrendous these deeds were.

Sometimes, in the course of daily living, there occur events that go beyond their own, immediate content. They are *critical incidents* that illuminate facets of the social order in which we exist. They highlight fundamental characteristics of that social order. They bring out into the open things we do not ordinarily notice, or prefer not to notice.

President Reagan's Bitburg visit was such a critical incident for American Jews. Here was an American President who was, and remains, a very good friend of American Jews. And yet he seemingly trampled upon the memory of the Nazi Holocaust against the Jews. Here appeared to be gross disregard for the suffering Jews have endured. Here was insensitivity to Jews, a lack of awareness of just how deeply and personally Jews still feel about the Holocaust. It mattered little that President Reagan later added a visit to a former concentration to his German itinerary, and there made a most moving speech about the Holocaust. It mattered little that, while at the Bitburg cemetery, he made no public speeches and that the visit, itself, was deliberately made to be short. The damage was done.

As a critical incident, the Bitburg visit aroused in Jews profound questions about their security in a Christian world. Not only did Jews remember the Holocaust, with its millions of Jewish victims, perhaps even more poignantly, they suddenly remembered Jewish helplessness in the 1930s, the years leading up to the massacre of the Jews. They remembered that the Roosevelt Administration — so humane in many of its social policies — was tardy and not altogether forthcoming when it came to practical measures to help the endangered Jews of Europe. Many American Jews suddenly saw themselves, again, as a vulnerable minority group.

On the positive side, the critical incident galvanized American Jews to act. They energetically made their concerns known. They did so far more effectively than their parents had done in the 1930s. And the President, on his part, demonstrated more realistic concern for Jewish sensitivities and fears than did Franklin Roosevelt. After all, we were not back in the 1930s, when Jews were fearful of expressing themselves publicly and politically, and when a President could quietly brush off the Jews of America.

And yet, after the critical incident of Bitburg, life for American Jews may not be the same again. Bitburg brought Jews back to a reality that they had preferred to ignore. Perhaps there are some Jewish concerns that even the most well-intentioned non-Jews of America may not share. Is this Jewish paranoia? Or is this a basic facet of being a minority group — in a land of minority groups — where each group retains some commitments, some perspectives, some concerns that other groups do not share? Perhaps even in a melting-pot society each ethnic group stubbornly retains some elements in its identity that other groups do not share. Without retreating into a ghetto mentality, this may be a facet of ordinary communal living in a multi-ethnic country.

II.

We need to take a deeper look at the *surprises*: We need to go beyond looking at how the surprises manifested themselves and ask ourselves: What are the reasons for the surprises?

Why was there such surprise, followed by mounting shock, when the Bitburg visit was announced? Why were Jews and veterans so surprised? And why, in turn, was the Reagan Administration so surprised by the response to its announcement of the planned visit?

The answer lies in a process of linkage and amalgamation among four diverse social issues.

First: The four issues.

(1) For the Reagan Administration, the Bitburg visit was centered on underscoring West Germany's role as a strong ally in the West's long-standing and continuing confrontation with the Communist East Europe bloc of nations, led by the Soviets. Since the Second World War this confrontation had become a core ingredient in the political life of Europe and America. In the wake of its "economic miracle," Germany had become the dominant economic power of Western Eruope. Germany had also become a very staunch political ally in the Western Alliance — despite occasional pointed reminders, by its erstwhile Western enemies, that her past required some atoning.

For the Reagan Administration, with its heightened agenda of confrontation with the Soviets, Germany was a most valued ally. In the recent past the German government had proven its political loyalty to the United States by permitting advanced American weaponry on its soil. Other Western allies — and quite a number of vocal German citizens — regarded these weapons with undisguised misgivings. For accomplishing the political loyalty to the United States, Chancellor Kohl, personally, needed to be thanked and supported. In short, the issue for the Reagan Administration was that the Bitburg visit was fundamentally one of thanking Germany for its support of the Western Alliance and courting it for further support in the future.

(2) For Chancellor Kohl, the President's visit centered on moving toward a "new" Germany — a Germany resting squarely on its considerable economic accomplishments and consequent stature as a world power. It was time to look ahead, rather than looking over one's shoulders to a past that the present generation did not create. The President's visit would underscore that war dead were war dead, regardless of the side on which they fought, and regardless of the particular units in which they served their country. Germany had been snubbed long enough when it came to honoring Western war dead. She had paid her dues politically (in her help to the Western Alliance) as well as economically. Personally, for Chancellor Kohl, the President's visit was also seen as a valuable source of support in forthcoming German elections. Kohl could use the glory of standing beside the American President, on German soil, honoring Germans who had given their lives for Germany. (In light of the subsequent events, this calculation

backfired.)

(3) The Bitburg issue for Jews, as I have already stated, centered on the Holocaust still being terribly real for today's Jews. For surviving victims, for families of victims and for all contemporary Jews, the Nazi Holocaust remains a burning issue — not something one can readily lay aside. The part played by the SS, in particular, is unforgivable and unforgettable.

As a critical incident, the Jewish response to the Bitburg visit demonstrates that the Holocaust remains a terribly raw wound. It has not healed with time. It may never heal. For Jews, the possibility that Germany's responsibility for the Holocaust — and the SS culpability in particular — might be sloughed off is repugnant. President Reagan's proposed visit to Bitburg seemed to do just that. It seemed to say, let us forget the past, including the Holocaust.

(4) For many American veterans who had fought against Germany, honoring of the notorious SS seemed profoundly blind to the atrocities committed by the SS. Indeed, the SS had carried out massive executions of American prisoners of war (just as they carried out even more massive executions of Russian prisoners of war and of Jews).

To be sure, since the end of World War II we have occasionally seen a perverse sense of camaraderie among former enemies. We have seen "re-union" affairs of airmen who were former enemies — who now toasted one another as good-old-boy gentlemen, basking in wasn't-it-grand-sport celebrations of their deadly encounters in the past. But the deeds of the SS went beyond this level of glorification of war. The deeds of the SS went beyond any rules of war that even some perverted gentlemen could accept.

Many veterans found the idea of honoring the SS dead utterly distasteful. It did violence to their fellow American soldiers who were victims of the exorbitant brutality of the SS.

Second: Linkage of the four issues.

For each of the four participating interest groups in the drama their respective issue stands out as being the crux of the matter. For each, theirs is the all-important issue for which the Bitburg visit is the critical event.

In actuality, all four issues soon became linked. No one could mention one issue without hearing about the other issues. The Bitburg visit became an amalgam of these issues — an amalgam that included them all, welded into one composite. But that amalgam of four issues was not a new alloy, where all the parts coexist in harmony, forming a new homogeneous entity. Quite the contrary. The new amalgam consisted of centrifugal forces, each going off in another direction, each leading to different interest groups. Yet all were forcibly linked in the Bitburg event.[1] None of the four interest groups fully accepted the others' priorities — although the veterans and Jews were roughly in agreement that the Bitburg visit should be cancelled, and the Reagan Administration agreed (publicly, at least) with Chancellor Kohl that the visit should go ahead as planned.

The basic reason for the various surprises is that each interest group as-

sumed that its issue had primacy. Each assumed that the other issues could be ignored. Each assumed that the other groups' issues were not *actively* linked to its
own primary issue.

At the beginning, when the Reagan Administration announced the Bitburg
visit, its officials were surely aware of the sensitivities of Jews and American
veterans. But they assumed that these concerns could be held in abeyance. They
could be kept far in the background. These issues were, in short, assumed not to
be *actively* linked to the need to reassure the Germans of American political
gratitude and support, which the Bitburg visit would symbolize. The Reagan Administration officials were wrong. They misjudged the degree of *active* linkage between their primary concern and the primary concerns of veterans and Jews.
They were surprised by the linkage they were forced to accept.

Chancellor Kohl, from his vantage point, was not merely concerned with his
political priorities (for Germany as well as for himself), he also assumed that
President Reagan could pull off the feat of helping to detach the Holocaust memories, once and for all, from the contemporary political and economic realities in
which Germany so clearly excelled. Kohl himself had tried to do this in his
speeches on a "new" Germany. He welcomed President Reagan in what, he believed, would be some very valuable help in cutting the linkage to the past which
he, Kohl, preferred to forget. He was surprised to find that President Reagan,
personally, was not quite so ready to forget the Holocaust. He was surprised, too,
to find that many citizens of his own country were prepared to accept a considerable amount of linkage to the other issues.

For American veterans the Reagan Administration represents friendly and
congenial officialdom. Many of the issues favored by traditional veterans' associations are favored by the President. These include emphasis on America being
strong militarily, and on honoring its armed services. The President's catering to
these issues made him attractive to official veterans' associations. The President
was their kind of man.

The surprise of the veterans was great when this President, of all people,
showed ignorance and insensitivity to some harsh military realities of World War
II. The memory of the murderous activities of the SS was still very much alive to
veterans who had the misfortune to have had contact with the SS. Although many
veterans shared the President's political posture of strong anti-communism, they
were unprepared to renounce linkage of the ghastly deeds of the SS to modern
realpolitik that sees West Germany as a fine, untarnished ally against the Soviets.
They were surprised that President Reagan could fail to see, and accept, the linkage between the deeds of the SS and the pain and heroism it had taken for the
American military to prevail against such a foe. It had happened during the President's lifetime. How could he have forgotten? How could he disconnect it from
his policies?

For Jews, the President's concentration on modern *realpolitik* seemed to disconnect him from a reality where many American Jews really live. Despite the

President's expression of support for Jews on many occasions, particularly his strong support for Israel, his Bitburg visit seemed to separate him from a most fundamental Jewish social reality. It was not only neglect of the specifics of the Holocaust, and its deep and ongoing meaning for Jews, that Jews found so surprising. For some Jews (I do not know how many) the President appeared to dissociate himself, and his Administration, from American Jewry.

The Holocaust is very central to contemporary Jewish life. To many Jews it is as basic an event as the Destruction of the Temple or the Covenant at Sinai. To some Jews the Holocaust calls their entire religiosity into question. To others it reaffirms it. To all it is very vital to their sense of identity as Jews. When President Reagan announced his Bitburg visit he seemed to separate himself from this core phenomenon in Jewish identity. Jews were surprised that the President could find it in his heart to separate a current American political activity from a reality that is so pervasive, so raw, and so immediate to American Jews.

When Jews expressed this sense of linkage of Holocaust memories to current American Jewish life they found a surprised President. He had not wanted to hurt Jewish sensitivities. He had believed that the Bitburg visit could be separated, benignly, from the Holocaust concerns.

Surprises do not arise out of thin air. They have their roots in social realities. In the case of the President's visit to Bitburg the surprises, themselves, served as critical incidents that illuminate real differences under which the American President, the German Chancellor, American veterans and American Jews operate.

---

[1]This type of phenomenon is very well known in modern research physics on elementary particles: In a specifically contrived event certain diverse forces come together in the form of high-speed collisions among elementary particles, they fleetingly but critically interact — coexisting only for the briefest moment — then they go off into different directions.

Somewhat comparably, what I am calling the Bitburg *amalgam* is an entity that came into existence for a brief moment. Its constituent parts are real, but they cannot coexist with one another for any great length of time. They are centrifugal forces going off in different directions.

In contrast to the fleeting Bitburg amalgam (and to the high-speed collisions of elementary particles in physics) there are other amalgams, in social and in physical phenomena, that are long-lasting and stable. The Nazi program was such a long-lasting amalgam. It existed for twelve years. That Nazi amalgam of programs included a racial program for destroying the Jews and other supposedly inferior races; a program for economic revitalization; and a program for restoring to Germany the political power and glory it had lost during the First World War. An individual German citizen might be attracted to only one of these components of the amalgam, such as its economic promise of full employment. But since the various parts of the amalgam were strongly linked together that citizen was apt to help implement the entire amalgam of programs, even those to which he or she had no great commitment. Yet it turned out that individual citizens might make a substantial contribution even to those programs to which they had little commitment. They did so because of their commitment to other components of the amalgam. For instance, an individual SS officer might make substantial contributions to inventing and using the murder technology for destroying Jews. He might do so out of commitment to advancing his personal career rather than commitment to hatred of Jews. This made his murderous deeds no less real. But it makes personal accountability for participating in horrors such as the Nazi Holocaust very complex. We see the result in Chancellor Kohl's claim that even SS soldiers were merely committed to doing their national duty. My answer to this line of reasoning is that SS officers and soldiers had considerable autonomy to act independently, just as did most Nazi bureaucrats. And where there is autonomy there is culpability.

(See, Fred E. Katz, "A Sociological Perspective to the Holocaust," *Modern Judaism,* Volume 2, 1982; and "Implementation of the Holocaust: The Behavior of Nazi Officials," *Comparative Studies in Society and History,* Volume 24, 1982.)

(Dr. Katz taught sociology at the State University of New York, Tel Aviv, Johns Hopkins, and the University of Toronto. Among his numerous publications are: Autonomy & Organization, 1968, Contemporary Sociological Theory, 1971, Structuralism in Sociology, SUNY Press, 1976.)

Bitburg—Who Spoke Out, Who Didn't
Present Tense
Summer 1985

By William Bole

At the height of the controversy over President Reagan's decision to visit the military cemetery at Bitburg, West Germany, last spring, Sister Carol Rittner telephoned a St. Lawrence University professor to ask whether he'd join a public appeal imploring the President to change his plans.

The professor wholeheartedly agreed, but Rittner withdrew the invitation when she found out he was Jewish. "I told him," quipped the liberal Catholic nun, who is a teacher and activist in Detroit, "that this is an 'anti-Semitic' ad. No Jews are allowed."

Rittner's appeal, joined by 143 prominent Christians, including black church leaders, appeared in an advertisement last April in *The New York Times.* The appeal illustrated the story behind the Bitburg story: who spoke out and who didn't— notably, the secular and Christian right.

At the same time that the major news media were referring to opposition by "Jews" and "veterans" (and "others," occasionally), scores of different religious, racial and ethnic organizations, which had worked with Jewish groups on a variety of issues for many years, were protesting loudly against the Bitburg visit—and the series of official explanations for it. Indeed, a virtual "rainbow coalition" of liberal

Christians, blacks, Hispanics, Asians and others joined in the effort to prevent an American President from laying a wreath at a cemetery where 49 Nazi SS soldiers were buried. Said Dr. Robert Huston, head of the United Methodist Church's Commission on Christian Unity and Interreligious Concerns: "The deeper tragedy of such errors of judgement is that perhaps they are a reflection of a new anti-Jewish mood or an implicit support for anti-Semitism."

The response, however, was different among other groups hailed lately by Jewish neoconservatives as the true friends and allies of the Jewish Community. Leaders of the New Christian Right—with the notable exception of the Reverend Jerry Falwell—refused to join in public appeals for a change in the President's plans. On the secular right, for the most part, there was either silence, expressions of disbelief as to what the fuss was all about—or worse.

On the other hand, cooperation with Jews during the dispute came from groups representing minority and other communities increasingly portrayed by neoconservatives as moving in directions that are hostile to Jewish concerns. The long list of national organizations that spoke out—most of them more than once—included the National Association for the Advancement of Colored People, the National Council of Churches, the National Council of Negro Women, the National Conference of Catholic Bishops, Church Women United, the Urban League, the Philadelphia Yearly Meeting (of Quakers), the United Methodist Church, Presbyterian Church U.S.A., Church of the Brethren and the United Church of Christ.

The flood of support by ethnic groups alone should have been enough to dismiss the "Jewish-and-veterans" label (which, in any event, was more accurate than Reagan's description of the controversy as media-generated). Among them were the Polish American Congress, the League of United Latin American Citizens, the Mexican-American Legal Defense Fund, the National Council of La Raza, the Ukrainian National Association, the Japanese Americans Citizens League, the Indochina Resource Action Center, the Organization of Chinese Americans and the Sons of Italy.

The protests were more dramatic at the local level. Several days before Reagan's visit last May, interreligious coalitions in 20 cities sponsored ceremonies prompted by the Bitburg affair at military cemeteries and war memorials, where they honored the "liberators" of World War II. In Philadelphia, dozens of local leaders, including black Baptist pastors (among them the Reverend Joseph Hall, a national board member of the Reverend Jesse Jackson's Operation P.U.S.H.), and representatives of church charities, the Quakers, the Order of Friar Minor, the Roman Catholic Archdiocese and Jewish groups joined in an "Appeal to the President."

Elsewhere, the Black-Jewish Coalition of Atlanta and the interfaith committee of Union Township, New Jersey, also voiced opposition in public appeals for the cancellation of Reagan's visit. Pastors of mainline Protestant churches spoke out from their pulpits on the two Sundays before the visit, in cities such as Miami; Ann Arbor, Michigan, and Tibertan, South Carolina.

The feeling that the White House had erred gravely throughout the Bitburg affair was so widespread that 83 members of the Republican-dominated Senate cosponsored a resolution opposing Reagan's plans. Along the way to passage of the resolution, there were, however, some interesting obstacles.

According to Dan Grady, an aide to Democratic Senator Howard Metzenbaum of Ohio, who spearheaded the resolution, the original draft was "much more sharply worded" and made "specific references to the SS," and to its victims and crimes. "But the Senate leadership wanted something that wasn't so hard-hitting," said Grady, "so they [Republicans] could cosponsor it." The result, he added, was a "classic Senate document," one with "the heart taken out of it."

Even so, the measure failed to garner the support of leading New Right Senators, including Jesse Helms of North Carolina, Strom Thurmond of South Carolina, and Steven Symms and James McClure of Idaho. A McClure spokesperson, H.E. Palmer, said the Senator opposed the resolution because he "favored the President's goal of reconciliation between the people" of this country and West Germany. Symms said through a spokesperson that he did not "want to tell the commander in chief what to do" on his European mission.

The stance taken by these and other New Right stalwarts was conspicuous not only because so many others spoke out against it, but because they did so with such intensity. "Unlike other times, it was not a case in which Jews had to solicit Christian names," said Rabbi A. James Rudin, director of interfaith relations at The American Jewish Committee. "They called us. They said this was what 'we want to do'. My phone was ringing off the hook."

As an example, Rudin noted that Dr. Arie Brouwer, the general secretary of the National Council of Churches, "immediately called us and didn't need any urging." He added that the council's educational programs on the Holocaust had helped increase public sensitivity about the Bitburg affair. Also, Brouwer, a Reformed Church minister, likes to point out that he has a 'Jewish' first name and is the son of Dutch immigrants whose birthplace, he says, served as a safe haven for Jews in the 18th and 19th centuries.

At an informal gathering with reporters in Washington two weeks after the visit, Brouwer noted that he has "good friends who were very involved" in the Dutch wartime resistance. Asked if his opposition to the wreath-laying ceremony didn't conflict with the Christian value of forgiveness, he replied, "It is not for us or President Reagan to forgive the Nazis for their sins. This is something the Jews have to work out."

Brouwer's staff aide for Christian-Jewish relations, David Simpson, was one of those who helped Sister Carol Rittner mobilize support for the *Times* advertisement. Said Rittner, who teaches courses on the Holocaust at Mercy College in Detroit: "I was aware of statements by non-Jewish groups, but they did not seem to be getting picked up in the media ... It was imperative that the Jewish community not be seen as standing alone on this issue."

Rittner said she feared that the Bitburg controversy might turn ugly, as did the 1981 dispute over the sale of AWACS surveillance planes to Saudi Arabia. There was the "potential," she said, for people to blame the controversy on Jews and "say the Jews are throwing their weight around."

So she drafted a statement and quickly got help in organizing the appeal from Simpson, Celia Deutsch, who is a Sister of Sion in Brooklyn, and three noted Christian writers on the Holocaust—Harry James Cargas, Franklin Littell and Robert McAfee Brown, who is a leading supporter of the movement to provide sanctuary to illegal Central American immigrants.

Not until she began soliciting support did Rittner learn of the intensity of feeling on the issue. Brouwer, one of those she contacted, said that "what outraged my moral sensibilities was the way it was handled. First," he said, "there was Reagan's early explanation, in turning down appeals to him to visit Dachau, that he didn't want to stir up old passions."

Then, his "equating of the SS with the victims of the death camps also showed an incredible lack of moral sense," Brouwer said. To that, Rittner added the belated decision by the White House to tack onto Reagan's itinerary a visit to Bergen-Belsen, seemingly "as an afterthought." The President's final statement that the trip was "morally right" sealed the disastrous series of events, she added.

In two days, Rittner and her supporters had more names than they could fit into a half-page ad, and had to cut about 30. "We could have easily had 250" sign, she said. One superior general of a religious order in Michigan telephoned to complain, "Why didn't you call us about it?" When the Reverend John Egan, a spokesperson for the Roman Catholic Archdiocese of Chicago, found out that he couldn't get on the list, said Rittner, he telephoned the White House in order to register the archdiocese's protest.

Meantime, the Sisters of Mercy, Rittner's religious order, asked its members, through a national telephone hotline, to "do something specific, call the White House or send a telegram. Identify yourself as a Christian, express opposition to the Bitburg visit and suggest we (the United States) do something else" to show friendship with West Germany, Rittner said.

Under the headline of "Open Letter to President Reagan," the ad appeared in the April 28 Sunday national edition of *The New York Times* (and cost over $20,000, which Rittner raised from individual Jews and Christians, including her father). The appeal began, "As Americans and Christians, we feel morally compelled to stand with our Jewish brothers and sisters and to express our profound disappointment over your decision to visit Bitburg Cemetery." It then suggested that Reagan go instead to the home of the late Konrad Adenauer, the first chancellor and leading architect of postwar Germany, or to the Flossenburg prison, where Protestant theologian Dietrich Bonhoeffer was hung for his part in a plot to kill Hitler.

Among those whose names appeared below the message were Monsignor Daniel Hoye, the general secretary of the National Conference of Catholic Bishops; Bishop Philip R. Cousin of the African Methodist Episcopal Church, who is President of the National Council of Churches; Wilburt Tatum, editor of The Amsterdam News, a black weekly in New York City, and heads of theological seminaries and local chapters of the Council of Churches.

Rittner said the list did not include any leaders of the religious right because they were not among her contacts. Even if they were, she claimed, it would have been unlikely that they would have joined the appeal.

A coalition of Jewish groups led by the National Jewish Community Relations Advisory Council—that placed an ad in the *Times* a week later—had unsuccessfully sought the support of well-known evangelical and fundamentalist leaders. Charney Bromberg, the council's associate director, had enlisted the aid of Rabbi Yechiel Eckstein of Chicago as go-between.

Eckstein heads the Holy Land Fellowship of Christians and Jews, promoting understanding between Jews and evangelical Christians. He has appeared on fundamentalist television talk shows, and has written articles about the concerns of Jews for such publications as the Reverend Jerry Falwell's *Fundamentalist Journal*. Last January, he became the first Jew to lead a workshop at the annual convention of the National Religious Broadcasters.

Nevertheless, he had little success when the Bitburg issue came up. One of those he contacted was the Christian Broadcasting Network's Pat Robertson, who, around the same time, had told Rabbi Alexander Schindler of the Union of American Hebrew Congregations, in a public debate in Washington, that he would do "anything" for the Jews. What he wouldn't do, however, was take a public stand on Bitburg. He "maintained that he was in contact with Patrick Buchanan, urging President Reagan no to go," Eckstein said.

Evangelist Billy Graham also declined, giving similar assurances of private contact with the White House. Rabbi Marc Tannenbaum of the American Jewish Committee, who had been in contact with Graham, said the evangelist had been deeply distressed by the Bitburg affair and had personally asked the President and Nancy Reagan not to go. Hyman Bookbinder, the committee's Washington representative, added that Graham's "intervention contributed to the decision to visit the home of Adenauer."

What disturbed Eckstein more, though, was the response of other evangelical Christians, who either declined his request to take a public stand or failed to answer his calls. They included Robert Schuller of the "Hour of Power" TV program; Charles Stanley, the fundamentalist President of the 15 million-member Southern Baptist Convention; Jim Bakker, of the "Praise the Lord" TV show; Ben Armstrong, executive director of the National Religious Broadcasters, and Billy Melvin, President of the Assemblies of God. With the exception of Schuller, all are listed as board members of the Washington-based American Coalition of Traditional Values, the most broadly representative association of religious right leaders.

The lone New Christian Right figure joining in the appeal was Jerry Falwell, who has been trying to cultivate closer ties to Jews. Yet, according to Duane Warde, a Falwell aide, Falwell's opposition to the President's visit brought him "a lot" of angry mail from his constituents and politically conservative friends.

Eckstein, who spends a good deal of time trying to persuade Jews that evangelicals want to enter into a genuine relationship with them, said the effort to win support from the religious right left him wondering, "Why does it seem like you have to pull teeth with the evangelical and fundamentalist community, but the liberals jumped on board so enthusiastically?"

One reason, he said, is that there is no "structure" of ties between evangelical Christians and Jews, as there is between Jews and liberal Christians. While liberal Christians may now, after two decades of interfaith dialogue, understand the meaning of the Holocaust, evangelical Christians "have not been exposed to this," Eckstein said, adding that their silence on Bitburg underscored the need to work toward a true "relationship between the two groups, and not a narrow political alliance on certain issues."

But "this [Bitburg] was not a hard or risky political issue. They should have come out with statements on their own, without solicitation, on a moral issue like this," he said. "I don't have an excuse."

The reactions from the secular right were even more disappointing.

William F. Buckley Jr. concluded in his widely syndicated column that "Reagan did the right thing. And he performed splendidly. And he is owed apologies he will never get."

Richard Viguerie, editor of *The Conservative Digest* and the direct-mail "whiz" of the New Right, took time out from his bid for the Republican nomination for Lieutenant Governor of Virginia to debate the issue with Senator Metzenbaum, sponsor of the anti-Bitburg resolution, on Public Broadcasting's "MacNeil/Lehrer NewsHour."

"If this is really a concern about the Holocaust, why isn't something done about an ongoing holocaust?"said Viguerie. "Isn't the best way to honor those who died, those 6 million people who died in the German Holocaust of 40-45-years ago, to prevent an ongoing holocaust in Afghanistan, the Miskito Indians in Nicaragua?"

In an interview from his car telephone after Reagan visited Bitburg, he said that the visit was needed to "heal the wounds" of West Germany, a key ally to the United States, and "to lay the past behind us." Viguerie said he only "wish[es] that the President had been more forceful about the hypocrisy" of those who opposed the trip.

"We need to be worried about holocausts of everybody, not just of one group," he said. "I'd like to see more emphasis placed on those dying today," he said, adding that he had been in touch with his colleagues on the New Right and that they shared his position.

"We're not making light, minimizing what happened. But we also recognize that if we're not careful we can all participate in a holocaust of 1985, courtesy of the Soviet Union ... What's the difference between communism and Nazism, except that communism is more effective? They kill more people than the Nazis did," he said.

"I don't understand the hypocritical feeling that we must keep the torch burning so everyone remembers the Nazis, but [we] don't see the same groups doing anything about the terrors of communism, which is much more threatening now," Viguerie said.

These reactions to Bitburg are important, particularly in light of forecasts by prominent Jewish neo-conservatives of an imminent rupture between Jews and their traditional friends and allies. In Irving Kristol's view, for example, blacks are allegedly moving in an anti-Semitic direction, and Hispanics and Asians, who are a growing force in such institutions as labor unions, have little reason to be concerned about Jewish issues. From the standpoint of "political expediency," he argues, Jews should forge an alliance with the religious right—which generally supports Israel—and play down their opposition to fundamentalist Christian goals such as prayer and Bible-reading in public schools that have little chance of being instituted.

Bitburg, however, illustrated the pitfalls of that narrowly political concept of alliances. For leading conservatives just couldn't understand why moral concerns about the Holocaust should outweigh the political and ideological goals of the President's visit to West Germany. At the same time, the period of the Bitburg affair and the months preceding it saw an improvement in the relationship between Jews and their traditional friends. One manifestation was the unprecedented coalition of 35 church social-action groups that joined the Union of Amercian Hebrew Congregations last fall in issuing a tough appeal on behalf of Soviet Jewish dissident Aleksandr Yakir. Another was the historic two-day conference held last spring by the U.A.H.C. and the N.A.A.C.P. during which the two groups announced a plan of joint action on a variety of issues, including black-Jewish discussions at the local level and a program that would involve sending black youths on visits to Israel and Jewish youngsters to Africa.

All this, of course, does not mean there is no longer any conflict between Jews and their old allies. Indeed, under certain circumstances—as was the case during the Israeli invasion of Lebanon in 1982—these ties could once again suffer serious damage. But on the Bitburg issue—a major test of sensitivity toward the Holocaust—the Jews' traditional allies came through; their purported "new" ones on the right were oddly quiet, if not insensitive.

Never Again?

Moment Magazine
June 18, 1985

By Leonard Fein

Who can deny the appeal of a pledge so powerful as "Never Again!"?
And yet, and yet…

What are we to understand from words that are spoken with equal passion by people of such unequal, and disparate, understanding? Meir Kahane says "Never Again!" and so do Ronald Reagan and Elie Wiesel. Can the wicked, the simple and the wise conceivably all mean the same thing? Surely they cannot. They agree, if at all, only in the way we all agree that war is hell, or that good must triumph over evil. Sweet, but so what?

If what the words mean is that there must never again be a Holocaust, no one will quarrel with them. Quite likely even Gorbachev, perhaps even Arafat, would agree. But then, "never again" becomes just a slogan, not a pledge, for it points in no particular direction. Nor is it clear that anything that matters to us is advanced by the sudden popularity of the slogan.

A slogan cannot be expected to contain within itself a policy; even a pledge does not. But we are entitled to be irritated when words that were meant to convey a solemn promise become the indiscriminate call of wise men and fools, of good men and bad alike. Conceding the sincerity with which they are spoken, we are still left with the fact that they mean nothing—or the wrong thing.

Standing at the gates of Birkenau, the death camp of Auschwitz, you learn that the camp stretches all the way to the horizon. And because it stretches all the way to the horizon, we do not know how far beyond the horizon it stretches.

There are horizons of space, and there are horizons of time. The absolute evil of the Nazis was not that they perfected the technology for mass murder. That was evil, but it was not absolute; in the 40 years that have now intervened, we have far surpassed their technological achievement.

No, their specific evil lay in the delight they took in stripping people of their humanity even before killing them. That is what we learn from all the memoirs, and that is what we learn from the photographs—not of the dead, but of modest families, fathers and mothers and their children, made to stand naked together before death.

The Nazis were specialists in dehumanization. In 1945, they were defeated, and we have now passed through a season of commemoration of that defeat. Forty years beyond the horizon of 1945 and the war's end, can we truly say that the forces of dehumanization were finally defeated in 1945? Looking about, it becomes clear that "never again" is a hope, not a description; "still, in our own day" is the awful and accurate truth."

Of course the President of the United States should not have thought to go to Bitburg, and surely not to have proposed an equivalence between the dead at Bitburg and the dead at Bergen-Belsen. The President, we are informed, was "wounded" by the controversy that his actions and statements provoked. Perhaps, then, it is time to let the matter rest, to classify it as an unfortunate error, to accept, as does, for example, Morris Abram, once President of the American Jewish Committee, now a member of the United States Civil Rights Commission, that the President has now committed himself "to the moral commandment 'never again' that this was, in short, just a terribly unfortunate lapse."

But this is the same President who, weeks before Bitburg, allowed as how the Contras of Nicaragua are "the moral equivalents of our Founding Fathers." And this is the same President who, weeks before Bitburg, suggested that most Americans believe the volunteers of the Lincoln Brigade, those who fought to save Spain from Franco's fascism, fought "on the wrong side."

These outrageous statements are a powerful indication that Mr. Reagan's "Never Again" at Bergen-Belsen and at the Bitburg air base were as inadequately understood as they were wholeheartedly asserted. There is no reason to gainsay Mr. Reagan's fundamental sincerity — but there is every reason to doubt that he understands where his "commitment" must point. For if it is to be taken seriously, it must point well beyond the kind of *Reader's Digest* sentimentality to which the President is so given; an anecdote is not an analysis, not even an argument. Yet Mr. Reagan's indiscriminate moral judgments must depend on anecdotes, for analytically, they crumble.

Is the President, then, as he is so often portrayed, merely a well-intentioned boob? That is most unlikely: No one as successful as he can be so casually appraised and dismissed. This President may not know history, but he knows how to make it. Curiously, however, any number of his most enthusiastic defenders ask us to see him as fundamentally naive. If one can damn with faint praise, then we have been witness, these past weeks, to the opposite, to praise with faint damnation.

That is what is implied by those who, while lamenting the President's itinerary, have insisted that Mr. Reagan is, after all, a good friend to the Jews, that in light of his record on Israel, on Ethiopian and Soviet Jews, and even on memorializing the Holocaust, we ought not hold the mistake of Bitburg against him. "We all want to be judged by our full records rather than our worse lapses," said Nathan Perlmutter, national director of the Anti-Defamation League, and "so should a President be judged."

Bitburg as lapse? This was not just a simple misstep, finally repaired by what Perlmutter calls "the President's gentle eloquence." Bitburg was a compound error; it began with the decision not to visit Dachau, and it ended only weeks later, after a nearly unbroken series of stubborn stumbles.

The point of Bitburg — the dumb politics of it aside — is that it was no exception at all to the Reagan rule. In its moral confusion, it was of a piece with what came before and with what is likely to come after. The President suffered here a unique embarrassment because this once, political ineptitude joined ongoing moral incompetence. The "lapse" was a lapse in political acumen only. And neither "gentle eloquence" nor still more aid to Israel can compensate for the continuing moral confusion from which the President so manifestly suffers.

Moral confusion and political myopia: In Bitburg, the President proposed that "freedom-loving people around the world must say, I am a Berliner, I am a Jew in a world still threatened by anti-Semitism, I am an Afghan, and I am a prisoner of the Gulag, I am a refugee in a crowded boat foundering off the coast of Vietnam, I am a Laotian, a Cambodian, a Cuban, and a Miskito Indian in Nicaragua."

The point these nine examples want to make is plainly a political, not a moral point. If a moral point had been intended, then surely the blacks of South Africa should have been listed, as also the citizens of Pinochet's Chile. Or are the Chileans really so much better off than the citizens of Castro's Cuba? (And what of the grim statistic that informs us that in the slums of this country, infant morality is now rising?)

What is the political point the President's inclusions and exclusions make?

It is the same point made by those who, seeing the evil of the Soviet Union, have eyes for no other evil. Some of those whose vision is so limited are very intelligent people, and their views are, these days, quite fashionable. Lately, some of them have taken to fulminating against those, who, they claim, think the United States and the U.S.SR are, somehow, morally equivalent.

But there are few people on the left of the political spectrum who are so morally inept as not to know the difference, the moral difference, the vast moral difference, between the two great powers. The purpose of the attacks is not to defeat a view that is widely held, but to discredit the whole of the left. And the mannerly McCarthyism of the new right demeans the argument it makes.

As to the argument itself, it has led during these weeks of debate over the President's debacle to a stream of columns and editorials that have held that the Holocaust was not, after all, so unique a tragedy, that the Gulag is as bad, or nearly as bad, and that Jews (and others) who would focus on yesterday's tragedy deflect our attention from today's agenda. To these counselors of amnesia, the defeat of the Soviet Union is the agenda, the whole of the agenda and nothing but the agenda.

But if that is all of the agenda, then it is a pointless hypocrisy to prattle on about "Never Again." For the assault on human dignity is not restricted to the U.S.S.R. It does not derogate from the evil of the Gulag to point to the evil of apartheid; it does not misapprehend the danger of the Gulag to observe that a 39 percent rate of unemployment among black teenagers in our own country is unacceptable, unconscionable. People who are insensitive to such travesties, to such tragedies, ought to be barred from saying "Never Again." They have not understood that the battle against dehumanization is a battle that must be fought, daily, on many different fronts — not least, the home front.

How comforting it would be to believe, as the President's defenders would have us believe, that Mr. Reagan's fiasco was merely a lapse in an otherwise acceptable record of defending human rights and human dignity. But there is no Reagan record in defense of human rights, at home or abroad; there is only Reagan rhetoric. For that reason, we are well-advised to suppose that Mr. Reagan and his advisors will remember Bitburg as a colossal tactical blunder—but will have learned nothing serious from the experience. Having learned nothing from it, their "Never Again" is revealed as an empty slogan.

And ours? On a good day, Never Again silence in the face of dehumanization. Never Again indifference.

From the St. Louis to Bitburg
Special Contribution

By Seymour Maxwell Finger

President Reagan's visit to Bitburg and the reaction to it brings out in sharp relief two important facts.

First, there remains among most non-Jews, even those who are friends of Israel, an insensitivity to deep Jewish feelings about the Holocaust. They simply do not understand the pain and deep emotional scars remaining from the brutal destruction of European Jewry.

Second, there has been a sea change in the attitude of American Jewry. During the Holocaust there was deep anguish and concern about the fate of European Jews, but a less self-confident American Jewish community felt almost helpless to influence events. Jewish organizations were relatively weak and under financed. They made repeated efforts to enlist the help of the Roosevelt Administration but found little interest or willingness to use the vast power and resources of the United States on behalf of European Jewry.

When the *St. Louis,* loaded with almost a thousand European Jewish refugees, was only a few miles off the Florida coast in 1938, Jewish organizations could not influence the American government to provide even temporary refuge. (The ship returned to Europe and the bulk of its passengers eventually died in Nazi concentration camps.) Even the limited power that Jewish organizations had was further weakened by divisions among them as to goals,—for example, Zionists versus anti-Zionists and non-Zionists, assimilationists versus Orthodox. As a result, there were from time to time united protests against particular ghastly events, such as the Madison Square Garden rally that followed the public revelation of Hitler's program to destroy all European Jews, but there was not a *united, sustained* drive for rescue.

By contrast, Reagan's visit to Bitburg was denounced by Jews and Jewish organizations all across the spectrum, including those who consider the President a friend. As Prime Minister Peres put it, "A mistake is a mistake and a friend is a friend." This is in sharp contrast with the reluctance of Roosevelt's Jewish supporters—an overwhelming majority of America Jewry—to criticize the wartime President. It also underscores the greater self-confidence and better organization of American Jewry.

But there is no reason for complacency. Far from it. Virulent anti-Semitism is still rife in the United States and around the world. Jews still constitute a tiny minority of the world's population. Israel is still bordered by Arab enemies who do not recognize its right to exist. Jews and Jewish organizations must learn from their tragic history, to be vigilant and to avoid mistakes. As a small minority they must reach out to friends and allies, while remembering—as the Holocaust and Bitburg show—that no one else will care about Jewish causes and the fate of Jewry as much as the Jews themselves.

(Prof. Seymour Maxwell Finger was executive director of the Commission to Report on Responses of American Jewry to Holocaust Commemoration. He is a former ambassador and lectures at CUNY.)

What Bitburg Revealed About the Jews
Special Contribution

By Dennis Prager

Bitburg focused most people's attention on Germany, Nazism, Chancellor Kohl, and President Reagan. In my view, however, Bitburg revealed more about the Jews than it did about anything or anyone else. It provided a particularly clear illustration of the Jews' role in forcing the world to confront evil. It demonstrated how the Jews only partially fulfill this role. And it revealed a significant difference between Judaism and Christianity.

I

To understand Bitburg, one must first understand the role played by Jewish suffering.

The Jews are the world's miner's canary. Canaries are taken down to mines because they quickly die upon exposure to noxious fumes. When the miner sees the canary dead, he knows there are noxious fumes to be fought. So it is with the Jews. Noxious moral forces often focus first on the Jews. But their ultimate targets are the moral values that the Jews represent. That is why non-Jews who share Jews' values have a vested interest in combating anti-Jewish forces. They make a fatal error when they dismiss anti-Semites as the Jews' problem.

Examples include the anti-Semitism or anti-Zionism of the Nazis, Idi Amin, Mouammar Qaddafi, the United Nations, and present day Islam. Each was first dismissed as the Jews' problem. By failing to understand the universal implications of anti-Semitism, moral non-Jews awoke too late to the threat posed by these anti-Semites.

Fifty-five million lives might have been saved had democracies understood the meaning of Nazi Jew-hatred. Five-hundred thousand Ugandans were eventually murdered by Idi Amin whose vicious anti-Zionism was ignored as a Jewish problem. Qaddafi, now regarded as the primary supporter of terrorism against Western democracies, first revealed his moral nature in his obsessive hatred of Israel. The transformation of the United Nations into a force inimical to democracy and human rights was rendered inevitable by its becoming an international vehicle for anti-Zionism. And the Muslim enemies of Israel are finally being perceived as the enemies as well of such Western values as individual rights, democracy, and freedom.

Anti-Semitism is not merely another hatred and it is much more than hatred of Jews. It is ultimately hatred of what the Jews, wittingly or not, willingly or not, have represented: the call to a higher moral law. Judaism and traditional Jews have always understood this. As the Talmud explains it, the Hebrew words for hatred and Sinai, *seenah* and *seenai*, are as related as they sound: the hatred of the Jews comes from Sinai. That is where the Jews received God's moral Law, and the world has never forgiven the Jews for imposing on it their ethical monotheism, their God of moral demands and moral judgment.

Non-Jewish students of anti-Semitism have often commented on this as well. As the Catholic historian of anti-Semitism, the Reverend Edward Flannery wrote, "It was Judaism that brought the concept of a God-given universal moral law into the world;" willingly or not, "the Jew carries the burden of God in history, [and] for this has never been forgiven."

And Ernest van den Haag in *The Jewish Mystique* summarized the roots of anti-Semitism in these words: "Most unpleasant, [the Jews'] invisible God not only insisted on being the one and only and all-powerful God . . . he also developed into a moral God. . . . The Jews have suffered from their own invention ever since."

Even anti-Semites have acknowledged this meaning of anti-Semitism. The father of German racial theory, Houston Stewart Chamberlain complained that "The Jew came into our gay world and spoiled everything with his ominous concept of sin, his law, and his cross." He was echoing Richard Wagner's words: "Emancipation from the yoke of Judaism appears to us the foremost necessity." And Hitler defined his mission as the destruction of the "tyrannical God of the Jews [and His] life-denying Ten Commandments."

The Jews have suffered for being the human representatives of God's moral demands. They have truly fulfilled Isaiah's description of them as God's "suffering servant." Whenever others reject God's moral law, Jews suffer. Of course other peoples have suffered at the hands of evil men and ideologies but the Jews and their suffering have repeatedly focused the world on its greatest evils.

The Jews therefore have a dual role with regard to evil: first, to confront the world with its greatest evils — never to allow "reconciliation" with evildoers, never to "forgive" them (unless the evil repent, which is impossible, for example, in the case of dead Nazis); second, to explain these evils, to explain that the Jewish suffering caused by these evils is a result of the denial of Sinai, the hatred of the ethical monotheism introduced by the Jews. For this reason, and only for this reason, does anti-Semitism has universal importance.

Bitburg helped to clarify precisely how well the Jews implement their dual role.

First role: confront the world with its evils

Most Jews, being quite human, as well as quite oblivious to their role in the world, have hardly sought to confront the world with its evils. They would just as soon let others play this role. But Bitburg showed once again that some Jews are not willing to leave this role to others. While many nations suffered terribly at the hands of the Nazis, it was the Jews, almost alone, who screamed bloody murder at any hint of forgetting Nazi evil.

The question is, Why? Why, if they do not identify with their calling to confront the world with its evils, do Jews so consistently do precisely that?

The answer, I believe, is that their role leaves them no choice.

For even though the Jews may not want to keep reminding the world to confront evil, they do so anyway—out of what they perceive as self-interest in not allowing the world to forget *their* suffering. But since the greatest forces of evil so often focus on the Jews, the Jews' suffering and their constant talking about it serve to an unparalleled extent to focus people's attention on those evils.

It was, in fact, a Roman Catholic, William F. Buckley, Jr., who once made this point most tellingly. In a public interview with Rabbi Joseph Telushkin and myself, he pointed out that if all Soviet Jews were allowed to leave the Soviet Union, as wonderful as that may be for the Jewish people, it would not be a positive development for the world. The reason, he immediately explained, was that in the West and at the United Nations, the Jews and Israel were really the only ones constantly confronting the world with Soviet evil. And why? Because the Jews were protesting on behalf of their fellow Jews. But if there were no Jews left suffering in the Soviet Union, Western Jewry would keep silent about the Soviets, and then no one would confront the world with Soviet evil.

In other words, the Jews' screaming about their suffering, even though done for selfish ethnic, rather than religious moral, reasons, serves a universal moral purpose.

The Holocaust is the quintessential example. Had the Nazis inflicted their Holocaust upon another people, most Jews, being normal human beings and oblivious to their religious/moral role, would hardly be screaming at the world "never again"—with the result that the world would not be talking all that much about Nazi evil. The Jews do not demand that the world remember the six million Ukrainians murdered by the Soviets, or the one out of every three Cambodians killed by the communists in Cambodia, or the genocidal destruction of Tibet by the Chinese communists, or confront the greatest evil of this moment, the Soviet destruction of Afghanistan. *And the result is that the world ignores these evils.*

Ideally the Jews would live up to their role and scream about these other horrors. But while the Jews may be failing in this role, they can hardly be criticized for demanding only that the world confront the evils done to their own—for other groups do not even do that. The apathy of Western Christians to the horrible persecution of fellow Christians in the U.S.S.R., the silence of the Catholic Church over the virtual decimation of the fellow Catholics in Lebanon, and the lack of worldwide Muslim opposition to the Soviet annihilation of Islam and Muslims in Afghanistan are simply incomprehensible to Jews.

Thus even though for most Jews it is self-interest, rather than a conscious fulfillment of their role, that motivates them to ensure that certain evils will not be ignored, it is still the Jews who most consistently demand that the world stare at evil's blinding light.

The confrontation at Bitburg was a classic reenactment of the Jewish role. Most people, including most fine, moral people who loathe what the Nazis did, and even groups that also suffered at the hands of Nazis, wanted to forgive and/or forget. The Jews said stare at evil, call it evil, remember evil. They said "reconciliation." The Jews cried "remember." Thus the Jews at Bitburg played their historical role.

Second role: Explain these evils

But they played it only half way. True, almost alone, the Jews insisted on remembering Nazi evil, but because they did so primarily out of self-interest (remember *our* suffering) rather than because of their religious role, they could offer no reasons why the world should remember Nazi anti-Semitism. Consequently, the world is perceiving the Jews' obsession with Auschwitz as obsession with themselves rather than as obsession with evil.

The Jews are telling the world to remember Nazism but they are giving the world no reason other than sympathy for the Jews to do so. Why should the world spend five more minutes on the Holocaust than on the mass murders of American Indians, Australian aborigines, Cambodians, Afghans, Ukrainians, Tatars, Armenians, or anyone else? By speaking as a suffering ethnic group rather than from our religious/moral role as spokesmen for ethical monotheism, we have little to say to the world about evil and solutions to it.

If we were to explain that Nazism is, in essence, the denial of the Jewish and Christian values of a God-based society with personal moral responsibility to that God and His moral law, then we Jews have a humanity-serving reason to keep humanity's memory focused on the Holocaust. If we would explain that the denial of God as the basis of ethics leads first to the destruction of Jews as the historical representatives of that doctrine and then to the destruction of all other decent people, then others, too, would become obsessed with the Holocaust.

Unfortunately, however, most Jews, in their alienation from Judaism and their adoption of secular values, find such notions bizarre, if not actually repugnant. That it is primarily a war on God that has led to Auschwitz, Gulag, Cambodia; that it is the Jews' role to bring mankind to ethical monotheism, to teach that God without ethics (Khomeini, Crusaders) and ethics opposed to God (Nazism, Marxism-Leninism) both lead to terrible evil; and that Jewish suffering has a universal religious/moral meaning are utterly alien ideas to most Jews whose secular worldview renders a Jewish one inscrutable.

But only such religious notions render the Holocaust meaningful—for both Jews and non-Jews. Otherwise the Holocaust is only a provincial, ethnic tragedy. Instead of teaching the world the universal meaning of Jewish suffering, we merely appear self-obsessed. We have to show how the Holocaust, how all anti-Semitism, threatens far more than Jews, not because of humanist platitudes such as all suffering affects all people, or no man is an island, or so long as one people is oppressed, all are oppressed, but because the Jews, as Catholic bishop Edward Flannery wrote, "carry the burden of God in history." And those who wish to supplant God with a *fuhrer* or with a Party, will seek to annihilate Judaism and/or the Jews. This is what Nazi and Soviet anti-Semitism are all about. This is why others should never ever forget the Holocaust.

Christians, for example, should be made aware of the anti-Christian essence of Nazi anti-Semitism. Psychiatrist Robert Jay Lifton who studied Nazi doctors explained Dr. Josef Mengele's Jew-hatred in *The New York Times:* According to an Auschwitz friend and fellow-SS physician, Mengele espoused the visionary SS ideology that the Nordic race... had been weakened by Christian morality of Jewish origin." As did Hitler and many pre-Nazi German anti-Semites (see, for example, Uriel Tal, *Christians and Jews in Germany,* Cornell, 1975), Mengele believed that Christianity was a Jewish aberration thrust upon an unwilling German race. That many despicable and foolish German Christians did not perceive the anti-God and anti-Christian components of Nazi anti-Semitism and did support Nazism tells us something about about those German Christians but nothing about the anti-Christian nature of Nazism.

If we showed Christians that modern anti-Semitism—from the Nazis to the Communists to the Muslims—is inevitably anti-Christian, we would enlist their passionate interest in the Holocaust and anti-Semitism generally. But instead of teaching that Auschwitz was built by an ideology that loathed the God of Judaism and of Christianity, most Jews continue to regard Christianity as if it were still calling for Crusades and inquisitions and still look to secular ideals for their salvation. Instead of teaching that Jews and Christians must fight *together* for ethical monotheism, many Jews continue to fight *against* Christianity and ethical monotheism. Instead of teaching Christians the divine role Jews and their suffering play, many Jews label Christians who do believe in the divine Jewish role fanatics and enemies.

In short, we must teach Christians and others the universal lessons of Auschwitz and Gulag. God is necessary for a moral order, His death must lead to additional holocausts, and the future of mankind is either Jerusalem or Moscow, ethical monotheism or totalitarianism, because people will be morally responsible for their actions either to Almighty God or to the almighty state.

Of course, most Jews would choke while uttering such words. Rather than teach the need for ethical monotheism, most Jews continue to preach humanism—*belief in humanity* after the Holocaust, *belief in humanity* after Gulag, *belief in humanity* after Cambodia—and a *secular* humanism, even though the most destructive and sadistic regimes in history have been anti-religious.

If we did teach these lessons of the Holocaust, *then* non-Jews would be likely to react positively to our very appropriate obsession with it. *Then* they would understand that the Holocaust is far more than a Jewish problem. Ironically, but as is often the case, it is the religious Jewish approach that has universal meaning and the secular ethnic Jewish approach that means nothing to non-

Jews. As of this moment the only reason we Jews have given for a non-Jew to feel strongly about the Holocaust is human empathy. But that is hardly enough for most people, and it certainly does not answer why anyone should devote more attention to Jewish sufferings than to any other.

II

One reason, then, why Jews do not teach the lessons of the Holocaust is their ignorance of and even opposition to religion and God-based explanations for anything. There is another reason. If Jews understood their obligation to push the world to stare at its most blinding evils, and to teach that these are consequences of ideologies that are anti-God, they would have to reach a conclusion that too few Jews are willing to confront: along with Nazism (which is essentially dead), communism has been this century's most systematic evil. If we understood what the Holocaust should teach the world and took our role seriously, we would have to confront the world with the evil that was — Nazism, and with the evil that is — communism.

Communism has murdered far more people than did Nazism (only because Nazism was destroyed, but this fact hardly invalidates the point, it merely argues for the destruction of communism whenever possible). It has destroyed far more national and religious cultures, subjugated more nations, ruined more lives, and tortured more innocents. And communism, even more explicitly than Nazism, is a war against God and Judeo-Christian Western civilization. But for reasons that are beyond the purview of this essay, Jews, while rarely (at long last) pro-communist, still often lead opposition to anti-communism.

Indeed, for many Jews there is a remarkable cognitive dissonance regarding communism and the Soviet Union. On the one hand, they protest vehemently against Soviet persecution of Soviet Jews; they know that outside of Nazi Germany no regime has ever as effectively warred on Judaism, and they are aware of the methodical torture of, among others, Anatoly Scharansky. Yet when the president of the United States calls those very same Soviets an "evil empire," they will scream that he is a war-monger and cold warrior, and demand to know who we are to judge them. And they will consider it *immoral* (not merely erroneous) to fund opponents of the burgeoning communist tyranny in Nicaragua, or for that matter to fight communism anywhere, and they will keep silent on Afghanistan whose decimation is nearing genocidal proportions.

Western Jews' policies regarding Soviet Jewry (recalling William Buckley's point) provide a classic example of the Jews unwittingly playing their religious/moral role, and of their playing it only half way. There are far more Christians in Soviet prison camps for being Christian than there are Jews for being Jewish. Yet, by and large, Western Christians ignore, or even worse, deny, as do the National and World Councils of Churches, how terribly Christians do suffer in communist countries. So it is often primarily thanks to the Jews screaming about the sufferings of Jews in the Soviet Union, that the West has often had to confront the evil of the Soviets. But just as we tell the world about the Holocaust but not about the meaning of Nazi evil, the Jews are telling the world about Soviet Jews, but not about Soviet evil.

So we play our role with regard to communist evil, as we did at Bitburg with regard to Nazi evil, provincially, and therefore only half way. But this is still half way more than Christians are doing about imprisoned Soviet Christians or Muslims are doing about Afghanistan.

I did not agree with the conservative defenders of the president's visit to Bitburg. The Jews were right, and the president and his defenders were wrong about ever having a "reconciliation" with Nazi evil, but their error emanated in part (the other part, the Christian view of forgiveness, will be discussed) from their very valid preoccupation with communist evil. They said that because of the contemporary battle against the Soviets, doing what our strategically most important ally in Europe wanted was more important than giving in on Bitburg. If we could support Stalin in fighting the Nazis, we could stand with Kohl and his dead SS men against the Soviets.

Thus, I believe that the moral scorecard at Bitburg read: Jews right about dead evil and therefore about Bitburg, Reagan and the conservatives right about living evil, but wrong about Bitburg.

III

Some years ago Simon Wiesenthal wrote an illuminating little book entitled *The Sunflower*. In it, he recounts how one day while he was an inmate in a Nazi concentration camp, he was picked at random to go to a nearby hospital. There a young Nazi soldier who had participated in atrocities such as burning Jews alive lay dying. The Nazi asked that a Jew, any Jew, be brought to him from the nearby camp. He wanted to ask a Jew for forgiveness before he died.

Wiesenthal was brought to the Nazi's room where he found a young man bandaged from head to toe. After recounting to Wiesenthal the atrocities he had perpetrated, he implored Wiesenthal to forgive him. Wiesenthal listened to the entire story, then left the room without forgiving the young man. Years later he sent this story to about two dozen major thinkers, and asked them to react. Was he, Wiesenthal, right or wrong?

Though Wiesenthal does not so note, there is one consistent pattern to the responses. All the Jews, whether religious or not, said Wiesenthal was right. All the non-Jews, whether religious or not, said he was wrong. I do not believe that the reason is in anyway related to the fact that it was Jews who were murdered. Among other things, that would be an insult to the very fine non-Jews who responded.

Bitburg, like *The Sunflower,* illustrated one of the most significant differences between Judaism and Christianity: their attitudes to forgiveness and therefore to evil.

When Elie Wiesel implored President Reagan not to visit Bitburg, he spoke as a Jew. Virtually every Jew who heard Mr. Wiesel understood him and could barely comprehend how anyone could not see the logic and righteousness of his position. To almost every Jew, it is axiomatic that one does not, indeed one has no right to, forgive murderers and torturers on behalf of their victims.

On the other hand, almost every Christian, lapsed ones included, understood the president, and could barely comprehend how Elie Wiesel and the Jews did not see the logic and righteousness of Mr. Reagan's position. To almost every Christian, it is axiomatic that one forgives. Period.

For more than three years I have been moderating a weekly radio show featuring a Protestant minister, Catholic priest, and rabbi. With different guests each week, a broad range of opinions is assured. Yet one issue consistently unites Protestants (from fundamentalist to most liberal) and Catholics and divides them from the Jews (from Reform to Orthodox) — forgiveness.

I have asked this question repeatedly to Christian clergy: "Do I understand correctly that it is the Christian position that if I hurt, even murder, another person, any person, you as a Christian are duty bound to forgive me?" Every one has said yes.

To virtually any Jew, this notion is simply immoral. Even Jews who are ignorant of Judaism's principles hold to the basic Jewish principle that only the victim can forgive the person who has hurt him. And those who are familiar with Judaism know that according to it, God Himself does not forgive unless the victim has already done so.

It is this profoundly differing view of forgiveness — which may reflect a profoundly different view of evil — that explains more than anything else, why President Reagan and his supporters on the one hand, and Elie Wiesel and the Jews on the other did not understand each other. President Reagan is a Christian. On this issue of forgiving evil, Jews and Christians so disagree that they simply do not understand one another.

This is not to say that for a Jew to understand the Christian position is to appreciate it any the more. One of the reasons I am so passionately committed to Judaism is precisely because of its obsession with good and evil (rather than, let us say, with love, forgiveness, and salvation). Its uncompromising attitude to the deliberate infliction of suffering on the innocent is Judaism's "light unto the nations."

At Bitburg, the Jews did not entirely fulfill their mission, while Christians who called for "reconciliation" with Nazi monsters were more consistent with theirs. But Bitburg showed once again that when it comes to having the world confront evil, it is still Judaism that leads the way.

(A respected author and radio commentator in Los Angeles, Dennis Prager reports on Jewish and world affairs.)

The Speech Ronald Reagan Should Have Given At Bitburg

Perspective
Spring, 1985

By Irving Greenberg

To The German People

This is the week of the fortieth anniversary of the surrender of Nazi Germany. Four decades ago, Germany was prostrate, war-damaged, and a pariah nation in the world. In these forty years, the people of West Germany have rebuilt a shattered country and economy, integrated and renewed the lives of hundreds of thousands of refugees and become an itegral part of the common European community. West Germany has become a flourishing democracy, a trusted, dependable ally of the nations of freedom in NATO and elsewhere. My visit to this nation at this time declares the appreciation and respect of all who treasure freedom, for your remarkable renewal, for earning legitimacy in this generation.

In laying a wreath at Bitburg cemetery, we sought to make a statement of an historic reconciliation between erstwhile enemy and warring countries. Our alliance for freedom, our common concern for peace, has overcome the anger and alienation of the war which ended forty years ago. It is a statement of gratitude to Chancellor Kohl and to the people of West Germany, for their steadfast willingness to share the burden and risk of Western defense.

One should never take allies for granted. We do not say it often enough, but let me say to you, here and now: the people of the free world do not take your friendship lightly, nor your dedication to freedom for granted.

To German Youth Born After 1945

Do not think that remembering the Holocaust is an attempt to impose collective guilt on the German people or on you. The Jewish people suffered for 1800 years from an untrue charge of deicide and unjust accusations of collective guilt, now repudiated by all of humanity. They and we repudiate any attempt to inflict such a collective guilt on you.

We ask you, the next generation, to join us in remembering. If you remember, you will understand how precious democracy is. The Nazis came to power when other Germans despaired of the Weimar Republic's ability to solve their economic and social problems. Now we understand that a democracy may fail to perform in the short run but it can eventually overcome its faults. In a dictatorship, there is no internal mechanism of correction. A few can decide to murder a people and there are no political checks or moral balances to prevent this monstrous policy from being carried out. Treasure freedom; with all its faults, it protects the humanity and dignity of all.

World War II was more than a tragic time. During that terrible conflict, the Third Reich embarked on an unprecedented, cruel war to kill an entire people — the Jews — and to degrade and cheapen their lives before death. Millions of other people — including the Allies in the war against the Third Reich — did not do enough to stop this war. Six million died. So shameful and painful is the record that those who still hate now try to deny the crime or its dimensions. But even good people are tempted to put it aside, especially in moments of happiness. This is wrong. We must resist temptation and cling to memory.

Those who strive to keep alive the memory of the Holocaust are not against reconciliation. As our religious traditions have taught us, the road to true reconciliation is through repentance and remembrance. The people of West Germany themselves have taught the world this lesson in paying reparations and in ongoing support for the state of Israel. The only way to prevent the recurrence is to continuously learn the lessons. Therefore, my tribute to the German war dead cannot be extended to those of the SS, who committed such terrible crimes. This is our way of placing such evil beyond the pale of future human action.

Chancellor Kohl has spoken of a collective shame at the terrible excesses of those days. That collective shame does honor to you. Whatever the pain of such recollection, it will give you the strength to build a better world and a healthier Germany. Thus you will honor the memory of all those who have died.

To The Veterans of the Allied Armies and Their Families and Friends

Acts of reconciliation involving tribute to the war dead of both sides are usually made after all who lived through the tragic events are gone. This insures that the friendship expressed to the living does not revive the pain still carried by the comrades-in-arms and those who suffered the loss of loved ones in those battles. Out of gratitude and desire to bring the German people closer, I personally sought to shorten the historic waiting time. We underestimated the continuing sense of loss felt by many people who respect the living Germans but remembered that their dead fell in battle with the German army and these war dead. No German should be offended at the natural sense of loss and grief which has been evoked by this visit.

To the veterans and families who carry the scars of those losses and those battles, I express my regret for their pain. Our reconciliation with Germany in no way minimizes our love and honor for those who risked their lives and those who gave the supreme sacrifice for their country. They died to make this a world of freedom and peace. The alliance celebrated in this visit advances their goals. It means that they did not die in vain.

To The Survivors

To the survivors and the Jewish people, I say: nothing can soften the pain of death. For those whose loved ones died in the normal course of history — even if it be in war — consolation comes sooner than for those who themselves and whose loved ones have suffered unspeakable cruelty. You still mourn those people whose death was inflicted for no other cause than their very existence. For implying that forgetfulness is part of reconciliation, for awakening the pain you feel, we ask forgiveness. Your protests saved us from forgetting even as your witness and example has spurred the world to recreate life.

To The World

There are those who will seek to exploit the feelings generated by our visit to divide, to set people against people, to dismiss justified suffering and moral anguish. The Holocaust itself is a terrible memory of evil, continuing to offer a model of cruelty and injustice for those who seek to act the same way. However, by the remarkable power of human repentance and memory, by the transforming force of love, it has evoked commitments to overcome the hatred of the past. It has restored Christianity to its gospel of love and Judaism to its commitment to perfect the world.

We cannot undo the crimes and the wars of the past, nor can we recall the millions to life. We can pledge to each other that the emotions evoked by this visit and by this historic anniversary shall be turned to the creation of mutual alliance and defense of peace. Let each other's pain drive us to greater efforts to heal humanity's suffering.

There is no lack of hunger, poverty, oppression and sickness in this world. A great sage once said: "In remembrance is the secret of redemption." Let us pledge to each other to turn memory into the driving force of that redemption for all humanity.

(Irving Greenberg is president of the National Jewish Resource Center. He was director of the President's Commission on the Holocaust (1979-1980) and is a member of the U.S. Holocaust Memorial Council.)

Some Lessons From Bitburg
Perspective
Spring, 1985

By Irving Greenberg

It will be some time until a final assessment can be made of the President's trip to Germany to commemorate the fortieth anniversary of VE Day, and the consequent decision to visit the Bitburg military cemetery. Much of the outcome will depend on future fallout from the entire controversy. I personally believe that the President's words about not imposing a guilt trip on the Germans, or his aide's comment about not "grovelling in a grisly thing" are more dangerous to the future struggle of remembering the Holocaust than any actions of the President. Much will depend on whether people will listen to his words in Germany, primarily, or to some of his other comments.

I.

It is not too early to learn something from the controversy. The first lesson is to stop the attacks of Holocaust commemoration within the Jewish community. Only a couple of weeks before the whole Bitburg issue blew up, the *Baltimore Jewish Times* ran another major story, with the oft-repeated panoply of quotes that too much attention is being paid to the Holocaust. One person quoted even suggested that the hundred million-dollar funding campaign for the national Holocaust memorial is "an obscenity." It is easier to get coverage by criticizing Holocaust commemoration than by supporting it. Apparently, even serious Jewish media continue to run such stories on the theory that man bites dog is news, without ever asking whether it might be unsanitary — or a poor model of behavior to offer to others.

It is hard enough to spit blood to work through these issues, just as it has been an agony for survivors to beat their heads against walls of indifference for thirty years. People find it hard to believe today that Elie Wiesel struggled in the Fifties and early Sixties as a reporter for Israeli and French newspapers, and for years could not even get his classic memoir of the Holocaust, *Night,* published. Emil Fackenheim once told me that he has had three or four, often savage attacks on him and his writing for "Holocaust-ism" for every one appreciative or thoughtful critique of his theological reflections on that catastrophe. Those who criticize "excessive" commemoration of the Holocaust are not "courageous anti-establishment" thinkers; they are running with the pack.

Nothing more clearly illustrates the premature nature of the claims that we are placing too much emphasis on the Holocaust than the blinding revelation in President Reagan's comments that even the basics of Holocaust memory are not yet understood. The fundamental difference between war and genocide — which means that one cannot equate German soldiers, let alone SS, to the victims; the natural desire to forget and be happy, which collides with the ongoing pain of memory and analysis; the fact that Holocaust commemoration is not a focus on death but a goad and entry into reaffirmation of life and ethics — are all lessons that need to be spelled out and repeated until they are understood by everyone.

II.

Elie Wiesel's words in the White House ceremony were truly memorable. "Your place is with the victims of the SS" will continue to morally reverberate down the corridors of time. However, overall, Jewish leadership failed to articulate a clear and simple message which would have responded to President Reagan's good intention of symbolic reconciliation.

Our primary message is and must be: true reconciliation comes through repentance and remembrance.

We — all those who work to remember the Holocaust — are for reconciliation. The natural revulsion of veterans or survivors at any visit to a cemetery, or at a clear statement of reconciliation with the German people, should not be allowed to obscure the truth that confronting the lessons of the Holocaust is the single most powerful generator of moral cleansing and fundamemtal reconciliation.

Repentance is the key to overcoming the evils of the past. When people recognize injustice, they can correct the wrongdoing and the conditions that lead to it. Memory leads to higher levels of responsibility and morality and reduces the anguish of the feeling that the dead may have died in vain. Repentance has liberated many Christians from past stereotyping and hatred of Jews, thus transforming Christianity into a true gospel of love — which it seeks to be. Repentance has liberated many Germans from the sins of the Nazi past. Those that resist are themselves implicated in the past, or give aid and comfort to those who still identify with those days and those evil forces in the German nation and soul.

Remembrance is the key to prevent recurrence. Goaded by the memory of the failures of the 1930s, the American government in 1979 organized a worldwide absorption program for two million boat people. As the then Vice President of the United States said, America was determined not to repeat the indifference toward Jewish refugees and the failures of the Evian Conference in the 1930s. Goaded by memory, America's Jews and Israel responded to the crisis of Soviet Jewry and, belatedly, of Ethiopian Jewry in far better fashion than they did to European Jewry in the 1940s.

Remembrance of the Holocaust is the best protection for German democracy. The Nazis were able to come to power because the Weimar Republic could not solve the economic and social crisis of the Thirties. In despair, people turned to dictatorship. The lesson of the Holocaust is that democracies can sooner or later correct their faults. But once people set up a dictatorship — which lacks internal checks and balances — a handful can unleash a process of mass murder without limit.

The key to purification of Germany is a universal recognition by Germans of the unprecedented horrors unleashed by the total war on the Jews. The memory of the Holocaust is the single most powerful condemnation, not only of the killers, but of those who, by respectable prejudice and stereotyping, isolate the victims and make them vulnerable to destruction. This is why those who long for the good old days are driven to deny the very fact that the crime ever happened. The memory of the Holocaust is the single most damning judgment of their past behavior, and the single greatest obstacle to any revival of neo-Nazism. The health of German democracy is dependent on the memory of the Holocaust.

III.

The very planning of the Bitburg visit as well as the decision not to visit Dachau which preceded it, was a grave setback for conscience and memory. Still, the furor about the trip proves that much has been accomplished in the past decades. The tremendous rise in public consciousness of the Holocaust reflected itself in extraordinary criticism and public attention. If only there had been such weeks of continuous headlines and controversy in 1944, would there not have been a bombing of Auschwitz? Would not hundreds of thousands have been saved? Sadly, now we are fighting over what is the proper homage to the dead. If we had had this kind of public consciousness and influence forty years ago, and used it right, we could well have saved lives. The accomplishment and the promise to the future is highly significant.

IV.

Once Holocaust commemoration becomes part of public life, even affiliated with a United States government agency, it does become involved in the daily flow of policy and politics. There will be grave errors made in the future as there have been in the past. Still, it is worth it. The millions whose lives will still be saved, the understanding of Israel's significance, are our consolation in moments of such moral anguish. Of course, memory is not a utilitarian value; there is a primary moral dimension to this work. Still, the Jewish community must be morally mature enough to recognize that the imperfections and faults of the political system do not delegitimize the fundamental rightness of the work of public commemoration.

Finally, in policy and political life, one does not burn bridges permanently. Overall, Ronald Reagan's record in commemorating the Holocaust has been very good. He serves as honorary chairman of the campaign to create a national memorial. He has held commemorations of the Holocaust in the White House and spoken passionately of the need to remember. His support for Israel — the single most powerful Jewish commitment that the Holocaust shall not recur, the haven where most of the survivors built their new lives — is exemplary. Our criticism of this particular callous misjudgment must not be allowed to falsify the total overall picture, which is a good one. And we shall have to work with him again.

(Irving Greenberg is president of the National Jewish Resource Center.)

Reflections On The Nature Of The Holocaust
Perspective
Spring, 1985

By David M. Elcott

The unanimity of Jewish response to Ronald Reagan's planned presidential trip to Germany well indicates the potential danger of opening debate about non-Jewish responses to the Holocaust. For the Jewish community today, the years of Nazi rule in Europe are not history — they are a searing, ever present reality of our collective and personal lives. An official American visit to a World War II German military cemetery in which those who murdered my family are buried seems morally unfathomable as well as wholly impolitic. President Reagan was thirty-three years old when the catastrophe of Hitler's reign ended. For him to relegate the reality of extermination camps to the faded childhood memories of contemporary Germans, Jews, and Americans is wrong and naively blind. I do not speak on behalf of the political sensitivity and timing of the President or his advisors. Yet it may be not only possible but critical for the Jewish community to try and listen more carefully to the implications of what Ronald Reagan is saying.

The President speaks for much of the basically good-hearted, all-American, non-Jewish society in which we live. Our attempts to dissuade him with thundering morality and guilt and overwhelming rhetoric prevent us from learning and understanding the evolving non-Jewish response to the Holocaust. It may be politically necessary to respond collectively as we do in public, but if we are truly to grasp and positively influence the way that non-Jews view us and our mission, then we must be willing to hear as well as to lecture.

The place of the Holocaust is central to Jewish self-definition in the twentieth century, but only part of the picture for the non-Jewish world. For the Jewish community, it often seems virtually impossible not to monopolize the suffering of the Holocaust. It is not just the quantity of Jews murdered, but the destruction of an entire people's culture in Europe and the dehumanization of Jews that preceded the gas chambers. Christian America can offer a sympathetic response, but has been given no right to connect empathetically.

Many profound thinkers in our community, from survivor and witness Elie Wiesel and historian Yehuda Bauer to theologian Yitz Greenberg, insist that the Holocaust is not the by-product of warfare or another example of attempted genocide. For them, the Holocaust was the Nazi attempt to totally exterminate the Jews while genocide was the policy to destroy Poles, Gypsies and other "undesirables." To speak in generalizations, much as the communist states have done, creates an easily dismissed, faceless slaughter. Wiesel argues that only through confronting the particular of Jewish destruction can one honestly universalize the Holocaust. This is a powerful and compelling message and a critical realization for the Jewish and non-Jewish world. But it is possible to offer an additional focus on analysis.

The Jews of Europe suffered unbearable destruction; we were not alone in our suffering. Along with the six million Jews perished millions of others — from union leaders and Christian theologians to communist organizers and avant garde artists. These additional millions of innocents were murdered in a conflict that pitted the briefly dominant forces of a great evil against a naive humanity. To say that the terror between 1933-1945 was Hitler's war against the Jews may conceal from us a truth that Hitler sought to remove God's presence from the world, to replace love with hatred, intellectual inquiry with slavish dogma, spiritual quests of divinity with a demonic adulation of raw human power. Jews represented in European culture a moral and ethical force as well as a litmus test of the justness and openness of European civilization. Their destruction cannot be simply explained as an outgrowth of innate Christian anti-Semitism or the idiosyncratic mania of one individual. For world history, the Jewish catastrophe was one scene from a multi-act play whose Wagnerian finale was an inferno for the entire ravaged continent.

From this, Simon Wiesenthal intuitively sensed another message of the Holocaust in his plea to the organized Jewish community following World War II, to speak of "eleven million victims" and not only six million Jews. While Elie Wiesel and the majority of Jews saw this as too dilutive of the Jewish Holocaust, in Wiesenthal's view, the rest of the world could not be allowed to dismiss this catastrophe as a conflict between Germans and Jews, ignoring any responsibility to deal with the implications for humanity. I suspect that the rawness of our pain and the guilt of the living overwhelmed the wisdom of Wiesenthal's logic.

We still bridle at the use of the word Holocaust for anything save the massacre of our people and risk judging the suffering of others in diminished terms next to ours. Even the non-Jews who died in Nazi camps or fought on behalf of our people have, for the most part, been afforded but footnote status. To mention Raoul Wallenberg today, forty years too late, only highlights the point. Harold Schulweis notes that, in the end, we hold aloft the names of our persecutors and have erased those who saved and suffered with us. He adds, ironically, that few can name the heroes who attempted to protect and nourish the Anne Frank family while all Jews know the pantheon of Nazi murderers.

Even those of us who lived safely in North America or were born following the war are often too quick to wrap the mantle of suffering safely around us as if pain must be a treasured and sacred possession of the Jewish people. That the Holocaust has and must alter Jewish consciousness is axiomatic. Those years of terror must become part of the personal experience of our people and its history. For our descendants, the Holocaust will be weaved into the fabric of Judaism as an integral component of Jewish memory. But there is also a message to the non-Jewish world beyond proclaiming Jewish suffering or how the whole world wants the Jews dead.

It is often seen as "un-American" to dwell on the collective pain of the nation. For most in our country, the Holocaust is a passing moment which should be placed behind us. American leaders are, on the whole, very poor historians. In fact, the non-Jewish leadership of this country during the past forty years has not dealt with many of the implications of Nazism and the American reaction to it. Yet Ronald Reagan seems to say (perhaps without the emotional and intellectual sophistication we need as an indication of sincerity) that he and other Americans are willing to look at the haunting photos of emaciated concentration camp victims and the charred remains of Jewish children, and still say "we." Assuming that Reagan excluded the SS murderers, defining young German conscripts as victims is an attempt to say that Hitler was no German hero, no model for the German nation, for Nazism distorted even the basest aspects of German culture and the core of humanity.

The President and the rest of the all-American, white Anglo-Saxon Protestants of the White House staff, with no personal connection to Hitler's victims and notwithstanding a greater natural affinity to the German than the Jew, are prepared to accept the deeper Jewish claim that the destruction of Jews was an attack on all humanity. They are willing, in a way perhaps far too facile for our emotional needs, to universalize the Jewish suffering and accept the memory of that pain as their own. They are willing to recognize that World War II was not the same as World War I; that this was not just another war of patriotic Germans against patriotic Americans, Russians, French and British.

The American non-Jew is an historical "revisionist," placing Hitler on the side of evil and all those living today united in support of justice and morality. This draws too simple a picture and the timing is off. Trying to universalize the Holocaust in this fashion may be more than a generation early, but the intended thrust is a positive one. One hundred years from now, it will be morally acceptable even for Germans to see Hitler as other, as the evil inclination potential of all human beings which must be suppressed and destroyed. We should be sensitive to the non-Jewish groping to understand the Holocaust and encourage it.

There is a model for such historiography in Jewish tradition. The sheer pain of slavery in Egypt was a uniquely Jewish experience. Yet Judaism has translated that experience into a remarkable universal lesson. We are told to diminish our joy of the Exodus by removing drops of wine as we recite the Passover rendition of the ten plagues of Egyptian suffering. The Egyptians are justifiably punished but, caught in an immoral and violent system, their pain, too, became part of the transcendent Jewish vision of messianic redemption. And the Assyrians, slayers of Israel, are allowed the opportunity of repentance. An angry Jonah, whose credibility as a prophet demands God's wrathful destruction of Ninevah, is rebuked by a God who seeks to offer all humanity access to God's love and divine goodness, even those who once subjugated us.

No one has the right to demand that the survivors allow the casual observer a place in their nightmare. The Holocaust at this moment in time is uniquely attached to those whose suffering was personal and real. But very soon the Jewish people will have to transform this reality into pure memory. Then we, in the self-defined Jewish tradition of bringing the world closer to Godliness, will have to share the Holocaust with the heirs of Ronald Reagan and even the descendants of the Germans who fought for the Third Reich. Only then will the eradication of Hitler's name be complete. Only then will the twelve-year eclipse of humanity and God's presence which we call the Holocaust emerge to illumine the greater universal truth of the triumph of life.

(David M. Elcott is a staff member of Perspective, *an opinon and policy paper of the National Jewish Resource Center.)*

The Bitburg Affair
And Its Implications for Black Americans
Reflections '84 Radio Program
May 12, 1985

By R. Blanchard Stone, Ph.D.

This week Reflections '84 discusses the aftermath of the Bitburg Affair and its implications for black Americans.

Historical conditions of racism have a way of revealing themselves even when meticulous attempts are made to hide them. The presence of black people in America has had a not yet understood way of clouding what would otherwise be an obvious situation. What the Bitburg Affair represents is a clash of two irresistible forces, meeting in a contest of wills, both committed to the justness of its respective cause. Who are these two irresistible forces? They are conservative America, and especially its right wing, and world Jewry, a people who understandably take symbolism very seriously. The ultimate conflict of views held by each of these two communities is not at all surprising. Conservatives have a concept of chosenness in a political sense and are becoming more fundamentalist in their spiritual beliefs and more oblivious to compromise. This point is important when evaluating the commitment in support of, or in opposition to, a given action. The Jewish people believe in the ultimate wisdom of their causes, their actions are divinely motivated by a covenant between God and themselves. On positions which they are convinced are just, there is little or no movement from their central position. Conservatives, at least the right wing variety, are unforgiving in their commitment to the destruction of their enemies and the causes they champion.

The Bitburg Affair, from a black perspective, might be viewed as Jessie Jackson's revenge. You will remember when the Jewish community had Jessie jacked up for his uncomplimentary designation of a Jewish section of town. Jessie's sins were laid at the alter of the National Democratic Party, causing Mondale a problem similar to the one experienced by Custer, when he had discovered the presence of another Indian. Jessie's problems with the Jews had to do with his Arab connection, and it seems Bitburg and Mr. Reagan's confrontations with the Jews involves the more serious Nazi connection.

Of all the tragedies suffered by the Jewish people, the Holocaust during World War II is the one most deeply etched into their consciousness. This is the event that caused a world to gasp in awe and disbelief at the tremendous amount of mortal pain inflicted upon a third of a race of people. Any tampering with this monument to the memory of a fallen people, will be seen as an effort to forget the past, and in the process rehabilitate those who bore direct responsibility for the Holocaust. This is the basis of the Jewish resentment of the Bitburg cemetery visit. There are several Jewish groups that monitor the level of anti-Jewish or anti-Semitic sentiment, detecting, where possible, if such sentiment may be on the rise. The purpose of such monitoring should be apparent to all who are aware of the tremendous loss suffered by Jewish people who, at the time of their suffering, had no homeland of their own. The emotional concern of the Jewish people is real and quite deep. The tragic plight of the Jews occurred in Europe and primarily in Germany, but it happened there because that's where the principals happened to have been at the time of their fateful engagement. The Jewish people correctly argue that tragedies are not confined to any one geographical location. The fascist thinking that fed the maniacal needs of Hitler is, today, present in America and only awaits a reincarnate of Adolph Hitler.

In Medieval Europe, in response to being continuously invaded, those invaded would build fortified, defensible castles, equipped with moat, draw bridges and towers. This was a sensible response to a threat of personal and group annihilation, a lesson black Americans are far too slow to learn. The lesson the Jews are clearly telling all who care to listen is that, "He who forgets his past is fated to repeat it." Black people must not think of a "past event" as meaningless history, or as an event that never needs recalling. According to the theory of cyclical events, physical and mental slavery is due to reappear on the world scene in less than 50 years. Just who these 21st Century slaves will be, or where they will be enslaved, is one of history's least well-kept secrets.

We have, in brief, attempted to show reasons for the deep resistance Jewish Americans showed to Reagan's visit, not to Germany, but to the German cemetery at Bitburg where a number of Waffen SS Troops are buried. The SS were the elite troop supporters of all military and political objectives of Nazism. Jewish Americans were not the only Americans to resent the cemetery visit, a majority of Americans seemed to have also thought the visit unwise. But a hard-core minority of conservatives believe that America should stand closer to Germany and believe Nazism to be preferable to communism. Congressional conservatives obviously have no abiding respect for the loss of millions of lives. If they did, they would not hesitate to ratify the anti-genocide treaty now nearing its expiration term. It will soon self-destruct for lack of ratification on the part of the United States Senate. The anti-genocide treaty commits a government to guarantee the safety of its minority citizens against the ravages and rages of its majority. Such a guarantee may appear quite frivolous to those not needing such a guarantee, but to those who have suffered under the rule of so-called civilized authority, such is basic to survival.

Did President Reagan bite off too much with Bitburg? Probably not. From the Reagan perspective, he had to go to Bitburg and lay the symbolic wreath of reconciliation. Why? Primarily because Helmut Kohl asked him to do so. What was so compelling about Chancellor Kohl's request was a veiled threat relating to the military balance of NATO and perhaps its very survival. West Germany is the linchpin of the NATO alliance. Only England has shown closer relations with the United States than Helmut Kohl's Germany. American missiles are stationed in Germany over the objections of a growing number of antinuclear adherents in that country. Mr. Reagan had little knowledge of who was buried in the cemetery or even why they were buried there. His primary goal was to appeal to the loyalty of the West Germans at the expense of domestic criticism. To Mr. Reagan, the geo-political considerations outweighed the hostility that might be vented as a result of the cemetery visit. As to Mr. Reagan's domestic problems, he felt this too would pass, and if perchance it did not, who loses? Not the President, for, under the current law, he's ineligible to succeed himself. Mr. Kohl and his conservative party needed to be reassured of America's continuing commitment to Germany. The West Germans were holding a bright light up to Mr. Reagan's face with the cemetery offer. If he had blinked, the Germans would have then probably insisted upon removal of the missiles and could have reverted to Willy Brandt's *Ost Politik*, or rapprochement. Any such move leaves NATO without a viable strategy against the Warsaw Pact, thereby triggering a crisis where nuclear weapons would be a likely option for the U.S. in scoring a "first strike" in any effort to knock the enemy out, a dead man's plan. World War III is for all practical purposes a "World War We."

Briefly, I've stated why Mr. Reagan had to go to Bitburg. Now, perhaps it should also be noted that Mr. Reagan wasn't just being loyal to an ally or obstinate as a conservative by his going ahead with the trip—he preferred to go. The more neoconservatives come to resemble the old fascists and Nazis, the more their criticism of these groups becomes muted. In a political sense, not all dinosaurs are extinct. This is the fear of Nazi rehabilitation that Jews are concerned about. The enemy of our time is communism, not fascism, nor Nazism, not even South Africanism. say the conservatives. The reunion of groups whose common interest is their mutual dislike or hatred of a particular race of people represents the return of what everybody thought had passed.

Is racism hereditary? Or is it simply passed from one generation to the next? This question should not be taken lightly. Racism is an ecumenical concern, not just a local one affecting minorities in America; the phenomenon is world wide.

An example of how racism can cloud an otherwise clear issue can be seen in the large numbers of voters who voted for Mr. Reagan in the past election, even though their vote would later spell harm to their most vital personal and group interests. Farmers, who are the center piece of middle America, answered the call of Mr. Reagan which was a conservative call, and implicit in that call was a "Now is the time for all good Americans to come to the aid of their party," an inference of racial solidarity. Watts puts it succinctly when he says, "In this country, there are but two kinds of people, liberals and Americans." Here, by inference, Americans are Republicans. Liberals are, by conservative accounts, the national spokesmen and representatives of blacks in America. Many Jewish voters, a number of which were identified as longtime liberal Democrats, voted in support of Mr. Reagan because of Jackson's Arab connection, and his failure to denounce Louis Farrakhan to the satisfaction of the Jewish community. Here was an example of the hound and the hare, running simultaneously, causing a severe fracture in the Democratic coalition. Unions, who had no logic whatever for their voting Republican, did so despite the endorsements by their leaders of the Democratic party. The lone exception was the Teamsters, whose boss endorsed the Reagan candidacy; now the Teamsters' boss faces his own sleaze factor.

Many voters in the previous election voted a fear, which is a negative factor, rather than their logic and their reason which are positive. If blacks and the Democratic party had not been so closely identified, the national voting patterns would have been far different from those which occurred. The Republicans wrapped Jessie and, symbolically, black people around the Democratic party and forced the party to wear the black factor as an albatross around its neck. The Democrats were pictured as liberals favoring the rights of blacks over those of our "own American citizens." America should look at historical Germany, and not in a detached manner, to see the incipient horrors of racism. As regards the issue of educating the world to the horrors of the past, black people stand in strong solidarity with their Jewish brethren in their efforts to keep the memory alive.

The primary purpose of Mr. Reagan's visit to Europe was to attend an economic summit in Bonn, Germany. The President asked his trading partners to take the ball and keep the economic momentum begun by the U.S. going forward. Mr. Reagan was seeking concessions from various of his allies to lower troublesome trade barriers in farm commodities and other products. This concern was directed toward France, which subsidizes its sizeable farm community. In a NATO related area, the conference in Geneva on arms' reduction was brought up topically with all NATO allies agreeing to the U.S. arms negotiating position. The economic problems, at least potentially, are proving more vexing than the ideological problems existing between the United States and the Soviet Union. Mr. Reagan had hoped that his presence at the Bonn Economic Summit would cause his Western allies to close ranks behind his economic suggestions, and the President might have been successful were it not for nationalist France. Mr. Mitterrand of France would not agree to the trade talks advocated by Mr. Reagan.

America seeks an international free trading zone, one that will allow the marketplace to determine the flow of international trade. Many countries subsidize certain of their national industries, such as agriculture in France, and until this administration, in the U.S. as well. This attempt to make governments superfluous is likely to have an unsalutary and an unsettling effect. America is attempting to have each nation lower its barriers to imports, thus allowing deficit trading nations, of which the United States is one, to more freely sell their products abroad. The potential of a trade war looms more likely than a shooting war with the Soviets. A trade war among allies would ultimately culminate in the dissolution of military and economic associations of the Western alliance. The European trip taken by Mr. Reagan will not be historically recorded for the European Economic Summit that was held. As a matter of record, there is nothing to record, for nothing was achieved short of the atmospherics that go along with heads of states greeting heads of states.

The trip will be remembered because of the ten minutes spent at the Bitburg cemetery were 48 Waffen SS Troopers are buried beside 2,000 regular German Army troopers. This stop, regardless of intentions of reconciliation between two World War II enemies, is being viewed as a moral selection, a decision to accept the Holocaust as history and cast its results into fashionable disrepute, then go on with the future. Germans, logically, would like to put Hitler behind them and all of his sins with him. Many Germans feel they have been victims of collective guilt. That is, ironically, an attitude of some against Jews, since many fundamentalist religions hold Jews collectively responsible for the death of Christ.

The issue of collective guilt condemns all of one class or group for the sins or crimes of any one or several of the same group. What about slavery? Did the responsibility for its sins end with the death of the last slave master, even though its negative effects still impact upon the descendants of this evil system? What was the white man's burden as relates to slavery? Collective guilt should apply in a situation where a heinous wrong was committed. And its lingering aftershock persists, without a significant public outcry. The Vatican, seat of the Roman Catholic Church, has exonerated Jews from any further guilt or responsibility in the crucifixion of Christ. Elie Wiesel, Chairman of the American Jewish Holocaust Commission and brilliant Jewish spokesman, says he does not believe in the collective guilt of the German people in the deaths of six million Jews, but he does believe that those who are guilty should remain guilty and should never be rehabilitated or accorded any measure of national or international respect. Bergen-Belsen is the death camp visited by Mr. Reagan in an effort to appease those who were most adamantly opposed to his visit to the Bitburg cemetery. This is the camp where Anne Frank, famous for her diary, was put to death. In this sense, Bergen-Belsen is one of several monuments to the Holocaust; it stands as a strong reminder and symbol of resistance to the oppression of the past.

What is most conspicuous about the lesson being proffered is its lack of applicability for black Americans, or black Americans' lack of sensitivity to a lesson in contrast. There are no monuments to slavery, save the lasting effects worn by its victims. It must have been assumed by someone at some time that the humiliating years suffered by blacks as slaves and as third class baggage in a nation that only recognizes the first class visas would have some lasting effects. The Holocaust of Europe was real and its pains are obviously deep, but the effects of slavery left more skeletons and wasted bodies and minds than any tragedy that has befallen man in the past 2,000 years. And yet there is no monument to slavery, an institution born of racism — that insidious disease that causes one man to totally reject the humanity of another.

Black people have, historically, been conditioned to forget; and Jews have been, historically, taught to remember so they would never again have to forget. When we forget a happening or an event, it's as though we never knew of its existence. Contrary to popular axiom, "What you don't know can't hurt you," it's more likely to be, "What you don't know will not only hurt you, but ignorance can, ultimately, kill." Whenever truth is ugly, only a lie can be beautiful. When we can find no solace in our past, we have a tendency to run from it, hoping the present will be our refuge from the past, and our future the hope of things to come. The present is a safe haven only if you have an appreciation of the past. History is replete with examples of people who have tried unsuccessfully to run from who they are, only to find such an evasion unsound, unwise and impossible. A thorough understanding of who we are is an indispensable requirement for personal liberation. Truth of the past is the only sensible approach to the realities of the present, our consciousness of the present is the harbinger of the future.

Black Americans have a need to understand the symbolism of the past and of the present. Every event portends a signal, however dimly lit such a signal may at first appear. America's current social signposts are pointing in a backward direction. America has gone only a short distance along the road of justice, and has made a u turn in its commitment to equality based upon justice and universal fairness. Affirmative Action is not a communist ploy aimed at overthrowing the government of the United States. Affirmative Action is the least any unapologetic nation can do to say to its descendants of slaves that, "We feel slavery to be an unconscionable act committed against human beings by other human beings." If Bitburg causes the world to reflect upon the horrors of the Holocaust and the excesses of the Waffen SS Troops under Hitler, the high numbers of nationally unemployed and imprisoned blacks should cause the nation to see the unfilled promise still lingering and fading in the many socio-economically deprived quarters throughout the nation.

It is absolutely essential for black people to build their monuments of joy and sorrow. They must learn to accept pain as a part of life, and use the painful experience as a lesson to minimize the chances of such painful experiences every happening again. The joys of life are to be added upon and extended in ways in which their benefits will be shared by those who are the least beneficiaries of them. There must be a conscious effort by black people to accentuate the positives and eliminate the negatives without losing the benefit of the experience of either. Education is the locomotive upon which ideas and concepts are put into motion. If education omits either the historical dark moments, or fabricates the bright moments, it will likely have an inconsequential impact upon the learning of the individual or of the affected group. This fact of educational reality cannot be disputed by any serious scholar of education. Any education that teaches you more about your neighbor than it teaches about yourself is a lesson intended for your neighbor and has an inconsequential message for others.

The freedom of a people is measured in relative terms. Equality and freedom are universally accepted as absolute conditions, unbridled by convention. Freedom is the absence of slavery, especially in a social, political and economic sense. Equality is the universal sameness of all things of a like or similar nature. In America, freedom and equality are victims of social cuts. Some people are freer and more equal than others. This has caused an entire society to weigh the rights of some against the rights of others, and if the arbiter of freedom and equality—the system—feels there is an imbalance, the scales are reset to compensate for the discrepancy. The problem arises when the scales of justice are set to measure the freedom and equality of black Americans. If the scales are not balanced by justice, freedom and equality will both become empty rhetorical refrains used to woo world opinion and not to correct or redress a historical imbalance. Education must become more to black people than it currently is. Intelligence, universal intelligence, is a mandatory requirement for all living beings in today's world, and especially the industrialized world.

The implications of Bitburg for black people are both varied and deep. From a historical perspective, Bitburg is a remembrance, from a Jewish and a victim's point of view, a very painful remembrance. The President's trip to Bitburg was, by his account, a reconciliation of former enemies, conservatives from America reaching across the ocean to embrace German conservatives. In this sense, international conservatism looms as a larger possibility; this hookup would not necessarily bode well for the developmental needs of black people, either at home or abroad. The larger lesson of Bitburg is to be seen in the almost universal solidarity of the Jewish people. Mr. Reagan was unable to convince a single Jewish person to stand at his side at Bergen-Belsen, where he went to commemorate the slaughter of 50,000 Jews. This was a definitive lesson in togetherness and, what's more important, a lesson in remembering. Black Americans, who are faced with a hostile Justice Department seeking to roll back the clock to a dark time in their historical pilgrimage, must not forget their pains as they must not over-celebrate what they feel to be their victories. Lessons are not lessons until they've been learned.

We leave you, as usual, with our thought for the week. For our thought of the week, we look, finally, at Bitburg.

The affair at Bitburg evokes a litany on man's inhumanity to man, on the excesses of the past and, most obviously, on the dangers of uncontrolled, overt racism. Bitburg has become one more symbol of a place where the past is buried, but whose memories have once again been resurrected. The lessons of Bitburg teach us that badges of superiority are only worn by inferior people. Any race that seeks to be "numero uno" at the expense of another, or other race(s), is engaged in a fatal game of racial roulette that will cause other so-called designated inferior races to accelerate their efforts to disprove and destroy the myth of racial superiority. Black people in America, without conceding anything in the way of intellectual ability, are not now, nor have they ever been in any fundamental way, equal to whites in America socially, politically, or economically. Black Americans, due to the nature of their American experience, have had a racial stigma placed against them that neither time nor commitment has seemed to diminish. Their physical presence causes a mood of indifference, a sort of indifference that is not always benign. Political participation of blacks evokes a mood of distrust on the parts of those who can only see black Americans as a domesticated people. The fact that America has come as far as she has is proof she is capable of going further in her rejection of petty and grand racism such as that existing in Africa. To be consistent in her condemnation, America must also deplore racism American style as well. When all is done to put race in the background, we then can say to Jew, Gentile and black people alike, "Free at last."

For Reflections '84, I'm R. Blanchard Stone

"Hunt of History"

The Bitburg Fiasco
Time
May 6, 1985

By Charles Krauthammer

When President Reagan and Chancellor Kohl of West Germany first discussed the idea, it seemed like a good one: a V-E day visit by the President to a cemetery in Germany where American and German soldiers lie side by side. It would be a ceremony of friendship and reconciliation.

It has, of course, become a disaster. It turned out that no American dead from World War II are buried in Germany. It would have to be a purely German cemetery. And it turned out that Bitburg, the one suggested by Chancellor Kohl, contained the graves of 47 members of the SS.

But even before the unraveling, and the storm that followed, was there anything wrong with the original scenario? Just a few months ago, after all, did not Kohl and President Mitterrand of France hold a moving reconciliation at the World War I battlefield at Verdun? When Kohl raised with Reagan the idea of a cemetery visit, he cited the Verdun ceremony as the model.

The analogy does not hold, and that Kohl and Reagan could miss the point is at the heart of the Bitburg fiasco. World War II was unlike World War I, or any other war. It was unique because Nazism was unique. Nazi Germany was not just another belligerent; it was a criminal state. Even that term is inadequate.

This does not make the 18-year-old who died defending the Nazi regime a criminal. Nor does it lessen the grief of his mother. But it does lessen the honor due him from the President of the United States. Even among the dead, we are required to make distinctions. It is not just grotesquely wrong to say, as the President said last week, that German soldiers are as much victims as those whom the Germans tortured and murdered. There is also a distinction to be drawn between Hitler's soldiers and the Kaiser's. Mitterrand's choice of Verdun, the awful symbol of World War I, shows a grasp of that distinction. The choice of Bitburg does not.

If the distinction seems subtle, after the discovery of *Waffen* SS graves the need for subtlety vanishes. Even if one claims that the ordinary German soldier fought for Germany and not for Hitler, that cannot be said of the Waffen SS. Hitler's 1938 edict declared them to be "a standing armed unit exclusively at my disposal." A further directive in 1940 elaborated their future role. After the war the Third Reich would be expected to contain many non-Germanic nationalities. The Waffen SS would be the special state police force to keep order among these unruly elements. They proved themselves during the war: 40 miles from Bitburg, the Waffen SS murdered 71 American POWs.

Of all the cemeteries of World War II, one containing such men is the most unworthy of a visit by an American President. The most worthy — the graves of

Allied liberators or of the Nazis' victims — were originally excluded from President Reagen's agenda. After the furor, the Administration hastily scheduled a trip to a concentration camp. It believes it has balanced things.

For the Jews, a camp; for Kohl, Bitburg; and for American vets, perhaps a sonorous speech. The picture now contains all the right elements. But the elements do not sit well on the canvas. They mock one another. What can it mean to honor the murdered if one also honors the murderers and their Praetorian Guard? This is photo opportunity morality, and so transparent that it will convince no one, offend everyone.

Peter Bönisch, a Bonn government spokesman, complaining about the uproar in the U.S. over the Bitburg visit, said, "We can't start denazification of the cemeteries." Exactly. That's the reason to stay away.

The President's lapse is not just moral but historical. At first, he declared that he would put the past behind him: reopen no wounds, apportion no blame, visit no death camp. But one cannot pretend that the world began on V-E day 1945. One has to ask the question: Where did the new Germany come from? Some concession had to be made to history. The President decided to make it. And he chose precisely the wrong history.

V-E day separates two German histories. The moral rebirth of Germany after the war was, and is, premised on a radical discontinuity with the Nazi past. The new Germany is built around the thin strand of decency, symbolized by people like Adenauer and Brandt, that reaches back to the pre-Nazi era. If history is what the President wants to acknowledge, it is this German history that deserves remembrance. For Kohl and Reagan to lay a wreath at Bitburg is to subvert, however thoughtlessly, the discontinuity that is the moral foundation of the new Germany.

It is a Soviet propagandist's delight: The Soviets play the Nazi-West Germany theme night and day. It is false. West Germany's honorable history is its refutation. Why then a visit that cannot fail symbolically to affirm the lie?

This is not just bad history, but terrible politics. It is all the more ironic because the only conceivable reason for the Bitburg visit in the first place is politics: alliance politics. Kohl had a problem. His exclusion from D-day ceremonies last year gave ammunition to those who complain that Germany bears equally the burdens of the Western alliance but is denied equal respect. Reagan wanted to use this ceremony to help Kohl.

Now, strengthening democratic and pro-NATO forces in Germany is a laudable end, particularly in light of domestic and Soviet pressures on Germany over Euromissile deployment. But surely there are less delicate instruments than V-E day for reinforcing NATO. And surely there are limits to alliance politics. At that point President Reagan is reluctant to change his plans because of the acute embarrassment it would cause the German government. But that injury is certain to be more transient than the injury to memory that would result from sticking to his plans.

The Bitburg fiasco is a mess, but even messes have a logic. This incident is a compound of some of the worst tendencies of the Reagan presidency: a weakness for theater, a neglect of history and a narrowly conceived politics.

Commemorating victory over radical evil demands more than theater, history or politics. Among the purposes of remembrance are pedagogy (for those who were not there) and solace (for those too much there). But the highest aim of remembrance (for us, here) is redemption. The President and the Chancellor did indeed want this V-E day to bring some good from evil. But for that to happen at Bitburg will require more than two politicians. It will require an act of grace, and that is not for politicians — or other mortals — to dispense.

It is perhaps just as difficult to find redemption at Bergen-Belsen, but there is a difference. There the blood of Abel cries out from the ground. We cannot answer that cry, but listening for it is in itself a redemptive act. To imagine that one can do the same over the tomb of Cain is sad illusion.

The Roper Report on Opinion About Bitburg
October 15, 1985

By Milton Himmelfarb

SUMMARY

The major findings of the poll on Bitburg that Roper did for the American Jewish Committee are these:
Three months after Bitburg began to make news, two of five Americans felt either particularly good about President Reagan or were most critical of him on account of Bitburg. Of these, two were critical for every one who felt good — 28 and 14 percent, respectively.
Approval was *not* linked to anti-Semitism, nor disapproval with its absence. On the contrary, the young and the educated approved of Bitburg more than average, and they tend to be low in anti-Semitism. The elder and less-educated approved less than average, and they tend to be higher in anti-Semitism.

To determine the aftereffects of Bitburg on American opinion, the American Jewish Committee asked the Roper Organization to do a poll in July 1985, three months after the controversy about President Reagan's planned visit had started. The chief findings of that poll follow.

1. Respondents were asked which of seven policies or actions of President Reagan had made them feel either "particularly good" or "most critical" about him. Among these was "his visit to the German military cemetery at Bitburg." About Bitburg the ratio of "critical" to "good" was 2 to 1, 28 per cent to 14 per cent. Only "aid to the rebels in Nicaragua" and "moves to cut back on federal social programs" had higher ratios of disapproval to approval, 3.9 and 2.8 respectively.

Table I

	Feel good about Bitburg	Feel critical	Ratio of "critical" to "good"
All	14%	28%	2.0
Non-Jewish whites	14	26	1.9
Blacks	12	35	2.9
Men	12	32	2.7
Women	15	24	1.6
Age			
18-29	16	20	1.3
60+	12	30	2.5
At least some college	17	27	1.6
Non-high-school graduates	9	31	3.4
Liberal	14	24	1.7
Moderate	12	30	2.5
Conservative	15	29	1.9

*The higher disapproval ratio of blacks may reflect a generalized disapproval of Reagan.

* Polls consistently show men to be more hawkish and women more dovish. Bitburg was probably seen as a ceremony for burying the hatchet, because doves approved more than hawks.

*The young were born years after the end of World War II. The old remember it well.

* The educated probably saw Reagan's visit as a contribution to international amity and the healing of old wounds, and therefore to be approved. The less-educated are more nationalistic.

*For probably much the same reason, the disapproval ratio of liberals was a bit lower than of conservatives.

There was a *negative* rather than positive correlation between approval of Bitburg and anti-Semitism.

Educated Americans are known to be less anti-Semitic than uneducated ones, but the uneducated disapproved of Reagan's visit more than twice as much as the educated. Young Americans are known to be less anti-Semitic than the elderly, but the elderly disapproved of the visit twice as much as the young.

The conventional wisdom, as expressed for instance in William Bole's "Bitburg—Who Spoke Out, Who Didn't" (*Present Tense,* Summer 1985), was that liberals were more anti-Bitburg than conservatives. This poll shows the opposite, conservatives a little more anti-Bitburg.

2. The second question was about remembering things that had been in the news some time earlier, and again Bitburg was one of 7 items. The average for "remember a lot" was 40 percent. The figure for Bitburg was strikingly higher, 58 percent. In combined "remember a lot" and "remember something about," Bitburg was first. As was to be expected, more of the educated than of the less-educated said they remembered a lot—65 percent and 44 percent, respectively.

The high rate of remembering Bitburg could be due to its having received greater and more sustained news coverage than the other items that were listed.

3. The third question asked whether "the Holocaust is something we need to be reminded of annually, or do you think that after 40 years Jews should stop focusing on the Holocaust?" Only eleven chose "to be reminded" to the ten who chose "Jews should stop focusing on the Holocaust."

Table II

	Be reminded of Holocaust	Jews stop focusing	Ratio of "reminded" to "stop focusing"
All	46%	40%	1.2
Non-Jewish whites	47	40	1.2
Blacks	31	45	.7
Men	45	40	1.1
Women	47	40	1.2
Age			
18-29	47	38	1.2
60+	44	43	1.0
At least some college	52	35	1.5
Non-high-school graduates	38	44	.9
Liberal	55	31	1.8
Moderate	49	38	1.3
Conservative	43	45	1.0

Liberals and the educated were most in favor of being reminded. More blacks

and less-educated opposed than favored it, and even those most in favor fell below a 2-to-1 ratio for being reminded. There would appear to be a widespread desire to involve a kind of statute of limitations on being reminded of the Holocaust.

4. This emerges even more clearly with respect to finding Nazi war
criminals—"continue" vs. "the time has come to put it behind us."

Table III

	Continue efforts to find Nazi war criminals	Put it behind us	Ratio of "put it behind us" to "continue"
All	41%	49%	1.2
Non-Jewish whites	41	50	1.2
Blacks	30	49	1.6
Men	43	49	1.1
Women	40	48	1.2
Age			
18-29	39	48	1.2
60+	38	53	1.4
At least some college	43	48	1.2
Non-high-school graduates	37	50	1.4
Liberal	42	49	1.2
Moderate	44	46	1.0
Conservative	40	50	1.3

In not one of these categories did more people want to continue than to dis-
continue the search for Nazi war criminals. The most opposed to continuing the
search were blacks, the less-educated, and the elderly.

Query: Do non-Jews interpret Jewish insistence on continuing the hunt for
Nazi war criminals as further evidence for what they think they know about Judaism? "Everyone knows" that the Jewish God is a wrathful and vindictive God, and
the Christian God is a God of love and forgiveness.

5. The fifth and last question asked whether each of nine groups "make too
much fuss," or "too little fuss," or "responds in the right way" in the pursuit of its interests. Four of these groups are proponents of causes or ideologies. One was economic or occupational; farmers. The remaining four were racial, ethnic, or
religious: Hispanics, blacks, Catholics, and Jews. Jews came out sixth among all nine
as making too much fuss, and third among the four racial, ethnic, or religious
groups.

There is a relatively narrow range around the 19 percent of all respondents
who thought Jews make too much fuss, between a low of 26 and a high of 31 percent. Much of this seems to be explainable by the greater or lesser attention that

Table IV

Make Too Much Fuss

	Pro-abortion groups	Anti-abortion groups	Blacks	Women's rights	Hispanics	JEWS	Environmentalists	Catholics	Farmers
All	57%	57%	53%	51%	31%	29%	20%	18%	12%
Non-Jewish whites	58	57	58	53	32	30	21	18	13
Blacks	48	56	14	36	16	26	12	18	6
Men	57	57	56	54	33	31	24	19	15
Women	56	57	50	49	29	26	16	17	10
Age									
18-29	56	58	49	49	27	27	12	18	11
60+	55	55	54	53	34	29	24	13	13
At least some college	57	61	47	46	26	30	20	19	13
Non-high-school graduates	56	50	55	54	32	26	19	15	12
Liberal	55	64	47	41	28	28	16	20	12
Moderate	58	59	51	52	32	29	20	14	11
Conservative	58	54	58	56	33	30	23	30	13

different kinds of people pay to the media, and therefore to reports on the "fuss" of various groups.

For the perception of the fuss made by other groups, other explanations are also plausible—ideology, identification, sympathy, annoyance, and the like.

About Jews, it may be useful to look more closely at the variation in the responses of non-Jewish whites, and especially to look at the ratio of "responds in the right way" to "makes too much fuss."

Table V

	Jews make too much fuss	Jews respond in right way	Ratio of "right way" to "too much fuss"
All Non-Jewish whites	30%	47%	1.6
Men	32	46	1.4
Women	28	48	1.7
Age			
18-29	28	48	1.7
60+	30	45	1.5
At least some college	32	51	1.6
Non-high-school graduates	26	41	1.6
Liberal	28	50	1.8
Moderate	30	50	1.7
Conservative	31	46	1.5

The ratio of favorable ("responds in the right way") to unfavorable ("makes too much fuss") for all non-Jewish whites is 1.6, and the range is again quite narrow, from a low of 1.4 to a high of 1.8. Oddly, education here has no effect, both the most and the least educated having the same 1.6 ratio. The greatest differences are between the liberals' 1.8 and the conservatives' 1.5, and between the women's 1.7 and the men's 1.4.

As in most other polls, so in this, anomalies or contradictions are not lacking. Blacks, the elderly, and the less-educated were high in disapproval of Bitburg. Why were they also high in disapproval of remembering the Holocaust and continued effort to find Nazi war criminals?

Similarly, "anti-abortion groups" tied for first in being seen as "making too much fuss," with 57 percent, while Catholics were next to last, with only 20 percent. But though not all anti-abortionists are Catholic, nor all Catholics anti-abortionist, surely there is considerable overlap between the two. Yet one group is condemned, so to speak, and the other is exonerated.

A parallel is to be found in the 1984 National Survey of American Jews, conducted by Professor Steven M. Cohen for the American Jewish Committee. Jews rated blacks, conservatives, Catholics, mainstream Protestants, and fundamentalists Protestants—which is to say, Christians—as highest in anti-Semitism, and Democrats as lowest. But who are nearly all Democrats if not, precisely, blacks, Christians, and conservatives? (A plurality of Democrats call themselves moderate, but of the remainder more call themselves conservatives than liberal.)

Finally, a word about some technical matters. The sample consisted of 1997 respondents, including 217 blacks and 54 Jews. The non-Jewish white sample was the only one large enough to warrant comparison between relatively small subgroups. (Roper provided data for many more subgroups than were singled out for inclusion in this report.)

Only the question about groups that "make too much fuss" was asked of the entire sample. Of the others, the questions about feeling good or critical about Reagan on account of Bitburg were asked of half the sample, and the question about remembering past news events was asked of the other half. Likewise, the question about being reminded of the Holocaust was asked of one half, and the question about continuing the effort to find Nazi war criminals was asked of the other half.

Chapter 16

The American Press

Before Bitburg

Why the President Should Go to Bitburg
Los Angeles Times
April 17, 1985

By Jody Powell

The President now says that, during his trip to Germany in May, he will visit both a Holocaust site and the Bitburg cemetery, where German soldiers are buried. That is as it should be. The President ought to stick with his decision to go to Bitburg and lay his wreath for reasons that are both practical and philosophical.

On the practical side of the ledger, there is the incontestable fact that the decision was his. Though the usual campaign to blame it on someone else is well under way, such delicate matters are not left to staffers. The President checked off on this schedule knowing that it would be controversial. To back off now would undercut his carefully nurtured image of consistency and determination in the face of adversity.

Much worse, it would be a nasty rebuff to West German Chancellor Kohl and to his people. Kohl was already stung by the rejection of his request to be included in last year's ceremonies marking the 40th anniversary of the Normandy landings. The Bitburg visit was intended, in part, as recompense for that exclusion. For the President now to cave in to domestic political pressure would be far more embarrassing for Kohl than if the Bitburg visit had never been scheduled in the first place.

It is hardly in our interest to humiliate publicly one of our better friends on the continent at a time when the Soviets are cranking up another of their "peace" offensives — this time with a fellow in charge who looks like an effective salesman.

But there is more to it than geo-political calculations. It seems to me that what Reagan decided to do next month in Germany is right and proper on its own merits. To say that is not to question the motives or the sincerity of those who feel so strongly that it is wrong. Nor is it even to dispute the essential points of their argument.

There are soldiers of the Waffen SS buried at Bitburg. Such units were guilty of atrocities that far exceeded the usual quota of modern warfare.

The Nazi government that plunged the world into war almost half a century ago was different from other governments, more evil and sinister than, say, the Japanese government of that period or the German Imperial government that we fought in the first Great War. Thus, the war that destroyed the government was also different, and those differences ought to be — must be — remembered.

But memory is mankind's curse as well as its blessing. It can bind us in its coils as well as strengthen, inform, and uplift. By what we choose to remember and how, we decide whether we will be the master of our memories or their slave.

We fought World War II to excise the Nazi cancer, not to destroy the German nation or to scourge all Germans with suffering and death. For an American President to place flowers at the graves of German war dead does not detract from the honor of those Americans who died to defeat Fascism or diminish the horror of the Holocaust — unless we decide to make it so.

That wreath will not express sympathy or understanding or forgiveness for the bestialities of Hitler and his henchmen. It will say something more basic: that terrible loss is shared by all sides in war.

It can, if we let it, express our ability to understand and sympathize with the grief of the widow and the orphan, however abhorrent we find the cause for which the husband and father died. It can remind us that in war the individual virtues of courage and sacrifice and loyalty to one's comrades are often unrelated to the larger issues of the conflict, that the costs of a government gone amok can be particularly horrible for its own citizens. It can express our sympathy with the enduring sorrow of a nation for the better part of a generation lost, a loss made even more bitter by the unworthiness of the cause. Such an expression would be nothing more nor less than a reaffirmation of the basic humanity that should unite us all.

About Cemeteries
Wall Street Journal
April 19, 1985

Does Ronald Reagan remember the Holocaust? The answer to that question is undoubtedly yes. But if you think a lapse in memory is the reason the President is in so much political trouble over his proposed visit to a German military cemetery, you haven't delved into the intricacies of this latest Washington *cause celebre*.

Let's start at the beginning. May 8 is the 40th anniversary of V-E Day. Mr. Reagan will be in West Germany that week for the Bonn summit, and the White House wanted some nice gesture toward host Helmut Kohl so he would feel less like a 40th anniversary wallflower. The cemetery visit would recognize that the Germans also paid a heavy price for Hitler's ambitions and that 40 years on, the German are entitled to shed at least some of their guilts.

The Bitburg cemetery, with graves of youths as young as 14 who died in that last futile effort to defend the homeland, bears ample testimony to what World War II cost Germany. But by searching carefully, you also can find among the 2,000 markers some 30 graves of vicious SS storm troopers. Departing White House staffer Michael Deaver is getting the blame for not knowing those graves were there, or if he did, not foreseeing that they carried a different and dangerous kind of symbolism. When the news broke, even the American Legion turned against a President it has usually admired and joined the critics demanding to know how the President could be so insensitive to history as to spend part of his German trip honoring Nazis.

It is not at all plausible that the President, who clearly hates totalitarianism of any stripe, had even the slightest thought of honoring Nazis. But an emotional reaction to even the tiniest suggestion of that is understandable, especially since it came in the context of his decision not to visit a concentration camp. Mr. Reagan has now responded to this sensitivity by planning a stop as well at a German Holocaust site. Modern Germans will not have total absolution from the massive crime of the Austrian-born dictator of henchmen. But the criticism of the President continues.

For some, the wounds of the Holocaust cannot be healed even by 40 years, and this is understandable enough given the horror of the event. But if Mr. Reagan can be accused of insensitivity, some of his critics might be equally guilty of political cynicism. Mr. Reagan intended a friendly gesture toward the West Germans, who are after all an important link in the resistance to totalitarianism today. Some of his attackers are a great deal less concerned about the Holocaust than about exploiting any weak spot they can find in Mr. Reagan's political armor. The primary audience for this political endeavor is American Jews, torn between their predominantly liberal politics of the past and the modern appeal of hawkish neoconservatism.

In Europe there is an even nastier game afoot. For 40 years, Russia has been calling the democratic politicians of West Germany neo-Nazis. Even the Holocaust monument at Buchenwald, in East Germany, conveys that message in not-very-subtle-fashion. Just last weekend, the East German Communist Party managed to stage a V-E Day commemoration ceremony at that site with much reference to the Western "Nazis" and no mention at all of Jews. Americans attuned to the plight of Jews today in the Soviet Union won't find that particularly surprising.

Mr. Reagan walked into this buzz saw innocently, hoping that with a bit of symbolism 40 years after the fact, he could lay some of the ghosts of the past to rest. But the ghosts are not so easily banished. For some it is because their horrors can never be erased. For others, it is because they remain politically useful.

On Anniversaries
Universal Press Syndicate
April 20, 1985

By William F. Buckley, Jr.

The hassle over the itinerary of Mr. Reagan when he journeys to Europe invites reflection on anniversaries and what they reveal.

Ten years after V-E Day, we had just finished telling the Soviet Union, our wartime ally, that we didn't give a damn what they thought about it, we were going to conclude a peace treaty with West Germany (our wartime enemy), which we proceeded to do. We had been intimate friends of Adenauer, the leader of West Germany, from virtually the beginning. We wrote some stiff laws — no Germans would be allowed to publish and circulate Nazi propaganda. We hanged a few criminals (and were a little unhappy about doing so, since there were jurists who said we were violating our own constitutional guarantees against ex post facto justice).

At the other end of the world we also did a spot of hanging, but then propped up the same emperor under whose divine benediction the Japanese bombed Pearl Harbor and launched their ravenous war against Manchuria, China, the Philippines and Southeast Asia. But a few years of Douglas MacArthur and we were the fastest of friends, and five years after V-J Day we were sending American troops to defend, to their death, the South Koreans and the Japanese against communist aggression from North Korea.

How much easier it is to reconcile oneself with countries one has defeated, than with countries that have defeated us. True, the Germans and Japanese, though defeated, came around quickly, but that was because, in order to reconcile themselves with their own defeat, it was necessary that they should publicly abominate their older leaders. So that it was all but impossible, a year or two after the war's end, to find a German who professed veneration for Hitler, or a Japanese who professed veneration for Tojo. And so we became friends with people we struggled so hard to kill, in a war that brought death to 55 million people.

But 10 years after the Vietnam War, we do not recognize the government of Vietnam. And our own government has not changed: They are still Republicans, and Democrats running Congress, not communists or Maoists.

No one, on the 10th anniversary of the fall of South Vietnam, is suggesting that we have anything in common with the people who conquered South Vietnam, Laos and Cambodia — and, incidentally, the United States. Nor were we wrong in predicting what would happen if the North Vietnamese took over the South. Peter Berger, the sociologist and philosopher, has said resonantly that anyone who can't tell the difference between authoritarianism and totalitarianism could not tell the difference between Saigon and Ho Chi Minh City.

But the introspection to which we have been given, on this 10th anniversary of our defeat in Southeast Asia, devotes very little time — have you noticed — to the awful betrayal of 1975. We no longer stood to lose American soldiers in 1975. They were long since gone. But Congress stood there. President Ford begged it to act. Congress all but laughed at the call to redeem the pledges we had so solemnly made to the South Vietnamese after — as well as before — the Treaty of Paris. The general fit of iconoclasm, brought on by the unpopular war and exacerbated by the apparent moral insouciance of Richard Nixon in the matter of Watergate coarsened our sensibilities, so that instead of worrying how to redeem promises made, we worried about executive initiatives that might be taken to redeem those programs. In 1973 we voted $2.3 billion in aid of South Vietnam's armed forces. In 1974, we cut the figure in half; in 1975, by another third. Southeast Asia learned what it can mean to rely on the United States. And other countries have learned, though most of them have no alternative than to hope that the United States will live up to its obligations.

"Finally, however tragic the outcome," writes Professor John Roche, who served Lyndon Johnson during his Vietnam years, "I will argue to my dying day that this was the most idealistic war we have ever fought, fundamentally a war for an abstraction: the freedom of a bunch of unfamiliar Asians at the end of the world." How strange those sounds, which antedated the period during which the America intelligentsia for the most part persuaded itself that the Vietnam War was the high moment of immorality. But that high moment came not while we were fighting, but when we abandoned our wounded. For that reason the focus will be on Europe this season, not on Saigon, or Da Nang, or any cemetery in South Vietnam where the bones lie of men who trusted us.

The False Choice of Bitburg

New York Times
April 21, 1985

It is finally clear how President Reagan came to his Bitburg blunder and why his defense of it grows more repugnant by the day. His perception of the planned tribute to Germany's war dead begins and ends with a false dichotomy, bitterly expressed this week by one of Chancellor Kohl's closest aides.

"What are we?" the aide asked. "Are we primarily friends and allies, or are we primarily the children and grandchildren of the Nazis? At some point one has to decide."

Why? Why must I decide, the President should have replied when Chancellor Kohl posed the same choice last fall, no doubt more subtly.

Why are today's Germans good friends and allies? Because some of them, and most of their fathers and some of their grandfathers, having brought the world to ruin 40 years ago, then accepted America's tutelage and generosity and made much of them. What is most admirable about the new Germany is the moral distance it has traveled from the old. To ignore the old is to ignore what is so remarkable about the new.

Mr. Reagan, however, fell for the false taunt. As one of *his* close aides recalls him saying during the trip planning: "I don't think we ought to focus on the past. I want to focus on the future. I want to put that history behind me."

So the President decided no visit to a Nazi concentration camp, a decision changed only when the uproar arose over Bitburg. But even now, the President insists on Bitburg über alles, because the Chancellor is said to want it and because the President regards most of the men buried there as also victims of the Nazi regime.

Yes, many German soldiers were misled, or simply drafted, into supporting Hitler's war of conquest. But they died as combatants in battle, not as innocents, infants and elderly, in gas chambers. There can be tragedy in the death of soldiers, but who cannot distinguish between that and the systematic slaughter of millions?

Hitler himself made a further distinction that Mr. Reagan would now ignore by laying a wreath where some SS troopers also lie. The soldiers who had to kill or be killed, Hitler dressed in green. But the SS who designed and ran his death camps, he dressed in black, and with the telltale insignia of crossbones. That some of these criminals lie at Bitburg is not just an awkward circumstance. It makes a tribute at their graves indecent.

When Mr. Reagan, pressed for explanations, ran out of reasons, he endowed this cemetery ceremony with strategic portent. There's no way to shift the wreath-laying out of Bitburg now, he argued, because "all it would do is leave me looking as if I caved in in the face of some unfavorable attention." Where friends and allies are concerned, you see, presidents cannot retreat because adversaries are always taking their measure.

Good allies in Germany would relieve a president of this shameful sense of duty. But whatever they do, the President is prizing strength in an ugly cause. There are times when stubbornness is not strength, only perversity.

Bitburg Ron's Waterloo
Philadelphia Daily News
April 22, 1985

By Jack McKinney

The continuing controversy over Ronald Reagan's scheduled visit to a German military cemetery may have pierced the President's "mantle of invincibility" and dissipated his "aura of authority," according to at least one former administration aide.

David Gergen, who was White House communications director during Reagan's first term, offered that bleak observation early yesterday on ABC-TV's "This Week with David Brinkley."

Only hours later, Gergen's warning was amply confirmed in the angry words of Menachem Rosensaft, as he denounced the "outrage" of Reagan's planned cemetery visit before an estimated crowd of 17,000 participants in the American Gathering of Jewish Holocaust Survivors, in front of Independence Hall.

Ironically, I can remember when Menachem Rosensaft saw Reagan as a man who could be counted upon to redress outrage, not commit it.

At the time, Rosensaft was confident that when the opportunity presented itself the President would do everything in his power to help justice overtake the most infamous surviving Nazi war criminal, Dr. Josef Mengele.

That was in late November, when Rosensaft, as founding chairman of the International Network of Children of Jewish Holocaust Survivors, had just returned from Paraguay, where he'd headed a four-member delegation seeking that government's cooperation in determining the whereabouts of Mengele.

According to my notes from a phone conversation I had with Rosensaft then, he was "quite sure of President Reagan's willingness to bring Mengele to justice."

All that was needed, Rosensaft added, was "enough public pressure on Congress to make this a priority."

But from his remarks yesterday, it was obvious that Menachem Rosensaft had profoundly revised his estimate of the power of public pressure on Congress, or even the power of Congress itself, to set Reagan's priorities in order.

Fortunately, Rosensaft spoke *after* Sen. Arlen Specter, R-Pa., described Reagan as "a solid friend of Israel and a solid friend of the Jewish people."

Having offered that obligatory partisan defense, Specter then stretched partisanship beyond the absurd by suggesting that the controversy over Reagan's plan to lay a commemorative wreath in the Bitburg military cemetery—where at least 47 Nazi SS men are buried—might have already "stimulated a much broader understanding of the Holocaust...."

But as he told me last November, Rosensaft does not see the criminality of the Holocaust as a "subject that is political." He organized the International Network of Children of Jewish Holocaust Survivors four years ago to help ensure that this horrendous chapter in history would never be polluted by politics.

Rosensaft's parents were survivors of the Auschwitz death camp. His father died 10 years ago, but his mother is still haunted by memories of seeing SS Capt. Mengele selecting column after column of inmates for extermination simply by waving a baton.

Only two years after the liberation, Menachem Rosensaft himself was born in the very refugee facility that was erected on the Allied-razed site of the Nazi's Bergen-Belsen camp—a site Reagan now proposes to visit as a sop to those who are righteously outraged at his obsequious Bitburg agenda.

"President Reagan has allied himself with those who seek to forget, or even deny, the Holocaust," Rosensaft charged.

"If he insists on going to Bitburg, we don't want him at Bergen-Belsen. His presence would violate the sanctity of that mass grave."

Then, sweeping his eyes across the breast tags bearing the names and concentration camps of the survivors assembled before him, Rosensaft added:

"Today must be a holiday for all surviving Nazis! Josef Mengele must be laughing!"

Bitter as his message was, Menachem Rosensaft received an ovation for having the honesty to deliver it.

Decline and Send No Regrets
The Washington Post
April 23, 1985

By Mary McGrory

President Reagan cannot go to Bitburg. It is out of the question for the leader of the Western world to lay a wreath in a war cemetery where Nazi storm troopers are buried.

As Elie Wiesel, the most eloquent voice among Holocaust survivors, told him at the White House: "That place, Mr. President, is not your place. Your place is with the victims of the SS."

It is not longer important if Reagan "offends" the German people or "insults" his host, Chancellor Helmut Kohl of West Germany.

"The issue," Wiesel said, "is not politics, but good and evil."

The reason that Reagan must not go was put, in powerful terms, by Gideon Hausner, prosecutor of Adolf Eichmann, the fiend who presided, enthusiastically, over the extermination of millions of European Jews. The visit, Hausner said, "will be a victory for Adolf Hitler from beyond the grave."

No apology is needed. Explanations would be superfluous. Reagan should simply say he has cancelled the visit because it is wrong.

It is wrong, because as Menachem Z. Rosensaft of New York, chairman of the International Network of Children of Jewish Holocaust Survivors, stated: "The visit will be exploited by revisionist historians, neo-Nazis and their sympathizers."

Reagan says his purpose is "reconciliation." He has been persuaded by his partner in the blunder, Kohl, that Germans feel left out. Apparently the two had an emotional Oval Office meeting last November, in which Kohl tearfully begged Reagan to visit a German war cemetery.

Reconciliation has been the official policy of the U.S. government for 40 years. Through the Marshall Plan, we lifted a prostrate nation from its knees, sheltered, clothed and fed it, restarted its industrial engines. For 15 months, from June 1948 to September 1949, the Berlin airlift gave daily, thundering reassurance of the U.S. commitment to reconciliation with our former enemy.

Kohl found it wounding to be excluded from the Allied observances of Normandy last year.

Reagan, who is sentimental and much moved by a hard-luck story from an individual, decided to meet Kohl's needs. He looks at Germany and does not see the country that started two world wars, the second of which brought western civilization to the brink of extinction, but a valiant, industrious, God-fearing nation, which stands as a bastion against the communist hordes across its borders and which accepts missiles and praises "Star Wars."

Reagan's initial decision not to visit a Nazi death camp was in character. He likes pleasant settings, upbeat events. Dachau is a downer. And as is often the case when he adopts a point of view, he was carried away into fantasy and misstatement.

"And I felt since the German people—and very few alive that remember even the war and certainly none of them who were adults and participating in any way…they have a feeling and a guilt feeling that's been imposed upon them, and I just think it's unnecessary," he said in March.

Reagan's wrong. Twelve million Nazi-era Germans are alive. He cannot transform all of them into "good" Germans.

Those appalled by the cemetery visit—and they include U.S. war veterans who remember Bitburg as the staging area for the Battle of the Bulge—do not want to relive the past or endlessly punish the Germans. But they think it is "necessary" to remember anti-Semitism. Tolerated, it means ugliness. As a national policy, it leads to the gas chambers and ovens.

Reagan forever disqualified himself as someone who grasped what World War II was about when he said most of the German troops buried in Bitburg were teenage draftees and equated them with the millions of Jews and others who perished in the Holocaust—"victims just as surely as the victims in the concentration camp," he gratingly called the soldiers.

Kohl is equally inept with analogy. He exhorted a group of down-in-the-mouth German bankers to emulate Dietrich Bonhoeffer, who was hanged by the Nazis. Equating interest rates with eternity reveals a brotherly obtuseness.

Reagan's rejection of Wiesel's plea indicates a deafness to moral suasion. He might instead think about the "negatives." The protesters have promised that death camp survivors, their children and U.S. war veterans will be at the cemetery gates to greet him, thus setting up the most gruesome photo opportunity of his presidency.

The stated purpose, reconciliation, is being drowned in a rising flood of long-buried passions from the death camp survivors, who feel as betrayed and abandoned as they did 40 years ago. The add-on trip to Bergen-Belsen is to them a monstrous stop, a try at "even-handedness" as outrageous as what they see as the first step in rehabilitating their tormentors.

Bergen-Belsen: Lest We Forget The Others
The Christian Science Monitor
April 25, 1985

By Douglas MacArthur II

It is welcome news that President Reagan has revised his European schedule so as to visit Bergen-Belsen, one of the worst Nazi extermination camps, as a mark of respect for 6 million European Jews who perished in the Holocaust. While some had actively resisted the Nazis, most suffered terribly and died only because of their race.

At the same time we should never forget the thousands of non-Jewish Europeans also killed in Hitler's concentration camps. They included Germans, and particularly the European resistance members who fought actively against Nazi Germany at appalling risk to themselves and their families who also disappeared. Without the immense contribution of the "resistance" in Nazi occupied Europe, the success of the Normandy landings, the countering of the German V-1 buzz bombs, and other important Allied successes would have been infinitely more difficult and costly in lives and resources. So for those of us who worked with the "resistance" in German occupied Europe, the President's visit to a Nazi concentration camp has also a special meaning. In my case it evokes unforgettable memories because I was present at the liberation of one such camp — Dachau.

It happened because earlier as a member of the United States Embassy at Vichy during the German occupation of France, I had been privileged to work with several resistance groups. They kept us informed of German troop and Luftwaffe dispositions in France and the movements of German submarines and surface vessels operating from French ports. They smuggled downed U.S. airmen through France to safety in Spain. They had deeply penetrated the Pétain-Laval puppet government and were able to keep us up to date on German economic and industrial demands, which helped to pinpoint German shortages and weaknesses.

Shortly before the Pearl Harbor attack they gave us a copy of a secret telegram from the French authorities in Saigon (which the Japanese had occupied following the fall of France) reporting Japanese military preparations there for what appeared to be an amphibious operation which was believed aimed at Malaya or the Philippines. Alas, we failed to put this information to useful purposes!

Our activities in Vichy were terminated in late 1942 following the Allied landings in North Africa when the Germans shut down our Vichy embassy. We were taken to Germany as hostages, but our internment lasted only until the spring of 1944, when we were exchanged and repatriated. Just a bit later, in the summer of 1944, I found myself happily in France once again, but this time as a member of General Eisenhower's staff in Normandy and headed in the right direction toward Paris.

While hemmed in on the Normandy beachhead, we could get little information about our Vichy resistance friends, but once Paris was liberated, it was easy, as five members of the CNR (National Council of Resistance) were comrades from our Vichy days. The news they gave us was bad. Many of our friends had been picked up in the Gestapo drive of the winter of 1943-44. Some had been tortured and shot, others deported to concentration camps to the east. There was nothing we could do.

However, by April 1945 the final Allied drive had begun to overrun Hitler's concentration camps. At Buchenwald our "T" force found three French comrades alive. They all were ill but survived. Our joy was great but our fears and those of de Gaulle's government about the fate of the hundreds of the still missing increased. So in late April as General Patch's Seventh Army advanced into Bavaria toward Dachau, General de Gaulle gave us a list of about 180 outstanding resistance leaders who were missing. It was suggested that I be present at the liberation of the infamous Dachau camp and arrange for the speedy repatriation of any survivors on the list. I arrived at General Patch's headquarters near Augsburg and was told Dachau was being liberated with only light resistance from a few diehard guards and that I was to go in with the first medical team as soon as the shooting stopped.

I will never forget the spectacle as we entered the camp area. It was worse than a nightmare! On a rail siding near the camp entrance were freight cars filled with skeleton-like corpses, dead from thirst and starvation. They had been moved from a camp farther west and then left to die locked in the freight cars. The door of one car had been forced open and about thirty crawled a few yards before collapsing and dying.

The living inmates were too weak to move, lying on wooden shelves that served as bunks in the barracks. Others were propped up against walls outside.

It was against this backdrop that I sought out the leader of the French contingent and had one of the most moving experiences in my life. The Nazis segregated inmates by nationality and only dealt with the leader, generally chosen by his fellows for his character and leadership. I finally found him and his name was Edmond Michelet. He had survived torture and almost two years at Dachau.

I looked at my list; his name was at the top. He had been a leader in the "combat" resistance organization and I had worked with some of his comrades, including de Gaulle's first defense minister, P. H. Teitgen, whom we knew only as "Tristan" in Vichy days.

I showed Michelet the de Gaulle list and said I could arrange to airlift him and 24 others to Paris the next day, where a hero's welcome awaited him. I shall never forget the reply of this living skeleton. He looked at me with pained eyes and said: "Monsieur, I am the leader of the French group. I shall only leave Dachau when the last Frenchman, be he resistance member or not, has been repatriated to France or has succumbed here, for many are dying and will never make it." In Dachau there were over 3,000 Frenchmen. Instead of going home to a hero's welcome, Michelet stayed there six long weeks until the last Frenchman had gone home or died. What can one say about the courage of a man like Edmond Michelet, a man who remained at monstrous Dachau all those weeks when honors and a loving wife and seven adoring children awaited him in France.

Shortly after Michelet's eventual return to Paris, de Gaulle appointed him minister for former prisoners and deported persons. He brought to that post the same great Christian spirit that motivated his life.

Epilogue: In 1948 I was transferred from Paris to another post and saw no more of Michelet. Almost 20 years later, in November 1967, when I was serving in Vienna my telephone rang. A voice speaking in French said: "Douglas, this is Michelet. Do you remember me?" Did I remember him? How could I ever forget him, then or now!

In remembering the Jewish victims of Holocaust, let us also not forget the Nazis' other victims.

(Douglas MacArthur II, a lecturer and consultant on international affairs, has been the U.S. ambassador to Japan, Belgium, Austria, Iran, and was present at the liberation of Dachau.)

Penetrating Bitburg
Universal Press Syndicate
April 25, 1985

By William F. Buckley, Jr.

Concerning the turmoil caused by the impending visit to the cemetery at Bitburg, a few observations:

Mr. Reagan's visit to Germany was originally conceived as a memorial to the ending of a world war in which the United States and its allies defeated Nazi Germany. In defeating Hitler, we made wonderful things possible. Immediately—and foremost among them in human importance—was the liberation of 300,000 Jews in concentration camps who, if the Allies had arrived say one month later, might have been dead. But there were other benefits: the liberation of entire peoples subjected to the hideousness of Hitler's rule. And, for America and its allies, it meant tne end of a war in which 50 million people had been killed. That epochal event—the end of the end of the war, the end of Hitler—was the commemorative objective of the Reagan visit.

The suggestion of co-celebrating the deliverance of Jewish survivors naturally arose, but that deliverance ought not to have taken center stage in the business of nations. We know that the chancellor of West Germany asked the President to visit a German military cemetery. Helmut Kohl meant to ask Ronald Reagan to confirm that German conscript soldiers should not be thought of as a killer class. Reagan agreed, and in agreeing did the conventional thing. De Gaulle and Adenauer, in a great feat of statesmanship, had agreed a generation ago to bury their historical hatchet. The approach by Sadat of Egypt to Begin of Israel was in that enlightened tradition.

It transpired that buried in the cemetery of Bitburg, amidst the 2,000 conventional German soldiers, were the bodies of 47 SS troopers. SS Nazis were the sadistic elite guard of Hitler's most evil designs. The advance man for Reagan, Michael Deaver, did not know that there were SS corpsmen buried among the thousands of regular German troops. What were the alternative courses of action?

- The visit to Bitburg could have been cancelled.
- The bodies of the SS men might have been removed to another site (not a difficult logistical feat).
- Mr. Reagan could have taken the position that the SS men's presence in the cemetery was not a decisive factor.

Mr. Reagan took the last of the alternative courses of action, but in explaining himself he used a vulnerable formulation. He said that the contentious corpses, in that they were young recruits of the Nazis' dying days, "were victims just as surely as the victims in the concentration camps."

Now in terms entirely logical, Reagan was quite right. If a drunken driver runs over first a dog, and then a child, a judge might well rule that the dog was just as surely a victim of the drunken driver as the child. Would he mean by such reasoning that a soldier killed in combat is someone whose fate one grieves over exactly as one grieves over a child (or his mother) being led into an execution chamber by a Nazi guard? Obviously not; though Mr. Reagan should have avoided a formulation that lent itself, by careless thinkers and polemical opportunists, to misunderstandings.

But the storm has centered on the suggestion that because Reagan is willing to visit a cemetery in which a few SS guards were buried, it follows that he is insensible to the distinctive horrors of the Holocaust. That position isn't defensible. We do not take totalist, eternal positions, else we would not acknowledge Germany, which was once Hitler's, as an ally. We shook hands with Stalin in order to defeat Hitler: there are surely as many gulag survivors legitimately infuriated that we should have done that as there are survivors of the Holocaust grateful that we did take the aid of Stalinist troops to hasten the end of Hitler.

454 THE AMERICAN RESPONSE

When one visits a cemetery intending to make a general point, one cannot exact a moral pedigree of every one of its occupants. Jack the Ripper is buried somewhere, one supposes, probably in consecrated ground. A pious gesture at the Tomb of the Unknown Soldier is not to be confused with an exonerative blessing on those unknown soldiers who, in life, were sadists.

A little-known scholar, Jack Jones, wrote 20 years ago that there is only one trenchant way to honor the memory of those who died in the Holocaust, and that is to pledge that we will struggle not to let such things happen again. But such things continue to happen. At the hands of those who preside over with great precision what the center of the current controversy has called "an evil empire." Eli Wiesel should applaud Mr. Reagan for continuing the struggle to keep us conscious of holocausts, major and minor, that continue their grisly course, as in Cambodia, as in Nicaragua, as in Afghanistan.

Bitburg is a Long Way From Arlington
New York Post
April 26, 1985

By Dorothy Rabinowitz

Who says April is the cruelest month? This must be the question they're asking one another at the Kremlin, for which May promises to be better still.

For it is in May that the Soviets will be receiving — if all goes as the President and Helmut Kohl say it will — a gift beyond imagining: the Bitburg trip.

Could the Soviet propagandists — those folk who have spent so many years portraying the U.S. as a friend of fascism — have conceived in their wildest dreams such an opportunity: that there would be granted to them actual footage of a U.S. President paying homage at the graves of Hitler's soldiers?

Nor could the rest of us have imagined that we would be hearing from official Washington such rejoinders — such explanations — as came this week.

This affair began, we are informed, because Chancellor Kohl cried in Ronald Reagan's office.

It proceeded with White House aide Michael Deaver and a retinue of 20 going to Germany, where — we are further informed — advance man Deaver was accorded the rare honor of a meeting with the chancellor.

The gratified Deaver proceeded apace to Bitburg, where a heavy snow prevented him, and his retinue of 20, from noticing SS insignia on the gravestones.

Deaver and party returned home thus secure in the belief that Bitburg posed no problems for a Presidential visit—and under the impression that American soldiers *too* lay buried at Bitburg.

Once the Bitburg plans were announced, it was discovered, alas, that the cemetery—where headstones were already being polished in honor of the Presidential visit—contained the bodies of some of Hitler's Waffen SS, and that it contained no bodies of American soldiers.

Thus ends the official outline of events—an outline, it seems necessary to say, that is not some product of satire but the exact reasons put forward in explanation of the Bitburg choice.

This alone should give us pause. Who among our officials in his right mind—and having the slightest acquaintance with history—would actually believe that American fighting men of World War II would lie buried in a German military cemetery?

Of the gravestones of the SS, snow-covered or otherwise, much has already been said—far too much—an uproar that obscures the truth that a Presidential visit honoring Hitler's regular troops—who fought side by side with the SS—would hardly have been more acceptable had there been no SS around.

What would have happened had the SS markings been visible at Bitburg, and in the unlikely event that this was a sight that would have troubled Deaver? Deaver, we are informed, would certainly have sought another military cemetery—one *without* SS graves.

Only there *are* no military cemeteries in Germany that do not have SS graves, as one West German has pointed out. This is as it should be: the inextricable mingling in death, as in life, of these two arms of Hitler, who fought together and died together, that the night of Nazism might fall on the world.

Not that such facts have any impact on White House spokesmen and others involved in "damage control."

Take Republican Congresswoman Marjorie Holt of Maryland, who told a reporter, "Every place we go, we bring people to Arlington Cemetery. . . I can't see any difference."

Then came a sortie from Donald Regan, speaking in private with a White House visitor who was urging cancellation of Bitburg, in reply to which urging the President's chief of staff repeatedly challenged, "Would you object if Chancellor Kohl visited Arlington?"

Here we have not just a congresswoman but the President's own chief of staff, neither of whom sees any difference, symbolically, between the burial grounds of those who died for Nazism—and Arlington.

What is wrong with these people?

In letters to the *Washington Post* and the *New York Times*, author William Shirer ("The Rise and Fall of the Third Reich") wrote with some emotion that, of the hundreds of German soldiers he talked to as a war correspondent in the last, as well as the earliest, days of World War II, he found not *one* who "considered himself 'a victim of Nazism'," not one of those teenagers (the kind cited in Reagan's address) who "did not express his utter loyalty to Hitler and the Third Reich," who did not "believe fanatically in Hitler's cause."

Such testimony, along with so much like it, will, from the looks of things, fall on deaf ears—for a while, at any rate. So, while everyone waits for Kohl to come to his senses, or the President to his, we shall continue to hear the maunderings about Arlington and Bitburg, and of the advance men's progress around Bergen-Belsen.

Even so, though it will be hard to convince the administration of this, some good has come of the Bitburg business. That good made itself evident in the strong popular reaction against the trip, a reaction which proves that—though our century's history, and its meaning, may have escaped all concerned at the White House—it has not escaped most Americans.

So clear was the evidence of this feeling—this memory of why the war against Hitler could not be considered a war like any other—this feeling that recalled why Gen. Dwight Eisenhower stared icily past the saluting Germans during the surrender in Reims—that it moved a West German official to recognize, with wonder, "how quickly history comes breaking through."

So it does. And for this convincing proof—which is a tribute to Americans—we can be grateful to the architects of Bitburg.

Liberalism Berserk
Universal Press Syndicate
April 27, 1985

By William F. Buckley, Jr.

Can you make any sense of it?

Forty years ago, after fighting a great war in which there were close to 1 million U.S. casualties, we defeated Hitler. We went on to sponsor, politically and economically, the democratic rebirth of one-half of the German state. The other half we let the Soviet Union take over, and it is today a state not significantly different from what it would have been if Hitler had continued to rule over it. There is no political vice practiced under Hitler that is not also practiced under the German pro-consuls of Stalin and his successors. The genocide is muted, though the anti-

Semitism is rife. (At the commemoration of Buchenwald last week, communist officials made no mention of the Jews as special victims of that camp.) In various forms, Gulag continues. No one puts at under 20 million the victims of Gulag; others arrive at plausible figures as high as 50 million.

There has not been a revival of Nazi sentiment in West Germany, and explicit pro-Nazism there is at the crank level, the equivalent of Ku Klux Klan activities in the United States. And yet there is a national furor over an American President, at the beckoning of a Christian Democratic West German chancellor, visiting a military graveyard containing the bodies of German soldiers, 3 percent of whom were members of the SS.

Two things are significant about Hitler and his death camps. The first is that Hitler was Hitler—reminding us of the long reach of human perversity. The second is that by act of sacrifice and will, we stopped Hitler.

Now although there is no revival of Hitlerism in Germany, there is Hitlerism abounding elsewhere, except that it goes by another name: communism. At this moment, the Soviet state is enforcing its will on the Afghan people by the use of Hitlerian-Stalinist methods: torture, genocide, starvation, the use even of chemical warfare. Minor efforts by neighboring Pakistan to provide refuge for some of Gorbachev's victims is met by direct threats against Pakistan by the Soviet Union. The U.S. government does little to help Afghanistan, and whatever we do, we do apologetically.

Meanwhile, in Nicaragua, the same people who gave us Castro in Cuba, and who pursue and kill Afghans who wish to be free, strike their salient. And the House of Representatives denies the motion to help that little band of dissidents who wish to contain the rising Hitlerism in their midst. So that at the same moment that we despise Reagan for consenting to visit an un-deNazified military cemetery of men dead 40 years, we decline to help men still alive, whose days are probably numbered, in Afghanistan and in Nicaragua.

Charles Krauthammer in *Time* magazine says, in protesting the visit to Bitburg: Can't we understand that Hitler's was a criminal state? Yes, we can understand that. But Hitler's state is dead, and another criminal state is very much alive, and against it there is no animus being fed by establishmentarian American moralists. They are too busy protesting the policies of South Africa. These are abominable. But South Africa would need to import East Germans to show them how to build a wall around its frontiers to keep black immigration down to controllable levels.

One month ago, an American officer doing routine things was shot dead by a Soviet soldier in East Germany. We got the opposite of an apology. The Soviets have said it might well happen again, it was right that it did happen, and that no reparations would be forthcoming. A year and a half ago the same government shot down an unarmed passenger plane, killing 269 people in cold blood; followed only by wild charges that the Korean airliner was a U.S. spy plane. That government continues to rule over Eastern Europe, and to press its aggressions against countries as far from one end of Moscow as Nicaragua, as far from the other end of Moscow as Cambodia.

The same American congressmen and senators who gasp for air in protest against the morally asphyxiative agreement by Reagan to make a gesture as far removed from overtones of forgiveness for those responsible for the Holocaust as a visit to a Civil War cemetery in the South is removed from an endorsement of slavery, blithely ignore the pleas of what one might call Nicaraguan Jews, asking for help in their own struggle to prevent the rise of Hitlerism in their own midst. Some dare call this moral idiocy.

Enough War Guilt
The Washington Post
April 28, 1985

For My Young German Friend's Sake, I'm Glad Reagan is Going

By June Tierney

I am glad President Reagan is going to Bitburg. I am an American who lived in Germany from the time I was in Kindergarten until 11th grade. I attended German schools, learned the language, made many German friends and learned something about how young Germans think about Hitler and the war.

For my friends' sake, I am glad the President declared last month that it was "unnecessary" to impose further feelings of guilt upon the Germans.

And whatever the drawbacks of the President's visiting that particular cemetery in Bitburg, it is an important gesture to my former classmates. I feel I owe it to them to tell the world how their heads would bow in shame at the mention of Hitler, and to describe the courage with which they accepted the responsibility for crimes they didn't commit.

Their sense of remorse surpasses anything I've seen displayed by my American peers when they're reminded of *our* nation's sins: the Indians massacred in the name of manifest destiny; the blacks enslaved to pick cotton, and the Japanese-Americans dispossessed and interned during World War II.

Young Germans do not need further reminders from us of their nation's war guilt. We Americans appear to have forgotten that we are allied with a new generation of Germans—Germans who have undergone 40 years of penance and are now, more than ever, in need of a signal that their nation's crimes, while they will never be forgotten, will not be held against them.

In 1969, my recently-divorced mother took me and my sister to Germany. It was supposed to be a three-month visit with my grandfather from Arizona who had a job in Munich with Radio Free Europe. But my mother liked Germany, and we ended up staying 11 years.

The day we arrived in Munich, we drove through the streets in a taxicab and my grandfather pointed out the *Friedensengel*, the statue of the "angel of peace." The angel's wing was bent, and grandfather explained, "That happened under Hitler, during World War II. The angel was hit by a bomb."

The name Hitler meant nothing to me, but I noticed how our cab driver suddenly gripped the steering wheel with both hands and fixed his eyes on the road.

I was about to ask who this Hitler was, but my mother preempted my question with a snap of her fingers, which meant, "We'll talk about it later."

That night, she tucked me into bed and told me about Adolf Hitler. I went to sleep, terrified by what I'd heard about an evil madman, who killed millions of Jews and single-handedly started a very big war.

Once I'd heard about Hitler, I wanted to know more. But by the time I entered second grade in a German school, I'd learned that my playmates weren't the people to ask about him. Hitler's name was more offensive to them than any dirty word I had learned on the playground. They would shrug at my questions and kick a hole in the ground until I changed the subject.

After World War II, West Germans accepted the blame. Its government decided that the best way of coming to terms with the past was to pass on to the next generation a legacy of guilt.

The concentration camps have been preserved because they are considered the supreme, irrefutable proof of German war guilt—*Kriegesschuld*. Each year, German educators send as many children as they can on field trips to the death camps. Participation is mandatory. Once the students have walked through the gas chambers and have inspected for themselves the charred furnaces, they are considered ready to assume their share of Germany's guilt.

Until then, though, German kids aren't invited to ask questions about Nazi Germany. As youngsters, they are conditioned by parental frowns never to mention Hitler's name without a sober expression on their face.

But behind their faces, I learned, was the same curiosity and fascination I felt about Hitler. Although it seemed to be forbidden, my German friends and I started looking for clues.

We looked for Hitlers in the phone book, but found none. The Führer's Munich headquarters had been around the corner from our apartment building. From the street, we could see the boarded-up sixth floor windows. We tried to go upstairs, but the staircase was blocked.

In school, we dared each other to draw swastikas on the blackboard and leave them there for the teacher to see. We wanted to watch her reaction. One day, my classmate Clemens was sent to see our principal because he persisted in asking why no one in the school was named Adolf. Clemens was also the kid who found the full lyrics to the Nazi national anthem—and taught them to the whole class. When we were caught singing it during recess, the class was severely reprimanded.

By seventh grade, however, pranks related to Nazism began losing their interest. As seventh graders, we were issued our first "adult" history books. Even though World War II is a 10th-grade history subject, we read the chapters toward the back of the book which dealt with Nazi Germany. They were accompanied by pictures of Hitler and concentration camps, which we spent hours gaping at in disbelief. Seventh grade was the year my classmates started asking their relatives specific questions about World War II—questions that could no longer be dismissed as childish audacity.

Barbara and Tina, two seventh-grade classmates, spent an afternoon at my house listening to Paul McCartney and the Wings, munching on pretzel sticks and gossiping about our math teacher.

He had a little black mustache and a tendency to turn very red when yelling at students for misbehaving. We were rehearsing a scene that week when he had yelled at us for sitting on a window ledge during recess.

Tina and I were giggling because we'd agreed that he must have been a member of the Hitler Youth—we figured that was where he had learned to trim his mustache and make his face turn red.

Our joke must have jarred a thought in Barbara. She had a strange, blank expression as she said, "You know, my father doesn't believe any of that ever happened."

I popped a pretzel stick in my mouth while Tina asked Barbara what she meant by "any of that." I gagged on my pretzel when Barbara answered, "I mean all that stuff about the Jews. I asked him about the concentration camps," she said, fingering her stringy blond hair and squinting with uncertainty.

"But he said they never existed. When I showed him the picture in our history book, he said it was a forgery." She added quickly, "But I don't believe him."

Barbara's story was eventually spread to every member of our class, prompting others to talk about what they were finding out at home. Some kids said their grandfathers refused to talk about the war and their experiences. Others reported that their fathers had shown them their red Hitler Youth scarves and the swastika armbands that had been part of their uniforms. One kid said his father had made him swear he wouldn't tell anyone about the autographed picture of the fuehrer that was kept at home.

Sometimes our teachers would overhear our speculations about the Hitler time, and start discussions in class about World War II. The talks always ended with a reminder that Germany alone was to blame for the war. My classmates would bow their heads and stare at their desks, while I would look around, unable to identify with their guilt, but aware than an oppressive mood had settled over the classroom.

In 1980, when I was 16, I had observed this phenomenon of bowed heads for a number of years. Still, I was unprepared for what I saw the day our class sponsor announced the annual 10th-grade field trip to Dachau, a concentration camp on the outskirts of Munich. It was time for the excursion that is meant to impress upon people like Clemens, Barbara and Tina the horror and magnitude of the crimes their people committed against humanity.

When the sponsor announced the trip, all heads in the room were bowed, except mine. This time, however, as I scanned the room, I saw some of my classmates look up at me in anger, as if I had caught them naked. For the first time, all of us were conscious that I was a foreigner—an American—who was intruding on their masochistic display of guilt and shame.

As the significance of the trip to Dachau was being explained, I saw my neighbor twisting a handkerchief around her fingers so tightly that her nails were turning blue. When the explanation was over, I raised my hand, intending to ask permission to be excused from the excursion, but I couldn't speak. I was still clearing my throat when the sponsor of the trip said, "Miss Tierney, you don't have to accompany us, unless, of course, you wish to . . ." I stayed home from school that day.

Are the West Germans making a mistake in imposing *Kriegesschuld* on each new generation? Some say it is necessary for a country to be acutely aware of its past. But others say it is a mistake—and perhaps politically dangerous—to make each generation responsible for the crimes of its predecessors.

John Gagliardo, a professor who teaches German history at Boston University, says that it is necessary for any country to be conscious of its past, but that is unfair and risky to make the heirs feel directly responsible. "Whenever you build a mandatory guilt feeling into a conscience, be it individual or national, you are creating a situation that demands release—release from the tension of always being guilty, of being irredeemable. Ultimately it leads to denial, because denying the past is easier than bearing the guilt."

Will young Germans go on feeling guilty? Or will they, at some point, find it more than they can handle and seek a release in nationalism?

In the summer of 1984, I returned to Munich and had a conversation that left me wondering if perhaps *Kriegesschuld* is pushing young Germans in just such a direction. The conversation took place over tea with my ninth-grade biology teacher, who almost flunked me for reading a magazine instead of taking notes on the reproductive cycles of amphibians.

She is a small, feisty woman of 42 who delights in arguments. Her turquoise eyes would sparkle while bartering with students who challenged her right to lecture against cruelty to animals when she was known to wear a fox wrap during the winter.

Her eyes were sparkling as we sat over tea and cherry strudel. She listened to me complain about Ronald Reagan's flag-waving campaign. "I think it's disgusting," I said. "It kills me to see how Americans are so tickled with his flag propaganda."

I wasn't looking at her when she answered me. "I think it's great to see America standing so tall again," she declared. I thought she was joking, but when I looked up, her eyes were solemn. Touching my arm lightly, she said: "I wish that you would infect our kids with some of that 'flagomania.'

Exasperated, I blurted out, "But isn't this what you wanted—a new Germany of citizens who are so ashamed of their past they they vow to kill themselves before they let it happen again?"

She pressed my arm urgently. She bowed her head and then almost whispered, "Oh yes. They've turned out the way we wanted them to. The problem is, we've been too successful. The guilt—it's more than they can bear. And you know, it's not really theirs."

What Transcends Bitburg
New York Times
May 2, 1985

By McGeorge Bundy

Seventy-two percent of the West Germans want President Reagan to go through with his visit to the Bitburg cemetery; 55 percent of Americans think he should not. It has taken 40 years to do it, but our leaders finally have managed to set majorities of their countries against each other. Or so it seems. Fortunately, the underlying reality is different, as we can see if we turn from the controversial visit and look at what people in both countries really care about.

These apparently opposing majorities may have different first thoughts, but they are not divided on fundamentals. What the West German majority wants is that an American President should recognize the enormous, tragic loss of life in the generation of young Germans who fought the war that Hitler made, and perhaps also the truth that among those who died there were millions of brave, decent men. Does an American majority object to such recognition? I doubt it.

What has turned Americans against the visit is the 49 graves of Waffen SS members and the pain that is thus created, among millions of Americans, Jews and non-Jews, by the thought that anyone, anywhere might wish to forget what the SS as a whole was and did. Do most Germans disagree? I am sure they do not. Nothing has been more remarkable in the extraordinary civic decency of the West Germans over these 40 years than their unflinching recognition of the Holocaust as Hitler's most monstrous crime, and of the guilt shared by all who had any part in it.

It is not the West German and America peoples, but a single insensitive arrangement, that has now put their shared values in apparent opposition. We may regret the insensitivity, but we must not let it divide us where we are not in truth divided. The President's wreath will be intended to honor decent men for decent reasons, and the German commitment to respect the memory of the Holocaust will not end because of a poor choice of cemeteries for this gesture.

I am sure Chancellor Helmut Kohl and President Reagan will do their very best to find the right words to express all that has brought us together since 1945—in dangers shared and surmounted, in understanding of what friendship is and requires, above all in our common commitment to a shared freedom. Meanwhile, it may help us all to keep in mind, that good things do not come free. In the words of Goethe, with which John F. Kennedy ended a speech in Paulskirche, in Frankfurt, 22 years ago: "He only earns his freedom and existence who daily conquers them anew."

One Last Try
Universal Press Syndicate
May 4, 1985

By William F. Buckley, Jr.

For the record, a forlorn attempt on the eve of the Bitburg ceremony to enunciate what ought to be accepted as the considerations that now sit on the table.

1. Was the Bitburg visit, in retrospect, worth it? The answer to that clearly is no. Given what has happened during the past fortnight, it would have been better if the invitation had never been issued; that if it had been issued, it had not been accepted.

2. But failed diplomacy is not an argument against diplomacy. Many of the same people who have been exhausting themselves in indignation over Mr. Reagan's acceptance of Chancellor Kohl's invitation to memorialize the reconciliation between Americans who were killed by Germans and Germans who were killed by Americans in a great war were furious with Ronald Reagan for not attending, in the name of diplomacy, the funeral services of Yuri Andropov, chief of govern-

ment of the Soviet Union.

Now Andropov was the head of the KGB over a period of 15 years. As such, he was responsible for cruelty as hideous, as relentless, as what was done by Himmler. One shouldn't evaluate ultimate evil on the basis of raw mathematical figures. If Prince Rainier rounded up every Jew in Monaco, stuck them in a crematorium, burned them and tortured their children, he would be as evil as Himmler even if there were only 50 Jews in Monaco. Gulag had shrunk by the time Andropov was put in charge of it, but it continued under him, and continues today, an awesome institutional presence, the backbone of Soviet discipline, the means by which an evil empire maintains peace at home.

So why do many civilized people want to send a president to lay a wreath on the grave of a man who grew up in the KGB and became its head? Because diplomacy becomes, at a certain level, the primary objective. If there is an act of horror Mao Tse-tung did not commit during the Cultural Revolution (and before), it testifies only to his occasional forgetfulness. But when Richard Nixon toasted Mao Tse-tung in 1972, the liberals in America cheered, in the name of Realpolitik.

3. When Reagan was asked by Kohl to visit a military cemetery to symbolize his agreement that not only German soldiers were buried there, but also a historical antagonism between the German state and the American state, Reagan agreed. The notion that burying the war with Nazi Germany was the equivalent of burying our detestation of Hitler and his works quite simply did not occur to him, and did not occur to Kohl.

4. Why? That, surely, is the most interesting question to ask at this juncture. Well, the reason it did not occur to anyone to suspect that a wreath laid at a military cemetery—even one that, it transpired, had in it the graves of 49 Waffen SS— mitigates in some way the hideousness of Hitler's crimes is, really, quite obvious. It is that no one seeks to mitigate that hideousness. Oh, sure, you can find someone maybe in Bavaria, someone in Indiana and someone in Bellevue, and maybe prop them up for an appearance on "60 Minutes," who will tell you that Hitler was OK. But these are not forces that shape international diplomacy. These are moral idiots.

The great paradox of the current commotion is that it suggests that the Holocaust is in some way defensible. If it is not defensible—which is the American position, as also the German position—then how is it that some speak and write as though the President's appearance at Bitburg has the effect of condoning the activities of the SS? How can one condone that which is uncondonable? If a bishop, or a consul officer, were to go to Jonestown and there lay a wreath on the graves of those wretched men, women and children who followed the Antichrist to a demonic death, would that have the effect of mitigating the case against Jim Jones?

5. Henry Kissinger and Richard Nixon advised Mr. Reagan to defy the hysteria and to proceed with the original design. These old soldiers know about Realpolitik, and have been applauded for their practice of it. We can all wish that the whole enterprise had not been crafted, if only because emotional grief and convulsion would have been avoided. But it is surely better, at this stage, to proceed to prove

that one can lay a wreath in a German military cemetery without legitimizing concentration camps. It would be good to reassure ourselves that nobody, anywhere, doing anything, could retroactively justify one of the supreme horrors of the century.

After Bitburg

Another 40 Years
New York Times
May 5, 1985

By Flora Lewis

BITBURG, WEST GERMANY — President Reagan's visit to the site of the Bergen-Belsen concentration camp and then to the German military cemetery here was to symbolize what has changed 40 years after the defeat of the Third Reich.

There was a series of amazingly clumsy mistakes and ugly undertones in arranging all this. But it has served to highlight both how far the world has moved and how much remains essentially the same.

In 1962, on the occasion of President Charles de Gaulle's dramatic trip of French-German reconciliation, the Social Democratic politician Carlo Schmidt, who had been an anti-Nazi exile, wrote: "If de Gaulle shakes hands with us, then our hands are no longer dirty. After everything that has happened, we could not after all grant ourselves absolution."

Twenty-three years later, Chancellor Helmut Kohl, who was 15 when the war ended, showed that the German craving remains. But no one can grant absolution, including President Reagan.

Alois Mertes, the Bundestag deputy from Bitburg, told Mr. Reagan: "We Germans have provided mankind with great and splendid accomplishments, but we have also committed terrible acts. However, it is not in keeping with Jewish and Christian ethics to apportion blame collectively. It is always the individual who bears responsibility." That should be accepted.

And it is why President Reagan was wrong to speak repeatedly of "one man's totalitarian dictatorship," "the awful evil started by one man." He never pronounced the name of Adolf Hitler, or the word genocide.

But it was not one man who killed so many millions. That myth should not be allowed to grow. It is not even quite true, as Mr. Reagan said, that "we can mourn the German war dead today as human beings, crushed by a vicious ideology." No one dies abstractly.

What must be true, for all, is Mr. Reagan's concluding pledge at Bergen-Belsen: "Never again."

The 40 years have transformed the world in many ways, especially Germany. It is hard now to revisualize the charred rubble fields of the cities, even though I saw them myself soon after the war. In the whole city of Cologne, near Bonn, 300 houses were left undamaged. In Düsseldorf, 98 percent of the homes were uninhabitable. Ravaged Berlin was left with 170 women for every 100 men.

It didn't require a conscious will for reconciliation or forgiveness to offer food to the old women who fainted from hunger on the street. It didn't matter what ideology they believed. Our own human instincts mattered, and still do.

Now, this is a prosperous country, capable of generosity to those who are starving in other parts of the world. It lives in freedom. But it is a troubled country, because of the past lying beneath the bright skyscrapers and beflowered city streets and the named and nameless graves, because of a present that keeps part of the Germans on the other side of an armored line, because of an uncertain future.

No one could have foreseen the well-being and friendships now enjoyed. They, too, are the result of many individual responsibilities. They were not inevitable. Neither is the future.

Mr. Reagan spoke a good deal about the "totalitarian darkness" that remains in the world. While he did not mention the Soviet Union, that was clearly his meaning. And he spoke of peace.

There have been some 140 armed conflicts since World War II, but the peace has been kept in Europe, so long the tinderbox of conflagration. Not all wars are caused by ideology. The human yearning for tranquility can still be outmatched by human greed, human stupidity, vengeful human fears and the appetite for power.

It is not enough to proclaim the best intentions and to denounce the adversary. Peace must be won by mutual effort, sober judgment, the prudence of the wise. It certainly doesn't help to compare the dismal, repressive Communist regimes of today to Nazi Germany. That sounds too much like another crusade.

If there is to be a celebration of 80 years of peace one day, and there must be or there will be nothing, it is the responsibility of leaders on both sides now. The lesson is the simple old one that war is hell.

Right Dumps Reagan on Bitburg

The Village Voice
May 7, 1985

By James Ridgeway

Washington — President Reagan's intransigence on Bitburg brings to mind his attacks on Walter Mondale last fall and the cynicism with which politicians in both parties exploit Jewish sentiments. A few days before the election, Reagan said Mondale lacked the "moral courage" to condemn anti-Semitism, and criticized Democrats for not passing a resolution at their convention condemning "this insidious cancer." The President raised eyebrows when he told one Jewish audience that the marines had been sent to Beirut to prevent another Holocaust of Jews, not, as it was commonly thought at the time, to prevent the slaughter of Palestinians by Christian Phalangists and to help Gemayel.

George Bush also plays fast and loose with "moral courage." Immediately before last year's Pennsylvania primary Vice-President Bush went after the three candidates for the Democratic nomination charging they had failed to issue strenuous condemnation of anti-Semitism. "Whom the Democrats pick is their business," Bush told the annual policy conference of American Israel Public Affairs Committee. "But some matters transcend party and concern the basic traditions of our republic."

He was talking about Jesse Jackson's refusal to dissociate himself from Louis Farrakhan. "But as shocking as I find Reverend Jackson's behavior," Bush continued, "I cannot understand why Walter Mondale and Gary Hart have not continued to speak out loudly and clearly against this."

In a last-minute pitch for the Jewish vote last fall, Bush attacked the Democratic party for being soft on anti-Semitism. Speaking to the annual convention of the Zionist Organization of America, Bush asked why the Democratic convention had not approved "what the overwhelming majority of the American people stand for: A resolution, a simple resolution, condemning anti-Semitism and dissociating their party from bigotry of all forms?"

On the matter of the President's visit to the Bitburg cemetery, the Vice-President, along with Jack Kemp, a leading contender for the Republican presidential nomination in 1988, is now uncharacteristically silent. "He is always very supportive of the President," Shirley Green, a deputy press secretary, said when asked for the Vice-President's thinking on Bitburg. "And he certainly has not in the past and I'm sure will not in this instance, second-guess the President. . . . ".

Kemp, on the other hand, sees nothing wrong with going to the town of Bitburg, but is against a visit to the cemetery. He thinks the President should visit the Konrad Adenauer Memorial, a more fitting way to commemorate the spirit of reconciliation between the two countries.

Reagan has been deserted by the right on Bitburg. "I think the President or his staff made an honest mistake," said Jerry Falwell. "Nevertheless, he made a mistake. I think he should admit that he was wrong, and I don't think it is an indication of weakness to do so." Falwell said he hasn't talked to the President about the visit, but "I recommend, 'Recant. Don't go.'"

While I can certainly understand President Reagan's efforts to celebrate the bond of democratic unity that we share with the West German people," says Jimmy Swaggart, the popular fundamentalist minister, "I must nonetheless disagree with the proposed visit to the Bitburg cemetery. Honoring our alliance is one thing. Participating in any ceremony that may even inadvertently bestow tribute or honor to those who personally participated in the Holocaust atrocities, however, can do nothing but reopen the tremendous wounds left by those experiences.

"It is a moral issue. And I, as a minister of the Gospel, cannot stand silently by, especially when it involves a President whom I have come to love and appreciate."

At the Heritage Foundation, the preeminent right-wing think tank, a spokeswoman said, "It's a little too political...We'll have to pass on that one."

Bitburg Bears Remembering
New York Times
May 6, 1985

It's over, but the Bitburg blunder, too, should not be forgotten. President Reagan's regret at having promised such a cemetery tribute was palpable. He walked though it with dignity but little reverence. He gave the cameras no emotional angles. All day long, he talked and talked of Hell and Nazi evil, to submerge the event.

No 10-minute gesture requiring all that explanation could retain much symbolic value. Not even Mr. Reagan's eloquent words before the mass graves of Bergen-Belsen could erase the fact that his visit there was an afterthought, to atone for the inadvertent salute to those SS graves.

What now needs remembering is how quickly even a ceremonial error can develop a political, indeed geopolitical life of its own, persuading the most powerful leaders that they are helpless hostages of history.

For all his pain at having to offend so many Americans, Mr. Reagan put it starkly: to abandon his promise to walk with Chancellor Kohl through the Bitburg cemetery would have looked as if he had "caved in" under pressure. And as Richard

Nixon and Henry Kissinger were summoned to testify, breaking even a small promise to an ally in the nuclear age would be a grievous sin.

This diplomacy of appearances insists that every presidential act has strategic significance: Since peace depends on nuclear weapons that can never be used, a President's willingness to use them rests entirely on threats and promises—on words; therefore, a President's words carry cosmic weight, his international promises must be impervious to pressure; indeed, the rougher the going, the more persevering a President must appear.

The theory is dangerous precisely because it rests on a foundation of truth. When practiced relentlessly, it can enshrine the most foolish commitments. And if pursued to absurd lengths, as in Bitburg, it makes strategic duty the enemy of democratic values. True strength resides securely between obduracy and complaisance. Strong leaders avoid both extremes.

Still, one could almost hear President Reagan's lesser rationalizations as he let Chancellor Kohl drag him through this "act of reconciliation." Had not the Chancellor stared down even stronger protests to plant Pershing missiles on his soil? Will not "Star Wars" get a boost from his gratitude for this political favor?

Yesterday's final travesty was the pretense that German-American reconciliation still required affirmation—four decades after the Marshall Plan and the Berlin Airlift. This alliance will survive the folly of Bitburg, just as it would have survived the cancellation of Bitburg, because it is now deeply rooted in the democratic politics and prosperity of all its peoples.

So too are the economic dysfunctions that worried all seven leaders of the industrial democracies at the Bonn meetings preceding Bitburg. No mere words and gestures of fellowship at the summit could move France's President Mitterrand to schedule a conference on trade barriers, which might threaten the protection of his farmers. And no mere lip service to interdependence could overcome the leaders' political fears and tampering with the world's monetary system.

It was a troubled summit in all respects. But what a blessing to find democracy at the root of the troubles.

'I Am a Jew…
New York Times
May 6, 1985

By William Safire

To President Kennedy's "Ich bin ein Berliner," a powerful and personal statement of identification with people struggling for freedom, President Reagan added: "…I am a Jew in a world still threatened by anti-Semitism, I am an Afghan, and I am a prisoner of the Gulag, I am a refugee in a crowded boat foundering off the coast of Vietnam, I am a Laotian, a Cambodian, a Cuban and a Miskito Indian in Nicaragua. I, too, am a potential victim of totalitarianism."

The poet-theologian John Donne made that point in his "no man is an island" passage, and Ernest Hemingway used a phrase from Donne in his title of a book about resistance to fascism, "For Whom the Bell Tolls." Many Jews will remember the lesson from the seder service that requires commemoration of the need for personal identification, during which it is recounted that an arrogant son asks, "What did the Almighty do for you?" and is castigated for not asking as a Jew, "What did the Almighty do for me?" To understand humanity, you have to be an active part of it.

Ronald Reagan, a month ago, had no real grasp of the moral priorities of the Holocaust or the fear of forgetting that prevent forgiveness. His journey to understanding—his own "painful walk into the past"—opened the minds of millions to the costs of reconciliation in a way that no other process could have accomplished. In driving home the lessons of history, his incredible series of blunders turned out to be a blessing.

At first, he did not want to go to a concentration camp. Too gloomy to be part of an upbeat trip. Like so many, he praised "remembrance" so long as it involved no personal pain.

The discovery of the SS graves in the scheduled cemetery visit saved him from the sin of avoidance. At that point, Mr. Reagan—and the world—had to go to a death camp and bear witness.

Then some invisible pedagogic hand led him to equate the victims of the death camps with the dead soldiers of the Third Reich. He soon learned, along with millions who had never given the matter any thought, that no reconciliation could ever come about by glossing over the enormity of the crimes committed by the Nazis and all the Germans who enthusiastically abetted them. Feeling sadness at the grave of soldiers is on a different order of magnitude from feeling agony at the slaughter of innocents.

The President absorbed the point. In an inspiring instructional penance in the Oval Office, he led a huge audience in listening to the testimony of Elie Wiesel, the quintessential survivor.

The invisible teaching hand would not let go. An ignoble motive (feat of appearing weak and subject to pressure) merged with a noble motive (the concern
about insulting a new generation of Germans) to send him to a place tainted with
the graves of storm troopers. This posed a test: Would he understand, and be able
to articulate both the need for remembrance and the requirement for reconciliation?

In part one of this amazing exam, he stood at Bergen-Belsen alongside the
German chancellor, a man of relentless repentance, "to confront and condemn
the acts of a hated regime of the past." The Jewish prayer for the dead speaks not
of the dead, but determinedly of faith in God; fittingly, the President stressed the
message of the doomed Anne Frank, "I still believe that people are really good at
heart." No horror photograph can be as affecting as that example of intelligent innocence and pure hope snuffed out: the ritual "never again" had context.

In the final part of the test, at the Bitburg cemetery, he acknowledged the presence of the Nazi graves first by turning his back on them, then by contrasting them
with the remains of young draftees, and left the judgment to Heaven. He did not
equate them with their victims or with the soldiers who fell in a moral cause. One
false note was an extended anecdote about the suspension of hostilities on a
holiday—as if the Wehrmacht had been made up mainly of sentimental boys—
but he drew the central lesson clearly: "that freedom must always be stronger than
totalitarianism, that good must always be stronger than evil."

That followed his uplifting "I am a Berliner, I am a Jew in a world still threatened by anti Semitism" passage, and for me redeemed the thoughtless early planning of this trip.

In seeking at first to sidestep the smouldering resentments the President
brought on a firestorm 40 years after a Holocaust, which in turn forced a forget-
ful world through a most necessary grief.

Despite Bitburg Blunders, Religious Leaders Work for Real Reconciliation

The Jewish Times
May 9, 1985

By Reverend Franklin H. Littell

While the German and American leaders have produced the most divisive series of incidents since soldiers of the two countries were shooting at each other, Jewish and Christian leaders in both countries are trying to accomplish a reconciliation worthy of the two peoples.

The Kohl/Reagan mismanagement of the situation has driven wedges between present-day Germans and Americans and present-day Christians and Jews that will wound for years to come—in spite of the efforts of people who know the difference between true reconciliation and its counterfeit.

In Germany, those media following the Kohl line have been trying to make "the Jews" the cause of the trouble. Some are subtle, taking the line that "of course we understand the Jews' feelings, but really they ought to have some respect for the feeling of others." Others more blatantly anti-Semitic, like the widely distributed *Bild* tabloid, blame "the Jews" and their great influence in America for the resentment over a botched itinerary. In Germany, few are aware that American veterans are offended, and almost none know that prominent American churchmen have also called upon the White House to undo the dreadful blunder that poor staffing made possible.

In America, those media following the Reagan line have supported the President's macho self-image and urged him to "tough it out." Those media who share the general shock and are critical have also joined the general chorus in blaming "the Germans." No major items have appeared on the keen criticism of the Social Democrats. None has called attention to the sinister influence of Alfred Dregger, the sabre-tooth right-winger who is Kohl's Pat Buchanan. None has pointed out the public praise given Reagan's "hanging tough" by the neo-Nazis. And none of the media has reported the fact that protests of the Bitburg observance, accompanied by affirmations of fraternity with the Jewish survivors, have come from some of the most distinguished intellectuals and Christian leaders in Germany. The faulty perception is allowed to stand that the stubbornness and stupidity of the Kohl government also represents "the Germans" on this issue.

Within the last two weeks prominent Christian leaders on both sides of the Atlantic have come into focus on the issues, motivated above all by the determination that there shall not here be another "abandonment of the Jews." Over the sponsorship of the Anne Frank House of Philadelphia, an "Open Letter to President Reagan" was published in a large advertisement in the national edition of *The New York Times*. Within the 48 hours after the financing was pledged and signatorics solicited, nearly 150 Christian leaders responded affirmatively—and many more missed the cut-off. The message was clear: A major moral issue is at stake. *Don't go to Bitburg.*

A group of prominent Christian leaders in Germany released a statement which was carried nationally over TV and radio and reported in most of the newspapers. The statement was initiated by Martin Stoehr, for 15 years a leader in Christian-Jewish seminars and conferences, and he was joined by Gertrud Luckner (venerable rescuer honored at Yad Vashem), Helmut Gollwitzer (Martin Niemoeller's aide in the early years and in maturity a world rank theologian), Eberhard Bethge (editor and biographer of Bonhoeffer, the Christian martyr to Nazism), and many others. Their message was blunt and unequivocal: an affirmation of fraternity with their Jewish brethren and a warning about the disastrous moral and political consequences of the Kohl-Reagan itinerary.

At first glance it seems that both Kohl and Reagan have painted themselves into a corner by depending upon staffs appallingly ignorant of the feelings in the partner country. It is hard to believe, however, that stupidity alone—even combined with incompetent staff work by advance parties—could manage a total no-win situation of this dimension. The question naturally arises: Who sand-bagged whom? Who took advantage of staff slovenliness and initial leadership indifference to create a situation in which every terrorist organization in the world is concentrating on Reagan's visit to Europe as a chance to drive a permanent wedge between West Germany and America, with the chance to throw blame on "the Jews" as an added bonus? Who created a situation, so cruel to decent Germans who have tried to atone for the past and build a democratic future, which would feature again the SS as representative of Germany? Who engineered a situation, so obscenely brutal toward Jewish survivors and so sublimely indifferent to the sensibilities of American veterans? Was it really nothing but incredibly poor staff work, its damaging effects confirmed by moral obtuseness on the part of the top leadership?

The Germans who have been working for Christian Jewish reconciliation since they emerged from under the Hitler dictatorship, and who have publicly confessed their co-responsibility for the crimes of a government they resisted as best they could, feel betrayed. And their feeling of betrayal by Kohl and Reagan is nothing compared with their feeling of betrayal by ambitious Jewish "spokesmen." For in fact the Jewish people is again betrayed by some of their own as well as assaulted by the heathen: the chief rabbi of Land Hannover and a prominent orthodox rabbi in Frankfurt issued public announcements welcoming Reagan to Bitburg, both of them saying they would be glad to accompany him into the cemetery(!). (I know their names, but I will not utter them.)

The Christian Germans who released the fraternal statement included some of those who fought through the bureaucratic ecclesiastial barbed wire and got the superb statement of the Synod of the Protestant Church of the Rheinland in January of 1980. Then they were immediately attacked in books and articles for "betraying the Christian faith" in repudiating conversionist activities targeting Jews. Like Christians everywhere who are post-Auschwitz, who are working for a reform of

Christian anti-Semitic teaching and preaching, they find themselves under attack for being "too friendly to the Jews." And now they find themselves undercut by public statements by Jewish "leaders" who, to most of the uninformed gentile public, look just as much "leaders" as anybody else…and are saying things that are easier to bear than the words that hit like hammers and burn like fire (as Jeremiah put it).

Enough! Enough! What a sick situation! Like the abandonment of the Jews which was the Holocaust itself, there is by now enough guilt to go around…And if we are going to be utterly honest about it, the shamefulness of the situation is not just the fault of superficial politicians with calloused consciences. Nor is it entirely the fault of the indifferent gentiles, with their easy consciences. In my own experience too, the teaching of the Holocaust and its lessons is made as difficult by some self-serving Jewish "leaders" as it is by the hardness of heart of the heathen.

Fortunately the small voices of the unworthy are drowned out in the theater of history by a clear word of truth such as that uttered by Elie Wiesel in the White House a few days ago. Once upon a time there was a ruler who liked to hear only pleasant things. And he surrounded himself with up-beat prophets who said only up-beat things. But one day there appeared a man of truth who said what the Lord wanted said: the denial of Truth is predictive of the destruction of a nation.

True reconciliation is not built upon media flim-flam or the deceptive calculations of politicians: it is a house of amity built upon the rock of Truth.

(The Reverend Franklin H. Littell is Professor of Religion at Temple University and is, also, Honorary Chairman and Founder of the Anne Frank Institute of Philadelphia [formerly The National Institute of Holocaust].)

Inquest
Universal Press Syndicate
May 9, 1985

By William F. Buckley, Jr.

A European reflecting on the machinery of American politics must be perplexed, though he cannot hope to be enlightened merely by picking up the phone and talking to a street-smart American. Because it is puzzling over here also. The President of the United States accepts an invitation that includes a visit to a military cemetery in which 49 SS soldiers are also buried, and confronts a political storm. But it isn't a political storm in which the overwhelming majority of Americans are engaged. But what emerges is a division between the people and their democratically elected representatives.

After total exposure to the issue, including a most unusual scene featuring the President of the United States being lectured to on foreign policy by someone on whom he had just conferred a medal, a poll (*Washington Post-ABC*) showed the American people roughly even (52 percent in favor) on the question whether Reagan should cancel the proposed visit. The poll, moreover, is properly examined with reference to the kinds of pressures experienced by the average American. Not many Americans are intimately aware of the delicacies of German politics — aware, for instance, of the leftward lurch of the Social Democrats during the past season, when the leadership went from demanding Pershing and cruise missiles (1979) to denouncing their deployment (1983). But everyone in America either knows, or from frequent television reports feels he knows, a Jewish survivor of the Holocaust: and the tendency is to wish to soothe those whose feelings stand to be hurt, in the absence of countervailing reasons for pursuing a course of action, personal feelings notwithstanding.

But while the American people were roughly divided, Congress was all but unanimous in opposition to the trip. Indeed, the vote in the Senate was unanimous: 82-0. Now, either the people who favored the trip were ill-informed, or else the senators were ill-informed. But certainly it follows that within Congress (the House voted 390 to 26 against), there was nothing like the division there was among the people who voted to send them to Congress.

Why? Opposition to the Bitburg visit was primarily, though by no means exclusively, voiced through Jewish organizations, the Jewish community taking the position, quite correctly, that their people were the special victims of Hitler. It is quite simply inconceivable that not a single senator on the floor that day sympathized with Mr. Reagan's position that he could not cancel the visit without affecting to our disadvantage German politics. Or, even, that there wasn't one senator there who felt that the President was entitled to follow his own sense of diplomatic priorities. But not one senator voted to back the President. It is as simple as that voters won't ever bring up, and seek to chastise, a senator who voted against the Bitburg trip.

But antagonists would be sure to bring up, in any future campaign, a senator's having voted in favor of the Bitburg trip. The senators were doing what was safer. They are politicians and are moved by political motives. Let Reagan assume all the blame, they were saying, as they raised their hands to condemn his decision to consummate the visit.

Do they now feel a little bit silly? Mayor Harold Washington of Chicago pronounced that if Reagan went to Bitburg, he would be "sowing the seeds of another Holocaust." What happens when you say something like that, and then look at yourself in the mirror? Revulsion?

The man who prosecuted Eichmann in Israel said that if Reagan went to Bitburg, Hitler would rise forward from his grave to proclaim a great victory. Do we have the feeling that that happened, after the events of last Sunday?

Would Hitler, looking down on the proceedings, take satisfaction from them? From being reviled as one of the worst totalitarian monsters in history?

Is there an American who watched television on Sunday who is less adamantly anti-Hitler than he was on Saturday?

Would it be fair, in fact, to go so far as to say that the events that climaxed with the Sunday visit renewed more ardently than anything done during the past 20 years the memory of the Holocaust?

And do we count for nothing the strengthened hand of the Christian Democratic Party in Germany, whose staunch backing of American foreign policy is crucial to the defense of the western frontier?

Reagan did the right thing. And he performed splendidly. And he is owed apologies he will never get.

Yet More Bitburg Lessons
Washington Jewish Week
May 16, 1985

The interests of the state of Israel and of the Jewish people are not always identical. While Jewish protesters stood outside the gates of Bergen-Belsen and the Reagan administration could not get a rabbi or a representative survivor to accompany them, the Israeli ambassador in Bonn attended the ceremony lest he offend his German hosts and American allies.

The Likud-led Foreign Office in Jerusalem approved the ambassador's attendance. At the same time, Likud ministers led the attack on what they termed Israel's "sluggish" and "muted" response to Bitburg.

Hearing Menachem Begin's claim that it was "one of the saddest days in Jewish history," one prominent survivor countered: "It was a proud day in American Jewish history. It was a sad day for the American President."

On the presidential tour of Germany, Jewish organizations, which proudly speak of community discipline, were unable to control responses. The timing of Reagan's decision gave Elie Wiesel — surely the most eloquent voice in the American Jewish community — presidential settings from which to protest Reagan's action.

No sooner had Wiesel completed his task, skillfully and respectfully, than the Inaugural Assembly of the American Gathering of Jewish Holocaust Survivors kept the issue in the forefront. Its most radical spokesman, Menachem Rosensaft, received an overwhelming endorsement from the crowd of 10,000 survivors gathered at the Liberty Bell in Philadelphia, when he denounced the President. The organizations were left in the position of responding to the community rather than leading it.

The Jewish establishment was so apprehensive over a high visibility in opposition to the President that no rabbi was invited to participate in the program at Arlington Cemetery. (A Presbyterian minister and a Roman Catholic priest were on the program.)

On the other hand, the call by Conservative and Reform leaders for a day of mourning and fasting was ignored in Washington. We know of only one synagogue whose rabbi canceled its breakfast program—much to the chagrin of its regulars. Another synagogue canceled an afternoon picnic so that members could attend the protest. No special services were held, and weddings went on as usual—including a rabbinic marriage attended by community elders.

Throughout the past month, the United States Holocaust Memorial Council, chaired by Wiesel, established its independence from the administration. Washington veterans cannot recall another federal agency—whose members are presidential appointees—protesting a presidential policy and getting away with it.

From Nuremburg to Bitburg
Universal Press Syndicate
May 16, 1985

By William F. Buckley, Jr.

The Bitburg visit leaves a very long wake, all of it conducive to useful reflection, among other things, on that loyalty of the military that can be said to transcend loyalty to civil authority.

The government of Adolf Hitler was legal if we define legal in terms of the positive law. It was in other respects never legal, not if in the term "legal" there inheres something more merely than de facto control of a country. We struggled with that one at Nuremburg, remember?

There we reasoned from the particular to the general. This is a practice not encouraged by legal philosophers, who wrote into the Constitution that there shall be no punishment for ex post facto offenses. Put simply, you don't get tried today for serving beer to a minor last December, when serving beer to a minor was legal. At Nuremburg, we struggled with something called "aggression" against humanity. We reasoned that there has got to be a law somewhere that says you don't, among other things, take 6 million Jews who have committed no offense whatever and liquidate them. So we hauled up a dozen top Nazis, faced them down with some tough prosecutors, and hanged them. To be sure, we contaminated the whole exercise by accepting as fellow judges Soviet officials who would not have hesitated to kill a million Jews, even as they had not hesitated in killing a million kulaks, if Stalin had simply ordered it. Still, a point was made.

A point with some resonance, because only a fortnight ago we were taking the position that no soldier who consented to serve in the Waffen SS was, really, a soldier: he was a criminal, and for that reason — the argument went — no American official should visit a graveyard in which also are included the remains of some of those criminals. Although the objectors to the Bitburg visit were unrealistic, the point they raised is not without current meaning. It has to do, of course, with the higher law, and most higher laws, for most people, are involved in some way with religion.

For that reason, Adm. James D. Watkins, who is chief of naval operations, wrote a spirited letter recently to the editor of the *Los Angeles Times*, objecting to the implications of a provocative story that had been published in the *Times*. Its flavor can be got from the headline: "Star Wars Called 'Moral'/Beirut Bombing Blamed on 'Antichrist'/Role of Religious Faith at Pentagon/Raises Questions, Doubts." The story spoke of Gen. John Vessey, chairman of the Joint Chiefs of Staff, and of Admiral Watkins, and of other prominent officials who have in public circumstances professed their faith in God. It drew attention to a fortnightly "prayer breakfast" held at the Pentagon, attended by those officers who wish to attend it. It quoted an anonymous chaplain as saying, "Many of the meetings are religious exhibitionism, I'm afraid."

But the reporter, Robert C. Toth, was on the one hand anxious to relay that the religious exercises did not mean very much, but anxious, also, to point out that they were in some way oriented toward public policy. For instance, Admiral Watkins was quoted as believing that Star Wars is "a morally sound course."

There are of course differences of opinion on the matter of the provenance of moral distinctions, and no doubt Admiral Watkins is explicitly guided by his belief in Christianity. But you have the coincidence that those whose anxiety about separation of church and state extends to worrying about generals who profess religious convictions are also, in most cases, the same folk who applaud the bishops when they convene to say, in effect, that a nuclear arsenal, to the extent that it exists because it might be used, is immoral. Admiral Watkins takes a view one would think would commend itself to those with the faintest grasp of right and wrong, namely that it is more nearly right than wrong to use bombs, instead of to kill people — which is the point of Star Wars, of course.

In an ideal world, those Hitler took into the SS would have risen against the monster. Some Germans in fact did, and July 20 — the day in 1944 they tried to assassinate Hitler — ought to be a part of Germany's sacred calendar. In the ideal world, people say no to an invitation to join the SS. In an ideal world, they say no to Hitler. Say no to Stalin. Say no to Gorbachev. Bitburg causes us all to consider these points, another reason to be grateful for the exercise.

Shambles And Reconciliation
Aufbau
May 24, 1985

By Hans Steinitz

The day of Bitburg has gone. But did it really? Can one let grass grow over this affair? Will we ever be rid of the bad aftertaste left by the day of Bitburg? Many Americans will say that a just and moral balance has been established. After all, President Reagan stayed only eight minutes in the soldier's cemetery of Bitburg, and spent almost fifty minutes in Bergen-Belsen where he made an absolutely dignified and touching speech. Equally dignified were his words spoke on the same day in the American military airbase near Bitburg.

And, as his visit to the former concentration camp was subsequently under American pressure fit into the program of his visit to Germany in order to calm down a political storm at home, so, too, was a visit and the placing of a wreath on Konrad Adenauer's tomb included, practically as a last-minute afterthought.

Has everything really been put to right again? To quote from the *New York Times*: "Ronald Reagan is America's oldest president. He is also the one with the shortest memory."

This episode was by far the most serious defeat he has suffered during his term of office. It would have been easy to avoid the entire catastrophe if only his planning staff had done its duty instead of concerning themselves with the private purchase of BMW automobiles at a diplomat's discount!

This incident clearly showed that everything that is usually considered Reagan's strengths is in essence just stubborness. He did not want to give in because he felt he would appear to be an insecure weakling and destroy the people's "perception" of him. This is why he unnecessarily turned almost the entire American people against him: veterans' organizations, the Jewish population, both Houses of Congress, dignitaries of religious denominations, with New York's Archbishop O'Connor and, yes, even Jerry Falwell of the "Moral Majority" in the lead — all of them, again and again, requested most urgently that he cancel the Bitburg visit.

But he stuck with his decision, allegedly because Chancellor Kohl wanted it (who, it should be noted, had his own domestic political reasons). Neither could he understand, as Willi Brandt put it, that "We Germans stand in opposition to our own past." As he repeatedly underscored, the President desired, with this gesture of honoring German war dead, to proclaim a decisive and highly visible act of reconciliation with the former enemy. This would offer proof of German-American friendship. He considered this action politically and, in the framework of NATO rearmament, strategically necessary.

There is no reason to object to this. *Aufbau* has always supported reconciliation (we called it bridge-building) with the new democratic regime of the Federal

Republic. But is this attitude a recent invention in 1985 and of the Ronald Reagan presidency? The reconciliation with the new and freedom-loving Germany started with President Truman and the Marshall Plan, followed by Konrad Adenauer, with President Eisenhower and his Secretary of State, Dulles. Later on the "Berlin Airlift" occurred during the blockade, soon to be followed by the outstretched hand of Ben-Gurion and the German restitution program — the most widely visible expression of German "bridge-building" to the Jewish community. Has the President with the shortest memory never heard of all this?

Admittedly, the President, faced with a totally messed-up situation, did find a halfway satisfying solution. This allowed him in the end, though rather cool and condescendingly, to dismiss the demonstrations against him by Jewish and veterans' organizations and also by German resistance fighters, with the remark: "Well, after all, it's a free country." Admittedly, too, it required the most intense pressure which Reagan ever experienced and which he might not have been used to, to move him reluctantly to visit Bergen-Belsen and Adenauer's tomb. Even if it satisfied a large part of the American people and American public opinion, we are obliged — as are all Jews of this country and the whole world — to pronounce, with much more intensity than Reagan did, a forceful "Never Again." Reconciliation, "Yes." Forgetting, "Never."

The annual conference of the seven Western industrial powers which preceded the day at Bitburg did not produce any success for the United States. It was not only French President Mitterand who replied negatively to all American suggestions. The others were not much more conciliatory. The only positive thing during this eventful week was the exemplary attitude of the German people and of the German press which once again, and perhaps more strongly than ever before, distanced itself from their Nazi and SS past. This represents a contribution to reconciliation which should not be underestimated and forgotten and which sweetens a bit the bitter memory of the day at Bitburg.

(Translated from the German by George Asher.)

(Heinz Steinitz is Editor Emeritus of Aufbau, the only German-Jewish newspaper in the United States.)

New SS Wreaths, Old Anti-Semitism
The New York Times
May 20, 1985

By Marvin Kalb

WASHINGTON.—The controversy over the Reagan visit to Bitburg is receding, no longer a front-page embarrassment. But do you hear an echo from the past?

I visited the cemetery the morning after President Reagan and Chancellor Helmut Kohl placed wreaths of reconciliation in front of its chapel. For years, the cemetery had been largely ignored; now, it was an instant shrine, a focus of political debate. Small flower pots marked many flat graves, 49 of them honoring Waffen SS troops. By the end of my visit, many hundreds of Germans and occasional Americans from the nearby Air Force base paused before the wreaths. Some took pictures. Mothers hushed children. A religious air seemed to saturate the scene.

But look and listen: all around there were the sights and sounds of the new Germany—and old. Six feet to the left of the President's wreath stood an equally impressive one. Across its banner: "To the Waffen SS who fell at Leningrad." No more than a foot to the right of the Chancellor's was another wreath: "For the fallen comrades of the Waffen SS."

These two wreaths had been placed in the chapel, out of sight, hours before the President arrived. They were restored to their original places of honor only hours after he left. In the ensuing tranquility, the Waffen SS could again be honored in the springtime sun.

A middle-aged visitor from Nuremberg said the Waffen SS were simply soldiers—young conscripts doing their duty. "Let them rest in peace. For us, a dead soldier is a dead soldier, not a hero."

A native of Bitburg, who looked to be in his 20's, expressed a view I was to hear with disturbing regularity. "We Germans and Americans had been cooperating very well"—he lowered his voice—"until the Jews began to make trouble."

Another Bitburg zeroed in on Elie Wiesel. "Imagine the nerve of a Jew lecturing President Reagan. I saw him on television, making trouble the way they all do."

An old woman complained that Mr. Reagan had spent only eight minutes at the cemetery. "You know why the visit had to be cut back? Because of the Jews." She stalked away to join a group of friends nodding in agreement.

A man with a cane stopped and said: "If they don't like it here, the Jews, let them go away. We were better off without them in Germany." There are only 28,000 left, he was reminded. "Too many," he replied.

The people of Bitburg are pleased that Mr. Reagan came to visit, that he didn't yield to pressure. But its clear they resent their new notoriety—and equally clear whom they consider responsible for the unwelcome change: the Jews and the media. The Jews are seen as a group separate from Germans and Americans--an indigestible lump, a foreign body. The media are seen as intrusive and irresponsible and, somehow, controlled by the Jews.

So it went. A few days later, a Munich newspaper editor explained that anti-Semitism is an "anthropological phenomenon" in Germany. The controversy seems only to have uncorked the venom once again. There is a sad irony. Bitburgers consider themselves remarkably enlightened. In 1933, when Hitler won a critical election, this conservative Catholic town voted overwhelmingly against him.

Is Bitburg an aberration? It is impossible to judge and dangerous to generalize. But a number of leading West German politicians and professors — several close to Mr. Kohl — think anti-Semitism was on the rise even before Bitburg. "The Jews were getting too impertinent," one politician said, citing among other things, their opposition to West German tank sales to Saudi Arabia. "We've listened to them much too long. It's enough."

The pursuit of reconciliation by way of Bitburg has been a failure. What should have been obvious from the beginning is that reconciliation is a long process — not a single photo opportunity, an event, a moment frozen in time. Bitburg, exposing clumsiness and poor political judgment in Bonn and Washington, in the process lifted the scab on dark corners of German history. There is a time to know when to leave well enough alone.

As I entered the cemetery, I noticed a sign: "Please do not disturb the peace and rest of the dead." Too late.

Part V

The German Response

Amazing as it may sound, the issue of the wreath-laying at Bitburg and the resulting Bitburg affair was made possible because of the absence of a national Holocaust memorial in Germany. The need for such a monument commemorating the victims of Nazism was suggested years ago by former German Chancellor Helmut Schmidt. However, the idea remained solely on paper. In January 1985 Oscar Schneider, Germany's minister of construction, sought and received a government permit to construct such a national monument that would properly commemorate all of the Nazi victims, Jewish and non-Jewish, among them the inmates of the concentration camps, soldiers killed in action, homeless German refugees, executed prisoners, and destroyed cities. Although this list reflects the classical political wisdom, the implementation of the monument remains to this day in the planning stage.

For many years Bonn used for occasions of wreath-laying by foreign dignitaries a surrogate for such a national memorial —a plaque located at the Academy of Art Museum which read:

TO THE VICTIMS OF WAR AND OPPRESSION

Eventually, due to construction, the site of this plaque was moved from the center of Bonn to the Northern Cemetery, located at the city's outskirts. In order to reach this place the foreign dignitaries and their hosts had to cross the city from the government center to its other side, which was time-consuming and presented a logistical problem. One of the reasons for this temporary solution was that Bonn is a temporary capital, and once Germany is reunited, Berlin will assume its traditional role as the capital.

The proposed project for the national monument encountered immediate opposition, which threatened to evolve into a wide conflict. In a special appeal to Minister Schneider, the representatives of the Central Council of German Jews voiced an objection to the ethics of this solution of erecting one memorial commemorating both "murderers and murdered." A similar position was taken by the representatives of the Association of German Expellees, representing some 12 million people. Meanwhile, pressure to proceed with the proposed memorial was coming from Chancellor Kohl, who wanted to see it completed before the federal election in 1987, in order to gain political support.

The problem escalated when demands were voiced by the two political major parties (the Christian Democrats [CDU] and the Social Democrats [SPD], the two leading churches [Protestant and Catholic]), and other organizations such as the Association for Erecting the National Monuments and Commemorations of the Victims of War and Violence. This association represents nine highly diverse organizations, including the German Red Cross, the Ring of the Association of German Soldiers, the Association for the Management of Military Cemeteries, and the Central Organization of the German Resistance Fighters. In order to find a compromise solution that would satisfy the various interests, Schneider plans to accept suggestions from the public concerning the inscription on such monument. The final decision concerning the construction itself and the inscription is to be made by a special committee that will include the president, the Chancellor, and other prominent personalities: "The memorial has to comply with the democratic reality and to express properly the difficult question of the German identity," stated Schneider.

German identity and its relation to the Third Reich indeed surfaced during the Bitburg affair and became the underlying issue for various groups and causes. The epicenter of this process of identity is the German perception of May 8, 1945. Theodore Heuss, the first president of the Federal Republic of Germany (FRG), succinctly expressed this dilemma: "Germans were redeemed and destroyed at the same time." This ambiguity is still alive and active in German political culture. For Americans this day is clearly defined as the moment of *capitulation* of the Third Reich. For Germans there are at least two schools of thought: the first sees a day of liberation and the second a catastrophy. While the first group harbors no nostalgic-idyllic attachments to the Nazi era, the second group sees the era primarily in terms of the lost war. This latter group sees Nazi Germany as a minute chapter in German history, an "industrial accident" *(Betriebsunfall),* and thus it stresses the limited implications of this period and the limited responsibility of future German generations for this war and its crimes. (See the penetrating analysis of Prof. Martin Stohr). This approach was vividly summarized by government spokesman Peter Boenisch: "This is the pits! That forty years after the war we still must run through those concentration camps!"[1]

This kind of political self-assertion finds its support among the right-wing sector of German voters. And it is to this particular sector of voters that Chancellor Kohl was appealing when he staged the reconciliation ceremony at Bitburg. The expression of German national pride stems from achievements in economics, technology, sports, and international activities such as the extensive foreign aid to the Third World, which exceeds that of the Soviet-block countries. Moreover, today's active political generation was fifteen to eighteen years old at the end of the war, and looks upon the time of its entrance into adult life with nostalgic feelings untainted by guilt or responsibility. The 50s constitutes for present German society a renaissance, a true rebirth of the polity following the devastations of war. It was a kind of incubator of adolescence, with its hopes and its struggles toward eventual economic rewards. This notion is reinforced in literature, movies, and television. Note, for instance, the film *The Marriage of Maria Brown* and the recent thirteen-hour TV movie *Heimat (Homeland).*[2]

Surprisingly, this notion of the "zero hour" — that modern German history began on May 8, 1945 — finds support from the church. Thus, at the ecumenical services commemorating that day, Joseph Cardinal Hoeffner stated:

> We should not continually torment ourselves by digging up past guilt and the wrongs we have committed against one another. We should not weigh one sin against the other. We should not use guilt as a weapon against each other. All our sins are taken away by the mercy of Jesus Christ who taught us to pray: "Forgive us our sins, as we forgive those who sin against us.

Thus, it was not surprising that the leaders of the German churches stood by Chancellor Kohl at the ceremonies at Bergen-Belsen and Bitburg, which were boycotted by the leading American clergy and by such supporters of President Reagan as Rev. Jerry Falwell and Rev. Billy Graham. It is interesting to note that Willy Brandt, Kohl's political opponent and a man who contributed so much to German-Jewish reconciliation, stated that personally he had no difficulty in deciding to participate in the wreath-laying ceremony at Bitburg.

Further evidence of the resistance of many Germans to confronting their historical responsibility for the crimes committed on their behalf can be seen in the case of the reaction of the community of Bergen, the town adjacent to the former concentration camp of Bergen-Belsen, to the idea of honoring the memory of Anne Frank, who perished there during the last months of the war. As in most cases, the conflict developed along political lines. In 1961 the SPD proposed to name a primary school for Anne Frank; however, this proposal fell through and the school was named after Eugen Naumann, a prominent representative of the German minority in Poland. This issue was raised again by the SPD in 1982, but again without success. After President Reagan's visit to Bergen-Belsen, a new campaign was begun by the Bergen SPD in July-August 1985. The Social Democrats proposed to name a street for Anne Frank, but this idea was rejected by the CDU and most vehemently opposed by the local residents, who refused to reside on a street that commemorated past crimes. Their resentments have been intentionally amplified through letters of a local newspaper whose editor, Gunther Ernst, also opposed the idea. This conflict reached the level of a local civil war. The underlying reason for this conflict was expressed by Hasso Holtz, the chairman of the local branch of the Free Democrarts: "The majority of the citizens do not want to be confronted permanently with the theme of Bergen-Belsen." Finally, a Bergen school was found, and it now bears the name of Anne Frank.

Approaching the issue of German historical responsibility, two sets of numbers illustrate the problem that is being faced by the present German generation which feels itself distant from the crimes committed by Nazi Germany. Out of 61.5 million German citizens 50 million were born after the war or were teenagers at the time of its end. These numbers were recited by Chancellor Kohl and President Reagan and were restated by Cardinal Hoeffner as an argument for lessening historical responsibility. The other set of numbers, brought out by Simon Wiesenthal, shows that out of 10.5 million members of the Nazi party, 9 million survived the war and, of these, 700 received sentences and 1,200 are now under indictment. This set of numbers points out the chronological/social proximity of the present generation to the one that unquestionably participated in committing the crimes. This aspect of the direct family ties between these generations was analyzed recently in an article entitled "Children of Culprits" in which the author traces four cases of the impact of Nazi fathers upon children who are now in their late thirties.[3] This political drive, represented by Chancellor Kohl and Dr. Dregger, to cap the past and relegate it to philosophical abstraction finds its way into the "historification"[4], away from the efforts to confront the past *(Vergangenheitsbewaltigung)* and toward the "release from the Past" *(Entsorgung der Vergangenheit).*[5] This trend is being supported by a growing sector of people who never before belonged to the radical right but whose nostalgic yearnings for the **Heimat** lost (historical and geographical, since the FRG lost one-third of its territory to Poland and East Germany) propel them to embrace nationalistic values. In order to retain this political patriotism/nationalism it is imperative to blur or deny responsibility for the Nazi crimes.

Among the overlooked actors in this drama is German Jewry. Today they constitute a tiny minority in a state that once declared a war of annihilation against them. After the war they returned to their destroyed *Heimat* to discover that even within the Jewish community they were a minority, dominated now by the East European Jews whom they once regarded as their less progressive cousins. In a way, this resurrected Jewish community was neither understood nor fully accepted by the other Jewish communities in the Diaspora and by Israel. The Bitburg affair left them with additional bitterness, especially toward the American Jewish leaders. When suddenly, after years of benign neglect, an international event was taking place within their territory (geographical as well as historical), the American Jewish leadership claimed it as their domain. While the German Jewish leaders saw the Bitburg affair within the context of German-Jewish relations in today's Germany, the American Jewish leaders, such as Rosensaft, perceived the Reagan-Kohl visits to Bergen-Belsen and Bitburg as purely political gestures that would desecrate the memory of the victims of the Holocaust rather than honor it.

Initially, the Central Council of German Jews had planned to participate in the ceremony at Bergen-Belsen, since only two weeks earlier, together with Chancellor Kohl, they had observed the Day of Remembrance for the victims of the Holocaust at that same site. However, two days before the ceremony, under pressure and threats from outside Germany, the representatives of the council gave in and decided not to take part in this ceremony. However, bitter feelings remained.

---

[1]"Das ist ja das letzte, dass man noch 40 Jahre nach Kriegsend durch die KZ's laufen muss."

[2]Forty-four prominent personalities were asked, "Do you love Germany?" and their answers present a highly vivid picture of the mixed emotions the question arouses. See *Lieben Sie Deutschland? Gefuehle zur Lage der Nation,* Marielouise Janssen-Jurreit, ed. (Piper, 195),. p.336; see also "Die Deutschen-wer sind wir," Marion Graflin Donhoff, *Die Zeit,* April 21, 1985, and "Sind die Deutsche Nationalisten," Heinrich August Winkler, *Die Zeit,* February 5, 1982.

[3]"Die Kinder der Taeter' Deutsche Geschichte als Familiendrama: Selbstzweifel, Zweispaltigkeit, Hass und Schuldgefuehle," Dorte von Westernhagen, *Die Zeit,* April 4, 1986, p. 7-9.

[4]"Spielraeume unter der Herrschaft des NS-Regime," Arnulf Baring, *FAZ,* August 6, 1985, p. 23.

[5]For a detailed analysis see "Die Entsorgung der Vergangenheit," Ein kulturpolitisches Pamphlet, Juergen Habermas, *Die Zeit,* May 17, 1985. pp. 56-57.

Chapter 17

The Response Of Religious Leaders

"I Reject Collective German Guilt": Cardinal Höffner
Cologne
May 8, 1985

By Joseph Cardinal Höffner

(Sermon given during an ecumenical service at Cologne Cathedral on the 40th anniversary of Germany's capitulation on May 8, 1945.)

Sisters and brothers,

Forty years after the end of the war we are still dismayed by what happened. In the Holy Scripture the number 40 designates a period of trial, scrutiny, effort, endurance and reflection. After a period of 40 years in the wilderness Moses said to his people: "Remember the days of old, consider the years of many generations."

Reflection

The courage to remember takes us to the root of the matter. The insane, misanthropic, evil and destructive National Socialist regime rode roughshod over human rights, persecuted Christians and systematically exterminated the sick and disabled, using the horrible term "human hulls" to describe them. The Second World War was unleashed. Unspeakable suffering was brought upon on neighboring peoples. Six million Jews were murdered. Apocalyptic events took place in the concentration camps and in the basements of Gestapo buildings.

This all would not have been possible without the programmed destruction of belief in God pursued over a period of years and without the befogging and deadening of people's consciences. The history of the world is at the same time the history of the human heart. Hunger for power and megalomania stem from the heart and lead to hate and murder.

Fresh Start

In the pastoral letter they published after the war, more precisely on August 23, 1945, the German bishops said: "Catholics, we are pleased that to such a large extent you remained free of the idolatry connected with brutal violence." However, the bishops added: "Nevertheless, horrible things happened in Germany before the war and horrible things were perpetrated by Germans in the occupied countries during the war. We profoundly deplore the fact that many Germans, including some from our own ranks, let themselves be deceived by the false doctrines of National Socialism. They remained indifferent to crimes against human freedom and human dignity. Many aided and abetted criminals through this attitude. Many became criminals themselves."

Guilt cannot be overcome by a flood of political and psychological analyses. The heart of man must be renewed. We ask God to forgive us for all our failures and for all our guilt in those years. Jesus Christ died for us sinners, "the just for the unjust". The redemption he has brought us is greater than all the calamity caused by man.

God's mercy presupposes turning away from sin and returning to God, the courageous beginning of a new life and the desire for atonement and reparation. God will then grant us his forgiveness. When a ship sails in the wrong direction it does no good to run back and forth on the ship. The ship itself must change its course. The warning to change our course applies to us all. In the Gospel Jesus warns us that as sinners we are not to exonerate ourselves of guilt. "I tell you Nay: but except ye repent, ye shall all likewise perish."

Reconciliation

The crimes and atrocities perpetrated by the National Socialist regime came back at us with the fury of pounding waves, sweeping over the guilty and the innocent alike. We are thankful to God that reconciliation with neighboring nations was more rapid and more profound after 1945 than after the First World War. The victims, i.e., the Poles, the French, the people of   Luxembourg, the Belgians, the Dutch and the British, as well as the Germans who were driven from their homes — they, too, were victims — had a strong hand in making this possible.

I have always rejected the idea of collective German guilt. This aside from the fact that of the 61.5 million people living in the Federal Republic of Germany today, some 50 million were either born after the war or were still children during the National Socialist period. However, we all feel a sense of responsibility for what

happened and for the consequences that live on today. This applies in large measure to the Church, which does not live apart from the people, but rather amidst
the people. The Church and the people go through history together, sharing guilt
and anguish, sharing the experience of God's mercy and sharing happiness over
that which is good.

We should not continually torment ourselves by digging up past guilt and the
wrongs we have committed against one another. We should not weigh one sin
against the other. We should not use guilt as a weapon against each other. All our
sins are taken away by the mercy of Jesus Christ who taught us to pray: "Forgive us
our sins, as we forgive those who sin against us."

Courage to Face the Future

When I look back to 1945 and think of the present I am filled with concern.
40 years ago—I was still young at the time—we had the courage to face the future
despite the heavy moral burden that weighed on our people. We said to ourselves
"where there is an end there is a beginning." Today it would seem to me that many
people have a disturbed attitude towards the future. There are reasons for this. The
horrible things that happened under the National Socialist regime seem not to
have been a lesson to many. Profound distrust and fear of one another divides the
power blocs. The arms race goes on. Today there continue to be wars, suppression,
criminal regimes, lack of freedom, torture chambers, forced labor camps, exploitation, as well as the famine death of women and children.

The young generation above all is tormented by the question as to whether
survival of mankind and nature will be possible. In the past, too, man perpetrated murders and waged horrible wars. Today, however, all of mankind and all forms
of life are endangered. This generates an apocalyptic fear of the end, indeed the
expectation of a horrible end in the near future.

Two attitudes are inadequate in today's world: First of all, as Christians it is not
enough for us to lock our Christian beliefs away in our hearts and to let things take
their course without any active involvement on our part. Secondly, it is not enough
for us to feel responsibility only within the Church. As Christians we must be present in the world and bear witness to the Gospel of Christ. . . .

Our service in the world is service to man. It is a commitment to the right of
man, even if unborn, to life. It is a commitment to human freedom and dignity.
As such, we reject any kind of discrimination against the human individual, any
act of violence against him based on race, skin color, social standing or religion.
Of course we cannot content ourselves with protests against injustice, poverty, famine, disease, misery, exploitation and want. It is our duty to give active, selfless help.
As Christians we are aware that the objective of Christian service is not to create
a paradise on earth, but rather a social order in which man is best able to fulfill
God's will and lead a life worthy of human dignity. "Come Holy Spirit that we may
see what is right. Light in us the fire of your love." Amen.

Ecumenical ceremony marking 40th Anniversary of Germany's capitulation (first row, left to right) Marianne von Weizsäcker, President Richard von Weizsäcker, Bundestag President Philip Jenninger, Ina Jenninger, Hannelore Kohl and Chancellor Helmut Kohl.

"People Inquire After Guilt; Forget Own": Bishop Lohse
Cologne
May 8, 1985

By Bishop Eduard Lohse

(Sermon given during an ecumenical service at Cologne Cathedral on the 40th anniversary of Germany's capitulation on May 8, 1945.)

    The peace of the Lord be with us all.
    During this hour let us direct our thoughts to the motto for today as written in the forty-second chapter of Jeremiah: "... we will obey the voice of the Lord our God .." Amen.
    What is of importance in this hour, 40 years after the end of the Second World

War? It is important that we honor God, listen to His Word, and answer Him with our prayers as well as with the deeds of our life. We thank the Churches in the countries that suffered heavily under the horrors of the war for sending representatives here to assure us of their brotherly solidarity and witness with us. "... we will obey the voice of the Lord our God ..."

This was said at the time of the prophet Jeremiah by people in Judah. With dismay they witnessed the conquest and destruction of Jerusalem, the holy city of Israel, by hostile armies. Most of the inhabitants were taken prisoner and sent to Babylon. An uncertain fate awaited the survivors of the war. They turned to the prophet Jeremiah, seeking his advice. They wanted to join forces with him in asking God to show them what they were to do. They vowed they would obey the voice of the Lord. In the hour of deepest degradation and nameless misery there is no other voice that can show the way that needs to be taken.

Those of us who are a little older remember May 8, 1945 from our own experience. For some it was the collapse of the country. For others it was a day of liberation. For many it was both at the same time. Dismay at the immeasurable amount of suffering caused was mixed with feelings of gratitude for having survived. The war left more than 40 million dead. Countless towns and villages in the countries immediately affected by the war lay in ruin, particularly in the Soviet Union, Poland, France and Germany. The horrifying reports about what had been perpetrated in the concentration camps and in the occupied countries in the name of Germany now made it manifestly evident to everyone the type of criminal regime that had started the war and mercilessly carried it through to the bitter end. The world was horrified by the murder of Jews. How could this all have come about?

The Holy Scripture tells us the truth, i.e. the commandments of our Lord God had been shamefully disregarded, at first quietly and secretly, but then in brazen disdain and godless arrogance. People had dishonored God and begun to worship false gods. "Thou shalt not commit adultery. Thou shalt not steal. Thou shalt not bear false witness against thy neighbour. Thou shalt not covet thy neighbour's house, thou shalt not covet anything that is thy neighbour's." Our people showed a blasphemous disregard for these clear commandments given to us by our God, teaching their soldiers to sing: "We will continue to march until everything is smashed. Germany is ours today and tomorrow it will be the entire world."

The Bible warns us not to be mistaken. God will not be scorned. What man sows he will also reap. Thus the inevitable happened. We were unable to free ourselves from the net in which we were caught. We had to be freed from a political system that rode roughshod over human dignity, rights and freedoms with lies and state terror. But at what price. Germany was divided up into zones of occupation. Countless soldiers became prisoners of war. Many refugees were unable to return to their homes. Many had to leave their homes. For many years a long line of suffering moved along the roads of misery. The grim harvest of death went on for some time.

In this time of degradation, shame, helplessness, and despair merciful God once again spoke His Word, and, with a timid voice at first, we began to answer:

"... we will obey the voice of the Lord our God ..." His Word alone was able to provide the mercy of a new beginning. Are we still aware of this today? A few months after the war representatives of the Evangelical Church in Germany met in Stuttgart with representatives of other churches and declared: "We accuse ourselves of not having professed our faith more courageously, of not having prayed more faithfully, of not having believed more confidently and of not having loved more ardently. Now a fresh start is to be made in our Churches."

Through God's mercy we were given a new beginning. For 40 years now we have lived in peace. We were able to rebuild our towns and villages and re-establish our livelihoods. Full of astonishment and gratitude we experienced gestures of reconciliation. The ties with neighboring nations are based on confidence that has grown up over time. Reconciliation over the graves has become reality and must never again be endangered. In the face of death conflict loses justification and meaning. In reverence we honor the memory of all those who died or were murdered in the war, those from other nations and those from our nation. May they rest in eternal peace.

We constantly encounter borders that separate people from one another. Particularly with regard to the East further steps towards reconciliation continue to be urgently necessary. Let me give one example. In 1982 as part of a delegation of our Church we visited the Christian Churches in the Soviet Union. In Leningrad on June 22 we recalled the day on which Hitler attacked Russia in 1941 and unleashed a ghastly war. We stood at the graves of 700,000 people who were killed in the course of the more than three-year siege of the city. That evening we attended a church service at Nicholas Cathedral, where the bishop welcomed us as Christian brothers and sisters and accepted us in the congregation gathered there. These are visible gestures of reconciliation.

We have had peace for 40 years. However, we are aware that peace is threatened. Years of new beginning were conceded to us. However, we are aware that the wounds caused by the war have not yet healed. A deeply incised border leads through our country. For many of us it represents an obstruction to reconciliation with our neighbors. Indeed it evokes defiant reactions. In these cases people tend only to inquire after the guilt of the other side and forget their own. Thoughts of this kind help to build walls instead of tearing them down. They harden our hearts and close them to others. A wonderful opportunity is contained in God's invitation to all of us to be reconciled with God, making a new beginning possible through his forgiveness.

Thus, we want to express our memories, our feelings and our concern for the future in halting words of gratitude for the fact that God in his goodness let us live. In the sign of the cross of Jesus Christ he provided reconciliation and renewal. Thus, in this hour we cannot speak any differently from the men who had come in profound despair to the prophet Jeremiah, no different from our fathers and mothers, sisters and brothers who, 40 years ago, amidst pain and tears, sought and by the grace of God found a new beginning and who say: "... we will obey the voice of the Lord our God ..."

Church Leaders Erred in Going To Bitburg
Dusseldorf
June 8, 1985

By Dietrich Goldschmidt

The Working Group of Jews and Christians of the German Evangelical Kir-
chentag has carried out a series of institutes at the Kirchentag. The objects of the
lectures and discussions were:
- The responsibility of Germans 40 years after Auschwitz,
- The self-understanding of Israel,
- The meaning of the Maidanek trial,
- The question of what we are able to do for Israel toward the solution of the
  Near East conflict,
- The consequences for theology and church of the new relationship between
  Jews and Christians.

The participants in the events heard the speech of Richard von Weizsäcker on
8 May* with relief and agreement. Nevertheless, they were alarmed afterward, as
they were before. The "spiritual-moral renewal," proclaimed for the Federal Republic, threatens to suppress an honest treatment of the events from 1933 to 1945 in
Germany and their pre-history. The commemorations in Bergen-Belsen and Bitburg on the occasion of 8 May in terms of the way they came about and the discussions pertaining to them let this be clearly known. To want to honor the
murdered in the same breath as those who covered Europe with war and annihilation denies their sacrifice any worth. In the comparison there lies at the same
time a falsification of history which leads the German people to a dishonest relationship with their own past and attaches heavy shadows to them.

We are ashamed that the church leadership and the synods let the Jews who
demonstrated against this development go it alone; the Jews who were carried away
by police from the doors of former concentration camps. Representatives of the
Protestant and Catholic church did not show solidarity with them, rather they took
part—in contrast to the Jewish representatives—in the ceremony at Bergen-Belsen.
Their appearance and their presence were incorrect in the eyes of both victim and
survivor. In the view of the silence of the church organs and the behavior of the
church representatives, we ask ourselves whether the Synodal Declarations on a
new, positive relationship to the Jews of the synods in the Rhineland, in Baden,
in Berlin and of the Reformed Church in northwest Germany were formed to remain paper documents instead of to lead to acts of solidarity with Jews in daily life.

Similarly, we are unsettled about the law over the so-called "Auschwitz-lies" and
about the relevant discussions concerning it. The equation and with it the equal-

---

* *West German Presidential address in connection with the 40th Anniversary of the end of the Second World War
in Europe.*

ity of treatment, of the offense of denying the crimes of Auschwitz with the offense of denying the crimes against Germans caused by the war; the legal treatment of these two offenses under the same category and deserving the same punishment illustrates a shameful, calculating mentality. This incident is a further proof that broad sections of our people seek still to close their eyes against the horror of past crimes and refuses to draw the necessary consequences.

Under the anxiety of the unstable, contradictory situation in the Federal Republic, all efforts to find at this moment an open and understanding relationship to the state of Israel and its citizens suffer. Indeed, Israel finds itself in an especially difficult economic, political and above all spiritual crisis at this time.

We expressly demand therefore:

1. That the government of the Federal Republic use all the ways and means at its disposal to further the peace process in the Near East to secure the right and possibility of the existence of the state of Israel, to which belongs especially:
    a. Furthering of direct trade with Israel as well as direct trade between the EEC and Israel;
    b. No sale of arms to the Arab nations or to Israel;
    c. Strengthening of cultural exchange with Israel, e.g. academic study in Israel, adult education in Israel and planned youth exchange by German subvention of the Israeli's travel tax.

2. The government of the Republic, the states and cities; the church and its communities; the mass media; the trade unions and the associations of trade and industry should do all that lies within their ability to insure that balanced and complete information about events in Israel and in the neighboring countries is broadcast. This means that antagonism toward Israel, anti-Zionism and anti-Semitism, newer designations than the classic "Jew hatred" must be countered with all available force.

(Translated by Dr. Allan Mittleman)

(Dietrich Goldschmidt, an officer of the commission which set up the Working Group of Jews and Christians of the German Evangelical Kirchentag, presented this report at the conclusion of the conference.)

Chapter 18

The Response Of Theologians

A State Visit as a State Funeral
Special Contribution

By Professor Martin Stöhr

In the summer of 1965, two thirds of the older citizens of the republic were in favor of letting bygones be bygones. Two thirds of the younger citizens, on the other hand, claimed wanting to know more about the war and the Nazi period. President Reagan's and Chancellor Kohl's visits to Bitburg and Bergen-Belsen contributed to ousting the history of the cemeteries to the cemetery of history.

I

President Reagan's visit to the Federal Republic of Germany took place 40 years after World War II ended. This date of commemoration could be avoided by some Germans by using two escape routes.

First, by refusing to analyze why the murderous National Socialist regime had been able to assume power in Germany. There are some who are most unwilling to ask this question, as the answers inevitably bring to light some aspects of pre-Nazi times that have by no means disappeared simply because the Nazis disappeared.

The second "escape route" from history utilizes the past historical experience, including that of its victims for a moral maxim: Jews were murdered for us to learn in the present. . . Jews are thus expropriated from their own history again.

Both German states would like to be among the ranks of the victors through their respective allies. Both of them creep under their tunics. Under the Soviets, the German Democratic Republic then feels as the incarnation of anti-fascism proper, because she is Communist. She may advocate a stiff anti-Zionism blended with anti-Semitic elements, even though she officially renounced anti-Semitism. The Federal Republic of Germany, as a U.S. ally, also renounced anti-Semitism officially. She does not cope, however, with the coalition partners of anti-Semitism such as nationalism, militarism, devotion to authorities, xenophobia, and the constraints of economic crises. These factors, coupled with anti-Semitism in all strata of society helped National Socialism come into power. Popular, everyday anti-Semitism still exists both in the Federal Republic of Germany and the GDR today. The small Jewish communities feel it. Opinion polls bring it to light.

II

Behind the incidents of May 1985, basic divergencies between the Germans are camouflaged behind semantic quibbles. On the one hand, there were some who said: This is a day of liberation. They had various hardships in mind, which they had been freed of—bombardments, the mass dying of soldiers on the front and of civilians at home, worrying about relatives, lack of food, and the pressures of Nazi-dictatorship. Others stressed emphatically: Foremost, the day of liberation means: The few surviving Jews, Sintis and Romas—peoples that had been doomed to total annihilation by *raison d'etat* and party ideology were liberated from the concentration camps.

In addition, the army of millions of forced laborers from Germany's neighboring countries, East and West, were liberated. They had been exposed to insidious death as a result of forced labor in the munitions industries. They belonged to the slave nations, on whose backs the superior German people of masters (*Herrenwolk*) planned on building their empire. Hundreds of thousands of resistance fighters— also from Germany—were liberated, who had risked their lives somewhere between Norway and Italy, France and the Soviet Union, in order to do away with the terror of the Nazi regime by force and subversion.

On the other hand, a second group referred to the end of the war in 1945 as a catastrophe, a defeat, the lost war of 1945. To them, the Nazi time was simply an epoch, an operating accident in German history. History was to continue after 1945 in much the same way as it had been prior to 1933. In this care, patriotic sentiments—which were not necessarily identical with National Socialist attitudes, yet, had supported them to a large extent!—played a great role. Additionally, the experiences during the war, which had brought death and destruction and—after 1945—hunger and flight (from East Europe) to many, thus directly affecting the lives of all families, contributed to the prevailing mood. The desire to forget was great. Peace of mind was to be attained through reconstruction, through proving oneself as a capable and efficient partner of the respective allies in East and West and by referring to Dresden, Hiroshima, and the Gulag, counter-claims could be made to justify past war crimes.

III

This discussion was preceded in 1984 by Chancellor Kohl's visit to Israel, which gave rise to heated debates both in Israel and in the Federal Republic of Germany. His government had deleted the HIAG, a veteran organization of the Waffen-SS from the list of unconstitutional organizations. The internal revenue service had recognized it as tax-exempt. Arms supplies to Saudi Arabia had been contemplated by Kohl and his predecessors. Kohl had made a point of stating that he was only fifteen by the end of the war and that the majority of the German population was born and raised after 1945, and that the time for a "normalization" in the relationship between Germans and Jews had come therefore. Many Germans loved to hear just that. Bitburg was approved of by the majority, because military honors, scapegoats, and a dissociation from the Nazi past were to be celebrated there. Who dared ask a U.S. ally embarrassing questions or probe into her past?

In a similar way, if for different reasons, a visit by the Greens, a new, socially critical, grass-root and ecologically oriented party was received in Israel. They had come to Israel naively, prepared to take the consequences of the Holocaust. In an "abstract", they drew a balance of history, without, however, taking into account the living part of it, i.e., the victims and survivors as actual, real, living beings, without seeing the living and the dead with their biographies. In contrast to the ruling conservative (CDU) and the liberal (FDP) parties, they will not tolerate former Nazis among their ranks, but they emphatically support the criticism of Israel as advocated by many Third World countries. In such a way, the Nazi era to them becomes in many cases a lesson to be learned. In this lesson of the "never again", there is no special room for Israel and the Jewish Diaspora with their still precarious existence.

IV

In 1979, Secretary Blüm (CDU) stated that the concentration camps could only have operated as long as they had because of the German army surrounding them. Pressured by his party friends, he had to renounce this "defamation" of the German army, even though all of the historical evidence proves that parts of the regular army, mainly in East Europe, actively participated in both defaming, registering, and capturing the Jews, even in the shooting of the Jewish population with the knowledge of their superiors. The problems around Bitburg was not so much the existence of SS graves, but rather the many other thousands of soldiers' graves. What had the soldiers died for? Whom had they served? How had they been mislead? The honor of the dead has certainly to be respected. If, however, all the dead of Bergen-Belsen and Bitburg are equally alike victims to the same causes, as Reagan and Kohl tried to suggest, then how can history be analyzed in an historically correct way? Can policies ever be developed, securing freedom and justice, peace and human rights for all, without analyzing the past and thus generating necessary differentiations, first? Policies which prevent that there will ever be a second Bergen-Belsen again, for any people whatsoever? Must I not ask: Who was whose victim? Who was the murderer, spectators, collaborator, resistance fighter, fellow traveler, who was the murdered one?

I do not say this to exonerate the SS in any way. To the contrary, whoever sees in the SS nothing but the eliminator of the Poles, Russians, and Jews (as German conservatives and U.S. movies tend to), makes light of the entanglement of all German institutions in the process of selection, suppression, and murdering, which included the army and the administration of the law, the universities and the administrative agencies, the churches and the cultural institutions, industry and the mass transport system.

It was the same spirit ruling the cowardice of those who looked away, or those who became a tool of the ruling powers, who did not want Auschwitz personally, but paved its way through books, building roads, through prejudice and obedience.

It must not be forgotten that the representatives of big industry (such as IG-Farben) were released by the allies soon after the Nuremberg trials. They had built factories in Auschwitz, to be sure, they had Jews and East European forced laborers toil themselves to death. Still, after the war, they were needed again for the economic reconstruction during the Cold War. Efficiency, rationality, and division of labor had turned industry and its collaborators into tools of the regime — even though their representatives were often enough not Nazis themselves.

As of 1950, the rehabilitation of the German army was started. New German soldiers were needed against the Soviet Union. Thus, a de facto, partial justification for the past war against the Poles and the Russians had been found. The CDU chairman in the German Parliament, Dr. Alfred Dregger, wrote to 53 U.S. senators directly before Reagan's impending visit: "On the last day of the war, May 8th, 1945, I — then 24 years of age — helped defend the town of Marklissa in Silesia with my battalion against the attacks of the Red Army." Here, as well as in the speeches delivered by Reagan and Kohl to German and American soldiers in Bitburg, the present-day friendly relations between the U.S. and the Federal Republic of Germany appear as a matter of continuity in the battle for freedom, in the battle against a merely exchangeable opponent: totalitarianism. It makes me sad to see that there is an affiliation (with honorary memberships!) between the 6th SS Mountain Division North and the 70th U.S. Infantry Division Association. Reconciliation is necessary. The mutual friendship between the peoples of Germany and America is a great achievement of the postwar era. To many Germans, the desire for reconciliation with the former enemies in the East is important also. We owe our liberation from National Socialism to the Allies and not to our own resistance movement. And due to the Allies we had a good teaching in democracy.

Still, the questions remains: Does anti-Semitism have to be replaced by anti-Communism? Anti-Communism has been a constant factor of ideological and political orientation in Germany ever since the Weimar era, through the Nazi period until the present day. After 1945, it was easy enough to dissociate oneself from anti-Semitism. An old scapegoat sufficed: Communism. It fulfilled all the require-ments needed to satisfy prejudice and scapegoating. It supplied a demarcation line, a clear outline of "good" and "bad", and it offered an explanation for all prob-lems under the sun. Anti-Semitism had had that function in Germany through-out the decades. It had turned the Jews into the scapegoats. Anti-Communism is now functionalized in the same way to fill the void. This, of course, does not mean to say that Communism may not be criticized or not be averted. In the language of the Nazis, the opponents of the Nazi regime were "Jewish-Bolshevist underlings." After 1945, the adjective "Jewish" was dropped, the scapegoat was given a chance to change or to continue existing. The defense of freedom today must not be a con-tinuation of defending Hitler's state and all its agencies.

V

When the Catholic bishop, in whose region Bergen-Belsen is located (the Prot-estant bishop had refused to appear in person, but had sent his substitute) prayed verses 2 to 8 of Psalm 85 in Bergen-Belsen with a Christological introduction, one thing became apparent: As during the Nazi period, this time again, the bishops and the Christians of all denominations did not stand by the Jews, who had them-selves been carried away by the German police in protest against Reagan's and Kohl's visit to Bergen-Belsen and Bitburg. They did not solidarize with the rabbis who had refused to come to Bergen-Belsen. Acts of state were celebrated there. Those in power love to surround themselves with religious decor on occasions like these and the Christians in front of their TV sets also with traditional associations, consisting of religious anti-Judaism and a way of thinking oriented toward punish-ment rather than compassion: The victims of Bergen-Belsen fell prey to God's wrath and their own malice.

Reading the speeches delivered in Bergen-Belsen today, their theological and historical imprecision becomes strikingly evident. In contrast to the Bible or the Talmud, no names were mentioned in Bergen-Belsen. Does that mean to say that the victims must be forever anonymous? Who were the dead victims?

In his speech, Reagan spoke of Jews, who were murdered, "because they prayed to their God. They lie side by side with many Christians, both Catholics and Pro-testants." Certainly, many Christians became victims. But to mention them in the same breath with the murdered Jewish people ignores the failure of the Christi-ans as it was voiced, e.g., by the Protestant Church in its Stuttgart Confession of Guilt in 1945. Other questions remain as well. There were thousands of atheist and communist, liberal and agnostic Jews — not only in Bergen-Belsen — who died. May the victims become subject to yet another selection? What about the resistance fighters from France, Belgium, and the Netherlands? What about the Russian prisoners of war?

Bergen-Belsen was started as an army training camp in 1935. In 1938, it be-came an ordnance depot as a result of the armament. In 1940, it housed Belgian and French prisoners of war. In 1941, Russian prisoners of war were transported there. Without food and shelter, they did not survive the winter. The SS established its provisioning office there. In 1943, the first Jews arrived, thousands of whom were sent to Auschwitz for extermination during the very same year. Over 50,000 people were murdered in Bergen-Belsen or left prey to death by hunger and epidemics. The millionfold mass extermination took place "under the protection" of war outside of the Reich's territory in the large camps of Auschwitz. Majdanek, Treblinka, Sobibor, and elsewhere. Only one thing is clear: Military force, equipment, and training only served as a preparation and camouflage of the mass murder. Why did the politicians visit the representatives of military force in Bitburg only, both dead and alive? Why was the courage of those resisting for their convictions not honored? Why was there no commemoration of the resistance fighters of all European nations? Was it because too many Socialists, Liberals, and Communists were among them? The Jewish resistance movement was a glorious chapter in European resistance against National Socialism. Jews were not victims only, they also defended themselves.

VI

Is German history subject to a singular development? Was or is Fascism or National Socialism, respectively, a conceivable factor in other countries? This does not only imply the following question: How did such an excess of ideologically preconceived, perfectly planned, militarily secured, and industrially executed genocide of the Jewish people come about? Why in Germany, despite the fact that there was anti-Semitism in many countries during the first decades of the twentieth century? This also implies a hypothesis: There is no mono-causal explanation for National Socialism. Thus, the question, why all occupational classes, all institutions, all Churches were prone to National Socialism, an ideology of Nihilism, which possessed no analytical or constructive political ideas of its own, is in need of an answer. Anti-Semitism became a tool, which combined many negative traditions of German history (Christian anti-Judaism, racism, nationalism, militarism, an education focusing on obedience and lack of criticism, disdain of democracy, an inability to cope with economic crises, xenophobia, etc.) and reinforced these factors with fanaticism, cowardice, venom, and canons.

At this point, the pre-National Socialist factors, which shaped the course of German history—apart from anti-Semitism—became evident. In terms of domestic affairs, this meant in those days: Conservatives and the critics of Capitalism alike placed their hopes in National Socialism. The first rightly so: The capitalist economic system remained unchanged under Hitler, even thrived. The critics of capitalism were mistaken and had themselves deceived, while revealing their weakness at the same time. Before 1933, they did too little to advocate for democracy as a way of life, did too little in support of a democratization of all spheres of life, and did too little to stand up for the notion, that an opponent, too, has unalienable rights.

During the time of the Great Depression, Eric Fromm conducted a sociological study, which remained unpublished then. According to his findings, both workers and the middle class were prone to authoritarian structures in the family, the educational system, and the state. Political ideas propagating strength and the exclusion of others met their approval, while they stated at the same time that they would not like to encounter such mechanisms of authority and exclusion at their workplace. When democracy was threatened outside the work world or destroyed, as in 1933, not many rushed to its rescue. It did not mean that much to them.

In addition, seven million jobless considered it more important to find work than to defend democracy, which, more often than not, they did not consider necessary in most important spheres of life (family, education, and nation). Hitler created new jobs through increased armament and prepared for his rule over the world, destroying it at the same time. He blamed the Jews for wanting to control the world as Bolshevists and capitalists. This nonsense was taken as an explanation and this substitute was something people believed in and practiced. As certainly as history does not repeat itself, it is justified to ask which attitudes and modes of behavior could become dangerous in the present world. I do not deny that I consider the Jewish people, both in Israel and in the Diaspora as a sensitive barometer for the threats our world is faced with.

VII

Bitburg and Bergen-Belsen — the former concentration camp was not included in the visiting schedule of the American President until very late — both reveal how fresh the scars of recent German history still are. Hitler believed that conscience was a Jewish invention. He had to expel the Jews from the face of the earth, to be freed from the memory of a conscience, in order to be able to destroy human dignity. He silenced millions. Their voices could be heard now, provided, politicians' interests in the actualities of the day, new scapegoats, the desire to forget and a civil religion will not silence them anew.

May 1985 contributed to defacing the victims by wrong equations, to drowning their specific voices, and to ignoring the urgent questions as to how the mass murdering of the Jewish people could happen. The massive protest against Bitburg in the U.S. and the lukewarm protest in Germany are promising indications that memory, however much put aside, cannot be repressed completely. In his impressive speech of May 8th, 1985, Richard von Weizsäcker (CDU), the president of the Federal Republic of Germany, encouraged all Germans to face German history honestly. This task also remains to be fulfilled by the next generation for the future generations to be able to live.

Translated by Renate Steinchen

(Prof. Martin Stöhr studied sociology and theology in Mainz, Bonn, and Basel. He has been Chaplain at the Technical University of Darmstadt and Director of the Protestant Academy of Arnoldshain since 1973. In 1983 he was awarded an honorary doctorate at the University of Heidelberg. The next year, he received the Hedwig-Burgheim-Award for the improvement of international relations.)

A Wasted Opportunity and A Salutary Lesson
Special Contribution

By Professor Rolf Rendtorff

Bitburg was a real shock for all those who had worked for so many years towards a serious rethinking of German and Christian history in order to establish a new approach to a common future of Jews and Christians all over the world. The two representatives of both our nations and their advisers in the backgrounds obviously did not understand anything of the historical and moral lesson we ought to have learned from the terrible past. It is not my task as a German to ask what happened (or did not happen) in the mind of the President of the United States when he had to listen to the imploring and ireful words of Elie Wiesel explaining to him that Bitburg was not the place for him to go. As a German I have to admit that probably it was the insistence of the German chancellor that prevented Reagan from changing the program of his visit to Germany. This man had demonstrated his total lack of sensitivity towards the German-Jewish history before, when during his visit to Israel he claimed to be too young to share any responsibility for what happened to the Jews during the times of the Nazi regime in Germany.

By this Chancellor Kohl showed what our real problem is: the attempt to escape from our history rather than to face it; the illusion to build a new society in this country by repressing the dark sides of our history, stressing only the nice and beautiful memories; to pretend that now, after forty years, everything will be forgotten if only the Germans will be nice fellows and reliable allies within the western world. He is the typical representative of a mainstream tendency in West Germany today.

Bitburg could have been an opportunity to open new horizons to a future built on the sensitive consciousness of the past and on the definite readiness to overcome the origins of the wrong development, and to fight any tendencies leading into the same direction. But now it becomes obvious that the chances of taking advantage of such an opportunity actually never existed. It is painful to admit, but I am afraid this is the truth. The minority of those who tried to build up a new consciousness was too small and our efforts have been too weak to achieve a fundamental change of thinking. That is the lesson we have to learn from the events and discussions around Bitburg.

But I hope this is not all we have to say. As a Bible scholar I try to learn from this important book that is the fundamental basis for both Jewish and Christian thinking and belief. In the Bible the period of forty years is mentioned several times. It indicates the change of generations be it for better or for worse. The Exodus generation was not allowed to see the Promised Land because of their lack of confidence in God's guidance; they had to stay in the wilderness for forty years until all men who had been responsible for the unfaithful attitude of the people had died, and only the next generation got the chance of entering the land and beginning a new epoch of the people's history (Numbers 14:20ff.). But there is also the opposite experience: After the death of Joshua, who had led the Israelites into the Promised Land, "there arose another generation who did not know the Lord or the work which he had done for Israel" (Judges 2:10). Thus Israel fell back into apostasy, and only after a deep crisis did they turn back to God who sent them a savior—and then the land had to rest for forty years. The change of generations is always a decisive point and it can become a turning point.

These Biblical experiences can illuminate our present situation. The majority of the generation who experienced the most terrible epoch of German history obviously was unable or unwilling to understand what happened—that from the depth of German and Christian tradition arose the most dreadful crime human history ever saw. Of course, most people in our country honestly condemn the murderous deeds. But they do not feel affected personally, and, in particular, they do not feel the need to reflect about the roots of these deeds in their own history. They want to carry on as usual and not to be bothered by uneasy reminiscences and by discussions about guilt and responsibility. Unfortunately, the political representatives too often are but the mirror of the average opinion and do not feel responsible for the changing of such inappropriate behaviour.

All this is true—but it is only half the truth. The other half is the fact that since the end of the Nazi regime there has been, and still is, serious discussion about how to deal with the complex of questions and problems involved, in particular, in all areas of education and the churches. Most of the younger teachers, pastors and priests and also the majority of journalists try hard to present a true picture of what happened, to discuss seriously the problems of guilt and responsibility and to ask again and again what has to be done in order to avoid a development which leads back into the dangerous trails of the past. Thus the next generation is educated in a quite different way. For most of them the idea to venerate the graves of SS men would be absurd. But probably it would not make any sense to them to visit a military cemetery at all. Fortunately the majority of them have no emotional ties to the militaristic German tradition nor to the Nazi ideology.

But there seems to be a gap: on the one side the yesterday-minded insensitive politicians who wish to represent an ideal world, on the other side the next generation almost without ideals and in its majority without a political commitment. They do not protest against events like Bitburg; they are simply uninterested. What happened forty years ago is distant past for them that does not have any discernable relation to the reality of their own present life.

Fortunately the picture drawn here is too rough. We had, and we have, politicians who are sensitive and have a consciousness towards the German past (remember Willi Brandt kneeling at the Warsaw ghetto!). We have people in all sectors of our society who are conscious and committed—educators, journalists, all kinds of academics, scientists, trade unionists and many others. And we have young people who are concerned with the German past and committed to work for a better future. But they always are a minority running the risk of being regarded by the majority as trouble-makers. Therefore, I feel it is dangerous for our society to be represented by persons like Chancellor Kohl who would prefer all these people to be silent. (Even worse was the inacceptable letter by Alfred Dregger to American senators! [see Chapter 6]) The bitter lesson we have to learn from Bitburg is: we still are, and obviously will remain to be, a minority suspiciously looked upon by the majority; and that the majority, as represented by the present chancellor, claims to be the true Germans of today.

And yet, we have to continue with our efforts and even to intensify them. Bitburg was a defeat for those Germans who try to learn from our history. But because we are convinced that this is the only way for our people to achieve a future which once and for all has to overcome the dangerous heritage of our past we have no choice but to continue. And we will do so — not least because we have American friends, Jews and Christians, who encourage us to continue. It is good to know that we work and fight together for a better common future.

The editor asked me to answer two questions: what the impact of President Reagan's visit to Bitburg was (a) on American-German reconciliation, and (b) upon the future developments of German-Jewish reconciliation.

The second question, which is my main concern, I tried to answer. But I wish to add that we are ashamed that some major activities during the visit came from non-German Jews, and not from German Christians as it should have been.

It was French Jews who demonstrated at Bergen-Belsen, and it was American Jews who organized a memorial ceremony for the martyrs of the "White Rose," young Christian fighters against the Nazi-tyranny. And while the Jewish representatives stayed away from the ceremony at Bergen-Belsen as a protest against the visit to the Bitburg cemetery, the German Church officials honored the ceremony by their Scripture readings and prayers. All this was anything but honorable for us. But we are glad that in the meantime we had the opportunity to welcome some American Jewish representatives at the Deutscher Evangelischer Kirchentag at Düsseldorf and to strengthen the ties by working together in this field of our common concern.

The other question is more complicated to answer and I can only express my personal views. First of all, I cannot see that there was a need for an American-German "reconciliation." There never existed a particular enmity between Germans and Americans (as it did, e.g., between Germans and French). Surely the Americans contributed most to the final victory against Germany. But there never were feelings of hatred on both sides (as it was, and partially still is, between Germans and Russians). Immediately after the disastrous defeat Germans experienced the American help by CARE parcels and the Marshall Plan. And when President Kennedy visited Germany in 1963 it was something like the beginning of the postwar era of American-German relations. Why reconciliation in 1985? Was it because the American President happened to be in Germany forty years after the war? Or was it because Chancellor Kohl wanted to have a particular show?

What really would be necessary is to study together the roots and origins of fascism and racism, of prejudices and discrimination of minorities, of national arrogance and hostility to foreigners. To affirm to the Germans that they are again good soldiers and reliable allies in the fight against someone else could be rather counter-productive. Probably this is one of the most crucial and most touchy points in the field of American-German relations.

In Germany today it is fashionable to denounce critical voices as "anti-American." But are those who are concerned about peace with our Eastern neighbours, who find it to be a task of particular urgency to look for ways towards reconciliation with the peoples of Eastern Europe who suffered so severely from the German invasion and occupation (while the Americans did not), anti-American? And are those people who are frightened about the vision of Star Wars and do not believe that this is the way to peace, who are afraid to become the victims of a "limited nuclear war" in Europe as some American strategists imagine, anti-American?

I could continue and hope my American readers will understand. In my view, American-German reconciliation could only exist if we work together towards peace between all nations and peoples and human beings. A coalition to fight other people, even if temporarily necessary, can never be a value on its own.

As for Germans, it is particularly dangerous to value their friendship in military categories. German militarism has brought such an amount of suffering to the world that everybody should be glad if Germans take all military affairs, at best, as a necessary evil but remain suspicious towards any development that could lead back to restore the bad German traditions we have overcome only with the help of our former American enemies.

Therefore, reconciliation never should help to reestablish those destructive forces of the German tradition.

Our American friends should understand and should help us never to turn back to any admiration of military power, be it for whatever purpose, but instead to develop forces of real reconciliation with Jews, Americans and all human beings.

(Prof. Rolf Rendtorff teaches Religion and Old Testament at Heidelberg University. In 1970-72 he was its Rector. Author of numerous scholarly works and an activist in German-Jewish reconciliation, he is co-founder and vice president of the German-Israeli Society, 1965-1977, co-founder and chairman of the German-Israeli Association for Peace in the Middle East since 1977, and chairman of the Commission on the Church and the Jewish People of the Protestant Church of West Germany.)

Christians and Jews After Auschwitz

By Professor Johann-Baptist Metz

A Moral Awareness of Tradition

I am no expert in the field of Jewish-Christian ecumenism. And yet my readiness to voice an opinion on the question of Jewish-Christian relations after Auschwitz is motivated not least by the fact that I no longer really know—faced with the catastrophe of Auschwitz—what being an expert can possibly mean. So already that name has been uttered which cannot and should not be avoided when the relationship between Jews and Christians in this country—or in fact anywhere else—is being formulated and decided. It is a name which may not be avoided here, nor forgotten for an instant, precisely because it threatens already to become only a fact of history, as if it could be classified alongside other names in some preconceived and overarching history and thereby successfully delivered over to forgetfulness, or—amounting in the end to the same thing—to selective memorial celebrations: the name "Auschwitz," intended above all here as a symbol of the horror of that millionfold murder done to the Jewish people.

Auschwitz concerns us all. Indeed what makes Auschwitz unfathomable is not only the executioners and their assistants, not only the apotheosis of evil revealed in these, and not only the silence of God. Unfathomable, and sometimes even more disturbing, is the silence of men: the silence of all those who looked on or looked away and thereby handed over this people in its peril of death to an unutterable loneliness. I say this not with contempt but with grief. Nor am I saying it in order to revive again the dubious notion of a collective guilt. I am making a plea here for what I would like to call a moral awareness of tradition. A moral awareness means that we can only mourn history and win from it standards for our own action when we neither deny the defeats present within it nor gloss over its catastrophes. Having an awareness of history and attempting to live out of this awareness means, above all, not evading history's disasters. It also means that there is at least *one* authority that we should never reject or despise—the authority of those who suffer. If this applied anywhere, it applies, in our Christian and German history, to Auschwitz. The fate of the Jews must be remembered as a moral reality precisely because it threatens already to become a mere matter of history.

Auschwitz as End Point and Turning Point?

The question whether there will be a reformation and a radical conversion in the relations between Christians and Jews will ultimately be decided, at least in Germany, by the attitude we Christians adopt toward Auschwitz and the value it really has for ourselves. Will we actually allow it to be the end point, the disruption which it really was, the catastrophe of our history, out of which we can find a way only through a radical change of direction achieved via new standards of action? Or will we see it only as a monstrous accident within this history but not affecting history's course?

Let me clarify the personal meaning I attach to Auschwitz as end point and turning point for us Christians by recalling a dialogue I shared in. At the end of 1967 there was a round-table discussion in Münster between the Czech philosopher Machovec, Karl Rahner, and myself. Toward the end of the discussion, Machovec recalled Adorno's saying: "After Auschwitz, there are no more poems"—a saying which is held everywhere today to be exaggerated and long since disproved—unjustly, to my mind, at least when applied to the Jews themselves. For were not Paul Celan, Thadeus Borowsky, and Nelly Sachs, among others—all born to make poetry as few others have been—destroyed by the sheer unutterability of that which took place at Auschwitz and the need for it somehow still to be uttered in language? In any case, Machovec cited Adorno's saying and asked me if there could be for us Christians, after Auschwitz, any more prayers. I finally gave the answer which I would still give today: We can pray *after* Auschwitz, because people prayed *in* Auschwitz.

If this is taken as a comprehensive answer, it may seem as exaggerated a saying as Adorno's. Yet I do not consider it an exaggeration. We Christians can never again go back behind Auschwitz: to go beyond Auschwitz, if we see clearly, is impossible for us of ourselves. It is possible only together with the victims of Auschwitz. This, in my eyes, is the root of Jewish-Christian ecumenism. The turning point in relations between Jews and Christians corresponds to the radical character of the end point which befell us in Auschwitz. Only when we confront this end point will we recognize what this "new" relationship between Jews and Christians is, or at least could become.

To confront Auschwitz is in no way to comprehend it. Anyone wishing to comprehend in this area will have comprehended nothing. As it gazes toward us incomprehensibly out of our most recent history, it eludes our every attempt at some kind of amicable reconciliation which would allow us to dismiss it from our consciousness. The only thing "objective" about Auschwitz are the victims, the mourners, and those who do penance. Faced with Auschwitz, there can be no abstention, no inability to relate. To attempt such a thing would be yet another case of secret complicity with the unfathomed horror. Yet how are we Christians to come to terms with Auschwitz? We will in any case forgo the temptation to interpret the suffering of the Jewish people from our standpoint, in terms of saving history. Under no circumstances is it *our* task to mystify this suffering! *We* encounter in this suffering first of all only the riddle of our own lack of feeling, the mystery of our own apathy, not, however, the traces of God.

Faced with Auschwitz, I consider a blasphemy every Christian theodicy (i.e., every attempt at a so-called "justification of God") and all language about "meaning" when these are initiated outside this catastrophe or on some level above it. Meaning, even divine meaning, can be invoked by us only to the extent that such meaning was not also abandoned in Auschwitz itself. But this means that we Christians for our very own sakes are from now on assigned to the victims of Auschwitz—assigned, in fact, in an alliance belonging to the heart of *saving history*, provided the word "history" in this Christian expression is to have a definite meaning and not just serve as a screen for a triumphalist metaphysic of salvation which never learns from catastrophes nor finds in them a cause for conversion, since in its view such catastrophes of meaning do not in fact exist at all.

This saving history alliance would have to mean, finally, the radical end of every persecution of Jews by Christians. If any persecution were to take place in the future, it could only be a persecution of both together, of Jews *and* Christians—*as it was in the beginning*. It is well known that the early persecutions of Christians were also persecutions of Jews. Because both groups refused to recognize the Roman Emperor as God, thus calling in question the foundations of Rome's political religion, they were together branded as atheists and haters of the human race and were persecuted unto death.

The Jewish-Christian Dialogue in Remembrance of Auschwitz

When these connections are seen, the question becomes obsolete as to whether Christians in their relations to Jews are now finally moving on from missionizing to dialogue. Dialogue itself seems, in fact, a weak and inappropriate description of this connection. For, after all, what does dialogue between Jews and Christians mean in remembrance of Auschwitz? It seems to me important to ask this question even though—or rather because—Christian-Jewish dialogue is booming at the present time and numerous organizations and institutions exist to support it.

1. Jewish-Christian dialogue in remembrance of Auschwitz means for us Christians first: It is not we who have the opening word, nor do we begin the dialogue. *Victims* are not offered a dialogue. We can only come into a dialogue when the victims themselves begin to speak. And then it is our primary duty as Christians to listen—*for once to begin really listening*—to what Jews are saying of themselves and about themselves. Am I mistaken in the impression I have that we Christians are already beginning in this dialogue to talk far too much about ourselves and our ideas regarding the Jewish people and their religion? That we are once again hastening to make comparisons, comparisons separated from concrete situations and memories and persons, dogmatic comparisons which may indeed be better disposed and more conciliatory than before but which remain equally naive because we are once more not listening closely? The end result is that the dialogue which never really achieved success is once more threatened with failure. And is not the reason for this that we are once again unable to see what is there, and prefer to speak about "Judaism" rather than to "the Jews"?

Have we really listened attentively during the last decades? Do we really know more today about the Jews and their religion? Have we become more attentive to the prophecy of their history of suffering? Or is the exploitation not beginning again, this time in a more sublime fashion because placed under the banner of friendliness toward the Jews? Is it not, for example, a kind of exploitation when we pick out fragments of texts from the Jewish tradition to serve as illustrations for our Christian preaching, or when we love to cite Hassidic stories without casting a single thought to the situation of suffering out of which they emerged and which is obviously an integral part of their truth?

2. No prepared patterns exist for this dialogue between Jews and Christians, patterns which could somehow be taken over from the familiar repertoire of inner-Christian ecumenism. Everything has to be measured by Auschwitz. This includes our Christian way of bringing into play *the question of truth*. Ecumenism, we often hear, can never succeed if it evades the question of truth: it must therefore continually derive from this its authentic direction. No one would deny this. But confronting the truth means first of all not avoiding the truth about Auschwitz, and ruthlessly unmasking the myths of self-exculpation and the mechanisms of trivialization which have been long since disseminated among Christians. This would be an ecumenical service to the one undivided truth! In general, Christians would be well advised, especially in dialogue with Jews, to show particular sensitivity in using the notion of truth. Too often, in fact, has truth—or rather what Christians all too triumphantly and uncompassionately portrayed as truth—been used as a weapon, an instrument of torture and persecution against Jews. Not to forget this for a moment belongs also to the respect for truth in the dialogue between Christians and Jews!

Something else has to be kept in mind, too: When we engage in this Christian-Jewish dialogue, we Christians should be more cautious about the titles we give ourselves and the sweeping comparisons we make. Faced with Auschwitz, who would dare to call our Christianity the "true" religion of the suffering, of the persecuted, of the dispersed? The caution and discretion I am recommending here, the theological principle of economy do not imply any kind of defeatism regarding the question of truth. They are rather expressions of mistrust in relation to any ecumenism separated from concrete situations and devoid of memory, that so-called purely doctrinal ecumenism. After Auschwitz, every theological "profundity" which is unrelated to people and their concrete situations must cease to exist. Such a theology would be the very essence of superficiality. With Auschwitz, the epoch of theological systems which are separate from people and their concrete situations has come to its irrevocable end. It is for this very reason that I am hesitant about all systematic comparisons of respective doctrines, however well-intentioned and gentle in tone; hesitant also toward all attempts to establish "theological common ground." Everything about this is too precipitate for my liking. Besides, did this common ground not always exist? Why, then, was it unable to protect the Jews from the aggressive scorn of Christians? The problems must surely lie at a deeper level. We have to ask ourselves the question: Can our theology ever be the same again after Auschwitz?

3. There is yet another reason why the Jewish-Christian dialogue after Auschwitz eludes every stereotyped pattern of ecumenism. The Jewish partner in this
sought-after new relationship would not only be the religious Jew, in the confessional sense of the term, but, in a universal sense, every Jew threatened by Auschwitz. Jean Améry expressed it thus, shortly before his death: "In the inferno [of
Auschwitz] the differences now became more than ever tangible and burned themselves into our skin like the tattooed numbers with which they branded us. All 'Ar-
ian' prisoners found themselves in the abyss *elevated* literally light-years *above* us, the
Jews... The Jew was the sacrificial animal. He had the chalice to drink—to its most
bitter dregs. I drank of it. And this became my existence as Jew."

Christianity and Theology after Auschwitz

The sought-after ecumenism between Christians and Jews does not, of course,
depend only on the readiness of Christians to begin at last to listen and to let Jews
express themselves as Jews, which means as the Jewish people with their own history. This ecumenism contains also a fundamental theological problem regarding
Christianity's own readiness, and the extent of this readiness, to recognize the messianic tradition of Judaism in its unsurpassed autonomy; as it were, in its enduring messianic dignity, without Christianity betraying or playing down the
christological mystery it proclaims. Once again, this question is not to be handled
abstractly but in remembrance of Auschwitz. Does not Auschwitz compel Christianity and Christian theology toward a radical inquiry into their own condition,
a self-interrogation without which no new ecumenical evaluation of the Jewish religion and of Jewish history will be possible for Christians? I would like briefly to
develop certain elements of this self-interrogation which seem important to me;
these contain, moreover, just as many indications of constantly recurring and
therefore quasi-endemic dangers within Christianity and its theology.

1. In the course of history, has not Christianity interpreted itself, in abstract
contrast to Judaism, far too much as a purely "affirmative" religion, so to speak, as
a theological "religion of conquerors" with an excess of answers and a corresponding lack of agonized questions? Was not the question of Job so repressed or played
down within christology that the image of the Son who suffers in relation to God
and God's powerlessness in the world became all too adorned with the features of
a conqueror? Does not the danger then arise of a christological reduction of the
world's history of suffering? I want to illustrate what this means by a brief quota-
tion from the German synodal document, "Our Hope": "In the history of our
church and of Christianity, have we not taken . . . Christ's suffering, in its hope-
inducing power, and then separated it too much from the one history of suffering of humanity? In connecting the Christian idea of suffering exclusively with his
cross and with ourselves as his disciples, have we not created gaps in our world,

spaces filled with the unprotected sufferings of others? Has not our attitude as Christians to this suffering often been one of unbelievable insensitivity and indifference²— as though we believed this suffering fell in some kind of purely profane sector, as though we could understand ourselves as the great conquerors in relation to it, as though this suffering had no atoning power, and as though our lives were not part of the burden placed upon it? How else, after all, is that history of suffering to be understood which Christians have prepared for the Jewish people over the centuries, or at least not protected them against? Did not our attitude in all that time manifest those typical marks of apathy and insensitivity which betray the conqueror?

2. Has not Christianity, precisely in comparison with the Jewish religion, concealed time and again its own *messianic weakness*? Does there not break through within Christianity, again and again, a dangerous triumphalism connected with saving history, something the Jews above all have had to suffer from in a special way? But is this the unavoidable consequence of Christian faith in the salvation definitively achieved in Christ? Or is it not true that Christians themselves still have something to await and to fear—not just for themselves, but rather for the world and for history as a whole? Must not Christians too lift up their heads in expectancy of the messianic Day of the Lord? This early Christian doctrine about expecting the messianic Day of the Lord—what level of intelligibility does it really have for Christian theologians? What meaning does it have—not only as a theme within Christian theology (one mostly dealt with in a perplexed or embarrassed way), but rather as a principle of theological knowledge? If this meaning were operative, or if Christians had rediscovered it in the light of Auschwitz, it would at once make clear that messianic trust is not identical with the euphoria about meaning often prevalent among Christians, something which makes them so unreceptive toward apocalyptic threats and perils within our history and allows them to react to the sufferings of others with the apathy of conquerors. And this meaning of the messianic Day of the Lord would make Christian theology perhaps more conscious of the extent to which the apocalyptic-messianic wisdom of Judaism is obstructed and repressed within Christianity. If the danger of Jewish messianism resides for me in the way it continually suspends all reconciliation from entering our history, the inverse danger in a Christian understanding of messianism seems to me to be the way it encloses the reconciliation given to us by Christ too much within the present, being only too prepared to hand out to its own form of Christianity a testimony of moral and political innocence.

Wherever Christianity victoriously conceals its own messianic weakness, its sensorium for dangers and downfalls diminishes to an ever greater degree. Theology loses its own awareness for historical disruptions and catastrophes. Has not our Christian faith in the salvation achieved for us by Christ been covertly reified to a kind of optimism about meaning, an optimism which is no longer really capable of perceiving radical disruptions and catastrophes within meaning? Does there not exist something like a typically Christian incapacity for dismay in the face of disasters? And does this not apply with particular intensity to the average Christian (and theological) attitude toward Auschwitz?

3. Is there not manifest within the history of our Christianity a drastic deficit in regard to political resistance and a corresponding excess of political conformity? This brings us, in fact, to what I see as the central point in the self-interrogation of Christians and of theology in remembrance of Auschwitz. In the earliest history of Christianity, as was already mentioned, Jews and Christians were persecuted together. The persecution of Christians ended, as we know, fairly soon, that of the Jews continued and increased immeasurably through the centuries. There are certainly numerous reasons for this dissimilar historical development in regard to Christians and Jews, and not all of them are to be used in criticism of Christianity.

Yet in making this observation, a question regarding our Christianity and its theology forces its way into my consciousness, a question that has long disturbed me and must surely affect every theology after Auschwitz: Has Christianity not allowed too strict an interiorization and individualization of that messianic salvation preached by Jesus? And was it not precisely this extreme interiorization and individualization of the messianic idea of salvation which placed Christianity—from its Pauline beginnings onward—at a continual advantage over against Judaism in coming to an arrangement with the political situation of the time and in functioning more or less without contradiction as an intermediary and reconciling force in regard to prevailing political powers? Has Christianity, perhaps for this reason only, been "in a better position?" Has the two-thousand-year-old history of Christianity contained less suffering, persecution, and dispersion than the history of the Jews for the very reason that with Christianity one could more easily "build a state?"

In a sense, Bismark was on the right track when he said that with the Sermon on the Mount "no one can build a state." But has it then been an advantage, I mean a messianic advantage, that Christians have obviously always been more successful than Jews in knowing how to accommodate their understanding of salvation to the exigencies of political power by using this extreme individualization and interiorization? Should we not have expected to find in the history of Christianity many more conflicts with political power similar to the history of suffering and persecution of the Jewish people? Does not Christianity, in fact, manifest historically a shattering deficit in political resistance, and an extreme historical surplus of political accommodation and obedience? And finally, is it not the case that we Christians can recognize that concrete destiny which Jesus foretold for his disciples more clearly in the history of suffering undergone by the Jewish people than in the actual history of Christianity? As a Christian theologian, I do not wish to suppress this question, which disturbs me above all in the presence of Auschwitz.

This is the question that compelled me to project and work on a "political theology" with its program of deprivatization (directed more toward the synoptics than to Pauline traditions), to work against just these dangers of an extreme interiorization of Christian salvation and its attendant danger of Christianity's uncritical reconciliation with prevailing political powers. This theology argues that it is pre-

cisely the consistently nonpolitical interpretation of Christianity, and the nondi-
alectical interiorizing and individualizing of its doctrines, that have continually led
to Christianity taking on an uncritical, as it were, postfactum political form. But
the Christianity of discipleship must never be politicized postfactum—through the
copying or imitation of political patterns of action and power constellations already present elsewhere. Christianity is in its very being, as messianic praxis of discipleship, political. It is mystical and political at the same time, and it leads us into
a responsibility, not only for what we do or fail to do but also for what we allow
to happen to others in our presence, before our eyes.

4. Does not Christianity conceal too much the *practical core* of its message?
Time and again we hear it said that Judaism is primarily oriented toward praxis
and less concerned with doctrinal unity, whereas Christianity is said to be primarily a doctrine of faith, and this difference is held to create considerable difficulty
for Jewish-Christian ecumenism. Yet Christianity itself is not in the first instance
a doctrine to be preserved in maximum "purity," but a praxis to be lived more radically! This messianic praxis of discipleship, conversion, love, and suffering does
not become a part of Christian faith postfactum, but is an authentic expression
of this faith. Ultimately, it is of the very essence of the Christian faith to be believed
in such a way that is never just believed, but rather—in the messianic praxis of
discipleship—enacted. There does, of course, exist a Christianity whose faith is
only believed, a superstructure Christianity serving our own interests—such a
Christianity is bourgeois religion. This kind of Christianity does not live discipleship but only believes in discipleship, and under the cover of merely believed-in
discipleship, goes its own way. It does not practice compassion, but only believes
in compassion and, under the screen of this merely believed-in compassion, cul-
tivates that apathy which allowed us Christians to continue our untroubled believing and praying with our backs to Auschwitz—allowed us, in a phrase from
Bonhoeffer, to go on singing Gregorian chants during the persecution of the Jews
without at the same time feeling the need to cry out in their behalf.

It is here, in this degeneration of messianic religion to a purely bourgeois religion, that I see one of the central roots within contemporary Christianity for our
failure in the Jewish question. Ultimately, it is the reason why we Christians, as a
whole, have remained incapable of real mourning and true penance, the reason
also why our churches have not resisted our society's massive repression of guilt
in these postwar years.

Presumably, there are still other Christian and theological questions posed
to us in remembrance of Auschwitz, questions which would open a way to an
ecumenism between Christians and Jews. We would certainly have to uncover the
individual roots of anti-Semitism within Christianity itself, in its doctrine and
praxis. A continual and significant part of this is that relationship of "substitution
within salvation history," through which Christians saw themselves displacing the
Jews and which led to the Jews never being really accepted either as partners or as
enemies—even enemies have a countenance! Rather, they were reified into an ob-

solete presupposition of saving history. However, this specific inner Christian research cannot be undertaken here; it would go far beyond the limits of this paper.
I must also rule out here any investigation of the roots of anti-Semitism in those
German philosophies of the nineteenth century which in their turn have lastingly
marked the world of theological ideas and categories in our own century.

What Christian theologians can *do* for the murdered of Auschwitz and thereby
for a true Christian-Jewish ecumenism is, in every case, this: Never again do theology in such a way that its construction remains unaffected, or could remain unaffected, by Auschwitz. In this sense, I make available to my students an apparently
very simple but, in fact, extremely demanding criterion for evaluating the theological scene: Ask yourselves if the theology you are learning is such that it could
remain unchanged before and after Auschwitz. If this is the case, be on your guard!

Revisions

The question of reaching an ecumenism between Christians and Jews, in accepting which the Jews would not be compelled to deny their own identity, will be
decided ultimately by the following factor: Will ecumenical development succeed
within the church and within society? Theological work for reconciliation remains
nothing more than a surface phenomenon when it fails to take root in church and
society, which means touching the soul of the people. Whether this ecumenism
successfully takes root, and the manner of its success, depends once again on the
way our churches, as official institutions and at the grass-roots level, relate to
Auschwitz.

What is, in fact, happening in our churches? Do not the "Weeks of Christian-
Jewish Fellowship" threaten gradually to become a farce? Are they not a witness to
isolation far more than to fellowship. Which of us are really concerning ourselves
about the newly emerging fears of persecution among the Jews in our country? The
Catholic Church in West Germany in its synodal decree, "Our Hope," declared its
readiness for a new relationship with the Jewish people and recognized its own special task and mission. Both the history behind the preparation of this section of
the synod's text and its finally accepted form could show how tendencies to hush
up and exonerate had a powerful impact. Nevertheless, if we would only take this
document really seriously even in this final version! "In that time of national socialism, despite the exemplary witness of individual persons and groups, we still
remained as a whole a church community which lived its life with our backs turned
to the fate of this persecuted Jewish people; we let our gaze be fixed too much on
the threat to our own institutions and remained silent in the face of the crimes perpetrated on the Jews and on Judaism."

Yet, in the meantime, has not a massive forgetfulness long since taken over?
The dead of Auschwitz should have brought upon us a total transformation; nothing should have been allowed to remain as it was, neither among our people nor
in our churches. Above all, not in the churches. They, at last, should necessarily
have perceived the spiritual catastrophe signified by Auschwitz, one which left nei-

ther our people nor our churches undamaged. Yet, what has happened to us as Christians and as citizens of this land? Not just the fact that everything happened as if Auschwitz had been, after all, only an operational accident, however deplorable a one. Indications are already appearing that we are once more beginning to seek the causes for the Auschwitz horror not only among the murderers and persecutors, but also among the victims and persecuted themselves. How long, then, are we to wear these penitential garments? This is a question asked above all by those who have probably never had them on. Has anyone had the idea of asking the victims themselves how long we have to drag out our penance and whether something like a general "limitation of liability" does not apply here? The desire to limit liability in this area is to my mind less the expression of a will to forgiveness from Christian motives (and indeed *we* have here hardly anything to forgive!) than it is the attempt of our society and of our Christianity(!) to decree for itself—at last—acquittal and, poised over the abyss of horror, to get the whole thing—at last—"over with."

Faced with this situation, one thing is clear: The basis for a new relationship between Christians and Jews in remembrance of Auschwitz must not remain restricted to the creation of a diffuse sense of reconciliation nor to a Christian friendliness toward Jews which is as cheap as it is ineffective (and is itself, in fact, not seldom the sign of an unfinished hostility to Jews). What must be aimed at is a concrete and fundamental revision of our consciousness.

To take one example: This new dialogical relationship we are seeking, if it is truly to succeed, must not become a dialogue of theological experts and church specialists. This ecumenism must take root in the people as a whole, in the pedagogy of everyday life, in Sunday preaching, in church communities, families, schools, and other grassroots institutions. Everyone knows that new traditions are not established in advanced seminars nor in occasional solemn celebrations. They will only emerge if they touch the souls of men through a tenacious process of formation, when they become the very environment of the soul. But what is actually happening here in our churches and schools? Not least in our churches and schools in the rural areas which are held to be so "Christian"? Certainly anti-Semitism in rural areas has varied causes; yet not the least of these are related to religious education. In my own rural area, in a typically Catholic milieu, "the Jews" remained even after the war a faceless reality, a vague stereotype; representations for "the Jews" were taken mostly from Oberammergau.

Some historians hold the view that the German people in the Nazi era were not, in fact, essentially more anti-Semitic than several other European peoples. Personally, I doubt this, but if it were true, it would raise an even more monstrous possibility, something already put forward years ago by one of these historians: Might the Germans have drawn the ultimate consequences of anti-Semitism, namely the extermination of the Jews, only because they were *commanded to*; that is, out of sheer dependence on authority? Whatever the individual connection may have been, there is manifest here what has often enough been established as a "typically German danger." And this is the reason why the question being dealt with here demands the highest priority being given by both society and the churches to an energetic educational campaign supporting critical obedience and critical solidarity, and against the evasion of conflict and the practice of successful conformism, opportunism, and fellow-traveling.

In this context I want to quote, without pursuing her argument further, the thoughts of a young Jewish woman, who worked as a teacher in West Germany, regarding the Week of Fellowship: "There are two expressions I learned in the school without having the least idea of their significance. One of them is 'in its juridical form', and the other is 'legal uncertainty'. Every event in the school, and I assume in all other institutions, has to be confirmed in its juridical form, even when this leads to senseless behavior.... Wherever I look, I see only exemplary democrats who, according to the letter and without any reason or emotion, observe laws and ordinances, instructions, directions, guiding lines and decrees. The few who protest against this and display some individualism and civil courage are systematically intimidated and cowed.... That is the reason why I do not fraternize with the Germans, why I reject the Week of Fellowship, and why my soul boils over at the empty babble about our dear Jewish brethren; the same people today who speak eloquently of tolerance would once again function as machines which had been presented with a new and different program!"

At the beginning, I mentioned that Auschwitz can only be remembered by us as a moral reality, never purely historically. This moral remembrance of the persecution of the Jews touches finally also on the relationship of the people in this country to the *State* of Israel. Indeed, *we* have no choice in this matter (and I stand by this against my left wing friends). *We* must at all events be the last people to now accuse the Jews of an exaggerated need for security after they were brought in the most recent history of our country to the edge of total annihilation; and *we* must be the first to trust the protestations of the Jews that they are defending their state, not from reasons of Zionist imperialism but as a "house against death," as a last place of refuge of a people persecuted through the centuries.

Ecumenism in a Messianic Perspective

The ecumenism between Jews and Christians in remembrance of Auschwitz, which I have been discussing here, does not lead at all to the outskirts of inner Christian ecumenism, but rather to its center. It is my profound conviction that ultimately ecumenism among Christians will only make progress at all, and certainly will only come to a good conclusion, when it recovers the biblical-messianic dimensions of ecumenism in general. This means it must learn to know and recognize the forgotten and suppressed partner of its own beginnings, the Jewish people and their messianic religion. It is in this sense that I understand Karl Barth's warning in his 1966 "Ecumenical Testament": "We do not wish to forget that there is ultimately only one really central ecumenical question: This is our relationship to Judaism." As Christians, we will only come together among ourselves when we achieve together a new relationship to the Jewish people and to its religion; not avoiding Auschwitz, but as that particular form of Christianity which, after Auschwitz, is alone permitted to us and indeed demanded of us. For, I repeat: We Christians can never again go back behind Auschwitz. To go beyond Auschwitz is, if we see clearly, impossible for us of ourselves; it is possible only together with the victims of Auschwitz.

And so we would arrive one day, although I suggest this cautiously, at a kind of *coalition of messianic trust* between Jews and Christians in opposition to the apotheosis of banality and hatred present in our world. Indeed, the remembrance of Auschwitz should sharpen all our senses for present-day processes of extermination in countries in which on the surface "law and order" reigns, as it did once in Nazi Germany.

Reprinted from Jenseits bürgerlicher Religion. edited by Johann-Baptist Metz (Mainz-München, 1980) pp 17-32.

(Prof. Johann-Baptist Metz teaches religion at the University of Münster and is the author of numerous scholarly works.)

Chapter 19

The Response Of Jewish Leaders

German Jewish Leader Addresses Kohl
Bergen-Belsen, West Germany
April 21, 1985

By Werner Nachmann

(Speech given by Werner Nachmann, Chairman of the Central Council of Jews in Germany, during a commemorative ceremony at the former Bergen-Belsen concentration camp.)

We have gathered "in the face of death."

Mr. President [West German President von Weizsäcker], Mr. Chancellor, ladies and gentlemen, dear Jewish friends.

We mourn the millions of dead and we stand here in indictment of a murderous tyranny.

Since the National Socialist dictatorship we know what man, who is seen as being created in the image of God both by the Jewish and the Christian religions, is capable of. We have seen that he is capable of giving up and warping his countenance and his soul. We must never again be unaware of this capacity man has to pervert himself. The dismay at the extent to which man is capable of being inhuman, in the final analysis dismay at ourselves, must always be present in our minds.

Since what happened did happen, we are deeply influenced by the experience that man is capable of misusing freedom of choice to the point of dehumanization. This is an experience we cannot forget and it will continue to be with us in the future. If this senseless organized murder is to have had any meaning at all, we must seek ways of preserving the image of God in man.

Each of us is confronted with this task. In some cases we will be asking people to seek an image that they have lost, one they yielded up in passive complacency, in a false desire for security and in a manic need to march along in step, renouncing their own identities because they shied away from the risks involved in freedom. Assertions to the effect that circumstances no longer permitted free decisions are not convincing nor useful as arguments for individual failure, weakness or obsequiousness. This is always preceded by the individual giving up his freedom of responsibility and of responsible action. It is the renunciation of this freedom that creates conditions resulting in the use of such arguments to justify individual actions.

Thus, the foremost task facing political leaders is to submit to the principle that man was created in the image of God and to see to it that this principle is applied. We have all undergone the bitter experience that resulted from disregard for this principle in our century. History has shown us what happens when an individual arrogates unto himself the power of law, abuses others in their abstinence from freedom, fascinates them with his excesses, deprives them of individual responsibility without significant resistance being offered, finally degrading them to followers and vassals.

We consider 1933 the date marking the beginning of human perversion and flagrant disregard for human dignity. However, without consideration for the period leading up to the 12 years of Nazi dictatorship it is impossible to explain the rapid breakdown of civilization and the equally rapid renunciation of the moral rights and obligations that had been recognized up to that point. Poisons must have accumulated over a period of many years without clear recognition of their pathological causes. Thus, we must extend our view beyond the Nazi period. Scholars and analysts have provided us with ample material.

However, if we are not constantly aware of the fact that renunciation of our own freedom of responsibility is a cause of delusion, our sense of judgement will be inaccurate and we will not do justice to the conclusions that need to be drawn from history for the present. To this extent it is our duty to accept history. Acceptance of history is first of all an individual process. It is something demanded of the individual, requiring him to accept it of his own free will, to shape it anew and, in doing so, to begin with himself. If we perceive ourselves to be responsible agents, we commit ourselves to the risks involved in availing ourselves of our freedom. If we avoid those risks, the danger will arise of our losing this freedom just as happened over 50 years ago.

As such, the tasks assumed by political leaders include making possible the venturous enterprise known as freedom, safeguarding the latitude in which it can take place as well as heightening awareness of it. If legitimate political leaders fail to fulfill this obligation and refuse to face history squarely by such evasive means as treating the National Socialist dictatorship as if it were an accidental occurrence, they are merely denying their own ability to assume responsibility today.

Bergen-Belsen, Auschwitz, Buchenwald, Dachau and Maidanek are places that remind us of unspeakable suffering, humiliation, degradation and agonizing death millions of times over. However, more than that, they are warning examples of history. Those who argue that we have now done enough looking back and we should now be looking ahead fail to recognize that we live from history and we are living more intensively from this period of history than ever before.

The Jews experienced the abysmal despair caused by this situation more profoundly and more painfully than others. Their camp numbers, tantamount to a government-ordered denial of human rights, were burned in more deeply.

Since then, Jews in particular, not just those who survived the extermination camps, not just those who were persecuted and had to flee, but all Jews have an obligation to keep history present whenever it is rejected or forgotten by others. They are mindful that they were not persecuted and tormented for any specific actions, but rather simply because they were Jews.

However, the task of maintaining an awareness of history and living with it cannot be left to the Jews alone. We all live in and with history. None of us can escape this fact. Of course we can desensitize ourselves to it. Still, this attempt at desensitization is nothing other than a renewed subterfuge aimed at renouncing freedom of decision. If we are unable to agree that the martyrdom and death of millions of persons was preceded by relinquishment of freedom then our meeting here today will have been meaningless.

I think we are in agreement that our actions must reflect our moral principles. Here and now. The beginning to which so many have stated their commitments is not arbitrary. We cannot choose the point in time like we choose the day on which we buy new clothes and throw away the old ones that have begun to bother us and then live the illusion that we have changed more than just our outer skin.

A new beginning is a constant challenge. It is a mandate of the moment, something we can either miss or consciously pass on to the next generation. But this would mean we had missed the point. After all, we have seen what happens when the moment is not seized upon and when decisions are left to others or postponed to an uncertain future. We now know how rapidly such failures may move us into the vicinity of the sources on which evil subsists.

Thus, it ultimately contradicts the interests of government and of the individual to want to assert oneself here and now through action without being clear on where we have come from and where the route we have decided on is to lead.

The forces responsible for the inferno caused by the war and the National Socialist regime jolted and changed the world. Not only the Jews, particularly the Jews in Germany, but rather all of us are no longer able to live and act like we used to, as if nothing had happened. We view with great concern tendencies aimed at treating the years of ideological insanity as a closed chapter of history to be relegated to the libraries.

Even more than on the attempt to flee from history manifest in this, we should reflect on whether experiencing the abysmal depths of the human spirit has affected the foundations of our spiritual awareness or whether we have only been tangentially affected.

We, the Jews in Germany, are in no small way aware of the value of this Federal Republic, created after 1945. At the beginning of this second German democracy we ventured to take a step considered by most to be either impossible or unfitting, i.e. that of returning, settling down and becoming German citizens again. We did this in order to reduce distrust and build bridges. In a constant dialogue with those in federal and state government office, with the democratic parties, with the representatives of the churches and the industrial associations, whose presence here we note with gratitude, we have accompanied the development of this polity, a system we approve of, with our constructive criticism.

We continue to consider it our duty to assume a warning role whenever we have reason to fear a decline in sensitiveness to this question and we feel that negligence, thoughtlessness and a loss of historical awareness have blurred people's perceptions of the past. Were this democracy to consider 36 years of stability a reassuring basis and a guarantee against any potential development it would be danger of being uncritical towards itself and of exceeding its limits. Intellectual unrest is a necessary part of its identity. This matter is something that must not cease to occupy our minds. To be sure, governments cannot order intellectual unrest. But they can make it clear on repeated occasions by means of their actions that they, too, need this kind of unrest and are tormented by it. In this way it would be possible for dismay at and dread of the monster in man to continue to have an effect.

The presence of history, something many would like to relegate to a foggy past in which things can no longer be properly made out, is documented here by men and women who survived Bergen-Belsen and the other extermination camps and who were freed from them 40 years ago. We are thankful to them for having overcome their trepidations and for having returned today to the site of their past suffering. In having done so they provide us with a physical manifestation of just how close the time was when human dignity was an alien concept. They are an embodied testimony to the presence of history and, at the same time, a determination to begin anew.

The traditional name used to designate Mosaic Law is "Halahah," meaning "path." Obeying the Law of Moses is thus to "walk the right path." We may stray from this path. We can also freely choose to leave it. But we always move along some path. In a speech given in the Reichstag Building in Berlin on January 30, 1983 the President, who has honored us with his presence here today, said with reference to Hitler's takeover of power in 1933: "It is our task to testify to the fact that freedom and responsibility are inseparable. Let us make use of them for human rights and human dignity in a situation of peace." Addressing himself to young Germans, he said that they were not responsible for what happened in the past, but that they were indeed responsible for what became of past experience in the future.

We turn to this young generation with conscientiousness and enthusiasm. We encounter many different types of young people. They include those distorted by hate, those who are disturbed, those who are arrogant, and those who are indifferent. We take them all seriously, no matter what camps they may be active in and what influences may attract them. More important, however, are those young people who feel concern as a result of this unrest and who are not satisfied with superficial statements and platitudes. It is a young generation that does not spare its fathers and grandfathers critical questions, once again exposing this period of history to the light of day, despite all those who felt that suppressing it was their salvation.

We call upon this young generation not to relax its efforts and not to accept evasive answers. None of them as yet have been given an answer as to why it was enough, here on this soil, to be the child of a Jewish mother to lose the right to respect and human dignity.

By asking this they will give themselves and us cause for reflection. By asking this they will refer us to history and to the fact that we must seize the moment, accept our responsibility and act accordingly.

In the proverbs of our fathers it is written: "You are not obliged to complete this task, but at the same time neither are you free to withdraw yourself from it."

A Jewish Voice On The Reagan Visit To Bitburg and Bergen-Belsen
ZDF-TV
May 6, 1985

(On the day following President Reagan's visit to Bergen-Belsen and Bitburg, the ZDF-TV network broadcast an interview with the Jewish theologian Pinchas Lapide, who had once been a government official in Israel. He later taught at the Bar-Ilan University and lives in Frankfurt today.)

Q: What did you feel personally when you watched the TV images from Bergen-Belsen and Bitburg?

A: Mixed feelings. As a Jew, who had lost seven members of his family in Auschwitz, I understand the pain of my fellow sufferers only too well. But after I had slept on it, the positive side prevailed. Positive because the ceremony in Bergen-Belsen was longer and came first. Positive because as a Jew freedom runs in my blood and, therefore, I am interested in the solidarity of the powers of freedom, which also is profitable for the state of Israel. To this belongs indispensably the friendship between America and Germany, which was confirmed there. Positive, also, because it was definitely proven during the Eichmann trial in Jerusalem that the Waffen-SS — represented here with 47 or 48 graves — was exclusively a combat unit with the Wehrmacht and had nothing to do with the concentration camps. For this reason David Ben-Gurion and the Israeli government accepted Rolf Pauls—he had been a major and had lost one arm in the Wehrmacht's campaign in Russia—as the first ambassador of the FRG in Tel Aviv.

So we should turn our views away from the pains of the past, which will continue to live on in all our hearts, and look towards the future. After all, we Jews have always, throughout the longest history of suffering of any people, understood how to learn of hope from failure and not to learn of hatred from pain, but compassion instead and to concentrate on the future. And for tomorrow only one commandment counts—reconciliation of this generation's sons, who are supposed to build a better world where no Auschwitz will be possible.

Q: Do you believe that what you just said about reconciliation can be conveyed?

A: I believe that to tear open old wounds, which also exist in my own heart, cannot help anybody, not the historical truth, nor peace and never reconciliation; to open old wounds after 40 years—and 40 years in the Bible is a period that is closed and calls for a new beginning—cannot, in my opinion, help reconciliation at all.

Q: But will your fellow-believers in America and Israel also accept this?

A: Now is the time to start over, even after a catastrophy that we name Auschwitz. I am absolutely sure that the majority of my fellow-believers, but especially our sons, are willing to start over. If not today, then the day after tomorrow.

(Prof. Pinchas Lapide lectures widely in Germany on Israeli politics, Jewish heritage and religion.)

(Translated by Renate Steinchen.)

Chapter 20

Press

Forty Years Later, Remembering Alone Is Just Not Enough
Die Zeit
April 19, 1985

By Eugen Kogon

The Wehrmacht's unconditional surrender eight days after Hitler's suicide is neither a disputed nor a disputable historical event.

The signing of the capitulation documents on 7 May 1945 in Reims and two days later in Karlshorst, Berlin, sealed the fate of the Third Reich's armed forces without negotiations.

It also brought the war to an end. That was what mattered for the remaining combat units and for civilians in areas the Allies had yet to occupy.

The civilian population no longer needed to seek refuge in air raid shelters or to pay any consideration to the Nazis.

Commemoration of the anniversary is in contrast most controversial and disputed. Why suddenly recall the event 40 years later? Why not 10, 20 or 25 years later?

These two days in May 1945 were not a common historic experience shared by the German people.

It was not as though white and black, red and gold flags had been flown on all buildings that were still standing all over the country to signify the end of the Nazis and a fresh start.

Millions of Germans only learnt indirectly that the Third Reich had capitulated. They had no idea that unconditional surrender was in keeping with a decision reached by the Allies in Casablanca in 1943.

There was to be no possibility of a repetition of claims made after the First World War that the Germans had been unbeaten on the battlefield.

These facts can now be read in all history books, yet they are still not common knowledge in the sense that everyone knows them to have been a fact and accepts them as a matter of course.

The difficulty is that defeat and freedom form a single unit. Defeat was the prerequisite of freedom; not just the defeat of the Nazi regime but the defeat of Germany and the Germans.

Many came to feel in the course of time that written confirmation of total military collapse was not an occasion for national remembrance.

At best, they felt, it might be an opportunity for considering a policy of revision and for at least hinting at wishes to that effect at some future date when the power position might have changed.

It is impossible to say how strong such wishes are and how powerful their influence on society still is, but it is certainly enough to ensure that the anniversary is not one on which a national consensus exists. The freedom that was to follow in the footsteps of capitulation was in itself contradictory. For Bonn the document signed in Reims paved the way for a fresh attempt at the parliamentary democracy and constitutional government that in many ways has been a success. In East Berlin the Karlshorst document is assessed in terms of a different viewpoint, the Soviet one. Germans in East and West have been integrated ideologically, economically and militarily in hostile pacts. So the anniversary of VE Day can hardly be seen, from the German point of view, as one of unity and unquestionable renewal.

The institutionalisation of the two German states and rearmament on both sides of the border steadily heightened this contradiction. How, given the progressive undermining of its originally intended meaning, can a uniform understanding be reached?

It is a matter of the anniversary's historic credibility and its contemporary significance now and in the future.

Both would be disregarded if official speeches, from Moscow via Paris and London to Washington, were merely to commemorate the Allied victory, which has by no means established humanely safeguarded international relations.

It would also be disregarded if the wartime Allies were merely to commemorate the 40th anniversary of the war's end as a preliminary to a fresh arms build-up, arguing that they alone ensure continued world peace.

The question is whether the contradiction between the document and the reality, perceptible a mere year after the capitulation was signed, clearly apparent from 1947 in the Cold War era and since taken to be inevitable, could still be resolved 40 years later if only the erstwhile belligerents so wanted.

The Germans would do well to grasp the initiative. They would be entitled to do so, if not duty-bound after everything that has been done with them and by them.

They would be well-advised to insist on the humane, civilizing prerequisites of freedom and to set about putting them into effect in their own national sector.

The position Germany has reached in 40 years is strong and respected. We could afford to put forward and even try to put into effect development proposals of a "productively utopian character." If only we would!

The circumstances of world history associated with VE Day must surely warrant the courage of any such attempt — just as German-Polish relations justified Willi Brandt falling on his knees in front of the Warsaw ghetto monument in 1970.

The more deeply we involve ourselves, as we have been doing for decades, in the consequences of the fateful decision to remilitarize, the less it suffices merely to remember the toll peoples paid to the Nazis.

Historic pointers to essential reforms need sounding out; it isn't enough to pledge that such exercises must never occur again. That alone fails to deeply impress many people in the Federal Republic of Germany.

The millions who died in wartime and terror are constantly recalled on other occasions. There is no shortage of democratic protestations. But do they change the world?

National Socialism, with roots not only in Germany, was a brutal attempt to reverse the European enlightenment that in four centuries had increasingly gained currency as a social principle.

Democratic civilization was to be replaced worldwide by racist rule, spearheaded by a greater German Reich.

For the Nazi war, once all other political means of gaining and maintaining power had been used, was the utmost test of whether their system worked.

The German capitulation, testifying to the defeat of the racist principle of government, was intended unconditionally to rule out the use of force for political ends in future.

What then happened was the exact opposite. The first and categorical imperative of civilization yielded to large-scale rearmament including the Germans.

Given developments in, say, arms technology that have come to threaten the very survival of entire nations, not to say mankind, and Germany's part in the pact system within which we have resumed a front-line role can only be one of constant, strenuous effort to achieve disarmament.

Not a word needs to be lost on the economic, social and cultural reform effects of a consistent reorientation from military security planning to the open problems of a peace economy.

They would open up entire horizons of hope and confidence.

The anniversary of the end of the Second World War could then be celebrated as Civilization Day and an occasion for taking stock of successes and failures, plans and initiatives, hostility and solidarity. Or is it just an illusion?

(Eugen Kogon, 82, is a survivor of the Buchenwald concentration camp. He is the author of a book, The SS State, *published in 1946.)*

No Bit* Please!
Der Spiegel
April 29, 1985

By Rudolf Augstein

We know from ancient time that the pomp of the rulers consumed about as much energy and health as the entire ruling altogether. At times ruling consisted of nothing but pomp. One should think that things have changed.

They haven't, though. Realizing that for four weeks or even longer the efforts of the entire government were focused on celebrating or not celebrating May 8th rather than on solving most pressing problems — pensions, unemployment, and most dangerous of all, space weapons — one may come to the conclusion that humans and mankind are not likely to change. Pomp and strutting about take as much time as good or bad government. It is part of the unnecessary and hence bad government.

Who, for heaven's sake, could possibly be interested in commemorating May 8, 1945, which was not observed 10 or 20 years ago? It was due to the good-for-nothing segment of our politicians, unwilling to be seen around without meaningless pomp.

Very well, the Soviet Russians have genuine political interests. In order to drive wedges of all sizes between their present-day enemies, they have to keep any memories of the war coalition alive through mouth-to-mouth resuscitation.

The Israelis, too, have — apart from emotions that have to be respected by all means — genuine political interests. They strive to keep the awareness of German

*Bit is the brand name of a beer brewed in Bitburg

guilt up, for material reasons and for the sake of armament. This may or may not be reasonable; however, it is politically legitimate.

Thus, both powers have good reasons for celebrating the last even numbered anniversary, as long as there are still both Nazi criminals and enough victims alive. President Reagan was a decade out in his accounts again when he came up with the revelation that such contemporaries were hard to be found these days. To make a long story short the 40]th anniversary is the last 10-year anniversary to possibly encounter any active interest.

The question arises, however, why we have to celebrate. If the others want to, let them go ahead and it does not hurt us in the least.

Presumably, this was the only war ever to have taken place which was unavoidable and had to be won at all costs by one side — the non-German one. It was a matter of national obligation to the Germans properly trained in patriotism to lose this war, only they remembered their lesson rather late.

But what is all this celebrating to us? One half of us was liberated for the other half to be incapacitated under a new dictatorship, which has become humanized only of late. The liberated half, by the way, is not sovereign and the non-liberated one isn't either. There is nothing to blame each other for, but there is nothing to celebrate, either.

Who was the squarehead to come up with the idea that the Federal Republic of Germany should join the celebration of the Anglo-Saxons' invasion of Normandy — one can only guess. Commemoration days of this kind could be broadcast on TV for the sake of information. The leading statesman of divided and amputated Germany, however, had no business on such an occasion.

The idea of holding hands in Verdun can only be devised by people who want to camouflage cosmetically that they are not able to manage their allegedly commonly shared politics. If the big catastrophe should actually come, then those holding hands now would realize that their interests are not only just different, but even opposing. Verdun is ideally suited for such a beauty treatment, if for no other reason than the impossibility of finding a gunner today, who fought in Verdun in 1916.

The observance of May 8th seems even more ridiculous, because this date does not just signify the liberation, but at the same time, also the enslavement of millions of people.

Shall we in all seriousness hold a seminar on the issue of who killed more people, Hitler or Stalin? Do we want to inquire into the war crimes committed by the Allies? Shall we make up a balance as to whether on key-date, May 8th, more people were liberated than enslaved?

No one would want to do that. There is not even a controversy on the issue of who wanted and started the war. It was the *Führer*, the Nazi riff-raff and the German people which, though not having been consulted, were misled. It is tragic — if the word does not sound too bombastic — for the non-tragedian sunnyboy Ronald Reagan to enter. No sooner had he spoken a true word — which may not even have been jotted down for him by someone else — than he faced the most difficult week ever since the beginning of his term on January 20, 1981. He had said the truth, which, however, no one should have done — he the very least.

Here, we encounter the problem of double standards. Arik Sharon may become Israel's Prime Minister — which he isn't, yet, but, but. . . . A cemetery, on the other hand, containing the remains of fallen SS soldiers — the highest of whom held the awesome rank of *Untersturmführer* (lieutenant) — must not be visited in a conciliatory mood.

Again, one would like to know the squarehead who had taken that idea into his head. No American President whatsoever has to visit a German cemetery. Who, after all, should profit from that?

But since it seems to have to be that way: Those who lie there are presumably, as Reagan said with a nice expression on his face, "Hitler's victims." Some had been called up, or were volunteers or semi-volunteers.

So far correct. But they cannot be equated, however, with those of "Hitler's victims (as Reagan said with his typical ignorance) who were deprived of all human dignity, cruelly tortured or gassed.

The humorous old man in the White House, who delights in space games like a little kid, is obviously racing into senility with the speed of light.

Considering that the most recent accident of a "Pershing 2" reoccurred, due to "a phenomenon universally not known, as yet," and that such "phenomena" will always be an integral part of space systems; further taking into account that this humorous old man has been more concerned with the Sandinistas in Nicaragua and with Bitburg rather than with SDI and the realization that the space hype has been taken over by the military industry a long time ago and has thus been made irreversible: All that in mind, Reagan may very well visit all the cemeteries of the world; we shall be nothing but perplexed.

It would fit into the history of mankind up to now, if more attention had been paid to the right color of the red carpet than to the first (and maybe last?) star war.

(Translated by Renate Steinchen.)

(Herr Rudolf Augstein has been the editor of West Germany's Der Spiegel *for the past 24 years.)*

"Herr Bürgermeister, We Love You So Much"
Der Spiegel
April 29, 1985

By Erich Wiedemann

"First the gentlemen from the TV station in New York, then the ZDF*. The press can wait." Mayor Theo Hallett is about to give his twelfth interview today. Whether the German nation likes it or not, their conscience is articulated by Theo Hallett of Bitburg these days.

"Where were we? Yes, I stress in all seriousness that I am not prepared to de-Nazify German soldiers forty years after their deaths. Frau Matthey, get us another beer!"

Frau Matthey comes through the door with a crate of beer. "What is that," roars Hallett, "what kind of an impression are the gentlemen to take home from Bitburg, if they get warm beer in the townhall?"

Frau Matthey smiles sheepishly. "I am sorry, Herr Bürgermeister, but the refrigerator is empty again." There seems no end to the chain of mishaps in Bitburg today.

Thursday morning, nine-thirty: A reception for the newly arrive American soldiers in the large conference hall. The mayor lectures on the determination of his compatriots, "not to take any further defamation of our soldiers by certain circles in the U.S."

Hallett looks around sternly. "The boys down there were 17, 18, 19, and twenty years of age. Is any of you seventeen? He is to stand up. Stand up, stand up."

No reply.

"Eighteen, nineteen, twenty?"

Nobody stands up.

Theo Hallett was a soldier himself. He experienced that the SS fought "often bravely and decently for their homeland." The rest of his statement drowns in a roar as a formation of F-15 interceptors hedgehops over the town. Frau Matthey brings in another coffee with a swig.

The Bitburgers of both sides of the Atlantic hardly have any problems with one another.

During the past thirty years, about 16,000 American children were born and 6,000 German-American marriages were contracted. In the one-hundred-meters-beer barrel—tumbling at the *Grenzlandfest* (Country-borderline-fair) the 36th Tactical Fighter Wing regularly participates with two or three teams.

A clear majority of the U.S.-Eifel inhabitants support their President and their mayor in the Bitburg controversy.

Theo Hallett always carries a greeting card with the signatures of eight officers from the Air Base in the wallet over his heart. It says, "Herr Bürgermeister, we love

*ZDF is Zweites Deutsches Fernsehen, one of the three German TV stations.

you so much."

A group of German and American women offered the mayor to transform the cemetery into a sea of flowers to set a sign. Hallet, however, declined for the time being. "If Reagan doesn't come," he says, "we could still do it."

Peter Siegmund, the owner of the inn *Zum Alten Deutschen* (To the Old Germany) articulates what many think. The hatred of the Jews was on the increase again. "That's typically Jewish that they will not let our boys rest in peace."

Bitburg sees itself as benign to Jews. The town chronicle reports that the substitute rabbi, Jacob Juda, succeeded in obtaining the rights to bury Jews on the Christian cemetery as early as 1900. The Holocaust did not exact many victims here. Most of the Bitburg Jews escaped to America before the SS could deport them.

Today, roughly a dozen Jews live in Bitburg. The most prominent of them is Max Rosenzweyg, the owner of a snackbar catering service, nicknamed Max Pommes (Max Fries) whose house is located directly beside the military cemetery. The fact that SS soldiers also lie there does not bother him. "They were soldiers like everybody else."

For 25 years, the American and French garrison commanders have been putting down wreaths on *Volkstrauertag* (Day of National Mourning), even though they knew that SS soldiers were also buried there. And nobody ever took offense at that.

During a protest meeting organized by the Bitburg peace movement against Reagan's visit, they will try to win over discontented, potential sympathizers for the progressive cause. Issues on the agenda are: "The Bitburg Air Base in the Nato concept (Air-Land-Battle, etc.)" and "The role of the Reagan administration in South and Central America." The *Geissblat* (Goat Paper), the central organ of the local eco-peace movement, already envisions this Eifel idyll as a standfast apocalypse. "Will Star Wars start in Bitburg?"

The "green" front has split up through the Reagan visit. "Many of the boys here simply don't understand why the Amis get so worked up over the SS," says Herbert Mertes, the owner of the local scene bar. "After all they did to the Indians . . ."

The opposition also faces its fair share of unresolved embarrassment. The German soldiers, said Social Democrat assemblyman Christoph Grimm two weeks ago, had gone to war for the "evil absolute," and whoever fought against them was "absolutely just." The SPD member of Parliament, Karl Haehser, eagerly tried to modify this statement the next day: In death all people were equal. The cross word, however, lingers on.

Thursday afternoon, an American TV reporter is caught on Kolmeshöhe by a group of tourists from Aachen as, with obviously dubious intentions, he is about to arrange pink carnations on an SS-grave. The cemetery visitors had just returned from a tour of a brewery. One of them walks up to the cameraman and screams at this face from an eight inch distance, "You want hatred, nothing but hatred! Fuck off, go home to America!"

Reconciliation across the graves has been adjourned until further notice.

(Translated by Renate Steinchen.)

Bitburg and Belsen:
Reagan Appeals For Reconciliation

Bremer Nachrichten
May 6, 1985

By Peter W. Schröder

President Reagan's visits to the site of the former concentration camp of Bergen-Belsen and the war cemetery at Bitburg had been planned as a demonstration of reconciliation.

But they turned out to be merely a tiresome obligation.

This was no repeat of John F. Kennedy's triumphant state visit to Germany.

President Reagan's visit marked a somewhat tragic chapter in German-American relations.

But after the embarrassing buck-passing of recent weeks there must be no more pointless recriminations. What is needed, in both Washington and Bonn, is harder work to limit the damage done.

There are many signs that the resilience of German-American relations will be clearly apparent before long. Despite the bids by Mr. Reagan and Herr Kohl to consolidate ties, the close relationship and friendship between the two countries are unlikely to sustain structural or lasting damage.

Over the past 40 years so many points of mutual dependence and common interest have accrued that not even the most hapless gestures could destroy them or even upset them in the long term.

Yet the excitement has not been for nothing. President Reagan is a factor in his country's home affairs, and the Democratic opposition in Congress is not alone in feeling he has made serious mistakes.

So, according to opinion polls, does about 70 percent of U.S. public opinion.

The President will have a price to pay in terms of political resistance. He can be sure of having difficulties in his way in policy on Germany (in the widest sense of the term).

It is largely academic whether U.S. criticism of the President's visit to Bitburg cemetery was justified or not. The practical consequences of his gestures in Bitburg and Belsen were much more important.

They were largely approved in Germany and largely rejected, partly with great indignation, in America. That alone is irritating enough.

The Germans are not going to steer clear of the backlash merely by feeling that domestic criticism of President Reagan in the United States is wrong and unwarranted.

American politicians will now be unlikely to resist the temptation to "punish" the President for "mistakes" made during his state visit.

They may, for instance, force him to embark on moves such as punitive trade measures or defense or finance policy changes to Bonn's disadvantage.

Such moves will be aimed first and foremost at President Reagan and not at the Federal Republic of Germany, but that is scant consolation for Bonn, which will be taking the beating.

We will see soon enough what extent such irritations might take. One can but hope President Reagan proves more skillful at warding off domestic political attacks than he has been at arranging the state visit.

The Bonn government would be well-advised to forgo justification campaigns to influence the domestic debate in the United States.

Words of advice from German politicians are virtually the last thing American politicians are prepared to put up with at present.

"This time with all sincerity, Nancy, tell me which hat fits me best: that of the military cemetery, the concentration camp or both?" (Words on box read 'Kohl's styles.')

Part VI

The Response From Israel

The response of Israel to the news of President Reagan's intended visit to Bitburg and Bergen-Belsen was as startling as it was diverse. Both Israeli leaders and the Israeli community differed drastically from their United States counterparts in the characteristics, intensity, and extent of their reactions to the Bitburg-Bergen-Belsen itinerary. One could well ask: How could the central polity of the Jewish nation not be in the forefront of opposition to the politicization of the Holocaust? How could they stand passively silent when American Jewry protested vigorously against the overt efforts to rewrite history?

The key to that discrepancy lies in the different pace of the Israeli confrontation with aspects of the Holocaust, a pace that contrasts with the approach taken by the rest of the world. In Israel, the repeated political exploitation of the memory of the 6 million murdered Jews has contributed to the gradual banalization of the Holocaust.[1] The differing approaches to this issue can be viewed in relation to the establishment of diplomatic relations with West Germany by the United States and Israel.

German-U.S. relations began the moment Nazi Germany surrendered to the Allies on May 8, 1945. The web of future relations between these two countries was characterized by a sense of magnanimity by the victor with respect to the defeated opponent. This point of view has spared American Jewry a head-on-confrontation over the Holocaust and its implications. On the other hand, the Israeli experience with the successor of the archenemy of the Jewish people was an agonizing one. It involved a large amount of soul-searching, questioning, and debate at each step of the way toward the establishment of diplomatic relations. For their part, the FRG was attempting to normalize diplomatic relations not merely with the Jewish state, but with the state which is located in a particular political setting, the Middle East, and from the first moment took this political fact as a cornerstone of its policies toward Israel. They refused to establish their embassy in Jerusalem for fear of antagonizing the Arabs. The first German ambassador sent as representative to Israel was Rolf Paulus, a high-ranking ambassador and a former officer of the Wehrmacht. His missing arm was a constant reminder of his military past, although he was highly effective in establishing relations between the FRG and Israel. He had served previously in Washington; however, his appointment evoked no response from the American Jewish community.

Such a reminder of things past was difficult for Israel, still struggling to establish itself as a nation and cognizant of its need to normalize relations with other countries. Soul-searching was constantly being forced on Israel by political and economic necessity.

This was true of the whole process of deciding to accept reparations from Germany and then determining how much should be apportioned, and of the decision to sell arms to, and later to manufacture military uniforms for, the Bundeswehr — the German Army!

Such decisions became part of an ineradicable lesson in the slowly evolving Israeli awareness concerning the difficulty of preserving moral purity within the domain of a political decision.

It could have been assumed that Israel would react vociferously to the announcement about the intended visit to Bitburg. After all, this could be construed as an issue related to the Holocaust, and Israel came into being as a viable country in part because of the Holocaust. The reality, however, proved different. The unrestrictive political use of the word "Holocaust" contributed to the negation of the Diaspora experience in general and the Holocaust in particular. One portion of Israel perceived this chapter of Jewish history as the weak one. This position is best exemplified in the inscription at Yad Va-Shem, the Israel National memorial to the Holocaust in Jerusalem, by a paratrooper: "Had I been there [during the Holocaust], this would not have happened."

This point of view may be difficult to comprehend unless one examines the educational curriculum in Israel. The subject of the Holocaust was only introduced into the educational system by the Ministry of Education in 1979 and ratified by the Knesset in 1981. To this one should add the fact that the subject is taught in two different ways.

In Israel there are two parallel government-controlled educational systems: parochial (religious) and secular. Each has its own textbooks and, therefore, its own method of teaching what the Holocaust was and what it meant to the world of Jewry. The textbook for the religious schools, by Morgenstern, stresses Jewish religious resistance against Nazi ideas. The secular textbook, by Gutman-Shatzker, stresses Zionist humanism and understresses the religious aspects. Coupled with these two factors is the fact that until late in 1982[2] no university taught teachers how to teach a course on the Holocaust. The young Israeli, therefore, does not have a unified concept of what the Holocaust was all about.[3]

In and of itself this lack of a set concept of the Holocaust might explain the absence of a concerted protest against Bitburg. Moreover, one must also take into account the matter of political expediency. After all, President Reagan's forthcoming visit to Bitburg and its symbolic implications were perceived in Israel within the encompassing web of Israeli-American relations.

At this time two specific issues dominated these relations:

1. An emergency loan of $1.5 billion was needed. Previously, the White House had voiced open opposition. When the Bitburg visit was announced, so, too, was the loan. Thus, the popular newspaper *Ma'ariv* on May 2 headlined a story 'The White House Will Remove Its Opposition to the Emergency Loan in Order to Soften the Anger over the President's Trip to Bitburg."

2. A letter sent by Secretary of Defense Caspar Weinberger on March 26, 1985, invited Israel to participate in the Strategic Defense Initiative ("Star Wars") research program. This invitation, besides promising much-needed research grants, also stressed the strategic affinity between the United States and Israel.

All this resulted in an official Israeli response to President Reagan's West German agenda that was muted for political expediency. Neither the Israeli ambassador to Washington nor the prime minister put forth a public complaint. Individually, however, several politicians — such as Gideon Hausner, the former state prosecutor at the Eichmann trial, Defense Minister Yitzhak Rabin, and members of parliament Dov Shilansky, and Haika Grossman — voiced objections. But even then, the overall tone was one of restraint in order to avoid the appearance of "one government preaching morality to another government."

Prime Minister Peres stated:

> We do not propose to respond to hate with hate. However, even death can't diffuse the difference between those buried as murdered and those buried as murderers ... I believe that the president is a true friend of the people and the State of Israel. Indeed, because of that undeniable fact, we feel the deep pain of his visit to Bitburg. There is a

place for reconciliation between nations, but there can be no reconciliation between epochs and generations. There is no reconciliation with the past. And no legitimization of the past.[4]

Peres's point of view, as the prime minister of Israel, clarified the coments made five days earlier when he had stated, "Ronald Reagan is a great friend who committed an error. The friend will remain, so will the error."[5]

Restraint was also the mood of the Knesset when Speaker Shlomo Hillel said, ". . . today we heard with great relief that President Reagan changed his itinerary." He was referring to the addition of Bergen-Belsen to the agenda.

Yet it was this decision that raised the ire of the survivors in the United States, who felt that a holy place was being defiled by political compromise. It was this mood that prompted Elie Wiesel, Simon Wiesenthal and many other prominent Jewish personalities to refuse the invitation from President Reagan to join him at the Bergen-Belsen ceremony. In fact, it was this mood that later caused Werner Nachmann, representing the Central Council of German Jews, to boycott the ceremony. Originally, this group, which is closely allied —politically— with Chancellor Kohl, had planned to be there, but a last-minute debate with, and pressure from, the World Jewish Congress caused it to change its policy. Thus, the Israeli ambassador to West Germany, on the instruction of his government, was the only official representative of world Jewry at the Bergen-Belsen ceremony.

In encapsulating the mixed views in Israel, a leading Israeli columnist suggested that Prime Minister Peres should have also attended: " . . . and by being there he would mobilize the world's public opinion concerning the lessons of the Holocaust, a goal that was not part and parcel of the planning of this visit."[6]

In explaining his government's stand, Ambassador Ben Ari stated that boycotting the ceremony would have been perceived as an insult to President Reagan.

However, once the ceremony was concluded and the dignitaries had departed, Ben Ari remained alone at the Bergen-Belsen memorial, offered a solitary prayer of mourning, and in the Jewish tradition placed beside the memorial three stones from Jerusalem.

---

[1]"Tzror Shel Mishgim" (A Bundle of Errors), Eliyahu Salpater, *Ha'Aretz,* May 3, 1985.
[2]"Outdated Ideas in Teaching Holocaust," Nili Mendler, *Ha-Aretz,* April 18, 1985.
[3]"The System of Annihilation Is An Interesting Topic," Miriam Goren, *Ha-Aretz,* April 17, 1985.
[4]*Ma'Ariv,* May 7, 1985.
[5]*Ma'Ariv,* May 2, 1985.
[6]"The Prime Minister Wasn't There," Moshe Zack, *Ma'Ariv,* May 6, 1985.

This Israeli cartoon by Dosh lists four words: (top) Confusion, (top right) Murdered, (bottom right) Victims, and (center) Reagan.

Chapter 21

Essays And Analysis

Was Hitler's War Just Another German War?
Special Contribution

By Professor Emil L. Fackenheim

"Ich hatt' einen Kameraden, einen besseren findest Du nicht . . ."

"I once had a comrade, you'll never find one better." Thus begins a dirge which is played by the military band, and sung by those present, whenever a German soldier is buried, and at a ceremony when those fallen in a war are remembered. It never fails to move. It never failed to move me, over fifty years ago when I was still a German as well as a Jew. The words of the song go on, how the two comrades march in the same step, how a bullet comes flying and who knows whether it is for the one or the other, and how, when the other falls, he, the surviving comrade, cannot even stop to shake his hand for the last time, for onwards he must march. *Ich hatt einen Kameraden* was sung at Bitburg.

I too once had a German comrade. We did not exactly do everything together, for he disliked sports. But we bicycled together, explored the country together, and played music together. Also, we discussed politics. For he was a genuine democrat, one of only two (not counting myself, the only Jew) in my high school class. His whole family were democrats. And I am convinced that he remained a sincere democrat and anti-Nazi to the end of his life. Yet Jürgen Wenzlau was killed on the Russian front, fighting Hitler's war.

I

If circumstances got me near the place where my friend lies buried I would be sure to visit his grave. I would mourn Jürgen. Yet if there were a public ceremony commemorating the German World War II dead at Jürgen's cemetery, I would absolutely refuse to attend. So should President Reagan have refused to attend; and, which is much more serious, Chancellor Kohl should not have invited him. All this even if not a single SS man were buried at Bitburg.

In a way, the presence of SS men's graves at Bitburg was unfortunate, for it clouded the issue. It was one thing for Frenchmen and Germans to join in commemorating the dead on both sides in World War I. But it was another thing entirely to do the same thing about the fallen of World War II. For that was not a war between two sides, "ours" and "theirs." It was a war for the survival of civilization itself. When U.S. Generals Eisenhower and Patton came to the murder camp of Ohrdruf, Eisenhower, on seeing what he saw, said that this was beyond the American mind to comprehend. Then he gave orders to the effect that as many U.S. soldiers as possible were to see this place. He remarked: "It is said that the American soldier does not know what he is fighting for. Let him come, see and understand at least what he is fighting against." Have Americans now forgotten what they were fighting against? Have Germans forgotten — have they ever learned? — that a total defeat of their armies in World War II was the necessary condition of the survival of civilization, and therefore of German civilization?

In saying what he did and putting it as he did General — later President — Eisenhower recognized that Ohrdruf and all it stood for and the war were not two things separate, but that they were firmly, if possible obscurely, interrelated. Does the present White House incumbent still recognize this fact? More importantly, is it recognized by the present German head of state? In his country there are thoughtful, conscientious young people who, taking upon themselves the responsibility for a German future, delve deeply into the German past, with a view to discovering how what did happen could have happened. Will Bitburg undermine their efforts, with its implication that, except for Auschwitz, Hitler's war was just another German war — and Auschwitz, perpetrated by just a few, was in German history as a whole an accident?

That Hitler's war was not just another German war was recognized at the time by Dietrich Bonhöffer. Bonhöffer was a great Christian and a leading member of the anti-Nazi Confessional Church. He also was a German patriot. Hence it was only after much agonizing that he was led to pray for the defeat of his own country, in which Caesar's throne then was occupied by the anti-Christ. (Murdered by the Nazis, he died a martyr for his convictions.) The Bonhöffers, however, were all-too-few. Martin Niemöller, too, was a great Christian, a leading member of the Confessional Church and a German patriot. For his opposition to Nazism he was imprisoned in the concentration camp of Sachsenhausen. Yet, when war broke out, Niemöller, who had been a submarine commander in World War I, offered his services to the *Führer*. Luckily for him, Hitler turned him down. Otherwise he, too, like Jürgen Wenzlau, might have been killed in the war and — which is worse —

killed fighting Hitler's war..

II

That the German second world war *was* Hitler's war — that it and Auschwitz are inseparable — is a lesson to be learned from a work written, aptly enough, by a German historian. Karl Dietrich Bracher's *The German Dictatorship* (New York: Praeger 1970) demonstrates that Nazi Germany was a dual system. The one, the inner core of the whole, was the SS state, a tightly organized system wholly dedicated to Nazi aims, among which was the murder of every available Jew. (Auschwitz was among the essential Nazi aims: arguably it was foremost.) The other was the traditional German system, the civil service, the railroads, the schools and universities, the clergy, the army. Quite deliberately, the second system was allowed independent existence to the very end of the war. But it was also increasingly used by the first system — manipulated, penetrated, perverted. (During the war the army, which prided itself on its Prussian-inspired code of honor, became gradually involved in Nazi crimes.) The traditional system remained largely non-Nazi. Here and there there were even anti-Nazi pickets, and sporadic acts of resistance. But since no part of the traditional German system ever resisted radically and systematically the Nazi use and manipulation of it, it enabled the SS state to do what this latter could never have accomplished simply by itself. Had the railway men gone on strike or simply melted away there would have been no Auschwitz. Had the German army resisted absolutely — the Wehrmacht could have overthrown the Nazi regime as late as in 1938 — there would have been neither Auschwitz nor World War II.

This is why no non-German head of state should ever again be asked to participate in a ceremony commemorating German soldiers fallen in World War II. It is also why Germans, alone in their commemoration, are faced with an unprecedented tragedy. Jürgen Wenzlau, a good man to the end — you'll never find a better comrade! — died fighting for the wrong cause, not only by the standards of "our" side, but by any decent standard of mankind.

III

In a secret speech delivered in 1944 to the SS elite, Heinrich Himmler asserted that all the seventy million Germans wished to get rid of the Jews, but that only they, the SS, had the guts to do it and to allow for no "decent" Jews who were to be spared. Himmler was correct enough about the SS elite. But he grossly slandered countless decent Germans who never accepted the Nazi philosophy.

Even so there was a true element in Himmler's assertion: the whole German people, or nearly all of them, were implicated in the process that led to Auschwitz. In every civilized state, a person is innocent until proven guilty; in the Nazi state everyone was suspect of "non-Aryan" guilt until he had proven his "Aryan" innocence. In every normal state, a person is punished for something he has done. In the Nazi anti-state a "non-Aryan" was "punished" by humiliation, torture and death for the "crime" of birth. Hence anyone within that anti-state proving his Aryan "innocence", prepared to prove it, or even just surviving on the presumption of it, was implicated, however innocently, in the process of abandoning the "non-Aryan" victims to their fate. Spider-like, the Nazi Reich sought to implicate in its own crimes the entire German people; and, lamentably but by no means unnaturally, it achieved a near-total success. It is true that some Germans escaped the spider's web — those clear-sighted enough to leave Nazi Germany in time, and those stout-hearted enough to oppose it absolutely i.e., in most cases, at the cost of their lives. But not many people are that clear-sighted, and few people anywhere are heroes. One ponders the success of the Nazi Reich — its twelve years were equal to a thousand — and is aghast. What is before our eyes can only be called a German tragedy, unequalled anywhere.

Germany once was the land of poets and philosophers. Once the philosopher Schelling wrote of "innocent guilt" in considering Oedipus, a tragedy merely on the stage, displayed for us who are mere spectators. When will the philosopher arise — he can only be German — who will consider a tragedy which unfolded on no mere stage, and of which none of us will ever be able to be mere spectators? One must hope that arise he will. For only from a confrontation with the tragedy of the German past can a true German future arise.

(Professor Emil Fackenheim is a renowned scholar on the Holocaust. He taught for many years at the University of Toronto, and presently teaches Holocaust Studies at the Hebrew University in Jerusalem, Israel.)

"Nobody Can Forgive On Someone Else's Behalf"
Special Contribution

By Professor Alexander Voronel

The controversy in the press around Reagan's visit to the military cemetery at Bitburg made me think: why am I not outraged by this act? If personalities such as Elie Wiesel would not have stepped into the matter, I, perhaps, wouldn't have paid any attention to the whole incident, taking it simply for political fault-finding by limelight-seeking groups. However, this controversy made me comprehend the difference between my point of view and that of the conventional approach of the West, and I realized that this difference does not only belong to me personally: it stems from a different experience, and a different perception of life.

I never studied the Holocaust. In my thoughts, the whole essence of it was pushed away, perhaps as a subconscious attempt to avoid the psychological trauma. Yet fleeting information about the Holocaust has gradually overtaken me since my childhood, and consequently it has become inseparable from my impressions of that childhood. I will try to analyze those impressions here.

In my child's consciousness, the Holocaust seemed to be exclusively a problem of dead old men, women and children. Childhood reminiscences do not admit the possibility of anybody but helpless people under German occupation. All adult men known to me at the time were in the army, and it is difficult for me to picture them as victims of the Holocaust. Partly because of this, the Holocaust, in my imagination, doesn't look like a premeditated and planned political operation, but rather as an exceptional case of brutality — an outburst of barbarity, savagery. And consequently, the responsibility for these savage acts, as for any other crime, must reside with the individual. However, we know that, in reality, the horror of the Holocaust is not in the fierce savagery of individuals, but in a carefully planned destruction of whole nations (not only Jews, but also Gypsies). Here my feeling fails me. Instead of growing more horrified, I suddenly turn to a familiar remembrance of my childhood, stripped of any horrible details.

In a small Siberian town, where we lived during the war, I remember thousands of tents on the outskirts of our town in which "Estonians" lived through the winter. This was the name given to the foreign-looking, tall, handsome people who were working in their neat uniforms at freezing temperatures of – 40 degrees Celsius. Even under these conditions they managed to maintain a brave appearance.

They were Latvians, Lithuanians and Estonians; exiled to Siberia and expected to die out. Indeed, every night several hundred of them were buried. By summer there was nobody left. Then, in their place came "Uzbeks" who looked much worse, but who died as well as the Estonians. The whole town knew and saw it, of course. At least they would say about the Estonians: "What a pity, such good-looking people." But they did not feel sorry for the Uzbeks because they were dirty and homely.

Numerous jokes were told about the Uzbeks' greed, wile, and stupidity. On the whole, their sins amounted to petty theft — selling dried apricots on the black market — and a poor command of the Russian language. This and their will to survive. This striving, and their dried apricots, protected their stay in our town for all the years of the war, to the extent that I believe some of them actually survived.

One year after the end of the war, at the age of fourteen, I was put into a labor camp on a political charge of promoting anti-Soviet propaganda. I did not think of it as an injustice because I had really tried, as much as I could at that age, to carry anti-Soviet propaganda. The time that my friend (also fourteen) and I were sentenced to was only three years, but at the end of the first few months we were convinced that we wouldn't last a year. We started preparing for a painless suicide, but within six months the Supreme Court reviewed our case. Although our families did pay a mighty bribe, the change in the court's decision was nevertheless an unheard of stroke of good luck. We returned to normal life, not completely believing in the finality of our lucky fate. The father of my friend and inmate had perished in a labor camp eight years earlier.

After only two years my friend was sentenced to another prison term. I had gotten off easy.

Over the years, my father, uncle, cousin and grandmother spent from one to ten years in jails and labor camps, where people were dying like flies. My grandmother remarked that it was lucky for me that I was put in jail so early in life because "it is better that you get your immunization early."

At this point I should say that I come from an average family of the technological intelligentsia, not only disinclined to breaking the law, but not even interested in politics. According to our standards, the family on the whole managed to play it safe. Surely nobody was shot. However, this conditioning during my upbringing could not contribute to my perception of the Holocaust as something extraordinary.

Perhaps I became hard-hearted in childhood.

I can't say that I wasn't personally touched by the Holocaust. Our relatives perished in Kharkov's ghetto. Upon our return to Kharkov after the war, we learned from our neighbors that Leo, the boy from a family I was friendly with, would secretly come running from the ghetto to get food for his mother and sister. The neighbors said that they offered to hide him, but that he couldn't leave his mother and sister and preferred to die with them. I imagined his life, and even his death, very clearly. More difficult for me was to imagine the life of their neighbors under these circumstances. I thought it was natural that invaders killed Leo and all the others. What else could one expect from invaders? But how did the neighbors manage to survive?

Why, nevertheless, in the matter of Nazi criminals and their crimes against our people, am I inclined to a position of compromise? The fact that since my childhood I was a witness to crimes that could be comparable in scope and brutality, should have set me in a vengeful mood.

However, looking at all these unprecedented crimes, so to speak, I clearly see that the cause — at least in the case familiar to me — has, first of all, its roots in a corrupted political and social system to which our resolve should be directed. Although the responsibility of single individuals at times turns out to be decisive, it must be examined only individually and in connection with the circumstances of the lives of those particular individuals. I do not know who was the commandant of the labor camp responsible for the genocide of the Estonians in our small town. But if he would turn out to be a Jew, I wouldn't consider that that would give the Estonians the right to spit on the grave of my grandfather. I know that even membership in an organization such as the KGB did not prevent single individuals (however rare) from accomplishing decent acts, even merciful deeds; whereas at the same time, some non-members of the communist party would rise in their frenzy to the level of voluntary executioners, deserving to be expelled from humanity.

Proceeding from this experience, I can easily imagine that my friend Leo ran out of the ghetto owing to the negligence, or even indulgence of the SS guard who closed his eyes on the flight of the boy who then was given away for execution by the same neighbors at whose place he sought to hide, and who so vividly described to me their compassion. Why, a German can't tell a Jewish boy from a Ukrainian one. One has to have a special eye.

Suppose that after the war this dunderhead Nazi was hanged (just at that time in Kharkov there was a public execution of several Nazi criminals, and I know the attitude of Soviet investigators towards the truth), or he simply got lost in Siberia, or got crushed by a tank, while a shrewd neighbor of Leo's sat snug beside his kitchen garden and survived even Stalin's purges. Must I now, forty years later, desecrate the grave of this supposedly unbending Nazi and send flowers to the grave of the supposedly virtuous neighbor? And what if this neighbor is the traitor and culprit?

Who in the whole world can give me an answer as to how it happened in reality?

Of course these suspicions of mine do not have the power of evidence and are based only on hypothetical possibilities and vast statistics of mass crimes committed in Nazi-occupied territory. But comrade Stalin took into consideration everything and put everybody left in occupied territory under suspicion, registering this fact in all their documents. Comrade Stalin not only worked out and executed his own grand criminal schemes, but also procedures of no less grand punishments and revenge for indirect aid to someone else's crimes. Direct collaboration was punished separately. Joseph Stalin held good and evil tight in his hands. It is a pity that his good always manifested itself in the shape of evil. That happened just as a consequence of the absolute nature of his decisions. Till his death, and even for some time after, all 50 million potential collaborators were trembling with fear nightly, expecting to be arrested, and remained second-class citizens in the eyes of all of the USSR's official agencies.

Do we want the same fate for the German nation that survived the war? Even to the present day without limitation of time?

Of course we cannot do anything to spite them in reality, but would we like to make them suffer such a total moral loss? I am not sure. I am almost convinced that the opposite is true. Divine justice was not given to us.

Does this mean that I think it possible to forgive them? No. Not at all.

The crimes of the Nazis, in many aspects, have analogies and parallels in the history of the human race. Their crime against the Jewish people is unprecedented. Even the massacre of the Armenians by the Turks, although on a similar scale, is radically different from the Holocaust in its primitive emotionalism. Other crimes of the Nazis, although unjustifiable, at least could be explained. Their crime against the Jews is inexplicable. The banality of motives of single executioners and the obvious pettiness of many initiators of this crime must not overshadow its unique nature and out-of-the-ordinary design. This event will remain among the phenomena which should be examined on a far wider background than a history of Europe in the middle of the 20th century can provide.

Comparable in many respects is the event described in the Bible: chapter 4 of

Genesis: ". . . Cain rose up against Abel, his brother, and slew him."

The similarity is not only in that Cain killed his brother, who did not defend himself—as opposed to the usual mortal conflicts—but in that the motive of the murder was exclusively idealistic: ". . . And the Lord had respect unto Abel and to his offering: But unto Cain and to his offering he had no respect." The argument was about invisible values, and divine justice remains inexplicable to us.

The mystery of the meaning of this crime is stressed by the mystery of the punishment: ". . . What hast thou done? The voice of thy brother's blood crieth unto me from the ground. And now art thou cursed. . . And Cain said unto the Lord, My punishment is greater than I can bear. . . everyone that findeth me shall slay me. And the Lord said unto him, 'Therefore, whosoever slayeth Cain, vengeance shall be taken on him sevenfold.' And the Lord set a mark upon Cain, lest any finding him should kill him. And Cain went out from the presence of the Lord. . . ."

Why this strange concern about the safety of the murderer on the part of the God of Vengeance? And doesn't the admonition, directed to Cain—yet before the murder—also sound strange: ". . . Why is thy countenance fallen? If thou doest well, shalt thou not be accepted? And if thou doest not well, sin lieth at the door. And unto thee shall be his desire, and thou shalt rule over him." God knew about the crime and let it happen. His reckoning with Cain is above any narrow understanding of an antithesis of crime and punishment. Indeed, the punishment removes the guilt.

We have a right to forgive or to punish only indubitably banal crimes. Eichmann, to his own relief, should be hanged because he was a miserable executioner, a pitiful accomplice to the Crime. Not only are we unable to punish real culprits, but we can't even discover them. As human beings, and not gods, we have no right to claim indiscriminately as culprits, neither whole nations (". . . whosoever slayeth Cain, vengeance shall be taken on him sevenfold"), nor even single categories of citizens (Nazis, communists) without clearly limited, generally accepted court procedures. Also, we cannot demand from the new generation of Germans (and, by the way, why has nobody ever mentioned the Austrians?) to admit indiscriminately that their fathers were carrion which deserved its dog's death from a bomb or a Russian bayonet. That would not be a moral victory. In addition, such is our Jewish history that if we want to go further in this irreconcilable guilt, we would have to condemn the entire human race. However, our ability to forgive and forget is still higher than that of worldwide standards. Maybe to be a chosen nation means to let other nations be as they are?

Perhaps some American Jews will object to all this, saying that this is exactly the mission of the Jewish Diaspora, to force nations to rise higher than they are now. To push them on a path of moral perfection beyond their present-day abilities.

Maybe there is a truth in that. But this is a matter of belief. Belief in a mission. Belief in the Diaspora. Belief that the influence of the Jewish Diaspora on surrounding nations leads to increase their morality.

All in all, Ronald Reagan came out of the situation with dignity, asking us to look at German soldiers who were killed in combat as also victims of an insane regime, based on an insane ideology. This definition, in itself, already excludes those who were actually conscientious culprits.

Well, he forgave *his* enemies. But his forgiveness does not in the least remove their guilt towards *us*. Nobody can forgive on someone else's behalf. But nobody has a right to condemn in absentia.

It seems to me that under the immediate influence of the Holocaust, Elie Wiesel and many others spontaneously adopted this apocalyptical world view, so that they subconsciously expected the realization of justice in actual political life after the war. In the course of the Holocaust, evil manifested itself so absolutely that the victory over it in World War II could be understood as a triumph of the good — also perhaps, absolute. And the war itself looked like some "final and decisive battle." In any case, the traces of this feeling tell very clearly in the absoluteness of their demands to the American and German governments in respect to Nazi culprits.

However, there isn't a single government in the whole world which could satisfy such demands. As unprecedented as they were, the crimes of the Nazis did not result in either unprecedented justice or even absolute righteousness of the winners. The Holocaust has receded into the past, but the Last Judgment still has not come.

The world after the Holocaust remains as imperfect as it was before. In a certain sense it has become even worse. If we want to we can discuss, forgive or not forgive the murderers, but we cannot erase this dreadful precedent. Its seductive influence on the minds of people who don't care about our forgiveness is certain. Its meaning for future history cannot inspire an optimism that would allow one to concentrate on the symbolic punishment of defeated criminals.

(Translated from the Russian by Nelly Slonim.)

(Professor Alexander Voronel, a former leading Jewish activist in Moscow, teaches physics at Tel Aviv University, and is the editor of the monthly "22". Among his publications is The Jewish Conscience *[Trepet Zabot Eudeiskikh].*

Morality, Pragmatism and Moral Pragmatism
Special Contribution

By Professor Benyamin Neuberger

The government of Israel cannot imagine that the gates of the cultured and peace-loving world will be opened to the German people, not only because their hands are still smeared with blood, but also when their plunder is still under their cloak.

(Moshe Sharett, 1950)[1]

I have certainly a racist approach. For me every German is a Nazi.

(Golda Meir, 1951)[2]

For a long time, all conduct between these two peoples will remain in the shadow of their memories. It is impossible to isolate the Holocaust within its narrow historical limits.

(Abba Eban, 1962)[3]

America gave us money, France arms for money, Germany arms without asking for money.

(Shimon Peres, 1968)[4]

(The official Israeli response to the Bitburg affair can't be fully understood without the analysis of the recent Israeli-German relationship, which sheds light on the interplay of morality and pragmatism in it.)

Relations between Israel and West Germany were a highly controversial and emotional issue in Israel in the 1950s and 1960s. Israel passed through three major political crises with regard to German-Israel relations: In 1952 the debate on the Reparations Agreement posed a threat to the very existence of Israel's young democracy; in 1959 the bitter controversy on the issue of arms sales to Germany led to the downfall of the coalition government and in 1965 the opponents of German-Israeli relations fought a lost battle against the establishment of full diplomatic relations.

The major crisis was that of 1952. The Reparations Agreement was opposed by the 'Right' ('Herut' and General Zionists) and the 'Left' (MAPAM and the Communists). Thousands of right-wing demonstrators threatened to storm and stone the Knesset. Menachem Begin, at that time leader of the 'Herut' opposition party led the onslaught on Israel's parliament. He urged Israel to prevent—by force if necessary—what he perceived as a sell-out of the Jewish People, their pride and dignity. Begin—himself a survivor of the Holocaust who saw his parents executed by the Nazis—was carried away by his emotional stand against any contact with Germany and Germans. Fervent hostility to any 'deal' with Germany was as strong on the 'Left' as on the 'Right' of the political spectrum. The socialist survivors of the Warsaw Ghetto Revolt, former partisans and inmates of the death and concentration camps in the kibbutzim led in 1958-9 the outcry against the sale of Israeli Uzi machine guns to the German army. While in 1952 the survival of the political system was at stake, the 'Uzi crisis' led only to the breakup of MAPAM/Ahdut

Haavoda-MAPAI coalition and to early new elections. In 1965 feelings against the establishment of diplomatic relations with Germany still ran high, but the opposition to this crucial step toward 'normalization' was substantially weaker in the 1952 and 1959 crises. The opposition of 'Herut' and MAPAM lacked the intensity of the 1950s and the General Zionists (Liberals) and Ahdut Haavoda abandoned their total opposition to relations with Germany. Since 1965 German-Israeli relations developed steadily. Here and there minor crises occurred on such issues as cultural relations, German relations with the Arab World or the German Statute of Limitations for Nazi war criminals. In general, controversies in the 1970s and 1980s lack the drama of 1952, 1959 and 1965. Nevertheless under the thin veneer of 'normalization' there is still a good measure of deep-felt distrust of Germany and the Germans. When in 1981 Prime Minister Begin lashed out against German Chancellor Helmut Schmidt, whom he accused of having been a "Nazi officer" avid for the sheer profit of arm sales to Israel's Arab enemies, the attack was popular with broad sections of the Israeli public.

The debates on German-Israeli relations in the 1950s and 1960s offer fascinating examples of the interrelationships of morality and politics, and of the role of emotions and *raisons d'etat* in international relations. The main protagonists in the debate sought support in the Bible, pleaded in the name of the six million Jews slaughtered in the Holocaust and felt strongly that only their attitude can assure the physical and moral survival of the Jewish State and the Jewish People.

The controversy of the 1950s and 1960s was widely perceived as representing the polarization between interest and morality, profit and conscience, or 'Realpolitik,' on the one hand and ideology on the other. The 'realists' argued that Germany was a rising political and economic power that Israel could disregard only at her peril, that Israel should not remain indifferent whether Germany sides with Israel or its enemies. They emphasized that Germany was not only important *per se* but also exerted influence as part of the Western World in NATO and the European Community. Prime Minister Ben-Gurion felt that "Germany as a force hostile to Israel endangers the friendship of the other countries of Western Europe and might even have an undesirable influence on the United States." Time and again the supporters of Israeli-German relations talked about 'realism', 'rationality', "interests of State" and the need to overcome emotional blocks. "A state must take a rational course," said Minister of Justice Pinhas Rosen—"as a people we could be an exception but not as a state."[6] Foreign Minister Moshe Sharett— a 'liberal dove' who was the 'moral conscience' of the Israeli establishment with regard to its policies toward the Arabs— stressed in the 'German debate' the need of the state to follow "every shift in the balance of forces around it and in the world at large."[7] 'Balance of forces' is certainly the classical 'realist' logic which collides with 'moralist' justice. On the occasion of the establishment of Israeli-German diplomatic relations Prime Minister Levy Eshkol conceded that "emotional blocks" are "understandable and legitimate"—yet Israel must follow a policy based on the "people's good" and the "people's military and political strength in its homeland."[8]

The "rational" state interests pursued by the realists were sometimes of a very 'practical' nature: the need for hard currency to prevent an economic collapse, the prospects of building a modern industrial infrastructure with the help of German reparations, the possibility to find in the German army a market for Israel's grow-ing arms production and the opportunity to secure through Germany a steady supply of Western arms for the Israeli Defense Forces.

The 'moralists' in the 1950s and 1960s were opposed to any talks, negotiations, agreements, deals and official relations between Israel and Germany. They regard-ed talks with the Germans as a betrayal of the six million Jews slaughtered in the Holocaust. Negotiations with the Adenauer administration were equivalent to ap-peasement of murderers and tantamount to "a spiritual and moral catastrophe."[9] They regarded the Reparations Agreement and Arms Deal as a moral sellout, a sur-render to materialism, which prefers material comfort to moral qualities, human dignity and national pride. Some of the moralists considered everything German taboo for eternity, others thought that the 'Nazi generation' has to die out first, that it was too early to forget and forgive. Moreover the moralists doubted the sincerity of the German metamorphosis after World War II. They viewed West Germany as essentially Nazi Germany in disguise, as a danger to world peace and Jewish survival. There is no doubt that the leading opponents of any German-Israeli relations were emotionally sincere in their dismay at seeing that the Jewish state was establishing working relations and making Realpolitik 'deals' with West Germany. While the centrist MAPAI supported 'realism', the opposition from both the 'left' and the 'right' represented 'moralism'.

The point I want to make in this paper is that the division between 'realists' who indulge in calculations of power and profit and 'moralists' who struggle in the name of values, conscience, 'purity' and morals is simplistic. It does not reflect the real debate and it does gross injustice to Israel's leaders in the 1950s and 1960s — in particular to Israel's first four prime-ministers Ben-Gurion, Sharett, Eshkol and Golda Meir.

Israel's leaders in the 1950s and 1960s adopted towards Germany a policy which can be aptly described as 'moral pragmatism'. That policy was pragmatic in form, but moral in content. It was firmly rooted in a moral assessment of what a Jewish State should do, what Jewish history demands, and was consonant with the responsibility of Jewish leaders after the Holocaust. Ben-Gurion had no doubts that a moral commitment to the six million murdered Jews involved a determination to make Israel strong and secure for the survivors. The Jewish struggle for survival, in his view, was continuing in Israel and the prime duty of an Israeli leader was to prevent another Holocaust. In the 1952 Reparations debate Ben-Gurion present-ed this view clearly: "If you want the overall reason in a single sentence, it was the final injunction of the inarticulate six million, the victims of Nazism, whose very number was a ringing cry for Israel to rise, to be strong and prosperous, to safe-guard her peace and security and to prevent such a disaster from ever again over-whelming the Jewish people."[10] Golda Meir put the Holocaust and Israeli-German postwar relations in the context of two thousand years of Jewish suffering and persecution: "Why was it placed upon us, a small people, to bear such a large part of the terrible cruelties that have befallen the world? There is only one answer. We were weak, we had no independence, we had no state. . .We must make ourselves strong in every way in order to save quickly. . .Jews from all over the world."[11] In her attitudes towards anything German Golda Meir was close to the 'moralist' camp, but during her term as Foreign Minister the sensitive military relations between Israel and Germany continued to develop and formal diplomatic relations were established. For Golda Meir it was a moral duty to override emotions and do everything possible to assure Israel's defense. The Israeli leadership of the day regarded economic relations as having a specific bearing on the security and survival of Israel. Thus even the 'dry' economic data of Israel's balance of trade deficit and the foreign exchange shortage assumed for Ben-Gurion, Sharett, Eshkol and Golda Meir a moral dimension which is usually absent in economic policymaking. German economic reparations and assistance were welcome because "the only thing to do was to establish Israel on such firm foundations that this (the Holocaust) could never happen again."[12] For the Israeli leadership the very fact that Jews for the first time in two thousand years will be receiving restitution for atrocities committed against them was of tremendous symbolic and moral significance. German Reparations to the Jewish State for atrocities against European Jewry also legitimized the Jewish-Zionist core value about the unity of the entire Jewish people and the Israeli claim to represent the past and future of all Jews. To dismiss these deeply seated feelings and convictions as sheer 'Realpolitik' does injustice to the main actors and to the complexity of the issue. The supporters of the government's policies thus saw nothing morally wrong in claiming a part of the property robbed from the murdered Jews. "Let not the murderers of our people be their inheritors as well," said Ben-Gurion.[13] Rosen spoke about our "sacred duty to rescue whatever is obtainable, to bring it here and to turn it to creative use."[14] Joseph agreed: "The Germans could not be left with vast stolen property. We had a natural duty to recover part of the enormous plunder."[15] NRP leader Moshe Haim Shapira also saw no moral wrong in a policy which simply meant to. try to get back "whatever we could reclaim" from the billions stolen by the Nazis."[16]

Ben-Gurion rejected the whole notion that his pragmatic policy towards Germany is less moral that the moralist boycott of Germany. His realism was based on moral grounds. He ridiculed the view that Germany was Neo-Nazi and that Adenauer was Hitler. Time and again he talked about the 'Other Germany' of Adenauer and the Social Democrats. He accused those who refuse to talk to any Germans — even to non-Nazis, anti-Nazis or those born after the War — of harboring a racist philosophy.[17] Prime Minister Sharett and Eshkol followed Ben-Gurion in questioning the morality of total opposition to any relations with any Germans. He demanded to relate to each German according to his deeds and attitudes and to the German State according to the principles and personalities of its leaders. He even defended his deeply held conviction that young Germans did not bear responsibility for the crimes of their fathers by invoking the Bible—"the fathers shall not be put to death for the children, neither shall the children be put to death for the fathers; every man shall be put to death for his own sin."[18]

Ben-Gurion's German policy may be termed 'moral pragmatism'. In 1977 the 'moralists' who had vehemently and even violently opposed any relations with Germany came to power in Israel. All the eyes were directed to Menachem Begin who in 1952 called to storm the Knesset in order to prevent the vote on the Reparations Agreement. Begin did not break relations with Germany, his government continued the pragmatic policies of his predecessors. Begin the prime minister engaged in personal talks with German politicians and diplomats, something Begin the opposition leader would have branded as betrayal of the Jewish people. The moralists turned out to be not averse to pragmatism, just the pragmatists had never actually betrayed morality.

(Professor Benyamin Neuberger taught at the University of Tel Aviv, Israel, and currently lectures at Beit Berl and the Open University in Tel Aviv. He is also a noted scholar on African affairs.

Notes

1. M. Sharett quoted in M. Brecher *Decisions in Israel's Foreign Policy* (New Haven, Yale University Press 1975) p. 67.
2. G. Meir quoted in Y. Auerbach *Foreign Policy Decisions and Changing Attitudes* (Ph.D Dissertation, Hebrew University 1980) p. 243.
3. A. Eban quoted in I. Deutschkron *Bonn and Jerusalem* (Philadelphia, Chilton 1970) p. 177.
4. S. Peres *ibid* p. 269.
5. D. Ben Gurion *ibid* p. 144.
6. P. Rosen quoted in M. Brecher p. 70.
7. M. Sharett *ibid* p. 68.
8. L. Eshkol quoted in Y. Auerbach p. 318.
9. M. Nurock *ibid* p. 85.
10. D. Ben Gurion *ibid* p. 69.
11. G. Meir *ibid* p. 69.
12. *Ibid* p. 69.
13. D. Ben Gurion *ibid* p. 65.
14. P. Rosen *ibid* p. 67.
15. D. Joseph *ibid* p. 70.
16. M.H. Shapira *ibid* p. 70.
17. D. Ben Gurion quoted in F. Shinar *Be'ol Korach Uregashot* (Tel Aviv, Shocken 1967) p. 103 (Hebrew).
18. D. Ben Gurion quoted in R. Vogel *The German Path to Israel* (London, O. Wolff 1969) p. 132.

"Israel Can Prevent This . . . Act"

Ha'aretz
May 6, 1985

By Shmuel Tamir

There are many graveyards in Germany for the millions of the German soldiers who died in the war, and the German government has invited President Reagan to pay tribute to German soldiers at Bitburg in his forthcoming visit. The purpose of the visit is clear: to show the German people, the American people, and the whole world that there is a *post facto* legitimization for the horrible war of the Third Reich: as if it were another "regular" war between nations that ended in an appeasement and not the war of which Churchill said, ". . . If the Allies will not win it, humanity will be sunk in a darkness of a thousand years."

When the President of the United States accepted the invitation he meant to demonstrate that due to the present friendship alliance with Germany, the United States is willing to forego the most sinful and horrible chapter in the German history on one hand, and the noble content of the holy war that the Allies waged against Germany on the other hand. By doing this the President of the United States showed a historical and moral bluntness, and very deeply insulted Jewish people, the American soldiers who were killed in the war, those who are still alive, and other Allied soldiers and citizens who endangered their lives in the Second World War.

This war was totally different in its essence and its goals from all the wars before it.

A historical and moral bluntness: For both Germany and the United States, this visit could, via their formal representatives, find many ways of making the relationship closer and even to demonstrate it with a total distinction between the past war and the present situation. However, what Reagan was requested to do, and accepted, has only one meaning: no more of the "other Germany's" apologies, but total reconciliation with the past. But such reconciliation harbors the nucleus of continuity.

Even worse, amongst hundreds, maybe thousands of military graveyards in Germany, there are so many in which only soldiers from the German army are buried — an army that in spite of its bloody criminals, is not identified automatically with the scum of humanity that was concentrated in the SS. The objective of the SS's existence was to be the arrowhead of the destruction of the Jewish people and to oversee tortures and the extermination of the nations of occupied Europe.

For Reagan's visit, the German government designated not a simple military cemetery, but a cemetery that has a special section for SS soldiers, the "elite unit" of the professional muderers. In front of their graves the President of the United States of America will stand silently. Those he will honor!

This horror has only one meaning: a sweeping purification — that includes

Germany and the most detestable Nazi war criminals, the persecutors of the Jewish people in Europe — by the Chancellor of Germany and the man who is head of what is called today the Free World.

And Israel is silent. A feeble word here, an apologetic expression there. But the government, the Knesset, the youth movements, the masses — are hardly heard. As a continuation of the official public indifference that disregards the alarm that came from the few before the Holocaust, as a continuation of the conspiracy of silence and the omissions of the official leadership of the "Yishuv"* and of the United States during the Holocaust, most of the leaders here, from the left and from the right, remember the Holocaust, first of all because of repatriation payments, but also because of fundraising, planting trees, etc. There was one Eichmann trial, and that concluded the blood-shed bill.

President Reagan is undoubtedly an important President, without illusions, who acts, basically, in the proper manner, in foreign as well as domestic policies. He is also a great friend of Israel, not only in a traditional vein but also from a correct strategic point of view. However, all of these aspects do not justify at all and do not reduce one single bit the shocking and terrifying act that he is about to perform.

Israel can prevent him from doing this. In this matter Israel's ability and power are a lot greater than it believes it is. Israel can prevent the President from this disgraceful act if it will give appropriate priority and energy to opposing it and if it will call up to this crucial campaign everyone who has a heart and eyes open.

Let's hope that the historical and moral senses of the Jewish state haven't been blunted, for he who abandons his past, is risking his future as well.

(Translated from Hebrew by Ronit Yoeli)

(Shmuel Tamir is a former Minister of Justice of Israel.)

---

* The Jewish population in Israel before 1948.

"Let My Cry Have No Resting Place"
Ma'ariv
June, 1985

By Hanokh Bartov

We all owe our thanks to Chancellor Kohl. Not for what he meant when he influenced President Reagan to visit certain sites in Germany and avoid some others. As has happened more than once before, intentions and consequences are totally different. For the big debate that ensued courtesy of the peculiar initiative and the poor White House cooperation we must be grateful, strange as it may sound.

The conciliation-summit held for the 40th anniversary of the defeat of the Nazi state — "The Thousand-Year Reich" — could have opened in a totally different atmosphere. The Federal Republic of Germany has been accepted as one of the major pillars, not only in the Western World — economically, politically, militarily — but also among us, the Jewish people and in the state of Israel. It is accepted as "another Germany."

I still remember that moment on the 35th floor of the Waldorf Astoria in New York 25 years ago, when a small group of Israeli journalists witnessed the first meeting between the founder and first Prime Minister of Israel, David Ben-Gurion, and the founder and first Chancellor of West Germany, Konrad Adenauer. In that meeting for the first time Ben-Gurion talked about "the other Germany."

That was many days ago. Much has happened since that date and all in the same direction; a distinction between Hitler's Reich — responsible for the historical Holocaust and with whom the Jewish people will never come to terms — and the "other Germany."

Each of these is a totally separate matter. It is the only way that a "normal relationship" between the two countries, the two peoples, can be maintained, though exacting a high emotional cost. This was the way the conciliation-summit of May '85 could have taken place.

To put matters into perspective, let us remember John Kennedy standing in front of the Berlin Wall and declaring, "I am a Berliner!" Let us also remember the German-French event which took place ten years ago, when Giscard d'Estang declared that "this will be the last ceremony in which victory over Nazism will be the main theme." Or, on the other hand, recall eight years ago in London, when leaders from seven Western states met in Downing Street and turned their backs to the tragic past.

What Chancellor Kohl tried to do this time — maybe just from a politician's lack of sensibility who knows where his electorate is — was totally different.

News about the debate between the Chancellor's and the President's offices began coming in quite a few months ago. They were quite astonishing in and of themselves. The news about the planned visit concentrated on the negative; Bonn refused vigorously the inclusion of a visit to a concentration camp (the difference between this and a death camp is only a matter of quantity).

It is only now that the other side, the positive one you might say, has been discovered. Kohl asked, demanded and achieved the President's consent to visit the Wehrmacht's soldiers' graves at Bitburg. In the public debate the fact that people from the Waffen SS were buried there was emphasized, as if it were only they who committed massacres. Detailed studies have proven beyond doubt that the whole German army was an active participant, especially on the Eastern front, in the massacre of Jews, Russian captives, and innocent citizens.

But the fundamental question arose, which the Chancellor certainly had no conscious intention of bringing to the center of the debate: Where *is* the "other Germany"?

When a visit to the Dachau camp is considered by Bonn as an offense to Germans' feelings in 1985, it is difficult to understand which Germans are being talked about. And when putting a bouquet of flowers on the graves of "death-angels" of the Third Reich constitutes a gesture which will appeal to the heart of Germany in 1985, one is shocked much more and one wonders even more about the validity of the distinction between that Germany and the present Germany, *the other.*

Thus it would appear certain individuals would be "positive" by forgetting crimes and concealing the criminals' traces and would rather concentrate on the present and the future.

However, with all the ensuing commotion, the main subject returned to the main stage. This is the subject that even 40 years after does not justify forgetting about — the criminal Nazi state. The Nazi state brought a horrible disaster on all of Europe — from which it recovered — but disaster upon the Jewish people from which it will probably never recover.

Bringing this subject back to the world's consciousness even on the 40th anniversary of the end of the war is very important. The people who had planned this event probably had assumed that most of the generation that experienced the horrid events of the Thirties and Forties had already passed away or had left active political life. I don't want to be accused of cynicism by reminding people that even when tens of thousands of Jews were murdered and cremated the Allies did not intensify their effort to save Jews.

Today this memory probably does not disturb them, nor do they search for it. They do not err by assuming that in ten, 20, and 50 years there won't be as much fuss made about such a visit as was made today.

But the opposite is happening in the state of Israel. The older and more established the state of Israel becomes the more the memory of the Holocaust will become the heart and soul of the Jewish people. For good reasons and for less than good reasons. Here we will neither want nor be able to forget.

The farther we shall go, and here lies the paradox, as years go by, the two dates — the date of the Third Reich's defeat and the date Israel was established — will become closer and closer till they become indistinguishable. At their inception they were two separate events, far away in place, in time, and in character.

From the very beginning there was some proximity in the calendar; even though the end of the war is always celebrated on the 8th of May, Independence Day, which is predicated on the Hebrew calendar, comes earlier and later. In between these two there are two remembrance days, the Holocaust and Valoure Day, and that for the Israeli Defense Forces' soldiers.

In the calendar, even today, the distance is very short: 40 years for Hitler's defeat, 37 for the state of Israel. It is already regarded as one historical moment. And who will distinguish between them when the years are 140 and 137? It is one historical moment, it is our very own double-consciousness.

How strange and puzzling, but thanks to Chancellor Kohl of the "Other Germany" and the crude intentions and amazing dullness of the President of the Great Power that feeds and supports us with love and willingness, the victory's 40th anniversary will be noted — two weeks after Israel's 37th Independence Day, as it ought to have been in the first place.

The first lesson we all got during the debate in Washington were important words pronounced not only by Jews but also by the Secretary of State, George Shultz. The second lesson issued from Chancellor Kohl, in a laudable speech at Bergen-Belsen. Although it is hard to understand why he "burst into tears" when trying to persuade President Reagan to visit graves of Hitler's soldiers, we should bless his words at Bergen-Belsen: "We have learnt the lesson of History . . . we will not deal lightly with the severity of the events that had happened." When this was said on the brothers' graves in the ears of the sons of the murderers' generation — let it be our partial comfort.

That verse from Job began Kohl's speech. He concluded with: "Earth, Conceal Not the Blood Shed on Thee."

There isn't a more appropriate ending to this lesson — to us here — than the second half of that same verse in Job (16, 18): "...And let my cry have no resting place."

And here is Dr. Moshe Anat's interpretation: Since Job is not asking for comfort but for justice — he had requested that there would not be a place [meaning a grave, that the cry will not be covered by a grave] to take his cry so that it would continue to echo in the world.

So what happened, like the case of the Bil'am story, is that this case has turned around and become a moralizing lesson in our times, perhaps a good one too.

(Translated by Ronit Yoeli.)
(Hanokh Bartov is a leading Israeli writer.)

"A Criminal Does Not Deserve To Be Honored"
Ma'ariv
May 3, 1985

(Interview with Prof. Israel Gutman, Director of Research at Yad Vashem and Professor at the Hebrew University, by Ya'akov He'alyon of Maariv, *a leading Israeli newspaper.)*

The most shocking scene, searing his memory forever, was the mocking laughter of two Germans at a 10-year-old boy who was holding a small child in his arms. The two children were naked, waiting in line to enter the gas chambers in Auschwitz.

He "projected" this scene in his shocking testimony at the Eichmann trial, in which he also said, "I tried furtively to steal a glance into their [the Germans'] eyes, because it was dangerous to give a direct look. Burning inside of me was the question as to whether there was any hesitation in their looks. And how children born to women could become smashers of babies' skulls."

It is very possible that those same Germans who were jeering at the children going to their deaths were members of the "Waffen SS," comrades-in-arms to the unit whose memory is about to be honored by the President of the U.S. on his visit to Bitburg.

Prof. Israel Gutman (62), a former resident of the Warsaw Ghetto and one of its rebels, was sent to Maidaneck and from there to Auschwitz. Upon liberation, "I was in such poor condition that my days were numbered." A former member of the kibbutz Lehavot Habashan, he is now a professor at the "Modern Judaism Institute" at Hebrew University and is the director of the "Center for Holocaust Research" at Yad Vashem. He has written numerous works and books; one of them, Warsaw — 1939-1943, *won him the "Yitzhak Sadeh Award" for Military Literature.*

We asked for his response to Reagan's unfortunate visit to the Waffen SS graves because we wanted to hear the voice of a Holocaust survivor who would look at both sides of the question.

Q: Did you have some kind of "personal touch" with the Waffen SS?

A: In the death camps, the people who ruled were the SS "death skulls." Toward the end of the war, the SS were taken out of the camps and were replaced by the Waffen SS. Placing the Waffen SS in the extermination camps indicated that the administration counted on them to execute the policy of cruelty and murder.

Q: The Germans claim, even now, in reference to Reagan's visit to the cemetery at Bitburg, that there is a misidentification, and that, as opposed to the SS, the Waffen SS were just fighting soldiers, like the Wehrmacht. Is this true?

A: The person who created the "death skulls" unit was the commander of the Dachau Camp. He was the one who established the regime of how the concentration and extermination camps were to be run, one of the most horrid and impossible specters ever. He is also the one who later went to the front and commanded a Waffen SS division.

Q: So upon what do the Germans base their claim?

A: They say that, as opposed to the SS which was a unit whose crimes had no precedent and whose people did not belong to the fighting forces, the Waffen SS was a fighting force. They also make a point of emphasizing that many of the people who belonged to this force did not volunteer for it, but were recruited into it without their consent. This argument does not refute the fact that the Waffen SS were assigned to "special duties."

Q: Why did the Nazi administration need a structure like the Waffen SS?

A: The Nazis considered them to be a nucleus that was loyal to the party. Himmler wanted to give the SS a powerful role. He wanted the SS to not only be loyal to the state but foremost to be devoted to their political affiliation. From an operational point of view the Waffen SS were actually subordinate to the Wehrmacht but they were part of the SS. The commanders, the training that they got in their units, the internal policies, all of these were dictated by the SS.

It is true that they were a fighting force, but on top of that, other missions were assigned to them: the actions against partisans and civilians, especially in certain territories in Eastern Europe. Some of their most horrid crimes have been mentioned these days. They murdered! It was known that they were the stormtroopers of the crimes and cruelty that this regime had performed. They were in charge of "operations." It was not by chance that in the Nürenberg trial verdict, the Waffen SS was included among the "criminal organizations," a definition that was not applied to the Wehrmacht.

Q: Considered among their crimes are the civilian massacre at the French village Oradour, the massacre of the American soldiers at Malmady and at the Arden's "Battle of the Bulge."

A: Of course, and also most cruel actions in Eastern Europe. They took part as an assisting force and were involved in quite a number of criminal actions such as: murder of Jews and political opposers, in the summer of 1941, in the Barbarosa operation, invading the Soviet Union, they killed hundreds of thousands of Jews in the areas of Vilna, Lithuania, Byelorussia.

Q: What would you say to President Reagan to prevent him from visiting Bitburg?

A: I would say that there is no need whatsoever to check if there is a soldier buried there who took part in one or another massacre. The fact is that SS soldiers are buried there and that's the symbol. These were people who belonged to units which symbolized Nazism and its crimes. The SS was the executer of these crimes.

Q: The German people today are so much insensitive that they don't perceive at all this symbol as horrible?

A: This case didn't come out of the blue, it is part of an ongoing process. At the beginning Germany said: the army is not one of the criminals; the SS is responsible for the crimes. Thus, the army was rehabilitated. Later, SS soldiers got organized and demanded rehabilitation for themselves too, due to a new "grading." They stated: we are the Waffen SS, we are not the "skulls of death." And now the rehabilitation is demanded by the "skulls of death" too. Well, the main point is not whether among the buried in that cemetery there are people who committed crimes. The important thing is that when Reagan is going there he is granting the SS, a criminal organization, rehabilitation. That means that he, as President of the U.S., sees them as victims who should be respected, be saluted!

Q: Two years ago you already expressed your concern of the process of blotting out the Holocaust.

A: In Germany there are historians, writers, intellectuals who are in a strong argument with the Chancellor: they oppose the tendency of blotting out the essence of Nazism and the general German responsibility to what had happened. But among German historians there is also another tendency, that is, trying to find a way to evade the responsibility. In post-World War I Germany there was a concept and feeling of vengefulness, claiming that it was accused falsely of crimes it had never committed, for which the Allies imposed sanctions on Germany to pay reparations. Some of the German historians at that time, even if they were not Nazis, had part in cultivating this concept. It was in this cultivated atmosphere that Nazism could have risen and influenced.

Right after World War II, similar claims, as if the Germans were not to blame, could not have been made. But today, after many years have passed, there is a tendency, claimed by the extremists, that there were no crimes, and there was no responsibility to the war, and there were no extermination camps, and no final solution — you know, the "school of denial of the Holocaust," as it is called.

Q: Does the denial of the Holocaust have any connection with Reagan's visit?

A: This is not the first time Kohl, who seeks rehabilitation, is stating that all the German victims, including the Waffen SS, are German victims, not victims of a Nazi war. And, therefore, the subject should be treated as part of German history, which should have the appropriate peace in the German tradition.

Q: You are placing a very serious accusation against him.

A: He has said these words!

Q: In other words, he is trying to blot out the German responsibility?

A: I wouldn't say that Kohl is trying to blot out Nazism and its crimes. He wants to be freed of the guilt, of the collective responsibility that Germany has. A law that was just passed in Germany shows that. The law forbids "the Denial of the Holocaust" and that denial is committing a crime. But the very same law also prosecutes those who deny that injustices had been committed against Germans in World War II.

Q: Meaning, retaining a "holy equilibrium?"

A: I will illuminate with a case: A habitual criminal crashes into a policeman. The gangster gets killed and the policeman gets killed. Both of them would be treated as victims? This is exactly what is interpreted from the law and from the visit to Bitburg.

Q: You mentioned activities of ex-SS members."

A: In the Waffen SS the SS traditions are kept, the loyalty, the comradeship, the fraternity, the Nazi-type discipline. A lot of literature is published in

Germany in which they figure as heroes. Thus, slowly, a myth is being created there and the yearning for the Nazi period. These are elements, if not of neo-Nazism, at least of glorification of Nazism.

Q: To what extent do these trends affect the young generation?

A: I don't know. However, the fact that Germany has had 40 years of a well-established democracy cannot be overlooked. After the war, many people predicted that these people and country are doomed to no changes, that they are "a sickness of humanity," certain that they would continue to threaten human society. All this has proved to be untrue.

Q: Isn't it possible that the danger is hidden? Maybe like a disease in the incubating stage?

A: The answer to this claim should be that Germany, in its own way, should be sensitive. They should educate, not by blotting out, but by revealing and unveiling the truth, with all the pain that goes with it. There is pain when children ask their grandfather or father, "Why were you a Nazi? Why were you in the SS? Why, at all, did you vote for Hitler? Why did you fight for him?" It causes a mental difficulty and it is possible that they are trying to find ways of escaping from it. From the point of historical responsibility it is the minimum the Germans should be doing.

Q: Therefore, you would not accept the claim that a state, after 40 years, has the right to cross out its past which it detests and is ashamed of?

A: I don't think that after 40, or even after 100 years, it is right and just to allow to be forgotten what the SS was, and what the concentration camps were, and the Nazi racism, and the murder of the Jews and prisoners of war. It is essential, because it creates defensive and deterring mechanisms which would prevent events from re-occurring. Today the large objection to racism is not coincidental. The great anxiety that racism left behind is still with us. When you are blotting out you tear off the historical truth and create a soil for growing new Nazi movements and Holocausts. As long as humanity remembers that Nazism led to a catastrophe that threatened the human race, it is a great deterrent force. It is not a coincidence that in the past 40 years neither meaningful Nazi movements nor new Hitlers have risen in Germany.

Q: And what about the political considerations that contribute to forgetfulness of the Holocaust?

A: There was no greater avowed opponent to communism than Churchill. But after the German invasion of the Soviet Union, he told them: "We are in one bundle." Today there is East and West. The Germans are part of the Western democratic world. Reagan wants to assure himself of a stronghold in Europe. Germany is a very important link in his strategic construction.

Q: That means that Reagan's visit to the cemetery is harlot's pay, that he's paying Germany?

A: I wouldn't call it harlot's pay. We cannot know how the decision was made. I also wouldn't judge if Reagan has a historical sense and understanding. In any case, he made a move that did not add to his popularity, even in his own country. I presume Chancellor Kohl wanted the visit this way, meaning that in this way Germany will become an ally, beyond give and take and what had happened in the world war, and that there is a symbolic act in the visit that erases events. Again, I cannot ignore the mixed emotions in Germany. It is difficult for them too. They are living in tragedy. Germans born after the war are left with an imprint, as that of Cain, just as Jews had one. The difference between them and the Jews lies in the fact that the imprint was put on us for no crime. As for them, there are severe historical facts. The Nazi victims are still living — this should not be forgotten!

Q: The mayor of Bitburg was quoted protesting the "public scandal" that is causing the "profanation of the soldiers' memory" — those buried in his town.

A: I don't know what is so profane. And I don't understand these words. If Reagan would not honor the victims, that means he is profaning? The profanation is honoring them! I know what profaning graves means. The Nazis also know very well how to profane. But Reagan is coming to honor them and that's what shouldn't be done. They should not be seen as victims.

Q: A Bonn government spokesman rejected the world's protest, saying that if the soldiers who are buried there were guilty, they had already paid with the most severe punishment: their death in battle.

A: I must repeat and state: Even if a criminal pays for his crime, he certainly does not deserve to be honored. Even death does not purify. They died for a cause that endangered the world, not for a just cause.

Q: Even so, objection to the visit of the Waffen SS graves is also heard in Germany?

A: Not all of Germany can be held responsible for the tendency to blot out. Even if most of its population wants the burden of responsibility off, there are circles in it that are warning, that would not let this matter rest, and that are standing on guard.

Q: Rudolf Augstein, *Der Spiegel*'s editor, has said that the major opposition came from Israel who would like, according to his words, to keep the guilt-fire burning for reasons of materialistic advantages.

A: That was the exact term which was used by the Holocaust deniers. The greatest opposers to any relations with Germany and to receiving any materialistic advantages from it were the most extremist about keeping the memory of the Holocaust. It is a libel! It hasn't started today that Jews have been falsely accused, that their motivation is the desire to profit from everything. These words have a smell of wicked anti-Semitism.

Q: Even though you are not known as a fan of Arik Sharon, what would you say about the claim that was heard in Germany, as if Israel has a double morality: on one hand, Sharon can aspire to lead the government, and on the other hand, we are "pestering the graves" in Germany?

A: (*With revulsion.*) I will not accept any sort of comparison between what happened here — and there were events that I could not agree with, condemned, and protested strongly against — and what happened with the Nazis. There is no similarity or anything in common. It is well known that in Germany there were many attempts to cling to the Lebanese war's events in order to achieve rehabilitation for what had happened in the Holocaust, attempts to straighten accounts.

In some sort of way the responsibility for the protest against Reagan's visit to Bitburg is cast upon the Jews and Israel. The protest did not begin among the Jewish people. On the contrary, the Jews joined it at first in a very modest manner, and their protest grew larger the larger it grew in the world. The first protesters were the war veterans in America, heads of churches, American Congressmen. These, as it is well known, are not delegates of the Jews.

Q: But the uproar that arose in the world did not persuade Reagan and the Germans to cancel the visit to Bitburg.

A: Perhaps in organizing the visit the Germans had an intention of making a certain experiment, sort of exploring, checking to see whether the past can be erased. After the uproar, they tried to create some sort of balance. At the beginning, Reagan didn't mean to visit Bergen-Belsen. They added this detail to the plan. And when the uproar grew stronger, an additional absurd attempt was made to calm it down. A German spokesman emphasized that Reagan would stay "longer" in Bergen-Belsen than in Bitburg—and Kohl himself went to Bergen-Belsen and said things he usually doesn't say, certainly not by chance. The lesson of this affair is that there are still many opponents who are attacking the attempts at blotting out.

Q: The official Israeli response was delayed and was hesitant. Some people say, cynically, that on the other side of the six million Jews stood the six hundred million dollars that we want from the U.S.

A: It *was* delayed and let's say the response wasn't very firm. It made me very sorry. Still, I'm also torn apart. The matter is very complicated. We are a state that is in constant struggle. Whoever wants to limit this to a matter of some dollars is oversimplifying and betrays the truth. Reagan is our friend in a consistent way and loyal to Israel's cause. Today we are not at the peak of our power so as to express things without taking into consideration what the President of the U.S. might think. Still, I would not say that I am pleased with the reactions, which were certainly very hesitant. I have wished that a big outcry had come from here. My complaints are mostly toward the Holocaust survivors who did not protest.

Q: Among them, you also did not protest

A: That's true.

Q: Well, maybe for you as well as for other Holocaust survivors the consciousness of the subject has decreased?

A: Undoubtedly. There is a general decrease, but it is also proportional.

Q: Peres called upon Germany to free Reagan from his commitment. Is Reagan so weak that he needs this kind of "releasing"?

A: The amount of consideration that is being asked from the U.S. toward this European pillar called West Germany cannot be underestimated. Kohl himself made it clear that cancelling the visit would hurt the current relations between his country and the U.S.

Q: So Kohl was the man who was supposed to release Reagan?

A: Kohl lost the ability to maneuver in this matter after it had gotten acceleration, in the way that happens to other diplomats, and he got into a very pressured mess, on both sides. And his own status isn't very strong.

Q: As for the Israelis, the youths' feelings toward the Holocaust, they often claim that they're "sick of it."

A: In Israel there is a tiredness evolving from the constant struggle with problems of survival. The constant stress sometimes creates some kind of numbness toward the Holocaust. But this is an external symptom, the thorny peel of the Israeli "Sabra." The sensitivity and the real feeling still exist and have not weakened. In the second and third generation the Holocaust consciousness and its historical significance have grown even stronger without the self-involvement complex.

(Translated from the Hebrew by Ronit Yoeli.)

"Ein Bergen-Belsener"
Ma'ariv
April 26, 1985

By G. Binyamin

Happy is the man that hath not walked in the counsel of the wicked, nor stood in the way of sinners, nor sat in the seat of the scornful . . . (Psalms 1:1)

For if you stand with sinners or live with the scornful, with evil men you must go. Evilness demands action. You see, it is not only those who scorn, waiting to show off, or sinners that do not sense nor feel, who have made President Reagan leave for Germany without dusting, God forbid, his soles in the gravel of the death-tows. But people of evil counsel know where they want him to go and where they do not want him to go. His visits to Bitburg and Bergen-Belsen are a voyage, but first and foremost the visit is a reward, one of forgiveness.

At the last moment Reagan changed his mind, and although the actual phrase "to go to Bitburg" may still be part of the ordinary dictionary, it will become the latest coined phrase that gives a bad reputation to those people that go or are sent by oral command, e.g., Jericho, Bedfordshire, and Coventry.

While it takes 20 attendants 14 days a year to wash the big Buddhah, Diobuchi of Kamakura's face, 100 spokesmen wouldn't have been enough to wash, in the

White House, pretty Ronnie's face from now till the end of his presidency had he followed his advisers' suggestions.

Pile the pages of the evidence of the Jews' sufferings, a voice came rising from his study, *and let me do my work undisturbed. I am — the dust!*

At the entrance to the Holocaust cellar next to King David's grave on Mt. Zion, close to the place where Jesus had, according to his students, his last meal, the survivors of Bergen-Belsen put up a *Yizkor,* a memorial on which was engraved: *Earth, Conceal Not the Blood Shed on Thee* (from Job 16:8). If Jesus were to come here, in a second return, he would be able to read this with the same fluency that we today read the Dead-Sea scrolls. He probably will go down to the cellar, look at the ashes of the Torah scrolls, on which is written that "the skies will vanish and the earth will disappear before one crownlet will fall off," and read through thousands of names — including Jesus, the holy name referred to by the President.

I wasn't at Bergen-Belsen, where the President will tour, but in Dachau, which he will not visit, ironically, on *Rosenmontag,* the last day of the Bavarian Alps' Carnival, which lasted that year, 72 days. On one of the monuments, nicely built, respectful — and I will not be misleading by saying aesthetic — I read in Hebrew: *And God should send fear into them, in order that Goyim will feel how fragile they are.*
feel how fragile they are.

Who really knew what? Do Gentiles know that we, the Jews, are human beings? But they, because they were created, after all, as humans, should treat us with a bit more mercy?

This way or another, I returned from the skeleton camps by foot and found a beautiful town. Churches, monuments — a few of them for the days of slaughter. Beside the monuments I saw luxurious cars, expensive restaurants, music conservatories, pedestrians, and since it was, as I said, *Rosenmontag,* girls and boys in costume, dolls, balloons, confetti, little clowns, Indians, Mexicans wearing sombreros, braided Chinese people, "temporary" blacks, who came up, singing and rejoicing in the S-Bahn car and made their way from the Mosulmanian's village, next to their town, into Munich.

Dachau's youth, that is not to be blamed, of course, for its fathers' deeds, coming out from the bones-gardens scenery, which are now Mark-masking parks, to a holiday of masks...

I have a song with me which I brought then from that place of the dead:

At the grave of the unknown prisoner,
That lived and died without shield,
I read some words of oath
On defiled land:
"Nie Wieder," "Never Again,"
"Nikogda Bolshe," "Phie jame."
I thought about every man who was killed
In all, all these bizarre deaths —
people of Odessa, Riga, Warsaw,
Prague

> *Before they swore to us*
> *In four languages . . . .*

I remembered what I had found, brought from "Psalms," and add to the draft:

> *"Words, words, words"*
> *Came a voice to me*
> *from across the curtain.*
> *Ashamed I am to recite Psalms here*
> *"Bozhe moi, Mon Dieu, Mein Gott,*
> *My God . . . ."*

Coming back home—far away from Marienplatz, Munich's fashion circle, between the "Alter Peter" and the "Rathaus," but also from Eikplatz, Eika's notorious parade circle, I exchange verse for verse:

> *While watching this scene*
> *I recalled seeing once before*
> *At the Gidi and Mitleh passes **
> *This ingathering of the exiles*
> *Long after Hitler.*
> *There they swore to me*
> *In a language uncruel*
> *But very authentic to me*
> *For it is Hebrew and only*
> *Hebrew*
> *That never — never again!*

Being in Berlin, President Kennedy said: "Ich bin ein Berliner!" I am curious to know what Reagan would be—"Ein Bitburger" or "Ein Bergen-Belsener."

---

* Passes between the mountains in the Sinai.

The Blot Of Bitburg

The Jerusalem Post
May 6, 1985

The original idea was to make the 40th anniversary ceremonies of the liberation of Europe, coinciding with the Western Summit in Bonn, into a joyous celebration of newly won freedom and amity, untainted by memories of Nazism and the Holocaust.

But that could not be done. In the event, the bizarre attempt to downplay, indeed to suppress, the moral dimension of the titanic struggle that had led to liberation only helped bring freshly to the fore the old passions the U.S. President had hoped to smooth over. In the end both Ronald Reagan and his German host, Chancellor Kohl, had to temper disrespect for the burden of history with due obeisance to its victims.

So at Bergen-Belsen yesterday Mr. Reagan and Mr. Kohl both offered tributes to the Jews incinerated by Hitler's death machine. Mr. Reagan spoke about the Jews murdered only because they had been Jews. And Mr. Kohl — continuing from a moving address at the site two weeks ago — said his compatriots had learned from history that there must not be another Holocaust.

Then the leaders of the United States of America and of the German Federal Republic flew to the Bitburg military cemetery, where they rendered homage to Nazi war dead, among them 49 members of the Waffen SS — the military arm of the notorious killer gang — whose own claim to fame was the gunning down of U.S. war prisoners. This gesture was supposed to signal the ultimate reconciliation between Germans and Americans.

It was Mr. Kohl who conceived the idea of the joint visit to Bitburg. He had his reasons, not least his exclusion from last year's rites commemorating the Allied landing in Normandy. But it was Mr. Reagan who endorsed the idea without weighing its implications, and without insisting that it be scrapped even when the presence of SS graves in the cemetery had been revealed. It was he who stuck to the Bitburg plan after rejecting the proposal — advanced, to his credit, by Mr. Kohl — that he should also pay a visit to the site of a former death camp, such as Dachau. And it was he who publicly suggested that the Bitburg dead were as much victims of Nazism as the Jews of the crematoria.

Only the uproar he raised among American Jews and veterans — which later spread to Capitol Hill — induced the President to add Bergen-Belsen to his schedule.

Mr. Reagan, no doubt, had his reasons, too. Although he failed to secure Mr. Kohl's unqualified support at the Bonn summit on Saturday, he cannot have failed to cement West Germany's tie to the Western Alliance under U.S. leadership. He must have struck a responsive chord among Germans who hate being held accountable, to this day, for Nazi crimes — and especially among those who believe their country deserves retroactive credit for having stood up to the communists in World War II.

These, however, are not good enough reasons for Jews, whether in or outside Israel, to feel any less appalled by yesterday's ceremonies. Mr. Reagan is a friend of the Jewish People, and of the State of Israel, as Shimon Peres has pointed out: and this explains why the official Israeli reaction to even his virtual legitimation of the SS has been so muted. The country cannot, now more than ever before, lose such a friend.

But it would be less than honest to pretend that, to most Israelis, Mr. Reagan's mistake, as it has been termed, is anything less than a colossal offense against the very moral imperative he so often invokes.

The memory of Bitburg may start fading away as soon as the exigencies of Israel's practical existence take center stage again. But the bitter taste will linger for a long time to come.

Frank Words to Ambassador Hansen
Ma'ariv
May 7, 1985

By Hanokh Bartov

Dear Mr. Ambassador of the Federal Republic,

I received the kind invitation for the reception that you and Mrs. Hansen are holding today in honour of Jerusalem's 12th International book fair. I had a sincere intention to go to Mishkenot Sha'ananim and rub shoulders with guests and the hosts. The book fair celebration is one of the distinguished symbols of the victory over Nazism, just as the burning of books side by side with burning peoples were the most horrid symbols of that criminal regime.

However, after Bitburg I am obliged to decline this invitation. Please allow me to explain why I am not just absent — who would know if I had come or not — but writing a private letter to you, Mr. Ambassador.

There are many things that are bursting in sight of the disgraceful ceremony that Chancellor Kohl forced upon President Reagan, like the false gathering of "combat-men's fellowship" between the American General Ridgeway and the General of the Luftwaffe, that are too difficult and too complicated to be described in words.

Thus, I shall restrict myself here to one point. You, too, were asked about it in your talk, in perfect Hebrew, on the radio talk show *Zeh Hazman*. I am referring to Kohl's efforts to restore the Wehrmacht's honor which was lost forever. He did not confine himself only to that, but also wanted to expand the "honor-restoration" to the Waffen SS forces, as it found its reflection in Reagan's arousing words: "The soldiers of the Wehrmacht were the Third Reich's victims just as much as the prisoners of the concentration camps."

Well, Mr. Ambassador, I do not know what's more deceitful and shocking — the attempt to distinguish between the "Waffen SS" and just "SS" or between these and the rest of the military divisions of the Third Reich.

Mr. Ambassador, you are probably more than I familiar with the many research works about the "criminal orders" that the Wehrmacht accepted and executed very enthusiastically. The commanding rank of the Wehrmacht issued four basic criminal orders before the invasion of Russia and those orders specifically stated: "To enable free activity to the SS's and the SD's murder units in the areas controlled by the army." Another order canceled the military law and enabled one to shoot, without any trial, anyone who was suspected as a partisan or a partisan-supporter. It also instituted massacre as "collective punishment." There was also the "Comissar's order" [the fourth order] which ordered one to kill immediately every captive that was identified as political comissar. The selection was done by the Wehrmacht and every comissar, commanding officer or a Jew, who was not shot on the spot was given to the "Einsatz Gruppen."

Things were so bad that generals scolded their people for "over-killing." I shall quote here from an order of the general commander of the 47th armoured corps, dated June 30th, 1941:

"In spite of my orders of the 25th. . . there are more irresponsible killings of captives and deserters without cause and without logic . . . we want to bring peace, tranquility and order to the land that has suffered terribly from a Jewish criminal group. The Führer's order calls for merciless actions against the Bolsheviks (political comissars) and all other partisans. People who were clearly identified as such would be taken aside and shot only with an officer's issuing orders . . . ."

The extent of the Wehrmacht's murders was such that the head of the Gestapo, Miller, stated on November 9th, 1941: "The commanders of the camps are complaining that 5 to 10 percent of the Russians that were marked to be executed arrive to the camps dead or half-dead."

In total: 3.3 million Russian captives out of 5.5 million were murdered and many of them — by the Wehrmacht.

I deliberately do not mention a word about the Wehrmacht's part in what was done to us, the Jews.

To us, to our generation, to our families.

A criminal regime can only function and exist with a similar army. A criminal regime has no existence without a criminal army, a criminal administration, a criminal law.

That is why there is no similarity between the armies that saved the world from a murderous regime and the army that served this regime till the last minute.

The day after tomorrow, the Lag Ba-Omer, the Israeli volunteers to the British army will assemble for a memorial meeting. I don't know how many of the 30,000 volunteers are still alive and how many will come. However, we who will come will come on behalf of all. I was one of those volunteers, Mr. Ambassador. We are still alive and our memories are alive as well.

I remember my friends buried in the military cemetery in Ravena, Italy. I also remember the remnants of humans we encountered as they were leaving the death camps.

There was no similarity. Neither between the living, nor between the dead. Perhaps it should be remembered that Hitler was the man who coined the phrase "Keine Kamaraden," meaning, there's no honor to enemy soldiers. Indeed, this order was always implemented. There is no place for equating the dead from the army which fought to defend humanity and those who fought to establish the Thousand Year Reich.

At Bitburg your chancellor sought to blot out this basic distinction. I recall your moments of perplexity in your radio talk with Ran Evron as a conflict between your duty to represent your government and your feeling, that a deed that has no forgiveness has been forgiven, identifying the murdered and their murderers as "victims."

My words are not aimed at you personally. On the contrary, perhaps your perfect knowledge of Hebrew may assist you in reaching the most latent chambers of the memories of our generation, its lamentation and grief. Maybe you would also express our stupefaction to the intellectuals in your country concerning their silence then and their silence today as well.

Between the day before yesterday in Bitburg and the day after tomorrow at the Israeli soldiers' convention, I protest with my absence the symmetry between a murderous regime and its organizations, and those who died as fighters for liberation of humanity from Nazism. And especially since it's the Jerusalem book fair, I shall not come. This is the least a Hebrew writer can do on such a day, even if all of us know well that no one cares.

(Translated from the Hebrew by Ronit Yoeli)

Part VII

Reaction From Around The World

The events surrounding the President's visit to Bitburg in an effort to stage a public act of symbolic reconciliation between the United States and the Federal Republic of Germany were of great interest to Western European countries on two counts:

1. They had gone through the agony of Nazi occupation; many had lost citizens in the war.
2. They participated at the European Economic Summit.

In particular, the British were up in arms about the visit. Usually, the British do not dwell upon the Holocaust, relying more upon its own Battle of Britain to fuel public opinion. Somehow, this time the issue of the Holocaust and the horrors of Nazi Germany became central to daily media coverage.

The Jewish press and the statements of British Jewish leaders were dwarfed by the quantity and intensity of articles and statements from the public including such religious notables as the Archbishop of Canterbury, Dr. Robert Runcie.

In France, former deportees and resistance fighters were forced to face those years of deprivation, many for the first time in years, by the announcement of the visit. The atmosphere in general is vividly reflected in the articles of lawyer-activist Serge Klarsfeld and Henri Bulawko, who represent the survivors, as well as in the eloquent speech of Simone Veil, the former president of the European Parliament, who experienced the Nazi camps firsthand.

The main articles in **Le Monde** were written by two well-known German personalities, von Stauffenberg, the son of the German general who opposed Hitler and was executed, and by Johannes Rau, the prime minister of the state of North Rhine-Westphalia and the contender for the Social Democratic nomination to challenge Kohl for the chancellorship.

Countries south of the equator were also well represented in the general media cry against the visit to Bitburg, among them Argentina and Australia. The Argentinean Jewish community, which has adopted German as its "lingua Judaica" produced several interesting and penetrating analyses of this affair, placing it in historical perspective. Another interesting historical analysis was provided by Isi J. Leibler, director of the Australian branch of the World Jewish Congress.

Unique in the Southern Hemisphere was the South African press in general and the Jewish community in particular. They did not refer to Bitburg. For some inexplicable reason, South African Jewry, which traces its forefathers to the Lithuanian community, that was ultimately annihilated by the Nazis, found no reason to raise the issue. Moreover, the South African Jewish Board of Deputies in its 33rd National Congress, May 30 — June 2, 1985, neither raised the issue nor had to entertain any resolutions for or against the visit. As far as they were concerned, the visit did not exist. What did exist was their one foreign issue, which was resolved as the "affirmation of its unbreakable bond and solidarity with the state of Israel and its inhabitants."

Non-Jews behind the "Iron Curtain" were not so reticent in making comment about the Bitburg affair. They used comment about this visit as a means to castigate the United States for its foreign policy in Europe and assaulted the position on disarmament.

Yet there was a difference, however slight or subtle, between comment from the Soviet Union and that from its satellite countries. While the former stressed the strategic goals behind Reagan's visit — such as the consolidation of NATO and support for SDI — the latter stressed their historical experience under the Nazi regime. This is understandable, because all of the Soviet satellite countries came under the domination of the Third Reich.

The Soviet Union, on the other hand, has refused to recognize the Holocaust. They do not have a single monument for the Holocaust or have any means by which to identify the policies of the Nazis specifically directed against the Jews. For example, the monument at Babi Yar (in Kiev) that was erected sixteen years *after* Yevtushenko's poem, "There Is No Monument at Babi Yar!" bears no inscription that identifies either the victims or the specific policies regarding the Holocaust. There is also a horrible irony in this monument that should not escape the attention of any Jew, or any man or woman of decency. The monument was placed there ostensibly to memorialize the murder of ninety thousand Jews in three days at Babi Yar, and in response to the outcry following the publication of the poem. Yet the monument is located at the wrong site, and pictures a soldier and a sailor defending a woman who is breast-feeding. There were neither soldiers nor sailors amidst the victims at Babi Yar.

Thus, it is no surprise that in the spring of 1986 the Soviets extended congratulations to one-time United Nations secretary general Kurt Waldheim upon his election to the presidency of Austria shortly after the release of information about Waldheim's Holocaust activities during World War II. They described the charges against him as the work of a conspiracy of Zionists and the U.S. government.

Not a single Soviet leader has ever uttered a word in commemoration of the Jewish victims of Nazism. It is impossible to imagine the screening of any film about the Holocaust in the Soviet Union or a television special such as the Greens' *Holocaust.* However, this absence of concern for Jewry did not prevent the Soviets from using the trip to Bitburg as a means to attack President Reagan's political goals.

Two satellite countries — Hungary and Rumania, who were victimized by the Holocaust — ignored the event. At the time much of the world was commenting, they were in the midst of expanding trade with the United States

This was the same Hungary in which Raul Wallenberg was kidnapped by the Soviets because his main occupation was saving Jews by granting them Swedish passports. To this day the Soviets refuse to acknowledge what has happened to him.

Obviously, responses from Jewish communities within the Soviet sphere were not allowed.

The Arab world also chose to ignore the issue. It is highly illuminating to read Abraham H. Foxman's letter to the Egyptian ambassador in which he mentions the Egyptian rendition of the event, which spoke of its abuse by the Zionists and other villains. There was no response. The silence was most eloquent.

Chapter 22

Great Britain—Press

Before Bitburg

Germans Won't Forgive Thatcher
The Guardian
April 5, 1985

Sir—Most of Mrs. Thatcher's "money back" from the EEC is coming out of West German pockets. I do not think they are likely to forgive or forget her criticism of President Reagan's proposed visit to Bitburg. Mrs. Thatcher in 1944 was the same age as the young Waffen-SS troops buried there after being killed in action. According to those who actually fought them, the Waffen-SS were elite soldiers bravely led and incomparably better armed than our own troops.

The EEC was founded mainly to prevent future wars between France and Germany. Instead of whining interminably about "England's money back," the English MEPs should lead the way towards full reconciliation between former enemies—

Yours faithfully,

Winnie Ewing MEP [Member of the European Parliament]
52 Queens Drive
Lossiemouth

Biting The Bitburg Bullet
The Guardian
May 1, 1985

Mr. Ronald Reagan talks on global television about the most "anguished" decision of his Presidency. Nonetheless, he mistily avers, it is "morally right" for him to go to Bitburg cemetery. And that's final.

On any reasonably calm assessment of this absurd affair, Mr. Reagan — anguish, morality and all — commands some sneaking sympathy. His West German hosts didn't do their Bitburg homework. His own advanceman, Michael Deaver, didn't spot the handful of Waffen-SS graves among the thousands stretched across acres. And by the time the facts of the matter came to light it was already too late: Mr. Reagan was stuck. Either he could mortally offend Chancellor Kohl or he could mortally offend a variety of vociferous Jewish and domestic political groups. But there was no way he could avoid offending anybody. A fellow in that sort of bind deserves some sympathy. Why, then, isn't he getting it? Why (quite apart from much European kertuffle) have square miles of American newsprint covered little else for almost a fortnight? There are issues and issues in politics: this is an issue, sure enough, but of the sugar frosted variety. It excites a measure of real emotion from some extremely articulate people. But it isn't, for a second, in the sense that — twelve months hence — ninety nine people out of a hundred will even be able to remember what it was all about.

To get the context you have to go back a twelve month. Then it was the fortieth anniversary of D-Day. And, naturally, another economic summit. Quite spontaneously, many of the men who participated in the allied landings in 1944 were anxious for a reunion. Forty years on wasn't perhaps a very natural celebration point. But fifty years on, most of them would be dead. The assembled statesmen of the world sensed a stupendous photo-opportunity: and none of them sensed it more eagerly than Mr. Reagan. This was the kind of facile TV theatre he had already made his own. The grand diplomacy of the London summit. The melodramatic return to his Irish O'Roots. And the commander in chief of modern freedom, jaw jutting, on a Normandy beach. An irresistible prospect. No politician even thought of resisting. But then came the reckoning. If you celebrate D-Day (miffing the Germans, and the Russians) how can you fail to celebrate VE-Day a year later? But what, actually, are you celebrating? Victory over the nation which is now your most important ally? The Yalta dismemberment of Europe? What? First the politicians hung back. Then logic and public opinion pushed them forward. But still they didn't know what they were celebrating.

Many weighty essays, of late, have been written on the unhealed scars of World War Two, the profound bitterness unleashed afresh by this single act of tactlessness. We don't for a second, underestimate the passions involved, or the way they can wash through politics. But honestly, chaps, that isn't what most of this is about, is it? Most of it is about the media — particularly the American media — who have loved and hated the growth of photo-diplomacy. Loved D-Day because there were terrific pictures: hated D-Day because it was all image manipulation by a White House professionally geared to just such PR antics. One banana skin, in such circumstances, may rapidly become a banana forest. Opposition politicians pour in the pineapples. Lobbyists do their absolutely predictable nut. A steaming tropical fruit salad ensues.

The honest response for Mr. Reagan, of course, would be to plead the simple truth. Look, you guys, none of this stuff is very important. None of it matters, or is designed to matter. But that, alas, is the one plea that can never be entered. Instead, there are only lashings of anguish and professions of seriousness that demean the serious business of politics. If one lesson lingers, though, there may yet be a flicker of gain. Until Bitburg, the outward video show of international diplomacy had come to seem so much more alluring than the tiresome business concerning real policies. No longer, perhaps. When the Big Top collapses it's time for the circus to start leaving town.

Misjudgment Over Bitburg
The Financial Times
May 2, 1985

The decision to include the German military cemetery at Bitburg in President Ronald Reagan's German itinerary rests upon poor judgment in both Bonn and Washington. The opposition that the proposed visit has stirred up in the Congress and elsewhere in the U.S. is proof enough of that. One may regret the hubbub, but one cannot ignore that it echoes hard if unpalatable political facts.

President Reagan and his host, Dr. Helmut Kohl, the German Chancellor, need not have worked themselves into the unenviable position in which they find themselves if they had avoided the theatrical celebration of reconciliation between wartime enemies. The tempers unwittingly stirred up will not advance a postwar reconciliation that has, by and large, been achieved, even if it must inevitably remain imperfect.

Both have been dragged to the surface at a time when detachment is needed to resolve the many issues of high importance, such as nuclear armament and disarmament or commercial policy, bedevilling transatlantic relations within the western alliance.

Sensationalist

Admitting so much does not absolve from blame those who have blown up the Bitburg issue beyond all proportion. They, too, have taken risks with the future of the alliance and with the cause of democracy in Germany and maybe even elsewhere. Moscow has seen its chance to fish in troubled waters. The West German left has had its say too.

So far nothing has been heard from the West German far right. But it would be blindness to ignore that continually picking upon the Germans of today for their people's past could eventually create a backlash. Germans can hardly be blamed for resenting an often merely sensationalist fascination of many media with Nazism which far oversteps the bounds of what might be explained as a justified vigilance.

A constant harping on the Nazi theme renders no service to Dr. Kohl and the other mainstream politicians in West Germany who have steered Germany down the middle of the road ever since its foundation. It can truthfully be said that their state has achieved a truer democracy and a greater degree of tolerance, than some of the Allies of the second world war.

Consultation

The honestly unconvinced might care to read the speech made by Dr. Kohl on April 21 at the site of the Bergen-Belsen concentration camp. It is a dignified speech in which he carefully avoided the trap of trying to offset Nazi inhumanity against the suffering of German people during the final rout. "We should not have learned anything from history if we were to weigh up atrocities against each other," he said.

Dr. Kohl also denied that the time had come to forgive and forget. The past should be remembered as a warning of what happens if people are spurned for their beliefs or for their racial origins, whatever they may be. President Reagan could save something from the debacle if he used his great powers of persuasion to make this very point to the world at large.

The Bitburg debacle is a reminder that no useful purpose is served by dwelling theatrically upon the past unless this really strengthens resolve everywhere to prevent a repetition of persecution and mass murder anywhere in the world.

Instead, today's energies should be devoted to realities of consideration and cooperation that hold together and strengthen the U.S. alliance with West Germany, and the western alliance as a whole. If that lesson is learned the Bitburg affair will have served some purpose.

The Past Is Not Prologue
The Economist
May 4, 1985

Verdun is not Bitburg. By linking hands for the cameras at a famous First World War battlefield last year, Dr. Helmut Kohl, the West German chancellor, and President Mitterrand of France conjured up a symbol of reconciliation between former enemies that spoke louder than a score of speeches. But well-meant plans to make a similar gesture with President Reagan at a German military graveyard went badly and predictably awry. The row about the Bitburg cemetery, whch turned out to contain the graves of soldiers of the Waffen-SS, cast a shadow over the seven-nation economic summit Dr. Kohl was to preside over in Bonn on May 2nd-4th.

Had Dr. Kohl, Mr. Reagan and their respective staffs done their homework properly, the row would probably never have occurred. Most West Germans seem to have liked the idea of marking VE-Day by a symbolic act of reconciliation with the United States. Even those who could see that the Bitburg graveyard was a silly place to make it backed up the Chancellor once the storm of protest from across the Atlantic began to blow. In a poll towards the end of April, 72% of those questioned thought Dr. Kohl was right to press ahead with plans for a brief Bitburg visit.

Yet the row, and the wounded West German reaction to it, are more than a matter of bad staffwork. West Germany's efforts to take part in VE-Day celebrations without abasing itself always risked embarrassment of some sort.

Not that soothing formulae or positive thinking have been in short supply. The words of West Germany's first president, Theodor Heuss, that in 1945 "we were redeemed and destroyed at the same time," have been widely and approvingly quoted this spring. Many West Germans will have agreed with Dr. Kohl when he said at the end of April that defeat gave Germans the chance to create a federal republic which was the freest state Germans had ever known.

Yet the past will not be buried, as today's West Germans seem the first to recognize. West German magazines have for months been carrying long, sombre accounts of the last days of the war. A television series mixing contemporary newsreel film with interviews of survivors who witnessed Germany's defeat masked none of the horrors. Ceremonies have been held at the sites of the concentration camps at Dachau and at Bergen-Belsen, where Dr. Kohl spoke of Germany's "never-ending shame."

That sense of guilt has entered deeply into the West German character. It is kept there in the classroom, where schoolchildren are taught about Nazism, and in school outings to the sites of the extermination camps. A close watch is kept on extreme right-wing groups, even though their following is negligible. No vigilance seems too small. West Germany's most populous state, North Rhine-Westphalia, last month banned car number-plates with the initials "SS" or others that might be taken for Nazi cryptograms.

The new Germany can still throw up jarring moments or casual remarks that jolt the unsuspecting visitor. A bluff, 55-year-old taxi driver told your correspondent that the fuss over Bitburg was due to the power of Jewish capitalism. Perhaps he had been reading the glossy, mass-circulation *Quick,* whose cover story on Mr. Reagan's West German visit was entitled "The Power of the Jews."

Other reactions in the West German press were less offensive, but no less scornful about the reaction the Bitburg plan was causing in America. In an editorial the *Frankfurter Allgemeine Zeitung,* a sober, conservative newspaper, blamed the American media for breathing new life into "the caricature of the ugly German." It noted sarcastically that the Nazis had always been good box-office for the American entertainment industry.

In part, such angry West German reactions simply reflect a crude misunderstanding of America: Christians and non-believers in the United States, as well as Jews, were affronted by the Bitburg plan. But the West Germans' reactions also laid bare a resentment that their allies — particularly the Americans — still do not fully understand them or their peculiar predicament. Many West Germans think that Americans do not grasp the complexities, of emotion as well as politics, of belonging to a divided nation. Only after much agonising did Dr. Kohl's government decide not to send a representative to the East German VE-Day celebration — an event as full of paradox as anything on the western side.

Quick to exploit these strains, the parliamentary floor leader of the ruling Christian Democratic party, Mr. Alfred Dregger, sent a sharp letter of criticism to American senators who had protested about the Bitburg visit. Mr. Dregger, a leader of his party's right wing, warned them not to stir up trouble between two anti-communist allies — thereby himself fuelling the fire. A minister of state at the foreign ministry, Mr. Alois Mertes, accused the senators of suggesting that every German soldier had been a Nazi. Behind it all Dr. Kohl detected a failure of Americans to teach their schoolchildren about the realities of today's Germany.

Workaday contact over 40 years has lessened the chance of this sort of muddle between West Germany and its west European allies. But in America there is plenty of room for misunderstanding West Germany. In one way, this is odd since so many things — a tendency to earnestness, the lack of a real upper class, fat weekend newspapers — make the two societies remarkably alike. In another way, it is not surprising. During the First World War, Germans in America, once one of the largest ethnic groups, put away their pictures of the Kaiser and anglicised their names. Today in the United States there are Irish-Americans, Italian-Americans, Mexican-Americans, Jewish-Americans. But although there are millions of Americans of German extraction there are no German-Americans. Put crudely, good German-American relations have to survive without a strong German lobby in America.

For many West Germans the graveyard fuss confirms a suspicion that friends apply a double standard to them. West Germany is a successful capitalist democracy and a full member of the western alliance; but still, West Germans often feel, their allies are ready to slap them down by reminding them of what Germany once was. Again, West Germany's allies from time to time urge it to take a part in world affairs better suited to its economic weight; but when West Germany does show fitful signs of stirring as a power, its friends, or so it suspects, recoil at the memory of Germans on the march.

As with many suspicions, there is a small core of truth here inside a husk of muddled feelings. The row over Bitburg is provoking West Germans to voice resentments they usually keep to themselves. What a pity that this came about as a result of a thoroughly avoidable miscalculation.

Hanging Out The Washing
The Guardian
May 4, 1985

By Erlend Clouston

Now this was almost worth fighting the Second World War for. "German Secret Weapons Portfolio. Large beautiful illustrations of Secret Weapons suitable for framing. These drawings, based on secret German blueprints, are strikingly reproduced on high quality art paper — a tremendous gift for the men of the house, whatever their age!"

Well, let's see. I would like lots of these. I would like the Sturmtiger 38cm Assault Mortar, the X-4 Homing rocket, the Thor Extra-heavy Siege Howitzer, the Dummy U-Boat, the Electric U-Boat. I am also curious to see the Curved Barrel Rifle, the Circular Winged Coleopter, and, why not? The Flying Saucer. What did you do in the war, Vater? I was developing the Curved Barrel Rifle, son, and shot myself in the foot.

Reconciliation is a wonderful thing. Reconciliation is the main reason I am at present studying the mail order catalogue of Samisdat Publishers, PO Box 11132, Buffalo, New York. Samisdat Publishers sort of present things from the other side's point of view: "Videocassette movies in your own home. Thrill to the destruction of another decade's old lie (The Anne Frank Diary Hoax), "... marvel at the magnificent architecture of Berlin and the longest military parade in German history" (Nazi Cinema). They do not seem to have any film of the Flying Saucer, but perhaps it was going too fast.

It is my friend Robert Faurisson who has been encouraging me to be reconciled. "Why," I asked Robert Faurisson, "should I be reconciled to a nation whose secondary education system had failed to make it 100 percent clear that uniform fetish is one thing, gassing people another?"

"But that is where you are wrong," cried Robert Faurisson, springing from the bed. "The Nazis were bad, but they did not have a planned extermination programme." Robert was springing from the bed because there were no chairs in the room. There were no chairs in the room for reasons not unconnected with the above statement. The French courts had imposed a whacking great fine on him because, in the process of developing his thesis, he had libelled another historian who did believe in the gas chambers. As the University of Lyon 2 had temporarily fired him from his job as Associate Professor of French Literature, he could not pay the fine. So he had hidden the chairs to prevent them being repossessed by the bailiff.

Robert Faurisson has distinct views. He will sell you a video tape outlining The Myth of the Gas Chambers. He laughs long and hard if you bring up Anne Frank's Diary. The old joke! He has just come back from Canada where he was a star defense witness in the trial of someone accused of spreading Nazi propaganda. S'easy, says Robert Faurisson. The Nazis did not have a planned extermination programme. Therefore there is nothing wrong in distributing Nazi propaganda.

Robert Faurisson is selling the Secret Weapon of all time: White-washed Nazis with Added Integrity. Well, let us give it a whirl.

Richard III has been (sort of) exonerated.

I have not personally inspected the sites of the gas chambers or bomb shelters (R.F.).

Rudolph Höss, first commandant of Auschwitz, was kind to animals. When his mother-in-law's canary died, he "tenderly put the birdie in a small box, covered it with a rose, and buried it under a rose bush in the garden." (Character witness at war crimes tribunal.)

Hitler's cook was Jewish (Fraulein Kunde).

Rudolf Höss writes in his autobiography (*Commandant of Auschwitz,* Pan, p. 186): "What would have happened to a group captain who refused to lead an air attack on a town which he knew for certain contained no arms factory and no military installation? An attack in which he knew for certain that his bombs must kill principally women and children? I am a soldier and an officer, just as was that group captain." But this witness is clearly a volunteer for the Curved Barrel Rifle Brigade, so I will ask him to stand down. Besides, Robert Faurisson believes the autobiography is phoney, the brainchild of Höss's Polish (communist) interrogators.

Copernicus had a bad time promoting his unorthodox views.

A man called Ditlib Felderer has produced some very complicated mathematics relating to the alleged size of the alleged piles of clothes of the alleged victims left outside the alleged gas chambers of the alleged death camp at Treblinka.

Personally I do not quite understand the alleged mathematics. But you will get the gist of the alleged argument from one of Mr. Felderer's asides: "It is a wonder that the (Exterminationists have). . . not come up with the suggestion the slope was used for skiing down by the Germans, or to push victims to their deaths, thus sparing them the gassing procedures." (*Journal of Historical Review,* Vol. I, No. 1.)

Then there are the plots. There are three plot theories. The first theory says the Holocaust was a good idea dreamed up by the Bolsheviks to camouflage the problems of the bankrupt Bolshevik state. The second says it was a good idea dreamed up by the Jews to blackmail Germany into solving the problems of the bankrupt Jewish state. The third says that the Holocaust was the answer to the problems of the Polish/American hotel industry. Ditlib Felderer says: "Concentration camp tourism is now a valuable source of foreign exchange for Poland. There is now a Holiday Inn at Auschwitz. . ." Actually it is in Kracow, 40 miles away. (Personally I find these theories slightly less watertight than a Dummy U-Boat, but then I am not a naval architect.)

Well, what do we make of that? I myself personally did not like to make up my mind before going down to London town to see Mr. Gerald Fleming. Mr. Gerald Fleming has just spent five years researching and writing a book called Hitler and the Final Solution. This book claims that Herr Hitler had little else in mind after he had seen a production of Wagner's "The Rienzi" than the destruction of European Jewry. And, knock me down with a Siege Howitzer, Robert Faurisson had read the book too.

Ask him these questions, he said.

And I did. And these are Mr. Gerald Fleming's replies.

Q. *Why is there not one autopsy report showing that the body of such and such a person is actually the body of someone who has been killed by poison gas?*

A. Because there were no bodies left for the Allies to perform autopsies on. The gassings stopped in late 1944.

Q. *If the Jews were to be exterminated, why were two German officers condemned to death in Budapest in 1942 for murdering a Jewess?*

A. That is a non-question. It could well be that if individuals committed a murder that was not within the secret liquidation process, they would have been court martialled.

Q. *If the Nazis were such fine planners, why has no one found a budget for this extermination programme?*

A. There is a budget for the administration of concentration camps. There is no budget specifically marked "For the Extermination of People." That would have been daft.

Q. *What about document PS 4025 or PS 4055? This is a collection of official papers. No. 4 was a note stating that Hitler intended to postpone the solution to the Jewish problem till the end of the war. I have a copy of it. It is dated March, 1942.*

A. Hitler is not referring to the extermination of the Jews. Hitler was referring to people of mixed marriages. Hitler insisted on keeping an eye on who should and should not be admitted to the German army, and therefore capable of claiming that he was a German. We have more documents saying that if these people submitted to sterilisation, the official could treat them more leniently.

Q. *Have you seen an order signed by Hitler ordering the extermination of the Jews?*
A. No.

Well, what do we make of that? I myself personally find Hitler and the Final Solution a shocker. It seems to be that Samidat Publishers of Buffalo have maybe overlooked the biggest Secret of all, but who can blame them? Ex-general Franz Halder told his historian daughter-in-law that Herr Hitler had told him: "You will never learn what is going on inside my head. As for those who boast of being privy to my thoughts — to them I lie all the time."

I will not go into all the evidence presented by Mr. Gerald Fleming. It would take too long and, besides, Mr. Fleming deserves all the royalties he can get. But he seems to make an awfully good case for saying that Hitler, for all his love of opera, was a very unpleasant twister with a terrific sense of his own importance.

This sort of puts me in a tricky position vis-a-vis Samidat publishers. Maybe I will tear up my cheque. Anyway, who needs a poster of a Homing Rocket? Perhaps I could settle for a poster of the Royal Family.

Reagan Goes Among The Ghosts
Telegraph
May 5, 1985

By Edward Steen

(Edward Steen trails President Reagan, who is visiting West Germany, through a postwar minefield of political sensitivities, involving the Nazi SS, concentration camps and Jewish protesters.)

The hero of VE-Day was the "Little Guy," reported an American radio correspondent in in May, 1945. "It's the little guy, the guy from two blocks down who smashed the might of Hitler's Wehrmacht, and he's right here directing the traffic."

But it takes large men to conquer a country as treacherous and ghostly as the past. Forty years on, President Reagan's fumbled State visit in West Germany has found him being led by his "friend," as both still insist he is, Chancellor Helmut Kohl, so far into unguessed-at minefields that it is more dangerous to retreat than to advance.

Kohl knows the phantoms quite well, and the various passwords like, "I myself was only 15 in 1945." He initiated this assault on the past by bringing forward the date of the 11th World Economic Summit (a police and politicos festival of little importance) to just before the anniversary of the end of the war. He held Reagan to an agreement to visit a German war cemetery, even after it was found to contain the graves of 49 soldiers of the Waffen SS. And then the fireworks began.

Considering he has tangled with the Germans in only two Hollywood movies, the American President is being as brave as John Wayne was in "True Grit."

To The Graves of Fallen SS

Today, fofllowing the much-adjusted programme, the friends are at the windswept empty site of the Belsen concentration camp where Anne Frank died. Then on to Bitburg and a cemetery where the 49 Waffen SS are buried along with 2,000 others and who were not spotted by the White House advance men.

This visit was to represent reconciliation, to honour the victory of democracy and nice guys (ones who accepted the Pershing missiles too). As the row broke, belated attempts were made to rope in some Jews, or at least German resisters. Berthold, a colonel in the West German army and the son of Count von Stauffenberg, who was executed after leading an attempt on Hitler's life, has reluctantly agreed to come.

But far from lying down and accepting defeat from Kohl and Reagan, the ghosts are everywhere, mocking and acting as gargoyles.

They leer at the cozy politicians with their "photo opportunities" and communiqués. The 49 graves are occupied mostly by dead teenagers; there is only one officer among them. But it is possible that Reagan's reconciliation today will take place over the graves of men who killed American POWs at Malmedy in 1944. "If we found one of them was buried here, what are we supposed to do with him then?" says the hard-pressed Mayor of Bitburg, Theo Hallet. His town of 12,000 German and 12,000 American troops and their families was "a model of German-American friendship — we do not need reconciliation. We achieved it 30 years ago." But he did not regret the rumpus. It could, he thought, lead to a catharsis.

But it is always a messy affair. Last week fresh white carnations — whose? — decorated the Waffen SS graves. A wreath in the Nazi colours had been placed nearby. In gold Gothic letters: "Born Germans, lived as fighters, died as heroes." (Actually not a few have Slavic names.)

A middle-aged Bitburger looked sourly on. "What do I think? What is someone supposed to think? *"Eine Schweinerei,"* he told me and pointed at the muddy track worn through the grass by sightseers and Press inspecting the graves that have figured in all the photos. The untidyness seemed to upset him most.

"They should leave us in peace after 40 years," said the landlord of the bar opposite Karl Marx's birthplace in Trier near Bitburg. The others tersely agreed that it would be an insult to Germany if Reagan did not go to Bitburg — a poll last weekend showed 72 per cent agreed with them. The visit could have a serious importance for Kohl's political career. Next Sunday's elections in North Rhine-Westphalia could be crucial to his future as leader of the Christian Democrats following a dismal failure in Saarland and not much to laugh about in Berlin.

The "they" so resented in Trier are forcigners poking around Germany's raw neurosis, above all the American Press. *Newsweek* blandly refers to "SS graves" and carried a photograph on its cover showing them decorated with West German flags.

Reagan's staff are not much more sensitive. Having failed to notice the Waffen SS problem, they threw in Belsen to "balance" things, then made matters worse still by having Reagan say no one was alive who had been involved in the Nazi period, and then that the German war dead were equally victims of Hitler's oppression.,

I am told on good authority that President Mitterrand was annoyed because the Americans did not consult him about Reagan's visit to the European Parliament in Strasbourg this week. The White House apparently did not know that Strasbourg was in France, imagining it to be "some kind of international city."

But it must be said that the whole Bitburg affair has been distorted by the fact that Reagan won power in the teeth of media opposition. Much put out by this, the Press and the networks seize any opportunity to ridicule him. However, the unpopularity of this visit in the United States is real enough, so is the large majority against it in Congress, and the 82 out of 100 in the Senate who tried to dissuade Reagan from going to Bitburg ("Well, they're all Jews, aren't they?" said

an old sourpuss at the cemetery), but Ronald Reagan will surely survive this imbroglio, absurdly being compared to the Iranian "hostage crisis."

Kohl, another popular "little guy," faces similar malice from his own Press.
He may look and sometimes sound like a provincial butcher, but he cannot be as
brutish as the powerful *Der Spiegel* magazine makes out: a man who tricked
Reagan into a politically opportune exercise to get his own back for being excluded from the celebration of the Normandy invasion last July. Didn't he
acknowledge, at Belsen a week ago, that Germany had a "historical responsibility
for the crimes of the Nazi tyranny" and that this was "reflected not least in our
never-ending shame"?

Simon Wiesenthal, the Nazi-hunter whom Reagan tried to include in the
ceremonies at the last moment, and Professor Elie Wiesel of Boston, another survivor of Auschwitz, have made clean and dignified protests.

Prof. Wiesel: "To suggest SS men were equal victims is an affront to history."
But there is an element of unseemly artificiality about the brouhaha, much of it
"got up by the Press." The deeds to Reagan's temporary home — where Queen
Elizabeth II also once stayed — at Gymnich Castle on the Rhine, turn out to
belong to a godson of Adolf Hitler, who then had to explain how his father lost enthusiasm for the Führer before 1945.

That said, there are certain skeletons in the German cupboard too. A
250-strong band of veterans from the Death's Head division of the Waffen SS
finish a three-day reunion at the Swabian ski resort of Nesselwang today, the day
of Reagan's Bitburg visit. Ex-soldiers of the Adolf Hitler Bodyguard and the 12th
SS Panzer "Hitler Youth" division meet at Nesselwang this weekend. One veteran
said: "If it had been George Wallace of Alabama, the Bitburg ceremony would have
happened years ago."

That does not necessarily make the old boys Nazis. Indeed, the Waffen SS,
whose veterans' association was taken off the list of banned organizations by Kohl
in 1983, is not to be compared with the SS pure and simple who guarded the concentration camps. Despite certain atrocities, they were combat troops rather than
full-time killers, and as the war became more desperate, many young men and
even foreigners were forced to join.

But a key part of the process of erasing the past is the half-lie, the having-it-
both-ways, which Adenauer's, now Kohl's, Christian Democratic Union Party
represents. It was the only means of uniting the good and not-so-good Germans
after the war, a process encouraged by the Americans' "little guys" who found they
could not run the country without using the old Nazis.

Its style has been to say one thing about "those dark times" and reminisce in
the *Gasthaus* about the grand old days when Germany was kicking the rest of the
world about. The cold war cemented this odd unity.

Coming To Terms With The Past

The ambiguity is clear enough in Kohl's new version of the "Auschwitz lie"
law which punishes anyone who denies there was slaughter of the Jews. But the

same law also forbids anyone to suggest the Germans did not suffer during the exodus from territory taken over by the Red Army.

There is a similar crassness about Kohl's parliamentary floor leader in the Bundestag, Alfred Dregger, who wrote to the U.S. Senate to point out that he and his brother had after all been fighting the Russians in the war. "A member of NATO even before it existed," mocked Willy Brandt, leader of the Social Democrat opposition.

It may be true that the full grotesquery of trying to tidy up Europe by exterminating Jews, Slavs, homosexuals, gypsies, cripples and anyone else who did not fit Hitler's ridiculous vision has never really sunk in here. Perhaps it is too terrible and too stupid for people to accept how obediently they or their fathers went along with all that.

The Holocaust Must Not Be Forgotten
The Times
May 5, 1985

By Rabbi Albert H. Friedlander

(As a child of 11, in 1939 Dr. Friedlander was arrested in Berlin, his home city. He escaped with his family to Cuba and later to the United States. He is now Dean of Leo Baeck College and rabbi of the Westminster Synagogue.)

The present climate of reconciliation and affirmation of political partnerships has tried to draw away from that aspect of the past.

Politicians and their advisers can and do forget the horrors of the death camps. President Reagan's intention to visit Bitburg tomorrow is a political blunder; his insistence upon the visit is an act of moral blindness. It causes hurt and anguish to all those touched by the evil of that time, to the Jewish and non-Jewish survivors who remember villages near Prague and Paris, ghettos in Poland, death camps in Germany and Austria. The SS were there. They burnt, gassed, shot and murdered the Jews, gypsies, Slavs, homosexuals, mentally ill — politically inconvenient opponents and victims of the Nazis.

Acknowledging the democracy of death, one may not blur the distinction between oppressor and victim, even if only one minute is spent in the military cemetery and an hour at a concentration camp memorial. Good intentions do lead to a special hell.

And yet, the world wants to forget. The anniversaries are not intended to conjure up the past, but to exorcise it. Europe is weary of the revenant shades who point to evils. Our society has applied new technology to the art of killing, and has dehumanized the victims by meaningless numbers and impersonal ways of meeting out death. "The Holocaust?" "Let us forgive and forget" is a central thought within our society, but addressed mainly to the Jews.

"Why not let go?" Jews are asked. "Must you be grim and unforgiving? Must we continue to mourn your six million when so manmy more have died since then? There have been more recent genocides, in Asia, in Africa, in Ethiopia, millions are dying of starvation. We have enough upon our conscience. Why not forgive and forget, like the rest of us?"

It is not easy to answer that question, particularly in a British environment where the average Briton remembers his own war against Hitler, the deprivations suffered, the relatives lost in the war.

The answer has to be given on several levels. Jews mourn their dead without requiring the outside world to share in their grief. Memorial candles are lit annually in Jewish homes to commemorate their loved ones. In a world where six million Jews were murdered, the community itself must remember the men, women and children who have no one to say these prayers for them. And so Jews remember and do not forget.

They remember the goodness in the midst of evil: the victims rather than the villains; the few who helped (there is an "Avenue of the Righteous Gentiles" in the Memorial Centre in Jerusalem) rather than the many who killed. But they cannot forget. Once the mind dwells on the Holocaust, can anyone really forget that event?

Can one be reconciled with the event by thinking of the victims as martyrs? It is an imposition of fading, insufficient structures of religion to ascribe martyrdom to the victims murdered in the death camps. Those we loved came to the edge of a wilderness. And it opened and drew them in. They were victims. We will revere them, we will remember them, we will mourn them. No Jewish or Christian theology of vicarious atonement can remove this grief from us; Jews will continue to mourn and remember.

Can we forgive? Who are we to usurp God's role? Some years ago, speaking to a German Kirchentag (church conference) in Nuremberg, I talked about the anguish of Auschwitz. A young girl rushed up to me after the lecture. "Rabbi," she said, "I wasn't there, but can you forgive me?" and we embraced and cried together.

Then an older man approached me. "Rabbi," he said, "I was a guard at a concentration camp. Can you forgive me?" I looked at him. "No," I said, "I cannot forgive. It is not the function of rabbis to give absolution, to be pardoners. In Judaism, there is a 10-day period of Penitence, between the New Year and the Day of Atonement, when we try to go to any person whom we have wronged, and ask for forgiveness. But you cannot go to the six million. They are dead, and I cannot speak for them. Nor can I speak for God. But you are here at a church conference. God's forgiving grace may touch you; but I am not a mediator, pardoner, or spokesman for God."

Can Jews practice conciliation in the contemporary world and thus align themselves with the contemporary climate? Again, difficulties confront us. A Hassidic story speaks of an isolated kingdom, where the grain harvest one year turns poisonous. Everyone who eats will become mad. Yet there is no other food available. Finally, the king turns to a trusted counsellor. "We must all eat, or we will die," he said. "But you, try to eat less. Preserve enough sanity to enable you to remind us, through the long dark period ahead, that we are mad. Tell us. Again and again. The time will come when we are sane again."

In an age of genocide and madness, Jews must continue to be the conscience which speaks to the world of Holocaust and death camps, of a guilt which touches everyone; all have eaten the poison. Apathy and ignorance killed many who could have survived. That is a harsh thing to accept, and gradations must be seen. But it is a religious truth that guilt must be acknowledged before it can be expiated. And then the work of reconciliation can begin. But one must know the world is damaged.

Bitburg — The Cost In Human Damage
The Observer
May 5, 1985

By Neal Ascherson

Take your seats for this week's meditation: the fortieth anniversary of the surrender of Nazi Germany. When I lived in Berlin, I had my own special seat for such May commemorations. It was a view undisturbed by parades or statesmen, seen from under a tree growing in the roofless palace which had once been the Museum of Prehistory.

It was a most peaceful place. The Berlin Wall blocked off its main entrance, and the Saxon voices of East German border guards occasionally broke the silence. There were no neighbours; the site of the Gestapo prison on Prinz-Albrecht-Strasse, next door, had become a dirty field. Only lovers and American intelligence patrols ever visited the great ruin. Underfoot, fragments of pottery from Schliemann's Troy crunched — the archaeology of a museum — and formed an accidental rock-garden for minor plants.

Tucked under a broken tile, I once found a heap of old newspapers. There was a copy of the upmarket weekly *Das Reich,* with a leader by Reichsminister Dr. Göbbels entitled 'War as the Measure of Human Worth.' And a tatter from a 1945 *Morgenpost,* referring to *'unser geniale Feldherr, Adolf Hitler'* — our genius of a warlord. . . .

The tree rustled its spring leaves where the cupola had once been. Germany did not merely lose that war, one tall tree ago, but lost it with a cataclysmic finality that has no precedent.

Today, as President Reagan gets through his bad moments at the Bitburg war cemetery, many Germans will be wondering whether 'reconciliation' and 'atonement' have turned out to be just more lost effort. 'They are going to squash Bitburg into 18 seconds,' blabbered a Presidential aide. Bigger mistakes have been made in even less time.

Afterwards, I suspect, it will be put around in Washington that the President really displayed courage — 'showed balls' — by going through with this and standing up to the Jewish lobby in the United States. But it is imagination, not courage, that he lacks.

There are, in fact, words which can be spoken in a cemetery which includes the graves of the Waffen-SS, and they are words about the elemental savagery latent in all nations and the temptation for all governments to harness it. But heads of government avoid this sort of talk at war memorials. I can think of only one statesman who would have known what to say at Bitburg — Willy Brandt.

The human damage — never mind the political damage — from this uproar is double. Enough has been written about the desolation and anger of those whose kin suffered under the SS, the Jews above all. But a deep and unkind hurt is done to German men and women, now old, whose young men lie in the war cemeteries and who now see them all slandered as murdering Nazis by foreign television teams scuttling among the graves. And the parents of the Waffen-SS dead: they did not deserve this. If Princess Michael did not recruit her father into Himmler's Black Order, no more did they pin the death's-head badges on their sons.

Lack of imagination again. In America, and in this country too, there is an enormous defect of imagination about the Third Reich and about its relevance to modern Germany. It's a defect with some honourable, decent roots in societies which have never known occupation, dictatorship or modern revolution. The French, in contrast, did not feel that their entire understanding of the human race was collapsing when they entered Nazi concentration camps in 1945. Their historical experience, like that of Russians, Poles, even Italians, to some extent protected them. But the Americans and the British, for all the wartime propaganda about Nazi atrocities, went morally naked into Buchenwald and Belsen.

There is a distinct generation of young British officers for whom the shock of witnessing Belsen was a crippling event. Their world simply had not allowed for this. Some became bitterly anti-German. Some (and I have known a few) became mentally unstable. In a new book about the German collapse (*In the Ruins of the Reich,* Allen & Unwin) Douglas Botting quotes a British captain who entered the place shortly after its liberation. 'I was very near a nervous breakdown. I was paralyzed by the whole thing. To me it was completely beyond tears — unless you feel you can cry when humanity dies. To my way of thinking it was humanity itself which had died this inglorious death of degradation and filth. . . .'

Those who have assumed the world was round and find that it is square can either work to make sense of their discovery or—feeling it too great a threat—explode it into fantasy. Our whole gigantic Nazi fiction industry (and I have even seen a comic about Treblinka) is really a violent effort of collective repression.

The British captain told Mr. Botting that 'I'm sure it could even have happened here, in England.' And this, precisely, is the perception which is being repressed. Nobody, seeing the garish garbage that is the average war movie, could imagine such things taking place in Cambridge, Eng., or Cambridge, Mass. When they did take place at My Lai, Vietnam, most Americans were at first incredulous.

Repression, all the same, has its function in the lands of the Protestant ethic. By inflating the Nazi past into unrecognisable nonsense, the Americans especially have managed to preserve their optimism and construct a close working relationship with West Germany which will survive, not entirely unspattered, the Bitburg stupidity.

To ask the dismayed Germans to understand the uses of 'repressive fiction' would be to over-tax them. Their defect of imagination is elsewhere. All nations are self-admiration societies, and cannot be expected to see themselves as collectively criminal—let alone for 40 years. The East Germans and Austrians have adopted easy psychological escapes: the Nazi horrors happened in another country, in capitalist Germany or in Austria forcibly annexed to the Reich...not here.

The West Germans, whose society has actually changed far more profoundly than theirs, can't play these convenient games. Instead, their cartoon self-image is the 'German Michel,' a trembling shrimp of humanity who wears a nightcap and feels outwitted by everyone. Michel expects foreigners to find him ugly and stupid. But the idea that somebody might fear him or see him as a threat is utterly beyond his grasp.

In the end, Bitburg does not matter that much. Reconciliation is a fact, achieved mostly by sheer forgetfulness but also—to a small and precious degree—by combining memory and imagination.

Herbert von Sulzbach is 91. He has given most of his life to helping the British and the Germans towards friendship, but in 1914 he was an artillery lieutenant in the Kaiser's army. A few months ago, the five survivors of the Ipswich branch of the Old Contemptibles—those who fought in 1914—held what they knew must be their last parade. They decided to ask a German, Herbert von Sulzbach, as their final guest of honour, and they found that he had been in action against their own battalion just 70 years before.

What do we celebrate on Wednesday, VE Day? Hitler's defeat, and Europe's liberation, and things like Ipswich. But if we are really trying to remember honestly, this day is about something more basic and marvellous than any of those, about the simple fact which the Russian and American soldiers yelled out as they spun drunkenly to balalaika music at Torgau on the Elbe. '*Voyna kaput!* — The goddam war is over!'

Belsen and Bitburg: Sorrow and Slapstick
The Times
May 6, 1985

By Frank Johnson

President Reagan stood at last in the cemetery at Bitburg yesterday. "Never again," he said later, in his speech at the U.S. military base nearby, referring to Nazism. "Never again," he had said earlier, in his speech at the site of the former concentration camp at Belsen.

He could be forgiven for investing the phrase with more than one meaning. Never again must a combination of an ignoramus of a White House public relations expert, a jovial, but wily German politician, and his own endlessly genial nature land him among the remains of 49 SS men — at least, not with him laying a wreath.

The proceedings lasted about seven minutes. They attained a haunting amalgam of the macabre and the slapstick. He and Chancellor Kohl looked understandably nervous as they got out of the disturbingly hearse-like American presidential vehicle that had brought them to the place.

As they entered the cemetery, there was much looking for the right path, and a certain amount of bumping into one another, as each one gestured to the other to go first — their wives and protectors stringing out behind them, and the entire scene being played out in silence.

They all made their way eventually up a gravel path. Flowers, put there by the town's people, stretched across a lawn. Some of the SS graves were said to have had fresh flowers too, put there by neo-Nazis, American television companies, the KGB, or any number of suspects. Mr. Reagan's eyes narrowed a little as he looked around him — perhaps keeping an eye out, as he must have done in at least one film or other, for the SS.

Here in Bonn we joined all Germany before the television screen. Only in that way does political ceremonial these days, in this as in any country, have reality. For Bitburg itself, visited the night before, was an implausible setting for an event which has aroused such fascination. It was reached through beautiful forests, the newcomer to this country being struck by how varied were the shades of green. Timbered villages passed by.

But Bitburg was not part of this idyll. It was a town of square, modern buildings. A hairdresser's called Figaro. One of those slightly clinical pedestrian precincts. At least one "sex shop." A Mexican take-away reminded us of the presence of the American forces nearby.

All over the town there were signs depicting a wrinkled, genial, elderly man. But, though he would have been about Mr. Reagan's age, he had been there long before Mr. Reagan's visit, and would long outlast it. For this was the advertisement for Bitburger Pils, upon whose reputation throughout drinking Germany

Bitburg's reputation had rested before all this.

Up by the cemetery, firemen, supervised by German bomb disposal experts, poked rods into the drains. Television technicians went about their incomprehensible work in the twilight. It rained steadily. Down in the town, the makers of Bitburger Pils were absent from the brewery, though various wastes from it drifted towards the forests. The drinkers of Bitburger Pils, however, jollied one another in the pubs, without a mention, until asked by the visiting foreigner, of the immortality conferred on their town, and on the presidential advance men who discovered it.

Their opinion, when solicited, was that the visit was a good thing, though not the circumstances surrounding it.

The following morning these jovial drinkers presumably looked on with the rest of the nation as Mr. Reagan, at Belsen, discharged that part of his day's duties about whose propriety we could all agree. Mr. Reagan arrived and was seen immediately to go into the rather sterile exhibition permanently at the site.

While we waited for him to come out, German television, to its credit showed some of that newsreel that transfixed the world when it was taken at the camp's liberation in 1945. New film from British archives showed some of the German guards, men and women, forced to stand before the mass graves while a wonderfully eloquent British officer, in Home Counties German, told them that responsibility lay "with you who allowed your Führer to carry out these murders."

Mr. Reagan emerged, moved through the easier of the day's ceremonies and speeches, and left for Bitburg. Two hours later he had to face the grimly absurd in the cemetery to which his own amiable folly had brought him. He did not spend much time manhandling the wreath, preferring to touch it quickly as it was put in place by two German soldiers. A Bundeswehr trumpeter sounded "I had a comrade," the German equivalent of the Last Post. The SS graves were a few feet to the right.

Not that the SS aspect has been understood abroad. The SS was indeed murderous as an institution. But many regular German soldiers were murderous, too, and many individual SS men were not.

It must have been one of the few wreath-layings of Mr. Reagan's life at which he had not made a speech. For oratory, he escaped to the familiarity of the U.S. base, and its Stars and Stripes and baseball results.

An especially admired speech-writer had been sent in to Mr. Reagan's rescue, or so it was said. This man of words had gone to work determinedly and abominably on Mr. Reagan's behalf. Some of us have a high tolerance of American presidential maunderings. But it did not seem right here — the ruthlessly sentimental patter better heard in Bitburg, Indiana, if there is one.

"I'm thinking of one special story," Mr. Reagan ominously confided, at about paragraph nine, "that of the mother and her young son living alone in a modest cottage in the middle of the woods. One night, as the Battle of the Bulge exploded not far away, three young American soldiers arrived at their door — standing in the snow, lost behind enemy lines . . ."

The story was very long and of bravura implausibility. Unlike most German stories about women living alone in the woods, she was not a witch. Instead she was someone who, when four German soldiers later reached her cottage, made them lay down their arms, and fraternise with the Americans.

"Next morning they all shook hands, and went their separate ways," said Mr. Reagan. "That was Christmas Day 40 years ago," was how ended this fusion of Hollywood and Humperdinck.

Afterwards, on the television, Israeli demonstrators ringed by German policemen, danced a hora in a Bitburg street. A young German with a banner spoke passionately against the wreath-laying. An SS veteran next to him said he sympathized "in my heart" with these protests but he had fought on the Russian front and never seen a concentration camp. This fighting was the reason why the Russians were not in Bitburg now.

Suddenly it was over. On the screen there was sport. Mr. Reagan's departure into Air Force One was the proof that it would never happen again.

The Price Kohl Pays For Bitburg
The Financial Times
May 6, 1985

By Rupert Cornwell

Those who have talked at length with Helmut Kohl in recent days bear witness to how much he has suffered over the decision. His stolidly reassuring face bears visible trace of the agonizing, too. The lines are more visible, the smiles less frequent. Equally though, every visitor has been struck by his unyielding inner conviction, that in the end he will be shown to be right.

The decision is, of course, Bitburg, and the chancellor's conviction is anything but universally shared. For who can tell now how the ceremony with President Reagan at the small German military cemetery will turn out — noble or excruciating, dignified or grotesque, perhaps a bit of each?

What is certain, on the other hand, is that his insistence on going ahead with it in the teeth of an outcry stretching from Israel to the U.S. has cast the West German leader in a very new light to many of his countrymen.

Ever since he took office in October 1982, it has been fashionable to mock Kohl as the "soft" chancellor, of few ideas other than a handful of provincial certainties, fundamentally indecisive and over-amenable, above all to the Americans. This same man's refusal to be budged has now cast a cloud over Bonn's relations with Washington, and drawn a good friend, and leader of West Germany's most important ally, into arguably the most embarrassing incident of Mr. Reagan's presidency.

The surprise has been considerable: but should it have been? Rightly or wrongly, Bitburg and its SS graves have now escalated into a giant test of the world's readiness to adjust to Germany's past.

On the face of it, either of the two previous Social Democrat chancellors, the intense idealistic Willy Brandt, or the cool, commanding Helmut Schmidt, might with their larger international prestige have seemed more suitable German ambassadors on such an occasion.

If West German self-respect demands that the nettle does now have to be grasped, then perhaps Kohl is the right man. "The most western of any Federal chancellor," it has been observed, and justifiably. He comes from Rhineland Palatinate, close to Luxembourg and France. His critics would say his commitment to European unity and especially to friendship with France is simplistic; but it is unquestionable.

By age, too, he is peculiarly qualified. Kohl, as he tirelessly repeats, is the first "postwar chancellor"; only 15 at the war's end and disinclined to be branded personally by crimes he was too young to have been aware of. If this, or to nurture the hope that one day Germany may be reunited, amounts to a new German "nationalism," then so be it, he would say. The country has achieved enough to be proud of since 1945. Anyone who claims that Helmut Kohl wants Nazi murderers forgiven should merely study his speech at Bergen-Belsen a fortnight ago.

The paradox remains that President Reagan's present discomfort has been brought about by the most instinctively pro-American of chancellors. Among his first recollections of "America" were U.S. soldiers in 1946 providing food for a 16-year-old schoolboy.

He has talked lately of his "love affair" with the U.S., his faith in the Western Alliance, his steadfastness in piloting NATO missile deployment in the face of bitter domestic opposition in 1983. Much of the Reagan philosophy is shared by the chancellor, above all where it touches the individual and free enterprise. All of this, Kohl believes, entitles him now to demand the Bitburg gesture of the president.

Should he have done so in the first place? Here we return to the other Kohl, of his second year in power in 1984, of muddle, misjudgment and pervasive incompetence. That at any rate was how it seemed to be slithered from the Lambsdorff affair to the Kiessling affair, ill-advised and insensitive to mood, in a sense. Bitburg has been more of the same. If things do go badly awry tomorrow, then the Chancellor's Christian Democrat party may pay a heavy price in the key North Rhine Westphalia state election on Sunday week.

Two political assets have long sustained Kohl, on the not infrequent occasions when the media have bayed for his head. One is the realisation that most mishaps, if doggedly ignored, will be forgotten of their own accord. The Kohl skin in that respect is elephantine. The other is an instinctive feel for the country's real mood, if not for that of the foetid greenhouse which is Bonn.

Helmut Kohl, it has been remarked, should never have risen higher than a small town mayor; but the small town mayor who can share constituents' problems over a glass or two of wine is arguably more in touch than the smooth-tongued statesman. The Chancellor has grown no more eloquent over the years, and his speeches still ramble interminably, but he does say what people think.

Bitburg once more captures the contrast. Polls say that 72 per cent of West Germans agree that he and President Reagan should go to Bitburg, and their support has hardened as controversy has thickened. That of course does not excuse the mishandling, still less now that the stakes are so high.

But the Chancellor typically is hunkering down. "When a hurricane suddenly threatens to destroy the landscape, I am not willing to accept that what I have been doing for decades is wrong. What I have to do is contain the storm and protect myself."

Helmut Kohl is practised in the skill—and now more than ever he needs to be.

"Nothing But War Could Have Beaten The Nazis," Preaches The Archbishop of Canterbury
The Daily Telegraph
May 9, 1985

The Archbishop of Canterbury, preaching at yesterday's V E-Day 40th anniversary service in Westminster Abbey, declared that "no other method than war" could have brought down the Nazi regime.

Dr. Robert Runcie, himself the holder of a wartime Military Cross, said he "profoundly disagreed" with those who questioned whether the war had been necessary or had achieved anything.

"The victory which closed down Belsen, Buchenwald and Auschwitz is in itself sufficient cause for thanksgiving," he told the huge congregation which included the Queen, the Prime Minister, representatives of wartime allies and other nations and people from many walks of life.

It had also given a 40-year breathing space in Europe, which had not been wasted. There had been genuine reconciliation. Old enemies had become friends in active reconciliation.

"May our celebration of this achievement provide the energy needed to work for the greater world-wide reconciliation on which lasting peace depends," he said.

"Most of us over 60 can remember where we were, that late summer Sunday in 1939, when we heard that the United Kingdom was at war with Germany.

"If we search our memories a little further we can remember something else: the mood of the time. There was a certain relief that the period of waiting was over. But there was very little jubilation.

"We already knew too much about war for that. Memories of the previous war were too fresh.

"After the Somme and Passchendaele we were not victims of any great illusion. We knew that war was ugly, but it was the lesser of two evils.

"One of the great nations of Europe was in the grip of a régime that set at nothing the liberty, the dignity, the life of all those who stood in the way of its notions of racial superiority and the expansion of its territory.

"Diplomacy had failed. By the summer of 1939 the choice was clear. Germany's European neighbours either had to submit to Nazism or resist it by force.

Heavy Cost

"Today we thank God that with the help of our allies that resistance culminated in a victory in which the Nazi régime perished.

"No historical inquiry has suggested that Nazism was less wicked than we thought it in 1939, or that any other method than war could have brought it down.

"The cost was heavy in a war which engulfed Europe, and extended far beyond it.

"Many of us will have personal memories of friends and relatives who died or who were maimed. The outstanding courage of those who were disabled is a constant reminder of the cost of our victory.

"It was a war which claimed victims among combatants and civilians alike — the very old and the very young.

"It is right that we should remember the pity of war. Today, in this place, it is fitting that we should remember the sorrows of the United Kingdom in particular — the lives lost or laid waste, the treasures obliterated.

"But it is also right to remember the good that can be set against the grief; part of the Christian answer to the eternal riddle of evil is that great afflictions call forth great virtues, public and private.

"Today we remember those virtues gratefully and humbly before God. We remember the steadfastness and unity of the nations that came together in the allied cause. So many of them we rejoice to see represented here today.

"We remember the qualities of our own sailors and soldiers and airmen: the loyalty they showed to their units and to their friends; their endurance of hardship and danger.

Proper Pride

"There is a proper pride which says: 'These people belong to us, and we to them, and we are glad of it, because they show what humanity can achieve.'

"Sacrifices there were on our home front, and we also remember the spirit that pervaded that. It was a sense of common cause transcending differences of status or interest.

"We recognized how precious our freedoms were and learned how much they cost. It was a summons to everyone to put a brave face on private pain, so that the face of others should not be clouded.

"Some people question now whether the war was really necessary, and whether anything was achieved by the victory. I respect their freedom to make such a judgment, but I profoundly disagree with them.

"It was not a panacea for every ill. But the victory which closed down Belsen, Buchenwald and Auschwitz is in itself sufficient cause for thanksgiving.

"But the war has also given us a 40-year breathing space in Europe, and the time has not been wasted.

"The peace settlement after World War I nourished deep resentments and a desire for revenge. We can all rejoice at the contrast which is provided by evidence of genuine reconciliation after World War II. Old enemies have become friends in active co-operation.

"The city of Coventry is a place where the reality of this reconciliation can be powerfully experienced. The charred ruins of the old Cathedral, destroyed by bombing in 1940, stand side by side with the new Cathedral.

Shared Emotion

"What often moves visitors most is the cross in the ruins, and the simple words: 'Father forgive.' It is a message which frequently brings British and German ex-servicemen together in shared emotion.

"Such experiences can dent the lazy cynicism about human beings and the capacities of the human spirit, which undermines our work for a wider peace.

"Of course, the victory of 40 years ago did not destroy all the world's evils. Every generation has its own problems to solve, and fresh forms of evil to resist.

"There is no retirement from the service of God, or from the struggle to establish His reign of love and justice upon earth.

"The organized life of groups and nations continues to be a struggle to dominate or to avoid domination. The dangers of this, at a time when our capacity for destruction is so immeasurably greater than it was in the Second World War, are obvious.

"Much has already been achieved in the reconciliation of ancient enemies. May our celebration of this achievement provide the energy needed to work for the greater world-wide reconciliation on which lasting peace depends.

"This service is a gift of thanksgiving offered to God, and we offer it in the Spirit of Jesus Christ who said: 'First be reconciled to your brother, and then come and offer your gift.'"

(Dr. Runcie, the Archbishop of Canterbury, is the spiritual leader of the world-wide Anglican Church, the official church in Great Britain.)

Not Sorry
The Jewish Chronicle
May 10, 1985

Jews had an unavoidable historical obligation to protest against President Reagan's visit to Bitburg cemetery, containing the graves of 49 SS men, and we have cause for pride in the young Jews from Europe who assembled there to do so. As Hugh Trevor Roper has stated so succinctly: "After the invasion of Poland, it was Heydrich's SS Einsatzkommandos which followed the German armies in order to exterminate, systematically, the Polish aristocracy, intelligentsia, Jews and 'similar trash.'. . . When Hitler ordered the invasion of the Soviet Union, he reckoned that the Wehrmacht might be squeamish. He therefore ordered it to stand aside and leave a free hand to the SS, which would perform its 'special tasks' of 'liquidating' all political commissars in areas otherwise under military control. And of course it was the SS which was to carry out, through 'mobile killing squads,' gas vans and extermination camps, the 'Final Solution,' the destruction of the European Jews. The horrible barbarities of Hitler's war were all the work of the SS. . . ."

However difficult for the non-Jewish world to grasp, forgiveness in all and every circumstance is not a Jewish virtue and it was inconceivable that there could be Jewish complicity in an act of reconciliation with Germany over the graves of SS men. Jews have achieved reconciliation with the Federal Republic at every level except that of forgiveness for the historic past — and this we can never offer, for six million reasons. Hostile commentators have depicted Jewish protests as a sort of "Jews against the world" phenomenon, which will only serve to encourage anti-Semitism. Others have welcomed President Reagan's decision to go ahead with the Bitburg visit as showing that he is not the "prisoner of the Jewish lobby" and can therefore be tougher with Israel. But, as we know, anti-Semites will always find sticks with which to beat Jews and anti-Zionists will never accept, as far as Jews and Israel are concerned, that the United States conducts its external affairs to suit its own national interests. The Bitburg protests were right. We do not have to say "Sorry" to anyone.

Why Don't The Jews Understand?
The Spectator
May 11, 1985

By Peregrine Worsthorne

As a committed and consistent pro-Semite — even to the point of defending Israel's incursions into Lebanon — I have to admit that the Jews come out of the Bitburg business very badly. Naturally everybody decent understands the depth of feelings about the Holocaust. But to use every devious trick of moral blackmail to try to wreck President Reagan's wholly laudable attempt, 40 years after the war, to do justice to Germany's miraculous regeneration seems to me quite inexcusable. Cannot the Jews realise the harm that would have been done to the free world by continuing to treat the Germans as permanent pariahs? Are they unable to appreciate the absolute priority that ought to be given to integrating Western Germany into Western Europe? For almost half a century in the Middle East, Western feelings of guilt have prodded us — quite rightly in my view — into supporting Israel, very often disastrously against Britain's own best interests. But for the Jews to try to use this same kind of moral blackmail to compel the West to allow its foreign policy to be equally distorted by guilt in regard to the very heartland of Western Europe, that really is over the odds: The Arabs have been complaining for years that the Jews are blind to any other good cause except their own. After Bitburg many of us pro-Semites will be slightly less eager to deny this charge than we were before.

With Friends Like Perry...
The Jewish Chronicle
July 5, 1985

By Philip Kleinman

Bitburg, the German war cemetery visited by President Reagan, was a subject I ignored at the height of the media furor about it, having more genuinely important matters to write about. If I turn to it now the reason is that the subject has continued to crop up.

My position, unlike that of my well-loved neighbour, Chaim Bermant, is that the event we have just been celebrating was the 40th anniversary not of the liberation of Germany from the Nazis but of the defeat of a nation which, with pitifully few noble exceptions, did its damnedest to murder and enslave everyone else. The whole German military machine, not just the SS, was a criminal organization. To pay tribute to its fallen members is inappropriate, despite the desirability of friendship with today's different Germany. I am happy that the thick-skinned Helmut Kohl, who dreamed up the visit for his own political ends, suffered a resounding defeat in this week's North Rhine-Westphalia elections.

Peregrine Worsthorne, however, writing in the last edition of the *Spectator,* said it was not the Germans but the Jews who "come out of the Bitburg business very badly." Despite calling himself a "pro-Semite" he accused "the Jews" of using moral blackmail to wreck Reagan's gesture and make the Germans "permanent pariahs."

Worsthorne, a "pro-Semite" whose friendship we might be better off without, was echoing the sentiments of David Watt in a more diplomatically worded article published a week earlier in *The Times.* Watt, however, however, focused on the American Jewish lobby rather than "the Jews" in general.

Now, many Fleet Street newspapers opposed the Bitburg visit. "Grave mistake," said the *Daily Mirror.* "Call it off," declared the *Daily Mail.* "Misjudgment," was the *Financial Times* verdict. "The President was wrong" editorialised the *Daily Telegraph,* though it changed its mind. *The News of the World* attacked the visit. *The Guardian* havered but did not think it a very good idea. Were these leaders all written by "the Jews"?

Bitburg was mentioned again in a "Heart of the Matter" programme on BBC television on Sunday, presented by David Jessel. His subject was anti-Semitism, and he asked on behalf of the gentile world (ignoring his own part-Jewish ancestry) whether "those of us who feel no complicity in the sin of genocide" have to have the Holocaust constantly brandished before "our guiltless eyes."

It was not a bad little documentary, but I thought that its 35 minutes could have been used to far better effect if less time had been spent on waffly interviews with a handful of Anglo-Jews and more time on one or two of the things they talked about. For example the writer Frederic Raphael, in by far the most powerful contribution, pointed out that Britain's record regarding the Holocaust was "by no means an honourable one" and that, as a matter of deliberate Foreign Office policy, Jews were prevented from escaping from Nazi Europe. Greville Janner alluded to anti-Semitic outbursts from fellow Labour MPs.

Those are two subjects really worth covering.

Chapter 23

France

White House Planners' Narrow Vision
Special Contribution

By Serge Klarsfeld

Bitburg appeared to us in France as a very unfortunate affair, above all, because it was obvious that Mr. Reagan did not plan such a visit, 40 years after the defeat of Nazism, in order to render homage to the SS. We believe that at the start of the preparations for the trip it was the intention of the American president to visit a camp of the victims of Nazism and that the name of Dachau had been mentioned in this context.

This project appears to have encountered a certain resistance on the part of Chancellor Kohl, because he wished, first, to avoid the possibility that Reagan's visit would have a symbolic connection to the criminal past of Germany, and secondly, because Bavaria, where Dachau is located, is the exclusive domain of his arch-political rival, Franz Josef Strauss. Kohl wished to avoid the chance that the main event of the visit might offer Strauss an opportunity to appear exclusively with Reagan. The itinerary was therefore replaced through the initiative of Kohl, by way of suggesting a visit to a military cemetery.

This, in our opinion, had already excluded the victims of Hitler. It should be noted that Germany is the most loyal and most deserving ally of the United States in continental Europe. Considering also the immense burden of the Holocaust, it would have been equitable to foresee a visit to a concentration camp followed by a visit to a military cemetery. Nobody would have been shocked at the necessity to

observe a certain distinction between the victims of Hitler: the distinction between a Jewish child gassed or made the object of medical experiments before
being hanged — as happened in the case of several dozen Jewish children in the
camp of Neuengamme near Hamburg — and a German soldier of 20 years, who
had never voted for Hitler and who was killed at the front. The first victim of
Nazism was, and still remains, the Jewish child. Even the military cemetery, by
itself, without the camp, represented an affront to us. But knowing that German
pressure had grounded the first American initiative, and that the idea of the
cemetery emanated from the Germans who pressured the U.S., did not represent
material for a scandal, but simply an inclination on the part of the Americans to
avoid causing trouble and pain to the chancellor by letting him formulate a program which should have been managed by Washington, not by Bonn.

This revelation of the presence of SS graves at the cemetery selected in Bitburg, however, was upsetting to our view. Again, we understood that the entourage of the president did not see the necessity for extreme prudence and tact in
order to prevent the exposure of the president to a possibly embarrassing situation. Undoubtedly, the personnel chosen by the White House for the preparation
of this important visit did not have the broad vision which was historically and intellectually required; nor did they have the sensibility to realize the meaning of a
trip which would express the feelings of a majority of Americans and of the citizens of the Western world, with respect to what they mostly resent and consider
regarding Germany: namely the horror of the Nazi crimes, an admiration for the
material rebuilding of Germany, the satisfaction of finally seeing a German state
become a great democracy, and a questioning of the future of a Germany divided
between two states, each one belonging to the great ideological blocs which divide
the world between them.

It was up to the White House to include in the Reagan team one or more
qualified academicians to think about all the problems implied by that visit to
Germany, and about what was required to make it a success: which means an
event which would create in the Western world a reflection of the horrors of the
Nazi totalitarian and racist regime, as well as of the benefits of democracy which
have positively transformed Germany, thanks in the main to the model provided
by American democracy.

Reagan's assistants did not ask Kohl those questions which they should have:
above all, are there SS men buried at Bitburg? A perfunctory visit to the snow-
covered cemetery was not enough. Yet the question had never been asked because
it was never formulated in the heads of the American emissaries. The moment it
became known that SS men were buried at Bitburg, and the entire world heard it,
Reagan's visit to Bitburg acquired an essentially symbolic character, even when,
in the fact of almost unanimous reproach, the face-saving visit to Bergen-Belsen
was introduced.

The visit to Bitburg acquired the significance of a pardon, not only directed
toward the German soldiers who died in combat for the fatherland — this by itself
represented, in our eyes, an understandable act insofar as it was directed toward

the young victims of the madness of men, and in particular, the German leaders of that time — but then assumed the significance of a pardon of members of an institution like the SS, which formed the military avant-garde of the Nazi regime in charge of the "final solution" of the Jewish question.

Even if it only concerned members of combat units of the so-called "general" SS, they were nevertheless part of an organization which had been identified with the massacre of the Jews. If one realistically wanted to express from both sides — within the framework of the Atlantic Alliance as well as within the bilateral relationship between Germany and the United States — the confidence of the Americans in the virtues of the German army, it would have been necessary or advisable to relate to the example given by General DeGaulle in 1963. When he wanted to seal the reconciliation between France and the Federal Republic, he did not do so by speaking at the tombs of German soldiers, but to the living German officers assembled to hear him talk of the German army.

The French president addressed the responsible leaders of a transformed army which had outlawed Prussianism and proclaimed the dignity of the individual.

Thus, a chain of errors and negligence from the American side was combined with pressure from the Germans, exercised by a chancellor who is the first belonging to the postwar generation. He affirms, more in his personal position than in the speeches he delivers — which are frequently excellent, but prepared by his staff — a lack of guilt regarding a past which he judges to be far away.

However, nobody demands from the Germans — in particular from the young ones — an obligation to have guilt complexes, but rather, only a demonstration of a sense of responsibility. Hitlerism is not simply an accident of German history. In order to heal the wounds inflicted by Nazism, it is necessary for the Germans to undertake difficult tasks which would clearly be in contrast to the acts committed by Hitler and his accomplices: for instance, calling the Nazi criminals to justice, explaining Nazism to the young people so that they can forever know its causes and thereby be able to condemn these acts and defend liberty in the world, engaging themselves with generosity in the fight against the suffering of people of the entire world, and standing with the Jewish state in defiance of the interests represented by the Arab oil monopoly and markets.

As it is, in a kind of turn-around and by a political blunder, the initial suggestion of Reagan to visit Dachau was transformed into a show of paying homage to the SS in Bitburg. In order to counteract the inevitable devastating effects of the visit to Bitburg, there remained only one issue to be raised: a protest movement, sufficiently energetic and strong and clear enough to reverberate through the entire world. It had to express the resolve of international public opinion to reject an honor of this kind, its seriousness and dignity verged on forgetting and pardoning the past.

We, in France, were saddened to find ourselves in this situation because many among us really sympathize personally and politically with Ronald Reagan, a man of character who has re-established the prestige of his country and reinforced the security of the free world. Regrettably, though, from the moment he endorsed the errors of his staff and didn't dare to oppose the German chancellor, we had no choice left.

Beate, my wife, and myself decided to join a protest of a group of militants of our Association of Sons and Daughters of Deported Jews in France at Bergen-Belsen several hours before the Bitburg ceremony. When Reagan arrived we planned to undertake a final, and as we knew, useless, effort of dissuasion in order to make the international media witness our demonstration. Many others went to Bitburg directly: we preferred to go to Bergen-Belsen which is much further away from Paris than Bitburg. At this camp, Jews suffered and were murdered. It is, therefore, closer to our hearts than a German military cemetery. Above all, at Bitburg, the enemies of America and Israel — the communists and leftists — planned to rally in order to protest against "imperialism and Zionism" and against the crimes of the Nazis.

Our motor car succeeded, during the night of the 4th to the 5th of May, to slip into the landing area of the presidential helicopter. We did not agree to leave the restricted area, in spite of the demands of the German police. They were forced, several moments before the arrival of the President, to attack the lines of us deportees and children of the deported in order to remove us by force. This violent police action against the militants, who wore the yellow star, was filmed by the regional television networks and transmitted to the entire world as were the slogans on our banners, like "Bitburg: the best argument for Soviet propaganda"; "Mr. President, your place is not in Bitburg"; "Don't break bread with the SS dead."

We believe that the efforts of all those who protested, each in his own way, whether Elie Wiesel at the White House or the militant Jews beaten by the German police, will have effectively demonstrated that the action of the president was not the expression of a unanimous decision. It was a monumental blunder and was contrary to the public opinon of the Western world.

Reagan's beautiful speech at Bergen-Belsen was certainly not prepared by one of his regular speech writers. The ceremony at Bitburg was performed with speed, restraint of action, and spectacular speeches which clearly went very far in demonstrating the bitterness of Reagan. It showed the resentment of the president with reference to Chancellor Kohl's neglect, and for having missed the opportunity of a visit of historic significance which left instead only the legacy of blunder and protest which accompanied it.

I must add that a similar error could not have happened if Israel had acted as one had the right to expect from the Jewish state. In fact, in the Fall of 1983, Chancellor Kohl had already expressed his wish to see the Waffen SS rehabilitated as regular combatants. His declaration had already aroused certain emotions in Israel. But in the beginning of 1984, when Kohl visited Israel officially, the red carpet was extended for him without any request or condition that he withdraw his statement.

At the entrance of Yad Vashem, where Kohl went to meditate, I personally saw Israelis beaten by Israeli policemen when they attempted to protest as Kohl's car passed. A truly depressing spectacle. If Kohl had received a refutation by Israel, the German chancellor would not have brought up the question with Reagan. If Kohl had refused, and Israel postponed or cancelled the visit, President Reagan would have been much more cautious in the preparation of his own trip, having been made aware of the delicate character of the problem.

In conclusion, I believe that the negative effects of Bitburg have been neutralized effectively by the protest actions of the international public opinion and fortunately, even by the Germans themselves — which is most reassuring.

(Translated from the French by George Asher.)

(Serge Klarsfeld is President of the Federation des Fils et Filles des Deportes Juifs [Sons and Daughters of the Jewish Deportees]. He also is a member of the Executive of CRIF [Council of Jewish Institutions in France].)

This Is Not An Isolated Incident
Special Contribution

By Henri Bulawko

For the serious historian it would be unthinkable to situate the beginnings of National Socialism and of the career of the Führer, Adolph Hitler, at 1933 — the year of his accession to the chancellorship of the Reich.

In order to understand this victory and the spread of anti-democratic and anti-Semitic theories it is necessary to go much further back to the age of Bismark, who in his time fought socialism as much as the parliamentary current. It is also necessary to underscore the "Prussian nationalism" having turned revanchist after the defeat of 1916 and to consider the serious economic crisis which shook the weak foundations of the young Weimar Republic, not to forget the West's fear of the October Revolution (Pope Pius XII justified the Roman Catholic Church's complacency vis-a-vis Hitler's Germany by his fear of Bolshevik expansionism).

As to anti-Semitism, which had found its expression in the Dreyfus affair in France and the Beylis affair in Russia, it had become a current political weapon in the period between the two wars. Hitler used it until it reached its climax in the "Final Solution" of the Jewish question.

To address the affair of the visit of President Reagan to the cemetery in Bitburg, while ignoring everything that preceded it, would mean reducing it to an ordinary soon-to-be-forgotten incident. In fact, it is the result of a deliberate policy conducted by the leaders of West Germany since the creation of the Federal Republic (with the exception of Willi Brandt who fought the Nazis unremittingly). To be sure, it was Chancellor Adenauer who acknowledged the crimes of the Nazis* and who, in 1952, signed the treaties of Luxembourg concerning the German reparations with Dr. Nachum Goldman for the Jews in the Diaspora and with David Ben Gurion for the state of Israel. These treaties allowed the state of Israel and individual victims of Nazism to receive reparations. But in certain cases there were restrictions depriving a good number of victims deserving indemnations from receiving any indemnity whatsoever.

The question also remains as to the choice Chancellor Adenauer made in selecting his partners. Instead of dealing with the survivors of the death camps and their families, he chose to confer the administration of the funds — available world-wide on behalf of the missing — to an organization created by the responsible American Jews located in New York.

Elie Wiesel in his role as a leader of the Former Jewish Deportees of France vigorously protested against those who established themselves as "inheritors."

Beginning the "Rehabilitation"

Once the Jews had been "compensated" materially, the Bonn government regarded all obstacles to its efforts of rehabilitaion as having been removed. The White House opened its doors as did the United Nations.

The Cold War transformed both parts of Germany into allies of one camp or the other. The German Democratic Republic, for obvious political reasons, fought the aftermath of Nazism (a number of the Führer's companions had sought refuge in the West). But, there, too, it became necessary to accept realities and the notion of the "little Nazis" was conceived permitting many of them to renew society.

In the Federal Republic the problem developed in a much more complex manner. Immediately after the war, before the revelations of the worst atrocities, the emphasis was on ignorance. It was not necessary to deny anything — that came much later — one simply claimed not to have known of anything that happened. The Nuremburg trials did not arouse any special emotions because much worse had been feared. But when the Allies transferred the task of judging the Nazi criminals to the judicial authorities of West Germany, all serious efforts at denazification were at an end.

The Question of the Nazi Criminals

One could write a whole volume on the question of the Nazi criminals, about the work of the Office for the Investigation of War Crimes in Ludwigsbourg

---

*It should be noted that the principal advisor of Adenauer in these matters was Dr. Hans Globke, who authorized the anti-Semitic laws of Nuremburg in the time of the Führer.

614 REACTION FROM AROUND THE WORLD

which is still active, about the way the trials have been conducted — frequently by judges who served under Hitler. The "failing memory" of the witnesses make a mockery of the acquittals of the murderers due to a lack of evidence.

Some figures will illustrate this matter. Let us remember first that the Allies' tribunal in Nuremberg estimated the number of those who participated directly in the "Final Solution of the Jewish Question" as more than one hundred thousand; some even quoted double this figure.

The same tribunal explicitly condemned the National-Socialist German Workers Party, the Gestapo, the SS and the Waffen SS as "criminal associations." Let us now look at the last report delivered in May 1985 by the Ludwigsbourg Office.

From 1945 to 1985, according to the report, 90,196 criminal actions have been started. They resulted in 6,478 convictions. One notices the bewildering difference between these two figures. In addition, it must be noted that the sentences were gradually and more frequently merely symbolic. (The torturers of Auschwitz were acquitted or released after the verdict for reasons of health in 1965.)

To be precise: of 6,478 sentences pronounced, 12 were for capital punishment (but the Federal Republic has abolished the death penalty); 60 were sentenced to life imprisonment, and 6,191 were sentenced to temporary prison terms.

The same report informs us that in January of 1985 there were still pending 134 active procedures against war criminals in Hanover, Hamburg, Düsseldorf, Hagen and Lüneburg. Let us make clear that if it hadn't been for the campaigns of Beate and Serge Klarsfeld of France, of Simon Wiesenthal in Vienna and of Tuvia Friedman in Haifa, the results would have been even worse

As far as pressure by the great Jewish organizations is concerned in this particular question, wherever it occurred it caused neither noticeable response nor effect.

The legalization of the SS and the Waffen SS recalls the passionate debate caused by the intention of the West-German authorities to introduce special laws outlawing war crimes. Under pressure, on March 25, 1965, the Bundestag decreed the application of these laws until the 31st of December, 1969. At that time, Prof. Vladimir Jankelevitch wrote: "Above all, the Holocaust represents an international crime and the Germans cannot reproach us for interfering in their affairs; these are not "their affairs." This affair is the affair of all the nations that have been victimized."

Germany, however, insisted on a different procedure. Insensibly, the associations of former SS men, reorganized in fraternal organizations, obtained legal status. They could now assemble freely, parade and sing their Nazi songs. Last year, the Waffen SS was freed from all restraints when the government of Chancellor Kohl accorded them the status of combat veterans.

One of the prosecuters at the Auschwitz trial, Henri Ormond, declared in his indictment: "The Waffen SS, contrary to what has been said about it, participated fully in the machinery of murder in Auschwitz. It is not true that it was simply a part of the Wehrmacht." These words were spoken in 1965. However, in 1985, Chancellor Kohl, the spokesman for a large section of German public opinion, decided otherwise and rehabilitated the Waffen SS.

The Law of the Auschwitz Lie

In April 1985, the West German Parliament adopted a law which aimed at forbidding denial of the Holocaust under the Nazi regime. At first glance, this is a response to the campaign waged in Germany and in the world by so-called "revisionist historians (some of whom are by no means historians) who deny the truth of the genocide, the existence of the gas chambers and the guilt of Hitler.

There always exists a "but" because this law is not limited to this issue. It condemns with the same fervor the dissemination of "lies" about any other victims of a suggested tyranny. Here we have an important step on the road to the banalization of Auschwitz.

However, in the piece quoted, Vladimir Jankelevitch declared: "Neither Auschwitz nor Treblinka resemble anything else, not because all things in general are different, but because above all nothing resembles Auschwitz." As if to echo this statement, Simon Veil, former president of the European Parliament, declared last May at Camp Struthof at the conclusion of the European meeting of the World Jewish Congress (May 16-19, 1985): "The children that disappeared in Argentina are not the children murdered in Auschwitz. Neither are the dead entombed in Dresden, nor the victims of Hiroshima, nor are those burned by napalm bombs in Vietnam the same as those gassed in Auschwitz — even though the pain, the human suffering is always the same and human life always has the same price."

Contradictory Signs

One could enumerate here the contradictory signs demonstrated during the evolution among the population in the Federal Republic of Germany. It has been said that the showing of the film "Holocaust" (a romanticized story lagging far behind the reality) had deeply shocked the audiences who viewed it. But the Israeli students who visited Germany about two years ago were bewildered by the ignorance of the young people they talked with about the events that occurred during the war. The grandparents pretended to have ignored everything; the parents preferred not to stir up this kind of memory, and the young ones mostly ignored this chapter.

There exists an evident contradiction if one thinks of the young Germans who want to work in the *kibbutzim,* but the truth is indisputable. Chancellor Erhardt said before Helmut Kohl that "one cannot eternally reproach the German people for the crimes of the past, especially when other crimes they say have been committed elsewhere."

As an answer to the "Holocaust" television program, a German counterpart called "Heimat" (14 hours in length) told of the life of a small German village between the two wars. It showed repulsive people who became Nazis, but also decent people who opposed them. This is the image of a beloved society which succeeded in freeing itself from evil in 1945. This would be more credible if the majority of the opponents of nazism hadn't been imprisoned in the concentration camps, making any acts of resistance very difficult. It suffices to view the film by Leni Riefenstall and the newsreels to conclude that the "marginals" and the depraved ones who followed Hitler can be counted in the millions.

We Now Come to Bitburg

These preliminary remarks explain the actions of Chancellor Kohl. Last year he wanted to participate in the ceremonies that marked the 40th anniversary of the Allied landings in Normandy (June, 1944). This project was aborted in particular due to French reticence. As compensation President François Mitterand invited Kohl to pay homage with him to the victims of the First World War at Verdun. All the same, this was less shocking.

In 1985, on the 40th anniversary of the victory of the Allies which put an end to Hitler's Third Reich, President Reagan decided to come to Europe. Germany was included in the President's itinerary. A visit to a concentration camp was, of course, foreseen, with Dachau in mind. Chancellor Kohl voiced opposition to this project which, according to him, would only serve to open the wounds which he wanted to see closed. President Reagan, in the name of the friendship between the two peoples, yielded.

But Chancellor Kohl was not satisfied. He insisted on a visit by President Reagan to a German military cemetery located at Bitburg in order to solemnly seal the new brotherhood-in-arms between Americans and Germans.

This was a very sensational project because it included in this brotherhood-in-arms the warriors of the Third Reich. It turned out that the cemetery of Bitburg also contained graves of the Waffen SS, and then the scandal began.

Protests were raised everywhere, and one witnessed a curious "hesitation valse" between President Reagan and Chancellor Kohl: The question was to go or not to go. Finally, Reagan yielded to Kohl's pleas. Obviously the protests by Jews and non-Jews counted less than certain strategic considerations. Not only were the Jewish protests — strengthened by the martyrdom of the European Jews — not listened to but the West German mass circulation magazine *Quick,* which is close to the CDU, ran the headline: "The Visit of Reagan to Germany: the Power of the Jews." One might believe that he had returned to a time 45 years past.

Bitburg and Bergen-Belsen

As we know, Reagan did go to Bitburg. But trying to appease the protests which mounted everywhere, he chose to add to his itinerary a visit to the camp of Bergen-Belsen which was a place of great suffering for many European Jews. In this way, he thought he could reestablish a balance. But, in fact, this gesture reinforced the revolt of the survivors. How can one put the victims of Nazism and the members of the Waffen SS on an equal footing? While Chancellor Kohl was talking about reconciliation, the response was not long in coming.

In the Knesset, as elsewhere, Deputy Speaker Chaika Grossman asked how one could speak of reconciliation between the victims and their executioners. Commenting on the visit to Bitburg, Simone Veil declared in her speech at Kanyr Struthof near Strasbourg: "I am thinking not only of the insult to millions of assassinated children, women and men, which is unsupportable and inadmissible when, by lack of will and ignorance of these children, these women, these men find themselves reduced to the same level of the victims of a system like their murderers."

And Afterwards

Weeks passed and Reagan returned home where other problems awaited him. Chancellor Kohl, on his part, went to speak at a congress of refugees from Silesia, many of whom dream of revenge. During this entire period, he was only concerned to please the German population — the German electorate which had started to grow cool to the forces which support him. As to the "Jewish power," he does not believe in it very much any longer because he could defy it without harm. Also, he is well aware that the majority of the inhabitants of the Federal Republic were born after the war.

So it follows according to him that one can draw the curtain over the past. If it is necessary, as he did in Bergen-Belsen, he can say a few strong words about the "Nazi tyranny." But one should not ask him for more.

It remains to be seen whether Judaism, either in Israel or in the Diaspora, considers it equally necessary to shelve the Bitburg affair. Considering that the Jews still recall what Amalek did to their ancestors, that for four centuries they have quarantined Spain for the crimes of the Inquisition which appear mild in comparison with the Nazi crimes, will they accept 40 years as sufficient to shelve the Holocaust, to file it away in their archives, which means in the "oubliettes" file of history.

This question must be asked now, at a moment when in Europe racism and anti-Semitism again raise their heads, profiting from a persistent economic crisis at a moment when terrorism in a very disturbing way declares its alliance with Nazis, old and new.

After the Nazis have killed the living Jews, can one then allow the memory of the millions of assassinated Jews to be erased?

The Image of The United States

One cannot say that the Bitburg affair marks a turning point in the way the United States is perceived here. In fact, the best informed observers have revealed that it was Helmut Kohl who won the game and who apparently found attentive ears among the counselors of the American President. It is obvious that during the discussions raised by "Star Wars," the role of Germany weighs heavier than that of the survivors of nazism. (One can perhaps paraphrase the famous remark of Stalin in regard to the Pope: how many divisions does he have?)

France, since de Gaulle, plays a very subtle game in order not to disturb the Western Alliance, while preserving her freedom of action with regard to defense. Washington counts less on the support of England — more on that of Germany. And the champions of the American strategy are ready to make gestures in order to maintain the Federal Republic as their principal ally. The Soviet Union is equally interested in Germany which represents one of its principal commercial partners and which, because of certain political turmoil, appears to be the weakest link in the Atlantic Alliance.

The leaders of the Jewish Community in France are unessential to these considerations. This can be noticed in the remarks by the Grand Rabbinate, by the speakers of the community at one anniversary of the Ghetto Uprising in Warsaw (April 1985).

Many have the feeling that the U.S.A., where investigations of numerous hidden Nazis have been started (as in Canada and in South America) does not completely understand the uniqueness of nazism. That was already the case when, in 1939, the refugees on board the last ship able to leave Hamburg (the S.S. St. Louis) were refused entry. Likewise, during the "Evian Conference on Refugees" (1938), organized through the initiative of President Roosevelt, when no visas were issued to save Jews who were able to leave the countries controlled by the Nazis.

The soldiers who liberated the Nazi camps were deeply shocked, and so was American public opinion. The democratic world as a whole developed a feeling of guilt.

Since that time, other wars have taken place and the media have directed the interst of public opinion to other tragedies. Politicians may try to enter Auschwitz in the "profit and loss" columns. Historians, swamped by events, might follow this approach. By no means can the survivors do the same. Their numbers inevitably diminish, but those still around should alert the world against the danger of forgetting the Nazi crimes, the most horrible crimes humanity has ever known.

(Translated from the French by George Asher.)

(Henri Bulawko is Vice President of the World Jewish Congress [French Section], Vice President of CRIF and President of the European branch of the World Federation of the Jewish Resistance Fighters and Deportees.)

Reagan at Bitburg — An Attack on History

Actualite Juive
May 3, 1985

By Jacques Melode

On the occasion of an official visit to the German Federal Republic as an official guest this month, the President of the United States, Mr. Ronald Reagan, is surprised that one takes exception to his project to visit the tombs of soldiers of the Wehrmacht buried at the cemetery in Bitburg. He has expressed himself publicly in the following terms: "The young German soldiers also were victims of Nazism though they were fighting in the German uniform."

When I was reading this statement I couldn't help to associate it with a caricature which appeared in one of the great American magazines a few years ago after the broadcast of the first episode of the famous *Holocaust* television series. The cartoon showed a group of former SS officers assembled in front of the television screen, one of them complaining: "What partiality! Not a word about the long cold nights which we had to spend on the guard towers of the concentration camps. What mockery!"

Everything has been said about the sinister project of the American president, who since mid-April has not ceased to repeat his blunders in proportion to the wave of furious expressions increasing in Israel and all over the world. Hasn't the head of the American government tried to balance the program of his visit to Germany by including the camp of Bergen-Belsen? Hasn't he pressured, in vain, his advisor on the commemoration of the Holocaust, Elie Wiesel, to silence his disapproval and indignation? All that while elsewhere in the world the ceremonies on occasion of the 40th anniversary of the liberation of the death camps by the Allied armies have produced more and more probing and convincing facts of the record of Nazi barbarism.

Seen from Israel, this sad Reagan event has been eloquently commented on by the Israeli Prime Minister Shimon Peres at Yad Vashem, the museum of Nazi horrors in Jerusalem created to serve as a bulwark against forgetting. Mr. Peres said, "One can reconcile oneself with the enemy, but never with the devil."

In fact, this is the true problem. The United States, desiring to strengthen its political and military position in Europe vis-a-vis the Soviet Union, must negotiate with the Germany of Chancellor Kohl the positioning in his country of a strategic system increasingly powerful in the form of nuclear missiles and of satellites designed to deliver, if necessary, the famous star war elements.

Germany is unquestionably the ideal partner for the United States in this planetary test of forces which pit President Reagan against the Kremlin. In order to demonstrate understanding and kindness, giving in to the inevitable blackmail is only one step and President Reagan is absolutely ready to take it. Thus reasoning, he undoubtedly does not take into consideration the damage resulting to the image of his country and to him personally. Are we witnessing here another episode of the permanent conflict between the reason of state and reason, between the too-subtle political moral and human moral, between compromise and compromising with conscience?

The United States does not hesitate to speak of a "New Germany" in opposition to Nazi Germany, and thereby also proceeds to get caught in the dangerous net of naivete and forgetfulness.

It is impossible to ignore the fact that the Germany of Chancellor Kohl is still infested with Nazis, old and new, proud of their existence and benefactors of a concealed complacency on the part of the authorities in the name of democracy, a democracy in whose name it was possible for Hitler to commit all of his crimes.

"It is necessary to accept one's history," Chancellor Kohl states, addressing himself to his compatriots without doubt in order to heal the complexes they retain from their rotten past. Well, no one knows better than the Jewish people how dangerous it is to throw one's past into the *oubliettes* — meaning to forget.

Never mind the compromise which Kohl and Reagan will arrive at. The fact alone that the problem should arise forty years after the liberation of the camps is revealing. Very much revealing of the incapacity of the leaders to grasp the most simple of realities: the history of a nation cannot be disassociated from its present. To render homage to the members of the SS does not only mean to absolve Nazism, but also and above all to justify all those who would like to see it reborn.

(*Translated from the French by George Asher.*)

Only A Minute Of Silence At Bitburg
Actualite Juive
May 3, 1985

By Henri Smolarski

"Ich hatt'einen Kameraden [Once I had a Comrade]. . .": the melancholy tune devoted to the dead at the cemetery of Bitburg. Neither the dead nor the living have been able to touch Ronald Reagan. Accompanied by Chancellor Helmut Kohl, he has bowed his head before a monument in this German cemetery where side by side dream the murderers of the SS and those of the Wehrmacht.

Neither the survivors among the deportees and the resistance, nor the Jewish organizations and their powerful voices, neither the protests from the House of Representatives or the Senate were able to prevent the head of the world's greatest democracy from reafirming the reconciliation of Germany and America over the graves of the young SS dead, whom Ronald Reagan called "the other victims of Hitler."

On the emotional level, for Ronald Reagan, the proclaimed friend of the Jewish people and of Israel (of which he is a vital supporter) this slip appears to be a blunder of the highest order. But on the political level, in spite of the President's statement in Bergen-Belsen invoking the Torah and Israel, the "blunder" is not simply a blunder and the error, referred to by Shimon Perez, is not simply an error.

Those who believe that the big powers are moved by deep emotions are full of illusions. So are those who believed that facing the graves of the SS, President Ronald Reagan would denounce the posthumous victory of Hitler, the renaissance of racism, of terrorism, of people's enslavement, and of torture as a system of government.

The Jews will be fuming. Fume! What do they have to complain about? It happened to be their chance, their good luck, that the interests of the state of Israel are identical with the primary interests of America. Anyhow, thinks Ronald Reagan, a short minute of silence in a far-away cemetery will not prejudice the excellent relations between Washington, the Jews and Israel.

All in all, the attitude of Ronald Reagan is completely coherent. His European strategy, his space defense initiative, his ideas on the reorganization of world trade with the aim of a better market for American products depend on a solid agreement with the Federal Republic of Germany. Therefore, as long as the past will no longer be an obstacle for a complicity between Germans and Americans, let us forgive, especially as it doesn't cost much and the benefits will certainly be substantial.

The gesture of Ronald Reagan has been well received by three quarters of German public opinion and the party of Helmut Kohl remembers that, after all, the Germans — SS or not — died for the Fatherland. In other words, to have died for Hitler and Auschwitz appears today to be equally honorable as to have died for freedom in the uniform of the American, the English, or the Russian forces. A Fatherland is a Fatherland. An idol is an idol.

In spite of the resistance by the Gaulists (opposed by Francois Mitterand) against the economic and strategic projects of Ronald Reagan, the "great seven" signed a unique declaration which evokes "with pain, the memory of all those who died because of the war, or have become victims of inhumanity and of tyranny." All now belong in the same bag or in the same tomb; the six million dead Jews, the resistance, the soldiers or the other so-called "victims of the war," the SS, the henchmen, the mechanics of the Holocaust.

The lesson of Bitburg is apparently a lesson of defeat. At the least one should have known in advance that between a slogan and an empire there can't be a fair game. Neither the Jewish community or its organizations, nor any lobby could have agreed with those German papers which questioned the American decision, and believed that the Jewish influence could have overcome the White House.

This supposed power of the Jews did not succeed in deflecting by one inch a bantering president from placing the victims and the henchmen on the same level.

Perhaps a stronger Jewish mobilization and, who knows, pressures on the part of Israel, could have opened a crack in the American determination. In spite of its toughness, there is hardly a great power that would be insensitive to a very strong pressure by world public opinion.

Let us therefore say that we have to do with a general repetition. Trying to prevent a president of the United States from bowing to the Nazi tombs was a *mitzvah,* an homage which we owe to the memory of a massacred people. Already other tasks, perhaps more urgent, await us and will not cease facing us. For instance, the struggle for the freedom of the Jews in the Soviet Union, and the struggle against the reason of state. And when will the general mobilization come?

(Translated from the French by George Asher.)

Tulips And Chrysanthemums Did Not Hide The Past
Actualite Juive
May 3, 1985

By Edwin Eytan

A German trumpeter played the traditional tune for soldiers fallen for the fatherland, *"I had a Comrade, "*while Ronald Reagan placed a wreath on the monument for the dead at the cemetery at Bitburg where 2,202 German soldiers are buried, among them 48 members of the Waffen SS. One kilometer away, at the crossroads of Hochstrasse and Franzmer-Benstrasse, several hundred demonstrators shouted: "Why, Ronnie, why?" Their cries, amplified by loudspeakers, did not reach the borders of the cemetery.

Thus, several hundred meters apart, two worlds clashed. Bitburg was to become the symbol for reconciliation. President Reagan and Chancellor Helmut Kohl, both in a somber and serious mood, could not help smiling when two generals, yesterday's enemies, today's allies, Matthew B. Ridgeway, 74, and the Luftwaffe acc, Johannes Steinhoff, 71, shook hands.

President Reagan could not see nor hear the demonstrators until the moment when his convoy of 47 cars passed around the "front" of them, a body of people that stretched for 150 meters. Conceivably, he noticed first a very young man perched on the roof of a building crying out in English, "Ronnie, why did you come? The SS killed my father!" Then, posters and cries, "Don't forget the murdered." The American President, relaxed, leaned to the left, to the side of the majority of the demonstrators, as if to see them better. He saluted them with a wave of his hand.

A few had arrived during Saturday night and early Sunday, from France, Belgium and Luxembourg, in cars rented in France by the Union of Jewish Students, and in a Belgian car sent by the European Union of Jewish Students which is located in Brussels.

Near one p.m., to general surprise, these demonstrators advanced through the village in closed ranks. In front of them, and facing them, helmeted officers of the Federal Police, visors down and carrying shields of transparent plastic, retreated step by step. A young officer allowed them to go to the front line saying: "There you will be seen by the President." The officer made them promise they would not engage in any violent acts and would not endanger the convoy. Mark Holter addressed the group of young Jews. "We must accept. We want the President to see us and the cameras of world-wide television to record our presence, here and today, showing that the past will never be forgotten."

For several days orders were received by the German authorities not to resort to violence unless there was an actual danger to the life of the President and the Chancellor. Most feared was an act of provocation by one side or the other. But everything went peaceably. The policemen continued to retreat to the line marking the passage of the convoy and there in a surprising gesture of conciliation took off their helmets and put them on the ground with their shields, In order not to be outdone, the demonstrators sat down on the ground.

The inhabitants of the village, which resembles a tourist poster, were glued to their windows. Some of them appeared stupefied to see their town, which is so clean and so lovely, without a scrap of paper, invaded by those who appeared to them as a yelling and vociferous mob who came to spoil the festivities. The majority of the houses displayed small American flags, but only a few Germans ventured out on the street.

All of Germany, or almost all, lived for several days in the shadow of the "affair," as the visit of the American President to Bitburg was cautiously called. The first reaction was a kind of manifestation of national solidarity. Almost five million Germans, or ten percent of its population, died during the Second World War, mostly in the ranks of the Wehrmacht. During the fourteen days of the Battle of Stalingrad, almost a million Germans perished. A haunting figure. Entire divisions marching to their death. Thus, almost every German family had been touched, For the majority of them, criticizing the visit to Bitburg or any manifestation against the principle of it would have lowered the dignity of those family members who died for the fatherland. The cemetery at Bitburg is identified on the maps as a "Cemetery of Honor."

Two days before the arrival of Reagan, the cemetery had the appearance of a flowery glade. The municipality had planted 62,400 panzies, chrysanthemums and tulips. But the majority of the graves had individual flower arrangements. The tombstones without inscriptions and those of the former Waffen SS were covered with jonquils. Obviously an anonymous hand wanted to pay special homage to these dead. On others, the families had lain wreaths or flowers as if the backlash of the Reagan visit had reawakened the memory of their fallen ones.

A resident of Tier, an elegant black-haired woman of about 56, came several times to place tulips, and even a candle, on the tomb of one of the Waffen SS, Josef Gavol, killed on the 14th of September 1944, at the age of 16 years and 11 months. As a young girl, 40 years ago, she had known this young man. And now, as she told the cemetery guard, her husband, her children and her grandchildren had encouraged her to come here.

This type of reaction crossed Germany like a wild fire. Except for the "Greens," all political parties did support the visit.

However, in an article discussed widely, one of the best-known intellectuals of the German Socialist Party, Peter Glotz, raised a problem hidden by the Germans during the last 40 years. According to him, nothing must be forgotten. The truth must not be hidden, he argued. The camps, the assassinations, and the support which the majority of Germans gave to Hitler until the capitulation of May 8, 1945, must be remembered.

"But," says Glotz, "It isn't less irresponsible to erase the memory of the acts committed by the Allies. For example, the useless bombardment of Dresden, teeming with refugee women and children a few days, which caused hundreds of thousands of casualties." Glotz quotes a statement by Egon Kogon, one of the first

German opponents of Nazism, who was detained for many years in concentration camps. On his return from Buchenwald, Kogon write: "A nation which has seen the burnt remains of its women and children scattered through the ruins of their bombarded villages cannot be expected to be moved by the mountains of nude corpses stacked in the concentration camps."

Bitburg's principal effect was an awakening of the phantoms of the past. The German-Jewish communities feared that a wave of anti-Semitism, verbal and polite, might unfurl throughout Germany.

Despite this apprehension, the Central Council of German Jews, under the presidency of Werner Nachmann, decided to boycott the ceremonies in Bergen-Belsen as a protest against the President's visit to Bitburg. Nevertheless, it asked the nearest Jewish community from the city of Hanover to round up a minyan so that the Kaddish could be said. The president of the Jewish community of Hanover, Michael Furst, pleaded throughout the night with his co-religionists. He needed only eight volunteers because it was known that two Jews would be in attendance: the Ambassador of Israel, Yitzhak Ben-Ari, and the Amnbassador of the United States, Arthur Burns. There was no minyan.

Several kilometers away, hundreds of Jewish demonstrators who came from France and America under the leadership of Serge Klarsfeld were unsuccessful in reaching their goal of Bergen-Belsen.

(Translated from the French by George Asher.)

"I Was Seven Years Old And A Prisoner Of The Nazis"
La Monde
May 6, 1985

By Frank Ludwig von Stauffenberg

On May 8, 1945, I was seven years old. I lived to the end of the war as a so-called *sippenha'ftling* — a prisoner because of reprisals against the family of a traitor interned with the brothers, sisters, spouses and children of other German resistance fighters. This internment was based on an alleged tradition of vengeance stemming from an old Germanic custom which extended the culpability to the children and parents of a "criminal."

At the time I did not understand. When I began to understand more about life, that period of time took on the form of an increasingly incomprehensible nightmare. The brutalities and perversions which I was forced to bear are not normal for a child. The victory of the Allies would protect the child-turned-adult, they said, forever.

Forever?

In England a princess has been accosted because her father had once belonged to a Nazi organization. With insane pleasure, a newspaper revealed with growing indignation that the brother-in-law of the Queen's husband, though dead for a long time, had been a Nazi dignitary. Who remembers in the face of such a scandal that the Prince-Consort had fought as a volunteer against Hitler's armies?

Boys Of Twenty Years

There is now a storm of protest in the world of the "rightness" of the President of the United States of America honoring the memory of defeated German soldiers — many of whom were also victims of the dictatorship.

No one examines or questions the undivided responsibility and the personal guilt of those 47 members of the Waffen SS, most of them youngsters less than 20 years old, who rest among several thousand other Wehrmacht soldiers. Isn't there in this indignation a trace of that same definition of collective family guilt of which I and my kin were made the victims?

I am proud when I think of my father though I could neither take part personally in his fight nor in the actions of his comrades for the right and dignity of Germany's name. That memory, above all, is a reason to be grateful. Thanks to their actions, I and my contemporaries were spared the compulsion, the seduction, the confusion and the complicity with the injustices and the violence of the Thousand Year Reich. I am grateful to the Allied armies which liberated us and who not only made it possible for us to survive but saved our youngsters from the tests which so many of our elders had failed.

I cannot help but react with disgust to the facile and belated gestures — which in our country and elsewhere today serve to spread retroactive condemnations from the comfortable safety of belonging to another generation or to another country. I experience growing uneasiness in the face of the spectacle of accusers who have identified once and for all the errors and the crimes of others while consciously or unconsciously regarding themselves as irreproachable and infallible. I am afraid, facing the clean conscience with which they seem to, or even sincerely believe in their ability to liquidate the past without having understood or learned anything. Pronouncing these judgments, dismissing the possibility of being guilty ourselves makes it impossible to assume a genuine responsibility.

Indeed, isn't it the true lesson so dearly paid for which we have to learn from the destiny of our people: that the rules of law and of liberty remain fragile if they are not supported by people who accept the burden of their responsibility.

(Frank von Stauffenberg is the son of Colonel Klaus von Stauffenberg who on July 20, 1944, placed a bomb in Hitler's general headquarters. He is a member of the Christian Social Union of Bavaria and at present represents his party in the European Parliament.)
(Translated from the French by George Asher.)

"To Know Where One Comes From"
Le Monde
May 16, 1985

By Heinz Kühn

If we want really to discover the truth of our historic destiny, we'll find the essence of what constitutes the true tragedy of our history — the knowledge that we have never succeeded in staging a revolution. I am using the word "revolution" in the sense given it by Ferdinand Lasalle, the founder of Social Democracy — namely the attitude by which a people uses its own dynamism and the force of its own sovereignty to change its historical direction.

In 1945 it was the military defeat and not a revolution springing from the popular will that freed us from Hitler's regime. Once more the democracy was carried to us on the point of the Allies' "bayonets."

On May 8, 1945, leaving behind the underground of the exile, I found myself free, legal, and amidst the joy of a freed people. During more than a decade we had appealed to our compatriots to save Germany by rejecting Hitler. Can we now undertake a democratic reconstitution of Germany?

Why do the Germans now facing May 8 present such a spectacle of disarray? On this 40th anniversary there should have been thousands of demonstrations, mass meetings of immense size which should have confessed the errors of the past, and above all there should have been reunions of men and women moved by the desire to know, to understand, to recognize finally the true facts of our history.

Bitburg should have been the last place upon which the advisers of Kohl and Reagan could have agreed, at least if they truly desired to celebrate the German-American alliance. After all, this cemetery only contains several young Waffen SS, hardly older at death than 18 years, buried among numerous soldiers. These members of the SS could have been conscripts. "Only a people that knows where it comes from can know where it goes to," was written by a historian. If we do not retain within us the conscience of our own history, we will find ourselves confused at each crossroad.

May 8, 1945, was the logical result of the errors preceding it. January 30, 1933, the day on which Hitler came to power, is part of the same logic as is March 23, 1933, when the majority of the Reichstag voted unlimited powers to Hitler in an action which represented the real birth of the Third Reich.

Neither words overflowing with unction or nobleness nor the evocation of everything positive we have accomplished since 1945 can relieve us from the chain of events as long as we, Germans, have not taken into account all that we have suffered and accepted throughout our long history because of our subservience and our lack of civil courage.

Copyright © 1985 Le Monde. Reprinted with permission.

(Heinz Kühn was forced to flee Germany when Hitler came to power. Born in 1912, he first fled to Czechoslovakia, then Belgium, where he participated in the Resistance during World War II. He is now a leading member of the Social Democratic Party in West Germany.)

(Translated from the French by George Asher.)

"You are not the only ones!"

Reconciliation Does Not Mean Forgetting
Strasbourg, West Germany
May 19, 1985

By Simone Veil

(This speech by Simone Veil, deputy of the European Parliament, was presented to the World Jewish Congress in Strasbourg, West Germany, shortly after President Reagan's visit to Bitburg.)

It is highly significant that the World Jewish Congress has chosen Strasbourg as the place to assemble for the commemoration of the 40th anniversary of the end of the Second World War and of the liberation of the concentration camps in Europe. Its choice has affirmed the importance which it attaches to the idea of a united Europe, as well as to the reconciliation of our peoples and the reinforcement of the democratic principles on which rest the democratic institutions of our countries.

This ceremony of remembrance to which you have honored me by your invitation reflects very well the spirit which animates and moves the survivors of the Holocaust.

To remember and not forget anything is not an expression of despair, anger or vengeance, but of hope that the memory of the past may serve as a lesson to the entire human community.

While remembering the millions of assassinated children, remembering those exterminated communities — exterminated at the same time when their synagogues were burned down and their cultural heritage destroyed — one must not shrink from recalling that everyone, forever, carries in himself part of the responsibility. By being silent in the face of authoritarianism, by accepting with complacency or indifference any display of racism means to forget the monstrous abberations which might be their consequence.

Those who cannot or do not want to understand our sentiments, those who remain deaf to our appeals for vigilance will without doubt be astonished that this day of remembrance has been devoted to the European union and that the World Jewish Congress is devoting its discussions and reflections to this subject. In this choice is reflected a moral and political engagement by your movement in which I see the clearest and most generous response to the ulterior motives and the ambiguities which so frequently mar the commemorations of the end of the war in Europe. Without having premeditated this response, it very properly shows a certain conception of Europe, a conception that is based on the will for reconciliation and on trust in the possibilities of a common defense of common democratic ideas.

Devoted as we are to the construction of such a Europe, we are aware of, and do not want to underestimate the exigencies for its success.

Exigencies imposed on the victims themselves required to overcome hate and distrust in order to engage themselves absolutely and without reservations in an undertaking based on friendship and confidence.

Exigencies imposed on those who by the simple fact of their relationship are obliged to disavow the past. For these, as well as for the others, the reconciliation could not mean forgetting.

The reconciliation must not be concerned only with the survivors, but with the six million women and men that were exterminated, and it is to them that we are responsible for our actions. The survivors of the camps? Are they not the trustees of the vow conveyed by their comrades in suffering: "That the world may know so that never again this should be possible."?

How can anyone imagine that a beautiful and solid union could be created if Europeans refuse to know their history. A Europe vitally democratic, capable of accepting its history, capable of enduring the corrosion of time to face the inevitable memories of the past, capable of assuming its responsibilities founded on its faith; its *raison d'etre,* and its strength to exist. The faith is not only in the memory; it is also the condemnation of a system, of its ideology as well as its methods employed without mercy in eradicating every trace of protest or resistance.

It will be equally necessary to throw light on the racist concepts in whose name this genocide was perpetrated, to study the inter-connection of facts, the development of theory to practice, how people seemingly normal participated in such projects and how others accepted them without protest or resistance. The investigations have to be undertaken without any prejudice, which does not mean without remembering, just as the absence of revenge does not imply forgetting. On the contrary, we believe that a true democracy can only be founded on the unbending condemnation of an abominable system; denying certain aspects, excusing those responsible and banalizing the wrongs would be a profound and important error for fostering friendship between European peoples. That is why the recent visit of President Reagan at the cemetery in Bitburg and certain remarks made at that occasion have greatly disturbed us.

I'm bringing up these events, not in a polemic spirit, but because the connections knowingly maintained during the course of this visit could have a grave impact on the future of Europe.

Contrary to what certain people might have thought about it, the handshakes over the graves are nothing but pretenses if the soul is not in it.

It is not simply the insult to the millions of assassinated children, women and men of whom I am thinking. I'm thinking of an insupportable and inadmissible offense caused either by a complete misunderstanding of history or a lack of resolution that these children, these women, and these men find themselves, together with their assassins, reduced to the position of victims of the system.

I'm thinking of the future of Europe and of the purification necessary by the rejection, without any ambiguity, of the past in order to draw on the forces of spiritual community that its unity requires today.

Undoubtedly there are people who try to erase everything and want to date history in 1945 or, even better, in 1950; the year which might be defined as "Year One of Europe." This would mean to make light of the realities and would be dangerous. History exists. It inscribes itself on the collective memory of the people, and is the only way to exorcise the past; not to forget it, but on the contrary, to know it well.

Those who are present here know very well that neither the survivors nor the orphans, nor the parents whose children were brutally torn from them on the fateful ramp of Auschwitz, have ever given in to the temptation of vengeance. Could it perhaps be that the immensity of the crime would render all personal vengeance futile or preposterous? To all those who by their complicity, their silence, or their passivity allowed the sinister Dr. Mengele to escape justice, we proclaim that the victims who had to submit to his abominable experiments — particularly the children, the twins which he treated like laboratory animals — recognize that sadistic assassin's right to the legality of the law.

Proving their attachment and their extraordinary confidence in justice which frequently behaves rather tolerantly, the Jews have nevertheless never failed in their respect of the democratic principle. They have also avoided all references to a collective responsibility. This is the outstanding proof that they have deliberately chosen to submit to the exigencies which their wish for reconciliation implies.

Taking the risk of shocking certain people, may I say that I have asked myself frequently by what miracle none of the survivors, in spite of the painful loss of children, parents, brothers, sisters and entire families have ever substituted themselves for justice even when some of those responsible for hundreds of thousands of murders were found to quietly cultivate their gardens as they had cultivated the flowers around the crematorium.

The process of turning the victim into the murderer might have allowed itself to foil the truth without having to out-maneuver the procedural quirks invoked by perverse lawyers.

Let us for a moment remember May 1945. Some people today appear to try to reject history or to adjust it. There are those who have killed themselves because the violence of their pain was such that it frightened to the extent that they couldn't do anything but to fall silent.

Perhaps it had to take forty years before we could say that our souls and our living hearts could not survive without reopening old wounds. Time is needed to do its part. It should be remembered that God required his people to wander through the desert for forty years before reaching the Promised Land.

Allow me now to mention some personal memories. There might also be those of my comrades but perhaps I would be listened to more than others.

In May 1945 the first reports of the realities of the camps, the first accounts of the survivors, arrived at a world which was unbelieving and speechless in the face of the enormity of the crime. The reality was too horrible to be perceived and understood as such. During the days and weeks while they awaited repatriation, which was then not considered a first priority, numerous survivors who had spent their last strength hoping to live until the liberation, died of exhaustion and lack of a minimum care before their return.

Let us also talk of the return of the repatriated. The flowers and the welcomes at the receptions did not hide the humiliation, the agony of having to report that the children, the parents, the brothers, and the sisters of those who questioned us, would not come back, that the waiting was useless. How can one talk of those months in the Spring of 1945 when so many were waiting for those who had disappeared into the smoke of Auschwitz? How can we think of our comrades in suffering coming from Poland, Czechoslovakia, Germany or Hungary, who at Bergen-Belsen or Theresienstadt waited for months or years for a country that would open its borders to admit them?

How can we visualize today the dangerous journey on which ventured the most determined and most courageous ones of the Holocaust survivors, embarking on those ships which could hardly keep afloat? They were resolved to face the guns of the British navy rather than to renounce their decision to reach Palestine.

About all that they do not talk anymore. But we have not forgotten it, and we maintain within ourselves our memories which might appear tainted with bitterness and anger. Why this discretion? Because we do not want our children and our grandchildren having to live in a world marked by hate. Because the reconciliation of which Europe is a symbol has been chosen by ourselves. We have decided to contribute as much as others, and perhaps more, to the work of reconciliation symbolized by Europe. It is indeed a miracle that those who have suffered the most, far from imprisoning themselves in hate or in the indifference of resignation, have frequently been among the pioneers of Europe. Without any doubt did they know that Europe represents the only hope of reconciliation with the German people and that this reconciliation was necessary to safeguard peace and democracy?

A great amount of courage and an immense faith in humanity was necessary to believe in this grand adventure.

Here we are far away from the Europe of milk and butter, and the ministers who discuss the Common Market and the price of grain. Some people at times scoff at Europe and don't see in it anything but pure mercantilism and national interests. For me, the reality of Europe is simply that it is here. We cannot forget it. And that is the reason why the visit to Bitburg has forced me to worry so much.

For a moment I ask myself if we haven't been taken; if in our desire to fight against all inclinations of returning to the ancient demons we have not shown a certain *naiveté*. The president of the Federal Republic of Germany, Mr. Richard Von Weizsäcker, gave us on May 8th the most beautiful of responses. Allow me to quote him:

"All of us, guilty or not, young or old, have to accept the past. All of us are involved in the consequences and we are being held responsible for them. Young and old, . . . we can and must help each other in order to understand why it is essential to maintain the memory. This is not a matter of erasing the past. That is impossible. To modify the past in hindsight or trying to believe it is non-existent is impossible. But whoever closes his eyes to the past cannot see the present. Whoever refuses to remember the barbarism will find himself again exposed to new risks of contagion.

"Often one deplores the absence of a political or active interest in favor of the European culture. But is this culture not in the first place the attachment to common values? Often one refers to them simply as a matter of style. Let us make sure that these values remain a credible and vibrant reality. . . . Europe must not be suspected or accused of complacency. It must be engaged in a permanent battle against everything that threatens to destroy forever the soul of the countries which are its constituencies. This is the continuing battle which we must wage for democracy.

"At all times the battles waged in the name of justice and freedom have mobilized the Jews. The persecution and the ostracism of which they were the object have, far from leading them to withdrawal and caution, to conformism or surrender, have on the contrary incited them to fight for the defense of all those whose rights have been violated.

"The attempt for a 'final solution' has only reinforced the zeal of this commitment. As the victims of the greatest, most barbarous crime in the history of mankind, our loyalty guides us to fight for all those who are victims, not only of racism, but of every attempt against their human rights. The recent decades have shown to all who doubted it that political ideology by itself constitutes a barrier against racism and anti-Semitism. This is a specific fight which must be fought with Europe as its leader. Born by the defeat of Nazism, by the victory over totalitarianism, it was only normal that the European community, as well as the Council of Europe, felt it to be their calling to defend human rights and to become the champions of this struggle."

Some contest the sound foundation of this debate or doubt its usefulness.

They tend to ignore the moral and psychological power of support it gives to all those in the world who are persecuted, discriminated against, tortured and detained for fighting for freedom. They also underestimate the invisible, but very real protection which the actions taken in the democratic countries give to the dissidents and the refuseniks in the Soviet Union, as well as the victims of the repression in Latin America. The authorities of the respective countries concerned are by no means indifferent to the impact of public opinion.

In my opinion, it is not a question of choosing between good and bad causes, between the victims of totalitarian regimes — according to the ideology they proclaim.

However, as far as we are concerned, we do not feel that special attention is paid to the situation of the Jews in the Soviet Union, the victims of discrimination — victims exclusively because they were born Jews.

Could anyone have imagined forty years ago that two and a half million Soviet citizens whose passports identify them as Jews — as did our identity cards

—could thus be put at the mercy of their country?

Emphasizing our devotion to the cause of human rights, I would like to warn against a trap into which some among us are risking to fall; namely, the trap of banalization. That we are the most ardent defenders of human rights appears to me to be legitimate because we know better than the others what it can cost to accept even a minimum of back-sliding, and how easy comes the progressive involvement that finally leads to disaster.

Just the same, we cannot accept each outcry of genocide or holocaust. The children who disappeared in Argentina are not the assassinated children of Auschwitz. Neither are the entombed dead of Dresden. Nor are the victims of Hiroshima or those burnt with napalm bombs in Vietnam the ones gassed in Auschwitz, even if human suffering is the same and human life always has the same price. We cannot accept that by a continuous and orchestrated propaganda, Israel can openly be accused of genocide for its military actions in Lebanon. This serves to silence the world of all responsibility and to silence the victims. These accusations have been embellished in all the media and in the drawing rooms of Paris.

We have been satisfied: yet it does not prevent the propaganda from continuing. However, beyond the responsibility which Europe must feel toward Israel — which has become the homeland of the children which Europe did not know how to save — the European community must not only maintain, but also intensify the already exclusive bond which it maintains with Israel. By saying that, I think, of course, of the actual community, but also and above all of the future community of 12 because we share this common faith in democracy.

One cannot but be convinced if one listens to the constantly open political discussions in Israel, to its free-wheeling television, not excluding the events during the war in Lebanon. The in-coming extension of the European community should not be seen as traumatized by Israel, but on the contrary, it should be seen as an enrichment. I certainly think of the economic problems to deal with, but above all of the political problems posed by the absence of diplomatic relations between Spain and Israel.

It wouldn't be admissible to appeal to the source of political cooperation in order to define the common positions with regard to Third World countries. Not all members entertain normal diplomatic relations with Israel. This is the reason why it appears very urgent that Spain establish such relations.

The World Jewish Congress devotes its celebration in Strasbourg to remembrance and reflections on democracy, human rights, and peace. This represents, I believe, the truth; the most ardent proof of the victory of Jewish humanism over the Nazi theories, and the victory of the victims over the executioners.

The Logic of Bitburg
Regards
June 5, 1985

By Marcel Lipmann

There are moments for emotion which are legitimate. And there are moments when indignation is very much justified.

The time has come to reflect upon and to analyze the pilgrimage of Reagan to Bitburg—which can be viewed as a scandal or a blunder. A scandal, certainly. But are there innocent blunders?

If one opts for analysis, it is necessary to accept the rules of this method. Analysis implies a total or global approach by introducing one party as a whole, and to bypass a partial perception. Furthermore, and perhaps foremost, it means to seek a logic behind the apparent incongruity of facts. Those who search and try to understand the "why" of the pilgrimage to Bitburg don't have a choice. They must reason in political terms with respect to a political gesture made by one of the most powerful political men of this world.

Reagan and The Talmud

One fact first: No one can seriously maintain that Reagan wanted to rehabilitate anti-Semitism. Because, in spite of the indecency of the pilgrimage, he has not forgotten the Jewish victims of Nazism. He has forgotten them so little that he allowed himself the luxury to invoke their scriptures. Didn't he declare at the cemetery of Bitburg:

"The Torah teaches us [notice the ineffable "us"] that it is only by suffering that the children of Israel have obtained three of the most precious treasures: the Torah, the Land of Israel, and Eternal Life." Here speaks a man who knows his classics.

In reality, for statesmen, the commemorations of the past are placed inevitably in a present-day perspective. They are functions of present-day preoccupations. Here is another proof in this respect. The war that tore apart the world between 1939 and 1945 interests Reagan much less than the Cold War that takes place today. And the pilgrimage to Bitburg is above all a maneuver in the Cold War, a gesture, an act of the Cold War. In fact, the silence of the President of the United States is as eloquent as his speeches. All his allusions to the Second World War, the battles, the tragedies and the sacrifices which it incurred, but not a single word about the part played by the Soviets in the victory over Nazism. Not a single one. Twenty million dead or 25 or 30, and not a word. Since the USSR is the present-day adversary, it is as an adversary that must be treated. Too bad for history.

Kohl "si", Brandt "no"

What about this pilgrimage? A political affair of today. Does one want additional proof? It can easily be found in the theme of the so-called "reconciliation" with the German people. For the past thirty years, the United States and the Federal Republic have been reconciled on the political, diplomatic, economic, strategic and tourist level — on all the possible levels. Well, what's the refrain of these songs in praise of the reconciliation of the two nations? It is as the *New York Times* succinctly defined them: "At Bitburg the bond of Kohl and Reagan was consolidated and with it the strategy of Star Wars." In fact, that is all that is behind it: that, and to repeat once more, the Cold War.

The armament politics of the White House, in particular the "Star Wars" project which has been widely challenged in Germany, is supported by the Christian Democrats. It is important to deliver to them the dividends of an investment and to reinforce the public judgment, not by reconciliation between the two people but by a political/military alliance between the two governments. That is the reason why at the same time Reagan identified himself with Kohl, he refused to meet with the anti-Nazi Willi Brandt, who is guilty of a very lukewarm attitude toward the foreign policy of the United States.

Viewed from this angle, the pilgrimage — or better, the undertaking — of Bitburg assumes a different significance. By affirming that there is no necessity for making a difference between the concentration camp inmates and the military — all of them innocent — and among the military between the SS and the others, Reagan wants to gain the support of the "average German" for his politics. For the "average German" and for his moral comfort, a dead soldier is by definition and by tradition a defender of the fatherland. And the rest — Nazism or anti-Nazism — that's but hollow ideology or low politics.

Is there, after all, a fundamental difference between the reaction of the "average German" of (very) average conscience, (very) average political awareness and the "average Frenchman," for instance? There isn't a village in France that does not have the monument to the dead on which are listed, classified by categories, the names of the victims of the war of 1914-1918, of the war of 1939-1945, and of the wars in Indochina or Algeria. The victims of a war of national defense, of a war in defense of democracy, or the fallen in the wars of colonial conquest — they are all considered to have "died for France."

The fields of Picardy, invaded by the Germans, and the rice fields of Indochina, invaded by the French, are all fields of honor fertilized by the average partiotism of which it is said that it does not ask many questions. There are certain differences between Hitler's war and the colonial wars. But, is there a deep, significant difference between the "average Frenchman" and the "average German" in their attitude toward their history?

Thank you, Mr. Reagan

Some concluding words. The speech given at the cemetery in Bitburg by the President of the United States has a didactic virtue which it would be wrong to overlook. It can serve to open eyes with respect to the meaning of the present Cold War. Confrontation between the superpowers? This can hardly be doubted. But seen from the side of the West—defense of freedom? How can one believe that in view of Reagan's rhetoric? "I am a Jew," he declared at Bitburg, "in a world still menaced by anti-Semitism; I am an Afghan, a prisoner of the Gulag, one of the boat people, a Laotian, a Cambodian, a Cuban, an Indian discriminated against by the Nicaraguan government." All those, President Reagan is. But in his immense heart that has room for so much compassion, he cannot find the smallest space for the dozens of thousands of martyrs assassinated by the extreme right in Guatemala, nor for the landless peasants in Brazil or elsewhere, neither for the oppressed blacks exploited and assassinated in South Africa. For this demonstration of the meaning which you attach to liberty and to human rights, thank you, Mr. Reagan.

(Translated from the French by George Asher.)

Chapter 24

Italy

Coming Back To Echterdingen
Bulletino De Milano
May 16, 1985

By Nedo Fiano

Lufthansa flight from Milan. The captain informs us that we have commenced our descent towards Stuttgart/Echterdingen Airport where we shall land in a few moments. "Passengers would please put on safety belts and refrain from smoking."

It is an announcement identical to many others. The voice of the hostess is sweet and sultry. A return to Echterdingen as a free man and with a 40-minute flight makes me jump back 40 years.

There I arrived on November 1944 with 500 other deportees from the camp of Stutthof/Danzig, after seven horrible days and nights in freight cars fit for livestock, across East and Southwest Germany with a modest ration of bread, a portion of margarine and a slice as long as a finger of synthetic salami. Death as a traveling companion.

During that transfer many among us died of hunger and thirst. Upon arrival at our destination, exhausted and filthy, we were obliged by the SS that accompanied us to carry the corpses of our companions all the way to the camp.

Today I look around me in this airport made of crystal, cement and aluminum, brightened by light, where a festive mass awaits the travelers upon their arrival. The musical background assists in embracing the city of Stuttgart. All the flags of Europe ruffling in the wind. I search, in vain, for a trace, even small, of that time long ago, anything, I don't know.

But this is a tranquil place, green, calm, where the war has the air of never having passed here. Is it possible that here were Stukas, Messerschmidts, Henkels, Dorniers, the spearhead of the Nazi war effort?

The posters of all dimensions, of all colors, of many nations, compete by offering cigarettes, hi-fi, cameras, whiskey, chocolate, trips and promises of a world of luxury, serenity, of love and beauty.

Where is the architect of this work? Why did he violate the airport of my memories and transform it into the City of "Balocchi" in Luna Park? Why this camouflage?

"But how is it that you know so well the name of this airport? Everyone simply calls it Stuttgart," asks with curiosity my traveling companion who, finally, I encounter at the airport exit. "I don't know. I must have read it somewhere," I answer.

I remember it was immense — in fact, this is the way I have described it for many years to my children — with the runways always bottled up with airplanes in arrival or awaiting departure that often we had to push on to the empty runways. We had no gloves and pieces of our poor hands often remained on the frozen structures of the airplanes. Then when the motors started and the propellers began to turn, there was an inferno of snow that entered violently into our eyes, noses, lungs and bones.

It is impossible to find something of that time long ago.

But I feel that I have already been here and that a part of me is still here. Maybe my youth.

My companion is a nobleman, Von Schmeling, originally from Berlin, who went to war at 17 years old, and returned — gravely injured — at 23.

"Were you also in the war?" he asks.

"Selbstverständlich!" I answer quickly.

Why should I talk to him about my deportation to Auschwitz, to Stutthof, to Buchenwald, and that two months of my deportation in Germany were spent here, just where we were talking?

These trees on the small hills, this sky, this sun, they were there then. And those three airplane hangars, maybe one — that one over there a little more run down — that's where we slept. . . Oh no, it is not possible, ours was destroyed by an Allied bombardment. I remember that during the nocturnal bombings that caused immense damage to the equipment and that lasted for more than an hour, I slept heavily, waking up in the morning as if nothing had happened.

I remember the airstrip where we worked (*"Schieben, schieben, schneller"!!*) and the hostile gray of the cement battered by the wind, snow, and by our sandals.

Day and night, non-stop, the airplanes returned from combat; the auxiliary forces placed the equipment on the ground. We were mutilated by hunger and our skin gray from the cold, almost dead, but no one noticed our existence. We were truly subhuman. Just objects.

I don't remember the difference between comrades. We were, by now, equals.

At the ticket office of the airport I feel I am part of a mass escape, with documents and false papers. I feel like a vigilante.

The clerk at the Lufthansa office looks at me with curiosity and asks, "Where did you learn to speak German so well?"

I look deep into her eyes but I don't know how to answer . . . how many things I could tell her: the memories (Cesare Terracina, the unforgettable Roman friend from Fossoli, of Auschwitz and of Stutthof, who I found dead in his bed after having made a cup of hot soup), the fear, the cold, the hunger . . .

I would like to say: "Leave work and come with me. I will tell you of my experiences. Come." Instead, I give her an enigmatic smile and repress my emotions.

In the beginning the Garrison at Echterdingen was made up of men from the Lufthansa. People, not angelic, but humane, who, very soon after, were replaced by the SS military.

Together with a prisoner from Hungary, I became an "official" singer with several advantages.

"Italian, sing Mama! Italian, sing O Sole Mio!"

And I then sang amidst smiling soldiers thinking of my mother in Venice.

Later I became part of a command that was in charge of burying dead soldiers in a forest near Stuttgart between the Black Forest and Swedish Alps.

We were six men and for two months we dug graves, two or three per week. It was hard work, but the prospect of finding bread as we passed by the small villages made the work seem less difficult. Upon re-entering the camp, we shared the booty we managed to hide.

I leave again for Frankfurt. The airplane has lifted off the ground.

"The captain welcomes you aboard and wishes you a good trip." From the window I see the small villages around Echterdingen, small houses with blue roofs, the streets, the bridges, the small piazzi, the trees. Probably just like the German aviators must have seen them in their time . . .

I passed by those villages many times during those days as a slave, pointed at by the golden-curled children that were by now fanatic Nazis.

The river still continues to flow, the birds still fly, the sun still shines like then.

I ask myself: What is left of me, of that deportee without hair, without hope? Maybe just my spirit, maybe.

The airplane has just about arrived in Frankfurt.

We are passing over a large stratus of clouds . . . I hear from afar, almost perceptible, the voice of Cesare over the murmur of jets. I call out, "Cesare, Cesare, do you hear me?"

The captain announces some news about our flight: altitude, velocity, pressure and temperature.

I gaze upon the passengers who are seated near me: their expressions are of those too young to remember, to know or want to know.

I hold on very dearly to the world that I remember. All of those phantoms.

Too bad the world forgets.

As Montherlant once said: "Men during their lifetime encounter indifference. It is not a vice: it is the bread that allows one to live."

Perhaps it is true.

(Translated from the Italian by Alesandro Giambelli.)

The Ingenuousness of Uncle Sam
Bulletino De Milano
May 16, 1985

(Ester Moscati and Mario Vigevani interviewed noted Italian author Primo Levi.)

"California is far away from Auschwitz," said Simone Veil concerning the U.S. President's visit to the cemetery at Bitburg. Why did Reagan not give any weight to the fifty SS officers buried there? Was it an act of "indifference," a vague "American" notion of what the significance of the Holocaust was as regards Europe, or maybe a lapse in the memory of the Head of State, the new ace of Washington-Bonn?

Q: What is your opinion of Reagan's visit to Bitburg?

A: As far as I am concerned, it was a very light gesture, an error from which Reagan could not retreat. I have just recently finished a trip to the U.S. to present my books, *The Periodic Table* and *If Not Now, When?*, and the Bitburg argument monopolized all of my encounters with all the correspondents of the world around the U.S. They were stupefied and scandalized. More than the administration in general, it was Reagan's image which was attached to this episode; he was seen as a pathetic character. On the cover of the *New Yorker* magazine, I saw this vignette: A Reagan who was senile and blank-faced, sitting in a chair reading a story of World War II while the book was upside-down. The visit to Bitburg was not a deliberate choice but a grave mistake in fate.

Q: If there had been a visit to the Wehrmacht cemetery, would it have been different?

A: Without a doubt. The soldiers at Wehrmacht were dedicated and desertion was just about impossible, and the same with insubordination. The SS, however, were not soldiers but professional exterminators.

Q: How do you judge the position of Kohl and his German government, who also knew the fact that at the cemetery at Bitburg there were SS?

A: I don't know how things came to pass exactly, but I say that Kohl made a very noble speech at Bergen-Belsen. From the American press I read that Bitburg is like a national, sacred burial ground where some soldiers from World War I are buried.

Q: The visit to Bergen-Belsen was arranged at the last moment in his program of visits, almost as if to repair the error of Bitburg. Was it an opportune choice?

A: The choice of Bergen-Belsen was an unhappy one and represented very little of the quality and quantity of the extermination. At Bergen-Belsen there were 50,000 inmates who died, the equivalent of two days of "work" in a concentration camp like Auschwitz. Many then died at Bergen-Belsen out of hunger and deprivation after having been transported there from other camps. More significant would have been a visit to Buchenwald.

Q: Was the political significance of the ceremony at Bitburg underlined? What do you think of these celebrations?

A: Celebrations always bore me, above all if they are aimed for political purposes. They would perhaps best be made in private, or in any event not by a head of state. In this case mistrust is certain, because celebrations serve to either make or destroy alliances.

Q: Reagan spoke about "turning a page of history" and of "mending old wounds."

A: Mending old wounds is possible, but without opening other wounds. This gesture has certainly revived the pain in many.

(*Translated from the Italian by Alesandro Giambelli.*)

Chapter 25

Sweden

Unable To Learn From History
April 30, 1985

His Excellency The Ambassador
of the United States of America
Strandvägen 101
115 27 Stockholm

Dear Sir:

The President of the United States has a lifelong record as a friend of the Jewish people. I do not only count his words, I count his deeds during the years of his presidency. No Jew shall ever forget this.

Asking Mr. Reagan to go to Bitburg, however, his German hosts are showing a complete lack of historical mind and political responsibility. Advising him to go, his aides in Washington have shown that they are unable to learn from history.

Let me use the words of Elie Wiesel and ask you to tell Mr. Reagan that Bitburg is not the place for the President of the United States — "your place is with the victims of the SS!"

Very truly yours,

Hans W. Levy
International Vice President,
B'nai B'rith International Council

Reagan in Bitburg
Goteborgsposten
April 30, 1985

Two hundred and fifty-seven of the 435 Congressmen of the United States Senate have made, in a letter to West German Chancellor Kohl, an appeal that he withdraw his invitation to President Reagan to visit the military cemetery in Bitburg. This shows how deeply the planned visit has stirred up the American opposition.

But the positions seem to be locked. Chancellor Kohl could have saved President Reagan from the awkward situation in which he's put himself with the assistance of unskilled advisors. But in West Germany that would have been seen as giving in to hostile foreign opinion and Kohl wants to avoid that, whatever the price.

SS Soldiers Honored

An opinion poll has shown the terrifying fact that 72% of the West German people think it's right that the visit to Bitburg should take place. The fact that the President of the U.S.A. then also will honor the SS men that are buried in the cemetery is something that the West Germans obviously find appropriate.

The memory of the horror in the concentration camps and the genocide carried out by SS forces on the order of the Hitler regime has been recently recalled. One of the most appalling crimes against humanity in history is still of a time not long past and people who survived the Holocaust are still alive. The German Federal Republic can't expect the rest of the world to have forgotten the evil deeds and think it right that the political leaders of the U.S.A. and West Germany officially honor fallen SS men in connection with the 40-year commemoration of the end of the Second World War.

The incredibly clumsy and insensitive actions of Washington as Reagan visits West Germany bears a large part of the responsibility for how the program has been formed. It will include both a long visit to the infamous concentration camp in Bergen-Belsen and a short visit to the graveyard in Bitburg.

The Visit Cancelled

The mayor of Bitburg has established the fact that the citizens of the town are embittered by the long and exhaustive protests against the cemetery visit. Local authorities will have a meeting this week to decide whether President Reagan and Chancellor Kohl are welcome, or if the visit should be cancelled.

Such an intervention would perhaps be welcomed by the parties involved, although what's happened can't be undone. The strong relationship between the U.S. A. and its most faithful ally in Western Europe has weakened. Last Thursday the Bundestag in Bonn discussed a proposal from the Green party suggesting that the visit to the cemetery be cancelled but there was no response. Not only the governing parties but also the Social Democratic opposition voted down the proposal. The Social Democrats welcomed the graveyard visit as Reagan will then "honor the dead German soldiers who were abused by a criminal government in an offensive war." But they disagreed with the choice of Bitburg.

The fact that a big West German magazine in a commentary writes that the wave of protests in the U.S.A. is proof of the Jewish influence over large TV-companies and the *New York Times* is an embarrassing confirmation that some Germans still don't realize what the protests are all about.

Copyright © 1985 Goteborgsposten. Reprinted with permission.

(Translated by Greta Johannsen.)

Nothing Turned Out The Way They Had Planned
Svenska Dagbladet
May 8, 1985

Nothing really turned out the way they thought it would — the brevity and the embarrassment which characterized the ceremonies in Bitburg and Bergen-Belsen showed that both Reagan and Kohl had understood that there was no longer a question of realizing the original plan.

The event in effect turned out to be simply a face-saving affair. But Bitburg will be remembered as a landmark diplomatic mission, in the most faithful of United States allies, which strangely enough turned out to be President Reagan's most controversial trip abroad so far. In the former concentration camp as well as in the military graveyard, the American President acted defensively: Reagan was forced to correct, reverse, almost excuse himself. Looking a bit perplexed, Chancellor Kohl stayed in the background.

Not until the last day, in Hambach Castle in front of about 10,000 enthusiastic West German young people, did Reagan become his usual winning and relaxed self and succeed in drawing attention to what was meant to be the theme of the whole trip — the future.

Kohl Driving

Helmut Kohl was the driving force behind what turned out to be the partial failure of a diplomatic mission. He insisted on making the Western world's top economic meeting, and Reagan and the commemoration of May 8, 1945, coincide, and has consequently turned 1985 into something which may be called a

West German "year of destiny." From the very beginning he took care of the formulation of the program from *Kanzleramt,* excluding the foreign ministry, with the experts who could have brought more finesse to it, if for no other reason, because it's their job.

It was also Kohl who persuaded Reagan that 65% of the West Germans of today were born after 1945 and have no memories of the year that continues to stigmatize German history. But as no collective guilt can exist, attention must eventually be drawn from the past towards the future. This new Germany, said Kohl, needs more self-confidence and optimism, it needs appreciation from its allies, not least from the U.S.A.

Helmut Kohl, born in 1930, is the first West German Chancellor who was not an adult during the war and he has often spoken of "the grace of the late birth." But in this matter he has sometimes proved to have difficulties separating the private man's personal, and the political leader's historical responsibilities.

During his visit to Israel, he irritated his hosts by establishing the fact that he was only 15 years old by the end of the war and didn't want to be reminded over and over again of a war in which he did not participate; he has hurt and irritated his Polish neighbors by appearing as the main speaker at the exiled Schlesian Peoples Day in Hanover last June, a decision that also added fuel to the fire of Moscow's absurd campaign against "revanchism" in Bonn. And last summer he contributed to the torpedoeing of Erich Honnecker's planned visit by explaining that he wanted to discuss with his East German guest ecology instead of historical and political stability problems that are a product of the German past.

But in the middle of all this ambivalence and impatience there is something representative. Here is something which is about more than Kohl personally and which is affirmed by a majority of the West German people of today: they are tired of being continuously confronted with the responsibility of the war, tired of all unspoken reservations of the world community, tired of being conditionally accepted as a state in the circle of other democratic states within the Western alliance. The new Germany wants to look forward instead of backward. This was the kind of absolution that Kohl had hoped to attain through Reagan's visit.

The visit to the war cemetery in Bitburg was therefore intended to play the same role as when Willi Brandt knelt down in the ghetto of Warsaw. But Helmut Kohl, who isn't Willi Brandt, wanted too much at once and besides, he overdid it by believing that a string of complicated knots could be untied by a single stroke of the gordian sword.

Furthermore Kohl — as well as Reagan — has shown an astonishing lack of historical insight and ability to comprehend the feelings of those who have every reason not to forget anything of the past.

The choice of symbol, Bitburg, was a gross mistake; the decision to honor also the victims of Nazism by visiting Bergen-Belsen worked as a compensation and an attempt to create a "balance" that does not exist and cannot exist. These things together created the final impression that, after all, there is very little learned from the history which they believed had taught them enough.

Helmut Kohl's "appeasement" toward the West is not going to become historical—like Willi Brandt's kneeling down in the ghetto of Warsaw. Kohl's understandable and sympathetic intention was supported by Reagan, who would have gladly contributed in order to strength Western alliances and to work against anti-Americanism in West Germany by instilling more self-confidence in the West German people and to show that the world likes them too. But the plan hasn't really succeeded: the West Germans will have to continue to live with the frustrations and contradictions risen from a history that is very alive and present.

(Translated by Greta Johannsen.)

The Swedish Press On Bitburg
Special Contribution

By Hans W. Levy

The first reaction in the press came on April 14. *Expressen,* which is the paper that has the largest circulation—a liberal afternoon paper with a solid pro-Jewish record, edited in the capital Stockholm and printed in different places in the country—had a short article "Reagan changes his mine—visits Dachau" that brings the whole story from the beginning. It is dated "New York" and other papers brought the same story.

The *Svenska Dagbladet (SvD),* the capital's second largest morning paper, read by liberal-conservative readers throughout the country and always picturing Jews and Israel in a sensitive sense, brought the same day the story seen from the horizon of the Jewish leadership in Frankfurt and Berlin. On April 18 the paper had an editorial on the case.

Not before April 21 *Göteborgs Posten,* the largest provincial paper (300,000 ex.), a liberal and strongly pro-Jewish and pro-Israel morning paper, brought the story in three columns over the whole page in three articles, of which the first was concentrating upon Elie Wiesel's speech to the President of the United States, the second was dated "Bonn" and the third "Tel Aviv".

Here I wish to add that one of the five persons Elie Wiesel was allowed to bring to the White House was his good friend Per Ahlmark, poet and journalist, former Vice Prime Minister in the Swedish Government, a gentile and an outstanding friend of Israel.

During the following days, the *Svenska Dagbladet* brought articles on Bitburg on April 26, 30, and on May 4, 6 and 8. On May 12 (a Sunday) there was a whole page plus 1 column on the Waffen-SS and on April 27 a biting cartoon (by Lurie). The *Göteborgs Posten* printed an editorial on April 30 and articles on April 27 and May 3, 5 (2 articles), 6.

I have not checked all Swedish papers, but in the above mentioned there has not been any news of a similar kind between the Austrian affair Frischenschläger/ Reder in January and the Bitburg affair in April.

I cannot tell you what the reaction has been of the general public. The people I have spoken to generally did not even know the word Bitburg. Those papers which always are interested in Jewish affairs gave Bitburg quite a good coverage, as you can see from my previous lines, and there was a follow-up article in both papers telling that the SS veterans praised Reagan.

I cannot find that we here in Sweden have learned any lessons from Bitburg. Please forgive me that I picked just the newspapers that are typical for the majority of our press. I possibly should add that there is no directly anti-Jewish press in this country, though the largest circulated morning paper in the country, the *Dagens Nyheter,* of Stockholm, ironically enough owned by Jews, often opens its pages to marxist so-called anti-Zionist authors; the general line of the paper is, however, liberal and not anti-Israel. The largest paper of the Labour (Social Democratic Party, that is in government) is *Aftonbladet* (evening paper) and *Arbette* (morning paper). Both have an ambivalent view on Israel and there is always a certain animosity. They are, however, not anti-Jewish and gave the Bitburg case about the same coverage as the papers I mentioned.

Let it finally be said, that I could not find any paper that supported the decision of your president. I myself have written a letter to your Embassy in Stockholm, of which I also enclose a copy.

(Hans W. Levy is the International Vice President of B'nat B'rith International Council.)

Chapter 26

Argentina

Big Stir About Reagan's Visit To Germany
Semanario Israelita
April 23, 1985

By W. W. F.

At the beginning of May, President Ronald Reagan will come to Bonn for the economic summit meeting of seven industrial nations. During his stay in the Federal Republic of Germany he will also bestow a wreath at the war cemetery at Bitburg, where the members of the Wehrmacht, who died in the Battle of the Ardennes, are buried.

Two factors were decisive for the polemic. First, the fact that these German soldiers were responsible for the deaths of thousands of North American GIs (there also were reports from Moscow about the shootings of U.S. war prisoners). And supposedly not only members of the Wehrmacht but SS men as well are buried in Bitburg. This fact led to vehement protests of U.S. war veterans, whose representatives spoke against honoring German soldiers. Second, was the strange declaration of President Reagan against the proposed visit to a former concentration camp on German soil. At this point there was massive protest by Jewish organizations about Reagan's position.

The White House couldn't ignore the arguments and Reagan himself felt forced to plan a visit to a former concentration camp in the Federal Republic.

As he said, in Chancellor Kohl's state visit agenda there had been explicitly planned a memorial celebration at a former concentration camp and also a visit to a synagogue had been mentioned as a possibility.

The fact that the U.S. President's trip coincided with the 40th anniversary of Nazi Germany's downfall had logically created a more tense climate than usual for the surroundings of a state visit. Because of this, Reagan's unfortunate statements — not the first verbal lapses of the President — were scrutinized more closely and the indignation of Jewish organizations was absolutely justified.

There are enough efforts going on to play down what happened under the Nazi regime, so there is no need for Reagan's attempt to mitigate the terrible incidents of this era.

According to him, "only a few persons from this epoch are still alive and remember the war." This is rude calumny of the memory of those who were killed by Hitler's hangmen. Furthermore, his suggestion that the time had come to "alleviate the guilt feelings forced upon the Germans" is completely unrealistic. As German politicans said then, there was a collective shame about the disaster that Hitler caused in the name of Germany and that no one could escape the historical responsibility of one's culture — neither for the good, nor for the bad.

The last thing we Jews should do is to acquire generalizations, because we have known from our own experience what it meant when "the Jews" allegedly carried the guilt for everything. Not "the Germans," but simply Germans were the ones who spread horror and cruelty over the civilized world and who started the Second World War.

But at the same time there had been different, decent Germans, who cannot be included into a general judgement. Because of that forgiveness is something everyone has to determine for themselves; but to forget, never!

(*Semanario Israelita* is the leading Jewish newspaper in Argentina.)

(*Translated from the German by Renate Steinchen*)

No Reason For Nostalgia:
Why Then The Nostalgia-Hurly-Burly?
Semanario Israelita
May 6, 1985

By Werner Kroll

Forty years ago the Third Reich capitulated. The worst gang of murderers in world history — that had succeeded in nestling in on a civilized nation and in spreading fire, death and unspeakable horror from the heart of Europe to all mankind — had lost its game. A good fifty million people had perished. About half the victims of this insane act of world incendiarism were unarmed civilians. To an end came twelve years of this gang's rule of terror and five years, seven months and eight days of World War.

The unforgettable Kurt Tucholsky had already at the beginning of the war described [Hitler's gang] so well in verse:

"There lives a trio of the future race,
A madman, a cripple and a sadist.
And they believe there is a need in this world
That just their dung survives as a race."

One year later, during his Swedish exile, Tucholsky chose to take his own life, probably foreseeing the inevitable course of disaster.

Today we must shiver at the thought that the majority did not believe him, that the suicide of this poet — one of the great contemporary spirits of the German language — was not meant to be a beacon calling for resistance, that mankind didn't condemn this "trio of the future race," did not stick up to them, when it was still possible.

But to look at it more closely and to say it more drastically, all that is history today, most bitter history, is actually not worth much more than last year's snow. Aside from this fact, the meaning of commemorative ceremonies with a lot of printer's ink and flashbacks can only be a single one: to learn a lesson from the past, but also to act accordingly. But there actually was not very much talk about this, at least not as a priority, as there was other talk on the occasion of this fortieth anniversary.

Among the 25 million dead civilians there were six million Jews who were assassinated in the gas chambers by Nazi-inhumans — calculated murder, cold-blooded slaughter; human beings were flayed in a way still inconceivable today. How could human beings treat other human beings like this? But probably this fact itself contains the explanation, at least partly, for what had happened: the Nazi-inhumanity regime realized acts which went beyond the most criminal fantasies as they were imaginable in most extreme cases then.

But this is only one part of the truth, even though an important one. The other part reaches into the present and was not a topic of the many speeches being held on the occasion of the 40th Anniversary of the Third Reich's capitulation. This other part of the truth was also not a topic of the numerous commentaries, at least not the ones which found a worldwide echo: the undeniable fact that the so-called Free World did not do everything to save human beings—Jews in most cases but also many other victims of inhumanitarianism—from the claws of killers, or to say the least, they did not help to the degree still possible then.

There had been more such possibilities than one is ready to admit today. Not only thousands of Germans and Christians of other nations—the small and helpless Denmark and singular personalities as the Swedish diplomat Raul Wallenberg who risked their lives in order to help the persecuted. These mostly unsung heroes showed that help was possible even under the Regime of Terror.

But the war opponents of the Third Reich failed then. They stood with their rifles aimed only at the ground—as the Soviets did at Warsaw when the ghetto-uprising was raging, as the British did when they blocked the exchange offer for one million Jews, as the North Americans and many other free nations did when they refused to take any more Jewish refugees and sent back their ships—they all passively observed as the murderers committed their crimes.

There was no talk about any of this and so these celebrations essentially, at least in my mind, don't mean anything except self-deception, these speeches nothing but empty phrases. In this respect Chancellor Helmut Kohl made a laudable and noticeable exception when in Bergen-Belsen he at least recognized that these incidents will forever impose a national disgrace and a historical responsibility on the Germanies.

It seems to me that the Jewish speakers—with a few exceptions—also avoided these subjects and these facts, and if this happened unconsciously it is even worse. What does it mean, this big stir about President Reagan's visit to the war cemetery at Bitburg? Is it only because some Waffen SS members are buried there?

Instead, it should be emphasized that nobody can sneak out of this historical responsibility and disgrace with just some beautiful words, a few tears and floral bouquets. None of today's representatives of these nations, which didn't commit murder themselves but didn't prevent it when that was still possible, may sneak out of their responsibility either. What does it matter, or to whom does it matter, today when North American Catholic bishops mock the bestowing of a wreath without adding a *mea culpa* concerning their own silence of the past?

On the other hand, what sense does it make to put moral pressure on a man like Reagan, to whom the Jewish people owe much gratitude for his marvelous position towards the distressed state of Israel even if one doesn't view the Bitburg celebration as a fortunate event and also has reservations against other aspects of Reagan's policy?

Why actually this whole hurly-burly about the 40th Anniversary of the Inhumanity-Regime's downfall? What difference does the number 40 make to all the previous anniversaries of this event? Who is served by this big show—do any of the victims live again because of it? What sense does it make to discuss whether the event should either be celebrated as the day of a Criminal Regime's surrender or as a day of liberation? What sense do the symbols of today's friendship and mutual ideas of former war enemies make — a fact that has been established for years beyond any doubt?

Admonition, symbol and lesson for the young generation? If it wasn't so sad one would have to laugh about this kind of silliness, about so much naivete and self-deception. Does anybody seriously believe that with this kind of solemn presentation, surrounded by scandal, one could atone for decades of neglect, where the truth was concealed or taught half-heartedly at best? Truth, which does not only include the crimes of murderers but also the failure of those who today so loudly and complacently state their disgust against things that they watched without interference?

Shouldn't the time have already arrived for an honest *mea culpa,* for the confession to be guilty by neglect for those most incredible crimes and in this way teach the young, and not only the Germans, never to be passive again when human rights are concerned, wherever they are trampled or threatened. Everything else is hypocrisy since no one can tell us or the young generations that the Nazis' acts of horror were only revealed on May 8th, 1945, when this regime surrendered.

Victory and peace nostalgia? There is no reason for it — and much less if one has to strike the balance with consternation that not only since the 8th of May, 1945 has there not been one day of peace in this world but also not even one day when human rights were not severely violated somewhere in the world; there has, also, not been a single day when there was no silence where active resistance was needed and could have helped. The prisoners of Zion in the Soviet Union — three quarters of a million Soviet Jews who want to travel abroad and to whom this right is violently denied; the children who are sent into death by the crazy Ayatollah Khomeini in the Gulf War against Iraq; the victims of cruel tyrants in Asia and Africa, the tyrannies that flay and bloodily oppress whole people in a good two-thirds of the UN-member-nations — is this the peace, is this the liberation to be celebrated? Impotence and silence — are these the lessons to learn from those terrible events, or is the world still paralysed by the evil spirit of those inhumanitarians who, on April 30th, 1945 (much too late!) committed suicide and in this way evaded worldly justice?

These are the anxious questions that have to move and worry us, because the nicest and even best intended speeches will bring no one back to life, while from the spiritual hell that still outlasts the 8th of May, 1945 only insights and lessons can lead into a better future. Better, for the victors as well as for the losers of that time, for Jews, Christians, Muslims and for everyone who thinks differently, for man and all of mankind!

(Translated from the German by Renate Steinchen)

The "Terrible Mentality of Counter-Charging"
Semanario Israelita
May 11, 1985

By Peter Gorlinsky

In the last session before the 40th anniversary of the May 8th surrender, the Bundestag in Bonn passed a law that settled the long and rather painful discussion about a threat of punishment against the so-called Auschwitz-lie. It so happened — not without the guilty participation of responsible politicians — that this legislative measure coincided with the continuing public discussion in the Federal Republic and elsewhere, especially in the USA and Israel, about President Reagan's agenda for his state visit to West Germany. The embarrassments, which had to be noted in this context, became even more embarrassing in this way. For in the eyes of not just a few contemporaries the foul compromise of the Bonn coalition to change the legislation would probably also give an oppressive explanation for the question, why Reagan's visit to a concentration camp memorial was only put on his itinerary under massive public protest. At first it was planned that the President should exclusively visit a German war cemetery, where also are buried half a hundred former members of the Waffen SS.

Compromise may indeed be an essential element in democracy, but there are problems that call for a crystal clear solution, which, in other words, can't be done justice by compromises. A defendant has either to be sentenced or acquitted. He cannot be imprisoned one day and released on the next. But the coalition parties have agreed on a foul compromise of just that kind. This happens if one tries to find a common denominator for serious supporters of an unequivocal punishableness denying the Nazis' murderous acts on one hand and determined opponents of this intention on the other.

Outside the coalition this trade-off deal is rejected unanimously — as the vehement debate in the Bundestag has demonstrated — and even within the CDU/CSU/FDP it is supported only with distinct uneasiness. The representatives of Jews in Germany have explained plainly that they prefer no law at all to this one. And they are shocked by this "terrible mentality of counter-charging" that equates the Nazis' acts of murder with the crimes against the refugees — even though this concerns facts that have to be judged differently in historical and moral respects, although both sides are highly reprehensible. Besides this, important legal shortcomings adhere to this foul compromise: so, in the future the denial of Nazi crimes can be officially prosecuted, but this only has to happen when a "public interest" is affirmed. But experience teaches that one should be prepared for surprises with lawyers, depending on their ideological convictions.

On his visit to the concentration camp Bergen-Belsen a few weeks ago, Chancellor Helmut Kohl declared that the Germans had understood the lessons of history and that they stood up to their historical liability. If this is true, the fight against the Auschwitz-lie cannot be followed up with inadequate means which also raise the suspicion that the systematic genocide should be played down in legislation. The members of the Bundestag had to come to a most difficult decision that will, according to the chancellor, ". . . last through history." The ratification of the bill about the Auschwitz-lie by the government coalition may do everything else but last through history!

Of course, Nazi terror can't be set off against Stalinist terror. But this shouldn't keep one from remembering the Stalinist terror in all its abomination; as in the examples of the concentration camps Buchenwald near Weimar and Sachsenhausen near Oranienburg on what is now East German territory. Buchenwald was liberated on the 11th of April, 1945 by U.S. troops. Only three months later Russian occupation forces moved into Thuringia. Sachsenhausen was liberated on April 22nd, 1945 by Red army troops. But the history of the two camps wasn't over at all. In August 1945 Buchenwald and Sachsenhausen were operative again — this time as "special camps" of the NKVD/MVD, i.e., the Soviet security agencies, which were also responsible for the "Gulag Archipelago" in Siberia then. Once again, political prisoners were kept here — this time for four and a half years.

They were by no means only Nazi-followers, nominal party-comrades, who were classified as "potentially dangerous Germans" in the sense of the then-valid de-Nazification regulations; "potential class-enemies," industrialists, landowners or so-called squires, members of the bourgeois intelligentsia, former war-prisoners from British and American camps, who the Russians found suspicious as "spies," and finally oppositional Social Democrats, bourgeois liberals and Christians — they all were interned and kept for years without any legal proceedings. They were not murdered as in the times of the SS, but NKVD/MVD agents let them die of starvation and other camp diseases.

Whoever honors the memory of those who died under the sign of the swastika in Buchenwald and Sachsenhausen cannot remain silent about the victims under the sign of the Red Star, if he wants to be credible. Humanity cannot be divided.

(Translated from the German by Renate Steinchen)

Chapter 27

The Soviet Union

Before Bitburg

Reagan Honors Killers of U.S. Soldiers, Says Soviet Party Newspaper
Pravda
April 16, 1985

By Yuriy Zhukov

It is reported from Washington that the itinerary of President R. Reagan's trip to Europe in early May has now been worked out. The itinerary, in particular, envisages the following: 5 May, 1000, departure from Bonn; 1050, arrival in Bitburg; wreath-laying ceremony at German military cemetery; church service at the base; picnic with American servicemen from the base taking part; speeches by Kohl and Reagan; joint military ceremony.

Thus, the U.S. President has nevertheless decided, despite storms of protest from American and West European war veterans, to honor on the eve of victory day the memory of Nazi soldiers, including SS men who, as the American television company CBS has reported, "took part in massacres of Americans" during the Wehrmacht's Ardennes offensive in 1944. (As is well known, 77,000 American soldiers died during those battles and the American troops found themselves in a critical situation; only the Soviet offensive quickly launched in the east at Churchill's request saved the Anglo-American allies from catastrophe.)

Washington is very clumsily attempting to justify the President's political gesture, which is viewed by war veterans in the United States and other countries which were members of the anti-fascist coalition as an insult to the memory of the tens of millions who died in the struggle against the fascist aggressors. The world public's indignation was intensified by the fact that the President has simultaneously refused to pay homage to the memory of the inmates of Hitler's Dachau concentration camp, since the proposed visit there would not have been to the FRG government's liking.

How then is one to explain such astonishing decisions by the U.S. President?

(Yuriy Zhukov is the most authoritative political commentator for Pravda, *the Communist Party's official newspaper.)*

"Blasphemy and Mockery"
Pravda
April 14, 1985

The White House has announced the itinerary of U.S. President R. Reagan's trip to the FRG, planned for May this year. Many people believed that he would take advantage of the opportunity to mark the 40th anniversary of the rout of fascism and honor the memory of those who died in the struggle against the Nazi plague. In particular, it was initially supposed that the President would visit the former concentration camp in Dachau near Munich, where 70,000 prisoners were killed and tortured by the fascist fanatics, but the President refused to visit Dachau. He stated: "Why stir up memories of the past?" In West Germany, he said, "None of those who . . . once took part in the war survives." So very different stops appeared on his itinerary. Instead of Dachau, there is a German military cemetery in Bitburg, where many Hitlerite troops are buried. A wreath is to be laid on their grave. Reagan will be accompanied on his visit by Chancellor Kohl, who is reported to have suggested the "change of itinerary" to the President. Kohl of all people should know that leftover [nedobityy] Nazis are not only alive but are also vigorously preaching fascism and revanchism in the FRG.

This decision has caused a storm of indignation in the United States. "Even the very memory of the victims of Nazism is being sacrificed to political considerations," *The Washington Post* wrote. "The President's decision is incredible," one veteran declared. "He is siding with those who wanted Hitler to win."

The American press reports that there are no graves of American soldiers at the cemetery in Bitburg. A group to prepare the President's visit has visited there twice and certainly must know that, among the other Hitlerites, it contains the remains of soldiers from SS subunits, some of whom took part in the mass killing of American prisoners during the Ardennes operation, which began with a tank attack from the Bitburg bridgehead. In Malmadi, near Bitburg, they tied up 84 captive American soldiers and shot them.

Some 77,000 Americans died during the Ardennes operation by Hitler's Wehrmacht, but Reagan is not planning to visit his compatriots' graves.

What is the explanation of this decision? It transpires that what will be marked on 5 May, the day of the visit to the cemetery in Bitburg, is not the 40th anniversary of the rout of fascism but the 30th anniversary of the FRG's entry into NATO. What is more, next year a new U.S. cruise missile base will open in Bitburg, which is why the White House is reluctant to "stir up the past" and has decided on this blasphemy. This bow by Reagan to the "Third Reich" cannot be regarded other than as a mockery of the memory of the millions who died at the hands of the fascists, both Americans and citizens of the other countries in the anti-Hitler coalition.

Ronald Reagan Paying Tribute To The Third Reich
TASS
April 30, 1985

By Yuriy Kornilov

Two reports from Washington simultaneously came off the teleprinters. The first one says that according to a spokesman of the White House, the President of the United States has no intention of altering the programme of his ten-day trip to Europe which includes the visit to the Nazi military cemetery in Bitburg, the FRG. The second report says that an American veteran of the past war, former commander of a company, J. Glickman, who was wounded in the Ardennes over 40 years ago, said that unless the programme of the President's trip starting April 30 is changed, he will return to the government the Purple Heart Order, a silver medal and other military awards with which he had been decorated for his part in the battles against fascists; the awards for which he paid with his blood.

The White House statement was welcomed perhaps only in Bonn and by the revanchist "Land associations" on the banks of the Rhine while the indignation of the American war veteran is shared by thousands, hundreds of thousands of people.

Now that the White House is faced with the mounting waves of indignation and protests, the Washington and Bonn sponsors of "Operation Bitburg" are maneuvering in every way, are trying to put a good face on the matter by means of propaganda gimmicks, moreover, to cover up an unsavoury political gamble. At first they were making assurances that they could not discern the signs on snow-bound tombs in Bitburg. But the snow has long since melted. However, the FRG authorities, the Bitburg burgomaster, showing surprising "lack of information," are swearing that they do not have "detailed data" as to who is buried at the cemetery. Then we shall take the trouble to remind to those gentlemen some facts that have already been published by the international press.

Buried in Bitburg is a certain Otto Franz Bengel, a sergeant of the Nazi troops, who had been presented by Hitler with an Iron Cross for the killing of ten American soldiers. Buried there is also Eugen Schüler, a member of the secret Nazi police from whose ranks Gestapo men and wardens of concentration camps were selected. Buried there are SS men who fought at the Ardennes and who were executing American prisoners of war in Malmedy, Belgium, punitive forces from the Second SS Armoured Division — butchers of Oradour, the French village, where nearly one thousand people, including women and children, were shot to death or burned alive. It is at those tombs that the American President is going to place wreaths.

In an effort to dampen the indignation, the White House talks about the "act of reconciliation" with which, according to Reagan , the 40th anniversary of the victory over fascism should be marked, rehashing the postulate that the Hitler soldiers buried at Bitburg were, allegedly, "victims of nazism" themselves. In this connection it would not be amiss to ask with whom this reconciliation should be? Should it be the reconciliation with aggressors and murderers who drenched Europe with blood, with inventors of gas chambers, creators of Dachau and other death camps in which hundreds of thousands of people were exterminated? By the way, the President of the United States refused to visit Dachau saying that he has no wish to reopen old wounds, as if his bowing to the tombs of fascists will not reopen the wounds of millions of fighters against nazism.

The "act of reconciliation" Washington-style looks very strange indeed. It looks not so much as reconciliation but as exoneration of nazism, the insult to the memory of those who gave their lives in the struggle against brown plague, as the French L'Humanite writes with full ground today. As to cynical attempts to exonerate fascist butchers as "victims of nazism," this is an old trite gimmick. Back at the trial at Nuremberg the Nazi war criminals, seeking to avoid the retribution they deserved, attempted to assert that they were only "fulfilling the Führer's orders." The American prosecutor, just as the prosecutors of other Allied powers, members of the anti-Hitler coalition, refuted the subterfuges of the butchers.

About half a century ago Hitlerite brasshats, many of whom are buried at Bitburg, launched their aggression. It is well known how that aggression ended. It is no secret, however, that far from everybody learning the lessons of history, mad Hitlerite ideas of world supremacy are now harboured by certain circles in the West who regard force as all but the sole "argument" of their foreign policy. It is a grim and alarming symbol that a base of the U.S. Air Force is situated close to the Bitburg cemetery where the chief of the White House is heading. It is precisely there that one of the launchpads is situated with the use of which those who are now striving to recarve the political map of the world intend to threaten sovereign countries and peoples with first-strike weapons. Are not the tributes to Nazis whose tombs are shadowed by U.S. nuclear missiles a direct encouragement to those circles and forces in the FRG who are pining for the Nazi past and are still dreaming of altering history?

Sacrilege is the only way to describe the tribute of the President of the United States to the "Third Reich."

(Yuriy Kornilov is the leading analyst of political affairs for TASS [Telegraphic Agency of the Soviet Union].)

After Bitburg

At Odds With History
Izvestiya
May 11, 1985

By Valentin Falin

That is what lay behind the apparently unremarkable phrase of the political declaration on the 40th anniversary of the capitalist countries at their Bonn meeting: 'The end of the war meant at the same time a new start.'" That was what was woven into the wreath which R. Reagan placed on the tombs of Hitler's warriors and SS members. As if those Bitburg flowers would not produce bitter—oh, so bitter—fruit for the whole world!

Essentially the Bonn declaration and the blasphemous "act of conciliation" over the ashes of the Nazis represent an attempt to rehabilitate German imperialism and militarism for all to hear and at the same time to retroactively whitewash the U.S. compact with it. "It was 40 years ago that our U.S.-West German friendship flowered on the ruins," the U.S. President said. He forgot to specify that it flowered on the ruins of the anti-Hitler alliance, which had "made the victory possible and undoubted for the Allied nations," as the Crimean Conference in Yalta statement said. It flowered on the soil of the betrayal of the behests of the anti-fascist struggle. It was in that corrupt soil that flowers were grown for Bitburg. In the past, Washington indulged its vices quietly, but the present head of the administration has an insuperable attraction for spectacle and scandal.

Just think about the sequence of R. Reagan's arguments: It is time "40 years later to put an end to the fireworks and victory celebrations." It is time to pay tribute to "the miracle thanks to which a 40-year period of peace ensued, a 40-year period of the existence of a union in which the countries of the axis and the countries of the alliance are taking part together in summer conferences...." He is praising the "miracle" of treachery.

Until now the peoples believed that liberation and peace had been brought to them by the defeat of fascism and the forces of aggression. The President demands that they believe that people are indebted to the compact between U.S. and German imperialism for their four peaceful decades.

He finds no need for justification. On the contrary, to refuse to honor the ashes of the Hitlerites would be to offend their West German friends and allies; to insult those who fought against the Bolsheviks during the war and who are ready to continue to fight them at the first call—that is what you hear from R. Reagan, G. Schultz, H. Kohl, and A. Dregger. Of course, friends and fighters against the "Marxists" and the Soviet army, especially fighters in uniform, must in no circumstances be insulted. Insulting the memory of the millions of victims of Hitler's aggression and terror, insulting the feelings of tens and hundreds of millions of people, and making a mockery of the most sacred oaths taken by the peoples in the struggle against fascism — you can have as much of that as you like, because for Reagan and company anti-fascists are strangers.

"After 40 years. . ." The White House chief is autocratically dealing with international law and establishing his own statute of limitations on the crimes against the world and mankind. No, not for the crimes of individual Hitlerite stooges. The United States long ago handed indulgences to all the fanatics useful and necessary to it. Back in 1945-46, they were transferred across the ocean in the thousands — all the Barbies, Mengeles, Rudolfs, and Raufs were reliably shielded and generously cared for.

The President's nature is eager for the mass remission of the sins of the entire Hitler reich. "We do not recognize collective guilt," he says, writing history to suit his own taste. There is no collective guilt, nor were there the criminal Nazi party, Gestapo, SS and stormtrooper detachments, Hitler's general staff, or other Nazi institutions and organizations, nor were there extermination camps or criminal German monopolies. The criminal regime was not so much criminal as eccentric. Indeed, what were we actually fighting in the world war? So far there is no answer. The ground is still being prepared for it. You need to be utterly depraved to seek a common denominator with German imperialism and the FRG and to invent a common enemy.

Let's concede that Washington is bursting with hegemonism and is afloat on a sea of militarism. What then, motivates Bonn? It is reported that the iniuative in honoring Hitler's warriors came from H. Kohl. He must have realized he was putting his best friend in a difficult position, but his ambitions still tipped the scales. He was so anxious to inherit only the profits from the past and renounce the debts. What a fine life it would be if it were the role that "real Germans" would teach their neighbors through evil and the latter humbly admonish the "real Germans" through good. Another motive was fear: would the United States not treat the FRG as it treated its allies in the anti-Hitler coalition? Exploit them and leave them exposed while itself taking cover behind a "strategic shield," and so much for high-flown Atlanticism? Nothing links people more strongly than a jointly perpetrated act of baseness. To all appearances, Bitburg was to be the Rubicon beyond which there would be no going back.

Victory day was the pretext not only for grateful remembrance of those who gave their lives for a just cause and for festive celebrations. Victory day is also a bequest to safeguard peace, to protect it against the intrigues of aggressors old and new and against attempts to "improve" that peace for themselves. Victory day is a day for considering the reasons for the tragedy which befell the peoples, a day when people draw lessons from the past. Broadly speaking, we can say that if you want to understand how World War II began, you should take a closer look at what present-day Washington is doing in various parts of the world, at how it is turning the past inside out, distorting the present, and undermining the future. We shall not forget that the revision of the results of the war begins with the revision of its sources, its outcome, the real contribution made by states and peoples to victory over the aggressors, and the repudiation of the principles and bright ideals which led the Allied nations 40 years ago to a common victory, to a common peace, a common security, and a common clear sky over their heads.

(Valentin Falin was the Soviet Ambassador to West Germany at the time of the Bitburg visit.)

Chapter 28

Eastern Europe

Czechoslovakia

Your Excellency
Rudé Právo, Czechoslovakia
April 29, 1985

U.S. Ambassador William H. Luers
United States Embassy
Prague,
Czechoslovakia

Your Excellency.

The Council of Jewish Religious Communities in Bohemia and the Central Committee of JRC in Slovakia beg you to inform the President of the USA Ronald Reagan about our profound exasperation concerning his incomprehensible intention to visit the German military cemetery in Bitburg, West Germany, where soldiers of the Nazi army and members of SS units are buried. Such a gesture would mean to sully the memory of millions of victims of the Nazi genocide, among whom were more than 200 thousand Czechoslovak Jews and an unforgivable offense to those, who in the rows of Allied forces fought in the Second World War for democracy, justice and liberation of nations from the fascist yoke. We therefore ask most emphatically that Mr. President Reagan should abstain from his intention to pay a visit to Bitburg's military cemetery.

Signed
Phil Dr. Dezider Galsky
President
Council of Jewish Religious Communities
Prague, Czechoslovakia

(This letter was published on the first page of the Communist Party's mass-circulated daily Rudè Pràvo *and later in the May edition of the Jewish monthly* Vestnik.*)*

"Homage" To Nazis, SS
Prague Radio, Czechoslovakia
May 3, 1985

By Antonın Kostka

The scandal has both stimulated and explained away many questions. Thus it has been unequivocally shown that attempts inspired by Washington to distort historical truth so far as World War II is concerned not only have not been a fortuitous matter of expediency but that, on the contrary, they form a part of a broadly based and organized campaign whose aim is to rehabilitate nazism and thus justify moves to revise the results of World War II. At the same time this case has also shown how profoundly mistaken the protagonists of these moves are in their estimation of public opinion. There is no doubt that had the people behind and around Reagan had only a slight notion about the scope of the wave of indignation and hatred this would arouse throughout the world, a wave in which the voices of hundreds of congressmen and such loyal allies as Mrs. Thatcher and the Israeli premier have partaken, they would have taken a totally different course and would not have risked the prestige of the President and, in fact, of the United States itself.

Now they have been given a hard lesson in that the memories and sacrifices made in the war and the hatred of fascism and the tragedy of war which it symbolizes, are still alive, strong, and widespread among all nations. Perhaps they will draw conclusions from this and correct their own policy.

The British newspaper *Scotsman* wrote the other day that Reagan apparently wanted by this gesture to reward Chancellor Kohl's loyalty. Kohl himself in his reply to 250 American congressmen, in which he rejected their request to alter the program of President Reagan's visit, declared that the cancellation of the visit to Bitburg would allegedly profoundly touch all Germans. Let us ignore Chancellor Kohl's arbitrary arrogation of the claim to speak on behalf of all Germans so as not to overlook the main thing — and that is that Reagan's homage to Nazis and SS men is a reward to the West German government for its unqualified support for the hegemonistic policy of the United States and its war preparations both on earth and in space. This really speaks for itself — a joint homage to Nazi soldiers and SS killers as a bond for a joint platform.

Among the circles favorably inclined toward Washington, explanations of various shades are now being put forward to the effect that this allegedly was an accidental faux pas which would have otherwise meant humanly well as a symbolic gesture of reconciliation, forgiveness, and the like. This is an unabashed lie. This not only because of the above-mentioned conspicuous connection between Reagan's pilgrimage to Bitburg and attempts to revise the results of the last war but because the glorification of the Nazi Wehrmacht is in the United States of the same date as the moves toward gaining superiority, toward a policy from a position of strength.

There is a monstrous logic in it. Who else can be a better example to the American army for the crusade against communism and socialism than the Nazi Wehrmacht itself, which after all was also trained and forged to fight communism in the name of Hitler's plans for world domination. It is also very symbolic that there is an American military base near Bitburg, part of which is made up of first strike nuclear devices.

The United States, burdened by the defeats in Korea and Vietnam, as well as the shameful "glory" of an aggressor against Grenada, needs suitable examples. It is the present West German Bundeswehr but above all the former Nazi Wehrmacht that is to become a source of experience, military traditions as well as fighting morale and example. Such is at least the view of the overwhelming section of those 257 generals and admirals of all four services of the United States Armed Forces who were recently polled by the journal *Newsweek*. This is at the same time the main reason why President Reagan has taken such a sudden and such a profound regard for the killers from the Nazi Wehrmacht and the SS criminals.

(This was broadcast in Czechoslovakian on Prague Radio and translated by Foreign Broadcast Information Service.)

Prague Jews Resolution
Vestnik, Czechoslovakia
July, 1985

(On the 5th of May 1985 at a session of the Board of the Council of JRC, together with the Representation of the Prague community, the following resolution was passed.)

"Together with the entire progressive world we, the Czechoslovak Jews, are immeasurably enraged by the decision of the U.S. President Ronald Reagan to pay a demonstrative visit to the military ceremony at Bitburg where there are also buried members of SS units and to honor their memory. We consider this a cruel disregard and an insult to all martyrs of the Nazi genocide.

"We also protest against those who are trying to mendaciously rewrite the history of these most horrible times by declaring the existence of concentration camps and the suffering of millions of Jews to be propaganda invention and who finally are trying to minimize the tremendous and decisive share of the Soviet people in the victory over fascism."

(This report was first broadcast on Radio Czechoslovakia and monitored by the Foreign Broadcast Information Service. Later, it was printed in the July edition of the Jewish monthly Vestnik.)

"To Forget Means To Perish"
October 28, 1985

By Dezider Galsky

Dear Mr. Levkov,

On the afternoon of the same 5th of May — in fact at the moment when Mr. President in spite of protests of Jewish organisations from all over the world *did* visit the military cemetery in Bitburg, Prague Jews gathered on the biggest Jewish cemetery in Prague for a solemn ceremonial: they unveiled a memorial to the memory of Czechoslovak Jews, who perished in concentration camps and on the battlefields of the Second World War. In my opening speech I again referred to those trends which are emerging here and there in the world and in connection with the 40th anniversary of the end of the Second World War that try to depreciate the tragedy of European Jews. It has recently come to our knowledge that in some countries articles or even books appear, in which some authors call in question the very existence of camps of extermination! In other countries again they commemorate victims of Nazism, but often conceal or distort the share of Jewish victims. So quite logically in my speech I deduced that the imprudent act of President Reagan willy nilly brought grist to the mill of such tendencies.

Shortly after the 5th of May, i.e., after the visit of Mr. Reagan to the cemetery in Bitburg, I was asked by the Czechoslovak Broadcast to express my feelings and take up an attitude toward the fact that the American President did not let himself be discouraged from this unbelievable act. In my speech, broadcast also in English, French and German, I again emphasized our view, expressed before, and concluded my speech thus: "For us who went through the Nazi hell, is any kind of a certain appeasement between representatives of Nazi Germany and democratic powers—i.e., between the murderer and his victims—absolutely unacceptable. We consider this a grave incomprehension of history. Of course, one cannot expect from a President to be a historian, but certainly he should have some feeling and understanding of history. After all, the last war was explicitly a war of the democratic world against the dictatorship, against a regime, whose programmatic aim was to annihilate whole nations and Jews in the first place. And that should be never forgotten. The memento of millions of victims of the Second World War is too vivid a warning."

Let me add for the purpose of readers of this letter one more—in a way personal—point: Among the victims from the Czechoslovak Jewry were not only those who perished in concentration camps or on the battlefields, but also hundreds of those who were shot dead on the spot by the members of SS units for one reason only: they were Jews. Such was also the fate of my own parents and other members of my family: on the 1st of December 1944 in a hut in Slovak mountains 30 people were shot dead by an SS unit, children, women, old people, who tried to hide from deportations.

Again it shows itself that even after 40 years it is highly topical to return to the occurrences of the Second World War; it would be an unforgivable crime against future generations not to commemorate our experiences—experiences of departing generations. We are the very last witness who are able to do so. Today, as always, that motto holds good: To forget means to perish.

Signed
Phil Dr. Dezider Galsky

Scandalous Tribute to SS
Rudé Právo, Czechoslovakia
May 6, 1985

Today's *Rudé Právo* carried an article entitled "Scandalous Tribute to SS," commenting on U.S. President Ronald Reagan's provocative visit to the Bitburg cemetery where he laid a wreath on the graves of Hitler's Wehrmacht soldiers and SS murderers from Oradourg.

The daily said that President Reagan and West German Chancellor Helmut Kohl ignored extensive protests of the world public, including FRG and U.S. citizens. *Rudé Právo* pointed out that in October 1946 SS units were already described as a criminal organization by the international military court in Nuremberg in which the United States, too, was represented.

"Reagan won loud applause in the camp of revanchists, who welcomed 'reconciliation' because the Bundeswehr allegedly can adhere to tradition of 'German military heroism,' as FRG Defence Minister Woerner said in a white paper," the newspaper maintained. It added that not a word was spoken of murders committed by the Nazis as these do not fit into the campaign aimed at preparing the public in West Germany and other West European countries for the possibility of a new world conflict, preparing a path for revision of the results of World War II.

Rudé Právo commented also on Ronald Reagan's speech at the U.S. military base near the Bitburg cemetery. It said that the U.S. President did not mention immense sacrifices of the people of the Soviet Union and other countries of the anti-Hitler coalition during World War II. On the contrary, he attacked the USSR and other countries whose policy does not correspond to the U.S. Administration's wishes.

(Translated by the Foreign Broadcast Information Service.)

Poland

Reagan's Bitburg Address Pleases Revanchists
Warsaw Radio, Poland
May 6, 1985

Some world statesmen have a very peculiar interpretation of the lessons of World War II. American President Ronald Reagan proved this yesterday by visiting—together with FRG Chancellor Helmut Kohl and despite numerous voices of protest from throughout the world—the military cemetery in Bitburg, where some SS men are buried. He laid a wreath there. Jan Gadomski reports:

"President Reagan did a bad turn to his faithful vassals in the ruling team in the FRG. Speaking about reconciliation, he paid homage to the memory of Nazi soldiers and fanatical guardsmen of the regime under the sign of the SS. By the same token, he traced for today's society in the FRG a beautiful Nazi heritage. Such a vision of history and the present day will please West German nationalists, neo-Nazis, and revanchists. Reagan evidently thinks that it is they who set the tone in the FRG."

Reagan wanted to unite the West Germans around his war program, but he revealed the division in the FRG and Western Europe, both in the assessment of recalling the war traditions of nazism and of a future war in space being prepared by him.

(Broadcast in Polish on Warsaw Radio and translated by Foreign Broadcast Information Service.)

Reagan's Bitburg Visit Seen Condoning SS Crimes
Zycie Warszawy, Poland
May 6, 1985

WARSAW—"Never will Ronald Reagan erase this scene from his political biography," *Zycie Warszawy* [leading Polish newspaper] wrote today. Excerpts:

"He committed so repulsive an act that it is incomprehensible in its political and moral indifferentism. He united against himself millions of people holding different political views both in the U.S. and Western Europe and the wave of indignation that he caused must have made Kohl and his fellow citizens aware that history must not be distorted for any political reasons.

"Reagan wanted to consciously make an attempt to absolve heirs to the

Third Reich, that is, the FRG, from moral and political responsibility for the crimes of genocide that have been and continue to be symbolized by the Waffen SS. Reagan tried to do this at the expense of tightening military cooperation within NATO and further activating the Bundeswehr in this alliance, and at the price of Bonn's even broader participation in pursuing the U.S. armaments policy in Western Europe.

"President Reagan's spectacular gesture caused an effect, reverse than planned, in the consciousness of Europeans and Americans and brought about universal recollection of the crimes of nazism and an almost equally universal condemnation of these crimes. But the world also got convinced how far the official America is ready to go to pursue its imperial military goals. In this sense, the wreath in Bitburg was a dangerous act and a sign of policy that must arouse gravest concern particularly in Poland," *Zycie Warszawy* said.

In the same connection, special correspondent of the *Rzeczpospolita* government daily in Bonn wrote:

"The victims of Nazi genocide, who survived the hell, protest against putting torturers and victims on the same footing.

"Reagan and his aides made the decision motivated by political needs and not by the requirements of historic truth. And those who could not put up with a thought that the American President made a calculated and politically motivated gesture protested and will continue to protest against that fact for a long time to come.

"Both sides used the visit to Bitburg for their ends, but world opinion was not misled, as is testified to by commentaries that came to Bonn from everywhere."

(Translated by the Foreign Broadcast Information Service.)

Murderers On Same Footing As Victims
Warsaw Television Service, Poland
May 6, 1985

The President of the United States is the first Western leader to put murderers on the same footing as their victims. The President's gesture is a serious political choice in the context of the revival of forces which history has cast aside and condemned. These views were being printed out on telex messages coming in from all over the world today and were being expressed by people who managed to escape a Hitlerite death. Voices from Poland are included in the voices of indignation. Ordinary citizens and Sejm deputies, members of the Patriotic Movement for National Rebirth and ZBOWID, and party and non-party people are talking about the presidential scandal. This is a subject of discussion at factories, shop lines, and in trams.

In the so-called declaration of the seven leaders in Bonn, published on the anniversary of the end of the war, the words "fascism" or "Hitlerism" have not been used once. President Reagan, by honoring SS men and Konrad Adenauer, has given an absolution of sins not only to murderous formations but also to revanchism and pan-Germanization. For us, this is not only a moral matter but also a political matter. Many official representatives of political spheres in the FRG continue to this very day to repeat after Adenauer not *Slask* but *Schlesien,* not *Gdansk* but *Danzig,* and not *Wroclaw* but *Breslau.* However, not a single Pole can fail to notice this and it does not matter whether he is a believer or not.

(Translated by the Foreign Broadcast Information Service.)

Yugoslavia

Dishonors Tombs Of Millions
Yugoslav Radio
April 29, 1985

By Milika Sundic

Confusion about Reagan's forthcoming visit to the FRG is gradually turning into a special kind of political scandal. Acting on Helmut Kohl's advice, Reagan agreed to lay a wreath on the tombs of German soldiers in Bitburg, where 47 members of Hitler's SS units are also buried, forgetting that in so doing he would dishonor the tombs of millions of those who lost their lives fighting against fascism. Kohl's insistence that Reagan should visit Bitburg, that is to say the German cemetery, can be understood to a certain extent, but not Reagan's assent. It is true that today's German generation should not be blamed for Hitler's crimes, but it is difficult to accept Kohl's explanation that German feelings will be hurt if Reagan abandons the idea. If the feelings of the Germans are so closely linked to the Third Reich and the World War II crimes, then there is something wrong with both Kohl and the Germans.

It is even more difficult to understand how a great power leader, a member of the anti-Hitler coalition, can repay his compatriots in this way, those who died in the war against Hitler's Germany, in other words, who were the victims of those to whom Reagan will pay homage in Bitburg. Western allies, in the first place the United States and Great Britain, have given up the idea of celebrating the 40th anniversary of the victory over fascism in the way in which it will be celebrated in Moscow because they did not want to offend the FRG. Such considerations, at least with regard to elucidating the course of World War II, also exist on the other side. In view of this, during recent days and months we have been convinced that the USSR also believes that its present allies should in no way be offended: the allies who were on the side of Hitler's Germany during World War II. Also, Yugoslavia's share in World War II is being equated with that of Bulgaria, Hungary, Romania and some other countries which did not even have resistance movements, let alone the divisions, corps and armies such as existed in Yugoslavia. And just to make it even more absurd, if something positive and true is ever written about the Yugoslav contribution to the victory over fascism, as the TASS agency did a few days ago, the Soviet press does not even mention it, which is further proof that considerations toward allies have been more important than the truth.

President Reagan is most probably not deceived, as some are claiming, because it is very unlikely that he did not realize from the very beginning what lay behind Kohl's protocol, which included a visit to Bitburg. Reagan places the fact that the FRG is on his side, even regarding "star wars," well above anything that his opponents think about this — and they include numerous congressmen, Jewish organizations and a vast majority of the U.S. public. All this could, of course, have been avoided, but when it concerns the allies, bloc interests and, ultimately, anti-communism, even the humiliation in Bitburg is not too high a price in return for all this. And there is no doubt that the price is so high that one should not be surprised as to why no one is preventing neo-Nazis in the FRG from holding their congress.

(Broadcast on Yugoslav Radio in Serbo-Croatian, this was translated by Foreign Broadcast Information Services.)

Reagan Bitburg Visit Leaves "Bitter Taste"
Yugoslav Radio
May 6, 1985

By Dragan Colovic

By laying a wreath to SS troops, with whatever justification, President Reagan has made a big political and moral error, because he has hurt to the quick millions of people who still have fresh memories of the horrible crimes the German Wehrmacht forces perpetrated in World War II. Therefore, it is very natural that this gesture by the U.S. President has been met by a storm of protests and indignation throughout the world, especially among those peoples that were the greatest victims of fascism and its crimes. The worst thing in all this is that such political reconciliation gestures, which are dictated by bloc interests, are being misused in the sense that one is trying to hush up facts about the horrifying consequences of Nazi crimes and thus to change the history of World War II, in which tens of millions of innocent people perished, including 1,700,000 Yugoslav victims.

One must not forget here, however, that along with all the aforementioned justified protests and bitterness aired throughout the world, and a few expressions of understanding for the gesture by President Reagan, there also exist attempts to justify and hush up present cases of genocide, occurring 40 years after World War II. In order to retain its pride, the world must not let it be forgotten that genocide has not disappeared even 40 years after the end of the most horrible slaughter in the history of mankind. The massacre of innocent women, children, and old people in the Palestinian camps of Sabra and Shatila and in other places in Lebanon and Palestine are still too fresh in our mind to be forgotten, as well as the crimes in South Africa that have not yet been stopped. It is not out of place here to ask who is hushing up or trying to moderate or even justify the consequences of the silent genocide of millions of Africans who are suffering mass starvation today, and why.

Along with the previously mentioned protests and indignation throughout the world, one is certainly encouraged by such gestures as that made by Austrian President Kirchschlaeger. When paying tribute to the victims of the Mauthausen concentration camp, among which there were also Yugoslavs, Kirchschlaeger said that the victims of an inhuman and organized mass political murder will never and must never be forgotten. Another is the gesture by the head of the SPD, Willy Brandt, who refused to appear at a reception given in the honor of President Reagan.

It is certain that peoples from which the Nazis and other death squads originated should not eternally bear the consequences of crimes of their fathers and grandfathers, because they are not to be blamed for them, but we all must know that there can be no reconciliation between innocent victims and their executioners, and there can be no reconciliation particularly with ideologies such as nazism and fascism, as well as with many present "isms" that jeopardize human dignity and the right to one's only life. Neo-fascism, nationalism, chauvinism, irredentism, and revanchism, which have no homeland or borders, are fed on and inspired by just such acts as the gesture by President Reagan that can lead to even more horrible and unprecedented pogroms. Therefore, despite the additional attempts of the U.S. President to mitigate the Bitburg episode, to explain that that symbolic act of reconciliation does not mean forgetting and forgiving the crimes, only a bitter taste remains. This and similar gestures can only stimulate insane forces to raise their heads again, 40 years after the greatest human tragedy in history.

(Broadcast on Yugoslav Radio in Serbo-Croatian and translated by Foreign Broadcast Information Services. Announcer Dragan Colovic is Yugoslav Radio's foreign political editor.)

SFRY Veterans' Paper Criticizes Bitburg Visit
TANJUG, Yugoslavia
May 9, 1985

BELGRADE—The Yugoslav veterans and entire public sharply condemn Reagan's visit to the Bitburg cemetery and express indignation and concern, especially because the U.S. President proclaimed a "reconciliation" that cannot and must not be "a deeply moral act," the newspaper of the Yugoslav World War Two veterans' organization *4 Jul* writes.

"Yugoslavia," it says, "respects international law, which specifies that war crimes cannot fall under the statute of limitations, no matter what justifications are attempted. Paying homage to Hitler's soldiers, the U.S. President in the grossest and most direct way drew an equation mark between the Nazi executioners and their victims," the Yugoslav newspaper writes in a commentary in its latest issue. "In this way, Reagan, intentionally or not, although, regrettably, the former seems to be the case, collectively amnestied Nazism, itself," *4 Jul* writes.

The newspaper writes that the planned, politically coloured and carefully timed decision was in essence aimed at strengthening the Western bloc and NATO's rivalry and confrontation with the opposite military-political alliance.

(This was broadcast by TANJUG, an English-speaking Yugoslavian radio station and released by the Foreign Broadcast Information Services.)

Three Themes
The Jewish Review, Yugoslavia
May-June 1985

During the months of April-May the attention of news media was focused on three themes. The first was Reagan's act of paying homage to German soldiers fallen in WWII and interred in the Bitburg cemetery. He was informed in advance that the graves of 49 members of the criminal SS troops are also in that same cemetery. This step was qualified as a historical mistake. The second theme concerned the endeavours to track down Joseph Mengele, the ill-famed war criminal, also known as the "angel of death" of Auschwitz. It appears now that he died in Brazil where he was found drowned. Experts confirmed this news but doubts still remained. And thirdly, a TWA Boeing 747 flying on the Athens-Rome-Boston route was hijacked. The sufferings of the hostages, the murder of one passenger and the driving away to unknown hiding place of passengers with Jewish sounding names are but new proofs that innocent people are yet threatened by terrorists and that racist and anti-Semite provocations are making their appearance felt in new dangerous forms.

During the period under review anti-Semite occurrences and provocations were registered in Argentina, Austria, England, France, the Federal Republic of Germany, Canada, Norway, Poland, U.S.A. and Yugoslavia, while events linked to the Holocaust and combating anti-Semitism were registered in Austria, England, France, the Federal Republic of Germany, Holland, Poland, South Africa, U.S.A. and Yugoslavia.

German Democratic Republic

Jewish Leader's Speech Recalls Liberation
Neues Deutschland, East Germany
May 6, 1985

EAST BERLIN — On 5 May a synagogue concert was held by Berlin's Jewish community in the Peace Temple on Rykestrasse in commemoration of the liberation of the German people from Hitlerite fascism 40 years ago. Participating as guests were Konrad Naumann, first secretary of the SED borough leadership in Berlin; Erhard Krack, mayor of Berlin; representatives of social organizations and churches; as well as the diplomatic corps.

In the beginning Dr. Peter Kirchner, chairman of the Jewish community in Berlin, made a speech in commemoration of the more than 6 million European Jews, among them 55,000 alone from Berlin, who were killed in the fascist concentration camps. He also reminded his audience of those who had fought the terror either in open combat or as sincere humanists by helping their Jewish neighbors escape or disappear. Dr. Kirchner personally thanked the representatives of the Soviet embassy for the liberation from fascism, for the liberation of the concentration camps and the city of Berlin. The speaker said that he failed to understand why the President of the United States would lay a wreath at an FRG cemetery where members of the Waffen SS are buried.

The synagogue concert was opened by Estrongo Nachama, senior cantor of the Jewish community of West Berlin, with "Memory of the Dead — El Mole-Rachamim."

(Neues Deutschland *is the daily newspaper for the East German communist party called Socialist Unity Party [SED].*)

Chapter 29

Other Nations

Egyptian Ambassador Questioned
May 13, 1985

His Excellency Dr. Abdel Raouf El-Reedy
Embassy of the Arab Republic of Egypt
2310 Decatur Place, NW
Washington, DC 20008

Your Excellency:

It was good seeing you last week and it is good to hear the news from the Middle East that Israel and Egypt seem on the road to improving relations. The substances and tone of the public statements are heartening.

There is nothing, however, more liable to undercut any progress than the kind of vicious anti-Semitic commentary that appeared in the establishment Egyptian press in reaction to the Bitburg controversy. Most vile was an article, without a byline, which appeared under the editorial in the section "Other Matters" in *Al-Akhbar* (May 6). Entitled "Zionist Propaganda and Reagan's Visit to Germany," it read:

> *The Zionist and Jewish organizations in the United States have exploited the visit — which Reagan is supposed to make to a German war cemetery in Bitburg — in the best manner for consolidating their old propaganda concerning the persecution which had been suffered at the hands of the Nazis, despite the many exaggerations, even regarding this persecution. It is strange that the Zionist propaganda about the burning of the Jews by the Nazis has become supposedly an established fact, although this was never*

dealt with scientifically. There are exaggerations regarding both the number of those Jews as well as the description of their cremation, as disseminated by the Zionist propaganda in order to awaken a guilt complex among the people of Europe; this, while ignoring the fact that the Jews in Germany, during the Second World War, constituted a thorn in Germany's back at a time when it was engaged in a difficult war. We do not intend here to defend Germany, but our only wish is to emphasize how the Zionist organizations are taking advantage of the situation in a most important manner in order to consolidate their old propaganda.

And there is more. Anis Mansour wrote in *Al-Ahram* on May 2 that nations hate the Jews because they try to impose their feelings on the entire world. He added: "It is not impossible that there will be an attempt made on the life of President Reagan, and that the assassin will be one of the minorities—Armenian, Turkish, or Irish—although the one who causes this and pays the fee will be one of the Jewish organizations."

Or an *Al-Ahram* article by Rajab al-Bana on May 6: "They want the wounds to remain open and the tortures suffered by the Jews in Hitler's camps to remain engraved in the memory of the world, while at the same time they demand that the world forget the tortures suffered and being suffered by the Arabs at their hands—and these are no less than what happened in Hitler's camps."

And Taha Abd al-Fatah in *Al-Akhbar* on May 8: "There is no lack of Jews who believe that they are above life's rules in contrast with the rest of mankind."

Mr. Ambassador, this is outrageous commentary, the most dangerous poison. It only serves to turn the people of Egypt against Israel, against Jews on the basis of lies. It also raises profound questions in Israel, and among Jews and other friends of Israel around the world whether Egypt is truly interested in peace with Israel, in a new era free of the old hatreds.

We urge you, Mr. Ambassador, to communicate with your government our concerns with regard to this new round of anti-Semitic outbursts in the Egyptian press.

Sincerely,

Abraham H. Foxman
Associate National Director
Anti-Defamation League of B'nai B'rith

(**Editor:** *The Egyptian Ambassador did not respond.*)

... YEAH, A CLOSE CALL ALL RIGHT, SO FOR MY VISIT...

... YOU'D BETTER TOSS IN A CONCENTRATION CAMP...

... NOT A NASTY, SERIOUS ONE...

... JUST SOMETHING IN THE LIGHT TO MEDIUM RANGE.

© 1985 BENSON ZONENA

Interview with Allan Rose
Montreal, Canada
September 18, 1985

(Allan Rose, Executive Vice President of the Canadian Jewish Congress, was interviewed by Ilya Levkov in Montreal, September 18, 1985.)

Q: The American Jewish community reacted actively to President Reagan's decision to visit the Bitburg cemetery. How would you characterize the reaction to this visit in Canada?

Rose: In the Jewish community there was a very strong reaction: they were against the planned visit. It was regarded as an obscenity that the President, commemorating the 40th anniversary of the ending of the war, should visit a cemetery where SS soldiers are buried. I hardly saw a piece in the Canadian press — English or French — which was in favor of the visit. We protested to the American Embassy, and it was known I think in the Canadian government that the Canadian government would in no way consider such a visit of any kind by our Prime Minister or anyone of that kind.

Q: Were there any official statements by the government?

Rose: There were no official statements by the government, but I should tell you that the Canadian 40th anniversary commemoration brought thousands of people together. Yet the Prime Minister unfortunately could not be there, because it was held on the day of the Economic Summit in Europe.

Q: Arthur Gunman, a spokesman for the opposition party, stated that there is no place to pay tribute to the Nazis in our time.

Rose: To that extent, yes, it was denounced. I think the general public was very strongly against it. There were a few people who said let bygones be bygones. But you must remember that Canada was in the war of September 1939, not the U.S. Canada suffered very grievous losses in the war and, therefore, there was a very strong reaction against it by everyone.

Q: Canada's record of opening its doors to Jewish refugees during World War II is not that highly respected. To what extent did this determine a Canadian response to the President or to downplay the public and the Jewish demands not to visit Bitburg?

Rose: I think that you're being much too kind to Canada. Actually, Canada was a country — if you read the book *None Is Too Many* — which made it a state policy not to accept refugees from Nazi oppression. It's a very sorry story, but Canada actually facilitated the admission of war criminals into Canada in concert with the U.S. and other governments. That's a very important point. Now I think that it's being stated by numerous representatives, and all the parties including the party in power, that the 40th anniversary was an opportunity, at least to the Jewish community, to say that what we did in the war was terrible. And to affirm that it will never happen again. I think that came across very clearly by representatives of all the parties. There were no group cleavages, or splinter groups, or objections.

Q: Canadian politics have carved out legitimate plans for a French ethnic nation, especially in Quebec. To what extent does the Jewish community exert pressure or have a legitimate place to influence the federal government?

Rose: As you know, Canada is officially a multi-cultural state, therefore, every Canadian is a hyphenated Canadian — French-Canadian, English-Canadian, Italian-Canadian, or, indeed, Jewish-Canadian. As former Prime Minister Trudeau said, "To be a Jew is to be a good Canadian and to be a good Canadian is to be a good Jew." That's true of all ethnicities in Canada.

We are regarded as proud Jews and proud Zionists who have made an enormous contribution to the well-being of Canada — to the new charters and constitution, and in regard to women's rights, the handicapped people's rights, even, indeed, to anti-discrimination of our French-speaking fellow citizens in Quebec. I think that Canada is a good place for Jews. The voicing of ethnic politics is not only legitimized, it is subsidized. For instance, the Quebec governor paid the provincial government for an international conference on Yiddish. We also get substantial sums of money for Yiddish and other programs on the Holocaust from the federal government.

Q: What proportion of the present Canadian Jews came from the ruins of the world war?

Rose: In round numbers, of 300,000 Jews about 50,000 are survivors or the children of survivors.

Q: The Jewish educational program in Canada has always stressed the learning of the Yiddish language and its culture, which in turn brings the Canadian Jews a bit closer to a world that is no longer known to others. To what degree does this contribute to the greater identity of the Canadian Jews with the Holocaust?

Rose: We have a Yiddish department in the Canadian Jewish Congress which we have turned into a *Kultur-kampf.* We think Yiddish is part of the heritage of the Jewish people. But you must remember that education in Canada is provincial, that is, state jurisdiction. Therefore, how much Yiddish is factored into the Jewish school system in Canada depends very much on conditions. For instance, in Montreal Jews have to learn four languages — French and English (the two official languages) plus Yiddish and Hebrew.

Q: My assumption is that youngsters, 15 and 16 year-olds, learn of the Yiddish culture in Europe that was destroyed by the Holocaust without taking courses in the Holocaust.

Rose: I think you're right. One embraces the other. Unfortunately, Yiddish has almost been wiped out by the Holocaust. We are not only trying to hand it down to the second generation survivors but to the younger Jews as well.

Q: You mentioned that Canada participated fully from '39 in action in World War II. What kind of process of reconciliation took place between Canada and Germany?

Rose: It's a very difficult question to answer. Canada is a member of NATO and the Federal Republic of Germany is a member of NATO. I think most Canadians regard the Federal Republic of Germany as a country substantially purged of Nazism and nationalism. I must tell you I think there is a very deep wound left from World War II, but I also think it's my generation that remembers that war. In 1979, when the statute of limitations for war crimes was due to lapse in Germany, Canada was the only country that protested it. So there is still a strong remembrance. On the other hand, there is a strong belief in Canada — there are a million and a half German-Canadians — that today's Germany will thrive as a democracy.

Q: I didn't know about such a large German contingent. To what extent are they organized and active?

Rose: We meet with the German Congress which has only just been organized. This tells you something about Germans. You see, there are old Germans and new Germans. The first Germans came here after the defeat of the British. Like the Americans, they came here as empire lawyers. These people are descendants of Hessian mercenaries. Then we have a group that came after 1815. After 1848, many liberal Germans came here. In southern Ontario you've got a very old German community. In Linenburg, fathers and grandfathers fought for the Canadian army in the two world wars against the Germans. We didn't have a substantial German migration after the war. And they are not well organized. Interestingly, what made them become organized was the 40th anniversary of the end of the war. In their minds, every time a movie is shown of Hitler or the atrocities in the camps, they revisit their trauma.

Q: Thus this Congress of German-Canadians has only just been organized. Of the million and a half, how many are from the post-1945 era?

Rose: I think a substantial number would not be interested in associating themselves with Germany.

Q: What is your analysis of the speeches President Reagan gave at Bitburg?

Rose: I think President Reagan is a very good friend of the Jewish people and of Israel, but he didn't understand the issue and the emotions involved. I think there was enormously sloppy staff work. I'm sure that they would have known what would happen, therefore, I think that it was right to register the protest. Morally, what I don't think was very intelligent to do is to keep on re-registering it. Morally, it was absolutely unacceptable and it has to be registered, but, unfortunately, although we can never forget the Holocaust, we have to live another day and the United States' President is not that important to the Jewish people.

Q: Would you say it was Reagan who spoke in those speeches and not a speech writer?

Rose: I would have thought so. I am not an American so it is difficult for me to comment.

Q: Chancellor Kohl gave a very moving speech at Bergen-Belsen which precluded reading the text, and three-quarters of us wondered if he would ask for reconciliation. But he didn't call for it. Instead, he used this to make a statement about how to perceive the present German government.

Rose: You mean the West German government? The speech did impress me more than Chancellor Kohl. However, while I don't think there was anything unscrupulous, I still hold the view expressed when Ben-Gurion met Adenauer at the famous meeting at the Waldorf-Astoria in 1960. There is no such thing as collective guilt, but I believe that there is collective responsibility. Therefore, I think that the Germans accept the responsibility for what happened. But only for the people who were involved, and those who remain silent. Young Germans can really be blamed for this. I am one of those people who think you can never forget. But, on the other hand, I think we have to be very careful to assume relationships with those who are totally innocent because they weren't born at the time.

Q: How would you classify the present perception in today's Germany with regard to the young, the old, and the middle-aged?

Rose: To compare Nazi peers of 1933 to 1945 with today is driving to the nuclear age in a stagecoach. It has no relevance. If somebody really wants to insult anyone in this country they call him a Nazi. It's perceived as indescribable evil. I think that what happened is reprehensible and regrettable. To have taken the attitude that we're committed to the visit is unacceptable. I agree with Elie Wiesel's statements at the White House: Once a mistake is made it doesn't mean to say that it can't be rectified. But I speak as a non-American.

Q: The debate about President Reagan's visit to Bitburg centers on two issues: the absolute morality and the element of compromise which is the ethics of politics. How do you see those two issues?

Rose: I don't accept that it is possible to compromise with the Nazi period or those who represented it. It's a moral and ethical question absolutely, and I don't think he should have gone. That's number one. I am in favor of having relations with a new Germany that is democratic. I don't know outside of Von Stauffenberg's memorial, or Adenauer's memorial, or the tombs of the Scholls of Munich if the memorial could have been done in any other place. But, it didn't have to be done at Bitburg. As I said earlier, that was utterly reprehensible.

Q: How did Canadian Jews perceive the protest of American Jews at Bergen-Belsen?

Rose: We were entirely supportive of them.

Q: You would have sent part of your constituents to join one of the groups or both? Weiss and Rosensaft?

Rose: We would have had no difficulty in joining them. I don't think there should be a co-mingling of what the Holocaust was and what happened to suit the immediate interest of Israel. The Holocaust stands as such an abomination that there could be no temporizing of it.

Q: Which are the Canadian groups that tend to support the so-called Jewish causes?

Rose: When you say Jewish causes, do you mean Israel?

Q: The Israel of the commemorated.

Rose: It's a difficult question to answer. Canada is a complex country. We recently did a survey which shows over 80 percent French and English are supporters of Israel. There may be criticisms of what they may be doing on the West Bank, but it's supported, that's number one. Number two is that all the political parties in this country, without exception, are supporters of Israel and have very close connections with the Jewish community. Indeed, they have Jews in them. The Director-General of the Conservative Party is Jewish. A former member of my staff, the Assistant Director-General of the Liberals, is Jewish, and the Director-General of the new Democratic Party is Jewish. The name of the conservative is Mr. Lampert. He is the Director-General of the Conservative Party. Mark Resnic, who is former Director of the Canada/Israel Committee, is now the Assistant Director-General of the Liberal Party. And there is Gary Kaplan, who is the Director-General of the new Democratic Party. This is the Social Democratic Labor Party.

Q: You mentioned you were a liberator.

Rose: I was an officer in the British army at that time. It was an accident of history that my tank happened to be in the line of approach of Celle which is the nearest town to Belsen, so we came across Belsen. I find it very difficult to talk about. But four years ago I gave a very substantial rendering of that period at the Liberators Conference in Washington.* [See below.] In the U.S. it was mainly the liberal groups, both political liberals and religious liberals, who voiced the objection to the President's decision to go. A conservative, without almost any exception, decided not to call the President.

Q: Did anything similar happen in Canada?

Rose: In Canada, the political ideology is different. Virtually all the parties belong to the center, including the Progressive Conservative Party, which is to the left of the Republicans. It belongs to the right center and, if you will, the liberals belong to the middle center. But basically, in my judgment, Conservative Liberals. When you take away the rhetoric there is very little difference. They believe this reconciliation comes through repentance and remembrance.

Q: What's your view of possible forms of reconciliation?

Rose: I think we have poor reconciliation between the Jewish people and the Germans. This will be difficult for the balance of this century. It would also depend on the Federal Republic's attitude toward Israel. It's unthinkable that the Federal Republic of Germany can sell leopard tanks to the enemies of Israel. After all, Israel is in a real sense the remnant of the Jewish people. There will always be this cleavage of morality with daily politics involved in that process of dialogue reconciliation with Germany.

Q: How do you see those two values that are usually absent in normal international intergovernmental politics?

Rose: Somewhere along the line we'll be objective. But who is not allowed the moral obligation or sense of high morality of innocent people who are uninformed people. Innocent because they didn't commit themselves — the bureaucrats and foreign minister in Berlin. Innocent because they didn't participate uninformed or informed. But still there are two levels to be guided by. I don't think there can be any relationships with the German people and the Jewish people without the Holocaust entering into it. Otherwise our relationship with the German people would be like that of the Italian people. They are innocent because, despite what Mussolini did, the Italian people were opposed to his anti-Jewish policies. Therefore, I don't think it is possible to have any discussions with Germans, or the German government, or German embassies, or German representatives, or even German-Canadians without this issue being addressed. But if you have to draw a graphic picture, it is in the shadow as a parallel issue.

Q: What should be the role of memory in the annals of Jewish history, and how is it applicable to the notion of the Holocaust?

Rose: In the 1940s we saw the destruction of the Jewish people and the birth of the Jewish state. I hope the history of the Holocaust will never disappear. On the other hand I think we have to be very careful. It's a warning that I always have to issue. There has been a tendency in the Jewish community here in Canada to relate everything to the Holocaust. If some minor thing happens, it's related to the Holocaust. There was a Soviet Jewry demonstration that I saw the other day. The audience was reminded that the buses were leaving for somewhere. Some said that the buses were waiting to go to Auschwitz! It is this kind of vulgarization of the Holocaust which I think is an extremely dangerous thing. It diminishes the Holocaust. It concerns me very much to compare the Soviet Union with the Nazis. We've got serious problems with Soviet Jewry and I am very much concerned with it. I deal with them every day. But nobody can be compared to the Nazis. They were beyond all comprehension. Therefore, I think we have to be very careful not to cheapen the Holocaust.

Q: To what degree is the Holocaust experience exclusively Jewish and not universal?

Rose: It happened to the Jews and because of Jews but many things can happen to others. It became a universal guide for an experience not to be repeated. The Ten Commandments also have things that should be done and things that shouldn't be done. It is both exclusion and inclusion. Jews are concerned. As far as non-Jews are concerned, it is terribly important to point out to them that if you look back at the period, the great politicians of the democracies are as much to blame for what happened by their cowardice, and the German people are as much to blame. I'm sure that Hitler and people of that kind of all nations are usually put into lunatic asylums. Now, that is a lesson to be learned for the non-Jews. It could start with the Jews but finish with the non-Jews. Thus, the quality of democracy is made up of resistance to racism of all kinds. That's a very strong lesson which people have got to learn. Generally speaking, it bears repeating that as go the Jews, so goes the rest of the world. At least the free world.

(see over)

Alan Rose's testimony at the Liberators of Nazi Concentration Camps Conference in the State Department, Washington, D.C., in October 1981.

Mr. Chairman, ladies and gentlemen.

I would like to say that I was twenty years of age [when I was] in the British Army, a sergeant in the 7th Armored Division. I think those of us in those last few days of war saw the epitome of heroism on the battlefields after the second front and the abyss of mankind when we came across Bergen-Belsen. I can hardly speak today without being gripped with the emotion that seized me thirty-five years ago.

We had triumphantly liberated Brussels and Antwerp, and the British Second Army and anyone who served in it will recall the tumultuous welcome and the touching remembrance of the Belgian people after the liberation. We had heard inferentially about what had happened in Europe, but if you're a sergeant sitting in a tank and worried about meeting a German panzer division, one's knowledge of what had happened was but sketchy at best.

The war was coming to an end. The invasion of Germany was about to begin, and the Second Army moved east through Aachen across the Rhine onto the great northwest German plain, headed toward Hamburg and Kiel. Eventually it cut off the German forces that were descending across western Germany toward Denmark. The town of Celle, which is adjacent to Bergen-Belsen, was taken after little resistance. I don't think that any human being could then conceive — certainly not I as a relatively innocent 20-year-old — what we saw as our tanks, almost by inadvertence, passed the gates and [saw] the rambling mass of buildings which was Bergen-Belsen.

I think it would require the words of an Elie Wiesel or the pen of a Churchill to really comprehend what happened that day. I had intended to be an architect, but I decided then to spend my time doing what I could to restore the remnants of Jewish life.

The horrors of Bergen-Belsen — the litter of people who had once been human beings — and the abysmal conditions have been described, and I don't really think there's too much point in redescribing them to those of my colleagues and others here who have seen them for themselves. It was for me an indescribable sight, but I think there are certain things that we should learn from these descriptions which I will not weary you with. But I have certain simple thoughts that I would like to share with you.

In my innocence at that time, I really believed that any presence of Fascism or anti-Semitism or racism of any kind surely must be expunged. Unfortunately, that is not so. As has been referred to this morning and last night, there is now an active school of revisionism which says, in fact, that the Holocaust never happened, that the camps never existed.

If the Holocaust never happened and the camps didn't exist, then all of us here are fraudulent, are we not, because we are being honored as liberators of camps. I think there is a particular duty incumbent on us who were privileged to liberate camps—if that is an understatement, and I come from a country of understatement—to perhaps devote our lives to refuting an abomination and an obscenity of this kind. I think it's particularly incumbent upon us—those who fought the war, those who were really the front-line soldiers, those who were the sharp end—to do that. It's a duty we owe ourselves as much as the victims.

The other thing that I remember vividly is that for the first time—having served for some years in the British Army—I, of all people, had to threaten my tank driver. He was prepared there with his submachine gun to wipe out all the guards that were inside or indeed any Germans, including the Bürgermeister of Celle who, I'm given to understand, thought that although the trains rumbled through Celle, the Bergen-Belsen camp was no more than a camp for the rehabilitation of wayward criminals.

The third thing I would like to say, and I'm sure you will understand me because I speak not only as a liberator but as a Jew, is that it never occurred to me in 1945, after the Jewish people had undergone the Holocaust—and after all, it's only existential that I was saved—that I could very well have been one of those who were in Bergen-Belsen and did not survive had my grandparents 100 years ago not come from Russia. Indeed, instead of sitting in a rather proud way as we did as tank commanders, I could very well have been any one of the people who were liberated. I never believed that I would have to go off and fight again in 1948 to defend the right of the Jewish State—which had been established not only by historical demand and mandate but by international law of the right for it to exist—as a member of the volunteer group that fought through all the countries of the Diaspora alongside our Israeli comrades.

So, I am both very happy and honored to have been spared to be among you, to be, as General Haig said, among comrades in arms. Today, we forget the divisions that there may be between countries, and we come together rather as old comrades, together with all the survivors and those who are interested in the Holocaust.

I am deeply honored that that has happened. But for all of us who passed through the Holocaust, whether as liberators or as liberated, it leaves an indelible mark on us, and I would hope an indelible mark on mankind.

The Australian Experience
Australia
Special Contribution

By Isi J. Leibler

As elsewhere in the Jewish world, President Reagan's visit to the Bitburg War Cemetery in early May 1985 was greeted with disappointment and even outrage in Australia, whose well-organized community of 90,000 Jews includes many Holocaust survivors and their off-spring. However, given the generally favourable reputation which President Reagan enjoys among the Australian Jewish Community, it is difficult to speak of any lasting harm or even impact which the Bitburg incident has had among Australian Jewry, and even a few months after President Reagan's visit, it seemed to have been swallowed up in the course of ongoing events.

The Bitburg visit was widely reported in both the print and electronic media in Australia, as are nearly all significant American events. (The Australian media is heavily dependent upon American wire services and television networks for their international news.) The criticisms voiced by many Jewish leaders in America were widely reported, almost always sympathetically. The Bitburg visit was also the subject of newspaper editorials and syndicated columns which, almost without exception, regarded the planned visit as a gross lapse of judgment by Reagan and not infrequently linked it with signs of a decline in Reagan's previously seemingly invulnerable public image and popularity. Typical of these comments were those by the widely-respected Melbourne *Age* (27 April 1985) that "The memories and passions of the Holocaust should not, must not be buried with the dead. . . President Reagan, in his shoddy political maneuvering. . . missed the point. . . the Holocaust should live in the memory of the whole world." Many other editorials made the same point. Australian newspapers had previously carried a good many stories on the Holocaust to coincide with the fortieth anniversary of the liberation of Nazi Germany, and most newspapers and columnists deplored the visit.

Perhaps the most controversial exchange to emerge came about when the president of the Returned Servicemans' League, (the major Australian veterans' organization, similar to the American Legion) Sir William Keys, publicly supported the Reagan visit. "If the President of the U.S. wishes to pay a tribute to people who were gallant in their own life, then I believe he should be allowed to do it without this confusion. In wartime, people in uniform. . . don't question the political decisions of their governments." Jewish groups immediately attacked Keys' statement. Gad Ben-Meir, president of the Australian Federation of Jewish Ex-Service Associations, wrote that "Never has history been so rudely dismissed; never has evil been so obscenely pampered." Several Jewish groups, including the Victorian Jewish Board of Deputies, passed resolutions deploring the planned visit.

Nevertheless, the Bitburg visit did not have the impact in Australia that it did in America, for a number of reasons. Firstly, the Australian Jewish community largely perceives Reagan very favourably and in a good light, recognizing that perhaps no previous American President has been as totally pro-Israel, anti-terrorist, or, indeed, sensitive to Jewish concerns. If symbolic acts and events are to be weighed, the highly creditable fighting of mindless anti-Israel resolutions in the UN by the Reagan administration will, for example, also have to be assessed along with Bitburg. If President Reagan was an anti-Semite, or even hostile to Jewish interests and concerns, this could have emerged long before Bitburg. Concomitant with this is the fact that whether hostility to the Bitburg visit in America was based upon or flowed from political dislike of President Reagan or his policies rather than outrage at the visit itself, would largely be absent from Australian political perceptions. Against this admittedly almost grotesque lack of judgment on the part of President Reagan must be set the rest of his Middle Eastern policies and highly sympathetic dealings with the Jewish community; since no Australian belongs to the Democratic party, it is Reagan's record of word and deed, rather than his perceptions as a party political leader, which largely determines attitudes here.

Secondly, much—indeed virtually all—of the harm done by the Bitburg visit lay in the sphere of the symbolic, especially in the seeming legitimation and normalization it gave to SS war criminals. In America, the symbolic importance of any act or statement by the President is systematically magnified by the vast publicity accorded to the president's every word and deed by the media, especially television, and by the fact that very much of political discourse in America is symbolic and based upon image, nuance, and intonation, rather than upon actual substance. Although the symbolic importance of Bitburg was fully and totally appreciated by Australian Jewry, and the visit deplored, naturally the Australian media is not preoccupied with this symbolic and imagistic side of the American Presidency, while the deeds and acts of the President are not seen in their ongoing context of forming the keystone of media accounts of public events.

Finally, Bitburg must be seen as one incident in the ongoing evolution of contemporary Jewish history. Even a few months after Reagan's visit, other events, intrinsically perhaps more important than Bitburg, have also occupied the world's headlines—the TWA hostage drama, continuing Shi'ite terrorism, the alleged discovery of the body of Josef Mengele, the release of 1100 terrorists from Israeli jails, the withdrawal from Lebanon, and so on. It seems doubtful if in future years Bitburg will seem as important as it did at the time; at least this is the Australian Jewish perspective on this event, the Australia's distance may well make for a more balanced view.

(Isi J. Leibler is President, Executive Council of Australian Jewry; Chairman, Asia Pacific section of the World Jewish Congress. He has established close ties with Prime Minister Bob Hawke and former Prime Minister Malcolm Fraser.)

Epilogue

Beyond Bitburg

The initial involvement of the U.S. government in the Holocaust issue that began in 1978 with the establishment of the Presidential Commission on the Holocaust has culminated, in the aftermath of the Bitburg affair, in the laying of the cornerstone of the Holocaust Museum in Washington. It will be interesting to see how this museum contributes to the general education of both laymen and political leaders to insure that such disastrous occurrences as the Bitburg affair are not repeated. Progress in this field will be an uphill battle, since American culture is permeated by numerous incorrect images and trivializations of the Holocaust. These are evidenced in the humor of comedian Lenny Bruce, or Zero Mostel's **The Producers,** or Leonard Cohen's poems "Flowers to Hitler," and more recently vis-a-vis the mythological presentation of the Nazi era in such fictional works as "Apt Pupil" by Stephen King. In this story a California teenager blackmails a former SS officer into telling in minute detail the evil deeds he committed during the Holocaust, which finally leads to a resurgence of his murderous behavior:

> "Maybe there is something about what the Germans did that exercises a deadly fascination over us — something that opens the catacombs of the imagination. Maybe part of our dread and horror comes from a secret knowledge that under the right — or wrong — set of circumstances, we ourselves would be willing to build such places and staff them. Black serendipity. Maybe we know that under the right set of circumstances the things that live in the catacombs would be glad to crawl out. And what do you think they would look like? Like mad Fuehrers with forelocks and shoe-polish moustaches, heil-ing all over the place? Like red devils, or demons, or the dragon that floats on its stinking reptile wings?"
>
> "I don't know . . . I think most of them would look like ordinary accountants . . . "

On the other hand, popular movies and the TV **Holocaust** mini series, although not always meticulous in historical detail, did reach millions of people with the right message. Thus, this television special was aired in West Germany with a minor change: the final episode was not the original one in which the protagonist's children are ready to embark on their journey to a safe haven in Israel, but rather focuses on the scene in which a child of the former SS officer discovers his father's uniform and demands to know what he did during the war.

The present unwillingness of people to remember the reasons of the Holocaust is succinctly presented in a recent Viennese joke that describes Sigmund Freud walking through the streets of Vienna and exclaiming in horror, "My God, there are so many amnesiacs and not a single patient."

On a general level the Bitburg affair left very minor marks on American-German relations. The role of Germany in the strategic alliance is quite stable. On another level the traditional dilemma remained without solution: how to maintain the idea of the uniqueness of the Holocaust and at the same time present it as a universal lesson. On a personal level the Bitburg affair reminds us all what a permanent scar the Nazi atrocities left upon Western civilization.

One of the major issues brought to the surface by the Bitburg incident was the inherent difficulty of maintaining an absolute separation between pure morality and traditional politics. In this case, supporters of moral causes were at times perceived to be at odds with each other because the emotional Holocaust subject leaves little room for compromise between dissenting friends. Thus, the issue becomes tantamount to a minefield, where any mistakes are magnified to catastrophic dimensions. A case in point is West German President Richard von Weizsaecker and his speech in the Bundestag entitled: "Let Us Look Truth In the Eye." Through this speech he became the beacon of German historical responsibility, its moral obligation to its own future generations and to other nations as well. Indeed, of all those in the German power structure, it was Weizsaecker who took the most striking public position, insuring that throughout this entire affair his political integrity remained beyond reproach. However, in his Christmas remarks to the German nation he called for the release of Rudolf Hess, now ninety-one years old, the last remaining Nazi leader interned in Berlin's Spandau prison. Weizsaecker cited humanitarian reasons as well as compassion *(Barmherzigkeit)* as justification for the release.

The Bitburg affair pointed out, among other things, the difficulties in classifying politicians as "pragmatists" or "moralists" based on any one isolated action or statement. President Richard von Weizsaecker, for example, called his fellow citizens to a clear and greater realization of their responsibility for the crimes committed by the Nazi regime, and then 'slipped' in tying the release of Rudolf Hess to the release of Andrei Sakharov and Nelson Mandela. Similarly, former Chancellor and Nobel Peace Prize laureate Willi Brandt, a man with an impeccable record of fighting against the Nazi regime and who had gone to his knees at the memorial to the Warsaw Ghetto uprising, stated that he personally would not have had any reservations about participating in the Bitburg wreath laying ceremony with Kohl and Reagan.

What lesson concerning the interplay of morality and politics can be drawn from this political hurricane called the Bitburg affair? One school of thought is characterized by the pragmatic/political approach taken by Israeli Prime Minister Shimon Peres: "Ronald Reagan is a great friend who committed an error. The friend will remain, so will the error." The same point of view was voiced by Morris B. Abram, who subsequently became Chairman of the Conference of Presidents of Major American Jewish Organizations, in his *New York Times* op-ed article, "Reagan Isn't Indifferent to Jews." *(See page 375.)*

Another school of thought, based on pure moral tenets, is represented by Elie Wiesel, Israel Singer, Menachem Rosensaft and others; it calls for uncompromising confrontation in such crises. The questions posed by Senator Frank Lautenberg's essay - - "Which Lesson Will Be Remembered?" *(see page 220)* — may constitute the heart of this dilemma. Perhaps future generations of Americans, Germans and Jews will look back upon the Bitburg affair and, as a result, will be able to avoid such conflicts by looking truth in the eye and letting it be the guiding light.

Beyond Bitburg

Brotherhood For The Minorities
Duisburg, West Germany
March 2, 1986

By President Richard von Weizsäcker

(Federal President von Weizsäcker spoke before 4,000 people in Duisburg, a city in the Ruhr Valley, marking Brotherhood Week, which is observed once every year in an effort to promote reconciliation between Germans and the victims of the terror of the Nazi regime. An excerpt from this speech follows.)

I.

"All men become brothers." Does this line from Schiller's "Ode to Joy" have any connection with reality? Is an event like Brotherhood Week a reflection of our everyday lives, our genuine feelings for one another, or a growing sense of concern?

Let us carefully seek answers to these questions.

As we are all aware, anti-Semitism extends far back into history. Almost all of the European nations have known it. It existed both outside and, to a very large extent, inside the Christian church and Christian theology.

Jews were continuously viewed with dislike, humiliated and robbed. They were isolated, persecuted and killed in pogroms.

The Jews in Diaspora around the world sought refuge in their faith. They refused to give it up. They remained loyal to its laws, commandments and customs, despite the persecutions they faced.

No other culture or mentality was able to separate this people from its beliefs. Many peoples have been absorbed by others in the course of the past two millennia. This has not been the case with the Jews.

If it were not for their religious faith, there would be no Jews today. Faith made Israel a nation of hope. Hope has provided it with support throughout its history and given it a sense of unity.

The faith of the Jews can be of help to others. It can bring them to reflect on their own beliefs. This is particularly true of us Christians.

When the Christians began persecuting the Jews, they forgot their own origins.

- They, themselves, had been persecuted for centuries because of their beliefs.

- They forgot the fact that the founder of their own religion was of Jewish origin. Jesus lived as a Jew among Jews. Did the Jews kill our Lord, as is so often said among Christians? No, we, the people of this earth, killed him.

- In their persecution of the Jews, the Christians forgot that the God to which the New Testament bears witness is the same God the Hebrew Bible speaks of. It is the Bible of Jesus. The God of Jesus is the God of Abraham, Moses and the prophets. The word of God, contained in the Holy Scripture, speaks to us, both Jews and Christians, here on Earth today.

- In their persecution of the Jews, the Christians forgot the central teachings of Jesus, based on Jewish religious traditions thousands of years old, i.e., the doctrine of divine and human love that does not know or accept any differences among men.

The fact that we Christians persecuted the Jews means that we forgot the brotherhood of man for which Christ died. As a religious Jew he bore witness to the fact that all men have only one father. The first words of the Lord's Prayer tell us this.

The Holocaust was an unimaginable and horrifying low point in the course of Jewish suffering. It taught us what forgetting the brotherhood of man can lead to. It took a Holocaust to motivate serious reflection on the relationship between Jews and Christians, as well as on how they might continue to live with one another. This reflective process was and continues to be difficult.

Who would wonder why many of the Jews who survived the Holocaust said that Christians should leave them in peace and that it was a bit strong to be urging them to engage in a dialogue? "Brotherhood Week" is a product of the dialogue between Christians and Jews after the war. We have every reason to be thankful for this. It helps us and we continue to need it.

II.

Anti-Semitic statements were made recently in our country. They were an insult and a source of concern to our Jewish fellow citizens and to Jews throughout the world. I would like to ask them, too, for forgiveness.

There is no excuse for these statements. They are incompatible with our view of man, of democratic humanity, of history, as well as our national honor.

No one should be taken aback by the fact that remarks of this kind are perceived with a high degree of sensitivity outside of Germany. After the war we gained the friendship of the democratic nations. Their confidence in us is based on the well-founded conviction that we are conscientiously aware of our recent past and that we base our actions on this awareness.

The consequences for our relations with our friends, both as a nation and as individual human beings, would be incalculable if there were a justifiable cause for concern regarding a reawakening of anti-Semitic sentiments.

This is the way the vast majority of our fellow citizens see it. As such, I would like to extend a heartfelt request for vigilance, understanding and assistance.

Many young people say to us: "This has to stop sometime. Stop bugging us with your past. Don't impose feelings of guilt on us." They don't say this with anti-Semitic sentiments, but rather with a need to cast off a burden. What should our response to them be?

They are not guilty of any involvement in the Holocaust. Guilt is and always will be individual. There is no such thing as the guilt of an entire nation and much less of following generations.

However, the murder of Jews, criminal offenses perpetrated by criminal individuals, had its roots in history and in mankind. This fact was made possible by widespread superficiality in intellectual and emotional responses, as well as by a traditional dislike for Jews that was broadly manifested in the way people thought, spoke, felt, and acted in their everyday affairs.

The younger generation is free to shape the era it lives in in accordance with its own insights and responsibilities. It will be able to do justice to this task:

- if it knows what happened,

- if it knows that this could not have happened without a long history of anti-Semitic prejudices,

- if it recognizes that every generation must protect itself anew against prejudice.

History passes on its heritage. It offers its teachings. No more and no less. It is not an automatically effective vaccination. Whether old or young, we are all human. No generation fails to be exposed to temptations.

Remembrance creates insights, knowledge and a sense of conscience. It creates a basis for self-awareness and self-confidence. Awareness of the past is not a burden, but rather a liberation.

The younger generation can deal with the challenges of life on its own. However, we, the older generation, can and must help. The most important thing is the example we set, the only effective means of education.

None of us has any reason to vent our feelings in irresponsible and shameless public tirades. We must not fail to react to unfeeling words that show little regard for whether or not they hurt other people.

The principle of not causing pain in others without justification takes priority over the thoughtless use of freedom of opinion. We of the older generation know that this principle must be respected most of all with regard to the Jews.

If something is talked about long enough, people end up believing it. We don't want to instill unnecessary inhibitions in our young people. We do not want to evoke resistance by applying pressure or suspecting sinister tendencies behind every case of youthful mischief. If we, the older generation, remain vigilant towards ourselves, then we will be able to defend against the forces of evil. The younger generation has the insights and the strength to do this.

III.

Brotherhood Week extends our perspective beyond the relations between Jews and Christians to the human foundations of government in general.

The religious and moral origins of the concept of brotherhood extend into the political sphere. The French revolution, the beginning of democracy in Europe, advocated brotherhood, alongside freedom and equality.

It is always worthwhile reflecting on the connection between democracy and brotherhood. Freedom and equality are demands that were fought for and are still being fought for. They are intended to be vital sources of strength for people in society.

Brotherhood, on the other hand, does not involve competition and conflict. It does not involve the satement of claims, the enforcement of demands or the winning of rights. It exists independently of democratic decision-making processes.

Wherever power and opportunity continue to be unequally distributed, brotherhood becomes an important and necessary part of democratic awareness.

Each of us encounters opportunities to test his capacity for brotherhood in his own human environment. This may involve a handicapped person in the family, at school or on the job. It may involve a young person with a prison record trying to make a new start in life. It may involve a lonely individual seeking contact with others. It may involve an older unemployed person with no chance of finding a new job. Or it may involve a refugee unable to return to his homeland.

For all of them formal freedom and equality may be a mockery if we fail to manifest brotherhood towards them.

In society, brotherhood is required in the way we deal with minorities. Any discrimination against a specific group in society is a violation of the concept of brotherhood.

Protection of minorities is not a political handout, nor is it a grandiose gesture on the part of democracy and something it could just as easily not do. On the contrary, it is part of the essence of democracy. We must not permit exceptions to this rule.

I take pleasure in noting that Sinti and Roma representatives have been invited to Duisburg this week. Before we will be able to speak of brotherhood in our relationship with them, we still have to work a lot on our own attitudes. The Sinti and Roma will help us in doing this.

Foreign workers and their families are the largest minority in our society and should be a major focus of our attention. Jews and Christians who come together for Brotherhood Week have a common source in the Scripture which can point them in the right direction. Moses recalls the time when Israel experienced what it means to be a stranger in a foreign country, saying:

"And if a stranger sojourns with you in your land, you shall not vex him. The stranger who sojourns with you shall be to you as the native among you, and you shall love him as yourself, for you were strangers in the land of Egypt" (Leviticus 19, 33/34).

The foreigner is our neighbor, our "Guestmate," as Martin Buber put it. You shall love him as yourself. Brotherhood is intended for him.

Like him, many others are waiting for this and asking whether we are willing to dedicate ourselves to them, to help them, to free them from their isolation, to include them in the same life everyone else is living, in brief to open ourselves up to them in a brotherly manner.

"From prejudice to partnership" is the theme you have given to this year's Brotherhood Week. We humans have many prejudices. Occasionally someone writes to me and asks why we always think of others. After all, we are Germans. What is involved is our name, our German values, and our pride.

Yes, to be sure, I feel the same way. However, what are our values?

The noblest minds our country has brought forth, and as a result of whose works the world today considers the Germans a cultural nation, did not shout, "Foreigners get out." On the contrary, in their time they propagated a message of brotherly love.

Goethe said of Lessing's "Nathan the Wise," a great literary work promoting human brotherhood:

"May the divine sentiment of tolerance and forbearance expressed in it always be holy and dear to the nation."

It is not just a matter of respecting someone else's sensitivity to pain. Accepting someone else, but remaining indifferent to him would be a type of tolerance bordering on disdain.

Freedom means freedom for those who hold a different opinion. This means that my freedom does not exist without the freedom of the others. I receive my freedom from them. This means the way I act towards them will determine both their and my freedom, both their and my human diginity.

Franz Rosenzweig, whose 100th birthday we are commemorating today, said: "My identity is based on my relationship with others." Countless people in our country know and are working in support of this. I would like to express my heartfelt thanks to them today. The trouble you went to and the mental effort you invested in preparing for Brotherhood Week are well worth it. Along with them I would like to thank all of our fellow citizens and the various groups in our society who lend their support to this idea and promote it in everyday life.

Young people and neighbors can take them as an example. We should all judge ourselves in terms of their standards in the test awaiting each and every one of us.

The Americanization of the Holocaust
Special Contribution

By Dr. Michael Berenbaum

(When President Carter created the President's Commission on the Holocaust, he appointed Dr. Michael Berenbaum of Georgetown University its Deputy Director.)

Facing the Holocaust

The Holocaust has become a symbol central to the identity of American Jewry. Annual Holocaust commemorations are broadly observed and well attended. Courses in the Holocaust are widely taught, resource centers and memorials are under development in many major cities, and serious scholarship is proliferating. Public occasions with Jewish content are incomplete without a required reference to the Holocaust, the memory of which is evoked to rally philanthropists and political activists, to challenge complacency, to undermine or fortify the Jewish establishment, to measure impending danger or bolster solidarity. Within the American Jewish community, the Holocaust has entered the domain of shared sacrality.

Perhaps a growing consciousness of the Holocaust was inevitable as the memory of the actual event receded and as those with direct memories of the war— or of the Jewish experience in Eastern Europe preceding the war—perished in the fullness of years. Only a generation more distant from the immediate catastrophe could dare to approach it. As the story of Lot's wife illustrates, a person cannot afford to look back while fleeing.

At a safer distance, however, the Holocaust can not be avoided. Few events in Jewish history are as basic or powerful. Few are as instructive. None is as destructive or as transformative.

"By the waters of Babylon, we sat down and cried as we remembered Zion," the poet tells us. The memory of Jerusalem's destruction was undoubtedly painful, but the place from which the event was recalled inevitably shaped the memory.

Our concern is less with the event itself than with its recall, less with history than metahistory. How does the place in which a tragedy is remembered shape the collective memory? The two great centers of Jewish life—Israel and America—deal differently with the legacy of destruction, which has permeated the folk religion of each society.

The Compound Identity of the American Jew

To understand the identity of American Jews, one must first address their

Americanism. Within the past half century, American Jews have developed an American identity and sought confirmation of their experience—legitimation for their Jewishness—within mainstream American culture. In the 50s, Will Herberg taught that America had three religious faiths—Catholic, Protestant, and Jew—and because the American experience made room for Judaism, the suburban migration of the first generation of American Jews enhanced rather than destroyed Jewish institutions. Similarly, the ethnic resurgence of the 60s gave a new affirmation of Jewishness at a time when its religious foundation was eroding. Black power made assertions of Jewishness solidarity more acceptable. Black studies forced the university to make room for Jewish studies, and the flourishing of Jewish studies that followed was possible only because—once university based—Jewish studies breached its ethnicity to become non-parochial and secular.[1]

In the seven years between the Six Day War and the Yom Kippur War, the Holocaust became a central part of Jewish consciousness. In the past dozen years, there has also been a determined effort to transmit this traumatic Jewish experience to the American people as a whole and thus enhance its importance to American Jews.

Predictably, the results have been dialectical. To confirm the Holocaust as a major Jewish experience—required that it attain recognition within American culture, yet the very act of reaching out toward a wider audience transformed the recollection and threatened its Judeo-centricity.

The attempts to introduce the Holocaust into the American experience have accelerated. In 1978, President Jimmy Carter created a Presidential Commission on the Holocaust charged with recommending a national Holocaust memorial. The commission's origin was political—as is almost every presidential action.[2] It came into being because Carter and his advisors recognized the importance of the Holocaust to the American Jewish community.[3] The date of Carter's announcement coincided with Prime Minister Menachem Begin's visit to Washington (in the middle of the congressional battle over the proposed sale of F-15 bombers to Saudi Arabia) and followed by less than a fortnight the widely successful TV mini-series on the Holocaust. One thousand rabbis were invited to the event.

The commission recommended a memorial museum where the story of the Holocaust could be retold, a program of educational outreach, and national days of remembrance to be observed across the country and in Washington, D.C. where a national ceremony would feature the President and other leaders. Though composed primarily of Jews, the commission made the deliberate decision to involve the greater American society. Intuitively, the commission understood that the role of the Holocaust within Jewish consciousness would be strengthened by secular sancta.[4]

A decade ago, there were less than a dozen courses on the Holocaust offered in American colleges and universities, yet the Holocaust is now the second most widely taught course of Judaic content—exceeded only by courses in the Hebrew Bible. The Holocaust is now taught in secondary schools throughout the country, in cities as large as New York and Philadelphia or as small as Great Barington, Massachusetts and Vineland, New Jersey. Television programs have proliferated; Green's *Holocaust* was joined by the mini-series on Wallenberg, Hershey's *The Wall,* and Felon's *Playing for Time.* All have attracted major audiences and have served as important, if flawed, vehicles for educating the American public. In the process, however, the memory and its message would change.

The Holocaust in Israel's Civil Religion

The Holocaust has also played a changing role in the civil religion of Israel as the demographic, political, and security conditions of the state evolved. Charles Liebman and Eliezer Don-Yehiya have argued that Israel's relationship to the Holocaust can be divided into three periods: 1948 to the Eichmann trial, the Eichmann trial to the Yom Kippur War, and the Yom Kippur War to the War in Lebanon.[5] In the aftermath of Lebanon, Israel will undergo yet another transition with respect to its understanding of the Holocaust.

For the first thirteen years after Israel's establishment as a state, Israeli leaders looked back on the Holocaust with fear and trembling—and, frankly speaking, with disdain. The only usable past—the only history of that period upon which they could base their future—was the heroic chapter of resistance. The fight for Jerusalem or the Negev came to be seen as an extension of the Warsaw Ghetto uprising. Historians sought to recapture a tradition of resistance defined as armed struggle against an enemy whose goal was genocide. Through oral histories and interviews, Israeli scholars successfully preserved the remnant of that history, not only in Warsaw but in other ghettoes, forests, and even the death camps. "Jews are fighters," was the lesson. Given only the means, Jews have the will to exact a high price in men and material from the enemy." The new Israeli heroes are not Diaspora leaders—neither *stadlanim* nor collaborators—but the proud representatives of a strong, independent people—so went the story.

With the Eichmann trial a native Israeli generation was forced to confront on a daily basis the twelve-year odyssey of Jewish extermination. Attorney General Gideon Hausner began the Eichmann trial by invoking Pharaoh, by reviewing three millennia of anti-Semitism, persecution, and pogroms, which culminated in the Holocaust.[7] The message was unequivocal. There could be no return to the lands of dispersion. Only a sovereign Jewish state could preserve the future.

The Passover *Haggadah* reads: "In every generation they rise against us to extinguish us." The traditional story continues, "but the Holy One, Blessed Be He, saves us from their hands." However, in the absence of a saving God, Jews turned to human means in order to protect themselves.

After the Yom Kippur War, the perilous condition of Israel came as a rude psychological blow to the Israeli national èlan. For seventy-two hours, the fate of Israel was dependent upon gentile rules; upon an American President, whose support for Israel was not matched by his love of Jews; upon a Secretary of Defense, who converted from Judaism; and upon the first Secretary of State of the United States who was—to use his own words—"of Jewish origin."[8] An independent people was humbled to discover themselves dependent on the good will of others in order to survive. Almost immediately in Israel, a new understanding developed of the desperate condition of Jews during the Holocaust coupled with a furious determination not to return to that condition.

Menachem Begin built upon this realization and constructed a usable past upon the twin pillars of anti-Semitism and the need for power. *Goyim* (literally, "the nations") hate Jews, Begin maintained. In traditional language, Esau hates Jacob. The Jews are a people that dwells alone. Power is essential. Powerlessness invites victimization. Jews must determine their own morality. The world's pronouncements toward the Jews masks — sometimes more successfully and sometimes less so — their genocidal intent. The desire to make the world *Judenrein* continues, and only a fool would allow himself to be deceived.

In the aftermath of Lebanon and its miscalculations — triggered in part by an inability to separate the politics of the 80s from the conditions of the 40s[9] — along with Israel's current economic dependence upon the United States, a new historical perspective can be anticipated. The questions Israel asks of the past will change; its responses may be more complex and more confused. Meir Kahane's unbridled hatred offers one reading of how Israel may grapple with the memory of the Holocaust. He copies the Nazis and echoes their myths. He longs for one nation, one folk. He wants to expel the alien and make Israel *Arabrein*. Yet, however pernicious Kahane's solution, in contrast to Hitler Kahane is a great humanitarian since he advocates expulsion with compensation — a far cry from Hitler's final solution.[10] The apocalyptic messianism of Gush Emunim offers a second option that threatens to overwhelm Labor's more secular reading of history.[11]

In short, Israel has retold the Holocaust story to mold and reinforce its national saga as it has developed over the past thirty-seven years.

Survivors and the American Dream

In America another reading of history has evolved. Two personal experiences in this regard might prove instructive. In 1983 I helped organize the American Gathering of Jewish Holocaust Survivors, which brought more than 20,000 survivors to Washington for a three day conference — the largest single sustained assembly in American Jewish history. The Gathering was convened on the fortieth anniversary of the Warsaw Ghetto Uprising to counteract the widespread and painful perception that Jews went compliantly to their deaths — like sheep to the slaughter — and to give new meaning to the word resistance — armed and spiritual. The organizers also wanted to express their commitment to Israel and speak to the American people.

This was not the first gathering of Jewish Holocaust survivors. Two years earlier, five thousand people from fourteen different countries came to Jerusalem. Amid the sacred shrines of old and new Jerusalem — the Western Wall, Yad Vashem, and the Knesset Building — as well as the Warsaw Ghetto Fighters' Kibbutz and Yad Mordecai — survivors assembled and formally transmitted their legacy to the next generation.[12]

When they met in Washington, by contrast, they were surrounded by other national shrines—the Capitol, the White House, the Washington Monument, Arlington Cemetery, the Lincoln and Vietnam Memorials. Much to the surprise of the survivors themselves, in speeches to large and formal sessions, in presentations to small seminars, and in conversations at informal meetings America became the dominant theme of the conference—or at least the survivors' unique sense of America.

There were expressions of pride and appreciation for America, the land of opportunity and liberty. "Our adopted country has been kind to us," said one Polish survivor, "and we in turn have contributed in some small way to build a strong and just society based on equality and justice for all." Another survivor said, "America embraced us when we felt rejected. America gave us the feeling of belonging when we were stateless." There were words of gratitude to America for defeating the Nazis, liberating the concentration camps, welcoming survivors, supporting Israel, and establishing a national Holocaust memorial.

Of course, there were also words of bitterness and sadness as survivors recalled long lines at U.S. consulates, quotas restricting refugees, ships turned away from American shores, gates closed to fleeing Jews, and bombs dropped everywhere but at Auschwitz. For unlike earlier immigrant generations, survivors are a reminder not only of the American dream but of America's failure to serve as a haven in the hour of greatest need.

During their three days in Washington, some survivors spoke of themselves as the embodiment of the American dream. Driven from their native lands by a tyrant, they came to America bereft of material possessions but fueled by a love of freedom. Through industry and initiative, they rebuilt their lives, raised children and grandchildren, and became an integral part of American life—adding to the rich mosaic of American culture their unique heritage of *yiddishkeit* and *menchlichkeit*. They portrayed themselves as incarnations of the simple values that are the essence of the American experience—courage and dignity, hope and defiance.

When survivors gathered in Jerusalem, they came as pilgrims to add their experience to the Jewish national saga, to which they felt inextricably connected. When they came to Washington, they offered their experience as part of the American drama, to which they also belonged.

Universalization and Dejudaization:

From 1979-81, I worked with a team of educational researchers, psychologists, historians, and sociologists on a study of four different Holocaust curricula—material developed by teachers and students in Great Neck, New York; Brookline, Massachusetts; Philadelphia, Pennsylvania; and New York City along with the written curricula of several other cities. In each of these four school systems, students and teachers were interviewed as well as the developers of Holocaust curricula.[13]

At that time, I had just completed writing a book on Elie Wiesel as a religious thinker within the context of post-Holocaust theology. In particular, I concentrated on the work of Emil Fackenheim, Richard Rubenstein, and Eliezer Berkovits along with Wiesel. I had also just begun my work with the President's Commission on the Holocaust.

Three debates affected my theological studies as well as the commemorative activities planned by the Holocaust Commission. They dominated the milieu in which I worked, taught, and wrote.

Theologically, the Holocaust appeared as the *mysterium tremendum* the awesome mystery—which cannot be penetrated. This insight forms the core of Fackenheim's theological work and was the basis of Wiesel's "Plea for the Survivors." Wiesel argued that the non-survivor can only approach the gates of the event and view it indistinctly from afar.

At the time, the President's Commission was engaged in a long and bitter debate concerning the uniqueness and universality of the Holocaust. Was the Holocaust an unprecedented event—a universe apart from the experience of the Armenians under Turkish rule, the slaughter in Biafra, the auto-genocide of Cambodia, and the suffering of non-Jewish nationals under occupation in Eastern Europe? Were Jews the only victims of the Holocaust? How should the Holocaust be defined?

Yehuda Bauer, the distinguished Israeli historian, argued that the Holocaust was the systematic, state-sponsored extermination of six million Jews as an international act of state undertaken in pursuit of what was considered a redemptive goal.[14] Simon Wiesenthal suggested another definition (which was adopted by Carter in the formal documents of the commission and its successor body, the United States Holocaust Memorial Council). "The Holocaust is the destruction of six million Jews and five million non-Jews by the Nazis and their collaborators during World War II."[15] Elie Wiesel sought language that would protect the uniqueness of the Holocaust and differentiate between the Jewish and non-Jewish victims of Nazism. The Holocaust, he argued, "was the systematic, bureaucratic extermination of six million Jews by the Nazis and their collaborators as a central act of state during the Second World War; as night descended, millions of other people were swept into this net of death."[16] "While not all the victims were Jews," Wiesel wrote, "all Jews were victims." In this way, he negotiated the labyrinth between those who argued for a Judeo-centric uniqueness and the national requirement of universality imposed by the President.

To Jews in Israel and in America, the Holocaust was a source of distinctiveness, albeit a horrible one, among peoples. Christianity had provided the Nazis with the choice of the Jew as victim, and Christian teaching and institutions did not have the moral force to resist Nazism. Modernity had also failed. The political, economic, bureaucratic,and demographic trends of modern Western society set the stage for the Holocaust. If a scientifically developed, culturally advanced, and philosophically sophisticated Germany could perpetrate the Holocaust, then Jews were different, a nation set apart—chosen, if not by the God of Israel, then at least by the enemies of that God.[17]

Under the circumstances, I was surprised to discover that in numerous public school systems throughout the United States, instruction in the Holocaust has become an instrument for teaching the professed values of American society: democracy, pluralism, respect for differences, individual responsibility, freedom from prejudice, and an abhorrence of racism.

High school students of the Holocaust and their teachers were essentially uninterested in the debate that consumed theologians and historians. They viewed the Holocaust as an extreme example of what can happen if the core values of American society were consistently abrogated.

All curricula had a common methodological assumption, which negated mystery. They saw the Holocaust as a human experience—committed and endured by human beings. As such, the Holocaust can be discussed and, yes, even understood by students in grades seven through twelve.

Holocaust curricula were not used, as some had feared, to differentiate between Jews and non-Jews. Instead, they became a means of reducing barriers between students. One black student spoke of telling the story of the Holocaust in his Brooklyn neighborhood and getting the following response: "God, we thought *we* had it bad." In Great Neck, with its large Jewish population, a study of the Holocaust reportedly sparked some of the most honest and personal discussions that students ever had.

The question of "universalizing" the Holocaust (of comparing it to other events or removing it from an exclusively Jewish context) was a recurrent issue. For example, such charges were leveled at William Styron's *Sophie's Choice*. In *A Double Dying*, Alvin Rosenfeld makes this accusation of Styron. Rosenfeld writes:

> *Sophie's Choice*...is another prominent example of the tendency to universalize Auschwitz as a murderous thrust against mankind. As such, it has the effect, and no doubt the intention, of removing the Holocaust from its place within Jewish and Christian history and placing it within the generalized history of evil, for which no one in particular need be held accountable.[18]

Rosenfeld objects to Styron's tendency—shared by other American writers and by the teachers interviewed in the study of Holocaust curriculum—to view the Holocaust from the perspective of their own experience; they place the Holocaust in categories alien to the event but native to the American soil. In Styron's case, Stingo's encounter with the Holocaust was shaped by his early experience of racism, domination, and violence—that is, by his personal history as a sensitive Southerner growing up during the war. Styron chose Rubenstein's *The Cunning of History* as his text because it approached the Holocaust from a perspective he understood; Rubenstein described the Holocaust as an expression of human slavery in the extreme—and thus in continuity with *The Confessions of Nat Turner*. At I. G. Auschwitz, slavery reached its most extreme manifestation. The slave became a consumable raw material to be discarded in the process of manufacture and recycled into the Nazi war economy (gold for the treasury, hair for stuffing mattresses, and the ashes of body fat to salt the winter roads).

Norbert Samuelson has suggested that the American Jewish image of the Holocaust has revolved around the passion, sentimentality and fervor of Elie Wiesel. Elizer Berkovits' work, *With God in Hell* seeks to reclaim the Holocaust for the pious believer. Arthur Miller's television script *Playing for Time* creates a character with which the secular Jewish left can identify, and William Styron appropriates the Holocaust for the gentiles.

As the study of the Holocaust passes out of the ghetto and into the mainstream of American culture, it will inevitably be reunderstood in different categories — and thus, in part, dejudaized.

In American high schools, as in Styron's work, the Holocaust was not "generalized" (not, for example, viewed as just another act of violence undifferentiated from all others); rather, it was regarded as distinct — unique because its scale and content was unprecedented even though it was analyzed within a secular context.

The authors of the curricula study concluded:

> As an event of this magnitude is incorporated into the American educational system, the lens through which the data is seen is necessarily an American one. The categories relate to the experience of American students throughout the country and also to their teachers. There is no way of resisting this tide, and indeed from our research, we find that the uniqueness of the Holocaust is underscored by this process of filtration and absorption. Indeed, its specialness is its own best witness, communicating itself most profoundly, most clearly and incontrovertibly.[19]

Optimism and the Reality of Auschwitz

Americans tend to be optimistic; the national ethos avoids the tragic or searches for a silver lining behind dark clouds. This hopeful tendency has reflected itself in the ways Americans deal with the Holocaust intellectually. Popularizers of the Holocaust have tended to look for *cheap grace,* for easy sources of consolation. They have sought to minimize the evil or to severely limit its implications.

Some have focused on the righteous gentile as a source of hope. Three cases come readily to mind: one a country, the second a village, and the third an individual — Denmark, Le Chambon, and Raoul Wallenberg. Each case is powerfully consoling, each simple in its common humanity. And each has entered the domain of legend.

The Danes explain that they did nothing extraordinary; they simply treated Jews as fellow citizens facing persecution from an oppressive, occupying army. The villagers of Le Chambon were raised on a tradition of hospice; Protestants in Catholic France — themselves persecuted, they just did what they had been taught to do when young Jewish children came knocking at their doors. Wallenberg was frustrated sitting on the side lines while the action was taking place elsewhere; he couldn't side with the despised Nazis or continue diplomatic business as usual.

No matter how touching these examples of humanity and heroism, righteous gentiles were numerically rare. There is an extraordinary imbalance between their accomplishment—however noble and glorious—and the needs.

As we look at the landscape of Europe, complicity and cowardice are the norm. Indifference was widespread. This reality does not demean the deeds of the few, but the flicker of hope that these exceptions generated is overwhelmed by darkness.

Instead of pointing to religious heroes and martyrs—a Bonhoffer, a Trochme, or a Niemoller—Christians must confront the uncomfortable fact that Church teaching allowed the Jews to be chosen as victims.

Religious practice measurably influenced the behavior of the perpetrators and the response of the bystanders. There was a direct correlation between the intensity of religious practice and the percentage of Jews killed in an occupied territory. Where Christians were most devout—in Poland, Slovakia, and the Baltic countries—the percentage of Jews killed increased (90% in Poland, 89% in Slovakia, 90% in the Baltic states—Latvia, Lithuania and Estonia).[20]

President Ronald Reagan also expressed this naive American optimism in his decision to visit Bitburg and in the statements he made at Bitburg and Bergen-Belsen. Reagan sought to narrow the scope of the Holocaust. It was proper, he thought, to pay tribute to German soldiers. They were honorable men who died on the battlefield for a dishonorable cause. Once he discovered that members of the Waffen SS were buried at Bitburg, Reagan further narrowed the scope of evil. Waffen SS were acceptable—after all, many of these men were conscripts eighteen or nineteen years of age—it was the SS elite volunteers, according to Reagan, who were actually to blame for killing Jews.

At Bitburg, Reagan spoke as if Hitler alone were responsible for the Holocaust. According to his speech, the entire apparatus of destruction rested on the shoulders of one man as good people were led astray. Reagan conveniently overlooked the assistance that the German military gave the SS *Einsatzgruppen* on the Russian front, not to mention the pervasiveness of Nazism within German society and the role of the SS in Western Europe. Not to be confused by facts, Reagan minimized, personalized, and limited the evil of the Holocaust.

America's optimistic tendencies are also reflected in a more sophisticated and serious way by Terrence Des Pres's *The Survivor.* In this moving study of Holocaust survivors—and survivors of the Russian Gulag—Des Pres poignantly describes the victims' suffering and their struggle. He does not hesitate to probe and graphically detail the survivors' anguish. Neither does he shy away from the unseemly—ruthlessness, aggressiveness, sexuality, and excremental assault. Yet in his final chapter on Radical Nakedness—at the lowest point of despair in the book—Des Pres detects what he terms the essence of human survival. Quoting a survivor, he states: "It wasn't the ruthlessness that enabled an individual to survive—it was an intangible quality, not particular to educated or sophisticated individuals... It is best described as an overriding thirst—perhaps, too, a talent for life, and a faith in life."[21]

Des Pres concludes:

> Much of the behavior of survivors may thus be traced to the "biosocial" roots of human existence; and not their behavior merely, but also the extraordinary stubbornness of will which characterizes action in extremity—the furious energy of a will impersonal and stronger than hope, which in an accurate, unmetaphorical sense can only be that of life itself.[22]

One cannot fail to be touched by the power of Des Pres' words and the awesome experience he describes. Yet, as Lawrence Langer has argued: "from the perspective of the victims, who far outnumber the survivors, the disorder of meaningless death contradicts the ordering impulses of time. Those who died for nothing in the Holocaust left the living with a paralyzing dilemma of facing a perpetually present grief."[23]

The Holocaust cannot be reduced to an order, to a system for survival or even to a sense of overriding meaning. The Holocaust defies meaning and negates hope. The scope of victimization reduces even survival to a nullity. The reality of Auschwitz should silence the optimists.

Conclusion

Two modern thinkers have sought to situate the Jew outside of history. For Franz Rosenzweig, Jews gaze at eternity untainted by history. For Joseph Soloveitchik, Jews are the recipients of an archetypal divine plan unchanging in time and space. For most others, religion—like life—is organic.

Some may argue that the Americanization of the Holocaust distorts the event. The Holocaust took place on the soil of Europe and to the body of the Jewish people. But only a part of memory involves the past. The past image is projected upon a screen of the present with which it interacts, and this new image in turn sheds light on the future. In addressing the authenticity of memory, we must examine both its source and its projection.

History reconstitutes itself in memory. Although American and Israeli Jews remember the same event as basic to their identity and even though the memory of that event cements the link between the two communities, their present reality and national sagas are so different that what is gleaned from the past for the future may increasingly diverge.

The tide of Americanization cannot easily be avoided because in order for Israeli scholarship to move beyond its shores, it must reach out to its western brethren. For Jews to solidify the place of the Holocaust within Jewish consciousness, they must establish its importance for the American people as a whole. The process cannot be reversed for the decision has already been made. By sharing our experience with the world, we have transformed it and it in turn has changed us.

FOOTNOTES

1. See Jacob Neusner, *The Public Side of Learning* (Chico:Scholars Press, 1985) pp. 27-39.
2. Michael Berenbaum, "On the Politics of Public Commemoration of the Holocaust," in *Shoah* (Fall/Winter 1981-82) pp. 9, 37.
3. President Jimmy Carter's advisors had deep roots in the Jewish community. The commission was originally suggested in a memo by Mark Siegel, who later left the White House to protest the sale of F-15s to Saudi Arabia. Stuart Eizenstat brought the project to Carter's attention.
4. *Report to the President: President's Commission on the Holocaust,* Washington: Government Printing Office, 1979).
5. Charles Liebman and Eliezer Don-Yehiya, *Civil Religion in Israel,* (Berkley: University of California Press, 1983) pp. 151-153.
6. *Ibid.* pp. 104-107.
7. Gideon Hausner, *Justice in Jerusalem* New York: Harper and Row 1966).
8. Henry Kissinger, *White House Years* (Boston: Little Brown, 1978).
9. Throughout the war Begin kept calling Beirut, Berlin. Ze'ev Schiff and Edhud Yaari report that Begin's basic commitment to the Christian population of Lebanon was a result of his identification with their fate.
10. Even Kahane's slogans evoke the memory of the Holocaust.
11. See Charles Liebman and Eliezer Don-Yehiya, *Religion and Politics in Israel* (Bloomington and London: Indiana University Press, 1984).
12. Sam Bloch, *From Holocaust to Redemption* (New York: American Gathering of Jewish Holocaust Survivors, 1983).
13. Mary T. Glynn, Geoffrey Bock with Karen C. Cohn, *American Youth and the Holocaust: A Study of Four Major Curricula* (New York: Zachor, 1982).
14. Yehudah Bauer, "Whose Holocaust?" in *Midstream,* Vol. XXVI, No. 9 (November 1980), p. 42.
15. This definition was expressed in the major address of President Jimmy Carter on the Holocaust and in the decision memo that led to the formation of the United States Holocaust Memorial Council. It is also found in the Executive Order announcing the formation of the Council.
16. *Report to the President,* p. 3.
17. This position is expressed by Eliezer Berkovits in *Faith After Auschwitz* (New York: Ktav Books, 1973).
18. Alvin Rosenfeld, *A Double Dying,* (Bloomington and London: Indiana University Press, 1980) p. 159.
19. *Op cit.* p. 126.
20. Helen Fein, *Accounting for Genocide* New York: Free Press, 1979).
21. Terrence Des Pres, *The Survivor* (New York and London: Oxford University Press, 1976) pp. 191-192.
22. *Ibid.,* p. 201.
23. Lawrence Langer, *Versions of Survival: The Holocaust and the Human Spirit* (Albany: State University of New York Press. 1982) p. 79.

The State of Contemporary German Nationalism
Book Excerpt

By Professor Walter Laqueur

When the Second World War ended it was widely assumed that the eradication of Nazism would be a long and difficult process. The Nazis were thought to have prepared for a protracted guerrilla campaign (by the so-called Werewolves) and also a political underground. Yet not a single Werewolf was ever seen; the plot had been a chimera. Nevertheless the spectre of a Nazi revival has not been put to rest in the last forty years. On the contrary, the underground survival of Nazi groups has not only provided inspiration to thriller writers (from the *Odessa File* to *The Boys from Brazil*), but has been the source of a flood of articles, books and movies under the general title 'Are the Nazis Returning?' On some occasions the question was transformed into a statement. This was, in part, the product of an excess of imagination, in part the desire to entertain. For a swastika on the cover of a thriller or a Nazi uniform in a movie were still powerful symbols and exerted a magic influence all over the world.

There was also political calculation: some circles had a vested interest in the survival of Nazism (or neo-Nazism). They had always maintained that the conditions which had produced Nazism still existed; that, in fact, post-war German society was morally so corrupt that it was bound to give birth to another neo-Nazi movement. Since Nazism had been right-wing (so the argument ran), the post-Hitlerian Right was a potential recruit to the new Nazism. With a little effort this argument could be further stretched so as to include the Christian Democrats and even many Social Democrats; for since the Nazis had been anti-communists, did it not follow that all anti-communists were neo-Nazis? These Nazi chasers were not interested in real Nazis but in groups which they defined as 'fascistoid', i.e. potential fascists. What Hermann Goering had said about Jews they applied to these groups — they would decide who was fascistoid. These critics pointed to the persistence of 'authoritarian structures', to the massive use of terror and propaganda in the *Bundesrepublic,* to negative attitudes towards modern art or homosexuality, and to social repression in general.

Exercises of this kind did not need to be taken unduly seriously because of their blatantly propagandist character. But the campaign did have its dangerous implications: it gratuitously gave publicity to a weak enemy who craved such publicity more than anything else, who could not have attracted it in any other way. Directly or indirectly it thus played into the hands of right-wing extremism.[2] The fact that much of this 'anti-fascist' campaign was instigated by communists and their fellow travellers, who claimed that they, and only they, had been the only consistent anti-Nazis from the very beginning, made many people doubt its bona fide character. Since attachment of the communists to the cause of democracy and liberty, or indeed their historical record relative to Nazism, was not en-

712 EPILOGUE: BEYOND BITBURG

tirely above suspicion, this campaign made some believe that a cause so bitterly attacked by the communists could not be all bad, a wrong conclusion but psychologically an understandable one. Thirdly, and equally importantly, the constant invocation of the neo-Nazi danger involved all the dangers of the 'cry wolf' syndrome: for even if the old Nazis were dying out and the young Nazis were few and far between, the danger of a major neo-Nazi revival, though improbable, could not be ruled out entirely. Constant vigilance was imperative, and through exaggeration and falsification this vigilance was undermined.

Many millions of Germans had belonged to the Nazi party and its various branches. Many more had believed in Hitler and Nazism. The war and the defeat had weakened or destroyed such beliefs, but this is not to say that they all became fervent believers in parliamentary democracy from one day to the next. The Allies dabbled in re-education, though it ought to be clear that they were ill-equipped for an assignment of this sort. It is relatively easy to replace one dictatorship by another. It is infinitely more difficult to make people think and act independently. The Allies engaged in de-Nazification, but the campaign soon ran out of steam. As the German elite in its overwhelming majority had belonged to the party, the Allies soon realized that as far as the middle and lower echelons of the bureaucracy were concerned, it was virtually impossible to run the country altogether without former party members. True, they would not employ leading Nazis, but for those who had not been prominent in politics before 1945 there were no particular handicaps to overcome to make a comeback after 1950. And so the state secretaries, bankers and professors returned, most of them now on their best democratic behavior. As far as they had been concerned, it had been a giant mistake or a tragic chain of developments, and they had joined to prevent worse crimes. It would have been nearer the truth if they had argued that few had been fanatical Nazis and that most had joined because everyone else did. But this plausible argument was not frequently heard.

To be fair to them, these former Nazis were, on the whole, loyal to the new regime, and did not try to undermine it from within. Whether the conversion was altogether genuine was not even of decisive importance; it was enough to know that no one in public office would dare to speak up for the 'good old days' or would try to justify Hitler. Some thought with regret about what they considered the positive aspects of Nazism, but everyone knew that it was finished.

Not all former Nazis were astute or lucky enough to make a comeback. Some found the new subservience to Western values morally wrong and aesthetically displeasing: how could one abjure one's gods just because the country had been defeated and occupied? It was among these men and women — and there were many hundreds of thousands of them — that Nazi views still found many sympathizers in the early post-war period, even though not much of this feeling surfaced. The old-timers did not arrange mass meetings or provoke street battles; they congregated in unobtrusive places and their views were given expression in internal newsletters of which few outsiders even knew. Most were ready to admit that Hitler may have committed some excesses: it had been a mistake to kill all the

Jews, some other way should'have been found to get rid of them. Of course the myth of the 'six millions' was a wicked lie: probably there were not more than a few hundred thousand. But it had been an error of judgment in any case, used now to besmirch the good name of the German people. They were willing to point to some other mistakes: on the whole they liked the pre-1939 Hitler better than the strategist of defeat.

They bitterly opposed Allied attempts to put all the blame on the German people, and they tried to show that Hitler had no more wanted the war than the Allies. If some excesses had been committed by the Germany army, Allied war crimes (such as the bombing of German cities) had been worse. The old faithful saw it as their duty to continue Hitler's fight against the contamination of German politics and culture by alien, sick elements, against the systematic destruction of traditional German values. They were in the forefront of the struggle for discipline and order, for a general amnesty to all 'political prisoners', and bitterly attacked the collaborationists and traitors (such as Adenauer) working for a new Germany so remote from their own ideals.

Such resentment may appear harmless enough in retrospect, the impotent rage of the defeated. But the country was still very poor, the economic miracle had not yet borne fruit, many millions of expellees who had lost everything streamed in from the East — more likely to blame the new order than the old for their plight. If Nazism did not have a real revival in the early 1950s it was mainly because even the most fanatical understood that the clock could not be put back, and that even an attempt to do so would result in total disaster. They had to accept that for the time being they had to lie low: perhaps in the future conditions would be more auspicious for the success of their cause. And so they would meet from time to time and reminisce about the good old days. Their heroes more often than not were military leaders, such as the Luftwaffe ace Colonel Rudel, rather than political figures. As the veterans grew older, they would collect Third Reich memorabilia, rewrite history and publish almanacs in which the months of the year were called *Wonnemond, Hartung,* and so on. Politically their influence was nil, for the new system worked and the economy improved. True, the new regime was in no hurry to confront the past; much that was inconvenient was swept under the carpet. Views which resembled Nazi doctrine could be heard from time to time in the 1950s among leaders of legal parties such as the BHE (the expellees), the German party, and even the far Right of the liberals and the CDU. The fact that Brandt and Herbert Wehner had been emigrants during the Hitler era was used in anti-SPD propaganda; about Erich Ollenhauer, another émigré, it was said that he was a half-Jew. The career of neither suffered, but the very fact that such arguments could be used publicly was a matter of concern.

The neo-Nazis derived little benefit from all this. For while the number of such organizations continued to grow their membership declined, the sects became even smaller and more sectarian. On two occasions in the 1950s and 1960s two major parties emerged to serve as a rallying point, the SRP and the NPD, of which mention has already been made. But even in their heyday, which lasted a mere two to three years, they were never a serious force — unlike, for instance, neo-fascism in Italy. The Italian MSI polled 9 percent of the total in the general election of 1972, while in the elections in Sicily and other southern regions the figure was 17 percent. The NPD polled between 7 and 8 percent in Bavaria, Hesse and Lower Saxony, but never overcame the 5 percent overall hurdle for representation in the *Bundestag*.

After the rapid decline of the NPD (1969-70) it was only a matter of a few years before the old Nazis would have ceased to exist. Even the younger ones among them, those who had been twenty when Hitler came to power, were pensioned off in the 1970s. Nazism had once been the party of youth; no major political initiatives, no great fresh impulses could be expected from these elderly, cautious and disillusioned former party members. The youth groups of the extreme Right were pathetically small, their representatives in the universities (BNS — *Bund nationaler Studenten*) almost non-existent. The attempts to revive the conservative *Korporationen* among the students, including those committed to duelling, were more successful. But even they did not amount to much and, in any case, could not possibly be equated with Nazism; they had, in fact, been banned in the Third Reich.

It could reasonably be assumed that neo-Nazism and the other groups of the extreme Right would wither away and eventually die out with the generation that had been the standard-bearer of Nazism. Such assumptions failed to take into account, however, the fact that in one form or another, extreme right-wing parties exist in every democratic society. For obvious reasons this trend was bound to be relatively weak in Germany, but there was no reason to believe that it would cease to exist altogether. One obvious cause for its persistence was the division of Germany, another the taboo on German nationalism during the first post-war decades. Just as democratic regimes in every European country are attacked from the far Left, they come under fire from the extreme Right by men and women claiming that there is no real freedom, that the democratic leaders are mere puppets who do not forcefully represent the nation's interests, that aliens have too much influence, that the Fatherland is in utmost peril and that only true patriots — those of the far Right — can possibly save it from ruin. It would have been a miracle if such views had not found some advocates in post-war Germany.

One specifically German form of right-wing dissent had been the belief that a third road in between (or rather different from) capitalism and communism was needed and that Germany was predestined to lead mankind in this direction. The idea of a national Bolshevism or of a national revolutionary movement has exerted a strong fascination for young Germans since the 1920s. It was not surprising therefore that some of the old ideas were rediscovered in the late 1960s and early 1970s, and reappeared in a somewhat modified form. This 'New Right' had certain features in common with the French *Nouvelle Droite* (GRECE), but in some respects it was quite *sui generis*. It was an attempt to combine incompatible ideas and concepts in which some genuinely believed. For others it was a mere public-relations stunt providing a left-wing, more attractive package for old-fashioned reactionary, or even fascist, ideas. Hitler's movement, after all, had also first appeared in a socialist disguise. Lastly, some suspected Soviet and communist influences behind the neutralist and anti-American slogans which, with varying intensity, were voiced by these circles. In view of the divisions on the New Right one could find proof for every one of these assumptions. Common to virtually all groups of this camp was their 'European orientation'. The most influential periodical of the far Right was called, not by accident, *Nation Europa*. They also advocated a new bio-humanism (more 'bio' than 'human') and a concern with the natural environment in contrast to the strong technological (and technocratic) element in both Marxism and capitalism. They rejected the old-fashioned Nazi race theories in their cruder form but smuggled some of them in through the back door in a more 'scientific' guise. There were marked differences in their ideas about the ideal social order. Some suggested a return to the corporationist and solidarist ideas first mooted in the 1920s. Others advocated a national socialism, not on the Nazi model but following the ideas first developed — they claimed — by Ferdinand Lassalle, a German Jew and a contemporary of Marx. Some even claimed to draw inspiration from the Chinese agricultural communes.

The leaders of this New Right belonged almost without exception to the post-war generation. They had studied with the same teachers who had influenced their left-wing comrades and it is not difficult to point to ideas among the 'New Right' which appeared in the writings of Herbert Marcuse and other gurus of this generation: the rejection of consumerism, the opposition to technocracy, the necessity to fight 'repressive tolerance', the critique of the manipulation of the media, of the American way of life, and, generally speaking, the frequent invocation of an anti-capitalist spirit which superficially sounded quite genuine. The spokesmen of the New Right frequently argued that while their starting-point had been on the old Right, they had more in common with their contemporaries on the Left than with their forefathers on the Right. With their ecological and anti-nuclear enthusiasm, their cultural anti-Americanism and their support for movements of national liberation in many parts of the world, the 'national revolutionaries' tried, in fact, to outflank their left-wing contemporaries. Some regarded Sinn Fein as a model for the German national revolutionaries, others suggested 'political Balkanization' in Germany and Europe as a solution to all outstanding questions.

While the national Bolshevism of the late 1920s expressed a mood that was fairly widespread at the time, it never became a political force. The same is true for the present-day national revolutionaries. Their inconsistencies are too blatant: truly European patriotism is incompatible with the chauvinist-racialist nonsense which has been part and parcel of the doctrine of the extreme Right in Germany. If their anti-capitalist and neutralist slogans are genuine and also their commitment to ecological revolution and participatory democracy, there is no need for a new party — the 'revolutionary Right' could find a new home in one of the existing parties of the Left as some of their precursors did in the 1930s. If, on the other hand, these left-wing professions are mere demagogy, the swindle will come out sooner rather than later.

Such attempts to merge left- and right-wing doctrines may have a certain fascination for intellectuals but the true militants of the extreme Right need more robust fare: a *Führer,* an enemy against whom violence can be directed, and some certainties. Nazism and fascism never tried very hard to conquer the intelligentsia, and consequently neo-Nazism has been more active among soccer crowds, motorcycle gangs and rock groups than among university students.

The number of right-wing extremist groups has continued to rise even in recent years (from sixty-nine in 1975 to seventy-four in 1982, among them twenty-two that were defined as neo-Nazi by the German authorities). But, to repeat once again, these figures reveal more about the fragmentation of the extreme Right than the number of its members which is now more or less static. For the first time some of the neo-Nazi groups have engaged in terrorist operations in recent years, such as the murder of foreign workers in Nuremberg and the attacks against U.S. soldiers near Frankfurt in December 1982. Far-Right paramilitary units have been established on a small scale and weapons collected.

The neo-Nazis have also shown eagerness to adapt themselves to modern forms of organization such as *Bürgerinitiativen.* They have sent out threatening letters to major employers demanding the dismissal of foreign workers. Some of the slogans daubed on the walls of German houses are barely distinguishable from those of the far Left (*Nie wieder Krieg* — Never again war. Smash this state, foreign troops out of Germany!). The periodical of the *Wiking Jugend,* which in one guise or another has been the main youth organization of the far Right for many years, published an article in 1982 to the effect that he who refuses to join the *Bundeswehr* does not object to national defense but merely refuses to serve in the 'international mercenaries' troop called NATO which is guided solely by American imperialist interests and which wants to make Europe an atomic battlefield. The conscientious objector was therefore merely doing his share to prevent the Holocaust prepared against the European peoples. With only slight changes such appeals could have been published by the extreme Left, which has led some observers to look for a hidden hand manipulating the extreme Right. Such penetration of the extreme Right is perfectly possible and has on occasion taken place in the past. But for anti-Western inspiration the extreme Right is in no need of loans from anyone; Nazism always waged war against Western liberal and democratic ideas.

There is one major political issue which neo-Nazism has all to itself and of which it has made the most: the campaign against foreign workers. There is resentment in Germany against the presence of these workers and their families, as there is in France and Britain. It is widely believed that they deprive German families of work and housing, that they have made Germany's streets unsafe. The extreme Right, again as in Britain and France, has tried to exploit these feelings, launching various campaigns against these foreigners. It is not that easy any more to find Jews in contemporary Germany, but there is no such difficulty in meeting Turks. At a time of economic crisis, anti-foreign feeling tends to become exacerbated. But it is still doubtful whether the neo-Nazis will derive lasting benefit from their campaigns against foreigners. They may trigger off some local riots, or score gains at some local elections. But those who join them in Turk-bashing will not usually stick with them at the next elections. The communists have been far more adept with various kinds of popular front tactics, but they too have not benefited much in the final analysis.

Neo-Nazism has been interpreted, just as have the New Left and the Greens, as a manifestation of a cultural crisis or, more specifically, a collective identity crisis, the sad remnants of so many unfulfilled post-war hopes. Some of the blame has been put, not without justification, at the door of the authorities, the political parties and society which did not squarely confront the Nazi period as it should have done in the 1950s and 1960s. It has been argued that massive indoctrination in a democratic society may be counterproductive. The emergence of Nazi symbols in the Punk-Rock scene seems to provide evidence to this effect. (This refers to the appearance of SS swastikas, rock groups with names like London SS or Nazi Dog, and songs with titles such as *Auschwitz Jerk* and *Blitzkrieg Boy.*) But such occurrences were equally frequent in Britain and should not be seen as a token of deep ideological identification with Nazism, about which little or nothing is known among Rockers and Punks. The main intention is to annoy adults rather than protest against a surfeit of anti-Nazi propaganda. The musings of isolated intellectuals and the exploits of Punk groups are of no great political consequence. What then is the present potential of neo-Nazism in Germany?

Empirical investigations in the early 1980s have shown that no fewer than 15 percent of all electors in West Germany had a 'complete right-wing extremist world view' (the SINUS study). If one adds the number of those not opposed to the democratic order in principle, but fascinated by strong men and in favor of law and order, such a picture could be frightening. But a closer look does not give that much cause for alarm. Such studies teach us more about the use and abuse of public opinion polls than about the true state of affairs. An examination of the scales on which the SINUS study was based show that the questions asked are such that many left-wing extremists and perhaps even some critical democrats could easily pass into the right-wing extremist camp or even the 'fascistoid' category.

It is more illuminating (and encouraging) to learn that over the last thirty years the number of Germans who believe in a democratic system has substantially increased and that, on the other hand, the number of those who think that Germany's golden years were before 1945, or that Hitler would have entered history as a great statesman had he not gone to war in 1939, has dramatically declined. A group of distinguished German social scientists discovered in the late 1950s that 30 percent of Germany's students belonged at least potentially to the extreme Right. But only a few years later German campuses were shaken by a student revolt in which the extreme Right was neither seen nor heard. Had it been a chimera?

The pretense of hostile feelings towards foreign workers is an indisputable fact of German political life; so is a longing for strong leadership and of attacks,

sometimes vicious, against the whole 'system'. Such attitudes exist in most Western countries and they are more deeply rooted than commonly believed. They
can be found even in circles which would indignantly deny harboring such views,
which had to be hidden in Germany for a long time and to a certain degree cannot
be openly voiced even now without fear of criminal prosecution. For this reason
there is need for constant vigilance. But seen in retrospect and taking into account
post-war conditions, auspicious in some respects for the spread of revanchism, it
is astonishing that there has been so little neo-Nazism rather than so much of it.
Can conditions be envisaged in which neo-Nazism might have a major revival in
West Germany? Certainly not at the present time: a new fascism, in the form of a
dictatorship, brutally aggressive against enemies at home and expansionist in its
foreign policy, seems ruled out. Prejudices, resentment, anti-democratic feeling
will not disappear in Germany and right-wing extremism in one form or another
will persevere. It is possible that the whole spectrum of German politics and the
orientation of the major parties may move a few degrees towards the Right or,
more correctly, towards national self-assertion. To a certain degree this has
already taken place, but to confuse this with a second coming of Nazism is to in-
vite ridicule. Germans are likely to commit all kinds of political mistakes in the
years to come, but not the one for which they had to pay so dearly in their recent
history.

How to explain the rediscovery in recent years of patriotism, the native land
and the old traditions, and how deep does it go? This has manifested itself in
debates on Germany's future (one nation or two) and also in a renewed interest in
German history such as on the occasion of the recent anniversaries of Prussia and
of Luther. After years of self-imposed silence and also perhaps a genuine lack of
interest, terms such as 'national interests', 'national aspirations' have returned
with a vengeance in left-wing speeches and literature. Figures in German history
who had been written off as hopelessly reactionary have been rediscovered and
partly rehabilitated in East Germany as much as in the West. There is a new concern with the fate of the German landscape, the old customs (*Brauchtum*), the old
architecture and the old songs. The far Right has observed with amazement (and
also a bit of concern) the emergence of a new patriotism on the hitherto cosmopolitan left — *Boden ohne Blut* (soil without blood) as one observer put it, alluding to
the famous Nazi slogan *Blut und Boden*.

Egon Bahr has said that it was wrong to give up the idea of the nation and be
surprised that the other Europeans did not follow suit. Hence his conclusion that
the nation cannot be suppressed in the long run. Theilhard de Chardin would
outgrow nationalism and the nation state, but he was not very successful in persuading even his own compatriots to become more internationalist in approach.
One could find even a certain logic in Günter Gaus's demand that the Bonn government should think (and act) more like de Gaulle. Gaus tended to be carried
away by his all-embracing German patriotism; he argued that the East Germans
were the most authentic Germans because they were poorer and unspoiled. The
Gaullist thesis was taken one step further by Rudolf Bahro, an East German

Marxist who had defected and become one of the pillars of the Green movement. He came out for a new Europe — Gaullist, Marxist and ecological at the same time, and by necessity anti-American in orientation. Pursuing this aim Bahro was willing to extend his hands to the far Right; 'after all, we are all Germans', as he put it. Bahro's demands were not supported by Bahr and Gaus simply because they had been exposed to the realities of world politics. They favored the continued existence of the military blocs, both NATO and the Warsaw pact, at least for the time being. At the same time they expressed the hope that as a result of *dètente* global tensions would decrease, gradually make the blocs redundant and bring German unity nearer.

A statement such as Egon Bahr's that the nation cannot be ignored or suppressed indefinitely would not be considered controversial or in any way menacing in other parts of Europe. The French and British, the Spanish and even the Italians, have seldom spent sleepless nights in search of national identity. Nationalism has not been a major theme for them simply because it is self-evident: there is no need to engage in self-conscious reflection and ideological justification.

But France and Britain are not divided, they need not engage in a quest for roots and identity. The reasons for the partition are, of course, well known, even though some have argued that it was simply a matter of bad luck, namely, losing the war. The embellishment of the Nazi era has not until recently found supporters among respectable German historians; some writers such as David Irving and David Hogan had their admirers but these were not found among the professionals. As time passes slight changes can be detected: *Geschichte der Deutschen,* by Helmut Diwald, a professor of history at Erlangen, is a case in point. The aim of this book was to confront various 'taboos': that everything in German history had been wrong, that the German past was all sick — claims which had hardly ever been made by any sane observer of the German scene. Diwald took it upon himself to restore national self-respect, and this voice calling in the wilderness had a first printing of 100,000 copies. The treatment of the Holocaust in this book became something of a scandal. Diwald said that, while the overall background of this mass slaughter was not yet quite clear, these were the most 'horrible crimes of our history' and that they could not be captured in words. Since the vocabulary was not adequate to express his feelings the author thought that he should not try to do so in the first place: he devoted little more than two pages to Nazi crimes, and almost thirty pages to the atrocities committed by the Allies *after* the war: 'What occurred in the way of crimes of violence and mass murder between the years 1945 and 1949 is scarcely describable or imaginable.' *

The issue at stake is not, of course, the Diwald case. Books written by eccentrics or expressing extreme views appear at all times and in every country. More interesting was the reception of this work: his admirers claimed that someone had dared at last to question the taboo of German war guilt. This was so essential because there was no future for the German nation unless it got rid of its guilt complex once and for all. This guilt complex had been fabricated by the victors, assisted by left-wing historians, theologians and philosophers. But these denunci-

* The section on the Holocaust in this book was rewritten in subsequent editions.

ations were unjust, for the extreme Left, starting from very different premises, had reached conclusions which were quite similar. For if Hiroshima was like Auschwitz, and My Lai comparable to Babi Yar, if the leaders of the Western democracies are the Hitlers of today, there is no need to get unduly excited about the record of Nazism.

The revisionist historians from the Right are not neo-Nazis. They only react violently whenever the question of German war guilt is brought up. They bitterly resent such *mea-culpitis* — a term which came into being in the 1920s following the debate on the responsibility for the outbreak of the First World War. They find it impossible to accept that the circumstances were not similar. True, public opinion in England and the United States became more hostile *vis-à-vis* Germany in the late 1930s, because Nazism was disliked and Hitler's successive conquests were regarded as a threat. But the idea that Chamberlain and the French governments of the day were warmongers rather than appeasers belongs to the realm of fantasy, and the fact that the U.S. entered the war only after Pearl Harbor and the German declaration of war makes the revisionist assignment even more difficult.

The question of war guilt and of the Nuremberg trials is central for the revisionists of the Right. This is the 'great lie' on which the thesis of the German *Fehlentwicklung* is based (the allegation that German history took a wrong turn). They also resent the negative judgments of foreign observers as well as German liberals and the churches about Bismarck, Prussia and Germany unity. The revisionists demand an unselfconscious and frank discussion of recent German history which, they are certain, will show that while Hitler wanted a strong Germany he probably did not want war; that while he committed major errors of judgment and even crimes, so did the Allies; that the extent of these crimes has been exaggerated and that the time has come to put them in proper perspective, and to let bygones be bygones. The revisionists are still few in number. But the reception of some of these works has been startling: the works of Diwald's German critics do not have a circulation of 100,000 copies.

The desire to see recent German history in a new and better light is psychologically and politically understandable. But it does not make for honest history and it leads to all kinds of strange aberrations. One further illustration should suffice. A distinguished sociologist developed a new theory of elites, according to which there had been a negative selection in recent Germany history. Those who had been brave enough to commit themselves politically had been eliminated; only the cowards remained alive. The author, born five years after Hitler came to power, seems to have persuaded himself that great courage was needed in the Third Reich to join the Nazi party.

But there is a new understanding for the Nazi era also on the far Left. Thomas Schmid, an ideologist of the 'autonomous' trend on the German Left, has complained about the 'imperialist de-Nazification of the god-damn Yankees who had prescribed democracy in our country'.[9] Those thinking that this was an elaborate joke in questionable taste soon learned that they were mistaken. For Schmid went on to argue that German horror and German fascination were one and could not be divided. He wanted to 'come closer' to both, and he was not impressed by rebukes of parafascism. He wanted a Left which was also German in character, hard, relentless in its struggle, capable of pressing the foe to the wall, a Left that did not get stuck in superficial common sense but went on to 'mysterious and unfathomable depths'. For this, too, was part of German political culture. Schmid complained that at international meetings every other country was represented as almost perfect — only the Germans had still to apologize for their existence. Such subservience was unacceptable, a view that is certainly shared by many young Germans. Thomas Schmid is not the elected spokesman of the German Left, and some of his colleagues were frightened by his excessive language. But it is also true that he expressed what others were thinking but had not dared to enunciate.

Schmid was born after the Second World War; another writer of the Left, Gerd Fuchs, is old enough to remember the last days of the war. His father had been a leading Nazi in the village and Fuchs quotes (with approval) the feelings of shock his mother suffered listening shortly after the war to the horrible things Thomas Mann had to say about German crimes. He writes angrily about the informers (against the Nazis) and the collaborators with the Americans among the local population. Fuchs argues that the Americans 'bought' Germany with their Marshall plan, their Vespas (*sic*), radio stations and the Cold War, and in a 'gangster-like way' divided Germany. He is exceedingly bitter about the lack of backbone on the part of his fellow citizens who accepted without even grumbling the right of the stronger.

Reading these personal recollections one is led to believe that Fuchs's ideological home is on the far Right but this is not so. For he also relates how he came to accept the 'economic interpretation of fascism' (meaning the Leninist version), and how, again, the Americans had criminally and systematically sabotaged any honest and genuine confrontation with fascism in Germany. This interpretation, as has been mentioned, lifts much of the responsibility for what happened before 1945 from the generation of Fuchs's father and puts it on 'objective circumstances' and/or the wicked essence of capitalism.

To provide yet another example: at a conference in Italy some years ago I made the acquaintance of a well-known German poetess who made no secret of the fact that she had little but contempt for the governments of the Western democracies but thought of North Korea, which she had just visited, as a shining example of socialism, of humanism and democracy. A few weeks later I happened to read some of her poems published during the Nazi era; they were not, alas, permeated with the same militant anti-fascist spirit.

It may be wrong to make too much of such cases; the last of this generation are now disappearing from the scene. There were similar cases in Italy after 1945; critics of 'liberal democracy' from the right have found a common language with the anti-democrats of the Right.

Nazism is out of fashion and will have no second coming in the foreseeable future. There are more attractive mixtures of nationalism and socialism such as the national revolutionary trend of which mention has already been made, the 'Left people of the Right'. The West German communists have disinterred their 1930 program for the 'national liberation' of the German people, and Lieutenant Scheringer, the much publicized *Reichswehr* officer who converted from Nazism to communism in 1931, became active again in post-war communist politics as a national symbol. General Remer, the Nazi officer whose action in support of Hitler was of decisive importance in putting down the anti-Nazi coup of 20 July 1944, came out with a passionate appeal in favor of a German-Soviet alliance forty years later. Rudolf Bahro has compared the intrusion of the Western lifestyle in Germany to the impact of the Spanish *conquistadores* on the poor *Indios*. Other German Marxists have reached the conclusion that the Allies' de-Nazification was the cultural counterpart of the integration of West Germany into the capitalist world market. The National Revolutionaries stand for an 'independent united and socialist Germany, committed to revolutionary change in the ecological field and to basis (participatory) democracy. It is for solidarity with the struggle of all oppressed peoples for freedom and independence against all kinds of chauvinism and imperialism.'[11] It would be wrong to dismiss these and similar statements as mere demagogy.

What are the basic differences between such doctrines and Soviet communism? The revolutionary nationalists point to their great emphasis on the revitalization of local dialects, songs, regionalism in general and, of course, a specific 'German socialism'. But these are not fundamental differences; after a short cosmopolitan interval the Soviet system became strongly nationalist and has remained so ever since. The national revolutionaries argue that for the first time in German history nationalism is not aggressive in character, is not directed against neighboring peoples; on the contrary, the love of peace is linked with the desire for self-determination.

Given Germany's diminished power, how could it be differently? Though advocating neutrality, the outlook of the national revolutionaries is hardly neutral: the West is the main enemy. Criticism of Soviet policy is seldom, if ever, found in their speeches and articles, partly because there is a greater kinship with the East, but also because such attacks would be risky. Unlike the West, the Soviets may not receive them in good spirit.

Heimat

The new patriotism is closely connected with the re-emergence of *Heimat,* which originally meant little more than the parental home. But gradually its meaning widened and it had a first blossoming in the mid-nineteenth century, a turning towards the past, part of a general anti-urban mood. *Heimat* was not, perhaps could not be, clearly defined. It meant, on the one hand, feeling at ease, at home, a place in which one could relax because there were no dangers. But it also meant the preservation of local traditions, such as a dialect, nature or monuments. *Heimat* was more than a symbol; it meant security and an emotional experience, familiar images, noises and smells, associations with family, one's youth, friendship and love. Then, even before the First World War, there developed a *Heimat* industry: novels naïvely extolling and embellishing its virtues and, in later years, *Heimat* films and hit songs which were immensely successful. Since many people had moved to a big town and thus lost their *Heimat* (for it was not at all clear whether a big city could ever be *Heimat*) all kinds of ersatz *Heimat* came into being to counter the effects of uprooting and alienation: little allotments on the fringe of town, weekend houses for the rich and camping sites or trailers for the less affluent.

But *Heimat* was not only fields and trees at sunset, it was also human beings, the need for contact. Hence the sprouting of the *Vereine,* voluntary associations to pursue ideals or activities of common interest, but also to spend one's time profitably and enjoyably, to find a home away from home, in short a second *Heimat.*

The fact that Nazism had promoted *Heimat* made it suspect for many years after the war; the very term was seldom used and the phenomenon ignored. Until recently one would have looked in vain for studies on *Heimat* in the publications of German sociologists. But whatever abuse had been made of it in the past, *Heimat* obviously corresponded with some deep longings. It was no mere nostalgia and it received fresh impetus as the result of the rapid modernization and urbanization after the Second World War which involved, of necessity, further uprooting of millions of people.

Heimat had never been out of fashion as far as the general public was concerned; it was rediscovered by the intellectuals only in the 1970s.

This may have been connected with the move of some intellectuals out of the big cities into the countryside or the far suburbs. There is no denying that the open country, the fields and forests have much to recommend them, and that great enjoyment can be found walking a lonely path far from the noise and the contaminated air of the big cities, watching the birds in the skies and ears of corn and grass bowing like waves in the wind. Life in small towns and villages also had other compensations: it was less hectic and anonymous, people knew each other, the schools were frequently superior to those in the big city, and people even took culture more seriously, perhaps because there was no *embarras de richesse.*

The small towns were bypassed by history, the philistine narrow-minded character of the *Kleinstädter* became a subject of anger, ridicule or at best pity among many of the educated. Then, in the 1970s, the advantages of backwardness were discovered: the inner composure, proximity to nature, closer family ties and friendships. There was romanticizing in this new mood, but having been exposed for so long to the growing drawbacks of big city life many did not mind this. They were even ready for a little *kitsch*; it was probably no coincidence that the *Gartenlaube* began to appear again in the wake of this nostalgia wave, the very same journal which once had been the essence of all that had seemed reprehensible and comic about small-town philistinism. The same happy ending stories were reprinted ('The Secret of The Silent Bells') and the same old drawings: in the garden, in the shade of a chestnut tree a young lady is seen knitting, seemingly oblivious of the young man, tall but tongue-tied, obviously in two minds about whether this was the right moment to confess his love. It was a touching reaction after two decades of breaking all conventions and the total demystification of sex. Life in the small cities and the village which had been 'fascistoid' almost by definition became acceptable again, indeed almost enviable. A small town could (perhaps) be *Heimat,* the grey concrete boxes of the big city would always remain alien. The less fortunate who could not leave the big cities tried at least to make the best of it by the infusion of a new spirit: the emphasis on neighborhood activities, street fêtes — a little awkwardly perhaps but full of goodwill.[13]

These new trends are in some ways natural and sometimes quite charming. Intellectuals rationalized them in post-Marxist terms: the need for *Heimat* was forward-looking, not reactionary. Even the new interest in Prussia was quite understandable, for not everything had been negative in the Prussian tradition. The rediscovery of a simpler life and a world which had been ignored or forgotten was part of a general trend found in many European countries, even the Soviet Union. The wish to preserve its traditions and customs had been, for instance, behind Norway's decision not to join the Common Market, and it could be found in one form or another in many other places. The new patriotism, as it ought to be called for want of a better term, is inward-looking rather than aggressive, it may be reactionary in the original sense of this term. But then the belief in infinite progress has waned.

How deep does it all go? The evidence is contradictory: everything considered, anti-Americanism is a marginal phenomenon in West Germany, less common than in Britain, France or Sweden. In West Germany 73 percent of the population felt overall favorably inclined towards America in 1982, in comparison with 63 percent in Italy, 55 percent in France and only 46 percent in Britain. When asked in 1954 whether good relations with America were more important than with the Soviet Union, 62 percent opted for America as against 10 percent for the Soviet Union. In 1981 the figure had risen to 65 percent; the same proportion felt spontaneous sympathy towards America and only 17 percent had contrary feelings. In 1957 only 37 percent had said that they liked Americans. But at the same time 45 percent of all Germans under the age of thirty prefer neutrality to the 40 percent who opt for an alliance with the United States. This is the generation which no longer remembers Nazism, the war and the early post-war period, neither the blockade of Berlin nor the CARE parcels, for whom the Cold War and threats to Germany's sovereign existence are relics from the distant past, of no meaning in present conditions.

In recent years there have been long and heated debates about the future of German nationhood—whether two nations have come into being because the partition has lasted so long, whether a *West* German national consciousness can be combined with the dream of national reunification, whether the two Germanies are cultural nations (*Kulturnationen*) but not nations in the traditional, political sense. The fact that so much heat had been generated on both the Right and the Left concerning this issue makes it appear as if the majority of Germans, old and young, regard this as the most important of all issues. Opinion polls however do not bear this out. Reunification once figured very highly on the scale of German priorities: for 47 percent it was the most important political task facing West Germany as recently as 1965. Ten years later only 1 percent still think so. In the early 1970s only 25 percent of Germans felt that they would remain one people in one nation. The majority believes that they will grow apart like Germans and Austrians. Significantly, the younger generation is even less interested in German reunification; of those over sixty questioned in 1976, 77 percent said they wished for German reunification very much indeed; of those under thirty, 52 percent said it was not so important. The trend is unmistakable, it is less clear how far it will progress in the near future, and whether and to what extent it is reversible.

How proud are Germans of their nation? About as much as other Europeans according to the polls, but less than the Americans.[14] Very slowly the new state, its appurtenances and symbols have been accepted by the majority of the population. The attitude to the national flag—that 'mere piece of cloth'—is typical. There was a surfeit of flags in the Nazi era and it is not surprising that sales resistance developed after the war. Asked in 1951 whether they felt joyful when seeing the black-red-and-gold flag of the Republic only 23 percent answered 'Yes, indeed' whereas 54 percent replied 'No'. It reminded me of a scene I had witnessed as a boy, a year or two before Hitler had come to power. On a Sunday afternoon my parents had taken me for an excursion on a steamer. As usual the national flag was hoisted on the aft deck but suddenly several swimmers jumped on board, tore the flag off and demonstratively used it to wipe their behinds—to the great amusement of the public. Even the twelve-year-old boy understood that a state in which the public applauded such scenes and no one dared to stand up for its honor was not likely to last.

In 1977 the same black-red-and-gold flag of the Republic received for the first time in the history of the FRG the approval of Germans. But a majority of those under thirty still did not know the opening words of their national anthem. The identification with the country and the nation is lower among young people than among their elders, and lowest of all among young people with a higher education.

In 1945 few people in their right mind would have worried about the prospect of a decline in German patriotism and the lack of willingness to defend the homeland. In modern European history German nationalism has so frequently meant striving for hegemony, the ambition to impose its will on others in Europe. Perhaps, as some have argued, an undivided German nation has been too large for Europe. But such are the paradoxes of history: the decline of national pride also has its danger for it means that there seems to be no good reason to stand up for the democratic order which has emerged since the war. Thus, paradoxically, not a few observers of the German scene have begun to worry about a possible loss of backbone; however critical young Frenchmen or Italians may be of their country and its institutions, only very few of them refuse to serve in its army, no French and Italian intellectuals have encouraged them in such action. All this on the one side of the ledger, and on the other the resurgence of a new kind of patriotism, a new emphasis on the national interest of the German people. No excessive importance should be attributed to the writings of essayists representing no one but themselves and small groups of like-minded people, to orators carried away by their own eloquence, by the specific occasion or by their audience. Even the demonstrations by highly committed and motivated minorities should be seen in the proper context. While the demonstrations for peace, for neutralism, against NATO and American policies have been the biggest in Europe, it is also true that a larger percentage of the young generation participated in such meetings in Denmark, Holland and Belgium.

But if Denmark decides to opt out of world politics is one thing; if Germany does is another matter. Denmark may get a free ride as far as Western defense is concerned, Germany cannot. Why has Germany moved in a direction different from the other major European countries? Much of it has to do with history and the well-known fact that the swings of the pendulum always go to greater extremes in this country than elsewhere. The results of public opinion polls are of interest, but one ought not to be hypnotized by them. They cannot predict substantial changes which may occur suddenly. A great deal of critical acumen has gone into finding out whether the views of the young generation have been shaped more by a feeling of fear, by the group dynamics of school and university, by deferred adolescence (the fact that young people now remain for a considerably longer time removed from real life and do not have to accept responsibilities), or whether perhaps the new 'telecracy' is of decisive importance — the fact that many key positions in radio, television and the cinema (the new culture industry) have passed into the hands of missionaries of 1968 vintage. Perhaps it has been a mixture of all these factors. Such studies are of interest but they do not explain the 'Falklands factor', the fact that Mrs. Thatcher, not an expert in social psychology or the theory of communication, received the backing of the great majority of her compatriots for the defense of an unimportant island 9,000 miles distant. True, many Germans found the British reaction difficult to understand, it seemed almost atavistic. But such atavisms happen to occur almost anywhere, suddenly, and with considerable force.

Seen in retrospect Germans since the Second World War have behaved with remarkable maturity, showing greater restraint than almost anybody expected at the time. They have acted reasonably and responsibly and it does not really matter that much whether such behavior was a marriage of convenience and prudence rather than an affair of the heart. Almost four decades have passed since the end of the war, new generations have grown up which no longer feel the need to behave as if Germany was still on probation. If France and Britain frequently put their own national interests first why should Germany not do so with equal justification? Why should they not have the right to behave a little irresponsibly from time to time? It is a legitimate question and in some ways such a reaction is natural and inevitable. Since the movement towards European political unity has come to a halt, the various nationalisms are bound to reassert themselves. But legitimate or not, this development entails certain dangers. Britain and France with all their nationalist escapades in recent decades have not, on the whole, exceeded certain boundaries. They bear much responsibility for the lack of progress on the road towards greater European unity, but they have kept, on the whole, to the ground rules of Western defiance. Neither Britain nor France is a divided country; but if West Germany should put reunification high on its political agenda this could have far-reaching repercussions.

A united Germany to be sure would not be a new superpower, a mortal threat to its neighbors; it would have global power status only in the realm of athletics and swimming — in other respects such risks are non-existent. The real danger is that any advance on the road towards German reunification is possible only on the basis of political concessions *vis-à-vis* the Soviet Union. This, of course, is not unknown to the protagonists of German unity in Bonn, and most of them argue that their goal will not be achieved in the near future and that their main concern now is not to set up any further obstacles, not to close any doors which may make it more difficult at some future date to achieve an aim which is, after all, part of the West German constitution. The road to German unity leads through Moscow; it is equally true that the Soviet leadership has no desire whatsoever to engage in experiments of this kind in the foreseeable future. But it may be enough to dangle some vague promises in front of some Germans to keep illusions alive in West Germany: decades have passed since Rapallo (which was never signed or followed up) and the allegedly missed opportunities to reunite Germany in 1952-3 (which belong to the realm of mythology). But these memories have been sufficient to provide inspiration for the advocates of an Eastern orientation to this day.

True, German unity despite the ritual invocations on various parts of the political spectrum does not figure very highly among the priorities of the present generation of Germans. But it is also true that unresolved national issues — and what could be more painful than the partition of a nation? — tend to re-emerge as major issues after lying dormant for many years. There are frequent examples in history, and it is clearly premature to write off the cause of German reunification as a major issue. Nor is German unity the only cause of a possible resurgence of 'Germany firstism'; the new nationalism, to repeat once again, is not militaristic, aggressive, or expansive in character but a passive count-me-out attitude, a resentment against too close an integration with the West — cultural, as much as political and military. Paradoxically it expresses itself at one and the same time in a certain lack of national pride and scruples about whether it is right to serve in the *Bundeswehr* — and on the other hand in the desire to establish closer relations with East Germany and to maintain friendly relations with East Germany's chief protector.

The era of a German *Sonderweg* pursued through military means is past and will not recur. But the Pied Piper can appear in many disguises and he can play more than one tune; a *Sonderweg* can also be followed by means other than war and this dream has not vanished: why make Germany the main battlefield of the future if it could attain safety through neutrality between West and East? It is a delusion, but those familiar with the attraction which myths have exerted in the history of nations — and German history is as good an example as any — will not dismiss the possibility that a myth of this kind may attract even more followers than it has at present. I feel confident that the re-emergence of German patriotism will continue but that either the instinct of self-preservation or a guardian angel will keep the Germans from committing yet another fateful error in their history. There is reasonable ground for optimism, but there are no certainties.

Copyright © 1985 Germany Today: A Personal Report. Little Brown & Co., pp. 143-174. Reprinted with permission.

The Waldheim-Kohl-Bitburg Axis
Reform Judaism
Fall 1986

By Menachem Z. Rosensaft

In the spring of 1985, Kurt Waldheim — then a respected former Secretary-General of the United Nations — publicly endorsed the ill-conceived visit of President Reagan and West German Chancellor Helmut Kohl to the Bitburg cemetery. Small wonder. As we now know, Waldheim has a great deal in common with the 49 members of the Waffen-SS who lie buried there. Presumably, he considered a formal tribute to the memory of dead Nazi soldiers to be no worse than electing a retired Nazi officer to serve as the chief executive of the United Nations.

One year later, Kohl returned the favor. By that time, the conservative Waldheim was the acknowledged front-runner in the campaign for the Austrian presidency. He also stood unmasked as a proven liar and an alleged war criminal who, for almost forty-one years, had concealed the fact that throughout the Second World War he had been, at best, an obedient and enthusiastic servant of Adolf Hitler and the Nazi regime. Nonetheless, in an interview broadcast on the Austrian state radio on April 26, 1986, Kohl, in effect, endorsed his "old personal friend" Waldheim as "a great patriot." This may well have been the first time in some five decades that a German chancellor chose to openly interfere in the internal political affairs of an independent Austria.

Kohl did not refer to any of the ever-mounting evidence against Waldheim. He did not mention that the United Nations War Crimes Commission had formally accused Waldheim of having committed atrocities in Nazi occupied Yugoslavia. For that matter, Kohl failed to utter even a single word of criticism against his "friend" for having deceived the entire international community.

Instead, the West German chancellor indignantly attacked the Jewish leaders and activists — most of whom had been born during or after the Second World War — who had uncovered and exposed the details of Waldheim's previously suppressed military record as a Nazi intelligence officer. "I sense an arrogance of the late-born," Kohl told the Austrian people, "which I find hard to bear." True to form, Kohl was far more offended by those who dared to remind Germans and Austrians of their reprehensible past than by the atrocities committed by his elders and contemporaries. It is not surprising, therefore, that Kohl remains self-satisfied about having been the architect of the Bitburg visit, even though its direct consequence has been a dramatic increase in blatant German anti-Semitism.

Ostensibly, President Reagan and Chancellor Kohl went to Bitburg in order to celebrate the spirit of "reconciliation" between their two nations. In reality, however, their motivation was entirely political in nature. Helmut Kohl sought votes among his country's reactionary elements, most of whom look back on the Third Reich with barely disguised nostalgia. And Ronald Reagan demonstrated once again his readiness to sacrifice even the most fundamental principles for the sake of yet another tenuous alliance with a kindred conservative politician. In addition, their wreath-laying at Bitburg has served as a virtual pardon for German anti-Semites, allowing them to re-surface and to reassert their baser instincts.

In January 1986, for example, Count Wilderich von Spee, a Christian Democratic mayor in Kohl's home state of North Rhineland-Westphalia, suggested that "a few rich Jews" should be slaughtered in order to balance his town's budget. In a similar vein, and at about the same time, Hermann Fellner, a member of the Bundestag, the West German Parliament, from the conservative Bavarian Christian Social Union, said publicly that Jews who seek reparations from German firms that had used them as slave laborers during the Second World War "are quick to show up whenever money tinkles in German cash registers."

Kohl's reaction to these and other equally loathsome incidents has been perfunctory at best, and, characteristically, he went out of his way to praise Fellner as "a splendid young man" who had simply said something "foolish." He certainly did not accuse either von Spee or Fellner of being "arrogant." In sharp contrast, West German President Richard von Weizsäcker denounced the new German Jew baiting. In a speech delivered on March 2 of this year, he declared that the recent anti-Semitic statements made in his country "were an insult and a source of concern to our Jewish fellow citizens and to Jews throughout the world. I would like to ask them, too, for forgiveness. There is no excuse for these statements. They are incompatible with our view of man, of democratic humanity, of history, as well as our national honor."

Ever since coming to power in 1982 — long before Bitburg — Kohl has endeavored to rehabilitate as many Germans who had served the Third Reich as possible. In 1983, for example, his government removed the veterans organizations of the Waffen-SS from a list of extremist right-wing groups on which the West German Ministry of the Interior is required to make an annual report to Parliament. Kohl has also blocked repeated demands by the opposition Social Democrats to ban the highly controversial reunions of former members of the Waffen-SS. Even though this infamous Nazi body was responsible for countless wartime atrocities — including the brutal liquidation of the Warsaw Ghetto — and provided guards for virtually all the concentration and extermination camps, Kohl has consistently depicted its men as simple soldiers who had no alternative but to follow orders. Twenty-five years after Adolf Eichmann used it as his principal defense, this hollow excuse is apparently becoming Helmut Kohl's alibi for the German nation.

Kohl is by no means alone in holding such views. In the course of his election campaign, Waldheim, who never once rejected the support of Nazis, neo-Nazis and other Austrian anti-Semites, disingenuously told his compatriots: "Don't let anybody turn your fathers and grandfathers into criminals." Like Kohl, he, too, wants the world to forget that only one generation ago, tens of thousands of German and Austrian fathers and grandfathers did commit the most brutal war crimes in history. And on June 8, 1986, some 54% of the Austrian people ratified this disavowal of the Austro-German collective responsibility for the Holocaust and all the Third Reich's other crimes against humanity by electing Waldheim.

Meanwhile, on what amounts to a parallel track, a number of highly respected German intellectuals have argued that, in reality, Nazi Germany was no different from, and no worse than, any other country. Thus, Rudolf Augstein, editor-in-chief of West Germany's influential *Der Spiegel,* wrote in January 1985: "Whether the anti-Hitler allies committed fewer crimes than Hitler is not at all certain. The one who initiated such crimes against humanity was, in any case, Stalin, in 1928. Hitler's crimes were not directed so much against his own compatriots as against foreign countries and against the numerically much stronger foreign Jews; within the Reich there were only 500,000 of them."

To be sure, these attempts to distort history by destigmatizing the Third Reich are not endorsed by all Germans. In his courageous speech in the Bundestag on May 8, 1985 — three days after Bitburg — President von Weizsäcker refuted the Augstein-Kohl perspective on Nazi Germany. "Hardly any country," he said, "has in its history always remained free from blame for war or violence. The genocide of the Jews is, however, unparalleled in history." Furthermore, he continued, "every German was able to experience what his Jewish compatriots had to suffer, ranging from plain apathy and hidden intolerance to outright hatred." Unfortunately, however, as historian Saul Friedländer has persuasively pointed out in various lectures and articles, President von Weizsäcker's attitude is the exception rather than the rule in contemporary German society.

Far from furthering any type of reconciliation, the Bitburg debacle succeeded only in lifting the forty-year old taboo on anti-Semitism which had restored Germany to respectability after the Holocaust. Moreover, most Jewish leaders have also failed to react appropriately to the post-Bitburg developments.

On the whole, they have not taken a sufficiently strong stand against the resurgence of anti-Jewish manifestations in West Germany. Even worse, despite Helmut Kohl's proven callousness with respect to his nation's Nazi past, many of them persist in regarding him as a legitimate partner for a dialogue on German-Jewish — as opposed to German-American — reconciliation.

Somewhere, somehow, something has gone seriously wrong. While it took the Jewish people almost five hundred years to re-establish formal relations with Spain after the Inquisition, we are now — only forty-one years after the Holocaust — coming dangerously close to the point where some Jews seem to be asking the Germans to forgive *us* for remembering, and for reminding them about, the crimes committed by *their* nation against the Jewish people. In recent years, a substantial number of Jewish leaders, intellectuals and organizational functionaries have adopted the position that German-Jewish reconciliation in and of itself — and at any cost — should be a Jewish priority. In so doing, however, they frequently fail to set any parameters for such reconciliation, and they disregard the fundamental fact that we, as the Nazis' victims or intended victims, have the absolute right and obligation to demand that any type of discussion on present-day or future German-Jewish relations be conducted only and exclusively on our terms.

Once and for all, it must be made clear to both German and Jewish leaders that there can be no reconciliation on the part of the Jewish people with any element or vestige of the Hitler regime. The evil of Nazi Germany was absolute, without any redeeming or redeemable features. Accordingly, no Jewish spokesman should even discuss the issue of German-Jewish reconciliation with any German leader or representative who does not unequivocally repudiate everything associated with Nazism or the Third Reich, or who wishes to exonerate or otherwise rehabilitate anyone who took part in any way in the annihilation of European Jewry. As far as the Jewish community is concerned, President von Weizsäcker, former Chancellor Willy Brandt, Johannes Rau (the leader of the West German Social Democratic Party) and Stuttgart Mayor Manfred Rommel are all decent and honorable representatives of the new, democratic, post-Holocaust Germany. Helmut Kohl, on the other hand, is not.

I do not mean to suggest that I am opposed to an ongoing German-Jewish dialogue which, eventually, may result in genuine reconciliation. However, any such dialogue must be predicated on complete truth and honesty. This is understood by those Germans and Jews who combine pilgrimages to Bergen-Belsen and Dachau with visits to the graves of anti-Nazi Germans such as Hans and Sophie Scholl, who were beheaded in 1943 for leading a student resistance group known as the White Rose.

Indeed, we now face a clear choice between two mutually exclusive alternatives. We can perpetuate the festering legacy of Bitburg, or we can remain true to the inflexible imperative of remembrance. And the latter goal is only achievable if the complex process of German-Jewish reconciliation is conducted in a moral rather than a purely pragmatic context.

Index of Authors

Index of Authors